OUTDOORS

COLORADO CAMPING

SARAH RYAN

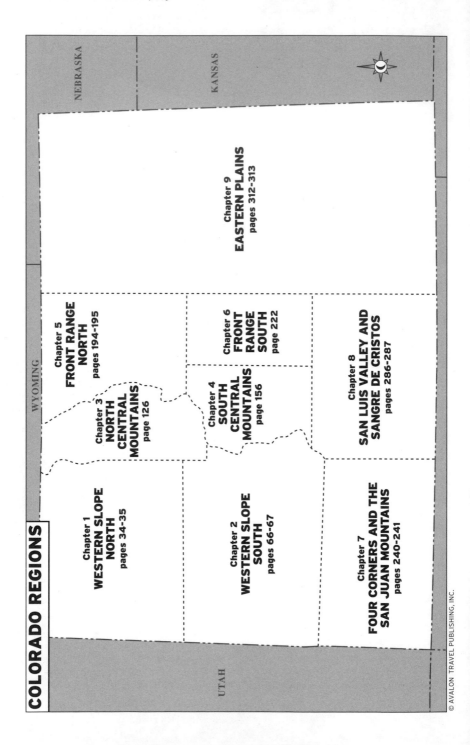

COLORADO REGIONS

NEBRASKA

KANSAS

WYOMING

UTAH

Chapter 9
EASTERN PLAINS
pages 312-313

Chapter 5
FRONT RANGE
NORTH
pages 194-195

Chapter 6
FRONT
RANGE
SOUTH
page 222

Chapter 3
NORTH
CENTRAL
MOUNTAINS
page 126

Chapter 4
SOUTH
CENTRAL
MOUNTAINS
page 156

Chapter 8
SAN LUIS VALLEY AND
SANGRE DE CRISTOS
pages 286-287

Chapter 1
WESTERN SLOPE
NORTH
pages 34-35

Chapter 2
WESTERN SLOPE
SOUTH
pages 66-67

Chapter 7
FOUR CORNERS AND THE
SAN JUAN MOUNTAINS
pages 240-241

© AVALON TRAVEL PUBLISHING, INC.

Contents

How To Use This Book

ABOUT THE CAMPGROUND PROFILES

The campgrounds are listed in a consistent, easy-to-read format to help you choose the ideal camping spot. If you already know the name of the specific campground you want to visit, or the name of the surrounding geological area or nearby feature (town, national or state park, forest, mountain, lake, river, etc.), look it up in the index and turn to the corresponding page. Here is a sample profile:

Campground name and map number →

Icons noting activities and facilities at or nearby the campground

1 SOMEWHERE USA CAMPGROUND

General location of the campground in relation to the nearest major town or landmark →

Scenic rating: 10

south of Somewhere USA Lake

Rating of scenic beauty on a scale of 1-10

BEST (

Symbol indicating that the campground is listed among the author's top picks

Each campground in this book begins with a brief overview of its setting. The description typically covers ambience, information about the attractions, and activities popular at the campground.

Campsites, facilities: This section notes the number of campsites for tents and RVs and indicates whether hookups are available. Facilities such as restrooms, picnic areas, recreation areas, laundry, and dump stations will be addressed, as well as the availability of piped water, showers, playgrounds, stores, and other amenities. The campground's pet policy and wheelchair accessibility is also mentioned here.

Reservations, fees: This section notes whether reservations are accepted, and provides rates for tent sites and RV sites. If there are additional fees for parking or pets, or discounted weekly or seasonal rates, they will also be noted here.

Directions: This section provides mile-by-mile driving directions to the campground from the nearest major town or highway.

Contact: This section provides an address, phone number, and website, if available, for the campground.

ABOUT THE ICONS

The icons in this book are designed to provide at-a-glance information on activities, facilities, and services available on-site or within walking distance of each campground.

A Hiking trails

A Biking trails

A Swimming

A Fishing

A Flatwater boating opportunities available (includes motorboats and personal watercrafts)

A Whitewater and/or kayaking

A Winter sports (such as downhill skiing, cross-country skiing, snowshoeing, snowmobiling, snowboarding, and ice-skating)

A Hot springs

A Pets permitted (restrictions or additional fees may apply)

A Playground

A Wheelchair access (Concerned persons should always call the campground to verify that their specific needs will be met.)

A RV sites

A Tent sites

MAP SYMBOLS

═══════ Expressway	(80) Interstate Freeway	✗ Airfield	
═══════ Primary Road	(101) US Highway	✗ Airport	
─────── Secondary Road	(29) State Highway	○ City/Town	
========= Unpaved Road	[66] County Highway	▲ Mountain	
··············· Ferry	Lake	♦ Park	
─ · ─ · ─ · National Border	Dry Lake	\⸍ Pass	
─ · · ─ State Border	Seasonal Lake	◉ State Capital	

INTRODUCTION

Author's Note

Natives and newcomers can agree on one thing: Colorado is a superlative state. It has more fourteeners (mountains with an elevation of 14,000 feet or higher) and microbreweries than any other state, the highest mean altitude of all the states, the highest suspension bridge in the world, the world's largest natural hot springs pool, the tallest sand dune in North America, the largest city park system in the country, the largest flat-top mountain in the world, and the highest paved highway in North America, to name just a few of the highlights.

Colorado offers unparalleled variety in scenery and outdoor recreation and 300 days of sunshine a year. There are 18 million acres of pubic land in Colorado, including 10 national parks and monuments, 15 national forests and grasslands, 40 state parks, and 37 wilderness areas. Visitors enjoy hiking and mountain biking on the Continental Divide, four-wheeling to ghost towns, rafting down raging rivers, soaking in hot springs, fly-fishing on Gold Medal waters, boating and waterskiing on reservoirs, touring the fall foliage, snowshoeing and skiing at world-class resorts, and camping, of course.

Colorado's campgrounds are incredibly diverse. From RV parks in the eastern plains to the tent campground at the base of Longs Peak, there is a dream destination for every type of traveler. And, indeed, the campers are as varied as the scenery. Colorado is an international destination, and you're likely to meet tourists from every part of the United States as well as Europe, South America, and Asia. And their interests are as varied as their hometowns: hiking, biking, wildlife viewing, sightseeing, climbing, and river running are just a few of the activities that draw millions of visitors to Colorado every year.

Whether you're a lifelong resident or a short-term visitor, you'll need a guide to Colorado's many campgrounds. *Moon Colorado Camping* includes over 480 public and commercial campgrounds in national parks, state forests, county and city parks, and on BLM and private land. The listings include practical information on facilities, reservations, and driving directions, as well as a narrative evaluation informed by first-hand knowledge and conversations with camp hosts, campers, and rangers. The listings also serve as an activity guide, with recommendations on hiking and biking trails, white-water runs, fishing opportunities, and winter sports, as well as nearby cultural attractions. Chapter introductions provide background information on the human and natural history of each region, describe the area's best features and attractions, and offer travel tips. Detailed maps and "Best Of" lists facilitate driving and decision making, and an extensive section on camping tips answers age-old questions like "What should I pack?" and "Is the water safe to drink?"

Researching *Colorado Camping* was a navigational challenge. My *Colorado Atlas & Gazetteer*—torn, creased, coffee stained, and covered in notes—is a testament to the more than 11,000 miles that I logged on Colorado's highways and back roads. I learned that in Colorado the shortcuts always take longer, but the views are worth the extra hours. In my experience, playing in Colorado is a story-making experience. My stories include waking up to a summer blizzard in Steamboat Springs, fishing on the Animas River, wandering through the ruins of Mesa Verde, surprising a herd of bighorn sheep on a lonely back road, sharing a rowdy dinner in Creede with through-hikers from the Colorado Trail, and celebrating my one-year wedding anniversary beside an alpine lake in Rocky Mountain National Park.

What will your story be?

Best Campgrounds

🄲 Best Campgrounds near Fourteeners
Silver Bar, Western Slope South, page 88.
Silver Bell, Western Slope South, page 88.
Silver Queen, Western Slope South, page 89.
Half Moon, North Central Mountains, page 146.
Elbert Creek, South Central Mountains, page 170.
Longs Peak, Front Range North, page 208.
Echo Lake, Front Range North, page 217.
Mueller State Park, Front Range South, page 232.
Matterhorn, Four Corners and the San Juan Mountains, page 249.
Molas Lake Public Park, Four Corners and the San Juan Mountains, page 252.
North Crestone, San Luis Valley and Sangre de Cristos, page 290.
Pinyon Flats, San Luis Valley and Sangre de Cristos, page 296.

🄲 Best Campgrounds for Hiking
Trappers Lake-Shepherd's Rim, Western Slope North, page 53.
Cold Springs, Western Slope North, page 55.
Saddlehorn, Western Slope South, page 76.
Avalanche, Western Slope South, page 85.
Silver Bar, Western Slope South, page 88.
Silver Bell, Western Slope South, page 88.
Silver Queen, Western Slope South, page 89.
Oh-Be-Joyful, Western Slope South, page 95.
Gold Park, North Central Mountains, page 150.
Moraine Park, Front Range North, page 206.
Pawnee, Front Range North, page 210.
Rainbow Lakes, Front Range North, page 212.
Burro Bridge, Four Corners and the San Juan Mountains, page 250.
Lost Trail, Four Corners and the San Juan Mountains, page 253.

🄲 Best Lakeside Campgrounds
Dutch Hill, Western Slope North, page 39.
Pearl Lake State Park, Western Slope North, page 40.
Trappers Lake-Cutthroat, Western Slope North, page 54.
Bear Lake, Western Slope North, page 56.
White Owl, Western Slope North, page 59.
Elk Run, Western Slope South, page 69.
Lost Lake, Western Slope South, page 94.
Silver Jack, Western Slope South, page 119.
Arapaho Bay, North Central Mountains, page 136.
May Queen, South Central Mountains, page 162.
Backcountry, South Central Mountains, page 183.
Haviland Lake, Four Corners and the San Juan Mountains, page 261.
Teal, Four Corners and the San Juan Mountains, page 262.

◖ Best Full-Service Campgrounds

Fruita, Western Slope South, page 75.
Early Settlers, Western Slope South, page 77.
Winding River Resort, North Central Mountains, page 132.
Stillwater, North Central Mountains, page 133.
Rocky Ridge, South Central Mountains, page 176.
Cherry Creek State Park, Front Range North, page 218.
Castle Lakes Resort, Four Corners and the San Juan Mountains, page 244.
Mosca, San Luis Valley and Sangre de Cristos, page 295.

◖ Best Tent-Only Campgrounds

Echo Park, Western Slope North, page 42.
Pioneer, Western Slope South, page 78.
Crater Lake, Western Slope South, page 87.
Cataract Creek, North Central Mountains, page 139.
Belle of Colorado, South Central Mountains, page 163.
Backcountry, South Central Mountains, page 183.

◖ Best Campgrounds for Stunning Views

Echo Park, Western Slope North, page 42.
Saddlehorn, Western Slope South, page 76.
Crater Lake, Western Slope South, page 87.
Lost Lake, Western Slope South, page 94.
Gothic, Western Slope South, page 96.
Dinner Station, Western Slope South, page 98.
May Queen, South Central Mountains, page 162.
Moraine Park, Front Range North, page 206.
Amphitheatre, Four Corners and the San Juan Mountains, page 243.
Molas Lake Public Park, Four Corners and the San Juan Mountains, page 252.
Lost Trail, Four Corners and the San Juan Mountains, page 253.
Pinyon Flats, San Luis Valley and Sangre de Cristos, page 296.

◖ Best Campgrounds for Weddings

Stillwater, North Central Mountains, page 133.
Tigiwon, North Central Mountains, page 145.
Ruby Mountain, South Central Mountains, page 185.
Moraine Park, Front Range North, page 206.
Mueller State Park, Front Range South, page 232.
Rosa, Four Corners and the San Juan Mountains, page 280.
Pinyon Flats, San Luis Valley and Sangre de Cristos, page 296.

🄲 Best Campgrounds for Whitewater

Gates of Lodore, Western Slope North, page 37.
Deerlodge Park, Western Slope North, page 42.
East Portal, Western Slope South, page 110.
Ruby Mountain, South Central Mountains, page 185.
Hecla Junction, South Central Mountains, page 187.
Narrows, Front Range North, page 200.
Ansel Watrous, Front Range North, page 201.

Camping Tips

WILDERNESS ETHICS AND SAFETY

The majority of campgrounds in this guidebook are developed campgrounds designed for tents and RVs. They may have paved roads, tent pads, new picnic tables, and composting vault toilets. They can accommodate families, wheelchairs, small children, and large groups. As our urban centers grow, they are increasingly busy throughout the summer and into the fall, and so they serve a dual purpose: base camp for exploring the great outdoors, and buffer zone for saving the great outdoors. Respect the wilderness you're there to enjoy by following Leave No Trace principles, an international program designed to assist travelers with their decisions while enjoying public lands. Leave No Trace is an educational program that teaches techniques for minimizing recreational impacts. To take part, look for the **Keep It Wild Tips** developed from Leave No Trace policies scattered throughout the Camping Tips section.

For a pocket-sized, weatherproof card and other free information on making ethical decisions while recreating on public lands, contact the Leave No Trace Center for Outdoor Ethics, P.O. Box 997, Boulder, CO, 80306, 800/332-4100, www.lnt.org.

Campsite Courtesy

The Forest Service, National Park Service, and state parks have done a great job of building convenient and accessible campgrounds in every nook and cranny of the state. In remote areas, you may have the campground to yourself, but in popular areas, you can count on having lots of neighbors, so campsite courtesy is essential. There are three common violations of campsite courtesy: noise, litter, and vandalism.

Be respectful of other campers by following posted quiet hours, which are usually from 9 P.M. to 6 A.M. While few things are as enjoyable as listening to musicians strum a guitar or pick a banjo around the campfire, replaying a Top 40 country hit over and over can put the rest of the campground in agony. Music should be played quietly, if at all. Gas-powered electrical generators are torture to tent camp-

Plan Ahead

- Learn about the regulations and any special concerns that apply to the area you're going to visit.
- Obtain maps, permits, and emergency contact numbers in advance.
- Plan your trip and give a copy of your itinerary to a reliable friend. Be clear about where you are going and when you should return.
- Plan your meals and do your grocery shopping in advance.
- Keep a handy checklist for gear, clothing, and food. Check it off as you pack.
- Check the condition of your gear and pack appropriate clothing for weather extremes.
- Run last-minute errands (including the bank and gas station) and pack the car the night before you leave.
- Double-check the weather forecast for any surprises.
- Get an early start and stay hydrated.

Keep It Wild: Keep the Wilderness Wild

Let nature's sound prevail. Avoid loud voices and noises; leave radios and tape players at home.

Treat natural heritage with respect. Leave plants, rocks, and historical artifacts where you find them. Do not cut down limbs or branches or remove leaves from trees.

Respect the animals that inhabit the area. Don't feed or harass animals that visit your campground. Animals need to stick to their natural diets or else they may become ill. Keep your camp area clean, especially if you're in or near bear country, so you don't tempt any animals to visit your site.

Control pets at all times or leave them with a sitter at home.

ers and should be used as little as possible and only during daylight hours. Late arrivals—or early risers—should be as quiet as possible.

Litter is a disturbing violation of the outdoors. Trash should be placed in trash cans or packed out when receptacles are not available. Well-meaning campers often leave garbage in the fire rings, but this trash attracts animals and may not burn. If in doubt, pack it out.

Here's a list of some humorous, and not so humorous, things we've seen at campgrounds that should probably be left at home: wading pools, armchairs, boom boxes, BB guns, sprinklers, fireworks and sparklers, disobedient dogs, house cats, hummingbird feeders, kegs, and satellite dishes.

Vandalism is equally upsetting. Carving names into trees leaves them susceptible to disease. Graffiti on picnic tables and vault toilets—or bullet holes in signs—redirects limited funds away from improvements to repairs.

Camping with Kids

Camping is an affordable family vacation, and it can be an enjoyable adventure—and learning experience—for kids of all ages. Infants can go camping as long as their physical requirements are kept in mind. Toddlers enjoy camping so much it can be hard to get to them to sleep. Elementary age children will unconsciously seize on the myriad learning opportunities of being outdoors. Teenagers can be more difficult to please—be sure to include them in the decision-making process, and they're more likely to have fun. Here are some tips for keeping young kids happy:

• Keep trips short and within the physical abilities of a child.

• Include children in the planning process. Show them maps and photos of the destination so they can get excited about the trip, too. Ask for their input on activities and outings.

• Plan frequent activities, outings, and games, while keeping in mind their short attention spans. For young children, plan naps as well. Be flexible to accommodate weather and moods.

• Keep the campground safe for kids. Be aware of fire and water hazards, and educate them on appropriate behavior in the woods and around wildlife.

• Pack appropriate clothing and gear. Children need layers, too, so be sure to bring long underwear, warm layers, rain gear, hats, and sunglasses. Bring a child's backpack with his or her own water and snacks, whistle, first-aid kit, magnifying glass, sun block and insect repellent, compass and watch, flashlight, hiking map, tube tent for taking naps, and disposable camera.

• Let them help around the campsite with setting up tents, pumping water, cooking meals, washing dishes, and planning activities.

• Keep it fun so they'll want to go again year after year.

Camping with Pets

Pets are family members and should be brought on camping trips, as long as a few simple rules are followed:

• Keep pets on a leash at all times. Loose pets disturb the homes and habits of native wildlife.

• Never leave pets unattended at the campground.

• Don't allow dogs to bark at or intimidate other campers or wildlife. If your dog can't be trusted in a campground, leave him or her at home.

Dress Yourself in Blaze Orange

I love fall. Golden aspens shaking in the wind, the first signs of snow, the crack of rifles in the backcountry … Colorado attracts hunters from around the world. The state has hunting seasons for deer, elk, pronghorn, bear, mountain goat, bighorn sheep, mountain lion, moose, turkey, prairie chickens, waterfowl, and small game. Seasons vary with location, weapon, and animal. In most areas, big game seasons begin in September and extend through January. If you're planning a trip to the backcountry in the fall or winter, call the Colorado Division of Wildlife at 303/297-1192 to check on local hunting regulations. If in doubt, be safe and dress yourself, your kids, and your pets in blaze orange.

Living with Wildlife: Bears

If you're camping in Colorado, you are playing in bear country. Black bears are the smallest and most common bear in North America, and they are the only bear known to live in Colorado at this time. Population estimates range from 8,000 to 12,000. Black bears can live for about 20 years in the wild. They run at speeds up to 35 mph, and they are strong swimmers and climbers.

Black bears vary in size and weight with gender, season, and food supply. Adult males average 275 pounds and adult females average 175 pounds. They are about three feet tall when standing on all fours and five feet tall when standing upright. Black bears can be identified by their tracks, droppings, claw marks on trees, and sound. The most common sounds are woofing and jaw popping. Black bears are solitary animals, but they use trails just as humans do. They are intelligent and curious. They have good vision but rely on smell and hearing to locate food and warn them about danger. In Colorado, the most common black bear habitats are areas of Gambel's oak and aspen near clearings with chokecherry and serviceberry bushes. They are omnivorous and will eat anything from plants, berries, and nuts to carrion and trash.

Most conflicts between bears and humans result from careless handling of food or garbage. Bears will eat almost anything, and once they discover that human settlements are a food source, they quickly become pests and often have to be tagged, removed, and sometimes put down. By adhering to the following guidelines, you'll save bears' lives, and possibly your own.

Keep your camp clean. Never leave food or coolers unattended. Keep food out of your tent, and don't eat and sleep in the same clothes. Burn grease off grills and camp stoves. Keep your eating area clean.

Store your food and toiletries safely. Store food and coolers in your car trunk or suspended from a tree (at least 10 feet off the ground and four feet from the trunk). Use bear-proof containers when available.

Dispose of garbage properly. Put trash in bear-proof receptacles and pack it out. Never burn or bury food. Bears will dig it up.

Sleep away from food areas. Move a safe distance away from your cooking and food storage sites to sleep.

Don't surprise them. Keep kids within sight at all times and dogs on a leash. Bears are most active at dawn and dusk, so take care

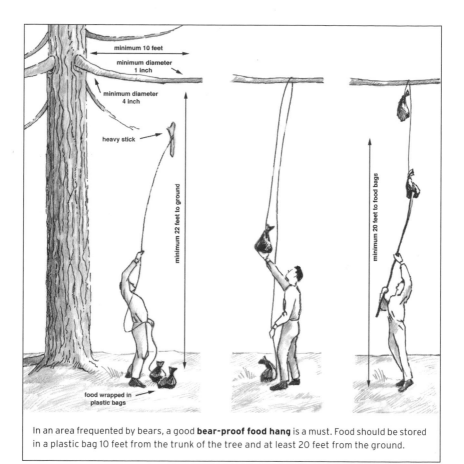

minimum 10 feet

minimum diameter
1 inch

minimum diameter
4 inch

heavy stick

minimum 22 feet to ground

minimum 20 feet to food bags

food wrapped in
plastic bags

In an area frequented by bears, a good **bear-proof food hang** is a must. Food should be stored in a plastic bag 10 feet from the trunk of the tree and at least 20 feet from the ground.

when hiking at these times and in areas with reduced visibility. Talk or sing to avoid surprising them.

Living with Wildlife: Mountain Lions

The mountain lion is one of North America's biggest cats and an important part of the Rocky Mountain ecosystem. In Colorado, population estimates range from 3,000 to 7,000 mountain lions, but sightings are rare. This powerful predator lives on big game, especially deer, but they will also eat elk, small mammals, pets, and livestock. They vary in size and weight. Adult males can be up to eight feet in length and weigh 150 pounds on average. Adult females weigh 90 pounds on average.

These solitary animals are most active from dusk to dawn, but they may hunt and travel during the day as well. In Colorado, lions are usually found in areas of piñon, juniper, ponderosa pine, and oak brush, and in areas with large deer populations. Lion/human interactions have increased as both human and lion populations grow, and as the lions' habitats begin to overlap with mountain subdivisions and urban areas. Lion attacks are extremely rare, but if you are traveling in mountain lion country, follow these rules to be safe:

• Make lots of noise when you are out at dusk or dawn.

• Travel in groups.
• Supervise children closely and keep pets on a leash.
• Never approach a mountain lion or its kittens.
• Stay calm if you meet a mountain lion. Stop or back away slowly. Appear larger by raising your arms or opening a jacket. Pick up small children so that they cannot panic and run.
• Throw stones and speak firmly if a lion acts aggressively. If you are attacked by a lion, fight back. Lions have been driven away by prey that fights back.

RULES, REGULATIONS, AND RESERVATIONS

National Parks and Monuments

Colorado has eight national parks, monuments, and recreation areas that allow camping: Rocky Mountain National Park, Mesa Verde National Park, Dinosaur National Monument, Black Canyon of the Gunnison National Park, Great Sand Dunes National Park, Colorado National Monument, Hovenweep National Monument, and Curecanti National Recreation Area.

The majority of these campgrounds have running water but no electricity. They range from walk-in tent campgrounds to RV parks in Curecanti National Recreation Area. Most campsites are limited to six people and two camping units. Leashed pets are permitted in campgrounds but are not allowed on trails or in the backcountry. Campfires are only allowed in fire rings. At smaller campgrounds, trash must be packed out. Quiet hours are enforced by rangers and camp hosts. Permits are required for backcountry camping.

Most of these campgrounds are first-come, first-serve, but reservations for the larger campgrounds at Rocky Mountain National Park can be made at 800/365-CAMP or at http://reservations.nps.gov.

National Forests

Colorado has 13 national forests and grasslands: Arapaho National Forest, Comanche National Grassland, Grand Mesa National Forest, Gunnison National Forest, Pawnee National Grassland, Pike National Forest, Rio Grande National Forest, Roosevelt National Forest, Routt National Forest, San Isabel National Forest, San Juan National Forest, Uncompahgre National Forest, and White River National Forest.

The campgrounds are maintained and operated by private concessionaires, and the rules vary with the concessionaires, but at most campgrounds, the campsites are limited to six–eight people and two camping units. Tents must be on pads if provided. Dogs must be leashed in the campground, and leashed or under voice command on trails. Campfires are limited to fire rings. Hammocks and laundry lines cannot be hung from trees. Dumpsters are frequently provided. Rules are enforced and facilities are cleaned by camp hosts at busy campgrounds. More remote campgrounds are occasionally cleaned and maintained by rangers and camp hosts.

Reserveable campgrounds are on the national reservation system. Reservations are accepted at 877/444-6777 and www.reserveamerica.com.

State Parks and Forests

In Colorado, there are 33 state parks with campgrounds. The majority of these parks have reservoirs, and the campgrounds are focused around the lakes. State park campgrounds usually have running water and frequently have electrical or full hookups. Laundry facilities and showers are also common. Camping fees include six people and one–two camping units. Pets must be leashed. Beverages that contain more than 3.2 percent alcohol are not allowed. Quiet hours are enforced by camp hosts.

Reserveable campgrounds are on a national reservation system. Reservations are accepted at 800/678-2267 and www.parks.state.co.us.

Colorado State Parks hire volunteer campground hosts. Hosts usually receive a free campsite and utilities in exchange for greeting campers, helping them check in, and keeping the facilities clean. To find out more, call 303/866-3437 or email parks.volunteer@state.co.us.

GEAR SELECTION AND MAINTENANCE

Tents

Purchasing the right tent requires planning, research, a little bit of introspection, and a whole lot of footwork. Before you look at tents, ask yourself the following questions:

What time of year and at what altitude will I be camping? A tent should keep you warm in the winter, cool in the summer, and dry year-round. Sporting goods companies now make summer, three-season, and four-season tents, and prices increase dramatically with the number of seasons covered. In my opinion, three-season tents offer the best compromise between price and adaptability.

How many people will use this tent? This is a key question. If you are young and childless, a two-person tent will often do the trick. If you are camping with the Brady Bunch, there are now tents with multiple rooms, windows, shelves, and even doggie doors. Every tent has a suggested capacity, but don't buy a tent without first setting it up and getting inside. Some people are more claustrophobic than the model camper.

Will I be car camping or backpacking? It's all about weight. If you're backpacking, you should buy the lightest tent you can afford. Car camping tents are heavier and slower to

With the world going high-tech, **tents** of today vary greatly in complexity, size, price, and put-up time. And they wouldn't be fit for this new millennium without offering options such as moon roofs, rain flies, and tent wings. Be sure to buy the one that's right for your needs.

Keep It Wild: Camp with Care

- Choose an existing, legal site.
- Restrict activities to areas where vegetation is compacted or absent.
- Camp at least 75 steps (200 feet) from lakes, streams, and trails.
- Always choose sites that won't be damaged by your stay.
- Preserve the feeling of solitude by selecting camps that are out of view when possible.
- Don't dig trenches or build structures or furniture.

set up; they're also larger and less expensive. You can take a backpacking tent car camping, but you can't take a car camping tent into the backcountry. If you are traveling alone in the backcountry, just need a tent for emergencies, or like having your own space, consider purchasing a bivy, a one-person tent that's barely more than a sleeping bag sheath.

Is quick setup important? Backpacking tents have fewer poles, and many of them are freestanding (they don't need to be staked to stand upright). These set up much more quickly than car camping tents. If you are backpacking, tend to arrive at camp after dark, or need to pack up quickly in the morning, purchase a tent that's easy to set up.

How often and how long will I use this tent? A good tent can last a lifetime if it's regularly maintained and properly stored. If you plan on camping frequently, buy the best tent you can afford. If you only go out once or twice a year, save your money for the perfect sleeping bag.

Once you've answered these questions, head out to the sporting good stores. Tell the salesperson what you need and how much you want to spend and then set up and climb inside every tent that interests you. Ask about warranties and repair policies. Keep a list of your favorites. Look for end-of-season sales and Internet bargains. With a little patience, you can get your first-choice tent at a discount price.

Sleeping Bags and Pads

A sleeping bag doesn't produce heat; it can only trap the heat your body generates. The heat is retained in the air trapped in the bag's insulation. More loft equals more air and that equals more warmth. Sleeping bags are sold by temperature rating, size, and shape, and their prices are determined by type of construction and material. Unless you are doing winter camping or mountaineering, you'll want a general purpose sleeping bag that will keep you cool in summer and warm in fall. Three-season bags usually do the trick.

Temperature Rating: This is the lowest temperature at which the bag will keep you warm. Because there's no universal standard, it's determined by individual manufacturers. Therefore, temperature ratings are consistent within brands but not necessarily between brands, and to complicate the matter further, individuals have different sleeping temperatures (women usually sleep colder than men). As a rule of thumb, figure out the coldest temperature that you'll experience and then pick a bag that's rated 10 degrees colder than that. Zero degree bags are a safe bet for the summers and falls in the mountains, and on warm evenings you can always unzip them. Three-season bags are usually rated to 20 degrees.

Size and Shape: Most bags now come in regular and long lengths. Some companies are also making specific bags for women that

Colorado's Fourteeners

In Colorado, there are 54 "fourteeners," or peaks that rise above 14,000 feet. The majority of peaks have walk-up routes, but some require technical climbing or mountaineering skills. Peak-bagging has become a popular activity in Colorado, and there are numerous guides to the fourteeners. The Colorado Fourteeners Initiative is also a valuable source of information. The mission of this nonprofit organization is to protect and preserve the integrity of these peaks through stewardship and public education. The Fourteeners Initiative offers several volunteer opportunities to help preserve and protect these peaks, including field projects, trail maintenance, and the Adopt-A-Peak and Peak Steward programs. To get involved, call 303/278-7535 or visit them online at www.coloradofourteeners.org.

The following list groups the fourteeners by mountain range:

Front Range: Longs Peak, Torreys Peak, Grays Peak, Mount Evans, Mount Bierstadt, Pikes Peak.

Mosquito Range: Quandary Peak, Mount Democrat, Mount Lincoln, Mount Bross, Mount Sherman.

Sawatch Range: Mount of the Holy Cross, Mount Massive, Mount Elbert, La Plata Peak, Huron Peak, Missouri Mountain, Mount Belford, Mount Oxford, Mount Harvard, Mount Columbia, Mount Yale, Mount Princeton, Mount Antero, Mount Shavano, Tabeguache Mountain.

Sangre de Cristo Range: Kit Carson Peak, Crestone Peak, Crestone Needle, Humboldt Peak, Ellingwood Point, Little Bear Peak, Blanca Peak, Mount Lindsey, Culebra Peak.

Elk Mountains: Capitol Peak, Snowmass Mountain, North Maroon Peak, South Maroon Peak, Pyramid Peak, Castle Peak.

San Juan Mountains: Wetterhorn Peak, Uncompahgre Peak, Mount Sneffels, San Luis Peak, El Diente Peak, Mount Wilson, Wilson Peak, Handies Peak, Redcloud Peak, Sunshine Peak, Mount Eolus, Sunlight Peak, Windom Peak.

---

are cut to accommodate narrower shoulders, wider hips, and colder sleeping temperatures. Extra air in a bag is difficult to heat and adds extra weight, but a small bag can make you claustrophobic. Pick the smallest bag that you can comfortably sleep in. Bags come in three cuts: mummy, rectangular, and semirectangular. Mummy bags are the narrowest and most efficient. Rectangular bags have room for tossing and turning but are not very efficient, and semirectangular bags are a good compromise between efficiency and comfort.

Construction: A quality sleeping bag has a hood with a drawstring (you should be able to draw it tight and still breathe) and a draft collar. Humans lose 50 percent of body heat through the head, so these features greatly increase the efficiency of a bag. You should

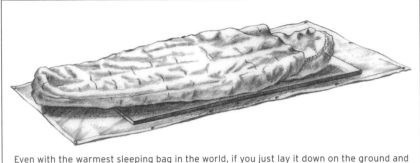

Even with the warmest sleeping bag in the world, if you just lay it down on the ground and try to sleep, you will likely get as cold as a winter cucumber. That is because the cold ground will suck the warmth right out of your body. The solution? A sleeping pad.

be able to wear a hat inside the hood. A good bag also has a comfortable foot box, a sturdy zipper with an insulated flap, and a lifetime warranty. Sleeping bags are built with baffling to keep the insulation material evenly distributed. Baffles should run horizontally across the body. Box, slant, and V-tube baffles have the best heat retention properties.

Materials: A sleeping bag consists of a shell and fill material. The shell is usually a synthetic material with a water-repellent finish. Waterproof shells are not recommended because they trap moisture inside the bag. Fills are down or synthetic, and this can be the hardest decision to make when shopping for a bag. Down is more expensive, but it is hands-down superior for the insulation-to-weight ratio. If you are backpacking, go with down. If you are car camping, synthetic is an excellent alternative. It is bulkier and heavier than down, but it's also less expensive, more durable, and it stays warm when wet (down doesn't). Synthetic fills come in a variety of brand names.

Sleeping Pads: Sleeping pads are essential for car camping and backpacking. They provide cushioning and extra insulation, and with a converter kit, they can pull double duty as a camp chair. Sleeping pads come in two types: foam and self-inflating mattresses. Foam pads are lighter, more durable, and less expensive. Self-inflating pads are more expensive and

require more care, but they are a heck of a lot more comfortable. Both types come in a variety of sizes and thicknesses designed for specific activities. As a backpacker, I don't mind carrying the extra weight of a full-length pad to keep my feet warm, but I won't go thicker than an inch. On the other hand, when I'm car camping I appreciate having the thickest self-inflating air mattress that I can afford.

Food and Cooking Gear

As soon as I know where I'm going and how long I'll be there, I plan my meals. Nothing keeps me happier on and off the trail. Whether you're car camping or backpacking, planning goes a long way when you're in the woods. Dehydrated, prepackaged meals are a great choice for saving weight in the backcountry, but I usually stick to the less expensive alternatives (couscous and oatmeal, for example) and throw in a few fancy meals for variety. Whatever you're packing, there are a few equipment essentials: lightweight nesting pots, a metal pot grabber, plastic bowls, insulated mugs, a lighter, spoons, a knife, and a strainer so you can do the dishes without leaving behind bits of food. In the front country, I also like to have a coffeepot, frying pan, and a "sink."

And, of course, you need a camp stove. Cooking over a fire is difficult, time-consuming, and not very environmentally friendly. In

Keep It Wild: Travel Lightly

- Visit the backcountry in small groups.
- Always stay on designated trails below tree line.
- Don't cut across switchbacks.
- Follow animal trails or spread out with your group so that no new routes are created when traveling cross-country where no trails are available.
- Read your map and orient yourself with landmarks, a compass, and an altimeter. Avoid marking trails with rock cairns, tree scars, or ribbons.

the backcountry, it's absolutely unacceptable. Camp stoves come in a variety of styles and sizes, but they all fall into two categories:

Liquid Gas Stoves: This is a good choice for backpackers and avid campers. The blow-torchlike flame is wind resistant, they operate at all temperatures and altitudes, the fuel bottles are refillable, and the stoves are easy to repair. This type of stove requires attention and maintenance, though. The fuel bottle has to be pumped so it's pressurized, and the stove has to be cleaned regularly. It can also be difficult to simmer with liquid gas stoves. Most of these stoves require white gas, but there are international versions that will run on any flammable liquid. These are best for traveling to Third World countries.

Gas Canister Stoves: These stoves burn butane, isobutane, and blended fuel. They are easier to operate, lighter, and better at simmering, but they do not work in extreme cold, and the fuel canisters must be disposed of. In the U.S., the canisters are usually resealable so you can separate the stove from the canister before it's empty. Avoid nonresealable canisters because they are dangerous and inconvenient.

Keep in Mind: Windscreens and repair kits are extremely useful, as are carrying cases to keep the stove from gunking up everything else in your backpack. A stove should have an adjust-

able flame. Push-button stoves are extremely convenient, but you should always pack a lighter. Never, ever use a stove in a tent. Not only are tents extremely flammable, but they can fill up quickly with carbon monoxide.

Water Treatment

Developed campgrounds usually have safe drinking water. If you're heading into the backcountry, you'll need to treat the water. The easiest option is to boil the water, but this takes time and fuel. In case your stove breaks down, you should always have iodine tablets for backup. Tablets require a little patience and taste a little funny, but they are foolproof and easy to use. Pump filters are used by the majority of backpackers. Ceramic filters are reliable, long lasting, and easy to replace. Be sure to air out your filter between uses.

MOUNTAIN WEATHER

Mountain weather changes quickly and sometimes unpredictably and can be affected by altitude and temperature, exposure to sun and wind, and topography. Prevailing westerly winds deposit more snow and rain on the peaks and western slopes, while eastern slopes are much drier. This is called the rain shadow effect. High and low pressure systems move through in cycles of three to five days each.

Pioneer Weather Indicators

- Cows lying in the field are a sign of rain.
- Geese fly low before bad weather arrives.
- Fish bite before rain.
- Smoke stays near the ground before a storm.
- Cottonwoods show the bottom of their leaves before rain.
- Woodpeckers call before rain falls.
- Dew on the grass means it won't rain.
- Rings around the moon are a sign of coming rain.
- Spiders spin long webs on hot, dry days and short webs when bad weather is coming.

Weather Fronts

The weather changes as warm and cold fronts move through. Fronts generally move at 30–50 miles per hour.

Cold fronts are associated with high pressure systems. They contain heavy, dense air that pushes warm air upward ahead of it. In general, the arrival of a cold front brings strong winds, low temperatures, poor visibility, and heavy but brief precipitation, followed by fine weather with occasional showers and clear skies.

Warm fronts are associated with low pressure systems. They contain warm, light air compared to cold air, which they will overrun. Rising temperatures and continuous rain and snow indicate an approaching warm front. The front is followed by high clouds, intermittent showers, and poor visibility.

Reading the Weather

Storms Approaching: Cirrus clouds thicken from the south or west and become altostratus clouds. Several layers of clouds move in at various altitudes. Lenticular clouds become ragged. A change in wind direction accompanies a rapid temperature change.

Local Thunderstorms: Scattered cumulus clouds grow rapidly in the afternoon. Cumulus or cumulonimbus clouds approach in a line. Large cumulus clouds hang over a summit or ridgeline.

Strong Winds: Blowing snow on ridgelines or peaks. Ragged clouds moving rapidly. Lens-shaped clouds above or on the downwind side of peaks and ridgelines.

Good Weather: A cloudless sky and fog or haze at the valley bottom in the morning. Cumulus clouds appear in the afternoon but do not increase in size or number. Clear skies.

Classifying Clouds

Clouds are formed when water droplets condense in the air.

High clouds occur from 16,500–45,000 feet. They include cirrus, cirrostratus, and cirrocumulus. Cirrus clouds are high, thin clouds of ice crystals that are common in the Rocky Mountains.

Middle clouds occur from 6,500–25,000 feet. They include altocumulus, altostratus, and cumulonimbus clouds. Altostratus appear as a thick, gray sheet of clouds. They are common in the Rocky Mountains. When they thicken, rain or snow is approaching quickly.

Keep It Wild: Sanitation

- Keep restroom facilities clean. Tidy up messes you make when brushing your teeth, shaving, or using toiletries.

- Do not put any kind of garbage in vault toilets. Trash – such as plastic bags, sanitary napkins, and diapers – cannot be pumped and have to picked out, piece by piece, by some unfortunate soul.

- If showers are available, bathe quickly so others can use the facilities.

- Use biodegradable soap for washing dishes and cleaning up. Scatter dishwater after food particles have been removed.

- Scour your campsite for even the tiniest bit of trash and any other evidence of your stay. Pack out all the trash you can, even if it's not yours.

- Never litter. Never. Or you become the enemy of all others.

- If bathrooms are not available, deposit human waste in "cat holes" dug six to eight inches deep. Cover and disguise the cat hole when finished. Make sure this is done at least 75 paces (200 feet) away from any water source.

- Use toilet paper sparingly. When finished, carefully burn it in the cat hole, then bury it. If no appropriate burial locations are available, such as in popular wilderness camps above tree line in granite settings, then all human refuse should be double bagged and packed out.

Low clouds occur from the surface to 6,500 feet. They include stratus, nimbostratus, and stratocumulus clouds. Stratus are low, gray clouds that become fog close to the surface. When they rain, they're called nimbostratus.

Vertical clouds extend from 1,600 feet up. They include cumulus, towering cumulus, and cumulonimbus clouds, often called thunderheads. Cumulus form at the tops of rising air. When they grow rapidly, they become cumulonimbus, which are common in the summer and bring lightning, heavy rain, and high winds.

Orographic clouds are formed by the interaction of air flow and mountainous terrain. They include cap clouds, which "cap" mountain summits, and lenticular clouds. These lens-shaped clouds form when strong winds blow over rugged terrain. They form on the lee side of mountains and ridges and may by stacked in layers like pancakes.

Lightning Strikes

Colorado ranks 10th in the nation in lightning casualties, so it's a good idea to learn to protect yourself from this natural threat. Most strikes occur in the early afternoon in thunderstorm season and in open, unprotected areas. Hikers in the high country are especially prone to lightning strike.

To protect yourself, follow the 30/30 rule. If the time between the lightning flash and the thunder is less than 30 seconds, seek shelter. Don't resume activities for 30 minutes after the last thunder.

What's a safe location? Buildings designed for year-round use are the safest locations. Avoid open shelters. Once you're inside, avoid

Keep It Wild: Campfires

- Fire use can scar the backcountry. If a fire ring is not available, use a lightweight stove for cooking.
- Where fires are permitted, use existing fire rings away from large rocks or overhangs.
- Don't char rocks by building new fire rings.
- Gather sticks from the ground that are no longer than the diameter of your wrist.
- Don't snap branches of live, dead, or downed trees, which can cause personal injury and scar the natural setting.
- Put the fire "dead out" and make sure it's cold before departing. Remove all trash from the fire ring and sprinkle dirt over the site.
- Remember that some forest fires can be started by a campfire that appears to be out. Hot embers burning deep in the pit can cause tree roots to catch fire and burn underground. If you ever see smoke rising from the ground, seemingly from nowhere, dig down and put the fire out.

metal objects and using water. If there are no safe buildings, wait inside a car with a hardtop roof. Never take shelter under a tree. If you're in an open area, crouch on the balls of your feet, at least as far away from a tree as it is tall. Reduce your contact with the surface as much as possible. If you have an air mattress, crouch on that.

Forest Fires

Forest fires are a natural force in the ecosystem. Many plants can't reproduce without fire. At lower elevations, fires used to occur naturally every 20–30 years, consuming young trees and forest litter. Beginning in the early 1900s, widespread fire suppression altered these natural cycles. Now, unplanned fires can be devastating because they burn too hot and too quickly and are difficult to control. The Forest Service and the Bureau of Land Management work together to reduce fuels near human development and use prescribed burns in more remote areas.

What's Eating Our Trees?

Large swatches of red evergreens and gray trees indicate spruce beetle infestations. Fighting beetle epidemics is expensive and labor intensive. Preventive measures include cutting and peeling infested trees, placing pheromone capsules on healthy trees to fool the beetles into avoiding the trees, spraying insecticides, and thinning forests.

FIRST AID

Dehydration

Drink water! Your body requires at least 8–10 cups of water a day, more during hot weather. Drink before you're thirsty. If your urine is dark, you have a headache, or you're nauseous, you could be experiencing severe dehydration. Drink water and replace your body's electrolytes by drinking energy drinks or fruit juice.

Giardia

Giardia is a microscopic organism that causes

intestinal disorders. It is widespread in Colorado and occurs in mountain streams and lakes that otherwise look safe and taste good. Symptoms include diarrhea, gas, loss of appetite, stomach cramps, and bloating. They occur a few days to a few weeks after infection and should be treated by a doctor. To avoid *Giardia,* boil your water for at least a minute or use an approved water filter.

Altitude Sickness

Acute Mountain Sickness (AMS) is the result of reduced oxygen levels at altitudes above 7,000 feet. Anyone can get AMS, even the physically fit. Symptoms include headache, fatigue, shortness of breath, sleeplessness, dizziness, nausea, coughing, diarrhea, or constipation. These symptoms will disappear as your body adjusts. To avoid AMS, take it easy and avoid strenuous exercise when you're adjusting to high altitudes. Drink plenty of water, avoid alcohol, and take aspirin. If you have a heart condition, lung disease, or diabetes, consult your physician before traveling in the mountains. If symptoms are severe or if there are signs of confusion or loss of muscular condition, see a doctor immediately.

Hypothermia

Hypothermia is the mental and physical collapse that results from lowered body temperatures. It's caused by exposure to cold and enhanced by water and wind. Symptoms include shivering, slurred speech, forgetfulness, irrational behavior, clumsiness, drowsiness or exhaustion, and a lack of concern about discomfort. Usually companions will notice hypothermia before the victim does.

To prevent hypothermia, stay dry and out of the wind. Build a fire and drink hot fluids. Make camp while you still have energy. Always dress in layers and pack adequate clothing for mountain weather and wilderness survival.

If a companion is suffering from hypothermia, seek medical help immediately. Remove wet clothing and replace them with warm, dry clothes or blankets. Give the victim warm, sweet drinks, but avoid caffeine and alcohol. Encourage the victim to move arms and legs to create muscle heat, and if he or she can't do this, place warm bottles in the armpits, groin, and neck and head areas. Do not rub the victim's limbs or place him or her in warm water—this could stop the victim's heart.

Keep It Wild: Respect Other Users

Horseback riders have priority over hikers. Step to the downhill side of the trail and talk softly when encountering horseback riders.

Hikers and horseback riders have priority over mountain bike riders. When mountain bikers encounter other users, even on wide trails, they should pass at an extremely slow speed. On very narrow trails, they should dismount and get off to the side so hikers or horseback riders can pass without having their trip disrupted.

Mountain bikes are not permitted on most single-track trails and are prohibited in designated wilderness areas.

It's illegal for horseback riders to break off branches that may be in the path on wilderness trails.

Horseback riders on overnight trips are prohibited from camping in many areas and are usually required to keep stock animals in a specific area where they cannot do damage to the landscape.

Frostbite

Frostbite is the freezing of the deep layers of the skin. The skin becomes numb and hard and turns pale and waxy white. It usually affects the fingers, hands, toes, feet, ears, and nose. The victim should be moved to a warm, dry area, and wet or tight clothing should be removed. Place the affected area in a warm water bath and monitor the temperature. Warm the tissue slowly. Warming should take 25–40 minutes. Do not rub the tissue or pour water over it. The affected area may become puffy and blister as it warms. When normal feeling returns, dry and wrap the area and keep it warm. If it might become cold again, do not warm the area as this could lead to more severe tissue damage.

Colorado Tick Fever

Colorado Tick Fever is an acute viral illness characterized by fever, headache, and body aches, as well as lethargy and nausea. The disease is rarely life threatening, and there are no vaccines. Humans contract tick fever from Rocky Mountain wood ticks. Adult ticks emerge in late February or March and are abundant on south-facing brushy slopes. To avoid tick fever, perform regular tick checks in the mountains and avoid areas of high infestation in April, May, and June.

Camping Gear Checklist

The Essentials
__Backpack
__Bear bag or bear canister
__Camp soap
__Compass
__Fuel
__Headlamp
__Insulated mug
__Knife
__Maps
__Matches
__Pack towel
__Pillow
__Plastic bags
__Pots and pans
__Rain gear
__Sleeping bag
__Sleeping pad
__Spare batteries
__Sponge
__Stove
__Sunglasses
__Tent
__Toilet paper
__Utensils
__Warm hat
__Water containers
__Water filter

First-Aid Kit
__Antibacterial ointment
__Aspirin
__Band-Aids
__Burn ointment

__Duct tape
__Elastic bandage
__Gauze pads
__Insect repellent
__Moleskin
__Notebook and pencil
__Sanitary pads or tampons
__Sunscreen
__Tape
__Thermometer
__Tweezers

The Extras
__A good book
__Aluminum foil
__Binoculars
__Camera and film
__Camp chair or hammock
__Can opener
__Cards or chess
__Extra blankets
__Field guides
__Firewood
__Fishing gear
__Grill
__Journal
__Kitchen towels
__Lantern
__Plates and bowls
__Portable table
__Spatula and serving spoon
__Spices
__Swimsuit

WESTERN SLOPE NORTH

© SARAH RYAN

BEST CAMPGROUNDS

❰ Hiking
Trappers Lake-Shepherd's Rim, **page 53**
Cold Springs, **page 55**

❰ Lakeside
Dutch Hill, **page 39**
Pearl Lake State Park, **page 40**
Trappers Lake-Cutthroat, **page 54**
Bear Lake, **page 56**
White Owl, **page 59**

❰ Tent-Only
Echo Park, **page 42**

❰ Stunning Views
Echo Park, **page 42**

❰ Whitewater
Gates of Lodore, **page 37**
Deerlodge Park, **page 42**

The Western Slope North region encompasses a
biologically, geologically, and culturally diverse area that reaches from the
northwestern corner of the state (where Utah, Wyoming, and Colorado
meet) east to the Continental Divide and south to the Colorado River.

The western half of the region contains the colorful plateau country that constitutes about a fifth of the state and extends into Arizona
and Utah. Wide rivers cut rainbow-colored canyons into sandstones
and shales laid down by Mesozoic rivers and seas and the erosion of
the Rocky Mountains. This is desert land, dotted by mesas, buttes,
and badlands, where the piñon, juniper, and sage thrive under endless
blue skies.

The most important rivers are the Yampa and the Green, and they
meet in Dinosaur National Monument, at a place called Echo Park. Dinosaur fossils were discovered there in 1909, and the monument was
created in 1915, and expanded in 1938 to its present size of 225,256
acres. There are only 15 miles of trails in the monument, so most visitors view the canyons from the road or the rivers. Rafting down the
Green and the Yampa is a feather in every whitewater lover's hat, and
a trip back in time to 1869, when the John Wesley Powell expedition
surveyed the Green and Colorado Rivers. In the process, Powell and
his men gave colorful names to the dangerous rapids of the Green,
including Disaster Falls and Hells Half Mile.

Modern-day rafters can join a private or commercial group to try a
paddle at these rapids and witness firsthand the canyons' fascinating
geology and ecology. Car-bound campers can also get a small taste of
the canyons at the Gates of Lodore, Deerlodge Park, and Echo Park.
Visitors interested in paleontology will want to drive over to the Utah
side of the monument to visit the rock quarry, or continue on the Dinosaur Diamond, a scenic driving loop that connects Grand Junction and
Dinosaur, Colorado, with Vernal, Green River, and Moab, Utah.

North of the monument, travelers will discover Browns Park, a
sparsely populated region that was once home to the infamous outlaw
Butch Cassidy. Cattle rustlers and petty thieves also lived there, such
as the three Irishmen who robbed a Wyoming saloon and then sat down
to enjoy their booty at the mouth of Irish Canyon. Irish Canyon runs

through the remnants of the Uinta Mountains, which contain Red Creek Quartzite. At 2.3 billion years old, it's Colorado's oldest rock.

Before its confluence with the Green, the Yampa River flows for about 260 miles from its headwaters in the Flat Tops, through Steamboat Springs, and across the Colorado Plateau. The Yampa is Colorado's most natural river. Except for a few small reservoirs near its headwaters, it flows unobstructed, providing habitat to endangered native species like the Colorado pikeminnow and the humpback chub. Yampa River State Park provides public access at 13 sites along a 172-mile stretch of the river.

Steamboat Springs is one of the best — and most laid-back — ski towns in Colorado. The home of "champagne powder," Steamboat's snowfalls are the envy of Colorado, but the fun doesn't stop in the summer. In addition to the hot springs, there is unparalleled hiking in Mount Zirkel Wilderness, a 250-square-mile wilderness area in the Park Range. Composed of Precambrian granite, schist, and gneiss, these mountains are noted for their glacial cirques, broad valleys, and alpine lakes.

Southwest of Steamboat Springs, the volcanic White River Plateau rises high above the Colorado Plateau, forming the Flat Top Mountains. Even by Colorado standards, the Flat Tops are idyllic, characterized by volcanic cliffs, alpine tundra, and countless lakes stocked with trout. Additionally, the flat topography makes backpacking a dream; there are 160 miles of trails in the wilderness area alone. The Flat Tops Scenic Byway is an 82-mile trip from Meeker to Yampa and a rewarding way to get a taste of the area. The byway passes nearby Trapper Lake, one of the most scenic and popular lakes — and campgrounds — in the area.

From the rainbow plateaus to the alpine lakes, the Western Slope merits a long visit, full of fishing, hiking, rafting, boating, and, of course, camping. Campgrounds range from remote BLM destinations to busy but enjoyable Forest Service sites and state park campgrounds with the works. In between all the driving and recreating, take time to meet your campground neighbors. Campers from all over the world travel to Dinosaur, Steamboat, and the Flat Tops, and they enjoy sharing their photos and swapping stories.

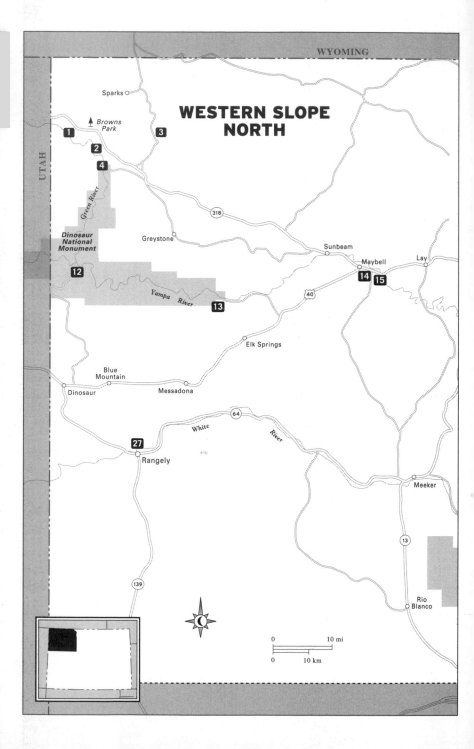

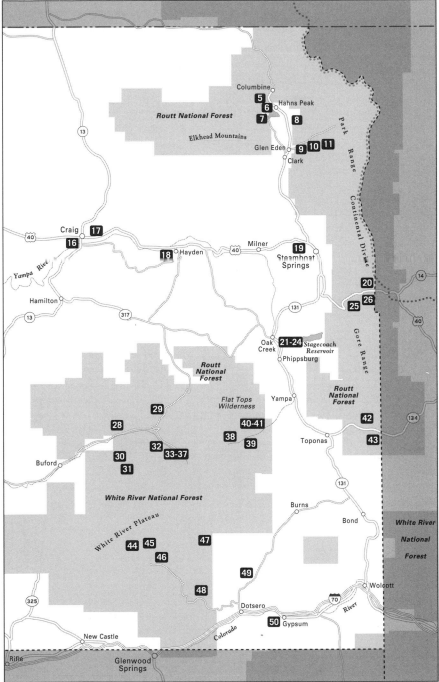

© AVALON TRAVEL PUBLISHING, INC.

1 SWINGING BRIDGE

Scenic rating: 8

in Browns Park National Wildlife Refuge

Browns Park, a remote valley that straddles the Colorado, Utah, and Wyoming borders, is miles from nowhere, but if you seek solitude, wildlife, or natural beauty, it is worth the drive. Browns Park was the wintering ground of the Utes and Shoshones because of its mild climate. In the 19th century, the park found favor first with trappers and traders and then with cattle ranchers. With the cattlemen came cattle rustlers. Browns Park soon had a reputation as an outlaw hideout. Most notably, Butch Cassidy and the Wild Bunch hid there between heists. Except for the creation of Dinosaur National Monument and Browns Park National Wildlife Refuge, not much has changed in the last hundred years. There is a small store (open seven days a week) at the town of Browns Park, but visitors should come prepared with lots of water and a full tank of gas.

The wildlife refuge was created in 1965 to provide marsh habitat along the Green River for migratory birds. Deer, antelope, coyote, and sage grouse also thrive there. The refuge is surrounded by BLM land and it adjoins Dinosaur National Monument. It's a dream destination for hunters, anglers, and birders who want to escape the crowds. Canoes and rafts can put in at the boat ramp. (Boaters who wish to continue into Dinosaur National Monument must secure permits months in advance.) There are also numerous hiking and mountain biking opportunities on the network of trails and 4WD roads, and endless opportunity for backcountry exploration on the BLM land. This campground is named for an old bridge that crosses the river. Cars are allowed on the bridge, but it takes a strong stomach to drive across.

Campsites, facilities: This primitive campground offers dispersed camping for tents and small RVs in a riparian zone. Stone fire rings are available at some sites. Vault toilets, a boat ramp, and a horse corral are available. Trash must be packed out. Leashed pets are permitted.

Reservations, fees: Reservations are not accepted, and camping is free. Open year-round.

Directions: From the intersection of Highways 40 and 318 (one mile west of Maybell), take Highway 318 north for 60 miles. Turn left on County Road 83, a well-maintained dirt road. The campground is on the north bank of the Green River in 2.8 miles. To reach the visitors center, continue on Highway 318 for 0.5 mile.

Contact: Browns Park National Wildlife Refuge, 970/365-3613, email: brownspark@fws.gov.

2 CROOK CAMP

Scenic rating: 8

in Browns Park National Wildlife Refuge

This campground's best features are its solitude and its proximity to the Green River, which is wide and wild at this stage on its journey to the Colorado River. In late spring and early summer, the river is flooded with runoff and spring rains. (It can be muddy, too, and therefore not much good for fishing. Conditions vary. Call the National Wildlife Refuge office for an update.) Occasionally, boaters traveling into Dinosaur National Monument will pass by, and in the fall, hunters arrive to look for deer and elk in the surrounding BLM lands. Otherwise, there is almost no traffic in this remote valley, which feels more like Wyoming or New Mexico than Colorado. (For more information on Browns Park, see the Swinging Bridge listing in this chapter.)

Campsites, facilities: This primitive campground has dispersed camping for tents and small RVs in a riparian zone. Stone fire rings are available at some sites. Vault toilets and a boat ramp are available. Trash must be packed out. Leashed pets are permitted.

Reservations, fees: Reservations are not accepted, and camping is free. Open year-round.

Directions: From the intersection of Highways 40 and 318 (one mile west of Maybell), take Highway 318 north for 52 miles. Turn left at the Browns Park National Wildlife Refuge, an unmarked dirt road. In 1.0 mile, turn right at the fork. The campground is on the left in 0.5 mile. To reach the visitors center, continue on Highway 318 for 8.5 miles.

Contact: Browns Park National Wildlife Refuge, 970/365-3613, email: brownspark@fws.gov.

3 IRISH CANYON

Scenic rating: 7

in Browns Park

Located in Browns Park, a remote valley with a Wild West history, Irish Canyon is a unique geological feature. Cold Spring Mountain juts 2,500 feet above the valley floor. The entrance to Irish Canyon is at the east end of the mountain, and approaching it feels like stepping back in time. The sensation is fitting—the colorful canyon consists of remnants of the ancient Uinta Mountains, including Red Creek Quartzite, which is the oldest rock in Colorado at 2.3 billion years. The canyon receives special environmental protection because of its geology as well its ecological and archaeological significance. Rare plants such as the Utah juniper-piñon and curl-leaf mountain mahogany grow there, and Native American rock art dating back to A.D. 400–1100 has been found in the canyon. More recently, this area was home to cattle ranchers and outlaws. The canyon is named for three Irishmen who robbed a Rock Springs, Wyoming, saloon and stopped at the entrance of the canyon to consume their booty. It is still a convenient shortcut to Wyoming.

Visitors to this campground are rare. Except for hunting season, you will likely have the haunting scenery to yourself. Nearby attractions include the Gates of Lodore in Dinosaur National Monument and wildlife viewing in Browns Park National Wildlife Refuge. In the tiny town of Browns Park, there is a small convenience store/gas station with a hilarious collection of "canned goods." Prices are high, though, and campers should come prepared with plenty of water and a full tank of gas. The campground is a gravel loop with numerous junipers, piñons, and wildflowers. All of the sites are equally appealing.

Campsites, facilities: There are six sites for tents, but it is possible to park RVs up to 25 feet next to most of the sites. Picnic tables, fire rings, grills, and vault toilets are provided. Trash must be packed out. Pets are permitted.

Reservations, fees: Reservations are not accepted, and there is no camping fee. Open year-round.

Directions: From the intersection of Highways 40 and 318 (one mile west of Maybell), take Highway 318 north for 42 miles. Turn north on County Road 10N. The campground is in 8.3 miles on the south side of the canyon.

Contact: Bureau of Land Management, 303/239-3600, www.blm.gov.

4 GATES OF LODORE

Scenic rating: 10

in Dinosaur National Monument

BEST (

The Gates of Lodore sounds and looks like a place out of *Lord of the Rings*. At this campground, the Green River leaves the high desert and enters the red rock Canyon of Lodore, named by a member of John Wesley Powell's 1869 expedition. The Gates are at the north end of Dinosaur National Monument, in the remote valley of Browns Park where it is easy to feel like you're camping at the end of the world. Kayaking and rafting groups on the

Green River make up most of the traffic at this campground. Watching them pack and repack as they prepare for the Class IV rapids ahead makes for an entertaining morning. (Permits are required for boating the canyon.) There is also 1.5-mile hike to the top of the canyon, with vistas of the canyonlands below and good wildlife-watching. Watch for bighorn sheep on north-facing canyon walls.

The campground parallels the river. Sites 11–20 are on the riverbank, and sites 1–9 are in the adjacent meadow. Sites 4–9, 19, and 20 are shaded by large cottonwood trees. When it rains, the dirt turns into mud, so avoid the barest tent sites.

Campsites, facilities: There are 17 sites for tents and RVs up to 35 feet. There are no hookups. Picnic tables, fire rings, and grills are provided. Vault toilets, drinking water, and a boat ramp are available. Trash must be packed out. Leashed pets are permitted in the campground and on the road but are not allowed in the river, on trails, or in the backcountry.

Reservations, fees: Reservations are not accepted. The fee is $8 per night. Golden Age and Golden Access Passports are accepted. Cash or check only. Open year-round, but in the winter, the drinking water is turned off and camping is free.

Directions: From the intersection of Highways 40 and 318 (one mile west of Maybell), take Highway 318 north for 40.5 miles. Turn left on County Road 34. Travel west on this dirt road for 7.5 miles to the campground entrance.

Contact: Dinosaur National Monument, 970/374-3000, www.nps.gov/dino.

5 HAHNS PEAK LAKE
🏃 🚴 🏊 🛶 🚗 🐕 ♿ 🚐 ⛰

Scenic rating: 7

north of Steamboat Springs

The Hahns Peak Lake campground is a smaller, quieter destination than the busy camp-grounds at Steamboat Lake State Park. The narrow lake sits between Nipple Peak to the north and Hahns Peak to the east. Mountain bikers enjoy the Nipple Peak Loop, a combination of forest service roads and trails. Hikers can climb Nipple Peak or stick to the West Side Trail along the lake. The campground contains two large loops in a lodgepole pine forest at the north end of the lake. The sites are about 100 feet apart and have ample room for big families to spread out. The first loop (sites 1–11) is closer to the lake, but the second loop seems to be more popular.

Campsites, facilities: There are 25 sites for tents and RVs up to 40 feet. There are no hookups. Sites 1–5, 7, 10, and 11 are pull-through. Picnic tables, grills, and fire rings are provided. Vault toilets are available. The facilities are wheelchair accessible. Leashed pets are permitted.

Reservations, fees: Reservations are not accepted. The fee is $10 per night. Golden Age and Golden Access Passports are accepted. Cash or check only. Open early June–mid-October.

Directions: From Steamboat Springs, take County Road 129 north for 28.3 miles. Turn left on Forest Route 486. The campground is in 2.5 miles.

Contact: Routt National Forest, Hahns Peak District, 970/879-1870, www.fs.fed.us/r2/mbr/.

6 SUNRISE VISTA
🏃 🚴 🏊 🛶 🚗 🐕 🚐 ⛰

Scenic rating: 8

in Steamboat Lake State Park

Steamboat Lake is a 1,055-acre reservoir at the base of Hahn's Peak in the heart of Routt National Forest. The surrounding mountains were the traditional hunting grounds of the Utes until 1881, when growing pressure from white settlers secured the long-sought exile of the Utes from Colorado to a reservation in eastern Utah. With the original residents gone, this area opened up to a flood of mining and ranching, and it still retains much of that early flavor. The Elk River valley to the south remains ranching land and will stay that way thanks to progressive landholders and conservation easements.

Steamboat Lake has a party reputation on weekends, but that shouldn't deter anglers, hikers, or mountain bikers. About half of the lake is restricted to wakeless boating; the other half is open to water sports of all kinds. In the quieter coves, and in the creeks that feed the lake, anglers will find cutthroat and rainbow trout. During the summer, hikers can enjoy meadows full of wildflowers, including harebell, mule's ear, lupine, and columbine; hardier souls can climb Hahn's Peak or Nipple Peak, or drive to trailheads that climb to the Continental Divide. Be prepared for inclement weather. This area receives vast quantities of precipitation, especially snow. (In the winter, there are 15 km of groomed trails around the lake. The campground is closed, but cabins and yurts are available for rent.) Sunrise Vista is the larger of the two campgrounds. All of the sites are pleasantly wooded except for the Arnica loop (1–50), which offers the least amount of privacy. The Yarrow loop (97–113) is closest to the water.

Campsites, facilities: There are 113 sites for tents and RVs up to 55 feet. The Larkspur, Lupine, and Yarrow loops (sites 77–113) have electrical hookups. Picnic tables, fire rings, grills, and tent pads are provided. Restrooms with flush toilets, vault toilets, and drinking water are available. The Dutch Hill campground and marina can be reached by a quarter-mile foot trail. Campers can use the showers, laundry facilities, and dump stations at Dutch Hill. At the marina, a convenience store, propane gas, vending machines, pay phones, and a boat ramp are available. Leashed pets are permitted.

Reservations, fees: Reservations are accepted (and recommended) at 800/678-2267 and www.parks.state.co.us. The fee is $12 per night for sites without hookups and $18 per night for sites with hookups. There is an additional $8 reservation fee. Campers must also purchase a Daily Parks Pass ($5) or an Annual Parks Pass ($55). The Aspen Leaf Annual Pass is accepted. Open Memorial Day–Labor Day.

Directions: From Steamboat Springs, drive north on County Road 129 for about 25 miles. One mile after the visitors center, turn left onto County Road 62. The entrance to Sunrise Vista is on the left in 0.4 mile.

Contact: Steamboat Lake State Park, 970/879-3922, email: steamboat.lake@state.co.us.

7 DUTCH HILL

Scenic rating: 9

in Steamboat Lake State Park

BEST (

Steamboat Lake attracts hikers, mountain bikers, anglers, water sports enthusiasts, wildlife lovers, and travelers who are ready to put up their feet and enjoy the view. A normal day at Steamboat Lake includes a hike up Hahn's Peak, a dip in the lake, and fishing for rainbow trout. Parents and kids will enjoy the interpretive programs at the visitors center and the five miles of easy trails surrounding the lake. Dutch Hill is the smaller of the two campgrounds at Steamboat Lake and the most attractive for tent campers. The Bridge Island loop (sites 166–200) is surrounded by water and offers breathtaking views of Hahns Peak and the Park Range. Sites 181–200 are walk-in sites. The Wheeler loop (sites 116–155) is very popular with RVers because of the electrical hookups and the mature trees. Sites 116–122 offer less privacy than any of the other sites in this loop.

Campsites, facilities: There are 44 sites for tents and RVs up to 55 feet, in addition to 19 hike-in tent sites and 10 cabins. The Wheeler loop (sites 116–155) has electrical hookups. Site 135 is wheelchair accessible. Picnic tables, fire rings, grills, and tent pads are provided. Restrooms with flush toilets and showers, vault toilets, drinking water, dump stations, laundry facilities, and a playground are available. A convenience store, propane gas, vending machines, pay phones, and a boat ramp are available at the marina. Leashed pets are permitted.

Reservations, fees: Reservations are accepted (and recommended) at 800/678-2267 and www.parks.state.co.us. The fee is $12 per night for sites without hookups and $18 per night for sites with hookups. There is an additional $8 reservation fee. Campers must also purchase a Daily Parks Pass ($5) or an Annual Parks Pass ($55). The Aspen Leaf Annual Pass is accepted. Open Memorial Day–Labor Day.

Directions: From Steamboat Springs, drive north on County Road 129 for about 25 miles. One mile after the visitors center, turn left onto County Road 62. The entrance to Dutch Hill is on the left in one mile.

Contact: Steamboat Lake State Park, 970/879-3922, email: steamboat.lake@state.co.us.

8 PEARL LAKE STATE PARK
🚶 🚵 🛶 ⛺ 🐕 ♿ 🚐 ⛺

Scenic rating: 10

north of Steamboat Springs

BEST (

Pearl Lake is a gem in the state park system. Tucked into a narrow north-south valley at the base of Farwell Mountain, this campground offers scenery, seclusion, and first-rate fishing. On an early summer morning, you might wake up to tendrils of mist curling over the lake, a dusting of snow on the ridgelines, and the sounds of 18-inch trout leaping out of the water. Pearl Lake is managed in conjunction with Steamboat Lake to the north, but it is much smaller and attracts a family crowd. There are two loops. The lower loop (sites 24–38) is lakeside, so these sites are most popular, but there is not a bad site in the park. The dense pine forest shelters every site, and the upper lollipop is located on a gentle hill

that is just 200 yards from the lake. Early in the season, the upper sites are preferable during wet weather. At the south end of the lake, there is a boat ramp and two short hiking trails. Only wakeless boating is allowed, and anglers must use flies or lures and are restricted to two 18-inch trout per day. The campground is closed in the winter, but the yurts are available by reservation.

Campsites, facilities: There are 38 sites for tents and RVs up to 55 feet and two yurts available by reservation only. Many sites are pull-through, but there are no hookups. Site 35 and Yurt 6 are wheelchair accessible. Picnic tables, fire rings, and grills are provided. Restrooms with flush toilets, vault toilets, drinking water, a boat ramp, and wildlife-viewing deck are available. Dump stations, showers, a laundry room, and interpretive programs are available at nearby Steamboat Lake State Park. Leashed pets are permitted.

Reservations, fees: Reservations are accepted (and recommended on weekends) at 800/678-2267 and www.parks.state.co.us. The fee is $12–14 per night. The yurts sleep six and cost $60 per night. Campers must also purchase a Daily Parks Pass ($5) or an Annual Parks Pass ($55). The Aspen Leaf Annual Pass is accepted. Open Memorial Day–Labor Day.

Directions: From Steamboat Springs, go north on County Road 129 for 22.8 miles. Turn right on County Road 209. Follow the signs for two miles to the park entrance. In 0.3 mile the road forks. Take the left fork to the campground or the right fork to the boat ramp.

Contact: Pearl Lake State Park, 970/879-3922, email: steamboat.lake@state.co.us.

9 HINMAN PARK
🚶 🛶 ⛺ 🚐 ⛺

Scenic rating: 6

north of Steamboat Springs

From Hinman Park, hikers can explore the Mount Zirkel Wilderness, an area of rugged granite peaks and glacial lakes. These mountains were carved by glaciers that left U-shaped valleys and high cirques. The South Fork Trail begins near the campground and connects with the Elk Park Trail. This trail crosses three drainages and is the best way to explore the lower elevations of the wilderness. Anglers will enjoy fishing on the Elk River, which the Forest Service has proposed for Wild and Scenic designation. The campground is in a pine forest beside a meadow. Sites 1, 3, and 5 border the meadow. Sites 9, 10, and 12 are on a steep hill that is not ideal for tent camping.

Campsites, facilities: There are 13 sites for tents and RVs up to 22 feet. There are no hookups. Sites 1 and 7 are pull-through. Picnic tables, grills, and fire rings are provided. Vault toilets and drinking water are available. Leashed pets are permitted.

Reservations, fees: Reservations are not accepted. The fee is $12 per night. Golden Age and Golden Access Passports are accepted. Cash or check only. Open early June–mid-October.

Directions: From Steamboat Springs, take County Road 129 north for 18 miles. Turn right on County Road 64/Forest Route 400. In 5.5 miles, turn right on Forest Route 440. The campground is on the right in 0.6 mile.

Contact: Routt National Forest, Hahns Peak District, 970/879-1870, www.fs.fed.us/r2/mbr/.

10 HINMAN PARK DISPERSED

Scenic rating: 8

north of Steamboat Springs

Hinman Park is a little valley hemmed in by the Elk River on one side and rocky outcroppings on the other. The vegetation is mostly sagebrush with evergreens along the river and some small aspen groves near the outcroppings. The north end of this valley has tantalizing views of the Park Range in the Mount Zirkel Wilderness. There are two pull offs that lead to campsites in the trees near the river. Hikers and bikers can explore the Hinman Creek Trail. Hikers who wish to explore the wilderness area can take the South Fork Trail (near the Hinman Park campground) to the Elk Park Trail, or drive up the road to the Slavonia trailhead. The Elk River has good but challenging fly-fishing.

Campsites, facilities: This is primitive dispersed camping. There are no facilities. Leashed pets are permitted.

Reservations, fees: Reservations are not accepted, and there is no fee for camping. Open mid-June–early November.

Directions: From Steamboat Springs, take County Road 129 north for 18 miles. Turn right on County Road 64/Forest Route 400. Dispersed camping begins in six miles.

Contact: Routt National Forest, Hahns Peak District, 970/879-1870, www.fs.fed.us/r2/mbr/.

11 SEEDHOUSE

Scenic rating: 7

north of Steamboat Springs

Located in the Elk River valley on the west side of the Park Range, the Seedhouse campground is popular because of its proximity to the Slavonia trailhead, the most heavily used trailhead in the Mount Zirkel Wilderness. Seedhouse is also adjacent to the Wyoming Trail, a 48-mile route from the Summit Lake campground (near Steamboat Springs) into the Medicine Bow Mountains in Wyoming. Anglers can attempt fly-fishing on the productive Elk River. The campground is a sprawling loop in a spruce-fir forest scattered with rocks and boulders left behind by the same glacial activity that carved this valley and the high cirques that are the main attraction of the Park Range. The sites are about 30 feet apart. Sites

14 and 15 overlook the Middle Fork of the Elk River.

Campsites, facilities: There are 24 sites for tents and RVs up to 25 feet. There are no hookups. Sites 5, 10, 13, 17, and 24 are pull-through. Picnic tables, grills, and fire rings are provided. Site 1 has an extra large picnic table. Vault toilets and drinking water are available. Leashed pets are permitted.

Reservations, fees: Reservations are not accepted. The fee is $12 per night. Golden Age and Golden Access Passports are accepted. Cash or check only. Open mid-June–late October.

Directions: From Steamboat Springs, take County Road 129 north for 18 miles. Turn right on County Road 64/Forest Route 400. In 8.5 miles, turn right into the campground.

Contact: Routt National Forest, Hahns Peak District, 970/879-1870, www.fs.fed.us/r2/mbr/.

12 ECHO PARK

Scenic rating: 10

in Dinosaur National Monument

BEST (

Dinosaur National Monument is a 210,000-acre classroom on the history of the earth. There are 23 exposed rock formations in the monument. The most notable, the Morrison Formation, is a treasure trove of plant and animal fossils. In 1909, paleontologist Earl Douglass discovered the dinosaur quarry which most park visitors come to see, but if you leave after just visiting the quarry, you have missed the best of the park. The auto tour from the visitors center to Harpers Corner features colorful canyons and stunning views. The tour takes four hours round-trip, but campers at Echo Park can turn it into a two-day (or more) adventure. Echo Park is located at the confluence of the Green and Yampa Rivers, in the shadow of the impressive Steamboat Rock. In the 1950s, conservation groups defeated a dam proposal at this loca-

tion. Today, the Yampa is Colorado's most naturally flowing river, with only a few small reservoirs near its headwaters. While enjoying the beautiful scenery at this campground, you can also expect to see (and camp with) kayakers and rafting groups traveling downriver toward Class IV rapids.

Campsites, facilities: There are 22 sites for tents (four are walk-in) and one group site. Picnic tables, fire rings, and grills are provided. Vault toilets, drinking water, and a boat ramp are available. Trash must be packed out. Leashed pets are permitted in the campground and on the road but are not allowed in the river, on trails, or in the backcountry.

Reservations, fees: Reservations are not accepted. The fee is $8 per night. The group site costs $15 for 8–20 people. Golden Age and Golden Access Passports are accepted. Cash only. Open year-round, but the road is impassable when wet and most of the winter. Call the park headquarters for travel conditions.

Directions: From Dinosaur, drive east on U.S. Highway 40 for two miles. Before the visitors center, turn north on Harpers Corner Drive. In 25 miles, turn right on Echo Park Road. In eight miles, bear left at the fork. Four-wheel-drive and high-clearance vehicles are recommended for this road.

Contact: Dinosaur National Monument, 970/374-3000, www.nps.gov/dino.

13 DEERLODGE PARK

Scenic rating: 10

in Dinosaur National Monument

BEST (

Deerlodge Park is located at the eastern end of Dinosaur National Monument, in the scenic valley of the Yampa River. This campground is mainly used by commercial outfitters and private groups setting out on rafting trips. Consequently, its heaviest use occurs during peak flows, usually in late May and early June. Backcountry hikers may also use this location as a jumping-off point for exploring the park. Permits are required for boating and back-country camping. The campground is very primitive and unpleasant if it's been raining. It can get quite muddy, and only site 7 has gravel to reduce the problem. Sites 1, 3, and 5 are right next to the road. (For more information on Dinosaur National Monument, see the Echo Park listing in this chapter.)

Campsites, facilities: There are seven walk-in sites in the riparian zone. RVs up to 35 feet can park near the camping area, but there are no hookups. Picnic tables, fire rings, and grills are provided at some sites. Vault toilets, drinking water, and a boat ramp are available. Trash must be packed out. Leashed pets are permitted in the campground and on the road but are not allowed in the river, on trails, or in the backcountry.

Reservations, fees: Reservations are not accepted. The fee is $8 per night. Golden Age and Golden Access Passports are accepted. Cash only. Open year-round, but in the winter, the drinking water is turned off and camping is free.

Directions: From Maybell, drive west on U.S. Highway 40 for 17 miles. Drive north on Twelvemile Gulch Road. The campground entrance is on the right in 12.2 miles.

Contact: Dinosaur National Monument, 970/374-3000, www.nps.gov/dino.

14 MAYBELL PARK
🐕 🚐 ⛺

Scenic rating: 1

in downtown Maybell

This campground is in the city park in a sleepy cow town. It is a large grassy square with a small camper services building. The campsites are laid out around the perimeter of the square, and they are all very close to the road. It's more suitable for RVs; there is no privacy for tent campers. There is not much to see or do in Maybell, but Dinosaur National Monument is 40 miles to the west, and Routt National Forest is to the east. This campground is a possible stopover if you just can't keep driving.

Campsites, facilities: There are 15 tent sites and 15 sites with electrical hookups for RVs of any length. Picnic tables and grills are provided. Restrooms with flush toilets and showers, drinking water, and a dump station are available. Leashed pets are permitted.

Reservations, fees: Reservations are not accepted. The tent fee is $10. Sites with electricity cost $15. There is an additional fee of $2 each for showers and using the dump station. Cash only. Open Memorial Day–Labor Day.

Directions: From Craig, take Highway 40 west for 30 miles to the little town of Maybell. The campground is in the town park on the north side of the highway.

Contact: Lorena Shaffer, 970/272-3021.

15 MAYBELL BRIDGE
🏊 🚣 🐕 🚐 ⛺

Scenic rating: 3

in Yampa River State Park

Yampa River State Park encompasses a visitors center and campground near Hayden, as well as 13 public access sites along a 172-mile stretch of the Yampa River. Maybell Bridge is a primitive campground mainly used for river access. It's also popular with hunters. The Moffat County–Routt County elk herds constitute one-third of Colorado's elk population. Craig (pop. 5,000) has 500 hotel rooms—and every one of those is booked during hunting season. For hunters without reservations, camping is the most reasonable option. Maybell Bridge is not scenic.

Campsites, facilities: There are seven sites for tents and RVs up to 30 feet, and three sites for tents only. Sites 5–8 have the best pull-ins for RVs. Picnic tables, grills, and tent pads are provided. Vault toilets and a boat ramp are available. Campers can use the shower and laundry facilities at the visitors center. Trash must be packed out. Leashed pets are permitted.

Reservations, fees: Reservations are not accepted. The fee is $7 per night. Campers must also purchase a Daily Parks Pass ($5) or an Annual Parks Pass ($55). Annual Parks Passes can be purchased at the visitors center near Hayden. The Aspen Leaf Annual Pass is accepted. Open year-round, weather permitting. Call ahead for road conditions.

Directions: From the intersection of Highways 40 and 13 in Craig, drive west on U.S. Highway 40 for 26.4 miles. Turn left before the bridge across the Yampa, at the Wildlife Viewing Area sign.

Contact: Yampa River State Park, 970/276-2061, email: yampa.river@state.co.us.

16 SOUTH BEACH

Scenic rating: 4

in Yampa River State Park

Yampa River State Park encompasses a visitors center and campground near Hayden, as well as 13 public access sites along a 172-mile stretch of the Yampa River. South Beach is a primitive campground mainly used for river access. A popular 33-mile float trip through Little Yampa Canyon begins here and ends at the Duffy Mountain take-out. The campground is located on a peninsula in the floodplain, next to a pump station. Overhead power lines cross the river about a hundred feet away. The surrounding red hills and sagebrush are pretty, but this campground is no beauty. There are plans for expansion in 2007.

Campsites, facilities: There are three sites for tents only. Picnic tables, grills, and vault toilets are provided. Campers can use the shower and laundry facilities at the visitors center. Trash must be packed out. Leashed pets are permitted.

Reservations, fees: Reservations are not accepted. The fee is $7 per night. Campers must also purchase a Daily Parks Pass ($5) or an Annual Parks Pass ($55). Annual Parks Passes can be purchased at the visitors center near Hayden. The Aspen Leaf Annual Pass is accepted. Open year-round, weather permitting. Call ahead for road conditions.

Directions: From Craig, drive south on Highway 13 for 3.1 miles. After crossing the Yampa, turn right at the wide pull off and the South Beach Public Access sign.

Contact: Yampa River State Park, 970/276-2061, email: yampa.river@state.co.us.

17 CRAIG KOA

Scenic rating: 3

in Craig

This KOA caters to hunters and road-weary families. Sandwiched between the Yampa River and the highway and railroad tracks, the scenery isn't appealing, but the facilities are excellent and the location is a great base camp for hunting in the Elkhead Mountains. The best way to see the area is the Black Mountain Auto Tour, a 100-mile self-guided trip into Routt National Forest. The tour features the largest elk herd in the state, fishing opportunities on Freeman Reservoir and mountain streams, short hiking trails to Black Mountain and Slater Falls, and panoramas of the Yampa Valley. (For more information, contact the Craig Chamber of Commerce at 970/824-5689.) Families will also enjoy the drive-in movie theater located nearby on U.S. Highway 40. The campground consists of several loops for RVs and grassy areas along the perimeter for tents. Tent sites A–I are located in a loop that is separated from the RV area and has shade trees. These sites offer the most privacy for tent campers.

Campsites, facilities: There are 92 sites with full hookups for RVs of any length and 15 tent-only sites. Picnic tables, grills, and tent pads are provided. Restrooms with flush toilets and showers, vault toilets, drinking water, dump stations, laundry facilities, a pool, hot tub, playground, and propane gas are available. There is also a gift store, horseshoe pits, and pet walk. Leashed pets are permitted.

Reservations, fees: Reservations are accepted at 800/562-5095. The tent fee is $23–27 per night for two people. The RV fee is $31 per night for two people. Each additional person over five years old costs $4 per night. The KOA Valu Kard is accepted. Open year-round.

Directions: From the intersection of Highways 40 and 13 in Craig, drive east on U.S. Highway 40 for two miles. The campground is on the south side of the road.

Contact: Craig KOA, 970/824-5105, www .koa.com.

18 YAMPA RIVER STATE PARK HEADQUARTERS

🚶 🚴 🎣 ⛵ 🏇 🛶 ♿ 🚐 ⛰

Scenic rating: 4

west of Steamboat Springs

Yampa River State Park encompasses a visitors center and campground near Hayden, as well as 13 public access sites along a 172-mile stretch of the Yampa River. The main campground at the visitors center makes a good base camp for exploring the Elkhead Mountains to the north, or a nice stopover between Dinosaur National Monument and Steamboat Springs. Hunters, anglers, and families enjoy this well-designed facility, which makes the best of its location (between the highway and the Yampa River) with a 1.75-mile nature trail and sheltering groves of cottonwood, willow, and Gambel's oak. Despite its proximity to the highway, the campground is quiet and feels almost rural. Summer interpretive programs feature local talent such as storytellers and musicians. The friendly rangers can offer advice on fishing and floating the Yampa. There is no put-in or take-out at this location, but a popular 33-mile float

trip through Little Yampa Canyon begins at the South Beach access site, which is 25 miles west on U.S. Highway 40. Another excellent day trip for anglers and wildlife lovers is California Park, located about 20 miles north in Routt National Forest. The 8,000-acre park has elk herds and trout streams, but it is closed to motor traffic May 15–July 1 to protect Colorado's largest population of Greater Sandhill Cranes. The campground is a large loop with little shade. Site 29, which sits beneath a giant cottonwood, is the only exception.

Campsites, facilities: There are 35 sites with electrical hookups for tents and RVs of any length, and 15 sites for tents only. Site 9 and all facilities are wheelchair accessible. Picnic tables, fire rings, grills, sun shelters, and tent pads are provided. Restrooms with flush toilets and showers, drinking water, dump stations, laundry facilities, a playground, and a group picnic area are available. Tepee rentals and group sites are also available. Leashed pets are permitted.

Reservations, fees: Reservations are accepted at 800/678-2267 and at www.parks.state.co.us. The fee is $12 per night for sites without hookups and $16 per night for sites with hookups. There is an additional $8 reservation fee. Campers must also purchase a Daily Parks Pass ($5) or an Annual Parks Pass ($55). The Aspen Leaf Annual Pass is accepted. Open May–November.

Directions: From Hayden, drive west on U.S. Highway 40 for three miles. The state park is on the south side of the road. The turnoff is clearly marked.

Contact: Yampa River State Park, 970/276-2061, email: yampa.river@state.co.us.

19 STEAMBOAT CAMPGROUND

🐕 🛶 🚐 ⛰

Scenic rating: 3

in Steamboat Springs

Steamboat Campground is the typical KOA-style RV park with a sprinkling of tent sites.

Campers won't stay here for the scenery, but they will stay here for the abundant recreation opportunities in the area. Steamboat (as it's usually called) is an outdoor lover's heaven, and the shopping ain't half bad either. There are public hot springs and a whitewater park in town, hiking and mountain biking trails in Routt National Forest, boating and fishing on Steamboat Lake and Pearl Lake—and that's just the summer. In the fall, hunters fill this campground, and in the winter, when the champagne powder starts flying, this could be the most affordable place to stay in town. If you don't have time to take it all in, at least ride the Silver Bullet Gondola up the ski mountain for vistas of the Continental Divide and the Yampa Valley.

Campsites, facilities: There are 100 sites for tents and RVs up to 70 feet and 36 sites for tents only. Full and partial hookups are available. Picnic tables, fire rings, and grills are provided. Restrooms with flush toilets and showers, drinking water, dump stations, a laundry room, a pool and hot tub, a playground, and propane gas are available. There is also a recreation room, miniature golf course, horseshoes, and a pet walk. Leashed pets are permitted.

Reservations, fees: Reservations are accepted at 888/451-2243. The tent fee is $24 per night for two people. The cost for RVs is $34–40 per night for two people. Each additional person costs $2.50 per night. Open year-round.

Directions: From downtown Steamboat Springs, drive west on U.S. Highway 40 for two miles. The campground is on the south side of the road, after the Snow Bowl Bowling Center.

Contact: Steamboat Campground, 970/879-0273, www.steamboatcampground.com.

20 DUMONT LAKE

🚶 ⛵ 🛶 🐕 🚐 ⛺

Scenic rating: 7

southeast of Steamboat Springs

Dumont Lake is the best campground on U.S. Highway 40 between Steamboat Springs and Rabbit Ears Pass. The campground is in a large meadow with abundant wildflowers. In the distance, the smaller peaks of the Park Range, including Walton Peak and Baker Mountain, are visible. Most sites are in the meadow. Sites 4, 11, 17, 14, 15, and 22 are screened by spruce and fir trees. Sites 8 and 9 have the best views. Hikers can walk or drive up Forest Route 311 to the Fish Creek Trail, which descends through subalpine meadows, past several lakes, to the popular Fish Creek Falls near Steamboat Springs. The campground is adjacent to a lake and a picnic area.

Campsites, facilities: There are 22 sites for tents and RVs up to 40 feet. There are no hookups. Sites 1, 2, 5, 7, 8, 16, and 19–21 are pull-through. Picnic tables, grills, and fire rings are provided. Vault toilets are available. Leashed pets are permitted.

Reservations, fees: Reservations are not accepted. The fee is $12 per night. Golden Age and Golden Access Passports are accepted. Cash or check only. Open late June–late October.

Directions: From Highway 131 in Steamboat Springs, take U.S. Highway 40 south for 16.3 miles. Turn left on Forest Route 315. The campground is on the left in 1.2 miles.

Contact: Routt National Forest, Hahns Peak District, 970/879-1870, www.fs.fed.us/r2/mbr/.

21 JUNCTION CITY

🚶 🚴 🏊 🛶 🚗 🐕 🚐 ⛺

Scenic rating: 6

in Stagecoach State Park

Stagecoach Reservoir is named for the stagecoaches that used to carry passengers and supplies over Yellow Jacket Pass, now County Road 14, between Oak Creek and Steamboat Springs. The reservoir is in a river valley green with native grasses, shrubs, and wildflowers. Woodchuck Hill and Green Ridge fill the horizon to the south, and there are glimpses of the Flat Tops to the west. The reservoir is three miles long and home to rainbow trout, as well as some brown and cutthroat. Most visitors come for the fishing and waterskiing. On the south shore, there's a five-mile hiking and biking trail, as well as fishing access and boat ramps. The one-mile Lakeside Trail on the north shore can be connected with the Elk Run Trail by walking on County Road 16 for a short distance. All of the campgrounds are on the north shore with excellent views of the lake, but traffic noise from Highway 14 is bothersome. Additionally, the campsites are surfaced with a gravel material that is practically impervious to tent stakes. If you don't have a mallet, you'll have to pitch your tent in the grass.

Junction City is adjacent to the wakeless boating area of the reservoir. The boat ramp and swim beach are a short walk away. The habitat is mostly sagebrush with a few planted trees. Sites 6–12, 16, 17, 19, and 20 are lakeside. Sites 9, 25, and 27 have a few shade trees.

Campsites, facilities: There are 27 sites for tents and RVs up to 35 feet. Electrical hookups are available. Sites 4, 16, 17, 19, 20, 22, 24, and 26 are pull-through. Picnic tables, fire rings, and grills are provided. Flush toilets, drinking water, a dump station, and picnic area are available. Campers can use the showers at the Pinnacle campground. A convenience store, boat rentals, boat ramp, and swim beach are available at the marina. Leashed pets are permitted.

Reservations, fees: Reservations are accepted at 800/678-2267 and www.parks.state.co.us. The fee is $18 per night. There is an additional $8 reservation fee. Campers must also purchase a Daily Parks Pass ($5) or an Annual Parks Pass ($55). The Aspen Leaf Annual Pass is accepted. Open mid-May–mid-October.

Directions: From Steamboat Springs, take U.S. Highway 40 south to Highway 131 south. In about six miles, turn left on County Road 14. The entrance station is in about five miles. Turn right 0.4 mile after the entrance station. In 0.3 mile, turn left into the campground.

Contact: Stagecoach State Park, 970/736-2436, email: stagecoach.park@state.co.us.

22 MCKINDLEY

Scenic rating: 6

in Stagecoach State Park

McKindley is the only tent campground at Stagecoach State Park. This small loop is on a hill overlooking the lake and the other campgrounds. The sites are just 10–20 feet apart, and the vegetation is mostly sagebrush, so there is no shade and very little privacy, but thanks to a small hill in the middle of the loop, campers can see only a couple sites at a time. The vault toilets at this low-use campground seem to be neglected by the maintenance crew. (For more information on Stagecoach State Park, see the Junction City entry in this chapter.)

Campsites, facilities: There are nine sites for tents and RVs up to 20 feet and one group site. There are no hookups. Sites 91 and 92 are pull-through. Picnic tables, fire rings, and grills are provided. Vault toilets are available. At the marina, a convenience store, boat rentals, boat ramp, swim beach, and restrooms with flush toilets and showers are available. Leashed pets are permitted.

Reservations, fees: Reservations are accepted at 800/678-2267 and www.parks.state.co.us. The fee is $7 per night. There is an additional $8 reservation fee. Campers must also purchase a Daily Parks Pass ($5) or an Annual Parks Pass ($55). The Aspen Leaf Annual Pass is accepted. Open mid-May–mid-October.

Directions: From Steamboat Springs, take U.S. Highway 40 south to Highway 131 south. In about six miles, turn left on County Road 14. The entrance station is in about five miles. Turn right 0.1 mile after the entrance station and stay to the left up the hill to enter the campground.

Contact: Stagecoach State Park, 970/736-2436, email: stagecoach.park@state.co.us.

23 PINNACLE

Scenic rating: 5

in Stagecoach State Park

Pinnacle is on a high flat area on the north shore of three-mile Stagecoach Reservoir, adjacent to a small knob with a short walking trail and a scenic overlook. The campground is essentially an RV park. It has rows of parallel pull-through RV sites that are not suitable for tent camping. Nevertheless, it's a popular campground and quite busy on summer weekends. It's adjacent to the marina, boat ramp, and swim beach. Sites 58–65 have the best lake views. (For more information on Stagecoach State Park, see the Junction City entry in this chapter.)

Campsites, facilities: There are 38 sites for RVs up to 35 feet. There are electrical hookups, and all sites are pull-through. Picnic tables, fire rings, and grills are provided. Restrooms with flush toilets and showers, drinking water, and a dump station are available. A convenience store, boat rentals, boat ramp, and swim beach are available at the marina. Leashed pets are permitted.

Reservations, fees: Reservations are accepted at 800/678-2267 and www.parks .state.co.us. The fee is $16 per night. There is an additional $8 reservation fee. Campers must also purchase a Daily Parks Pass ($5) or an Annual Parks Pass ($55). The Aspen Leaf Annual Pass is accepted. Open mid-May–mid-October. A few sites remain open in the winter without water.

Directions: From Steamboat Springs, take U.S. Highway 40 south to Highway 131 south. In about six miles, turn left on County Road 14. The entrance station is in about five miles. Turn left 0.4 mile after the entrance station. The campground is on the right in 0.1 mile.

Contact: Stagecoach State Park, 970/736-2436, email: stagecoach.park@state.co.us.

24 HARDING

Scenic rating: 5

in Stagecoach State Park

Harding parallels a narrow inlet on the north shore of Stagecoach Reservoir. The views aren't as panoramic as at the other campgrounds, but there's also no noise from Highway 14. The campground is in a sagebrush meadow with very few trees and no shade. Sites 66, 67, 69, 72, 74, and 76 are closest to the water. (For more information on Stagecoach State Park, see the Junction City entry in this chapter.)

Campsites, facilities: There are 18 sites for tents and RVs up to 25 feet. There are no hookups or pull-throughs. Picnic tables, fire rings, and grills are provided. Flush toilets, drinking water, and a dump station are available. A convenience store, boat rentals, boat ramp, and swim beach are available at the marina. Leashed pets are permitted.

Reservations, fees: Reservations are accepted at 800/678-2267 and www.parks.state.co.us. The fee is $12 per night. There is an additional $8 reservation fee. Campers must also purchase a Daily Parks Pass ($5) or an Annual Parks Pass ($55). The Aspen Leaf Annual Pass is accepted. Open mid-May–mid-October.

Directions: From Steamboat Springs, take U.S. Highway 40 south to Highway 131 south. In about six miles, turn left on County Road 14. The entrance station is in about five miles. Turn left 0.4 mile after the entrance station. The road ends at the campground in 0.2 mile.

Contact: Stagecoach State Park, 970/736-2436, email: stagecoach.park@state.co.us.

25 MEADOWS

Scenic rating: 6

southeast of Steamboat Springs

The Meadows is a stopover campground

between Steamboat Springs and Walden. This part of the Park Range is characterized by low peaks, meandering streams, and large meadows. The campground contains two loops in a dense spruce-fir forest near an open riparian zone. Sites 1, 28, 29, and 31 border the meadow. The campground isn't especially scenic, but as a stopover, it stays about half full during the summer. There are no hiking trails nearby.

Campsites, facilities: There are 30 sites for tents and RVs up to 40 feet. There are no hookups. Sites 8, 10, 15, 20, and 25 are pull-through. Picnic tables, grills, and fire rings are provided. Vault toilets are available. Leashed pets are permitted.

Reservations, fees: Reservations are not accepted. The fee is $10 per night. Golden Age and Golden Access Passports are accepted. Cash or check only. Open early June–late October.

Directions: From Highway 131 in Steamboat Springs, take U.S. Highway 40 south for 11.4 miles. Turn right on Forest Route 297. The campground is in 0.2 mile.

Contact: Routt National Forest, Hahns Peak District, 970/879-1870, www.fs.fed.us/r2/mbr/.

26 WALTON CREEK

Scenic rating: 5

southeast of Steamboat Springs

Walton Creek is a low-use stopover campground between Steamboat Springs and Walden, about four miles west of Rabbit Ears Pass. This part of the Park Range is characterized by low peaks, meandering streams, and large meadows. The campground is a small loop beside a meadow with scattered spruce and fir trees. All of the sites are within sight of the road, so traffic noise is bothersome and there is not much privacy. Sites 6 and 8–13 are in the meadow. Sites 12 and 13 are farthest from the road. There are no hiking trails nearby.

Campsites, facilities: There are 14 sites for tents and RVs up to 22 feet. There are no hookups. Site 13 is pull-through. Picnic tables, grills, and fire rings are provided. Vault toilets and drinking water are available. Leashed pets are permitted.

Reservations, fees: Reservations are not accepted. The fee is $12 per night. Golden Age and Golden Access Passports are accepted. Cash or check only. Open early June–early October.

Directions: From Highway 131 in Steamboat Springs, take U.S. Highway 40 south for 13.4 miles. The campground is on the right.

Contact: Routt National Forest, Hahns Peak District, 970/879-1870, www.fs.fed.us/r2/mbr/.

27 RANGELY CAMPER PARK

Scenic rating: 2

north of Rangely

This campground is a paved loop in a mature stand of cottonwoods. It is shady and clean, but there is little to recommend it. It's a decent stopover for road-weary families, or a base camp for rock hounds and mountain bikers who want to explore the BLM lands that surround this tiny town. In Cañon Pintado, south of Rangely on Highway 139, there are numerous petroglyphs. Highway 139 is the quickest route from Dinosaur to Grand Junction.

Campsites, facilities: There are 25 sites for tents and RVs of any length. Sites 1, 3, 7, 8, 9, and 13–15 have electrical hookups. Picnic tables and grills are provided. Restrooms with flush toilets and showers, drinking water, a dump station, volleyball court, horseshoe pits, and group picnic area are available. Leashed pets are permitted.

Reservations, fees: Reservations are not accepted. The fee is $12 without hookups and $14 with hookups. Cash only. Open May–October.

Directions: From Dinosaur, take Highway 64

south to Rangely. Turn left on Nicholson Avenue and then right on East Rangely Avenue. The campground is at the end of the road.
Contact: Rangely Recreation Center, 970/675-8211.

28 NORTH FORK

🚶 🚲 🎣 🐕 🚐 ⛺

Scenic rating: 7

east of Meeker

North Fork is the most accessible campground on the Flat Tops Scenic Byway, an 84-mile driving route between Meeker and Yampa. This campground is a convenient stopover, and it appeals to ATV owners and mountain bikers because the nearby trails travel north (instead of into the wilderness to the south). The Lost Creek Trail has good trout fishing, and the Lost Park Trail traverses important elk habitat. The more difficult Long Park Trail has views of the White River Valley. It connects with the Deadhorse 4WD Loop and is popular with snowmobilers. This isn't the most scenic camping in the area, but it's a good place to slather on the mosquito repellent and put your feet up in a hammock. The campground never fills up and is very slow midweek. The sites are widely spaced, and dense underbrush provides ample privacy while aspen trees offer shade.
Campsites, facilities: There are 40 sites for tents and RVs up to 60 feet. There are no hookups. Sites 2, 7, 10, 22, 25, 27, 31, 34, and 39 are pull-through. Picnic tables, grills, and fire rings are provided. Site 39 has a tent pad. Site 2 has an extra-large picnic table. Vault toilets and drinking water are available. Leashed pets are permitted.
Reservations, fees: Reservations are accepted at 877/444-6777 and www.reserveusa.com. The fee is $14 per night (includes two vehicles). Additional vehicles cost $5 per night, and there is an $8 reservation fee. Golden Age and Golden Access Passports are accepted.

Cash or check only. Open late May–early November.
Directions: From Meeker, take Highway 13 east for less than two miles. Then take Flat Top Road/County Road 8 east for 32.5 miles. The campground is on the left.
Contact: White River National Forest, Blanco District, 970/878-4039, www.fs.fed.us/r2/whiteriver/.

29 VAUGHN LAKE

🎣 🚤 🐕 🚐 ⛺

Scenic rating: 7

west of Oak Creek

Vaughn Lake is a small, stocked reservoir on the eastern side of the Flat Tops Scenic Byway. The primitive campground is in an aspen grove overlooking the lake, which is surrounded by meadows and spruce-covered hills. The sites are large and well spaced, but the spurs are very rough and a few require high clearance. Site 1 is totally isolated and the most scenic. The other sites are near the road. Nearby Ripple Creek Pass has panoramic views of the Flat Top mountains, formed over millennia by volcanic activity, glacial activity, and erosion.
Campsites, facilities: There are six sites for tents and RVs up to 18 feet. There are no hookups. Site 4 is pull-through. Picnic tables, grills, and fire rings are provided. Vault toilets are available. Leashed pets are permitted.
Reservations, fees: Reservations are not accepted. The fee is $5 per night. Golden Age and Golden Access Passports are accepted. Cash or check only. Open mid-June–mid-November.
Directions: From Oak Creek, take County Road 25 west for seven miles to Forest Route 16 and go left. In 17.5 miles, turn left on County Road 8. The campground is on the right in 7.5 miles.
Contact: Routt National Forest, Yampa District, 970/638-4516, www.fs.fed.us/r2/mbr/.

30 EAST MARVINE

Scenic rating: 7

east of Meeker

The Flat Tops Scenic Byway is an 82-mile drive (half of it on unpaved roads) through the northern half of the White River Plateau. The drive is scenic, especially at Ripple Creek Pass, but to really enjoy the Flat Tops, one needs to set up camp and hike into the 235,214-acre wilderness. This is an area of subalpine meadows and alpine tundra interrupted by volcanic cliffs and peaks and dotted with picturesque lakes. The East Marvine Trail begins about 2,000 feet below the plateau and climbs through aspen, pine, and spruce-fir forests past Rainbow Lake to the rolling tundra of the plateau. A side trail climbs Big Marvine Peak and offers panoramic vistas of the wilderness. This 10.5-mile trail can be done as an out-and-back day hike or linked with the Marvine Trail for an overnight loop. These trails are very popular pack trips, and the numerous lakes present good fly-fishing opportunities.

The campground at the trailhead is on the east side of the narrow Marvine Creek valley. The sites are shaded by aspen and spruce and overlook a small meadow. It's a short walk to the creek, where anglers can fish for small brookies. This pleasant campground rarely fills up.

Campsites, facilities: There are seven sites for tents and RVs up to 50 feet. There are no hookups. Site 1 is pull-through. Picnic tables, grills, and fire rings are provided. Vault toilets, drinking water, and horse corrals are available. Leashed pets are permitted.

Reservations, fees: Reservations are not accepted. The fee is $13 per night or $15 per night with a corral (includes two vehicles). Additional vehicles cost $5 per night, and an extra corral costs $7 per night. Golden Age and Golden Access Passports are accepted. Cash or check only. Open late May–early November.

Directions: From Meeker, take Highway 13 east for less than two miles. Then take Flat Top Road/County Road 8 east for 29 miles. Turn right on County Road 12. Stay left at the top of the hill and continue 4.8 miles to the campground.

Contact: White River National Forest, Blanco District, 970/878-4039, www.fs.fed.us/r2/whiteriver/.

31 MARVINE

Scenic rating: 7

east of Meeker

Like nearby East Marvine, this campground attracts mostly hikers and horseback riders. The East Marvine and Marvine Trails begin 2,000 feet below the plateau and climb through valleys full of aspen and spruce-fir forests to the rolling tundra and picturesque lakes of the plateau. Slide Lake, Pine Island Lake, and Marvine Lakes all lie near the trail, offering numerous opportunities for the backcountry angler. Above Marvine Lake, the trail passes through a ghost forest killed by a budworm epidemic in the 1940s. These dead trees are important habitat for birds and insects, but snags can be dangerous, so hikers should stay on the trail. The East Marvine and Marvine Trails can be hiked separately or turned into an overnight loop.

The campground is in a small valley forested by aspen, spruce, and fir. Sites 1, 2, 4, 8, 17, and 18 are on the edge of a meadow, and the other sites are in the trees. This campground attracts regulars who return every year, many of them with horse trailers in tow. Boy Scout troops also frequent this campground, which is busier than East Marvine.

Campsites, facilities: There are 18 sites for tents and RVs up to 60 feet. There are no hookups. Sites 2, 4, 5, 11, 14, 17, and 18 are pull-through. Picnic tables, grills, and fire rings are provided. Vault toilets, drinking water, and horse corrals are available. Leashed pets are permitted.

Reservations, fees: Reservations are not accepted. The fee is $13 per night or $15 per night with a corral (includes two vehicles). Additional vehicles cost $5 per night, and an extra corral costs $7 per night. Golden Age and Golden Access Passports are accepted. Cash or check only. Open late May–early November.

Directions: From Meeker, take Highway 13 east for less than two miles. Then take Flat Top Road/County Road 8 east for 29 miles. Turn right on County Road 12. Stay left at the top of the hill. The road ends at the campground in five miles.

Contact: White River National Forest, Blanco District, 970/878-4039, www.fs.fed.us/r2/whiteriver/.

32 HIMES PEAK

Scenic rating: 7

east of Meeker

Himes Peak is on the North Fork of the White River, not far from the famed Trapper Lake area. Himes Peak attracts anglers and hikers. The high-use Big Fish Trail leaves from the campground and accesses several fishing spots: Bigfish, Boulder, Gwendolyn, Robinson, McBride, and Doris Lakes. The trail also passes Bessie's Falls and climbs onto the Flat Tops Plateau. The Ripple Creek Fire burned this area several years ago, but the burned forests are actually quite scenic in late summer when red and purple wildflowers carpet the forest floor. The campground was unscathed by the fire, and the lush green meadow and aspens make an interesting contrast with the ghostly ridge across the valley. The jagged knife-edge of Himes Peak soars several thousand feet overhead. The sites are 20–50 feet apart, so privacy varies. Aspen, spruce, and fir provide ample shade. This campground is moderately busy all week during the summer.

Campsites, facilities: There are 11 sites for tents and RVs up to 36 feet. There are no hookups. Sites 1, 7, and 11 are pull-through. Picnic tables, grills, and fire rings are provided. Vault toilets are available. Leashed pets are permitted.

Reservations, fees: Reservations are not accepted. The fee is $13 per night (includes two vehicles). Additional vehicles cost $5 per night. Golden Age and Golden Access Passports are accepted. Cash or check only. Open late May–early November.

Directions: From Meeker, take Highway 13 east for less than two miles. Then take Flat Top Road/County Road 8 east for 39.2 miles. Turn right on Forest Route 205. In 4.3 miles, turn right at the campground sign and continue 0.4 mile to the campground.

Contact: White River National Forest, Blanco District, 970/878-4039, www.fs.fed.us/r2/whiteriver/.

33 TRAPPERS LAKE– HORSETHIEF

Scenic rating: 7

east of Meeker

A drive along the Flat Tops Scenic Byway isn't complete without a side trip to Trappers Lake, the birthplace of the wilderness concept. In 1919, landscape architect Arthur Carhart was sent by the Forest Service to survey the lake for a summer resort. The beauty of the lake ringed by volcanic cliffs inspired him to recommend saving this wilderness in its natural form for all visitors rather than transforming it into a summer destination for a few. The Forest Service heeded his recommendation, marking the genesis of the wilderness movement that Aldo Leopold spearheaded. The north shore has campgrounds and roads, but the rest of the shoreline is wilderness. The trail system around the lake features the Carhart, Still-water, Trappers Lake, and Wall Lake Trails, which offer numerous opportunities for day hiking and backpacking in the Flat Tops Wilderness. In addition to excellent native trout fishing (Trappers Lake is a spawn-taking station for the Division of Wildlife), these trails access the rolling tundra of the 11,000-foot Flat Tops plateau, the stunning Chinese Wall, the Devils Causeway, and panoramic views of the wilderness. The trails also pass through a ghost forest of spruce killed in the 1940s by a budworm epidemic. Hikers should be wary of snags in this area.

There are five campgrounds in a circle on the north shore of the lake. Horsethief is the wrangler's campground. It is ringed by the cliffs of the Flat Top plateau and the ghost forest. The campground is in a hummocky meadow with many wildflowers. The sites are not very private, but a few live trees provide scattered shade.

Campsites, facilities: There are five sites for tents and RVs up to 60 feet. There are no hookups. Picnic tables, grills, fire rings, and tent pads are provided. Vault toilets, horse corrals, and a dump station are available. The facilities are wheelchair accessible. The water system was inoperative for several years, but the Forest Service plans on restoring it by 2006. Leashed pets are permitted.

Reservations, fees: Reservations are not accepted. The fee is $15 per night (includes two vehicles). Additional vehicles cost $5 per night. Golden Age and Golden Access Passports are accepted. Cash or check only. Open mid-June–early November.

Directions: From Meeker, take Highway 13 east for less than two miles. Then take Flat Top Road/County Road 8 east for 39.2 miles. Turn right on Forest Route 205. In 7.5 miles, veer right and cross the one-lane bridge. The campground is on the right, one mile after the bridge.

Contact: White River National Forest, Blanco District, 970/878-4039, www.fs.fed.us/r2/whiteriver/.

34 TRAPPERS LAKE–SHEPHERD'S RIM

🚶 🛶 🚤 🎣 ♿ 🚐 ⛺

Scenic rating: 8

east of Meeker

BEST (

Shepard's Rim features a striking contrast. Set in a dense spruce-fir forest, the campground is ringed by the ghost forest that a budworm epidemic created in the 1940s. In late summer, the forest floor is covered with wildflowers, so sites with views of the North Fork valley are prized. Sites 7 and 8 have the best views to the west. Site 16 and the four overflow sites have excellent views of the cliffs of the Flat Tops plateau. The campground is flatter than nearby Buck's, and the sites are more private. The Himes Peak trailhead is adjacent. (For more information on Trappers Lake, see the Trappers Lake–Horsethief listing in this chapter.)

Campsites, facilities: There are 20 sites for tents and RVs up to 36 feet. There are no hookups. Sites 5, 6, 10, 12, and 13 are pull-through. Picnic tables, grills, and fire rings are provided. Sites 1, 3, 5, 7–9, and 12 have tent pads. Vault toilets and a dump station are available. The facilities are wheelchair accessible. The drinking water system was inoperative for several years, but the Forest Service plans on restoring it by 2006. Leashed pets are permitted.

Reservations, fees: Reservations are not accepted. The fee is $15 per night (includes two vehicles). Additional vehicles cost $5 per night. Golden Age and Golden Access Passports are accepted. Cash or check only. Open mid-June–mid-November.

Directions: From Meeker, take Highway 13 east for less than two miles. Then take Flat Top Road/County Road 8 east for 39.2 miles. Turn right on Forest Route 205. In 7.5 miles, veer right and cross the one-lane bridge. The campground is on the right, 1.2 miles after the bridge.

Contact: White River National Forest, Blanco District, 970/878-4039, www.fs.fed.us/r2/whiteriver/.

35 TRAPPERS LAKE–BUCK'S
🏕 🛶 🚐 🐕 ♿ 🚌 ⛰

Scenic rating: 6

east of Meeker

Buck's is the least appealing of the five campgrounds on the north shore of picturesque Trappers Lake. The campground is in a dense spruce-fir forest, and the sites are close to each other and the campground road. It's a bit hilly, so flat tent sites can be hard to find. The trees obscure views of the surrounding cliffs. Only site 5 offers glimpses of the Flat Tops. (For more information on Trappers Lake, see the Trappers Lake–Horsethief entry in this chapter.)

Campsites, facilities: There are 10 sites for tents and RVs up to 36 feet. There are no hookups. Sites 1, 3, 7, and 9 are pull-through. Picnic tables, grills, and fire rings are provided. Sites 3 and 4 have tent pads. Vault toilets and a dump station are available. The facilities are wheelchair accessible. The drinking water system was inoperative for several years, but the Forest Service plans on restoring it in 2006. Leashed pets are permitted.

Reservations, fees: Reservations are not accepted. The fee is $15 per night (includes two vehicles). Additional vehicles cost $5 per night. Golden Age and Golden Access Passports are accepted. Cash or check only. Open mid-June–early September.

Directions: From Meeker, take Highway 13 east for less than two miles. Then take Flat Top Road/County Road 8 east for 39.2 miles. Turn right on Forest Route 205. In 7.5 miles, veer right and cross the one-lane bridge. The campground is on the left, 1.1 miles after the bridge.

Contact: White River National Forest, Blanco District, 970/878-4039, www.fs.fed.us/r2/whiteriver/.

36 TRAPPERS LAKE– CUTTHROAT
🏕 🛶 🚐 🐕 🚌 ⛰

Scenic rating: 8

east of Meeker

BEST (

Cutthroat and Trapline are identical twins. Adjacent to Trappers Lake, these campgrounds are in a dense spruce-fir forest that obscures the lake but permits glimpses of the volcanic cliffs that ring the lake. The sites are about 50 feet apart and very private. Sites 5, 6, and 7 have the best views. Sites 10 and 11 are runners-up. Cutthroat is the most popular campground at the lake, but these campgrounds never fill up. (For more information on Trappers Lake, see the Trappers Lake–Horsethief entry in this chapter.)

Campsites, facilities: There are 14 sites for tents and RVs up to 36 feet. There are no hookups. Sites 1, 2, 3, and 12 are pull-through. Picnic tables, grills, and fire rings are provided. Sites 1, 2, 8, and 13 have tent pads. Vault toilets and a dump station are available. The drinking water system was inoperative for several years, but the Forest Service plans on restoring it by 2006. Leashed pets are permitted.

Reservations, fees: Reservations are not accepted. The fee is $15 per night (includes two vehicles). Additional vehicles cost $5 per night. Golden Age and Golden Access Passports are accepted. Cash or check only. Open mid-June–early September.

Directions: From Meeker, take Highway 13 east for less than two miles. Then take Flat Top Road/County Road 8 east for 39.2 miles. Turn right on Forest Route 205. In 7.5 miles, veer right and cross the one-lane bridge. The campground is on the right, 1.3 miles after the bridge.

Contact: White River National Forest, Blanco District, 970/878-4039, www.fs.fed.us/r2/whiteriver/.

37 TRAPPERS LAKE–TRAPLINE

Scenic rating: 8

east of Meeker

Cutthroat and Trapline are identical twins, except that Cutthroat is more popular. Adjacent to Trappers Lake, these campgrounds are in a dense spruce-fir forest that obscures the lake but permits glimpses of the volcanic cliffs that ring the lake. The sites are about 50 feet apart and very private. They are also flat, so there's room to spread out. (For more information on Trappers Lake, see the Trappers Lake–Horsethief entry in this chapter.)

Campsites, facilities: There are 13 sites for tents and RVs up to 36 feet. There are no hookups. Site 11 is pull-through. Picnic tables, grills, and fire rings are provided. Sites 1, 2, 4, 7, 8, and 11 have tent pads. Vault toilets and a dump station are available. The drinking water system was inoperative for several years, but the Forest Service plans on restoring it by 2006. Leashed pets are permitted.

Reservations, fees: Reservations are not accepted. The fee is $15 per night (includes two vehicles). Additional vehicles cost $5 per night. Golden Age and Golden Access Passports are accepted. Cash or check only. Open mid-June–early September.

Directions: From Meeker, take Highway 13 east for less than two miles. Then take Flat Top Road/County Road 8 east for 39.2 miles. Turn right on Forest Route 205. In 7.5 miles, veer right and cross the one-lane bridge. The campground is on the right, 1.3 miles after the bridge. It is the last campground on the circle.

Contact: White River National Forest, Blanco District, 970/878-4039, www.fs.fed.us/r2/whiteriver/.

38 COLD SPRINGS

Scenic rating: 9

west of Yampa

BEST (

The Bear River Recreation Area contains 10,000 acres of national forest that abuts the Flat Tops Wilderness, the second-largest wilderness area in the state. The Bear River Area is managed jointly by Routt National Forest and the Department of Wildlife, so the fishing in the reservoirs (Stillwater, Bear Lake, and Yamcolo) and the river has an excellent reputation. Cold Springs is the most remote of the three campgrounds in this area, but it's also the most rewarding. This little loop is high up the Bear River valley, and every site has views of the Flat Tops and the stunning Chinese Wall, a 600–1,000 foot cliff. Equally impressive is the Devil's Causeway, a rock ridge that divides the Williams Fork and Bear River drainages. It's about 50 feet long and four feet across at its narrowest and requires a tough stomach to scramble across. The East Fork Trail accesses this area and can be turned into an overnight loop with the Stillwater Trail. In addition to fishing on the reservoir, the river, and the alpine lakes, the campground has a kid's fishing pond fed by two cascades. The campground fills up on weekends but is very slow midweek. It attracts regulars who enjoy the hiking and fishing.

Campsites, facilities: There are five sites for tents and RVs up to 20 feet. There are no hookups. Sites 1, 3, and 5 are pull-through. Picnic tables, grills, and fire rings are provided. Vault toilets and drinking water are available. Leashed pets are permitted.

Reservations, fees: Reservations are not accepted. The fee is $10 per night. Golden Age and Golden Access Passports are accepted. Cash or check only. Open early June–early October.

Directions: From Yampa, take County Road 7/Forest Route 900 south for 16.6 miles. Turn right into the campground.

Contact: Routt National Forest, Yampa District, 970/638-4516, www.fs.fed.us/r2/mbr/.

39 HORSESHOE

Scenic rating: 8

west of Yampa

Horseshoe is in the Bear River Recreation Area, which contains 10,000 acres of national forest that adjoin the Flat Tops Wilderness, the second-largest wilderness area in the state. The Bear River Area is managed jointly by Routt National Forest and the Department of Wildlife, so the fishing in the reservoirs (Stillwater, Bear Lake, and Yamcolo) and the river has an excellent reputation. At 10,000 feet, Horseshoe offers high-altitude camping for tents and small RVs. The views aren't as amazing as at Cold Springs, but they are still a tantalizing glimpse at the volcanic cliffs of the Flat Tops. The loop is right next to the road, and the small sites are 25–50 feet apart. Privacy could be a problem, but this campground is not heavily used. Several trails begin between the campground and Stillwater Reservoir, including the East Fork Trail, which climbs to the Devil's Causeway, a rock ridge that's 1,500 feet high and four feet wide at its narrowest. Hikers can also take the North Derby and Bear River Trails into the wilderness.

Campsites, facilities: There are seven sites for tents and RVs up to 25 feet. There are no hookups. Sites 6 and 7 are pull-through. Picnic tables, grills, and fire rings are provided. Vault toilets and drinking water are available. Leashed pets are permitted.

Reservations, fees: Reservations are not accepted. The fee is $10 per night. Golden Age and Golden Access Passports are accepted. Cash or check only. Open early June–mid-November.

Directions: From Yampa, take County Road 7/Forest Route 900 south for 16.2 miles. Turn right into the campground.

Contact: Routt National Forest, Yampa District, 970/638-4516, www.fs.fed.us/r2/mbr/.

40 BEAR LAKE

Scenic rating: 8

west of Yampa

BEST (

Bear Lake is a lovely lake in the Bear River valley, not far from the Flat Tops Wilderness area, the second-largest wilderness in the state. The lake is enclosed by the volcanic cliffs of the Flat Tops, and the valley is lush with aspen, spruce, and fir. The area is managed jointly by Routt National Forest and the Division of Wildlife, so the trout fishery has an excellent reputation. Bear Lake is open to electric and hand-powered boats, and there is a boat ramp on Yamcolo Reservoir for larger boats. The Mandall Lakes Trail begins opposite the campground and climbs onto the Flat Tops Plateau. Several more trails begin at Stillwater Reservoir. The campground was renovated in 2003 and is the best campground in the valley for families and RVs. It's divided into two wooded loops. The east loop (sites 24–43) has more aspens and is more open. The sites are 50–75 feet apart and fairly private. Sites 13, 34, and 35 are double units. Site 33 is a triple unit. Sites 14–18, 26, 28, 33, and 34 have the best views of the Flat Tops.

Campsites, facilities: There are 41 sites for tents and RVs up to 30 feet and two walk-in tent sites. Site 3 and the facilities are wheelchair accessible. There are no hookups. Sites 11, 17, 18, 25, and 26 are pull-through. Picnic tables, grills, fire rings, grill tables, and tent pads are provided. Vault toilets, drinking water, and a fishing pier are available. Leashed pets are permitted.

Reservations, fees: Reservations are not accepted. The fee is $10 per night for a single site, $20 per night for a double, and $30 per night for a triple (includes two vehicles). Additional vehicles cost $5 per night. Golden Age and Golden Access Passports are accepted. Cash or check only. Open early June–early October.

Directions: From Yampa, take County Road 7/Forest Route 900 south for 13.5 miles. Turn left and continue 0.5 mile through the day-use area to the campground.

Contact: Routt National Forest, Yampa District, 970/638-4516, www.fs.fed.us/r2/mbr/.

41 BEAR RIVER DISPERSED

Scenic rating: 9

west of Yampa

Dispersed camping is so popular in the 10,000-acre Bear River Recreation Area that the Forest Service has developed a system for managing the sites. For a small fee, you can camp away from the crowds with a grill and fire ring to boot. The Forest Service plans on gradually adding picnic tables to these sites as well. There are 31 sites from the Forest Service boundary to the Cold Springs campground, a distance of about 12 miles. Settings range from sagebrush flats, to meadows, to aspen groves and spruce-fir forests. Sites 16–23 are near the Yamcolo Reservoir, and sites 24–26 are near Bear Lake. The views improve the higher you go. The Bear River is an excellent trout fishery with lake fishing on the Yamcolo, Bear Lake, and Stillwater Reservoirs, and backcountry fishing on alpine lakes in the Flat Tops Wilderness, which adjoins the recreation area. The fly-fishing is excellent on the rivers and streams. The 200 miles of hiking trails in the wilderness area are accessible from several trailheads near Stillwater Reservoir.

Campsites, facilities: There are 31 dispersed sites for tents and RVs up to 60 feet. Grills and fire rings are provided at some sites. Leashed pets are permitted.

Reservations, fees: Reservations are not accepted. The fee is $3 per night for one camping unit and $2 per night per additional camping unit. Golden Age and Golden Access Passports are accepted. Cash or check only. Open early June–early October.

Directions: From Yampa, take County Road 7/Forest Route 900 south for 13 miles. Dispersed camping extends from the Forest Service boundary to Cold Springs campground.

Contact: Routt National Forest, Yampa District, 970/638-4516, www.fs.fed.us/r2/mbr/.

42 LYNX PASS

Scenic rating: 7

east of Yampa

The Lynx Pass–Gore Pass area on the west side of the Gore Range is very popular with mountain bikers. Several mountain bike routes (on trails and Forest Service roads) explore the large, open meadows and forested ridgelines of this area. Popular routes include the Morrison Divide and Teepee Creek Trails and the Rock Creek, Gore Pass, and Gore Creek Loops. (Trail descriptions and maps are available from the Forest Service.) The Morrison Divide and Teepee Creek Trails are also good for hikers. Moose may be sighted near streams. The campground is a roomy loop in a forest of spruce, fir, and pine. The sites are about 100 feet apart and there are few users, so privacy is excellent. Sites 1 and 2 border a meadow with an aspen grove.

Campsites, facilities: There are 11 sites for tents and RVs up to 18 feet. Site 3 and the facilities are wheelchair accessible. There are no hookups. Sites 1, 2, 5, and 6 are pull-through. Picnic tables, grills, and fire rings are provided. Vault toilets and drinking water are available. Leashed pets are permitted.

Reservations, fees: Reservations are not accepted. The fee is $10 per night (includes two vehicles). Additional vehicles cost $5 per night. Golden Age and Golden Access Passports are accepted. Cash or check only. Open early June–mid-November.

Directions: From Yampa, take Highway 131 south for nine miles. Go east on Highway 134 for 8.6 miles. Turn left on County Road 16/Forest Route 270. The campground is on the left in 2.9 miles.

Contact: Routt National Forest, Yampa District, 970/638-4516, www.fs.fed.us/r2/mbr/.

43 BLACKTAIL CREEK

Scenic rating: 6

east of Yampa

Blacktail Creek is on the west side of the Gore Range, just a mile from Gore Pass (elevation 9,527 feet). The Lynx Pass–Gore Pass area is very popular with mountain bikers. Several mountain bike routes (on trails and forest service roads) explore the large, open meadows and forested ridgelines that characterize this region. Popular routes include the Morrison Divide and Teepee Creek Trails and the Rock Creek, Gore Pass, and Gore Creek Loops. (Trail descriptions and maps are available from the Forest Service.) Moose may be sighted near streams. Highway 134 is also very popular with road cyclists. The campground is in a forest of pine, aspen, and spruce near the headwaters of Blacktail Creek. Sites have partial shade and are 75–100 feet apart. This campground is more popular than nearby Lynx Pass, but there is still ample room for a big family to spread out.

Campsites, facilities: There are 11 sites for tents and RVs up to 18 feet. Site 3 and the facilities are wheelchair accessible. There are no hookups. Picnic tables, grills, and fire rings are provided. Vault toilets and drinking water are available. Leashed pets are permitted.

Reservations, fees: Reservations are not accepted. The fee is $10 per night (includes two vehicles). Additional vehicles cost $5 per night. Golden Age and Golden Access Passports are accepted. Cash or check only. Open early June–mid-November.

Directions: From Yampa, take Highway 131 south for nine miles. Go east on Highway 134 for 14.5 miles. The campground is on the right.

Contact: Routt National Forest, Yampa District, 970/638-4516, www.fs.fed.us/r2/mbr/.

44 SUPPLY BASIN

Scenic rating: 9

north of Glenwood Springs

Supply Basin is on the southern half of the White River Plateau, an area remarkable for its rolling meadows and numerous lakes. This small, primitive campground is on the shore of an unnamed lake, with views of sprawling Heart Lake. The campground feels on top of the world. It is quite remote, and the rough road deters many campers, but this part of the plateau is popular with ATVers because of its distance from the Flat Tops Wilderness, where ATVs are not allowed. The network of 4WD roads and lakes is perfect for exploring in a Jeep. There are no hiking trails nearby, but the plateau makes off-trail hiking fairly easy. All of the sites in this campground are close to the water, but sites 4 and 6 are right on the shore. Site 5 is screened by spruce and fir trees and has the most privacy. (For more information on the White River Plateau, see the Coffee Pot Spring listing later in this chapter.)

Campsites, facilities: There are eight sites for tents and RVs up to 25 feet. There are no hookups. Picnic tables, grills, and fire rings are provided. Vault toilets are available. Leashed pets are permitted.

Reservations, fees: Reservations are not accepted. The fee is $6 per night. Golden Age and Golden Access Passports are accepted. Cash or check only. Open early July–early October.

Directions: From I-70, take the Dotsero exit (Exit 133). Go north on County Road 301 for 1.6 miles. Turn left on Coffee Pot Road/Forest Route 600. In 27.4 miles, turn left on Forest Route 601. The campground is on the left in 1.2 miles.

Contact: White River National Forest, 970/328-6388, www.fs.fed.us/r2/whiteriver/.

45 DEEP LAKE

Scenic rating: 8

north of Glenwood Springs

The White River Plateau is an area of rolling subalpine meadows and alpine tundra dotted with small scenic lakes and interspersed with spruce-fir forests and aspen groves. This area is unique in Colorado for its openness. It's also home to thriving elk herds and the 235,000-acre Flat Tops Wilderness. Deep Lake is on the southern edge of the plateau, far from the trails of the wilderness area, which makes it popular with four-wheelers and ATV owners, and the lake attracts anglers. The campground contains two loops on the east side of Deep Lake. The scenery is excellent: rolling meadows, a steep canyon, spruce-fir forests, and wildflowers. The sites are 50–75 feet apart in meadows and trees. Privacy varies widely with the number of trees. Sites 9, 28, 30–32, and A–C have the best lake views. (For more information on the White River Plateau, see the Coffee Pot Spring listing later in this chapter.)

Campsites, facilities: There are 37 sites for tents and RVs up to 35 feet. There are no hookups. Sites 6, 17, 18, 20, and 21 are pull-through. Picnic tables, grills, and fire rings are provided. Wheelchair-accessible vault toilets are available. Leashed pets are permitted.

Reservations, fees: Reservations are not accepted. The fee is $6 per night. Golden Age and Golden Access Passports are accepted. Cash or check only. Open early July–late October.

Directions: From Glenwood Springs, take I-70 east to Exit 133. Go north on County Road 301 for 1.6 miles. Turn left on Coffee Pot Road/Forest Route 600. The campground is on the right in 28.5 miles.

Contact: White River National Forest, 970/328-6388, www.fs.fed.us/r2/whiteriver/.

46 WHITE OWL

Scenic rating: 9

north of Glenwood Springs

BEST (

White Owl is my favorite of the five campgrounds on Coffee Pot Road. The campground encircles White Owl Lake, a shimmering little fishing hole surrounded by lush meadows and spruce-fir forests with glimpses of the Flat Tops to the north. The sites are well spaced and screened by trees, and they are all close to the lake and have excellent views. Sites 5, 8, 10, and 11 are the best tent sites. Site 1 is perfect for large groups and RVs. There are no hiking trails nearby, but the plateau is suitable for off-trail hiking. Bikers and ATV riders enjoy the network of Jeep trails that connect the lakes.

Campsites, facilities: There are 11 sites for tents and RVs up to 20 feet. There are no hookups. Sites 1 and 8 are pull-through. Picnic tables, grills, and fire rings are provided at all sites. Sites 5 and 8 have tent pads. Vault toilets are available. Leashed pets are permitted. (For more information on the White River Plateau, see the Coffee Pot Spring listing later in this chapter.)

Reservations, fees: Reservations are not accepted. The fee is $6 per night. Golden Age and Golden Access Passports are accepted. Cash or check only. Open early July–late October.

Directions: From I-70, take the Dotsero exit (Exit 133). Go north on County Road 301 for 1.6 miles. Turn left on Coffee Pot Road/Forest Route 600. In 26.6 miles, turn left at the White Owl Lake sign. The campground is on the left in 0.6 mile.

Contact: White River National Forest, 970/328-6388, www.fs.fed.us/r2/whiteriver/.

47 SWEETWATER LAKE

🏃 🏊 🚣 ➡️ 🐕 🚐 ⛺

Scenic rating: 8

north of Glenwood Springs

At an elevation of 7,700 feet, Sweetwater Lake is a lovely, low-altitude destination on the eastern edge of the White River Plateau. The campground is at the east end of the lake and has impressive views of Sweetwater Canyon. The fishing is good, and electric-motor or hand-powered boating is allowed in the lake. There is also an extensive network of trails departing from the campground and the end of Sweetwater Road: Turret Creek, Cross Creek, Wet and Dry Sweetwater, Ute-Deep Lake, and Rim Lake Trails are all possibilities. Generally, these trails feature gradual climbs through sagebrush and scrub oak hills, aspen groves, pine forests, and subalpine meadows to the Shingle and Turret Peaks area in the Flat Tops Wilderness. There is excellent wildflower viewing, and the Cross Creek Trail provides access to a small cave with pictographs drawn by the Utes about 200 years ago. Many of these trails were originally Ute hunting trails.

The campground is on a steep hill overlooking the lake. The terraced sites are screened by scrub oak, but they are small and close to the campground road. Sites 3, 4, 8, and 9 are walk-in sites. Sites 8–10 have wonderful lake views.

Campsites, facilities: There are nine sites for tents and RVs up to 25 feet. There are no hookups. Site 7 is pull-through. Picnic tables, grills, and fire rings are provided. Wheelchair-accessible vault toilets and a fishing pier are available. Drinking water is available at the Sweetwater Lake Resort. Leashed pets are permitted.

Reservations, fees: Reservations are not accepted. The fee is $8 per night. Golden Age and Golden Access Passports are accepted. Cash or check only. Open early May–mid-November.

Directions: From I-70, take the Dotsero exit (Exit 133). Go north on County Road 301 for 6.9 miles. Go west on Sweetwater Road/County Road 40 for 10 miles. Turn left on an unmarked road. The campground is in 0.2 mile.

Contact: White River National Forest, 970/328-6388, www.fs.fed.us/r2/whiteriver/.

48 COFFEE POT SPRING

🐕 🚐 ⛺

Scenic rating: 8

north of Glenwood Springs

The White River Plateau is capped by erosion-resistant volcanic rock which has preserved the high plateau while surrounding sedimentary rocks have been carried away by erosion. The escarpment is an area of rolling subalpine meadows and alpine tundra dotted with small, scenic lakes and interspersed with spruce-fir forests and aspen groves. This area is unique in Colorado for its openness, and it's home to thriving elk herds and the 235,000-acre Flat Tops Wilderness. Coffee Pot Spring is on the southern edge of the plateau, far from the trails of the wilderness area, which makes it popular with ATV owners. Several 4WD roads begin nearby, but there are no hiking or mountain biking trails, although off-trail hiking is relatively easy on the plateau. The nearby Deep Creek Overlook is simply amazing. From the top of the plateau, you can look down a deep canyon with walls of sandstone and shale. The campground is a small loop on a sloping meadow full of colorful wildflowers. The campsites are on the edge of an aspen grove. Sites 5–8 and 10 are in the trees, and the other sites are in the meadow.

Campsites, facilities: There are 10 sites for tents and RVs up to 20 feet. There are no hookups. Picnic tables, grills, and fire rings are provided. Vault toilets are available. Leashed pets are permitted.

Reservations, fees: Reservations are not accepted. The fee is $6 per night. Golden Age and Golden Access Passports are accepted. Cash or check only. Open early June–late October.

Directions: From Glenwood Springs, take I-70 east to Exit 133. Go north on County Road 301 for 1.6 miles. Turn left on Coffee Pot Road/Forest Route 600. The campground is on the left in 16.6 miles.

Contact: White River National Forest, 970/328-6388, www.fs.fed.us/r2/whiteriver/.

49 LYONS GULCH

Scenic rating: 4

north of Dotsero

This is a primitive campground on the west bank of the Colorado River. It's screened from the road by cottonwoods and dense undergrowth. Rafters and kayakers can float 2.2 miles from the Cottonwood Island put-in to Lyons Gulch, or put in at Lyons Gulch and float 3.8 miles to the Dotsero take-out. There are scenic views up the valley, and it's a treat when the train passes on the tracks across the river, but proximity to the road limits this campground to a stopover.

Campsites, facilities: There are two walk-in tent sites. Picnic tables, grills, and fire rings are provided. Vault toilets are available. Leashed pets are permitted.

Reservations, fees: Camping is free, and reservations are not accepted. Open year-round.

Directions: From I-70, take the Dotsero exit (Exit 133). Go north on County Road 301 for four miles. The campground entrance is on the right.

Contact: Bureau of Land Management, 970/945-2341, www.blm.gov.

50 GYPSUM

Scenic rating: 5

east of Glenwood Springs

Gypsum is a primitive BLM campground on the shores of the Eagle River, about five miles upstream of the confluence with the Colorado River. The campground is a humble, inexpensive stopover. Accessibility is the biggest plus and the biggest drawback. Convenience, and the absence of a camp host, make this campground a prime site for weekend parties that leave the Dumpster, and the toilets, overflowing. Ughh. If you do need to stop here, the best sites are 1 and 2. They're located in a large cottonwood grove on the riverbank. Sites 3–8 are on a slight rise overlooking the river, surrounded by sagebrush. Sites 3 and 4 are well screened. Sites 5–8 are less private. Sites 7 and 8 have excellent views of the river. Activities here include fishing and river running. Rafters and novice kayakers frequently boat from Edwards to Eagle, but the river can be run to Dotsero, as well.

Campsites, facilities: There are eight sites for tents and RVs up to 35 feet. Sites 5, 7, and 8 are double-occupancy sites. There are no hookups or pull-throughs. Picnic tables, grills, fire rings, and vault toilets are provided. Leashed pets are permitted.

Reservations, fees: Reservations are not accepted. The fee is $10 per night. Golden Age and Golden Access Passports are accepted. Cash or check only. Open mid-May–mid-November.

Directions: From Glenwood Springs, take I-70 to Exit 140/Gypsum and turn right off the ramp. From the roundabout, take the frontage road west for 1.2 miles and turn left into the campground.

Contact: BLM Glenwood Springs, 970/947-2800.

WESTERN SLOPE SOUTH

© SARAH RYAN

BEST CAMPGROUNDS

The Western Slope South region begins in the valley
of the Colorado River, where the wide waterway curves north around the
edge of the Uncompahgre Plateau. The foundation rock of the plateau
was once part of Uncompahgria, one of the island mountain ranges of
the Ancestral Rockies that rose around 200 million years ago. Over millennia, those peaks were completely eroded away and covered by layers
of sandstone and shale. Regional uplift began again about 28 million
years ago, lifting the Uncompahgre Plateau nearly 7,000 feet above
the surrounding area. Today, the plateau is a forested highland that's
25 miles wide and nearly 100 miles long, and at the edges, the plateau
gives way to colorful cliffs, canyons, hogbacks, and cuestas.

These canyon lands are the centerpiece of Colorado National Monument, a natural amusement park for hikers and photographers who
can enjoy 41 miles of trails. The best introduction to the park is the
23-mile Rim Rock Drive, which offers views of many of the monument's
geological attractions.

The Black Ridge Canyons Wilderness reaches from the eastern
edge of Colorado National Monument to the Utah/Colorado border
and encompasses three major canyon systems which offer unparalleled backcountry desert experiences. These rugged canyons are home
to desert bighorn sheep, mountain lions, and native fish species. The
Colorado River is the northern boundary of the wilderness area and
the best way to explore it. A rafting or canoeing trip can be combined
with day hikes up Rattlesnake, Mee, and Knowles Canyons.

Grand Junction, the largest city in western Colorado (pop. 48,000
and growing), sits at the eastern end of the Grand Valley, at the confluence of the Colorado and Gunnison Rivers. (Both the valley and
the city derive their names from "Grand River," the former name of
the Colorado River.) As elsewhere in Colorado, these rivers dictate
industry and recreation. The valley is a productive agricultural zone,
with 15 wineries and numerous orchards. The distinctive outline of the
Grand Mesa dominates the horizon southeast of Grand Junction. Like
the Uncompahgre Plateau, the foundation of this 6,000-foot mesa
was once a part of Uncompahgria. Millennia of erosion, deposition,

and volcanic activity created an uplift of sandstone and shale capped by erosion-resistant lava. The lava was deposited during a volcanic period that began about 40 million years ago and ended about 5 million years ago. This period also formed the White River Plateau, West Elk Mountains, and the San Juans. Today, the appealing Grand Mesa is a vast plateau of shady aspen forests and fishing lakes, interspersed with loop hikes and 12 public campgrounds.

East of Grand Mesa on I-70, Glenwood Springs is a popular year-round destination because of its large public hot springs. It's also the gateway to the White River National Forest. Encompassing 2.3 million acres, the national forest includes the Flat Tops and Elk Mountains, as well as 10 fourteeners and eight wilderness areas. South of Glenwood Springs, Aspen is famous not just for Hunter S. Thompson and legendary skiing, but also for the Maroon Bells–Snowmass Wilderness. The reflection of the Bells in Maroon Lake might be the most photographed sight in Colorado. This glacial lake is accessible to all ages and fitness levels, but it is only a glimpse of the wonders of these mountains. Backcountry visitors can enjoy backpacking loops over nine 12,000-foot passes and six fourteeners. The most accessible are Castle Peak and Snowmass Mountain.

Returning to Grand Junction, the traveler can also follow U.S. Highway 50 south out of town to the Black Canyon of Gunnison National Park, a remarkable addition to the national park system. Carved by the Gunnison River during the last Ice Age, it is the deepest, narrowest canyon in the country. At its deepest point, it is 2,425 feet deep (twice the height of the Empire State Building), and at the Narrows it is just 1,300 feet across. There are campgrounds on the North and South Rims. For the best nightcap ever, camp on the North Rim and drive the North Rim Road at sunset.

Because Colorado never ceases to change, Curecanti National Recreation Area, just east of the national park, is a drastically different landscape of arid hills, wide reservoirs, and windswept campgrounds. The West Elk Mountains to the north of the recreation area form a remote landscape of volcanic spires and buttresses flanked by aspen forests.

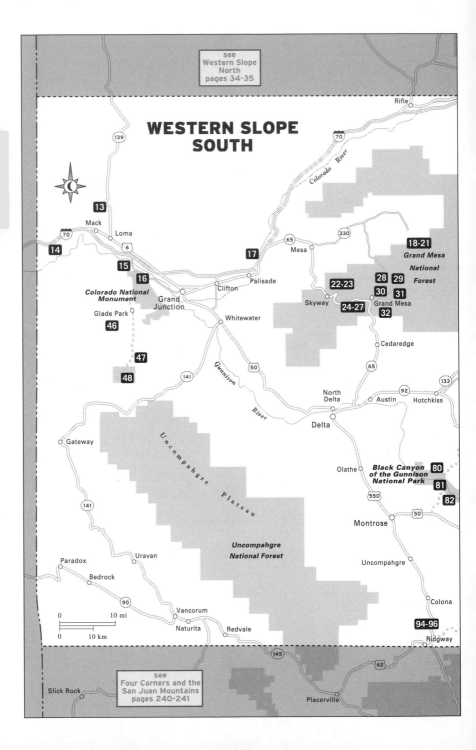

see
Western Slope
North
pages 34-35

WESTERN SLOPE SOUTH

Rifle

139

70

Colorado River

13

Mack

Loma

70

14

6

65

330

Mesa

17

18-21

Grand Mesa

15

National

16

Clifton

Palisade

22-23

28   29

Forest

Colorado National Monument

Skyway

30

31

Grand Mesa

Grand Junction

24-27

32

Glade Park

Whitewater

46

Cedaredge

65

47

141

Gunnison

50

48

North Delta

92

133

Austin   Hotchkiss

River

Delta

Gateway

U n c o m p a h g r e   P l a t e a u

Black Canyon of the Gunnison National Park

Olathe

80

81

550

82

141

50

Montrose

Uncompahgre National Forest

Paradox

Uravan

Uncompahgre

Bedrock

90

Colona

0   10 mi

Vancorum

0   10 km

Naturita   Redvale

94-96

Ridgway

145

62

see
Four Corners and the
San Juan Mountains
pages 240-241

Slick Rock

Placerville

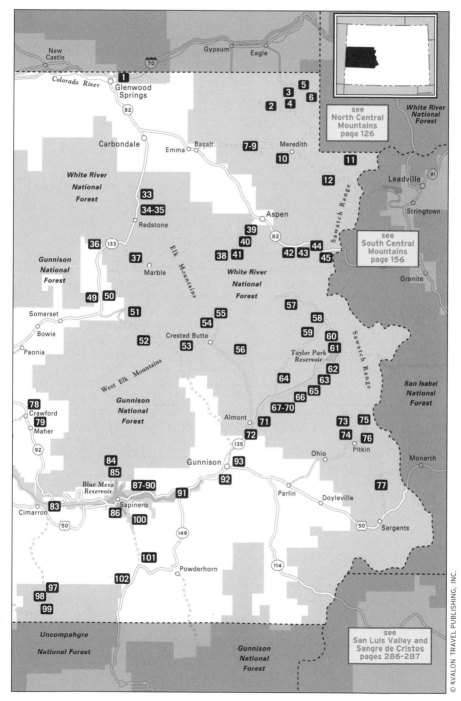

1 GLENWOOD CANYON RESORT

🚶 🚴 🎣 🚣 〰️ 🐕 🧗 🚐 ⛺

Scenic rating: 4

near Glenwood Springs

This resort is in the impressive Glenwood Canyon just east of Glenwood Springs. The campground is a weekend destination for families interested in rafting the Colorado River. The resort organizes half-day and full-day Class III whitewater trips. Kayakers can also boat this section of the river. Hikers can attempt the difficult 12-mile No Name Trail, which begins across the interstate, or stick to the mellower Glenwood Canyon Trail, which connects Glenwood Springs to Dotsero and is also open to bikers. Hikers shouldn't miss the Hanging Lake Trail, a 1.2-mile climb through Deadhorse Creek Canyon to a lake and Bridal Veil Falls. In Glenwood Springs, the Hot Springs Lodge is famous for its enormous open-air pool. A shuttle will take campers to the hot springs. Due to the variety of activities and proximity to the interstate, this campground is busy throughout the summer, and reservations are recommended. The sites are very close together with little privacy. Sites 1–45 are next to the river and shaded by large cottonwoods.

Campsites, facilities: There are 20 sites for tents and 40 sites for RVs up to 45 feet. Full and partial hookups are available. Picnic tables, grills, and fire rings are provided, and tent pads are provided at the tent sites. Restrooms with flush toilets and showers, drinking water, dump stations, a laundry room, playground, and boat ramp are available. Leashed pets are permitted.

Reservations, fees: Reservations are accepted at 800/958-6737. The tent fee is $28 per night, and the RV fee is $38–42 per night (includes two people). Additional people cost $5 per night. RV sites are open year-round. Tent sites are open from May to October, weather permitting.

Directions: From Glenwood Springs, take I-70 east to Exit 119. Follow the signs 0.1 mile to the campground entrance.

Contact: Glenwood Canyon Resort, 970/945-6737, www.glenwoodcanyonresort.com.

2 LEDE RESERVOIR

🚶 🐕 ⛺

Scenic rating: 6

south of Gypsum

LEDE Reservoir is tucked into a narrow valley that receives few visitors. The east shore is bordered by a meadow, and the west shore is bordered by a dense evergreen forest. The water levels fluctuate dramatically so there are no fish in the lake. On the north side of the reservoir, Antones Trail begins as an old Jeep road. The trail climbs for a half mile to a ridge-top meadow at an elevation of 10,000 feet. There are excellent views from the meadow of Mount of the Holy Cross and the Sawatch Range. This trail is closed to bikes and motorized vehicles.

Campsites, facilities: There are four sites for tents. Picnic tables and fire rings are provided. A vault toilet is available. Leashed pets are permitted.

Reservations, fees: Reservations are not accepted. The fee is $6 per night. Open June–October.

Directions: From the Gypsum roundabout, drive south on Highway 6 for 0.5 mile. Turn right on Valley Road/Gypsum Creek Road/Forest Route 412. In 19 miles, the road ends at the reservoir. The first 15 miles are fairly smooth. The last five miles can be very rough depending on recent weather.

Contact: White River National Forest, 970/328-6388, www.fs.fed.us/r2/whiteriver/.

3 ELK RUN

🚶 🚴 ⛵ 🛶 🐕 ♿ 🚐 ⛺

Scenic rating: 8

in Sylvan Lake State Park

BEST (

Sylvan Lake doesn't look like much on the map, but this beautiful little reservoir should not be missed. Tucked into a narrow valley and surrounded by national forest, the 40-acre lake is an angler's paradise full of brook, brown, and rainbow trout. The small boat ramp and still waters are perfect for launching a canoe. Elk, mule deer, beaver, and hummingbirds also live around the lake, and the wildflowers are outstanding. There are several options for hikers and mountain bikers. A short level trail circles the lake, and there are more nearby trails on East and West Brush Creek. Hikers and bikers can also try Sneve Gulch Trail, which begins in the parking lot and climbs 2.5 miles to an overlook with views of the lake.

Elk Run is the larger of the two campgrounds. It has two gravel loops. The top loop, sites 1–17, has slightly better views of the lake. There are very few trees in the campground, but the sites are far enough apart (50–100 feet) to afford some privacy. Sites 25, 27, and 29–31 are next to the creek.

Campsites, facilities: There are 34 sites for tents and RVs up to 35 feet. Sites 13 and 16 are wheelchair accessible. There are no hookups. Half of the sites are pull-through. Picnic tables, fire rings, and grills are provided. Restrooms with flush toilets and showers, drinking water, dump stations, a group camping area, and a boat ramp are available. Leashed pets are permitted.

Reservations, fees: Reservations are accepted (and highly recommended) at 800/678-2267 and www.parks.state.co.us. The fee is $12–14 per night. There is an additional $8 reservation fee. Campers must also purchase a Daily Parks Pass ($5) or an Annual Parks Pass ($55). The Aspen Leaf Annual Pass is accepted. Open June–October.

Directions: In Eagle, take Capitol Street south through town for 1.2 miles. Turn left on Brush Creek Road/County Road 307. The visitors center is in 9.6 miles. Bear right at the fork, and the campground entrance is in five miles. After the self-service station, turn left to enter Fisherman's Paradise or right to enter Elk Run.

Contact: Sylvan Lake State Park, 970/928-2021, email: sylvan.lake.park@state.co.us.

4 FISHERMAN'S PARADISE

🚶 🚴 ⛵ 🚐 🐕 ♿ 🚐 ⛺

Scenic rating: 6

in Sylvan Lake State Park

Fisherman's Paradise is a long, narrow grass strip overlooking fabulous Sylvan Lake. The views are unbeatable, but privacy is in very short supply. These 12 sites are just five feet apart from each other, and there are no trees or screens. (RVs can use the large parking lot next to the sites.) For avid anglers, the exposure is a small price to pay to have the 40-acre lake so close. Sailboats, electric boats, and hand-powered boats can all use the boat ramp. Hiking and mountain biking trails encircle the lake and explore East and West Brush Creek and the surrounding White River National Forest. The wildlife and wildflower viewing are also excellent. This is a truly idyllic place to wile away a weekend, but it's not secret. Reservations are a necessity during summer weekends.

Campsites, facilities: There are 12 sites for tents and RVs up to 35 feet and nine cabins. Site 46 is wheelchair accessible. There are no hookups or pull-through sites. Picnic tables, fire rings, and grills are provided. Vault toilets, drinking water, dump stations, and a boat ramp are available. Showers are available at nearby Elk Run. Leashed pets are permitted.

Reservations, fees: Reservations are accepted (and highly recommended) at 800/678-2267 and www.parks.state.co.us. The fee is $12–14 per night for camping. Cabins cost $60–120 per night. There is an additional $8 reservation fee. Campers must also purchase a Daily Parks Pass ($5) or an Annual Parks Pass ($55). The Aspen Leaf Annual Pass is accepted. Open year-round.

Directions: In Eagle, take Capitol Street south through town for 1.2 miles. Turn left on Brush Creek Road/County Road 307. The visitors center is in 9.6 miles. Bear right at the fork, and the campground entrance is in five miles. After the self-service station, turn left to enter Fisherman's Paradise or right to enter Elk Run.

Contact: Sylvan Lake State Park, 970/928-2021, email: sylvan.lake.park@state.co.us.

5 YEOMAN PARK

Scenic rating: 8

south of Eagle

Yeoman Park deserves a long visit from RV and tent campers alike. The campground is on the edge of a wetland meadow with an active beaver colony, and lies partly within a mature spruce forest. The campground is far enough from the crowds to feel like a secret, but it's still easily accessible by passenger car. Adults love the beauty of this quiet valley, and kids love chasing butterflies and exploring the wetlands. (The only drawback is the occasional early-morning ATV activity.) There's brook and rainbow trout fishing on East Brush Creek, and two short trails (Yeoman Park Discovery Trail and Browns Loop) begin at the campground. Two longer trails also begin here. The Ironedge and Lake Charles Trails can be combined into an 11.5-mile loop with views of the Elk Range, the Fryingpan Wilderness, Castle Peak, and the Flat Tops. Anglers should bring their poles. Cutthroat trout can be found in both Lake Charles and Mystic Island Lake. If the snow falls early enough, winter campers can go cross-country skiing, snowshoeing, and snowmobiling. The 10th Mountain Division Huts are located nearby.

Loop A (sites 1–15) sits on the border of an evergreen forest and a wide meadow. Site 1, at the end of the loop, is the most private, and it's next to the Discovery Trail. Sites 6, 8, 9, and 11 have beautiful views of the valley. Loop B (sites 16–24) also occupies the border between forest and meadow, but the sites are more varied. Site 19 is a walk-in tent site on a hill with good views of the creek. Sites 20–22 are very exposed, but they also have the best views in the campground of Craig Peak to the south.

Campsites, facilities: There are 23 sites for tents and RVs up to 30 feet. There are no hookups. Sites 4, 5, 9, 12, 13, and 20 are pull-through. Picnic tables, grills, and fire rings are provided. Tent pads are available at sites 1, 5, 6, 9, 12, and 22–24. Vault toilets and a fishing platform are available. The facilities are wheelchair accessible. Leashed pets are permitted.

Reservations, fees: Reservations are not accepted. The fee is $8 per night (includes two vehicles). Additional vehicles cost $5 per night. Golden Age and Golden Access Passports are accepted. Cash or check only. Open May–November.

Directions: In Eagle, take Capitol Street south through town for 1.2 miles. Turn left on Brush Creek Road/County Road 307. The visitors center is in 9.6 miles. Bear left at the fork onto East Brush Creek Road/Forest Route 415. In six miles, turn right and cross the bridge to enter the campground.

Contact: White River National Forest, 970/328-6388, www.fs.fed.us/r2/whiteriver/.

6 FULFORD CAVE

Scenic rating: 7

south of Eagle

A 0.7-mile trail climbs from the campground to the entrance of Fulford Cave, the eighth largest cave in Colorado. Spelunkers will discover crevices and pillars, stalactites and stalagmites, narrow gorges and running water. The hiking is also excellent. Hikers can access the Ironedge and Lake Charles Trails, which can be combined into an 11.5-mile loop with views of the Elk Range, the Fryingpan Wilderness, Castle Peak, and the Flat Tops. Anglers should bring their poles. Cutthroat trout can be found in both Lake Charles and Mystic Island Lake. The camping isn't half bad either. The campground is a small loop in an aspen grove high above East Brush Creek. Sites 1 and 4 are next to the drop-off to the creek. Sites 2–4 are very close together, but there are rarely crowds at this remote campground. Site 6 is the most private site, but it doesn't have a tent pad. Site 4 has a double-sized tent pad.

Campsites, facilities: There are seven sites for tents and RVs up to 20 feet. There are no hookups or pull-throughs. Picnic tables, grills, fire rings, and tent pads are provided. Vault toilets are available. Leashed pets are permitted.

Reservations, fees: Reservations are not accepted. The fee is $8 per night (includes two vehicles). Additional vehicles cost $5 per night. Golden Age and Golden Access Passports are accepted. Cash or check only. Open May–November.

Directions: In Eagle, take Capitol Street south through town for 1.2 miles. Turn left on Brush Creek Road/County Road 307. The visitors center is in 9.6 miles. Bear left at the fork onto East Brush Creek Road/Forest Route 415. In 6.3 miles, stay right at the fork. The campground is in one mile. The road is narrow and badly rutted for the last mile.

Contact: White River National Forest, 970/328-6388, www.fs.fed.us/r2/whiteriver/.

slopes. It's a popular weekend destination for boaters and sailors. There is also good fishing for rainbow, brown, and Mackinaw trout. There are two trails nearby for hiking and mountain biking. Ruedi Trail climbs steeply eight miles to the top of Red Table Mountain and has great views of the Fryingpan Valley and the Hunter-Fryingpan Wilderness area. The Rocky Fork Trail follows Rocky Fork Creek for 7.5 miles and offers good stream fishing.

Little Maud is the first of three campgrounds in the Ruedi Complex. It's a mid-sized loop with aspen and spruce in the outer campsites and an open meadow in the center. A small creek runs near the campground. The sites are about 50 feet apart, and there is not much shade. Sites 7–11 have good views of the lake. The campground fills up on the weekends.

Campsites, facilities: There are 22 sites for tents and RVs up to 40 feet. There are no hookups. Picnic tables, grills, and fire rings are provided. Vault toilets, drinking water, dump stations, and a boat ramp are available. Leashed pets are permitted.

Reservations, fees: Reservations are not accepted. The fee is $16 per night (includes two cars). Each additional car costs $5 per night. Golden Age and Golden Access Passports are accepted. Cash or check only. Open May–September.

Directions: From Basalt, take Fryingpan Road east for 14.7 miles. Turn right at the Ruedi Creek sign and then left down the hill to the first campground on the right.

Contact: White River National Forest, 970/925-3445, www.fs.fed.us/r2/whiteriver/.

▨ LITTLE MAUD

Scenic rating: 6

at Ruedi Reservoir

Ruedi is a 1,000-acre reservoir in the Fryingpan Valley, surrounded by steep, thickly forested

▨ MOLLIE B

Scenic rating: 6

at Ruedi Reservoir

Mollie B is the second of three campgrounds in the Ruedi Complex and the closest to the lake. (For more information on the reservoir, see the Little Maud listing in this chapter.) The campground is in a meadow with a creek. The sites are 30–50 feet apart, and there is very little shade except at sites 25, 26, 28, and 30, which are in a small aspen grove. Sites 33–37 are next to the shore.

Campsites, facilities: There are 25 sites for tents and RVs up to 40 feet. Site 27 is wheelchair accessible. There are no hookups. Sites 26, 34, and 46 are pull-through. Picnic tables, grills, and fire rings are provided. Flush toilets, drinking water, dump stations, and a boat ramp are available. Leashed pets are permitted.

Reservations, fees: Reservations are accepted at 877/444-6777 and www.reserve-usa.com. The fee is $16 per night (includes two cars). Each additional car costs $5 per night. Golden Age and Golden Access Passports are accepted. Cash or check only. Open May–September.

Directions: From Basalt, take Fryingpan Road east for 14.7 miles. Turn right at the Ruedi Creek sign and then left down the hill to the second campground.

Contact: White River National Forest, 970/925-3445, www.fs.fed.us/r2/whiteriver/.

9 LITTLE MATTIE

Scenic rating: 6

at Ruedi Reservoir

Little Mattie is the last of three campgrounds in the Ruedi complex and the farthest from the lake. (For more information on the reservoir, see the Little Maud listing in this chapter.) The other campgrounds are loops, but Little Mattie is a long lollipop that parallels Pond Creek. It has a lot more vegetation than the other campgrounds. Site 1 has a great view of the lake. Sites 2–4 are in dense thickets. Sites 15–19 are in a pleasant aspen grove.

Campsites, facilities: There are 20 sites for

tents and RVs up to 40 feet. There are no hookups. Sites 7–9 are pull-through. Picnic tables, grills, and fire rings are provided. Vault toilets and drinking water are available. Dump stations and a boat ramp are available at Little Maud. Leashed pets are permitted.

Reservations, fees: Reservations are not accepted. The fee is $14 per night (includes two cars). Each additional car costs $5 per night. Golden Age and Golden Access Passports are accepted. Cash or check only. Open May–September.

Directions: From Basalt, take Fryingpan Road east for 14.7 miles. Turn right at the Ruedi Creek sign and then left down the hill one mile to the last campground.

Contact: White River National Forest, 970/925-3445, www.fs.fed.us/r2/whiteriver/.

10 DEARHAMER

Scenic rating: 4

at Ruedi Reservoir

Dearhamer is a small loop at the east end of Ruedi Reservoir. (For more information on the reservoir, see the Little Maud listing in this chapter.) The sites are just 10–20 feet apart. There are some cottonwoods for shade, but no privacy. Mostly RVers use this campground. It's also a good campground for anglers who want to fish on the reservoir and the river. The Fryingpan, a Gold Medal river, enters the reservoir next to the campground. The Miller Divide Trail begins near the campground. Open to hiking and mountain biking (but not motorized vehicles), the trail traverses four miles to Rocky Fork Creek. There are excellent views of the Fryingpan Valley. This is also prime elk and deer habitat.

Campsites, facilities: There are 13 sites for tents and RVs up to 35 feet. Picnic tables, grills, and fire rings are provided. Vault toilets, drinking water, and a small boat ramp are available. Leashed pets are permitted.

Reservations, fees: Reservations are not accepted. The fee is $15 per night (includes two cars). Each additional car costs $5 per night. Golden Age and Golden Access Passports are accepted. Cash or check only. Open May–November.

Directions: From Basalt, take Fryingpan Road east for 22.6 miles. Make a sharp right at the end of the reservoir and then bear right immediately into the campground.

Contact: White River National Forest, 970/925-3445, www.fs.fed.us/r2/whiteriver/.

11 ELK WALLOW

Scenic rating: 7

east of Ruedi Reservoir

Situated in a wide valley on the North Fork of Mormon Creek, Elk Wallow's primary attraction is remoteness. This small, primitive campground overlooks a series of beaver ponds and offers excellent wildlife-watching. Bighorn sheep, bald eagles, waterfowl, deer, and elk live in this valley. A short drive up the road is the boundary of the Holy Cross Wilderness and the south end of the Tellurium Lake Trail. The campground is in a small evergreen forest and has a big granite outcropping that's perfect for stargazing. The sites are shaded and 30–50 feet apart. There is ample privacy.

Campsites, facilities: There are seven sites for tents and RVs up to 30 feet. There are no hookups or pull-through sites. Picnic tables, grills, fire rings, and vault toilets are provided. Drinking water is not available. Trash must be packed out. Leashed pets are permitted.

Reservations, fees: Reservations are not accepted. The fee is $7 per night (includes two cars). Each additional car costs $5 per night. Golden Age and Golden Access Passports are accepted. Cash or check only. Open May–November.

Directions: From Basalt, take Fryingpan

Road east for 26.8 miles. Turn left onto Forest Route 501. In three miles, turn right into the campground. There is no sign.

Contact: White River National Forest, 970/925-3445, www.fs.fed.us/r2/whiteriver/.

12 CHAPMAN

Scenic rating: 7

east of Ruedi Reservoir

This extra-large campground feels much smaller than it is because many of the loops are not visible to each other. This is a pretty, peaceful campground with lots of butterflies, birds, and wildflowers. The diminutive Chapman Reservoir is good for fishing, hand-powered boats, and swimming. The fishing is excellent on the Fryingpan, a Gold Medal river. There is a one-mile nature trail for hiking.

Chapman fills up on holidays, but the rest of the summer there are always first-come, first-served sites available. Loop A (sites 1–6) is on a hill in an evergreen forest. All of the sites are walk-ins. Loop B (7–9) are also walk-in sites. Loop C (10–14) is a small loop between the river and a meadow. Site 14 is walk-in. Loop D (15–22) is the least private loop, but it is also right next to the river. Loop E (23–41) is in an evergreen forest next to the pond. Loops F, G, and H are on the far side of the river. In Loop F (42–56), most sites are in a meadow, and there are some next to the river. Loop G (57–70) combines the river, aspen groves, and a meadow. Loop H (71–83) is in an evergreen forest next to the river and offers views of Seller Peak and Wildcat Mountain. There are lots of trees and privacy.

The group site is a long walk from the rest of the campground. It offers dispersed tent camping in an evergreen forest and can accommodate up to 60 people. It is very private and scenic with views of the Sawatch Range, and it has a picnic area and horseshoe pits.

This is the perfect destination for a family reunion or outdoor wedding. The group site is available by reservation only and is usually booked every summer weekend.

Campsites, facilities: There are 84 sites for tents and RVs up to 50 feet. There are no hookups. There are pull-through sites in Loops G and H. Picnic tables, grills, and fire rings are provided. Vault toilets and drinking water are available. Leashed pets are permitted.

Reservations, fees: Reservations are accepted at 877/444-6777 and www.reserve-usa.com. The fee is $15 per night (includes two cars). Each additional car costs $5 per night. Golden Age and Golden Access Passports are accepted. Cash or check only. Open May–November.

Directions: From Basalt, take Fryingpan Road east for 33.2 miles. Make a soft right into the campground.

Contact: White River National Forest, 970/925-3445, www.fs.fed.us/r2/whiteriver/.

13 BOOKCLIFF

Scenic rating: 5

in Highline Lake State Park

Highline Lake is a reservoir in the agricultural town of Loma. The park has a following of regulars who enjoy the roomy campsites, which are large enough to set up several tents and a volleyball net. The camping area is grassy and shaded by mature trees. Except for the Book Cliffs to the north, the scenery is not impressive, but this is an ideal weekend trip or stopover for families with small children. Kids can romp on the sandy swimming beach or go mountain biking on the flat 3.5-mile trail that circles the lake. Water sports and fishing are also popular pastimes. There are two lakes for fishing: Highline Lake, which has largemouth bass and bluegill, and the smaller Mack Mesa Lake, which has trout. Mountain bikers who are exploring the adjacent BLM lands will appreciate the facilities and convenience of this park. Winter sports include ice fishing and waterfowl hunting.

Campsites, facilities: There are 27 sites for tents and RVs up to 35 feet. Site 19 is wheelchair accessible. There are no hookups. Picnic tables and grills are provided. Restrooms with flush toilets and showers, drinking water, dump stations, laundry facilities, a playground, vending machines, and a boat ramp are available. In the summer, there is a small store at the marina and personal watercraft rentals. The group picnic area is available by reservation. Leashed pets are permitted.

Reservations, fees: Reservations are accepted (and recommended during the summer) at 800/678-2267 and www.parks.state.co.us. The fee is $12 per night. There is an additional $8 reservation fee. Campers must also purchase a Daily Parks Pass ($5) or an Annual Parks Pass ($55). The Aspen Leaf Annual Pass is accepted. Open year-round.

Directions: From Grand Junction, drive west on I-70 to Loma. Go north on Highway 139 for five miles. Turn left on Q Road. In 1.3 miles, turn right on 11.75 Road. The park entrance is in 1.3 miles.

Contact: Highline Lake State Park, 970/858-7208, email: highline.park@state.co.us.

14 RABBIT VALLEY

Scenic rating: 9

in Colorado Canyons National Conservation Area

The Colorado Canyons NCA encompasses the northern canyon lands of the Uncompahgre Plateau as they descend to the Colorado River. Visitors to this area will find the high desert and colorful landforms that one usually associates with southern Utah, but there are no visitors centers or manicured trails here. The adventure is in the backcountry—in remote destinations like Rattlesnake Canyon, Horse-thief Canyon, and Ruby Canyon. Most of the visitors to this area are mountain bikers, rafters, and ATVers. The Rabbit Valley campground is a stop on Kokopelli's Trail, a 142-mile mountain bike trail from Loma, Colorado, to Moab, Utah. This trail is technically challenging and requires a lot of preparation and planning. For bikers who want a taste of the trail, there are several shorter loops in the area. Trail conditions and maps are available at the bike shops in Fruita (see next listing). Fruita is also the last place to stock up on water and biking gear. Visitors who don't want to enter the backcountry can try the Trail Through Time on the north side of the interstate. This 1.5-mile hiking trail tours a working dinosaur quarry. There are two more primitive campgrounds in Rabbit Valley (Castle Rocks and Knowles Canyon), but these are only accessible by 4WD vehicles.

Campsites, facilities: This is a primitive campground. There are five walk-in tent sites around a large dirt parking lot. Small RVs can access this area, but the road is very rough and high-clearance vehicles are recommended. Picnic tables, fire rings, grills, and vault toilets are provided. Leashed pets are permitted.

Reservations, fees: Camping is free. Reservations are not accepted. Open year-round.

Directions: From Grand Junction, take I-70 west to Exit 2. At the top of the ramp, turn south. From the Rabbit Valley Recreation Management Area sign, proceed 0.5 mile to a fork. Take the right fork. The campground is on the right in 0.6 mile.

Contact: Bureau of Land Management, Grand Junction Office, 970/224-3000.

15 FRUITA

Scenic rating: 5

in Colorado River State Park

BEST (

Fruita is a very modern park that caters mostly to RVs. It is a large, flat loop with very little privacy, but the walk-in tent sites are partially screened by landscaping. Families and retirees love this park because of the facilities and the convenience. It is next to the highway and less than a mile from the entrance to Colorado National Monument. It is also walking distance to the Dinosaur Journey Museum. Hiking opportunities abound in the monument, and there are endless mountain biking trails in the surrounding BLM lands. Grand Junction and the Grand Valley wineries are an easy day trip, and the Grand Mesa Scenic Byway is also nearby. Adventurous souls can schedule horseback riding and rafting trips with local outfitters. It's also a great stopover on the road to Utah.

Campsites, facilities: There are 13 walk-in tent sites with tent pads. There are 49 sites for tents and RVs of any length. Sites 1–12, 25, and 36–44 have full hookups. Sites 13–24 and 26–35 have water and electric hookups. Sites A–F are for group camping and rent as one unit. They can accommodate 36 people. Most sites are wheelchair accessible. Picnic tables, fire rings, grills, and shelters are provided. Restrooms with flush toilets and showers, vault toilets, drinking water, dump stations, laundry facilities, and a playground are available. There is also a group picnic area, bookstore, amphitheater, and swim beach. Leashed pets are permitted.

Reservations, fees: Reservations are accepted at 800/678-2267 and www.parks.state.co.us. The tent fee is $12 per night. The RV fee is $16–20 per night. There is an additional $8 reservation fee. Campers must also purchase a Daily Parks Pass ($5) or an Annual Parks Pass ($55). The Aspen Leaf Annual Pass is accepted. Open year-round.

Directions: From Grand Junction, take I-70 west to Exit 19/Fruita. Go south on Highway 340 for one mile. The park entrance is on the right.

Contact: Colorado River State Park, 970/858-9188, email: colorado.river.park@state.co.us.

16 SADDLEHORN

👤❄️🏠🚐🏕️

Scenic rating: 9

in Colorado National Monument

BEST (

Colorado National Monument is one of Colorado's secret destinations. Most Coloradoans drive by the monument on their way to Utah, never realizing that the canyons and rock monuments they're seeking are just south of the interstate. As a result, the park is uncrowded, and there's always space for late arrivals in this first-come, first-served campground. The monument protects 32 square miles of canyons and plateaus on the northern end of the Uncompahgre Uplift. The high country here rises 2,000 feet above the Colorado River and the towns of Fruita and Grand Junction. As you might guess, the views are spectacular. Visitors can spend hours at the overlooks watching the weather move across the Grand Valley and the Book Cliffs to the north. It's a paradise for photographers and hikers. There are seven trails that are less than a mile, and six backcountry trails that are four to nine miles long. The most popular is Monument Canyon Trail, which descends 600 feet through layers of Mesozoic sandstone and passes the Coke Ovens monoliths. There are campfire programs and guided walks for visitors who want to learn more about the geology and ecology of the park. The trails are open to cross-country skiing in the winter. Mountain biking is not allowed in the park, but the monument is surrounded by BLM land with world-class mountain bike trails.

Campsites, facilities: There are 51 sites for tents and RVs up to 35 feet in Loops A and B. The most attractive sites are on the outside of the loops; these sites have more privacy and better views. There are no hookups. Loop C is reserved for school groups. Picnic tables and charcoal grills are provided. Wood fires are prohibited in the park. Restrooms with flush toilets and drinking water are available. Leashed pets are permitted in the campground but are not allowed on trails.

Reservations, fees: Reservations are not accepted. The fee is $10 per night for up to seven people. Cash or check only. The park entrance fee is $5 per vehicle (good for seven days). Golden Age and Golden Access Passports are accepted. Open year-round.

Directions: From Grand Junction, take I-70 west to Exit 19/Fruita. Go south on Highway 340. In 2.4 miles, turn right on Rim Rock Road. The campground entrance is on the left in four miles.

Contact: Colorado National Monument, 970/858-3617, www.nps.gov/colm.

17 ISLAND ACRES

👤🚴🏖️🏊🛶🎣🏠🏄♿🚐🏕️

Scenic rating: 4

in Colorado River State Park

Colorado River State Park actually consists of five sections along the Colorado River from the campground at Fruita (the western anchor) to Island Acres (the eastern anchor). The middle three sections are for day use only. The scenery changes dramatically on the drive from Fruita, at the base of Colorado National Monument in the Grand Valley, through the crumbling hills and sandstone cliffs carved by the river. Island Acres is surrounded by the Little Books Cliff Wild Horse Range, where the BLM manages a herd of over 300 wild horses. It's in a deep canyon, just a hundred yards from the interstate, so it's a convenient stopover with deluxe facilities. It has three stocked fishing ponds and a swim beach, as well as a short trail for hiking and biking. Grand Junction and the Grand Valley wineries are an easy day trip, and the Grand Mesa Scenic Byway begins nearby. Kayakers take over when the river hits 20,000 cubic feet per second and enormous waves occur upstream of Cameo dam. In the winter, the campground and lakes are open for ice fishing and ice-skating.

There are three loops between the interstate and the river. Loop A (sites 1–34) has electric hookups and more shade trees than the other loops. Loop B (sites 35–40) is for tent camping only. The sites are very close together and not appealing. Loops C and D (sites 41–80) are closest to the highway and have few mature shade trees. The sites are about 30 feet apart. There is limited privacy and shade.

Campsites, facilities: There are six tent-only sites and 74 sites for tents and RVs of any size. Sites 1–34 have electric hookups, and sites 41–80 have full hookups. Sites 17–19, 39, 41, 56, and 80 and the facilities are wheelchair accessible. Picnic tables, fire rings, and grills are provided at all sites. Some sites have sun shelters and tent pads. Restrooms with flush toilets and showers, vault toilets, drinking water, dump stations, a laundry room, pay phones, vending machines, and a playground are available. There is also a group picnic area, swim beach, stocked fishing ponds, and interpretive programs. Leashed pets are permitted.

Reservations, fees: Reservations are accepted at 800/678-2267 and www.parks.state.co.us. The tent fee is $12 per night, and the RV fee is $16–20 (up to six people). There is an additional $8 reservation fee. Campers must also purchase a Daily Parks Pass ($5) or an Annual Parks Pass ($55). The Aspen Leaf Annual Pass is accepted. Open year-round.

Directions: From Grand Junction, take I-70 east to Exit 49. Go north on the Frontage Road for 0.3 mile to the campground entrance.

Contact: Colorado River State Park, 970/464-0548, email: colorado.river.park@ state.co.us.

18 EARLY SETTLERS

🚶 🚴 🛶 🚤 🐕 🎣 ♿ 🚐 ⛺

Scenic rating: 6

in Vega State Park

BEST (

The main attraction at Vega State Park is the 900-acre reservoir at an elevation of 8,000 feet. Vega means "meadow" in Spanish, and

the land under the reservoir was once fertile ranchlands. The surrounding hillsides slope gently out of the lake, facilitating fishing access and hiking. To the south, the Grand Mesa rises 2,000 feet above the lake and provides endless four-wheeling and mountain biking opportunities. From the campground, bikes and ATVs can take Park Creek Road into Grand Mesa National Forest. Mountain bikers also come to the park in September for the annual Wrap Yourself in Gold Mountain Bike Tour. Participants can choose from three biking events of varying length and difficulty. Hikers can take an easy trail along the shore to the Aspen Grove campground. The lake offers good trout fishing and waterskiing, sailing, and windsurfing.

Early Settlers is a large paved loop in a meadow of wheat and wildflowers at the west end of the lake. It is the most modern and the busiest campground at the park. There are very few trees, and privacy is poor for tent campers. All of the sites have nice views of the hills to the north, but the lakeside sites (111–114, 117, 118, 120, and 122) are the best.

Campsites, facilities: There are 33 sites for tents and RVs up to 40 feet. Sites 101, 104, and 119 and the facilities are wheelchair accessible. Water and electrical hookups and pull-through sites are available. Picnic tables, fire rings, grills, and tent pads are provided. Sites 101, 104, 106, 108–111, 119, 124, 127, 129, and 132 have sun shelters. Restrooms with flush toilets and showers, vault toilets, drinking water, dump stations, a playground, and a boat ramp are available. Leashed pets are permitted.

Reservations, fees: Reservations are accepted at 800/678-2267 and www.parks.state.co.us. The fee is $16 per night. There is an additional $8 reservation fee. Campers must also purchase a Daily Parks Pass ($5) or an Annual Parks Pass ($55). The Aspen Leaf Annual Pass is accepted. Open May–October.

Directions: From Collbran, take County Road 330E east for 6.5 miles. Turn right on

County Road 64.5 and continue 3.3 miles to the entrance station. Take the first right after the station. The campground is on the left in one mile.

Contact: Vega State Park, 970/487-3407, email: vega.park@state.co.us.

19 PIONEER

Scenic rating: 8

in Vega State Park

BEST (

Pioneer is a real treat for tent campers. This new loop is on a hillside overlooking Vega Reservoir, and it winds through dense bushes and scrub oaks with pockets of wildflowers. The sites are well screened from each other, and sites 126, 135, and 138–141 have excellent views of the lake. On the other side of the parking lot, there is an ATV staging area for Park Creek Road, which climbs into Grand Mesa National Forest. This route is very popular with mountain bikers. Hikers and anglers can take a trail from the Early Settlers to Aspen Grove campgrounds. The lake has good rainbow trout fishing. It's also a popular water sports destination. The cabins at this campground are open year-round and are very popular in the winter, when the lake is open to ice-skating and ice fishing, and cross-country skiers and snowmobilers enjoy exploring Grand Mesa. (For more information on Vega State Park, see the Early Settlers listing in this chapter.)

Campsites, facilities: There are 10 walk-in tent sites and five rustic cabins. Sites 134 and 135 and the facilities are wheelchair accessible. Picnic tables, fire rings, grills, tent pads, and wheelbarrows are provided. Vault toilets and drinking water are available at the campground. Restrooms with flush toilets and showers, a playground, and a boat ramp are available at the Early Settlers campground. Leashed pets are permitted.

Reservations, fees: Reservations are accepted at 800/678-2267 and www.parks.state.co.us. The fee is $12 per night. There is an additional $8 reservation fee. Campers must also purchase a Daily Parks Pass ($5) or an Annual Parks Pass ($55). The Aspen Leaf Annual Pass is accepted. The tent sites are open May–October, and the cabins are open year-round.

Directions: From Collbran, take County Road 330E east for 6.5 miles. Turn right on Country Road 64.5 and continue 3.3 miles to the entrance station. Take the first right after the station. The campground is on the right in one mile.

Contact: Vega State Park, 970/487-3407, email: vega.park@state.co.us.

20 ASPEN GROVE

Scenic rating: 7

in Vega State Park

Aspen Grove is a pleasant campground on the eastern end of the 900-acre reservoir, at the base of the Grand Mesa. The campground has two loops separated by a group picnic area with a large pavilion. The first loop (sites 200–208) is in an open meadow close to the water. The second loop (sites 209–227) is in a dense thicket of tall bushes and scattered trees. The first has better views, and the second is much more private. Sites 200, 202, 204, and 205 are closest to the lake. Because there are no hookups, this campground is much less popular than Early Settlers, but it's an excellent choice for both tent campers and RVers. A foot trail connects the two campgrounds, and mountain bikers and ATVers can take forest roads into Grand Mesa National Forest. The lake has good rainbow trout fishing, and canoes and kayaks can be carried down to the water. (For more information on Vega State Park, see the Early Settlers entry in this chapter.)

Campsites, facilities: There are 27 sites for

tents and RVs up to 40 feet. Sites 203, 212, and 214 and the facilities are wheelchair accessible. There are no hookups, but most sites are pull-through. Picnic tables, fire rings, grills, and tent pads are provided. Sites 200, 203, 212, and 214 have sun shelters. Vault toilets, drinking water, and a group picnic area are available. Restrooms with flush toilets and showers and a dump station are available at the Early Settlers campground. Leashed pets are permitted.

Reservations, fees: Reservations are accepted at 800/678-2267 and www.parks.state.co.us. The fee is $12 per night. There is an additional $8 reservation fee. Campers must also purchase a Daily Parks Pass ($5) or an Annual Parks Pass ($55). The Aspen Leaf Annual Pass is accepted. Open May–October.

Directions: From Collbran, take County Road 330E east for 6.5 miles. Turn right on Country Road 64.5 and continue 3.3 miles to the entrance station. Take the first right after the station. The campground is on the left in 2.8 miles.

Contact: Vega State Park, 970/487-3407, email: vega.park@state.co.us.

21 OAK POINT

Scenic rating: 6

in Vega State Park

On the north shore of 900-acre Vega Reservoir, Oak Point is the only campground in the park with views of Grand Mesa towering 2,000 feet above the lake. Except for this feature, it's the least appealing of the campgrounds in the park. It hasn't been renovated, so the sites are smaller and closer together than at the other campgrounds. There are three distinct areas in this long loop along the shore. Some sites are surrounded by Gambel's oak, but sites 301–324 and 333–337 are in a meadow with no shade and limited privacy. Sites 306, 307, 309–313, 327, and 332–336

are lakeside. Anglers and water sports enthusiasts will appreciate the boat ramp at the campground. The lake has good fishing for rainbow trout and some cutthroat. (For more information on Vega State Park, see the Early Settlers entry in this chapter.)

Campsites, facilities: There are 39 sites for tents and RVs up to 25 feet. There are no hookups or pull-throughs. Picnic tables, fire rings, and grills are provided. Vault toilets, drinking water, a dump station, boat ramp, and swing set are available. Leashed pets are permitted.

Reservations, fees: Reservations are accepted at 800/678-2267 and www.parks.state.co.us. The fee is $12 per night. There is an additional $8 reservation fee. Campers must also purchase a Daily Parks Pass ($5) or an Annual Parks Pass ($55). The Aspen Leaf Annual Pass is accepted. Open May–October.

Directions: From Collbran, take County Road 330E east for 6.5 miles. Turn right on Country Road 64.5 and continue 3.3 miles to the entrance station. The campground is on the right two miles after the station.

Contact: Vega State Park, 970/487-3407, email: vega.park@state.co.us.

22 JUMBO

Scenic rating: 7

in Grand Mesa

Grand Mesa is exactly what the name describes—a huge mesa that's about 50 miles across and 4,000 feet tall. The mesa was once part of an enormous basin that filled with 5,000 feet of shale, limestone, and sandstone. Volcanic activity covered the basin with 400 feet of basalt, and then the whole Colorado Plateau uplifted. After the uplift, the surrounding sediments that weren't capped by basalt eroded away. Weaknesses in the underlying sediments made the basalt unstable, resulting in cracks and depressions that became lakes. Glaciers added to those cracks and depressions, helping to create the 300 ponds, lakes, and reservoirs that speckle the Grand Mesa today.

The Utes tell a very different story to explain the lakes. Their legend says that Grand Mesa was once home to an enormous eagle who swept down on misbehaving children and carried them away. The eagle took a chief's son, and the chief climbed up to the nest to retrieve his son. The boy was gone, so the chief took the eagle's eggs and threw them into the jaws of a giant serpent. The eagle attacked the serpent, tearing it to pieces in the air. Where the pieces of the serpent fell, they left holes that later became the lakes.

The Grand Mesa Scenic Byway passes through five life zones on its way to the top of the mesa: Lower Sonoran, Upper Sonoran, Lower Montane, Montane, and Subalpine. The top of the mesa is mostly covered with spruce-fir forests interspersed with small meadows and hundreds of lakes. The mesa receives huge amounts of snow, making it one of the lushest environments on the western slope. Five major creeks drain the mesa: Plateau, Buzzard, Kannah, Surface, and LeRoux. Settlers began developing the mesa for irrigation in the 1880s, and today it remains an important source of water for farming and power utilities. The mesa is a patchwork of public and private property, and there are several vacation lodges and developed areas on the mesa.

As you might expect, fishing reigns on the Mesa. There are rainbow, cutthroat, brook, brown, and lake trout and splake. The majority of ponds and lakes are stocked. Boating regulations vary, but most boating is limited to hand-powered boats and electric motors. Swimming is not recommended because of the water temperatures and the amount of hooks in the water. Four-wheeling and ATVs are also extremely popular on the mesa. A network of 4WD roads crisscrosses the forest and provides access to remote lakes.

Supplies are available at Mesa Lakes, Ward Lake, and Twin Lakes, but bring plenty of

insect repellent. In the words of one camp host, "The mosquitoes are free." And there are lots of them.

Campsites, facilities: There are 26 sites for tents and RVs up to 35 feet. Sites 9, 10, and 20 are wheelchair-accessible. Most sites have electric hookups. Sites 1, 2, 5, 25, and 26 do not have hookups. There are no pull-through sites. Sites 25 and 26 are walk-in tent sites. Sites 17 and 24 are double-wide. Picnic tables, grills, and fire rings are provided. Vault toilets and drinking water are available. Leashed pets are permitted.

Reservations, fees: Reservations are not accepted. Golden Age and Golden Access Passports are accepted. Cash or check only. Open May–September.

Directions: From I-70, take Highway 65 east for 25 miles. Turn right at Jumbo Reservoir and right again to enter the campground.

Contact: Grand Mesa National Forest, 970/874-6600, www.fs.fed.us/r2/gmug/.

23 SPRUCE GROVE

Scenic rating: 6

in Grand Mesa

Spruce Grove is in the Mesa Lakes area on the west side of the mesa. As one of the only campgrounds that's not on a lake, it tends to be less crowded than nearby Jumbo. It's a gravel loop in a dense spruce-fir forest about 150 yards from the highway. Sites 1, 2, and 13–16 are within sight of the road. Sites 1–6 have a gentle slope that makes it hard to find tent sites, but sites 7–16 are flat. (For more information on Grand Mesa, see the Jumbo listing in this chapter.)

Campsites, facilities: There are 16 sites for tents and RVs up to 22 feet. There are no hookups. Sites 1, 2, and 5–16 are pull-through. Picnic tables, grills, and fire rings are provided. Vault toilets and drinking water are available. Leashed pets are permitted.

Reservations, fees: Reservations are not accepted. The fee is $10 per night. Additional vehicles cost $5 per night. Golden Age and Golden Access Passports are accepted. Cash or check only. Open Memorial Day–Labor Day. Directions: From I-70, take Highway 65 east for 25.7 miles. The campground entrance is on the right.
Contact: Grand Mesa National Forest, 970/874-6600, www.fs.fed.us/r2/gmug/.

24 ISLAND LAKE

Scenic rating: 6

in Grand Mesa

Island Lake is one of the larger lakes on the mesa. Its north shore is rimmed by high red cliffs, and the campground at the western tip overlooks meadows that slope away to the south. The campground is separated from the water by the road, but it's a short walk to the boat ramp and fishing pier. The majority of sites are shaded by spruce and fir trees; other sites border a large meadow. Sites 29 and 33–37 have the best views. Mountain bikers and ATV riders can take Forest Route 115 to Granby Reservoir and beyond. Cross-country skiers will enjoy the Powderhorn to Sunlight Trail, which runs along the south shore of the lake. It's a short drive to the west trailhead for the Crag Crest National Recreation Trail. This 10.3-mile loop traverses the "crest" of the mesa and has panoramic views of the Book and Roan Cliffs to the north, the West Elk and San Juan Mountains to the east and south, and the Uncompahgre Plateau and La Sal Mountains to the west. (For more information on Grand Mesa, see the Jumbo listing in this chapter.)
Campsites, facilities: There are 41 sites for tents and RVs up to 45 feet. There are no hookups. Sites 3, 4, 6, 7, and 14 are pull-through. Picnic tables, grills, and fire rings are provided. Vault toilets, drinking water, a boat

ramp, fishing pier, and fish-cleaning station are available. Leashed pets are permitted.
Reservations, fees: Reservations are not accepted. The fee is $12 per night. Additional vehicles cost $6 per night. Golden Age and Golden Access Passports are accepted. Cash or check only. Open Memorial Day–Labor Day and without services after Labor Day. Directions: From I-70, take Highway 65 east for 33.3 miles. Turn right at the Island Lake sign and continue 0.6 mile downhill. The campground is on the right.
Contact: Grand Mesa National Forest, 970/874-6600, www.fs.fed.us/r2/gmug/.

25 LITTLE BEAR

Scenic rating: 7

in Grand Mesa

Little Bear is the second campground on lovely Island Lake and the more scenic one. It's strung along the south shore of the lake, in a spruce-fir forest scattered with boulders probably left behind by a glacier. Like most of the Grand Mesa campgrounds, Little Bear isn't very busy during the week, but it fills up on weekends. Sites 10–12, 14, 19, 22, 23, and 25–27 have excellent lake views. Sites 28–30 are also next to the lake, but the dam obstructs their views. From the Island Lake campground, ATVs and mountain bikes can take Forest Route 115 to Granby Reservoir and beyond. It's a short drive to the west trailhead for the Crag Crest National Recreation Trail. This 10.3-mile loop traverses the "crest" of the mesa and has panoramic views of the Book and Roan Cliffs to the north, the West Elk and San Juan Mountains to the east and south, and the Uncompahgre Plateau and La Sal Mountains to the west. (For more information on Grand Mesa, see the Jumbo entry in this chapter.)
Campsites, facilities: There are 36 sites for tents and RVs up to 22 feet. There are no

hookups. Sites 3, 4, 6, 16, 20, 24, 29, and 30 are pull-through. Picnic tables, grills, and fire rings are provided. Vault toilets, drinking water, a boat ramp, fish-cleaning station, and fishing pier are available. Leashed pets are permitted.

Reservations, fees: Reservations are not accepted. The fee is $12 per night. Additional vehicles cost $6 per night. Golden Age and Golden Access Passports are accepted. Cash or check only. Open Memorial Day–Labor Day.

Directions: From I-70, take Highway 65 east for 34.5 miles. Turn right on Forest Route 116. The campground is on the right in 0.8 mile.

Contact: Grand Mesa National Forest, 970/874-6600, www.fs.fed.us/r2/gmug/.

26 WARD LAKE

🎣 🚐 ❄️ 🏕️ 🚙 ⛰️

Scenic rating: 8

in Grand Mesa

Ward Lake is a medium-sized lake surrounded by spruce-fir forests that go right down to the water. Although there is a resort at one end, only one private residence is visible from the campground. The campground is in a mature but thin forest with lots of wildflowers. This is a very popular campground on weekends. The visitors center and Discovery Trail are within walking distance. In the winter, cross-country skiing trails circle Deep Slough and Ward Creek Reservoirs. Sites 6–11 and 14–27 have lake views. Sites 8, 9, 22, 23, 25, and 26 are right on the shore. Sites 1–3, 5, 12, and 13 are near the road. (For more information on Grand Mesa, see the Jumbo entry in this chapter.)

Campsites, facilities: There are 27 sites for tents and RVs up to 20 feet. There are no hookups. Sites 3, 5, 10, 14, 19, 22, 23, and 25 are pull-through. Picnic tables, grills, and fire rings are provided. Vault toilets, drinking water, and a boat ramp are available. Leashed pets are permitted.

Reservations, fees: Reservations are not accepted. The fee is $12 per night. Additional vehicles cost $6 per night. Golden Age and Golden Access Passports are accepted. Cash or check only. Open Memorial Day–Labor Day and without services after Labor Day.

Directions: From I-70, take Highway 65 east for 34.6 miles. Turn left on Forest Route 121. The campground is on the right in 0.5 mile.

Contact: Grand Mesa National Forest, 970/874-6600, www.fs.fed.us/r2/gmug/.

27 COBBETT LAKE

🏃 🚴 🎣 🚐 🏕️ 🚙 ⛰️

Scenic rating: 6

in Grand Mesa

This is a small campground on the shore of a small lake, but it attracts big RVs and it's busy all summer. Only nonmotorized boats are allowed on Cobbett Lake. Sites 1–3, 5, 7, and 8 are next to the lake, but they are also very close together. Sites 16–20 overlook a smaller lake to the north, but they are also close together. At the visitors center across the lake, there is a short interpretive hiking trail, and the west trailhead of the Crag Crest National Recreation Trail is a short drive away. This 10.3-mile loop traverses the "crest" of the mesa and has panoramic views of the Book and Roan Cliffs to the north, the West Elk and San Juan Mountains to the east and south, and the Uncompahgre Plateau and La Sal Mountains to the west. Half of the loop is open to mountain bikes and horses. (For more information on Grand Mesa, see the Jumbo entry in this chapter.)

Campsites, facilities: There are 20 sites for tents and RVs up to 30 feet. There are no hookups. Sites 8, 10, 15, and 18 are pull-through. Picnic tables, grills, and fire rings are provided. Vault toilets and drinking water are available. Leashed pets are permitted.

Reservations, fees: Reservations are accepted at 877/444-6777 and www.reserveusa.com. The fee is $12 per night. Additional vehicles cost $6 per night. There is an $8 reservation fee. Golden Age and Golden Access Passports are accepted. Cash or check only. Open Memorial Day–Labor Day.

Directions: From I-70, take Highway 65 east for 34.5 miles. The campground entrance is on the left before the lake.

Contact: Grand Mesa National Forest, 970/874-6600, www.fs.fed.us/r2/gmug/.

28 COTTONWOOD LAKE

Scenic rating: 5

in Grand Mesa

In 2005, a timber sale ruined this campground. Almost every site was left with fresh tree stumps and reduced privacy. To top it off, heavy machinery wreaked havoc on the roads, which led to drainage issues and flooded sites. Hopefully, the Forest Service will fix these problems, but even then this wouldn't be a first choice. The sites are very close together, and there are no lake views. Cottonwood Lake and the boat ramp are within walking distance. (For more information on Grand Mesa, see the Jumbo listing in this chapter.)

Campsites, facilities: There are 42 sites for tents and RVs up to 30 feet. There are no hookups. Sites 2, 6, 10, 13, 15, and 17 are pull-through. Picnic tables, grills, and fire rings are provided. Vault toilets are available. Leashed pets are permitted.

Reservations, fees: Reservations are not accepted. The fee is $12 per night. Additional vehicles cost $6 per night. Golden Age and Golden Access Passports are accepted. Cash or check only. Open Memorial Day–Labor Day.

Directions: From I-70, take Highway 65 east for 34.6 miles. Turn left on Forest Route 121. In 11.5 miles, turn left on Forest Route 257. The campground is on the left in five miles.

Contact: Grand Mesa National Forest, 970/874-6600, www.fs.fed.us/r2/gmug/.

29 BIG CREEK

Scenic rating: 7

in Grand Mesa

This campground is on the west shore of Big Creek Reservoir, a large lake with views of Leon Peak, the highest point on the mesa. This part of the mesa receives more precipitation than the western half, as well as fewer visitors. Campers who do drive out here usually stay for four or five days. Most sites are in a spruce-fir forest. Sites 1, 2, 4–9, 12, 13, and 15 have lake views. Sites 13, 14, 16–18, and 24–26 border a large meadow. (For more information on Grand Mesa, see the Jumbo listing in this chapter.)

Campsites, facilities: There are 26 sites for tents and RVs up to 30 feet. There are no hookups. Sites 9, 11, 12, 17, and 24 are pull-through. Picnic tables, grills, and fire rings are provided. Vault toilets and drinking water are available. Leashed pets are permitted.

Reservations, fees: Reservations are not accepted. The fee is $12 per night. Additional vehicles cost $6 per night. Golden Age and Golden Access Passports are accepted. Cash or check only. Open Memorial Day–Labor Day.

Directions: From I-70, take Highway 65 east for 34.6 miles. Turn left on Forest Route 121. The campground is on the left in 9.3 miles.

Contact: Grand Mesa National Forest, 970/874-6600, www.fs.fed.us/r2/gmug/.

30 CRAG CREST

Scenic rating: 8

in Grand Mesa

Crag Crest is on the north shore of Eggleston Lake, the largest lake on the mesa. It was a pretty, hilly spot with excellent views and privacy, but a timber sale in 2005 may have spoiled some of the sites. Nevertheless, it's the best campground for hikers because it's adjacent to the eastern trailhead of the Crag Crest National Recreation Trail. This 10.3-mile loop traverses the "crest" of the mesa and has panoramic views of the Book and Roan Cliffs to the north, the West Elk and San Juan Mountains to the east and south, and the Uncompahgre Plateau and La Sal Mountains to the west. Half of the loop is open to mountain bikes and horses. (For more information on Grand Mesa, see the Jumbo listing in this chapter.)

Campsites, facilities: There are 11 sites for tents and RVs up to 30 feet. There are no hookups. Picnic tables, grills, and fire rings are provided. Vault toilets and drinking water are available. Leashed pets are permitted.

Reservations, fees: Reservations are not accepted. The fee is $10 per night. Additional vehicles cost $5 per night. Golden Age and Golden Access Passports are accepted. Cash or check only. Open Memorial Day–Labor Day.

Directions: From I-70, take Highway 65 east for 34.6 miles. Turn left on Forest Route 121. The campground is on the left in 3.4 miles.

Contact: Grand Mesa National Forest, 970/874-6600, www.fs.fed.us/r2/gmug/.

31 WEIR AND JOHNSON

🏃 🎣 🚤 🐴 🚐 ⛺

Scenic rating: 6

in Grand Mesa

This campground is on the east side of the mesa beneath Leon Peak, the highest point on the mesa. The campground receives heavy precipitation, so there are usually pockets of snow on the ground until mid-July. It's in a lush spruce-fir forest between Weir and Johnson and Sackett Reservoirs. Sackett is closed to motorized boats. Trail 717 climbs to Loon Lake and other ponds. The sites are just 20–50 feet apart, and the campground is

usually busy despite its remote location. Sites 5–7 are walk-in sites on the shore. (For more information on Grand Mesa, see the Jumbo listing in this chapter.)

Campsites, facilities: There are 12 sites for tents and RVs up to 22 feet. There are no hookups. Picnic tables, grills, and fire rings are provided. Vault toilets and drinking water are available. Leashed pets are permitted.

Reservations, fees: Reservations are not accepted. The fee is $10 per night. Additional vehicles cost $5 per night. Golden Age and Golden Access Passports are accepted. Cash or check only. Open Memorial Day–Labor Day and without services after Labor Day.

Directions: From I-70, take Highway 65 east for 34.6 miles. Turn left on Forest Route 121. In 8.7 miles, turn right on Forest Route 126. The campground is in 2.7 miles.

Contact: Grand Mesa National Forest, 970/874-6600, www.fs.fed.us/r2/gmug/.

32 KISER CREEK

🎣 🚤 🐴 🚐 ⛺

Scenic rating: 7

in Grand Mesa

Kiser Creek is one of the smaller, more private campgrounds on the mesa. It is less popular because it doesn't overlook a lake, but it's a short walk to Baron Lake and Reed Lake. The campground is in a shady spruce-fir forest on a hill overlooking a large meadow. Campers can choose between camping in the trees or in the meadow. The sites are 50–100 feet apart. (For more information on Grand Mesa, see the Jumbo listing in this chapter.)

Campsites, facilities: There are 12 sites for tents and RVs up to 16 feet. There are no hookups. Sites 4, 6, 7, and 9 are pull-through. Picnic tables, grills, and fire rings are provided. Vault toilets and drinking water are available. Leashed pets are permitted.

Reservations, fees: Reservations are not accepted. The fee is $10 per night. Additional vehicles cost $5 per night. Golden Age and Golden Access Passports are accepted. Cash or check only. Open Memorial Day–Labor Day.

Directions: From I-70, take Highway 65 east for 34.6 miles. Turn left on Forest Route 121. In 2.4 miles, turn right on Forest Route 123. The campground is on the left in 0.1 mile.

Contact: Grand Mesa National Forest, 970/874-6600, www.fs.fed.us/r2/gmug/.

33 AVALANCHE

Scenic rating: 8

south of Carbondale

BEST (

Avalanche is a small campground in a stunning setting at the base of Mount Sopris and the western entrance to the Maroon Bells–Snowmass Wilderness. Area. This area doesn't have the Aspen crowds, but it does have hiking, backpacking, and trail-riding access to the Maroon Bells and some gorgeous wildflower meadows in late summer. The popular Avalanche Lake Trail begins at the campground and travels 11 miles to an alpine lake in the shadow of Capitol Peak (14,130 feet). This trail connects to the Hell Roaring Creek, East Creek, and Capitol Creek Trails.

The primitive campground is a small loop beside Avalanche Creek in a forest of evergreens and cottonwoods. Most of the sites are quite large and 50–100 feet apart. Sites 1–6 and 11–13 are next to the creek. Sites 11–13 are overflow sites, so they are a long way from the toilets, but they are next to a meadow and have great views. Site 7 is the smallest and least appealing site.

Campsites, facilities: There are 13 sites for tents and RVs up to 25 feet. There are no hookups. Picnic tables, grills, and fire rings are provided. Vault toilets and drinking water are available. Leashed pets are permitted.

Reservations, fees: Reservations are not accepted. The fee is $14 per night.

Golden Age and Golden Access Passports are accepted. Cash or check only. Open mid-May–mid-November.

Directions: From Carbondale, take Highway 133 south for 10.5 miles. Turn left on Avalanche Creek Road/County Road 10. In 1.8 miles, there is a shallow ford which passenger cars can usually cross, but drivers should check the water levels first. The road ends about one mile past the ford at the campground. This is a narrow dirt road which is not recommended for trailers.

Contact: White River National Forest, 970/945-2521, www.fs.fed.us/r2/whiteriver/.

34 REDSTONE I

Scenic rating: 6

south of Carbondale

Redstone is a clean and pleasant stopover on the way to or from Carbondale. The two loops, Algiers and Osgood, are terraced, slightly wooded, and well screened from the Highway. Redstone I is more spacious and has better views than Redstone II. This is one of the few national forest campgrounds in this area with hookups and showers, so it's very popular with RVers. The main activities are fishing on the Crystal and shopping or eating in Redstone. Redstone, population 200, was founded by utopian industrialist John Cleveland Osgood, who built an inn to house his single employees and cottages for his married employees. The inn and many of the cottages have been preserved. This cute town is full of shops and cafés and is a pleasant one-mile walk from the campground. Advanced kayakers can paddle the Class III–IV section of the Crystal River from Marble to Redstone when water levels permit.

Campsites, facilities: There are 20 sites for tents and RVs up to 40 feet. Water and electric hookups are available at all sites. Sites 10, 17, and 20 are pull-through, and sites 1, 2, 6,

7, 18, and 19 are double sites. Picnic tables, grills, fire rings, and tent pads are provided. Restrooms with flush toilets and showers, vault toilets, drinking water, a playground, and horseshoe pits are available. Leashed pets are permitted.

Reservations, fees: Reservations are accepted at 877/444-6777 and www.reserveamerica.com. The fee is $26 per night. Golden Age and Golden Access Passports are accepted. Cash or check only. Open May–September.

Directions: From Carbondale, take Highway 133 south for 14.3 miles. Turn left on County Road 3. Redstone I is on the left and Redstone II is on the right.

Contact: White River National Forest, 970/945-2521, www.fs.fed.us/r2/whiteriver/.

35 REDSTONE II

Scenic rating: 6

south of Carbondale

Redstone II is very similar to Redstone I (see the listing in this chapter). It's a terraced loop on a hill overlooking the Crystal River and Highway 133. There is some traffic noise from the road, but the wooded site is fairly well screened. The sites are 20–30 feet apart and not very private, but they are large and clean. The main activities are fishing and shopping.

Campsites, facilities: There are 19 sites for tents and RVs up to 40 feet. There are no hookups. Sites 3, 4, 8, 10, and 13–15 are pull-through. Sites 3, 4, 14, and 15 are double sites. Picnic tables, grills, fire rings, and tent pads are provided. Vault toilets, showers, and drinking water are available. Leashed pets are permitted.

Reservations, fees: Reservations are accepted at 877/444-6777 and www.reserveamerica.com. The fee is $19 per night. Golden Age and Golden Access Passports are accepted. Cash or check only. Open May–September.

Directions: From Carbondale, take Highway 133 south for 14.3 miles. Turn left on County Road 3. Redstone I is on the left and Redstone II is on the right.

Contact: White River National Forest, 970/945-2521, www.fs.fed.us/r2/whiteriver/.

36 McCLURE

Scenic rating: 6

south of Carbondale

McClure is a half-forgotten campground in the Gunnison National Forest, about a half-hour drive from Carbondale. It's a pretty campground full of quaking aspen and the bubbling sounds of Lee Creek. There's not much to do here except sit back, relax, and enjoy the solitude. The sites are large, flat, and heavily wooded. Site 1 has views of Sheep Mountain and the Muddy Creek valley. Sites 15 and 17 are on the edge of a small meadow, so they have room for multiple tents.

Campsites, facilities: There are 19 sites for tents and RVs up to 35 feet. There are no hookups. Sites 2, 7, and 14 are pull-through. Picnic tables, grills, and fire rings are provided. Vault toilets and drinking water are available. Leashed pets are permitted.

Reservations, fees: Reservations are not accepted. The fee is $10 per night and includes two vehicles. Additional vehicles cost $5 per night. Golden Age and Golden Access Passports are accepted. Cash or check only. Open May–September.

Directions: From Carbondale, drive south on Highway 133. The campground is on the left 1.6 miles after McClure Pass.

Contact: Gunnison National Forest, 970/240-5300, www.fs.fed.us/r2/gmug/.

37 BOGAN FLATS

Scenic rating: 7

south of Carbondale

Bogan Flats is in a beautiful location on the banks of the Crystal River, between the Maroon Bells–Snowmass and Raggeds wilderness areas. There are two main attractions: fly-fishing on the Crystal and visiting the historic town of Marble (five miles away). The Marble Quarry produced the stone for the Lincoln Memorial and the Tomb of the Unknown Soldier. Local artists still use this pure white stone for sculptures. The nearest hiking trail is the nine-mile Raspberry Creek Loop which begins in Marble. Jeep trails for four-wheeling and mountain biking are also accessible in Marble. Advanced kayakers can boat the Class III–IV section of the Crystal from Marble to Redstone.

This campground is packed on weekends, so make reservations if possible. The sites are about 50 feet apart, and many are wooded. Sites 1–9, 12, 13, 15–19, 21, and 23–26 are next to the river. Sites 1–5 have views of Ragged Peak. Sites 12 and 15 are very large. The group site is upstream of the main campground. It is very private and an excellent group destination.

Campsites, facilities: There are 38 sites for tents and RVs up to 35 feet and one group site. Sites 24 and 28 are wheelchair accessible. There are no hookups. Sites 6, 19, 24, and 31 are pull-through. Picnic tables, grills, and fire rings are provided. Vault toilets and drinking water are available. Leashed pets are permitted.

Reservations, fees: Reservations are accepted for sites 8–38 at 877/444-6777 and www.reserveamerica.com. The fee is $15 per night (includes two vehicles). Additional vehicles cost $5 per night. The group site costs $75 per night. Golden Age and Golden Access Passports are accepted. Cash or check only. Open late May–early September.

Directions: From Carbondale, take Highway 133 south. Turn left on Forest Route 314. In 1.5 miles, make a sharp left into the campground.

Contact: White River National Forest, 970/945-2521, www.fs.fed.us/r2/whiteriver/.

38 CRATER LAKE

Scenic rating: 10

in the Maroon Bells-Snowmass Wilderness

BEST (

Crater Lake Trail is a popular, easy day hike to a subalpine lake at the foot of Pyramid Peak and the Maroon Bells. From this location, hikers can make day trips to Buckskin Pass, Snowmass Lake, and West Maroon Pass, or backpack a larger loop around the fourteeners. This is amazing, easily accessible backcountry camping. There are 12 designated campsites dispersed around the west shore of the lake to reduce impact on the habitat. These sites are very far apart and private. The sites vary from forest to meadow habitat. Sites 1, 2, 7, 9, 11, and 12 are small and only suitable for one tent. Sites 3–6 and 8 can accommodate larger groups. Site 9 is on a hill with excellent views.

Campsites, facilities: There are 12 primitive tent sites. Campfires are not allowed. Gas stoves are required for cooking. Leashed pets are permitted.

Reservations, fees: Reservations are not accepted. Open year-round, but access is limited by weather and avalanche danger.

Directions: From Aspen, take the Maroon Bells Road to the overnight parking area at Maroon Lake. Hike the Crater Lake Trail (1.8 miles one-way) to the bulletin board. Take the left fork to the lake and the campsites.

Contact: White River National Forest, 970/925-3445, www.fs.fed.us/r2/whiteriver/.

39 SILVER BAR

Scenic rating: 7

near Aspen

BEST (

The Maroon Bells are among the most photographed mountains in the country because of their beauty and accessibility. The Maroon Creek valley, formed by glaciers and landslides, provides easy access to a wilderness area with nine passes, six fourteeners, and countless wildflower-filled meadows and alpine lakes. Hundreds of thousands of tourists visit the Maroon Bells every summer for picnics, hiking, backpacking, and trail riding. To reduce the impact on the valley, the road is closed to passenger cars during the day from mid-June–September. A public bus takes visitors from the Aspen Highlands Ski Area to Maroon Lake and other popular trailheads. Additionally, there are only three campgrounds in the valley with a total of 24 campsites. Reservations are HIGHLY recommended from mid-June–late August.

All of the trails in the valley begin a short drive away from the campgrounds. The easiest day hikes range from 1.0–3.6 miles round-trip. They are the Maroon Lake, Falls Loop, Maroon Creek, and Crater Lake Trails. Longer backpacking trails are the Maroon-Snowmass, East Maroon, and West Maroon Trails, which feature high passes, alpine lakes, and mountain meadows. The Maroon Bells are composed of fragile shale and siltstone, which breaks easily, making them famous for their treachery. Many experienced mountaineers have died while attempting to climb these fourteeners—be cautious while hiking in these mountains. Maroon Lake is stocked with trout and is a popular fly-fishing destination. Road cyclists should not miss the long ascent up Maroon Creek Road.

Silver Bar is the smallest and most-overlooked campground on the road. It doesn't have views of the peaks, but there is plenty of privacy in this campground designed mainly

for tents. Site 4 is the least private spot, but it also receives the most sunshine early in the morning, which is a big plus.

Campsites, facilities: There are four sites for tents with parking for RVs up to 30 feet. Sites 1–3 are short walk-ins. There are no hookups or pull-through sites. Picnic tables, grills, fire rings, and tent pads are provided. Vault toilets and drinking water are available. Leashed pets are permitted.

Reservations, fees: Reservations are accepted at 877/444-6777 and www.reserveusa.com. The fee is $15 per night. There is an additional $9 reservation fee, and campers must purchase a $10 vehicle pass (good for 5 days). Golden Age and Golden Access Passports are accepted. Cash or check only. Open May–October.

Directions: From the Aspen roundabout, take Maroon Creek Road south for 4.6 miles. The campground is on the left across from the entrance station. Stop at the entrance station to purchase a car pass.

Contact: White River National Forest, 970/925-3445, www.fs.fed.us/r2/whiteriver/.

40 SILVER BELL

Scenic rating: 8

near Aspen

BEST (

Silver Bell is the middle campground in the beautiful Maroon Creek Valley. Between the creek and the views of the Maroon Bells, this is a jaw-dropping location. Sites 1–10 are next to the water. Sites 1–4 are very private walk-ins with excellent views. Sites 8–13 are walk-in sites at the end of the campground. They are more exposed to the weather and less private, but they also have the best views of the Bells. Sites 1, 5, and 7 can accommodate RVs. Site 14, right next to the road, is the worst site. (For more information on the Maroon Bells, see the Silver Bar listing in this chapter.)

Campsites, facilities: There are 14 sites for tents and RVs up to 30 feet. Sites 2, 3, 4, and 8–13 are walk-in. Picnic tables, grills, fire rings, and tent pads are provided. Vault toilets and drinking water are available. Leashed pets are permitted.

Reservations, fees: Reservations are accepted at 877/444-6777 and www.reserveusa.com. The fee is $15 per night. There is an additional $9 reservation fee, and campers must purchase a $10 vehicle pass (good for 5 days). Golden Age and Golden Access Passports are accepted. Cash or check only. Open May–October.

Directions: From the Aspen roundabout, take Maroon Creek Road south for 4.6 miles to the entrance station. After purchasing a car pass, continue 0.3 mile to the campground on the left.

Contact: White River National Forest, 970/925-3445, www.fs.fed.us/r2/whiteriver/.

41 SILVER QUEEN

🚶 🛶 🐕 🚗 ⛺

Scenic rating: 8

near Aspen

BEST (

Silver Queen, the last campground on Maroon Creek Road, is a quiet, relaxing destination. This small campground in an aspen grove is surrounded by red cliffs and offers amazing views of the Bells. Site 1 is near the entry but very private. Sites 2 and 3 are near the creek and also very private. Site 4, next to the toilet in the middle of the loop, is the worst site. Sites 5 and 6 have the best views of the peaks. (For more information on the Maroon Bells, see the Silver Bar listing in this chapter.)

Campsites, facilities: Picnic tables, grills, fire rings, and tent pads are provided. Vault toilets and drinking water are available. Leashed pets are permitted.

Reservations, fees: Reservations are accepted at 877/444-6777 and www.reserveusa.com.

The fee is $15 per night. There is an additional $9 reservation fee, and campers must purchase a $10 vehicle pass (good for 5 days). Golden Age and Golden Access Passports are accepted. Cash or check only. Open May–October.

Directions: From the Aspen roundabout, take Maroon Creek Road south for 4.6 miles to the entrance station. After purchasing a car pass, continue one mile to the campground on the left.

Contact: White River National Forest, 970/925-3445, www.fs.fed.us/r2/whiteriver/.

42 DIFFICULT

🚶 🛶 🐕 🚗 ⛺

Scenic rating: 6

near Aspen

Aspen is flooded during the summer with tourists from around the country and the world, and the hype is justified. The Snowmass–Maroon Bells, Collegiate Peaks, and Hunter-Fryingpan wilderness areas are all accessible from town. In a state famous for hiking, Aspen has some of the best trails around. For a small taste, try the Difficult Creek Trail, which leaves from the picnic area. Fishing is also excellent on the Roaring Fork, a designated Gold Medal river. And don't miss the drive up to Independence Pass (elevation 12,095 feet) or a visit to the ghost town of Independence. The campgrounds on Highway 82 are also the best place to stay if you're planning a visit to the Maroon Bells but didn't manage to make a reservation six months ahead of time. Set up camp here and explore the area. Difficult is the largest public campground near Aspen. It contains two paved loops in an aspen and cottonwood grove. The sites are about 30 feet apart. They can feel cramped, but dense vegetation (including wild roses) provides ample privacy.

Campsites, facilities: There are 47 sites for tents and RVs up to 40 feet and one group site for 50 people. There are no hookups. Sites 5–7, 11, 14, and 17 are pull-through. Picnic tables, grills, and fire rings are provided. Vault toilets and drinking water are available. Leashed pets are permitted.

Reservations, fees: Reservations are accepted for sites 1–25 and the group site at 877/444-6777 and www.reserveusa.com. The fee is $15 per night. The group site costs $50 per night. Golden Age and Golden Access Passports are accepted. Cash or check only. Open May–September.

Directions: In Aspen, from the Independence Pass sign at the east end of town, drive east on Highway 82 for 4.3 miles and turn right into the campground.

Contact: White River National Forest, 970/925-3445, www.fs.fed.us/r2/whiteriver/.

43 WELLER
🏃 🚴 🛶 🏕 ♿ 🚐 ⛺

Scenic rating: 6

near Aspen

Weller is on Highway 82 about halfway up Independence Pass. This is a good starting place for road cyclists who want to bike the pass but aren't ready for the whole climb. Anglers can fish on the Roaring Fork, a Gold Medal river, and on Weller Lake. The Weller Lake Trail is about a half mile long and begins on the other side of the highway. Many more hiking trails are available nearby in the Hunter-Fryingpan and Collegiate Peaks wilderness areas. Nearby Weller Slab is a popular Aspen rock-climbing area with routes ranging in difficulty from 5.7 to 5.10. The campground is a small paved loop in a beautiful aspen grove with well-spaced, wooded sites. This is a quiet, relaxing location to pitch your tent.

Campsites, facilities: There are 11 sites for tents and RVs up to 35 feet. Site 5 is wheelchair accessible. There are no pull-throughs, and this campground is not recommended for large RVs or trailers. There are no hookups.

Picnic tables, grills, and fire rings are provided. Vault toilets and drinking water are available. Leashed pets are permitted.

Reservations, fees: Reservations are not accepted. The fee is $13 per night (includes two vehicles). Additional vehicles cost $5 per night. Golden Age and Golden Access Passports are accepted. Cash or check only. Open May–September.

Directions: In Aspen, from the Independence Pass sign at the east end of town, drive east on Highway 82 for 7.3 miles and turn left into the campground.

Contact: White River National Forest, 970/925-3445, www.fs.fed.us/r2/whiteriver/.

44 LINCOLN GULCH
🏃 🚴 🐕 🚐 ⛺

Scenic rating: 7

near Aspen

Lincoln Gulch is at the northern edge of the Collegiate Peaks Wilderness, which encompasses eight fourteeners, more than any other wilderness area in Colorado. Lincoln Creek Road penetrates 10 miles into the wilderness and remains open to bikes and vehicles. Several trails are accessible from this road, including the New York Creek, Tabor Creek, Petroleum Lake, and Grizzly Lake Trails. Grizzly Lake is a 3.6-mile trail to an alpine lake at the foot of Grizzly Peak, a former volcano on the Continental Divide. Lincoln Creek Road to Ruby, an old mining camp, is a moderately challenging mountain bike ride. Local climbers frequent the cliff near the campground, which has 5.8 to 5.11 routes.

At first sight, Lincoln Gulch is not very impressive, but there's more than meets the eye at this small campground with interesting rock formations. Maybe it's the solitude, maybe it's the setting, but there's a little bit of magic in the air. The sites are large but not very private because of the clearing in the middle of the loop. Fortunately, Lincoln

Gulch rarely fills up. Sites 1 and 2 are next to the creek. Sites 5 and 7 are the best spots.

Campsites, facilities: There are seven sites for tents and trailers up to 16 feet. There are no hookups. Picnic tables, grills, fire rings, vault toilets, and drinking water are provided. Leashed pets are permitted.

Reservations, fees: Reservations are not accepted. The fee is $13 per night. Golden Age and Golden Access Passports are accepted. Cash or check only. Open May–September.

Directions: In Aspen, from the Independence Pass sign at the east end of town, drive east on Highway 82 for 9.2 miles. Turn right on Lincoln Creek Road/Forest Route 106. It is 0.4 mile downhill to the campground. This road is very rough and narrow with steep drop-offs. Trailers and RVs are not recommended, and 4WD is a must if the road is muddy or wet.

Contact: White River National Forest, 970/925-3445, www.fs.fed.us/r2/whiteriver/.

45 LOST MAN

Scenic rating: 6

near Aspen

Just four miles from Independence Pass, Lost Man is a great base camp for exploring the Aspen area. Lost Man Trail begins across the road and traverses nine miles of the rugged Hunter-Fryingpan Wilderness. (This trail is an arc which connects at both ends with Highway 82 and requires a short shuttle.) The serrated 13,000-foot peaks and forested valleys of this area don't receive the heavy traffic of the Maroon Bells Wilderness, but they are very rewarding for hikers and backpackers. Campers can also explore the ghost town of Independence, two miles up Highway 82, where the Aspen mining boom started on July 4, 1879, with the discovery of the Independence gold lode. Anglers can try their luck on the Roaring Fork River.

The campground is a small gravel loop in a pine forest. It is heavily wooded, and the sites are 50–100 feet apart. Site 1 is next to the entrance and has no privacy. Sites 3 and 4 are next to the creek. Site 7, over 100 feet from the road, is the most private campsite. At an elevation of 10,500 feet, Lost Man is cool all summer and is the last campground on this road to open.

Campsites, facilities: There are 10 sites for tents and RVs up to 30 feet. There are no hookups. Sites 7 and 8 are pull-through. Picnic tables, vault toilets, and drinking water are provided. Leashed pets are permitted.

Reservations, fees: Reservations are not accepted. The fee is $12 per night. Golden Age and Golden Access Passports are accepted. Cash or check only. Open May–September.

Directions: In Aspen, from the Independence Pass sign at the east end of town, drive east on Highway 82 for 13 miles. The campground is on the right, across from the Lost Man trailhead.

Contact: White River National Forest, 970/925-3445, www.fs.fed.us/r2/whiteriver/.

46 MIRACLE ROCK

Scenic rating: 5

southwest of Colorado National Monument

This is a primitive campground and picnic area at the Miracle Rock trailhead. It's not a destination in itself, but it could be a stopover for travelers taking the back roads to Utah. Miracle Rock is a 12,000-ton rock balanced on a pedestal that is one foot wide, an interesting example of the erosive power of wind and water in this sandstone canyon country. The only other nearby attraction is The Potholes, a series of swimming holes and waterfalls on the Little Dolores River. (Visitors should ask for directions at the Glade Park store.)

Campsites, facilities: This primitive campground can accommodate four groups. Only walk-in tent camping is available, but the parking area can accommodate RVs up to 30 feet. Picnic tables, grills, fire rings, and vault toilets are provided. Trash must be packed out. Leashed pets are permitted.

Reservations, fees: Reservations are not accepted. Camping is free. Open early May–late October.

Directions: From the Colorado National Monument visitors center, take Rim Rock Road south for 6.6 miles. At the "Glade Springs 5 mi." sign, turn right. In Glade Park, turn right on DS Road. In eight miles, turn left on 9.8 Road. The campground entrance is on the left in 1.2 miles. Visitors should contact the BLM office for road conditions.

Contact: Bureau of Land Management, Grand Junction Office, 970/224-3000.

47 MUD SPRINGS

🚶 🚴 🐕 ♿ 🚐 ⛺

Scenic rating: 8

south of Colorado National Monument

Mud Springs is on Piñon Mesa, a part of the 100-mile-long Uncompahgre Plateau. The campground is on BLM land, just south of the Grand Mesa National Forest, in a setting of meadows and aspen groves. Cool breezes and afternoon showers make this the perfect place to escape the heat of the canyon lands to the north. This is a popular destination for church groups, wedding parties, family reunions, handicap organizations, and scouting troops, all of whom benefit from the remote location. There isn't a bad campsite here. They are all very private and screened by aspen. The surrounding land is crisscrossed by 4WD roads and pack trails that are also suitable for hiking and mountain biking. Fishing is available at the Enoch and Fruita Reservoirs located four miles north of the campground. (Swimming is not recommended because of ranching activities in the area.) Glade Park is the last place to buy supplies or, surprisingly,

watch a movie. During the summer, the Glade Park Volunteer Fire Station shows movies under the stars on Friday nights for $1 per person. All proceeds benefit the fire station.

Campsites, facilities: There are 10 sites for tents and RVs up to 30 feet and two group sites. There are no hookups. The facilities and group sites are wheelchair accessible. Picnic tables, fire rings, grills, and a horse corral are provided. Vault toilets and drinking water are available. Leashed pets are permitted.

Reservations, fees: Reservations are not accepted. The fee is $5 per day for two vehicles. Cash only. Open mid-May–mid-October.

Directions: From the Colorado National Monument visitors center, take Rim Rock Road south for 6.6 miles. At the "Glade Springs 5 mi." sign, turn right. At 4.8 miles, you will pass the Glade Park Store and Post Office. Continue straight on Glade Park Road for another seven miles to the campground entrance on the right.

Contact: Bureau of Land Management, Grand Junction Office, 970/224-3000.

48 HAY PRESS

🚶 🚴 🏊 🐕 🚐 ⛺

Scenic rating: 6

south of Colorado National Monument

Haypress is just 16 miles from Colorado National Monument, but it feels worlds away from the hot canyon lands. This is ranching land, where cool breezes blow through aspen groves and fields full of wildflowers. Haypress is the only official campground in this part of Uncompahgre National Forest, which is popular with hunters, horse owners, and ATV riders. (Many of these groups choose backcountry camping over Haypress.) Fishing is available at the Fruita Reservoir (stocked with rainbow trout), but swimming is not recommended because of ranching activities. Glade Park is the last place to buy supplies or, surprisingly, watch a movie. During the summer, the Glade Park Volunteer Fire Station shows movies under the stars on Friday nights for $1 per person. All proceeds benefit the fire station.

Campsites, facilities: This primitive campground can accommodate three dispersed groups. Picnic tables, grills, and vault toilets are provided. All trash must be packed out. Leashed pets are permitted.

Reservations, fees: Reservations are not accepted. Camping is free. Open May 15–November. The road is not maintained after October 15.

Directions: From the Colorado National Monument visitors center, take Rim Rock Road south for 6.6 miles. At the "Glade Springs 5 mi." sign, turn right. At 4.8 miles, you will pass the Glade Park Store and Post Office. Continue straight on Glade Park Road for 8.8 miles to a fork. Stay right. The campground entrance is on the right in 2.5 miles. This is a long, dirt road that may be impassable when wet. Visitors should contact the BLM office for trail maps and road conditions.

Contact: Uncompahgre National Forest, 970/874-6600, www.fs.fed.us/r2/gmug.

49 SPRUCE

Scenic rating: 6

in Paonia State Park

Paonia State Park features a 334-acre reservoir in a narrow valley with views of the Ragged Mountains. There are two campgrounds and a total of 15 campsites. Spruce is north of the reservoir, between Muddy Creek and Highway 133, in a mature spruce grove. During runoff, Muddy Creek earns its name, making fishing impossible. When the water clears, anglers fish for northern pike from the shore and boats. The nearest hiking is in the Raggeds Wilderness area, accessible via County Road 12, which intersects Highway 133 beneath the dam. Spruce is a primitive campground with ample shade and well-spaced sites. Sites 8–10, 14, and 15 are next to the creek.

Campsites, facilities: There are eight sites for tents and RVs up to 35 feet. There are no hookups. Site 15 is pull-through. Picnic tables, fire rings, and vault toilets are provided. Drinking water is not available. Groceries, drinking water, and a restaurant are available at Crystal Meadows Ranch below the dam. Leashed pets are permitted.

Reservations, fees: Reservations are accepted at 800/678-2267 and www.parks.state.co.us. The fee is $7 per night. Cash or check only. Campers must also purchase a Daily Parks Pass ($3) or an Annual Parks Pass ($55). The Aspen Leaf Annual Pass is accepted. Open May–September.

Directions: From Highway 133 and Highway 187, take Highway 133 north for 20 miles. Turn right at the campground sign.

Contact: Crawford State Park, 970/921-5721, email: crawford.park@state.co.us.

50 HAWSAPPLE

Scenic rating: 6

in Paonia State Park

Paonia State Park features a 334-acre reservoir in a narrow valley with views of the Ragged Mountains. During runoff, the reservoir is muddy and unappealing. The rest of the summer, it's popular with water-skiers and boaters. Anglers fish for northern pike from boats and the shore. The nearest hiking is in the Raggeds Wilderness area, accessible via County Road 12, which intersects Highway 133 beneath the dam. Hawsapple is a primitive campground without much shade except at site 7, which is secluded in a small grove of trees. Sites 5 and 6 are on the waterfront, and boats can moor at Site 6. Sites 5–7 also have views of Mount Gunnison.

Campsites, facilities: There are seven sites for tents and RVs up to 35 feet. Site 1 is wheelchair accessible. There are no hookups. Sites 4–6 are pull-through. Picnic tables, fire rings, and tent pads are provided. Vault toilets and a boat ramp are available. Drinking water is not available. Groceries, drinking water, and a restaurant are available at Crystal Meadows Ranch below the dam. Leashed pets are permitted.

Reservations, fees: Reservations are accepted at 800/678-2267 and www.parks.state.co.us. The fee is $7 per night. Cash or check only. Campers must also purchase a Daily Parks Pass ($3) or an Annual Parks Pass ($55). The Aspen Leaf Annual Pass is accepted. Open May–September.

Directions: From Highway 133 and Highway 187, take Highway 133 north for 19.2 miles. Turn right at the Paonia State Park sign. After the bridge, turn right on Country Road 2. Follow the right fork into the campground.

Contact: Crawford State Park, 970/921-5721, email: crawford.park@state.co.us.

51 ERICKSON SPRINGS
🥾🛶🐾🚐🏕️

Scenic rating: 7

east of Paonia

Erickson Springs is a pleasant stopover on the West Elk Loop Scenic Byway, with the bonus of an amazing hiking trail out the back door. The 16-mile Dark Canyon Trail traverses the Raggeds Wilderness. The first portion along Anthracite Creek offers excellent stream fishing and numerous waterfalls. After climbing the Devils Stairway (1,200 feet in less than a mile), the trail enters Horse Ranch Park, an area of quaking aspen stands and meadows full of wildflowers. Connecting trails access the town of Marble and Oh-Be-Joyful Pass.

The campground is separated from Anthracite Creek by the road, but it's a beautiful, overgrown mess of wildflowers, cottonwoods, spruce, and brush. The vegetation offers a lot of privacy, and the sites are well spaced and shaded. The only sites without shade are 11 and 12.

Campsites, facilities: There are 18 sites for tents and RVs up to 35 feet. There are no hookups. Sites 2, 3, 5, 7, 11, and 13 are pull-through. Picnic tables, grills, fire rings, and tent pads are provided. Vault toilets and drinking water are available. Leashed pets are permitted.

Reservations, fees: Reservations are not accepted. The fee is $10 per night (includes one vehicle). There is a $5 fee per additional vehicle. Golden Age and Golden Access Passports are accepted. Cash or check only. Open May–September.

Directions: From Highway 135 in Crested Butte, take Whiterock Avenue/County Road 12 west for 18.7 miles. Before the bridge, turn right at the campground sign. The entrance is on the right in 0.25 mile.

Contact: Gunnison National Forest, 970/641-0471, www.fs.fed.us/r2/gmug.

52 LOST LAKE
🥾🚲🛶🚗🐾🚐🏕️

Scenic rating: 9

west of Crested Butte

BEST (

Lost Lake is on the West Elk Loop Scenic Byway, and whether you're coming from Paonia or Crested Butte, it's worth every minute of the drive because you usually have to hike to reach a place like Lost Lake. This subalpine lake sits in a cirque at the base of East Beckwith Mountain, between the Raggeds and West Elk wilderness areas. The campground is in a forest of aspen, spruce, and fir on the north shore of the lake, and many of the sites have amazing views of the Beckwith Mountains. Campers enjoy fishing and boating on the lake, as well as hiking and mountain biking the Three Lakes Trail. This 2.1-mile trail circles Lost Lake and offers great views of the Ruby Range. It connects to the Beckwith Pass Trail, which hikers can take through aspen stands and parks full of wildflowers into the West Elk Wilderness.

Sites 1, 2, 3, 5, 7, and 8 are separated from the lake by the campground road, but they have great views. Sites 4 and 6 are on the lakeshore and also offer excellent views. Sites 8–11 are in a wooded area at the end of the loop and lack views. The sites are 100–200 feet apart and very private. This is a very popular campground. The best way to get a spot is to arrive midweek.

Campsites, facilities: There are 11 sites for tents and RVs up to 21 feet. There are no hookups. Site 4 is pull-through. Picnic tables, grills, and fire rings are provided. Vault toilets are available. Leashed pets are permitted.

Reservations, fees: Reservations are not accepted. The fee is $10 per night (includes one vehicle). There is a $5 fee per additional vehicle. Golden Age and Golden Access Passports are accepted. Cash or check only. Open late June–September.

Directions: From Highway 135 in Crested Butte, take Whiterock Avenue/County Road 12 west for 9.7 miles. Turn left on Forest Route 706. The campground is on the left in 2.4 miles.

Contact: Gunnison National Forest, 970/641-0471, www.fs.fed.us/r2/gmug.

53 LAKE IRWIN

🏃 🚲 🏊 🚗 🐕 🚐 ⛺

Scenic rating: 8

west of Crested Butte

At 10,000 feet, on the edge of the Raggeds Wilderness, Lake Irwin is in a jaw-dropping setting. The campground sits on the northern tip of the reservoir, in a spruce and fir forest, and offers views of the Ruby Range, Anthracite Range, and Mount Axtell, among other peaks. Hikers with strong lungs will have a heyday. The Dyke Trail leaves from the western shore of the lake and climbs to meet the Silver Basin Trail in the Raggeds Wilderness.

The trail is open to mountain bikes until it enters the wilderness area. After that, it travels through pristine high mountain basins where a long loop is possible by connecting with the Dark Canyon Trail. The lake is stocked with rainbow trout and there are native brookies. But there's one problem: Lake Irwin is no secret, and the campground is packed all summer long. With a few exceptions, the sites are small and very close together, so the camping is cramped.

The following sites have great views: 1, 2, 11–18, 30, and 31. Sites 1–6, 8, and 10 overlook the lake. The best sites for privacy and scenery are 10–12.

Campsites, facilities: There are 32 sites for tents and RVs up to 30 feet. There are no hookups. Sites 2, 8, 12, 20, and 31 are pull-through. Picnic tables, grills, and fire rings are provided. Vault toilets and drinking water are available. Leashed pets are permitted.

Reservations, fees: Reservations are accepted at 877/444-6777 and www.reserveusa.com. The fee is $14 per night (includes one vehicle). There is a $7 fee per additional vehicle. Golden Age and Golden Access Passports are accepted. Cash or check only. Open mid-June–mid-September.

Directions: From Highway 135 in Crested Butte, take Whiterock Avenue/County Road 12 west for 6.8 miles. Turn right on Forest Route 826. The campground is on the right in 2.6 miles.

Contact: Gunnison National Forest, 970/641-0471, www.fs.fed.us/r2/gmug.

54 OH-BE-JOYFUL

🏃 🏊 🛶 🐕 ⛺

Scenic rating: 9

north of Crested Butte

BEST (

Oh-Be-Joyful, besides having the best campground name in Colorado, is a tent camping gem. It offers free, dispersed camping in an evergreen grove on the east bank of the Slate

River, upstream of the confluence with Oh-Be-Joyful Creek. Understandably, it's very popular, and all of the designated sites are full for most of July and August. If you have a 4WD vehicle and can ford the Slate, there's more camping on the west bank. Hikers can take the Oh-Be-Joyful Creek Trail up to Oh-Be-Joyful Pass and down into Buck Basin, Swan Basin, Silver Basin, and Gold Basin. These pristine basins are in the Raggeds Wilderness area and offer unparalleled scenery and wildflowers. This is backpacking paradise. Expert kayakers boat the creek and the river when the levels are right, but this is a very advanced run. Mountain bikers might explore the Forest Service roads, but, because of the wilderness area, there are no trails nearby.

Campsites, facilities: There are nine tent sites. There are no hookups or pull-throughs. Picnic tables, grills, and fire rings are provided. Vault toilets are available. Trash must be packed out. Leashed pets are permitted.

Reservations, fees: There is no fee for camping, and reservations are not accepted. Open June–September.

Directions: From Elk Avenue in Crested Butte, take Gothic Road north for 0.8 mile. Turn left on Forest Route 734/Slate River Road. In 4.6 miles, turn left at the Oh-Be-Joyful sign onto Forest Route 754. The campground is about a quarter mile down this 4WD road.

Contact: Gunnison National Forest, 970/641-0471, www.fs.fed.us/r2/gmug.

55 GOTHIC

Scenic rating: 9

north of Crested Butte

BEST (

This itsy-bitsy campground is in a stunning location on the East River between Avery Peak and Gothic Mountain, north of the historic town of Gothic and a few miles south of the Maroon Bells–Snowmass Wilderness. Crested Butte is the Wildflower Capital of Colorado, and the drive to Gothic campground explains the designation. It's gorgeous. Bring a camera and butterfly net, and you will have hours of enjoyment in fields of purple, yellow, and red wildflowers. As if that weren't enough, Gothic Natural Area, a virgin stand of Engelmann spruce, is just up the road. On the way there, you'll pass the Washington Gulch trailhead, which ascends Rock Creek through beautiful scenery. The town of Gothic, once one of the wildest towns in Colorado, is now the home of the Rocky Mountain Biological Laboratory. To take part in a Historical Stroll or Botanical Investigation, call 970/349-7231 or email enviro-ed@rmbl.org. Mountain bikers can take Gothic Road up to Scholfield Pass. You'll share the way with four-wheelers, but the rough road deters many visitors. Fly-fishing is excellent on the East River.

The four campsites are in a stand of Engelmann spruce beside a small creek. The trees provide shade and privacy, and the sites are about 100 feet apart. They can only accommodate tents, pop-ups, and very small RVs. You might be the lone camper on a weekday in July, but arrive early on weekends to secure a spot.

Campsites, facilities: There are four sites for tents and RVs up to 20 feet. There are no hookups or pull-throughs. Picnic tables, grills, fire rings, and tent pads are provided. Vault toilets are available. Trash must be packed out. Leashed pets are permitted.

Reservations, fees: Reservations are not accepted. The fee is $8 per night (includes one vehicle). There is a $4 fee per additional vehicle. Golden Age and Golden Access Passports are accepted. Cash or check only. Open June–September.

Directions: From the Town Hall in Mount Crested Butte, take Gothic Road/County Road 317 north for 6.4 miles. The campground is on the left. The road is deeply rutted for the last 100 feet before the campground.

Contact: Gunnison National Forest, 970/641-0471, www.fs.fed.us/r2/gmug.

56 CEMENT CREEK

Scenic rating: 7

southeast of Crested Butte

Cement Creek is the most accessible campground in the Crested Butte area. This small loop occupies a clearing on the banks of Cement Creek, in the shadow of Cement Mountain. The campground is more open and sunny than many canyon campgrounds and has a profusion of wild roses. It's usually quiet, but it always fills up on weekends, mostly with mountain bikers. Several trails on the north side of the road access the Elk Mountains. Walrod Gulch begins nearby and connects with Double Top Trail, which in turn connects to Block and Tackle and Hunter Hill Trails. Several challenging mountain bike loops can be made on the flanks of Double Top Mountain. Skiers might be interested to know that Cement Creek was the site of Pioneer Ski Area, one of Colorado's first ski mountains. It operated 1939–1952. The chairlift was partly assembled from trams from nearby mines.

Sites 2–9 are next to the creek and shaded. Site 9 is a walk-in. Sites 11–13 are in the clearing. The roomy sites can easily accommodate large family groups.

Campsites, facilities: There are 12 sites for tents and RVs up to 28 feet and one walk-in tent site. There are no hookups. Sites 2–6 are pull-through. Picnic tables, grills, fire rings, and tent pads are provided. Vault toilets and drinking water are available. Leashed pets are permitted.

Reservations, fees: Reservations are not accepted. The fee is $12 per night (includes one vehicle). There is a $6 fee per additional vehicle. Golden Age and Golden Access Passports are accepted. Cash or check only. Open May–September.

Directions: From Gunnison, take Highway 135 north. Turn right on Forest Route 740/Cement Creek Road, 10.5 miles after Al-

mont. The campground is on the right in 3.7 miles.

Contact: Gunnison National Forest, 970/641-0471, www.fs.fed.us/r2/gmug. National Forest, 970/641-0471, www.fs.fed.us/r2/gmug.

57 DORCHESTER

Scenic rating: 9

northeast of Gunnison

Dorchester is the most remote campground in Taylor Park, and consequently the least used. It occupies the border between a coniferous forest and the expanse of sagebrush that characterizes most of the park. The campsites have shade and privacy plus excellent views of the Sawatch Range. Sites 9 and 10 overlook the Taylor River. Mostly hikers, tent campers, and few anglers come to this very quiet campground. Trail 760 ascends from the campground to Lily Pond and is open to hikers and mountain bikers. Another popular hike or multiday backpack trip is the Timberline Trail, which begins near Pothole Reservoir and follows the timberline for 31 miles to Mirror Lake. The trail is the western border of the Collegiate Peaks Wilderness, but because it's not in the wilderness, it's open to bikers and motorized traffic.

Campsites, facilities: There are 10 sites for tents and RVs up to 28 feet. There are no hookups or pull-throughs. Picnic tables, grills, and fire rings are provided. Vault toilets and drinking water are available. Leashed pets are permitted.

Reservations, fees: Reservations are not accepted. The fee is $10 per night (includes one vehicle). There is a $5 fee per additional vehicle. Golden Age and Golden Access Passports are accepted. Cash or check only. Open May–September.

Directions: From Main Street in Gunnison, take Highway 135 north for 10.2 miles. In Almont, turn right on Forest Route 742 and drive up Taylor Canyon to the reservoir. The campground is 17 miles past the dam on the left.

Contact: Gunnison National Forest, 970/641-0471, www.fs.fed.us/r2/gmug.

58 NORTH TAYLOR PARK

Scenic rating: 10

northeast of Gunnison

At an elevation of 9,500 feet, Taylor Park is a broad basin rimmed by the Sawatch Range and brimming with the scent of sagebrush. In 1937, a 2,033-surface-acre reservoir was completed in the park to provide irrigation water to the Uncompahgre Valley. Many visitors stay at the designated campgrounds (Lakeview, Rivers End, Dinner Station, and Dorchester), but almost as many prefer dispersed camping. From Italian Creek to the end of Forest Route 742, there are 75 primitive campsites along the creeks and in the forests of the park. These campers come for the first-rate fly-fishing and the four-wheeling. An attendant at the Dorchester cabin can offer information on camping and fishing regulations as well as the history of the park.

Campsites, facilities: There are about 75 dispersed primitive sites for tents and RVs. Vault toilets are available at Pothole Reservoir. Leashed pets are permitted.

Reservations, fees: There is no fee for dispersed camping, but campers are limited to 14 days.

Directions: From Main Street in Gunnison, take Highway 135 north for 10.2 miles. In Almont, turn right on Forest Route 742 and drive up Taylor Canyon to the reservoir. The dispersed camping begins north of the inlet.

Contact: Gunnison National Forest, 970/641-0471, www.fs.fed.us/r2/gmug.

59 MOSCA

Scenic rating: 7

northeast of Gunnison

Mosca is on the western shore of Spring Creek Reservoir, a small but scenic lake in the Elk Mountains. The campground contains several small loops on steep, forested hills. Fishing and canoeing on the lake make this a great family destination, but if you crave a little solitude, Mosca isn't for you. The campground is packed with families in July and August (despite the washboard road), and the sites are small and fairly close together. Sites 6–9, 11, and 13 are close to the water. Sites 8 and 9 are short walk-ins. Sites 3, 10, and 13 are family sites.

Campsites, facilities: There are 16 sites for tents and RVs up to 30 feet. There are no hookups. Sites 2, 4–7, 11, and 13–15 are pull-throughs. Picnic tables, grills, and fire rings are provided. Vault toilets and drinking water are available. Leashed pets are permitted.

Reservations, fees: Reservations are not accepted. The fee is $12 per night (includes one vehicle). There is a $6 fee per additional vehicle. Golden Age and Golden Access Passports are accepted. Cash or check only. Open May–September.

Directions: From Gunnison, take Highway 135 north to Almont. Turn left on Forest Route 744. The campground is on the right in 11.3 miles.

Contact: Gunnison National Forest, 970/641-0471, www.fs.fed.us/r2/gmug.

60 DINNER STATION

Scenic rating: 10

northeast of Gunnison

BEST (

This is the kind of campground that people visit as children and return to every year for the rest of their lives. It's perfect. On one side, the lovely Taylor River flows by. On the other, the Sawatch Range looms impressively above Taylor Park. Most of the campsites are in a coniferous forest that provides ample privacy and shade. The fishing is excellent. Four-wheeling is the second most popular pastime. There are seemingly endless Forest Service routes in the park and the surrounding mountains. Hiking and mountain biking trails are accessible within a 15-minute drive.

Sites 0–5, 7, 11, 12, 13, and 17–22 are by the river. Sites 17–22 are not in the woods, so they have limited shade and privacy but excellent views. The views are also excellent from sites 0–5 and 13–16.

Campsites, facilities: There are 22 sites for tents and RVs up to 35 feet. There are no hookups. Sites 0, 1, 2, 11, and 12 are pull-through. Picnic tables, grills, and fire rings are provided. Vault toilets and drinking water are available. Leashed pets are permitted.

Reservations, fees: Reservations are accepted for 12 sites at 877/444-6777 and www.reserveusa.com. The fee is $12 per night (includes one vehicle). There is a $6 fee per additional vehicle. Golden Age and Golden Access Passports are accepted. Cash or check only. Open year-round.

Directions: From Main Street in Gunnison, take Highway 135 north for 10.2 miles. In Almont, turn right on Forest Route 742 and drive up Taylor Canyon to the reservoir. The campground is 10.2 miles past the dam on the left.

Contact: Gunnison National Forest, 970/641-0471, www.fs.fed.us/r2/gmug.

61 RIVERS END

Scenic rating: 8

northeast of Gunnison

Rivers End is at the inlet of 2,033-surface-acre Taylor Reservoir. Anglers will be very happy at this campground. The stream fishing is excellent from the inlet up, especially at Italian Creek, and the stocked lake contains rainbow, brook, brown, lake, and cutthroat trout, as well as kokanee salmon. This area is also very popular with four-wheelers. The campground consists of three small loops on a rise above the river. Without trees, it is very windblown, but the views of the Sawatch Range are jaw dropping from every campsite. Sites 10–18 also have views of the lake. Bring a tarp to provide some shade and your camera so you can capture the sunsets.

Campsites, facilities: There are 15 sites for tents and RVs up to 35 feet. There are no hookups. Sites 10–18 are pull-through. Picnic tables, grills, and fire rings are provided. Vault toilets and drinking water are available. Leashed pets are permitted.

Reservations, fees: Reservations are not accepted. The fee is $12 per night (includes one vehicle). There is a $6 fee per additional vehicle. Golden Age and Golden Access Passports are accepted. Cash or check only. Open May–September.

Directions: From Main Street in Gunnison, take Highway 135 north for 10.2 miles. In Almont, turn right on Forest Route 742 and drive up Taylor Canyon to the reservoir. The campground is 6.3 miles past the dam on the right.

Contact: Gunnison National Forest, 970/641-0471, www.fs.fed.us/r2/gmug.

62 LAKEVIEW

Scenic rating: 8

northeast of Gunnison

The broad basin of Taylor Park was one the summer hunting grounds of the Utes, who called it "the Valley of the Gods." In the late 1800s, it saw numerous gold towns boom and bust. The dam was completed in 1937, and since then, the 2,033-surface-acre reservoir has provided irrigation water to the Uncompahgre Valley, as well as recreation opportunities. At an elevation of 9,000 feet, the park is worth a visit whether or not you have time to camp. The impressive Sawatch Range forms the eastern boundary of the park, and the Taylor River and numerous creeks meander through the bottomlands.

Lakeview is a large campground that's very popular with RVers. Situated on a steep hill overlooking the reservoir and the Sawatch Range, the campground offers amazing views, but you have to put up with a lot of neighbors. There are four loops. The first loop (sites 47–68) is the electrical loop, and it has very few trees. The second and third loops (sites 1–29) are in a coniferous forest, but many sites still have great views. The last loop is highest on the hill. It's heavily wooded and seems to attract a lot of campers, although there are no views of the park.

Campsites, facilities: There are 68 sites for tents and RVs up to 40 feet. Electrical hookups are available at sites 47–68, and many sites are pull-through. Picnic tables, grills, fire rings, tent pads and lantern posts are provided. Vault toilets and drinking water are available. The facilities are wheelchair accessible. A marina with a boat ramp and boat rentals is 0.2 mile down the road. Leashed pets are permitted.

Reservations, fees: Reservations are accepted at 877/444-6777 and www.reserveusa.com. The fee is $16 per night (includes one vehicle). There is an $8 fee per additional vehicle and a $4 fee for electricity. Golden Age and Golden Access Passports are accepted. Cash or check only. Open May–September.

Directions: From Main Street in Gunnison, take Highway 135 north for 10.2 miles. In Almont, turn right on Forest Route 742 and drive up Taylor Canyon to the reservoir. The campground is 1.4 miles past the dam on the right.

Contact: Gunnison National Forest, 970/641-0471, www.fs.fed.us/r2/gmug.

63 LOTTIS CREEK

Scenic rating: 7

northeast of Gunnison

Lottis Creek flows from the Fossil Ridge area into the Taylor River. The campground is the last one in the canyon before entering Taylor Park. It's also the best first-come first-served campground in the canyon, so it stays fairly busy all summer, but there are usually available sites. It's popular with families and anglers. Hikers also stay here and use the South Lottis Creek Trail, which begins in the campground, to explore the Fossil Ridge Wilderness.

The campground has two wooded loops on either side of Lottis Creek and one group loop across the road beside the Taylor River. The traffic noise is less pronounced than at earlier campgrounds in the canyon. The first loop follows Lottis Creek away from the main road. The sites are about 100 feet apart. The second loop is larger, and the sites are closer together. Sites 5–10, at the back of the loop, are the quietest. Sites 21–29 are next to the creek. Sites 25–27 are designed as a family site. In the group loop, there are four sites that must be reserved together.

Campsites, facilities: There are 29 sites for tents and RVs up to 35 feet and one group site. Sites 15 and 16 and the facilities are wheelchair accessible. Electrical hookups are available at sites 3, 5, 12, and 13. Sites 2, 3, 5, 8, 12, 15, 17–21, and 25–27 are pull-through. Picnic tables, grills, and fire rings are provided. Vault toilets, drinking water, and a small amphitheater with electricity are available. Leashed pets are permitted.

Reservations, fees: Reservations are not accepted for the main campground, but they are required for the group site. Reservations are accepted at 877/444-6777 and www.reserveusa.com. The fee is $14 per night (includes one vehicle). There is a $7 fee per additional vehicle and a $4 fee for electricity. The group site costs $60 per night. Golden Age and Golden Access Passports are accepted. Cash or check only. Open May–September.

Directions: From Main Street in Gunnison, take Highway 135 north for 10.2 miles. In Almont, turn right on Forest Route 742. The campground is on the right in 16.7 miles.

Contact: Gunnison National Forest, 970/641-0471, www.fs.fed.us/r2/gmug.

64 SPRING CREEK

Scenic rating: 6

northeast of Gunnison

Spring Creek is a pretty little canyon campground located near Gunnison. It's a convenient stopover or a nice weekend destination. Although the campground is very close to the road, noise is not as much of a problem here as in Taylor Canyon because Spring Creek sees a lot less traffic, in part because of the washboard road. The fly-fishing on Spring Creek is excellent. Public access begins at the campground and extends upstream for 10 miles. Rainbow, brown, brook, and native cutthroat trout are found in the numerous pools, some of them right next to the campground. The campground is a loop beside the creek, forested with spruce, pine, and aspen. Sites 1–3, 5–7, and 9–11 all have adequate shade. Sites 11 and 12 are next to the road. The rest of the sites border the creek.

Campsites, facilities: There are 12 sites for tents and RVs up to 35 feet. There are no hookups. Sites 2, 3, 6, 7, 9, 11, and 12 are pull-through. Picnic tables, grills, and fire rings are provided. Vault toilets and drinking water are available. Leashed pets are permitted.

Reservations, fees: Reservations are not accepted. The fee is $10 per night (includes one vehicle). There is a $5 fee per additional vehicle. Golden Age and Golden Access Passports are accepted. Cash or check only. Open May–September.

Directions: From Main Street in Gunnison, take Highway 135 north to Almont. Turn left on Forest Route 744. The campground is on the right in 1.8 miles.

Contact: Gunnison National Forest, 970/641-0471, www.fs.fed.us/r2/gmug.

65 COLD SPRING

Scenic rating: 6

northeast of Gunnison

Cold Spring is a little nicer than its neighbor Lodgepole, but they share the same problem: proximity to the road. During the day, campers can anticipate lots of traffic noise. All of the sites are visible from the road and vice versa. However, Cold Spring has denser vegetation than Lodgepole, including wild roses, which helps the sites feel more private. Sites 1, 3, and 6 are next to the road. Sites 4 and 5 are the best sites. From Lodgepole campground to Lottis Creek campground, the river is open to public access. The fishing is excellent, although wading can be difficult. Kayakers can put in on this stretch of river as well.

Campsites, facilities: There are six sites for tents. Small pop-up campers can also fit in the spurs, but trailers are not recommended. There are no hookups. Site 5 is pull-through. Picnic tables, grills, and fire rings are provided. Vault toilets are available. Leashed pets are permitted.

Reservations, fees: Reservations are not accepted. The fee is $8 per night (includes one vehicle). There is a $4 fee per additional vehicle. Golden Age and Golden Access Passports are accepted. Cash or check only. Open May–September.

Directions: From Main Street in Gunnison, take Highway 135 north for 10.2 miles. In Almont, turn right on Forest Route 742. The campground is on the right in 15.4 miles.

Contact: Gunnison National Forest, 970/641-0471, www.fs.fed.us/r2/gmug.

66 LODGEPOLE

Scenic rating: 5

northeast of Gunnison

As the name suggests, Lodgepole campground is in a lodgepole pine forest. It is cool and shady, but the pines do not provide much privacy. All campsites are visible from the road and vice versa, and the road separates the campground from the river. The traffic noise and lack of privacy make this campground my last choice in the canyon. If you do have to stay here, sites 6–8 are farthest from the road. Site 10 is the best site because huge boulders shield it from the cars. Public fishing access begins at Lodgepole and extends upstream to Lottis Creek campground. The 12-mile Summerville Trail begins one mile downstream and climbs into the Fossil Ridge Wilderness. Kayakers can put in on this stretch of river as well.

Campsites, facilities: There are 17 sites for tents and RVs up to 35 feet. There are no hookups. Sites 4, 9, and 12–16 are pull-through. Picnic tables, grills, and fire rings are provided. Vault toilets and drinking water are available. Leashed pets are permitted.

Reservations, fees: Reservations are accepted at 877/444-6777 and www.reserveusa.com. The fee is $12 per night (includes one vehicle). There is a $6 fee per additional vehicle. Golden Age and Golden Access Passports are accepted. Cash or check only. Open May–September.

Directions: From Main Street in Gunnison, take Highway 135 north for 10.2 miles. In Almont, turn right on Forest Route 742. The campground is on the right in 14.3 miles.

Contact: Gunnison National Forest, 970/641-0471, www.fs.fed.us/r2/gmug.

67 GRANITE

Scenic rating: 6

northeast of Gunnison

Granite is in a small clearing of sagebrush and pine trees between the Gunnison River and the highway. There are fascinating cliffs across the road, and heaps of wildflowers, but there's also a ton of traffic noise. Nonetheless, this campground can be full all weekend because of the whitewater and fishing in the area. The Taylor is an excellent trout fishery, and the whitewater from the South Bank put-in to Almont is a mellow Class II–III that's perfect for beginners. The nearest hiking and mountain biking trail begins at the North Bank campground. Trail 424 travels nine miles into the Doctor Park area. In the campground, privacy is limited. Site 1 is farthest from the parking lot, but it's also very close to the road. Site 2, the nicest site in the campground, has lots of shade and privacy. Sites 3 and 6 also have shade and some privacy. Sites 4 and 5 are completely exposed and very close to the parking lot.

Campsites, facilities: There are seven walk-in tent sites. Picnic tables, grills, and fire rings are provided. Vault toilets are available. Leashed pets are permitted.

Reservations, fees: Reservations are not accepted. The fee is $8 per night (includes one vehicle). There is a $4 fee per additional vehicle. Golden Age and Golden Access Passports are accepted. Cash or check only. Open May–September.

Directions: From Main Street in Gunnison, take Highway 135 north for 10.2 miles. In Almont, turn right on Forest Route 742. The campground is on the right in 7.4 miles.

Contact: Gunnison National Forest, 970/641-0471, www.fs.fed.us/r2/gmug.

68 ONE MILE

🚶🚴🐟🚣🐕♿🚐⛺

Scenic rating: 6

northeast of Gunnison

One Mile is on a steep slope above the highway and the Gunnison River. As one of the few campgrounds with electricity in Taylor Canyon, it's very popular with RVers, so reservations are recommended on weekends. The campground is a paved loop in a forest of pine, aspen, and wild roses with several resident hummingbirds (and Texans). Like all of the Taylor Canyon campgrounds, its main drawback is traffic noise, but fortunately none of the sites is really visible from the road and vice versa. The canyon is popular with kayakers, rafters, and anglers. Trout fishing is excellent, although much of the river is on private property, so anglers should watch for signs. The whitewater ranges from tough Class IIIs to mellow Class IIs. Guided rafting trips are available at Three Rivers Resort. Hiking and mountain biking are available on Doctor Park Trail, which begins at nearby North Bank campground, across from the South Bank river access. The sites are large and 50–100 feet apart. Sites 24 and 25, at the end of the loop, have the most privacy.

Campsites, facilities: There are 25 sites for tents and RVs up to 35 feet. Site 21 and the facilities are wheelchair accessible. Electric hookups are available at all sites. Sites 2, 4, 6, 8, 9, and 13–19 are pull-through. Picnic tables, grills, fire rings, and lantern hooks are provided. Tent pads are provided at sites 3, 10, 15, 16, 18, and 23–25. Vault toilets, drinking water, and gray-water dump stations are available. Leashed pets are permitted.

Reservations, fees: Reservations are accepted at 877/444-6777 and www.reserveusa.com. The fee is $16 per night (includes one vehicle). There is an $8 fee per additional vehicle and a $4 fee for electricity. Golden Age and Golden Access Passports are accepted. Cash or check only. Open May–September.

Directions: From Main Street in Gunnison, take Highway 135 north for 10.2 miles. In Almont, turn right on Forest Route 742. The campground is on the right in 8.3 miles.

Contact: Gunnison National Forest, 970/641-0471, www.fs.fed.us/r2/gmug.

69 NORTH BANK

🚶🚴🐟🚣🐕🚐⛺

Scenic rating: 6

northeast of Gunnison

Like all of the Taylor Canyon sites, you can't get away from the sound of traffic at North Bank, but it's full on weekends with rafters, kayakers, and anglers. The stretch of whitewater from the South Bank put-in to Almont is an easy Class II–III that's perfect for beginners. The five-mile stretch above South Bank is more challenging. Anglers can fish from the campground for about a mile in each direction. The Doctor Park Trail begins in the parking lot and is open to both hikers and mountain bikers. The sites are 25–50 feet apart and not large. Sites 1, 3, and 5–7 are next to the river. Sites 9–16 are in a loop that's away from the road and very shady. It's the best area for tent campers.

Campsites, facilities: There are 17 sites for tents and RVs up to 35 feet. There are no hookups. Sites 1–7 and 15–17 are pull-through. Picnic tables, grills, and fire rings are provided. Vault toilets and drinking water are available. Leashed pets are permitted.

Reservations, fees: Reservations are not accepted. The fee is $12 per night (includes one vehicle). There is a $6 fee per additional vehicle. Golden Age and Golden Access Passports are accepted. Cash or check only. Open May–September.

Directions: From Main Street in Gunnison, take Highway 135 north for 10.2 miles. In Almont, turn right on Forest Route 742. The campground is on the left in 7.6 miles.

Contact: Gunnison National Forest, 970/641-0471, www.fs.fed.us/r2/gmug.

70 ROSY LANE

Scenic rating: 7

northeast of Gunnison

For scenery, privacy, and river access, Rosy Lane is the best campground in Taylor Canyon. It's also the most beloved—the camp host, Ray Zimball, has spent over 16 summers looking after this campground, and he doesn't put up with any misbehaving. Like Zimball, many of the campers are regulars who return every summer for the peace and quiet and good fishing. Hiking, mountain biking, and whitewater are available a little over a mile downstream at the North Bank campground and South Bank river access. The campground is a paved loop in a forest of pine, spruce, and aspen beside the Taylor River. Across the river, there are impressive granite cliffs with so much mica in them that, according to Ray, "on a full moon you could read a newspaper by the light." Sites 3–9, 11, 13, and 14 are by the river. Sites 1, 2, and 15–19 are near the highway. Site 14 is a family site with two picnic tables and fire rings. Sites 4–7 are the best tent sites.

Campsites, facilities: There are 19 sites for tents and RVs up to 35 feet. Site 8, the facilities, and the fishing trail are wheelchair accessible. Sites 8–11 have electric hookups and site 8 also has water. Sites 1, 2, 4, 6, 13, 15, and 17–19 are pull-through. Picnic tables, grills, and fire rings are provided. Tent pads are provided at sites 3–5. Vault toilets and drinking water are available. Leashed pets are permitted.

Reservations, fees: Reservations are accepted at 877/444-6777 and www.reserveusa.com, but about 40 percent of the sites are nonreservable. The fee is $14 per night (includes one vehicle). There is a $7 fee per additional vehicle and a $4 fee for electricity. Golden Age and Golden Access Passports are accepted. Cash or check only. Open May–September.

Directions: From Main Street in Gunnison, take Highway 135 north for 10.2 miles. In Almont, turn right on Forest Route 742. The campground is on the left in 8.8 miles.

Contact: Gunnison National Forest, 970/641-0471, www.fs.fed.us/r2/gmug.

71 TAYLOR CANYON

Scenic rating: 6

northeast of Gunnison

This campground is within the Almont Triangle, an area of south-facing hills that are critical habitat for bighorn sheep, elk, and mule deer in the winter, when it's possible to sight bighorn sheep in the cliffs across from the viewing area in the campground. The campsites are located beneath a similar cliff face in a forest of spruce and aspen. The highway separates the campground from the Taylor River. The small sites are 15–30 feet apart and not far from the road, but this is a comfortable stopover with excellent fishing and white-water opportunities nearby. The Lower Taylor, from South Bank to Almont, is a Class II–III run that's perfect for advanced beginners. Sites 3–5 are closest to the parking lot.

Campsites, facilities: There are 11 walk-in sites for tents. There are no hookups. Picnic tables, grills, fire rings, and tent pads are provided. Vault toilets and drinking water are available. Leashed pets are permitted.

Reservations, fees: Reservations are not accepted. The fee is $7 per tent per night. Golden Age and Golden Access Passports are accepted. Cash or check only. Open May–September.

Directions: From Main Street in Gunnison, take Highway 135 north 10.2 miles to Almont. Turn right on Forest Route 742. The campground is on the right in 2.9 miles.

Contact: Gunnison Parks and Recreation, 970/641-8060.

72 ALMONT

Scenic rating: 6

northeast of Gunnison

Almont is a historic stagecoach town turned fishing and rafting resort. In the summer, there are hordes of Midwesterners and Texans in wet shorts and swimsuits returning from rafting trips on the Taylor and Gunnison Rivers. The campground is on the banks of the Gunnison, less than a mile downstream of the town. With the incessant hum of traffic and pretty but not spectacular scenery, it's just a stopover between Gunnison and Crested Butte. Rainbow and brown trout inhabit the river, but even anglers are likely to prefer the roomier campsites in Taylor Canyon. Sites 6–10 are for tents only. Sites 6, 9, and 10 are down by the river and more private. Site 3 is the best RV site.

Campsites, facilities: There are five sites for RVs up to 28 feet and five tent sites. There are no hookups. Site 3 is pull-through. Picnic tables, grills, and fire rings are provided. Vault toilets and drinking water are available. Leashed pets are permitted.

Reservations, fees: Reservations are not accepted. The fee is $10 per night (includes one vehicle). There is a $5 fee per additional vehicle. Golden Age and Golden Access Passports are accepted. Cash or check only. Open May–September.

Directions: From Main Street in Gunnison, take Highway 135 north for 9.3 miles. Turn right at the Almont sign.

Contact: Gunnison National Forest, 970/641-0471, www.fs.fed.us/r2/gmug.

73 GOLD CREEK

Scenic rating: 7

east of Gunnison

It's a long drive to Gold Creek, but the tantaliz-

ing views of the Fossil Ridge Wilderness area will please every hiker and backpacker. The South Lottis Trail follows South Lottis Creek to the Lamphier Lakes, where good fishing is available, and continues over Gunsight Pass to the Taylor Park area. Hikers and anglers can also follow the Fossil Ridge Trail for four miles to Boulder Lake. Mountain bikers can follow the Fairview Peak Trail to an altitude of 13,200 feet and then continue into the Taylor Park area. Horseback riders also use this campground frequently. The wooded campsites have Gold Creek on one side and a small meadow on the other. Sites 1 and 2 are on top of each other, as are 3 and 4. Walk-in sites 5 and 6 are about 100 feet from the loop and are forested. Horse trailers and corrals can be set up across the road.

Campsites, facilities: There are four sites for tents and RVs up to 25 feet and two sites for tents only. There are no hookups or pull-throughs. Picnic tables, grills, and fire rings are provided. Vault toilets are available. Leashed pets are permitted.

Reservations, fees: Reservations are not accepted. The fee is $8 per night (includes one vehicle). There is a $4 fee per additional vehicle. Golden Age and Golden Access Passports are accepted. Cash or check only. Open May–September.

Directions: From Gunnison, take U.S. Highway 50 east to County Road 76. Go north on County Road 76 for 8.7 miles to Ohio City. Turn left on Forest Route 771. The road ends at the campground in 6.8 miles. The last 1.5 miles are rough but do not require 4WD.

Contact: Gunnison National Forest, 970/641-0471, www.fs.fed.us/r2/gmug.

74 COMANCHE

Scenic rating: 5

east of Gunnison

This itsy-bitsy campground is in an aspen grove right next to the road. There's no reason to stay here except that it's a convenient stopover between Gunnison and Salida. The campground can only accommodate tents and pop-ups. Sites 1–3 are on top of each other. Site 4 is more private.

Campsites, facilities: There are four sites for tents and RVs up to 15 feet. There are no hookups or pull-throughs. Picnic tables, grills, and fire rings are provided. Vault toilets are available. Leashed pets are permitted.

Reservations, fees: Reservations are not accepted. The fee is $8 per night (includes one vehicle). There is a $4 fee per additional vehicle. Golden Age and Golden Access Passports are accepted. Cash or check only. Open May–September.

Directions: From Gunnison, take U.S. Highway 50 east to County Road 76. Go north on County Road 76 for 8.7 miles to Ohio City. Turn left on Forest Route 771. The campground is on the right in 1.2 miles.

Contact: Gunnison National Forest, 970/641-0471, www.fs.fed.us/r2/gmug.

75 QUARTZ

Scenic rating: 6

east of Gunnison

The area around the tiny community of Pitkin is very popular with ATV owners and Texans. Forest Service roads explore ghost towns and the Continental Divide, and the weather is very mild. Quartz campground, on the banks of North Quartz Creek, is popular with tent and pop-up campers, and it sees a lot less use than Pitkin campground. It's in a forest of aspen, spruce, and fir, and its main features are wilderness and solitude. The small sites are about 50 feet apart. Sites 1–5 are next to the open wetland area along the creek. Site 10 has the most privacy.

Campsites, facilities: There are 10 sites for tents and short RVs. There are no hookups or pull-throughs. Picnic tables, grills,

and fire rings are provided. Vault toilets and drinking water are available. Leashed pets are permitted.

Reservations, fees: Reservations are not accepted. The fee is $10 per night (includes one vehicle). There is a $5 fee per additional vehicle. Golden Age and Golden Access Passports are accepted. Cash or check only. Open May–September.

Directions: From the Silver Plume General Store in Pitkin, drive north on Forest Route 765. The campground is on the right in 3.6 miles.

Contact: Gunnison National Forest, 970/641-0471, www.fs.fed.us/r2/gmug.

76 PITKIN

Scenic rating: 6

east of Gunnison

Located in the Sawatch Range, on the west side of the Continental Divide, Pitkin is considered an ATV mecca. A network of Forest Service roads extends from this revived railroad town into the mining district to the north. Popular destinations are the Alpine Tunnel, Cumberland Pass, and the ghost town of Tincup. (The Alpine Tunnel is a railroad tunnel through the Continental Divide that was built in 1881 and abandoned in 1910.) Anglers can fish on Quartz Creek or take the kids to the fishing pond across the street. The mild weather also attracts many vacationers, especially west Texans, who can drive to Pitkin in a day. This campground is a short walk from town, where campers can pick up ice cream and other summer necessities. It's in a spruce/fir forest on the banks of Quartz Creek. The large sites are 50–100 feet apart. Except for ATV traffic, it's a quiet place. Sites 10–14 are on the creek and reserved mainly for tents. Sites 1 and 4 are also on the creek and can accommodate RVs.

Campsites, facilities: There are 22 sites for

tents and RVs up to 35 feet. There are no hookups. Sites 8, 9, and 15–23 are pull-through. Site 21 and the facilities are wheelchair accessible. Picnic tables, grills, fire rings, and lantern posts are provided at all sites. Tent pads are provided at sites 5–14. Vault toilets, drinking water, a gray-water dump station, and a very small amphitheater are available. Leashed pets are permitted.

Reservations, fees: Reservations are not accepted. The fee is $14 per night (includes one vehicle). There is a $7 fee per additional vehicle. Golden Age and Golden Access Passports are accepted. Cash or check only. Open May–October.

Directions: From the Silver Plume General Store in Pitkin, drive north on Forest Route 765. The campground is on the right in 0.5 mile.

Contact: Gunnison National Forest, 970/641-0471, www.fs.fed.us/r2/gmug.

77 SNOWBLIND

🚶 🚵 🎣 ❄ 🐕 🚐 ⛺

Scenic rating: 7

east of Gunnison

Hardly anyone knows about Snowblind, which contributes immensely to the charm of this little campground on the banks of Tomichi Creek. Few people visit this remote area between Gunnison and Monarch Pass, but the open meadows and scenic vistas from nearby Waunita Pass are beautiful. Those who do visit this campground can set up camp in one of four loops and spend a week or two without neighbors. Hikers and mountain bikers can explore the Canyon Creek and Horseshoe Creek Trails, which climb to Stella Mountain and Tomichi Pass. Mountain bikers can explore the Old Monarch Pass Road. Waunita Hot Springs, 7.5 miles to the west, are open to the public in the fall. Sites 4–7, 16–18, and 19–21 are next to the creek, which offers fair fishing. Sites 22 and 23 are next to the road.

Campsites, facilities: There are 23 sites for tents and RVs up to 35 feet. There are no hookups or pull-throughs. Picnic tables, grills, and fire rings are provided. Vault toilets and drinking water are available. Leashed pets are permitted.

Reservations, fees: Reservations are not accepted. The fee is $10 per night (includes one vehicle). There is a $5 fee per additional vehicle. Golden Age and Golden Access Passports are accepted. Cash or check only. Open mid-May–mid-September.

Directions: From Gunnison, take U.S. Highway 50 east to Sargents. From Sargents, continue east for 1.3 miles and turn north on Forest Route 888. The campground is on the left in 7.8 miles.

Contact: Gunnison National Forest, 970/641-0471, www.fs.fed.us/r2/gmug.

78 CLEAR FORK

🚶 🚵 ⛵ 🎣 🚤 ❄ 🐕 🚸 ♿ 🚐 ⛺

Scenic rating: 6

in Crawford State Park

Crawford State Park is in an agricultural valley with a mild climate 12 miles north of the Black Canyon of the Gunnison. The park includes 337 acres of land and a 400-acre reservoir. It's a weekend getaway for locals and a convenient stopover on the West Elk Scenic Byway Loop. When the reservoir is full, the park is packed on the weekends, mostly with families. The sandy swimming beach, lake fishing, and gravel trails are perfect for small kids. A half-mile trail connects Clear Fork to the swimming beach, and another trail connects the campgrounds. The lake is stocked with largemouth bass and catfish. Water sports include waterskiing, scuba diving, and boating. Winter sports include ice fishing, cross-country skiing, and snowshoeing.

The campgrounds were renovated in 1997, and the facilities still look very new. Clear Fork is a lakeside loop with very few trees.

The five tent-only sites (50–54) and sites 63–66 are in the middle of the loop and about 20 feet apart without trees or shade. Sites 55–59 are very small. Sites 46–49 are on the shore. Sites 46, 60, and 61 are very large and perfect for big family groups.

Campsites, facilities: There are 15 sites for tents and RVs up to 35 feet and five tent-only sites. Sites 62 and 63 are wheelchair accessible. There are no hookups. Sites 63–65 are pull-through. Picnic tables, fire rings and grills are provided at all sites. Sun shelters are provided at sites 46–49 and 60–63. Restrooms with flush toilets and showers, drinking water, a swim beach, and playground are available. Dump stations and a boat ramp are available at Iron Creek campground. Leashed pets are permitted.

Reservations, fees: Reservations are accepted at 800/678-2267 and www.parks.state.co.us. The fee is $12 per night. There is an additional $8 reservation fee. Campers must also purchase a Daily Parks Pass ($5) or an Annual Parks Pass ($55). The Aspen Leaf Annual Pass is accepted. Open year-round.

Directions: From Crawford, take Highway 92 south for 1.5 miles. The campground entrance is on the right.

Contact: Crawford State Park, 970/921-5721, email: crawford.park@state.co.us.

79 IRON CREEK

Scenic rating: 6

in Crawford State Park

Crawford is a small state park that's popular with families because of the swimming beach, lake fishing, and gravel trails. A one-mile trail connects Iron Creek to the swimming beach and the other campground. The lake is stocked with largemouth bass and catfish. Water sports include waterskiing, scuba diving, and boating. The campgrounds were renovated in 1997, and they still look very new. Iron Creek is a loop on a small peninsula in a sagebrush habitat. There are excellent views of Needle Rock, Castle Rock, and Saddle Mountain. The sites are 50 feet apart; sun shelters provide most of the privacy. Sites 20, 22, 24, 26, 28, 30, 32, 34, 35, 37, 39, and 41 are lakefront sites, but a steep embankment limits access to the lake.

Campsites, facilities: There are 35 sites for tents and RVs up to 35 feet. Sites 1, 33–36, and 44 are wheelchair accessible. Full hookups are available at all sites. Half of the sites are pull-through. Picnic tables, fire rings, grills, and tent pads are provided at all sites. Sun shelters are provided at sites 1, 2, 6, 7, 10, 14, 33–35, and 44. Restrooms with flush toilets and showers, drinking water, dump stations, and a boat ramp are available. Leashed pets are permitted.

Reservations, fees: Reservations are accepted at 800/678-2267 and www.parks.state.co.us. The fee is $16 per night. There is an additional $8 reservation fee. Campers must also purchase a Daily Parks Pass ($5) or an Annual Parks Pass ($55). The Aspen Leaf Annual Pass is accepted. Open April–November.

Directions: From Crawford, take Highway 92 south for two miles. The campground entrance is on the right.

Contact: Crawford State Park, 970/921-5721, email: crawford.park@state.co.us.

80 NORTH RIM

Scenic rating: 7

in Black Canyon of the Gunnison National Park

North Rim campground is much smaller than the South Rim facility; it is also more popular because of the spectacular views, especially at sunrise or sunset. (For more information on the Black Canyon, see the South Rim listing in this chapter.) The North Rim Drive has six overlooks and takes about two–three hours to drive. There are three hiking trails on the North Rim. The longest trail in the park, North Vista, begins at the campground and travels west to Exclamation Point (three miles round-trip) and then Green Mountain (seven miles round-trip). Bring your camera to capture the panoramic vistas and inner-canyon views. Intrepid hikers can explore the inner canyon via S.O.B. Draw, Long Draw, and Slide Draw. These steep, strenuous scrambles drop 1,800 feet in one mile. Wildlife viewing is excellent, especially for bird-watchers who might see peregrine falcons, canyon wrens, great horned owls, and mountain bluebirds. The campground is a small loop in a piñon-sage habitat. It occasionally fills up during the summer, but midweek there's plenty of solitude.

Campsites, facilities: There are 13 sites for tents and RVs up to 35 feet. There are no hookups. Picnic tables, grills, and vault toilets are provided. Drinking water is available mid-May–mid-October. Leashed pets are permitted.

Reservations, fees: Reservations are not accepted. The nightly fee is $10. Cash or check only. The park entrance fee is $8 for seven days. Golden Age and Golden Access Passports are accepted. Open spring–fall.

Directions: From Crawford, take 38.50 Drive west to Amber Road. Turn right on Amber Road and in less than a mile turn left on Black Canyon Road/North Rim Drive. In 10 miles, stop at the park entrance station and then follow the signs one mile to the campground.

Contact: Black Canyon of the Gunnison National Park, 970/641-2337, www.nps.gov/blca.

81 SOUTH RIM

Scenic rating: 7

in Black Canyon of the Gunnison National Park

Geologist Wallace Hansen wrote: "Some are longer, some are deeper, some are narrower, and a few have walls as steep. But no other canyon in North America combines the depth, narrowness, sheerness, and somber countenance of the Black Canyon of the Gunnison." It took the Gunnison River two million years to carve the 48-mile canyon out of Precambrian gneiss. On average, the river drops 96 feet per mile through the park, and before the dams upstream of the park were built, it was laden with rocks and debris that helped carve the canyon. Most visitors are only able to peer over the rim at the colorful cliffs and spires; a lucky few go rafting or kayaking on the Gunny. Hiking in the park is very limited due to the steep walls of the canyon. Most hikers will explore the Rim Rock, Oak Flat, Cedar Point, and Warner Point Trails, which range in length from one–three miles round-trip. An excellent half-day trip from the campground involves driving the South Rim Road, stopping at the overlooks, and stretching your legs on the nature trails. Intrepid hikers can head into the inner canyon on the Gunnison, Timichi, and Warner Routes. These are very steep, difficult scrambles. Fishing is available at East Portal. Winter sports include cross-country skiing and snowshoeing on South Rim Road.

This campground is densely wooded with Gambel's oak and serviceberry. As a result, the sites are very private, especially in Loop A, which has many walk-in sites. Loop B attracts mostly RVs. Loop C features views of the mountains. This campground rarely fills up, although reservations are recommended on holidays.

Campsites, facilities: There are 88 sites for tents and RVs up to 37 feet. Two sites and the facilities are wheelchair accessible. Electric hookups are available in Loop B, and pull-through sites are available in all three loops. Picnic tables and grills are provided at all sites. Tent pads are provided in Loop B. Vault toilets, drinking water, dump stations for gray water, an amphitheater, and campfire programs are available. Leashed pets are permitted.

Reservations, fees: Reservations are accepted for Loops A and B at 877/444-6777 and www.reserveusa.com. The nightly fee is $10 for sites without electricity and $15 for sites with electricity. Cash or check only. The park entrance fee is $8 for seven days. Golden Age and Golden Access Passports are accepted. Loop A is open year-round. Loops B and C are open spring–fall.

Directions: From Montrose, take U.S. Highway 50 east for 7.5 miles. Turn north on Highway 347. The entrance station is in 5.8 miles, and the campground entrance is on the right, 0.2 mile after the station.

Contact: Black Canyon of the Gunnison National Park, 970/641-2337, www.nps.gov/blca.

82 EAST PORTAL

🚶 🎣 🛶 🐎 🚐 ⛺

Scenic rating: 6

in Curecanti National Recreation Area

BEST (

Curecanti National Recreation Area contains three reservoirs: Blue Mesa, Morrow Point, and Crystal. Blue Mesa is the main storage reservoir, Morrow Point Dam generates power, and Crystal Dam moderates the releases from Morrow Point. East Portal is located downstream of Crystal Dam, making it the most western campground in Curecanti (but it must be accessed through the Black Canyon of the Gunnison National Park). From 700 yards below the dam to the North Fork, the Gunnison River is considered Gold Medal Water. Anglers can fish for brown and rainbow trout in nearly absolute solitude. An unmaintained trail from the end of the campground reaches about a half mile into the inner canyon. It's great for fishing access and a nice short trail for families with kids. Expert kayakers put in here for a 27-mile adventure down the Black Canyon to Gunnison Forks. Permits are required for kayaking and overnight backcountry use.

The campground has two loops. The first is a small, gravel loop with five sites. There is some shade but no privacy. The second loop, "The Bowl," has 10 walk-in sites in a grove of box elder and narrowleaf cottonwood. The sites are close together, but the combination of shade and limited use makes it very pleasant.

Campsites, facilities: There are five sites for tents and RVs and 10 walk-in tent sites. Vehicles longer than 22 feet (including the trailer) are prohibited on East Portal Road. Picnic tables, grills, fire rings, and tent pads are provided. Vault toilets and drinking water are available. Leashed pets are permitted.

Reservations, fees: Reservations are not accepted. The fee is $10 per night. Cash or check only. The park entrance fee is $8 for seven days. Golden Age and Golden Access Passports are accepted. Open Memorial Day–Labor Day, weather permitting.

Directions: From Montrose, take U.S. Highway 50 east for 7.5 miles. Turn north on Highway 347. The entrance station is in 5.8 miles. After the station, turn right on East Portal Road. This is a long, steep, very narrow road. Vehicles longer than 22 feet (including the trailer) are prohibited. In 5.3 miles, turn left at the campground sign. The road ends at the campground.

Contact: Curecanti National Recreation Area, 970/641-2337, www.nps.gov/cure.

83 CIMARRON

🚶 🎣 🚗 🐎 🚐 ⛺

Scenic rating: 5

in Curecanti National Recreation Area

Cimarron is the only campground in Curecanti that offers access to Crystal Reservoir and the Cimarron River. Hand-powered boats can be carried down to the reservoir via the Mesa Creek Trail, a 0.8-mile trail with a footbridge across the reservoir that provides access to the north shore. (Boaters should inquire at the visitors center about dam releases, which can cause strong currents.) Fishing on the reservoir includes rainbow, brown, brook, and cutthroat trout, as well as kokanee salmon and yellow perch. Kids and history buffs will enjoy the outdoor exhibit at the visitors center which includes corrals and stock cars from the Denver and Rio Grande Narrow Gauge Railroad and explains the early importance of the railroad to the ranching communities of the west.

The campground is surrounded by badlands and a granite ridge. The sites in this loop are about 25 feet apart. There is not much privacy or scenery, but the campground consistently attracts a small crowd of anglers.

Campsites, facilities: There are 21 sites for tents and RVs up to 30 feet. Sites 12, 15, 17, 19, and 21 are pull through. There are no hookups. Picnic tables, grills, vault toilets, and drinking water are provided. Leashed pets are permitted.

Reservations, fees: Reservations are not accepted. The fee is $10 per night. Golden Age and Golden Access Passports are accepted. Cash or check only. Open year-round.

Directions: From Montrose, take U.S. Highway 50 east for 19.3 miles. In Cimarron, turn left at the Cimarron Campground sign. The campground is across the bridge on the left.

Contact: Curecanti National Recreation Area, 970/641-2337, www.nps.gov/cure.

84 SOAP CREEK

🚶 🛶 🐎 🚐 ⛺

Scenic rating: 7

north of Curecanti National Recreation Area

Soap Creek is a remote and scenic campground. It provides southern access to West Elk Wilderness area which, despite its size (176,092 acres), is mostly used only by hunters in the fall. Trail 451 leads from the campground into the mountains and reaches Cow Creek in two miles, West Elk Creek in 13 miles, and Rainbow Lake in 18 miles. The campground is a gravel loop in a mature pine

forest. Sites are 10–50 feet apart and heavily wooded. Sites on the outside of the loop are more private. Sites 3–5, 7, 9, 10, and 12–14 are next to Soap Creek, which offers good trout fishing. With a decent pair of binoculars, campers can spot mountain goats on the dramatic cliffs of Pearson Point. Site 17 has especially good views of the Point.

Campsites, facilities: There are 16 sites for tents and RVs up to 35 feet and five walk-in tent sites. There are no hookups. Sites 9 and 10 are pull-through. Picnic tables, grills, and fire rings are provided at all sites. The walk-in sites have tent pads. Vault toilets, drinking water, and a horse corral are available. Leashed pets are permitted.

Reservations, fees: Reservations are not accepted. The fee is $14 per night. Cash or check only. Golden Age and Golden Access Passports are accepted. Open May–September.

Directions: From the intersection of U.S. Highway 50 and Highway 92, go west on Highway 92 for 1.5 miles. Turn right on Soap Creek Road. (This dirt road can be hazardous after precipitation.) In 8.8 miles, turn right at the tent sign and continue downhill for 1.7 miles to the campground.

Contact: Gunnison National Forest, 970/641-0471, www.fs.fed.us/r2/gmug.

85 PONDEROSA

🚶 🛶 🚐 🐎 🚐 ⛺

Scenic rating: 6

in Curecanti National Recreation Area

Ponderosa is a big surprise after the stark landscape and mega-campgrounds of the Blue Mesa Reservoir. Located at the northern tip of the Soap Creek Arm of Blue Mesa, Ponderosa has three loops at different levels in the canyon. The environment changes dramatically from sagebrush at lake level to a ponderosa pine forest at the highest loop. Most of the campground has excellent views of the cliffs looming over the reservoir. Sites 1–7 are high above the water in a loop around the horse corral. Horse riders can access the West Elk Wilderness area via Forest Route 721/Trail 443. Sites 8–29 are closer to the water. Sites 11–16 and 26–28 are walk-in tent sites. Sites 8–23 are also good tent sites. Sites 24–29 are closest to the water, but they lack privacy and shade.

Campsites, facilities: There are 19 sites for tents and RVs up to 30 feet and nine walk-in sites. There are no hookups. Some sites have extra parking available. Picnic tables, grills, vault toilets, and drinking water are provided. A boat ramp and horse corral are available. Leashed pets are permitted.

Reservations, fees: Reservations are not accepted. The fee is $10 per night. Cash or check only. Golden Age and Golden Access Passports are accepted. Open May–October.

Directions: From the intersection of U.S. Highway 50 and Highway 92, go west on Highway 92 for 1.5 miles. Turn right on Soap Creek Road. The campground is on the right in seven miles. This dirt road is hazardous when muddy.

Contact: Curecanti National Recreation Area, 970/641-2337, www.nps.gov/cure.

86 LAKE FORK

Scenic rating: 5

in Curecanti National Recreation Area

Curecanti National Recreation Area contains three reservoirs: Blue Mesa, Morrow Point, and Crystal. Blue Mesa Reservoir is the uppermost reservoir and the largest lake in Colorado. It is 20 miles long and has 96 miles of shoreline and a capacity of 941,000 acre feet. Stocked with over three million fish a year, the reservoir has some of the best deep-water fishing in the state. Lake trout and kokanee salmon thrive in the cold, deep waters. Boating, waterskiing, and windsurfing are also popular. (Personal watercraft are prohibited.) The reservoir contrasts boldly with the surrounding landscape of arid mesas and canyons. The weather can be harsh, and strong winds are common. Boaters should be alert for storms.

Another attraction is the Morrow Point Boat Tours, accessible via the Pine Creek Trail, which is a short drive from the Lake Fork campground. On the tour, park rangers interpret the geology and history of the area. The tour operates twice daily from Memorial Day–Labor Day. Reservations are required.

There are a few tent sites at Lake Fork, but the campground is designed for RVs and boaters. It is basically a large parking lot with picnic tables. It's quite exposed and windblown, and there is no privacy here.

Campsites, facilities: There are 85 sites for RVs of any length and five walk-in tent sites (52–56). Sites 1–14 can also accommodate tents. Most sites and facilities are wheelchair accessible. There are 16 pull-through sites and no hookups. Picnic tables, grills, and wind screens are provided. Restrooms with flush toilets and showers, vault toilets, dump stations, a boat ramp, fish-cleaning station, and amphitheater are available. Leashed pets are permitted.

Reservations, fees: Reservations are accepted for the upper loop at 877/444-6777 or www.reserveusa.com. The fee is $10 per night. There is an additional $9 reservation fee. Golden Age and Golden Access Passports are accepted. Open mid-April–November.

Directions: From Montrose, take U.S. Highway 50 east for 36.7 miles. Turn left on Highway 92. In 0.2 mile, turn right into the campground.

Contact: Curecanti National Recreation Area, 970/641-2337, www.nps.gov/cure.

87 RED CREEK

Scenic rating: 5

in Curecanti National Recreation Area

Red Creek is the smallest campground at Curecanti and it's rarely used, in part because there is no fishing or boating available at the campground. The individual sites are two small dirt spots beside the river and are not very appealing. At the end of the road, there is a large gravel parking lot and stairs that lead downhill to dispersed tent camping in a cottonwood grove beside the creek. There is not a lot of flat space for pitching a tent. The main activity here is backcountry hiking in Sapinero Wildlife Area. Gunnison National Forest and several pack trails can be accessed via Red Creek Road.

Campsites, facilities: There are two individual tent sites and one group site for tents and RVs up to 22 feet. There are no hookups. Picnic tables, grills, vault toilets, and drinking water are provided. Leashed pets are permitted.

Reservations, fees: Reservations are accepted for the group site at 877/444-6777 and www.reserveusa.com. The individual fee is $10 per night. The group fee is $25 per night. Golden Age and Golden Access Passports are accepted. Open May–October.

Directions: From Gunnison, take U.S. Highway 50 west for about 19 miles. Turn right at the Red Creek sign. Bear left at the fork into the campground. The individual sites are on the left beside the creek. The group site is one mile past the gate.

Contact: Curecanti National Recreation Area, 970/641-2337, www.nps.gov/cure.

88 DRY GULCH

Scenic rating: 5

in Curecanti National Recreation Area

Dry Gulch offers tent camping in a large cottonwood grove beside an intermittent stream. It is small and not very appealing, but it may be attractive to horse owners who want to explore the BLM lands north of the campground. Windsurfers will appreciate the proximity to the Blue Mesa windsurfing area, about a mile east on U.S. Highway 50. The sites are 15–30 feet apart. There is not much privacy, but there are also very few visitors here.

Campsites, facilities: There are nine tent sites. Picnic tables, grills, and fire rings are provided. Vault toilets, drinking water, and a horse corral are available. Leashed pets are permitted.

Reservations, fees: Reservations are not accepted. The fee is $10 per night. Cash or check only. Golden Age and Golden Access Passports are accepted. Open May–October.

Directions: From Gunnison, take U.S. Highway 50 west for about 17 miles. Turn right at the Dry Gulch sign.

Contact: Curecanti National Recreation Area, 970/641-2337, www.nps.gov/cure.

89 EAST ELK CREEK GROUP

Scenic rating: 6

in Curecanti National Recreation Area

East Elk Creek is the best group site in Curecanti. It offers dispersed tent camping in a large cottonwood grove. After the stark landscape of Blue Mesa, this green hollow feels like an oasis. It's very sheltered and shady and is a great place for kids to play. Fishing access is available a short walk away on a small arm of the reservoir. The windsurfing area is also nearby. North of the campground are some very interesting rock formations. There are no hiking trails in this area, but backcountry scrambling is an option.

Campsites, facilities: There is one group site for up to 50 people. A picnic shelter and tables, grills, vault toilets, and drinking water are provided. Leashed pets are permitted.

Reservations, fees: Reservations are required and are accepted at 877/444-6777 and www.reserveusa.com. The fee is $50 per night. Open May–October.

Directions: From Gunnison, take U.S. Highway 50 west for about 16.5 miles. Turn right

at the East Elk Creek sign. The campground is on the far side of the creek in 0.5 mile.
Contact: Curecanti National Recreation Area, 970/641-2337, www.nps.gov/cure.

90 ELK CREEK

Scenic rating: 6

in Curecanti National Recreation Area

Curecanti National Recreation Area contains three reservoirs: Blue Mesa, Morrow Point, and Crystal. Elk Creek is located between the Cebolla and Iola Basins of Blue Mesa Reservoir. (For more information on Blue Mesa Reservoir, see the Lake Fork listing earlier in this chapter.) This is the biggest campground in Curecanti. The location and facilities are perfect for water sports enthusiasts and anglers who usually troll the deep waters for kokanee salmon and lake trout. Ice fishing continues in the winter on Iola Basin. Snowmobiling, ice-skating, and cross-country skiing are also available on the frozen surface of Blue Mesa. (Check with park rangers for ice conditions.)

The campground is surrounded by sagebrush and mesa country, which contributes to beautiful sunsets, when the arid mesas are outlined against the dark blue sky. The sites are 30–50 feet apart. There are no trees and very little privacy, but tent campers will appreciate the walk-in sites, which are close to the water and slightly downhill (and out of sight) of the RV area. Pappy's Restaurant serves up good burgers and fish and chips.

Campsites, facilities: There are 145 sites for tents and RVs of any length and 15 walk-in tent sites. Loop D has electric hookups and 20 pull-through sites. Most facilities are wheelchair accessible. Picnic tables, grills, and fire rings are provided. Restrooms with flush toilets and showers, vault toilets, drinking water, dump stations, a marina and boat ramp, a restaurant, and naturalist programs are available. Leashed pets are permitted.

Reservations, fees: Reservations are accepted at 877/444-6777 and www.reserveusa.com. The fee is $10 per night or $15 per night for sites with electricity. There is an additional $9 reservation fee. Golden Age and Golden Access Passports are accepted. Open year-round.
Directions: From Gunnison, take U.S. Highway 50 west for about 16 miles. Turn left at the Elk Creek Visitor Center.
Contact: Curecanti National Recreation Area, 970/641-2337, www.nps.gov/cure.

91 STEVENS CREEK

Scenic rating: 6

in Curecanti National Recreation Area

Stevens Creek overlooks the Iola Basin of Blue Mesa Reservoir. (For more information on Blue Mesa Reservoir, see the Lake Fork listing earlier in this chapter.) This is mesa and sagebrush country. It's arid and the weather can be harsh, but the reservoir is irresistible to boaters and anglers looking for trout and kokanee salmon. Fly-fishing is also available on the Gunnison, two miles east of the campground. Hikers can drive four miles east to the Cooper Ranch and Neversink Trails, which offer good bird-watching and more river access.

Stevens Creek is smaller and quieter than its massive neighbor Elk Creek. It has good RV camping and the best tent camping on Blue Mesa Reservoir. Loop A is the middle loop and thus least private. Loop C is on a separate peninsula and is the most private. Sites 1–11 overlook the water. Loop B is occasionally closed to protect breeding birds.

Campsites, facilities: There are 52 sites for tents and RVs up to 40 feet. There are no hookups or pull-through sites. Most facilities are wheelchair accessible. Picnic tables, grills, fire rings, and tent pads are provided. Vault toilets, drinking water, a boat ramp, fish-cleaning station, amphitheater, and dog walk are available. Leashed pets are permitted.

Reservations, fees: Reservations are accepted at 877/444-6777 and www.reserveusa.com. The fee is $10 per night. There is an additional $9 reservation fee. Golden Age and Golden Access Passports are accepted. Open May–October.

Directions: From Gunnison, take U.S. Highway 50 west for about 12 miles. Turn left at the Stevens Creek sign, before the Blue Mesa RV Park.

Contact: Curecanti National Recreation Area, 970/641-2337, www.nps.gov/cure.

92 GUNNISON KOA

Scenic rating: 4

in Gunnison

The Gunnison KOA, located southwest of downtown, contains two grassy loops ringed by cottonwoods with a large pond for fishing and paddleboats. This campground is a bit off the beaten path, so it's not as busy as many KOAs. The back loop has nice views of nearby cliffs, and sites 38–48 border the pond. Tent camping is available in the middle of the loops and the outer edge of the pavilion loop. Gunnison is a destination city with a mild climate and excellent recreation opportunities. Surrounded by national forest, visitors can wear themselves out with rafting, fishing, hiking, mountain biking, sightseeing, and shopping.

Campsites, facilities: There are 88 sites for RVs up to 45 feet and 28 tent sites. Full and partial hookups are available, and many sites are pull-through. Picnic tables, grills, and fire rings are provided. Restrooms with flush toilets and showers, drinking water, dump stations, laundry facilities, a playground, and propane gas are available. There is also a store, horseshoe pits, shuffleboard, stocked fishing ponds, boat ramp, bike rentals, and paddleboat rentals. Leashed pets are permitted.

Reservations, fees: Reservations are accepted at 800/562-1248. The tent fee is $20 per night for two people. The RV fee is $27–35 per night for two people. Each additional person costs $2 per night. The KOA Valu Kard is accepted. Open late April–late October.

Directions: From Highway 135 in Gunnison, take U.S. Highway 50 west for one mile. Turn left on County Road 38. The campground is on the right in 0.5 mile.

Contact: Gunnison KOA, 970/641-1358, www.gunnisonkoa.com.

93 TALL TEXAN

Scenic rating: 4

in Gunnison

Tall Texan is just two miles north of downtown Gunnison and offers easy access to Gunnison National Forest, Crested Butte, and Taylor Park Reservoir. The location and mild climate keep this campground busy all summer long. The camground is in a cottonwood grove across the street from the Gunnison River. Like most RV parks, the sites are on top of each other. The tent sites are on a grassy strip next to the playground. There is no privacy here, but plenty of shade. The majority of residents seem to be kids and snowbirds.

Campsites, facilities: There are 97 sites for RVs up to 40 feet and six tent sites. Full and partial hookups and pull-throughs are available. Picnic tables and fire rings are provided. Restrooms with flush toilets and showers, drinking water, dump stations, laundry facilities, a convenience store, playground, and propane are available. Cable TV, a recreation room, and pavilion are also available. Leashed pets are permitted.

Reservations, fees: Reservations are accepted at 970/641-2927 or by email at ttcampground@juno.com. The tent fee is $15 per night for two people. The RV fee is $21–25 per night for two people. Each additional person costs $2 per night, and cable costs $2 per night. Weekly and monthly rates are also available. Open May 1–October 15.

Directions: From Main Street in Gunnison, take Highway 135 north for 2.5 miles. Turn right on County Road 11. The campground is on the right in 0.1 mile.

Contact: Tall Texan Campground, 970/641-2927, email: ttcampground@juno.com.

94 PA-CO-CHU-PUK

🚶 🚲 🏊 🛶 🎣 🚤 🐕 🛝 ♿ 🚐 ⛺

Scenic rating: 6

in Ridgway State Park

Ridgway is a popular destination with residents and out-of-staters because it is the northwestern gateway to the San Juans. From here, campers can make day trips to Telluride, Silverton, Durango, Mesa Verde National Park, Black Canyon of the Gunnison, and Colorado National Monument. And when campers don't feel like driving, they can enjoy water sports and fishing on the park's 1,000-surface-acre reservoir and the Uncompahgre Reservoir. There are also 14 miles of maintained gravel and concrete trails in the park. As a bonus, the park stays fairly cool all summer because of its altitude (6,650 feet) and frequent afternoon thunderstorms.

Pa-Co-Chu-Puk is one of three campgrounds at Ridgway. It is at the north end of the park, beneath the dam. Loop F (200–236) and Loop G (237–280) are the RV loops. They are located in a barren meadow without shade trees and are almost identical except that Loop G is closer to the river. Sites 200–215 are very close to the highway. Loop H (281–295), which contains the walk-in tent sites, is fantastic. This loop is on a hill across the river in a mature ponderosa pine forest. It is cool and shady, and all of the sites are fairly private. Carts are provided at the parking lot to help campers carry in their gear.

Campsites, facilities: There are 15 walk-in tent sites and 81 sites with full hookups for tents and RVs up to 40 feet. The facilities, most trails, and sites 230, 280, and 281 are wheelchair accessible. Picnic tables, fire rings, grills, and tent pads are provided. Restrooms with flush toilets and showers, vault toilets, drinking water, a playground, and a laundry room are available. Vending machines, a group picnic area, fish-cleaning station, pay phones, volleyball courts, horseshoe pits, and campfire programs are also available. Dump stations are provided at the south entrance of the park. Leashed pets are permitted.

Reservations, fees: Reservations are accepted (and recommended on weekends) at 800/678-CAMP or www.parks.state.co.us. The fee is $12 per night for tents and $20 per night for RVs. There is an additional $8 reservation fee. Campers must also purchase a Daily Parks Pass ($5) or an Annual Parks Pass ($55). The Aspen Leaf Annual Pass is accepted. Open mid-May–mid-October.

Directions: From the intersection of Highways 50 and 550 in Montrose, drive south on U.S. Highway 550 for 18.4 miles. Turn right at the Ridgway State Park entrance. After purchasing a camping permit at the entrance station, bear right into the campground.

Contact: Ridgway State Park, 970/626-5822, email: ridgway.park@state.co.us.

95 ELK RIDGE

🚶 🚲 🏊 🛶 🎣 🚤 🐕 🛝 ♿ 🚐 ⛺

Scenic rating: 7

in Ridgway State Park

Ridgway is a very popular state park because of its convenient location, balmy weather, and variety of family-oriented activities. Elk Ridge is one of three campgrounds at Ridgway, and since it is the most popular, reservations are highly recommended. It is situated at the south end of the park, on top of a hill overlooking the 1,000-acre reservoir, in a piñon-juniper forest. Fishing opportunities include stocked rainbow trout, native brown trout, and kokanee salmon. Waterskiing, sailing, and personal watercraft are all allowed on the lake. Three maintained hiking trails are accessible from the campground, and the swim beach is a 0.7-mile walk downhill. The campground is divided into two loops: Loop D (80–118) and Loop E (119–187). Sites 80–95 offer glimpses of the water through the trees. Sites 134–165 and 184–186 have great views of snow-clad Mount Sneffels to the south. The hike-in tent sites (151–160) also have good views of the San Juans, but they are not as private as many of the RV spots. Additionally, there are steep drop-offs near these sites, so they are not recommended for campers with small kids.

Campsites, facilities: There are 10 walk-in tent sites and 88 sites with electric hookups for tents and RVs up to 40 feet. The facilities, most trails, and sites 105, 107, and 136 are wheelchair accessible. Picnic tables, fire rings, grills, and tent pads are provided. Restrooms with flush toilets and showers, vault toilets, drinking water, dump stations, laundry facilities, and a playground are available. At the marina, vending machines, fish-cleaning stations, pay phones, a boat ramp, convenience store, and propane gas are available. Naturalist programs are offered at the visitors center. Leashed pets are permitted.

Reservations, fees: Reservations are accepted (and recommended on weekends) at 800/678-CAMP or www.parks.state.co.us. The fee is $12 per night for tents and $16–18 per night for RVs. There is an additional $8 reservation fee. Campers must also purchase a Daily Parks Pass ($5) or an Annual Parks Pass ($55). The Aspen Leaf Annual Pass is accepted. Open mid-May–mid-October.

Directions: From the intersection of Highways 50 and 550 in Montrose, drive south on U.S. Highway 550 for 22 miles. Turn right at the second Ridgway State Park entrance. After purchasing a camping permit at the entrance station, make the first left and drive up the hill into the campground.

Contact: Ridgway State Park, 970/626-5822, email: ridgway.park@state.co.us.

96 DAKOTA TERRACES

Scenic rating: 6

in Ridgway State Park

Ridgway is a very popular state park because of its convenient location, balmy weather, and variety of family-oriented activities. Dakota Terraces, at the southern entrance, is one of three campgrounds at the park. What it lacks in privacy (there is none) it makes up for in lake access. It is a short stroll from the campground to the swim beach and marina. Anglers will find stocked rainbow trout, native brown trout, and kokanee salmon in the lake, and water-sports enthusiasts can enjoy waterskiing, riding personal watercraft, and sailing. There are also 14 miles of maintained gravel and concrete trails in the park. As a bonus, the park stays fairly cool all summer because of its altitude (6,650 feet) and frequent afternoon thunderstorms. Dakota Terraces is divided into three loops. Loop A (1–25) is the most attractive loop because it has great views of the San Juans to the west, and mature trees shelter several campsites. Loop B (26–55) and Loop C (56–79) are not as appealing. Loop C does not have mountain views, and it is closest to the highway. There are also 14 miles of maintained gravel and concrete trails in the park open to hiking, biking, and cross-country skiing.

Campsites, facilities: There are 76 sites with electric hookups for tents and RVs up to 40 feet and three yurts. The facilities, most trails, and sites 44 and 46 are wheelchair accessible. Picnic tables, fire rings, grills, and tent pads are provided. Sun shelters are provided at sites 4, 6, 8, 9, 25, 35, 38, 40, 42, 46, 49, and 78. Restrooms with flush toilets and showers, vault toilets, drinking water, dump stations, laundry facilities, and a playground are available. At the marina, vending machines, fish-cleaning stations, pay phones, a boat ramp, convenience store, and propane gas are available. Naturalist programs are offered at the visitors center. Leashed pets are permitted.

Reservations, fees: Reservations are accepted (and recommended on weekends) at 800/678-CAMP or www.parks.state.co.us. The fee is $12 per night for tents and $16–18 per night for RVs. Yurts cost $60 per night for up to six people. There is an additional $8 reservation fee. Campers must also purchase a Daily Parks Pass ($5) or an Annual Parks Pass ($55). The Aspen Leaf Annual Pass is accepted. Open year-round.

Directions: From the intersection of Highways 50 and 550 in Montrose, drive south on U.S. Highway 550 for 22 miles. Turn right at the second Ridgway State Park entrance. After purchasing a camping permit at the entrance station, make the first right into the campground.

Contact: Ridgway State Park, 970/626-5822, email: ridgway.park@state.co.us.

97 BIG CIMARRON

Scenic rating: 5

southeast of Montrose

Big Cimarron is the first campground on the road to Silver Jack Reservoir and the least appealing. If you're not trying to save money, keep driving to the larger campground beside the reservoir. If you do stop, you'll find a narrow campground that parallels the Cimarron River. The main attraction here is fishing for trout. Anglers and boaters can also head north to Beaver Lake or Silver Jack. Hikers, mountain bikers, and four-wheelers can explore Alpine and Middle Fork Trail. (For more information on these trails, see the Silver Jack listing in this chapter.) This quiet campground is in an aspen and evergreen

forest. The large sites are far apart but not well screened, and there are no views of Cimarron Ridge. Site 3, in a small aspen grove, is the most private. Site 11 is large enough to accommodate multiple tents.

Campsites, facilities: There are 10 sites for tents and RVs up to 20 feet and one walk-in site. There are no hookups. Picnic tables, grills, and fire rings are provided. Vault toilets and drinking water are available. Leashed pets are permitted.

Reservations, fees: Reservations are not accepted. The fee is $8 per night and includes two vehicles. Additional vehicles cost $4 per night. Golden Age and Golden Access Passports are accepted. Cash or check only. Open May–September.

Directions: From Montrose, drive east on U.S. Highway 50 for 20 miles. Turn south on Cimarron Road/Forest Route 858. This winding dirt road is passable for passenger cars most of the summer. In 15 miles, turn right at the campground sign.

Contact: Uncompahgre National Forest, 970/240-5300, www.fs.fed.us/r2/gmug/.

98 BEAVER LAKE

Scenic rating: 6

southeast of Montrose

Beaver Lake is a quiet campground beside a fishing pond. There are two loops in an evergreen and aspen forest. The sites are small and some feel cramped, but this is a good campground for families with small kids who will enjoy learning to fish on Beaver Lake. A gravel trail around the lake facilitates fishing access, and hand-powered boats are allowed on the lake. Anglers can also cast for trout in Cimarron River. The fishing is best below the Silver Jack dam. Hikers, mountain bikers, and four-wheelers can explore Alpine and Middle Fork Trail. (For more information on these trails see the Silver Jack listing in this chapter.) There are views of Cimarron Ridge from the campground, but not from the actual campsites. The best sites are 6–11, and sites 6 and 9 overlook the pond. Sites 1–5 are shaded but smaller.

Campsites, facilities: There are 10 sites for tents and RVs up to 20 feet and one walk-in site. There are no hookups. Picnic tables, grills, and fire rings are provided. Vault toilets and drinking water are available. Leashed pets are permitted.

Reservations, fees: Reservations are not accepted. The fee is $10 per night and includes two vehicles. Additional vehicles cost $5 per night. Golden Age and Golden Access Passports are accepted. Cash or check only. Open May–September.

Directions: From Montrose, drive east on U.S. Highway 50 for 20 miles. Turn south on Cimarron Road/Forest Route 858. This winding dirt road is passable for passenger cars most of the summer. In 15.7 miles, turn right at the campground sign.

Contact: Uncompahgre National Forest, 970/240-5300, www.fs.fed.us/r2/gmug/.

99 SILVER JACK

Scenic rating: 8

southeast of Montrose

BEST (

Silver Jack is a little-known treasure in the Uncompahgre National Forest. There are rarely crowds at this spacious campground near the dam, and the views from the overlook of Courthouse Peak, Turret Peak, and Cimarron Ridge are breathtaking. The campground contains three paved loops (Ouray, Chipeta, and Sapinero) in a dense aspen forest, but it feels much smaller because the loops are so well hidden from each other. The sites are 50–100 feet apart. In Ouray Loop, sites 8–12 have excellent views of Cimarron Ridge. Activities include nonmotorized boating and fishing for trout on the 250-acre reservoir,

plus hiking, mountain biking, horse riding, and four-wheeling in the national forest. The Alpine Trail begins just past the campground and traverses 17 miles on the flat-top ridges of High Mesa and Big Park to Alpine Guard Station. The Middle Fork Trail begins five miles past the campground at the end of Middle Fork Road in the Uncompahgre Wilderness. Most of the 10-mile trail climbs gently alongside the Middle Fork of the Cimarron before climbing steeply to meet the East Fork Trail. Both trails are scenic and lightly used.

Campsites, facilities: There are 60 sites for tents and RVs up to 30 feet. Sites 4, 18, 21, and 41 are wheelchair accessible. Many sites are pull-through, but there are no hookups. Picnic tables, grills, and fire rings are provided. Vault toilets and drinking water are available. Leashed pets are permitted.

Reservations, fees: Reservations are not accepted. The fee is $14 per night and includes two vehicles. Additional vehicles cost $7 per night. Golden Age and Golden Access Passports are accepted. Cash or check only. Open May–September.

Directions: From Montrose, drive east on U.S. Highway 50 for 20 miles. Turn south on Cimarron Road/Forest Route 858. This winding dirt road is passable for passenger cars most of the summer. In 17 miles, turn right at the Silver Jack sign. The campground is the first left.

Contact: Uncompahgre National Forest, 970/240-5300, www.fs.fed.us/r2/gmug/.

100 GATEVIEW

Scenic rating: 6

in the Curecanti National Recreation Area

Gateview is in a craggy canyon of volcanic tuff and Precambrian granite, on a steep slope above the Lake Fork of the Gunnison. A short trail behind the toilets climbs up to the tent sites, which are surrounded by Ponderosa pine, Gambel's oak, and sagebrush. Except for the roaring of the river and the occasional jackrabbit or bighorn sheep, silence reigns in this canyon, and this remote campground sees little use. Most visitors are kayakers or anglers. The river offers excellent trout fishing for seven miles downstream of the campground, and the white-water run from Red Bridge campground to Gateview campground has Class III–IV boating with some good play spots. Hand-powered boats can be carried down a short trail to the Lake Fork Arm of Blue Mesa Reservoir. Campers may also be interested in the history of settlement in this valley. The first narrow gauge railroad passed through this canyon in 1889 on its way to Lake City. Nearby communities like Powderhorn and Gateview thrived until the last train in 1933.

Campsites, facilities: There are five walk-in tent sites. Picnic tables, grills, fire rings, and food lockers are provided. Vault toilets and drinking water are available. Leashed pets are permitted.

Reservations, fees: Camping is free and reservations are not accepted. Open year-round.

Directions: From Lake City, take Highway 149 north for 20.6 miles. Turn left on County Road 25. The campground is on the right in 7.2 miles.

Contact: Curecanti National Recreation Area, 970/641-2337, www.nps.gov/cure.

101 RED BRIDGE

Scenic rating: 5

north of Lake City

Red Bridge is a classic BLM campground: small, remote, and quiet, with good recreation nearby. The campground is in a spruce grove on the east bank of the Lake Fork of the Gunnison. The scenery includes glimpses of Cinnamon Ridge and a lush valley bottom surrounded by arid hills. The river

offers excellent trout fishing for two miles upstream and five miles downstream of the campground, and the white-water run from Red Bridge to Gateview campground has Class III–IV boating with some good play spots. The river used to be boatable from The Gate to Red Bridge, but private landowners have put up obstacles which may make this route impassable. Check with the BLM for current conditions.

Sites 3–7 are in a spruce grove beside the river. There is plenty of shade but no privacy because the sites are right next to each other. Sites 1 and 2 are across the road and have no shade. This campground fills up on the weekends with families and anglers.

Campsites, facilities: There are seven sites for tents and RVs up to 20 feet. There are no hookups or pull-through sites. Facilities are wheelchair accessible. Picnic tables, grills, and fire rings are provided. Vault toilets are available. Trash must be packed out. Leashed pets are permitted.

Reservations, fees: Reservations are not accepted. The fee is $5 per night. Golden Age and Golden Access Passports are accepted. Open early May–late October.

Directions: From Lake City, take Highway 149 north for 20.6 miles. Turn left on County Road 25. The campground is on the left in 2.3 miles.

Contact: Bureau of Land Management, 970/242-8211, www.blm.gov.

102 THE GATE

Scenic rating: 5

north of Lake City

The Gate is an easy-to-miss stopover on the road between Gunnison and Lake City. It's a small campground beside the Lake Fork of the Gunnison, just upstream of the geologic feature for which it's named. The river runs through volcanic tuff that has fractured into fascinating cliff shapes. There is decent trout fishing for two miles upstream from the campground. The river used to be a mellow Class II white-water run from The Gate to Red Bridge, but private landowners have built obstacles to prevent access, so boaters should check with the BLM before getting on the river. The campground is in a grove of spruce trees and willow bushes. Sites 1, 7, and 8 have the most shade.

Campsites, facilities: There are eight sites for tents and RVs up to 21 feet. There are no hookups or pull-through sites. Picnic tables, grills, and fire rings are provided. Vault toilets are available. Trash must be packed out. Leashed pets are permitted.

Reservations, fees: Reservations are not accepted. The fee is $5 per night. Golden Age and Golden Access Passports are accepted. Open early May–late October.

Directions: From Lake City, take Highway 149 north for 20.6 miles. Turn left on County Road 25. The campground is on the left in 2.3 miles.

Contact: BLM Gunnison, 970/641-0471, www.blm.gov.

NORTH CENTRAL MOUNTAINS

© SARAH RYAN

BEST CAMPGROUNDS

This region contains two intermountain valleys –

North Park and Middle Park – the western half of Rocky Mountain National Park, and the high peaks and deep reservoirs of Summit County. Hikers, bikers, riders, four-wheelers, and hunters visit in the summer and fall, and skiers and snowmobilers take over Summit County in the winter and spring.

North Park is a wide expanse of fertile ranchlands ringed by the Park Range to the west, Rabbit Ears Range to the south, and the Medicine Bow Mountains to the east. The headwaters of the North Platte are located in the Park Range, and this river flows north through the park into Wyoming. Along the way, it absorbs the Illinois, Michigan, and Canadian Rivers. All that water makes this valley an important stopover for migrating birds. The sagebrush flats, meadows, and riparian zones of the Arapaho National Wildlife Refuge provide a sanctuary for about 8,000 waterfowl every fall, as well as moose, mule deer, and antelope year-round.

Moose were introduced to North Park in 1978, and the herd is now about 600 strong. Every summer and fall, tourists line the road along Cameron Pass to take photos of these surprising animals. There is also a viewing deck in the Colorado State Forest, which contains 70,000 acres of multiuse forest on the west side of the Medicine Bow Mountains. Colorado State Forest is a year-round destination for hiking, fishing, hunting, four-wheeling, cross-country skiing, and snowshoeing. There are four campgrounds in the state forest; the North Michigan and Bockman campgrounds delight visitors with excellent views of the Medicine Bow.

Middle Park is due south of North Park. The two valleys are separated by the low volcanic peaks of the Rabbit Ears Range. This is Grand County, a summer destination that families return to year after year. It includes the eastern half of Rocky Mountain National Park, the headwaters of the Colorado River, the Indian Peaks Wilderness, and the Arapaho National Recreation Area (ANRA). There are five campgrounds in ANRA, and they are packed all summer with RVs and water-sports lovers. Grand Lake is also a winter destination for snowmobilers.

The Colorado River begins its long journey in Rocky Mountain

National Park and flows west through Middle Park. After Kremmling, the river enters Gore Canyon, nine miles of unforgettable Class V whitewater. Downstream of the Gore, the Pumphouse run is more family friendly. This 11-mile stretch has Class II/III boating that's popular with beginning and intermediate kayakers, anglers, and commercial rafting companies.

Grand County also includes the Fraser Valley and the resort town of Winter Park. Winter Park is a great ski mountain and a mountain-biking mecca. Since the inauguration of the Fat Tire Classic in 1990, the valley has been flooded every summer with spandex-clad bikers. There are trails for all ages and abilities in the valley and the surrounding Arapaho National Forest. If you like climbing, don't miss Moffat Road or Rogers Pass Trail.

The Continental Divide and the Williams Fork Mountains separate Grand County from Summit County, home to a few of Colorado's best ski resorts: Arapahoe Basin, Keystone, Breckenridge, and Copper Mountain. This region also includes a small portion of Eagle County. There is excellent camping and fly-fishing along the Eagle River and U.S. Highway 24, part of the Top of the Rockies Scenic Byway. From Hornsilver, Blodgett, and Gold Park campgrounds, hikers can explore the Holy Cross Wilderness, named for the fourteener Mount of the Holy Cross. The wilderness area is in the Sawatch Range. It has more than 25 peaks over 13,000 feet and countless lakes, waterfalls, streams, and wetlands, all fed by spring snowmelt. The Eagle River Valley is also home to Camp Hale, the former training ground of the 10th Mountain Division, the skiing soldiers who fought in the Italian Alps in World War II. There is now a campground at the former base.

The Colorado Trail is also a major draw to this region. After passing through the Eagle River Valley, it climbs over the southern tip of the Gore Range and the northern tip of Ten Mile Range, crosses the Blue River a few miles south of Dillon Reservoir, and follows the Swan River over the Continental Divide and into South Park. This 470-mile trail embodies the multiuse ethic of Colorado recreation. Hikers, bikers, riders, and four-wheelers hop on and off the trail at its frequent road crossings.

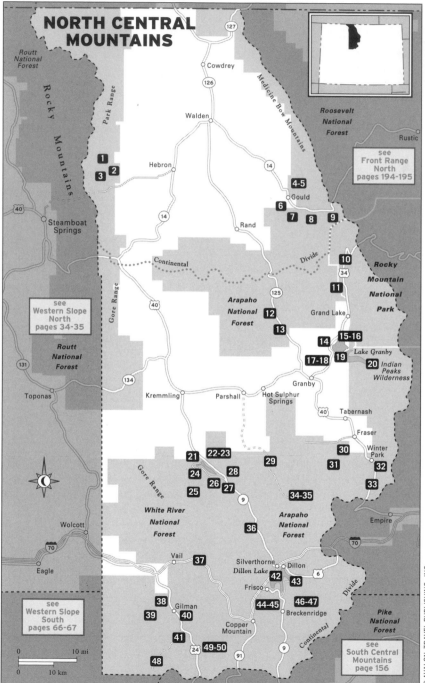

NORTH CENTRAL MOUNTAINS

■ TEAL LAKE

Scenic rating: 7

southwest of Walden

Teal Lake is on the west side of North Park, one of Colorado's four large intermountain valleys. North Park is ringed by the Park Range, Front Range, and the Rabbit Ears Range. Teal Lake is on the eastern flank of the Park Range, just outside the Mount Zirkell Wilderness, a rugged landscape bisected by the Continental Divide. The Newcomb Creek Trail begins nearby and climbs the north flank of Round Mountain to the Continental Divide Trail. The campground is on the northern tip of Teal Lake, a small stocked lake surrounded by tall lodgepole pines. The large sites are about 50 feet apart and privacy is good. The campground can fill up on weekends, but it's quiet midweek. Most campers are there for fishing and four-wheeling. Sites 1, 3, 4, 8, and the group site are lakeside.

Campsites, facilities: There are 17 sites for tents and RVs up to 22 feet and one group site. There are no hookups. Sites 1, 3, 4, 9, 11, 13, 16, and 17 are pull-through. Sites 4 and 11 and the facilities are wheelchair accessible. Picnic tables, grills, and fire rings are provided. Vault toilets, drinking water, and a boat ramp are available. Leashed pets are permitted.

Reservations, fees: Reservations are accepted for the group site at 877/444-6777 and www.reserveusa.com. The fee is $10 per night or $20–40 per night for the group site. Golden Age and Golden Access Passports are accepted. Cash or check only. Open May–September.

Directions: From Walden, take Highway 14 west. At Hebron, turn right on County Road 24. In 11.3 miles, turn right on Forest Route 615. The campground is on the right in 2.8 miles.

Contact: Routt National Forest, 970/723-8204, www.fs.fed.us/r2/mbr.

■ GRIZZLY CREEK

Scenic rating: 6

southwest of Walden

Grizzly Creek is on the west side of North Park, one of Colorado's four large intermountain valleys. North Park is ringed by the Park Range, Front Range, and the Rabbit Ears Range. Grizzly Creek is on the east side of the Park Range, just outside the Mount Zirkell Wilderness, a rugged landscape bisected by the Continental Divide. The nearest trailhead is the Newcomb Creek Trail, which begins about four miles north of the campground. The campground is a dirt loop on a small hill in an open aspen grove. The sites are 50–75 feet apart. There are no views, but it's a pleasant place to enjoy the sunshine. Sites 1, 2, 6, 10, and 12 have been blocked off.

Campsites, facilities: There are 12 sites for tents and RVs up to 18 feet, but five sites appear to be closed. There are no hookups. Picnic tables, grills, and fire rings are provided. Vault toilets and drinking water are available. Leashed pets are permitted.

Reservations, fees: Reservations are not accepted. The fee is $5 per night. Golden Age and Golden Access Passports are accepted. Cash or check only. Open May–September.

Directions: From Walden, take Highway 14 west. At Hebron, turn right on County Road 24. The campground is on the right in 11.2 miles.

Contact: Routt National Forest, 970/723-8204, www.fs.fed.us/r2/mbr.

■ HIDDEN LAKE

Scenic rating: 7

southwest of Walden

Hidden Lake is on the west side of North Park, one of Colorado's four large intermountain valleys. North Park is ringed by the Park Range, Front Range, and the Rabbit Ears Range. Hidden Lake, on the east side of the Park Range, is part of a chain of small lakes surrounded by a dense conifer forest. The lake has a gentle shore that's excellent for fishing. The sites are about 50 feet apart. The lakeside sites (1–4) are large and appealing. The other sites are small and close to the road.

Campsites, facilities: There are nine sites for tents and RVs up to 22 feet. There are no hookups. Sites 1, 7, and 8 are pull-through. Picnic tables, grills, and fire rings are provided. Vault toilets and drinking water are available. Trash must be packed out. Leashed pets are permitted.

Reservations, fees: Reservations are not accepted. The fee is $10 per night. Golden Age and Golden Access Passports are accepted. Cash or check only. Open May–September.

Directions: From Walden, take Highway 14 west. At Hebron, turn right on County Road 24/Forest Route 60 and go west for 12 miles. Turn left on Forest Route 20. The campground is on the left in 4.3 miles.

Contact: Routt National Forest, 970/723-8204, www.fs.fed.us/r2/mbr.

◢ NORTH MICHIGAN

Scenic rating: 7

in State Forest State Park

The Colorado State Forest contains 71,000 acres on the west side of the Medicine Bow Mountains and ranges in altitude from 8,500–12,000 feet. The forest is managed for recreation, logging, and wildlife. The state park system manages the recreational opportunities in the forest, including the busy campgrounds. Visitors come for the hiking, fishing, mountain biking, and four-wheeling, and to see the ungainly members of the thriving moose herd. Since 1978, 36

moose have been relocated to North Park, and the herd is now about 600 strong. Hikers and bikers will want to drive to the Montgomery Pass and Ruby Jewel trailheads. Winter visitors can enjoy snowshoeing and cross-country skiing.

The campground has two loops on opposite sides of the North Michigan Reservoir. The north loop (sites 201–213) is stretched along the whole north shore of the lake. Sites 201–205 are next to the dam and road and are very unappealing. Sites 206–213 are on the shore near the middle of the lake. Sites 207–209 are for tents only and are on a small spur at the east end of the lake. The other loop is on the south shore of the lake. Sites 214–230 are in a dense spruce forest on a steep section of the shore. Sites 231–241 are separated from the lake by the forest, and they don't have views. Sites 242–248 have great views of the ridgeline.

Campsites, facilities: There are 48 sites for tents and RVs up to 35 feet. Sites 211, 213, 215, 217, 219, 221, 222, and 225 are for tents only. Site 207 and the facilities are wheelchair accessible. Sites 221 and 237–241 are pull-through. Picnic tables, grills, and fire rings are provided. Tent pads are provided at the tent-only sites. Vault toilets, drinking water, and a boat ramp are available. Leashed pets are permitted.

Reservations, fees: Reservations are accepted at 800/678-2267 and www.parks.state.co.us. The fee is $12–16 per night (includes six people). Vehicles must also have a Daily Park Pass ($5) or Annual Parks Pass ($55). The Aspen Leaf Annual Pass is accepted. Credit cards are accepted at the visitors center. Five sites are open year-round.

Directions: From Walden, take Highway 14 east for 19.3 miles. Turn left on County Road 41. To reach the south loop, turn right in 1.2 miles. To reach the north loop, stay straight for another mile.

Contact: State Forest State Park, 970/723-8366, www.parks.state.co.us.

5 BOCKMAN

Scenic rating: 8

in State Forest State Park

Bockman is located in the Colorado State Forest, on the west side of the Medicine Bow Mountains. It's the former site of the Bockman Lumber Camp, the largest logging camp in Colorado's history. The campground contains a large loop in a spruce-fir forest surrounded by grasslands and a short walk from a wetland where anglers can fish in the beaver ponds. Hikers will want to drive to the Montgomery Pass and Ruby Jewel trailheads, but bikers can take the forest routes to those trails. About half of the sites are in the meadow and the other half are in the forest. The majority of sites have excellent views of the Medicine Bows. The sites are about 75 feet apart, and privacy is good. (For more information on Colorado State Forest, see the North Michigan listing in this chapter.)

Campsites, facilities: There are 52 sites for tents and RVs up to 35 feet and one group area with six sites. There are 13 pull-through sites but no hookups. Picnic tables, grills, fire rings, and tent pads are provided. Vault toilets and drinking water are available. The facilities are wheelchair accessible. Leashed pets are permitted.

Reservations, fees: Reservations are accepted at 800/678-2267 and www.parks.state.co.us. The fee is $12–16 per night (includes six people). Vehicles must also have a Daily Park Pass ($5) or Annual Parks Pass ($55). The Aspen Leaf Annual Pass is accepted. Credit cards are accepted at the visitors center. Open May–October.

Directions: From Walden, take Highway 14 east for 19.3 miles. Turn left on County Road 41. In 3.7 miles, turn right at Bockman sign. The campground is in 1.2 miles.

Contact: State Forest State Park, 970/723-8366, www.parks.state.co.us.

6 ASPEN

Scenic rating: 6

near Gould

North Park is one of four large intermountain valleys in Colorado. (The others are Middle Park, South Park, and the San Luis Valley.) North Park is enclosed by the Front Range to the east, the Park Range to the west, and the Rabbit Ears Range to the south. Wyoming lies to the north. The Michigan, Canadian, Illinois, and North Platte Rivers flow through this fertile ranching valley. Aspen campground is in the southeast corner of the valley, in the Routt National Forest, near the Colorado State Forest State Park. The state park campgrounds are quite busy all summer, so campers who want a small, quiet destination should head over to Aspen. This small loop is wooded with pine and aspen and borders a wetland. It's popular with hunters and ATV owners because of its proximity to BLM land and the Arapaho National Widlife Refuge.

Campsites, facilities: There are seven sites for tents and RVs up to 22 feet. There are no hookups. Picnic tables, grills, and fire rings are provided. Vault toilets and drinking water are available. Leashed pets are permitted.

Reservations, fees: Reservations are not accepted. The fee is $10 per night. Golden Age and Golden Access Passports are accepted. Cash or check only. Open May–September.

Directions: From Walden, take Highway 14 southeast to Gould. Turn right on County Road 21/Forest Route 740. In 0.7 mile, turn right at the fork. The campground is on the right in less than 0.1 mile.

Contact: Routt National Forest, 970/723-8204, www.fs.fed.us/r2/mbr.

◻ THE PINES

Scenic rating: 6

near Gould

The Pines is in the southeast corner of North Park, one of four large intermountain valleys in Colorado. (The others are Middle Park, South Park, and the San Luis Valley.) North Park is enclosed by the Front Range to the east, the Park Range to the west, and the Rabbit Ears Range to the south. Wyoming lies to the north. The Michigan, Canadian, Illinois, and North Platte Rivers flow through this fertile ranching valley and provide habitat for waterfowl and migratory birds. The Pines is near the Arapaho National Wildlife Refuge and a large amount of BLM land, so it's popular with hunters and ATV owners. The campground is a small dirt loop in an evergreen forest beside the South Fork of the Michigan River. There are no views from the campground, but the park is quite scenic. Sites 1–4 are next to the river. Site 6 has the most privacy.

Campsites, facilities: There are 11 sites for tents and RVs up to 22 feet. There are no hookups. Sites 4, 6, and 9 are pull-through. Picnic tables, grills, and fire rings are provided. Vault toilets and drinking water are available. Leashed pets are permitted.

Reservations, fees: Reservations are not accepted. The fee is $10 per night. Golden Age and Golden Access Passports are accepted. Cash or check only. Open May–September.

Directions: From Walden, take Highway 14 southeast to Gould. Turn right on County Road 21/Forest Route 740. The campground is on the left in three miles.

Contact: Routt National Forest, 970/723-8204, www.fs.fed.us/r2/mbr.

◻ RANGER LAKES

Scenic rating: 6

in State Forest State Park

Ranger Lakes is one of the most popular campgrounds in the Colorado State Forest, a year-round destination in the Medicine Bow Mountains. Visitors to this campground enjoy easy access to the highway and the moose viewing areas near Cameron Pass. (For more information on Colorado State Forest, see the North Michigan listing earlier in this chapter.)

The campground is a short walk away from the Ranger Lakes fishing area. The loop is in a dense spruce-fir forest. The sites are just 10–30 feet apart. Sites 112–131 are especially close together. There are no views at the campground, which is not especially appealing, but it's very popular due to the hookups and the fishing ponds.

Campsites, facilities: There are 32 sites for tents and RVs up to 40 feet. Electric hookups are available. Site 107 and the facilities are wheelchair accessible. Picnic tables, grills, fire rings, and tent pads are provided. Vault toilets, drinking water, dump stations, an amphitheater, and campfire programs are available. Leashed pets are permitted.

Reservations, fees: Reservations are accepted at 800/678-2267 and www.parks.state.co.us. The fee is $12–16 per night (includes six people). Vehicles must also have a Daily Park Pass ($5) or Annual Parks Pass ($55). The Aspen Leaf Annual Pass is accepted. Credit cards are accepted at the visitors center. Open May–September.

Directions: From Walden, take Highway 14 east to Gould. The campground is one mile after the visitors center on the right.

Contact: State Forest State Park, 970/723-8366, www.parks.state.co.us.

⑨ CRAGS

Scenic rating: 6

in State Forest State Park

Crags (named for the stunning rock formations of the Nokhu Crags) is about two miles west of Cameron Pass on the road to Lake Agnes. This is the most undeveloped campground in the Colorado State Forest, a year-round destination for hikers, bikers, and skiiers. Hikers and bikers can explore the Michigan Ditch and American Lakes Trails. From Lake Agnes and Michigan Lakes, hikers can continue south into the Never Summer Wilderness and Rocky Mountain National Park. (For more information on Colorado State Forest, see the North Michigan listing earlier in this chapter.)

The campground is in a dense spruce-fir forest. The road is not recommended for RVs, so it's mostly tent campers who use the campground. The sites are small but fairly private. Sites 9, 10, 18, and 20 are on top of one another. Sites 16 and 17 have views of Cameron Pass.

Campsites, facilities: There are 26 sites for tents and very small RVs. Picnic tables, grills, and fire rings are provided. Vault toilets and drinking water are available. Leashed pets are permitted.

Reservations, fees: Reservations are accepted at 800/678-2267 and www.parks.state.co.us. The fee is $12 per night (includes six people). Vehicles must also have a Daily Park Pass ($5) or Annual Parks Pass ($55). The Aspen Leaf Annual Pass is accepted. Credit cards are accepted at the visitors center. Open May–September.

Directions: From Walden, take Highway 14 east for about 30 miles. Turn right at the Crags sign and follow the signs 1.5 miles to the campground.

Contact: State Forest State Park, 970/723-8366, www.parks.state.co.us.

⑩ TIMBER CREEK

Scenic rating: 7

in Rocky Mountain National Park

Rocky Mountain National Park is a renowned destination for hikers, climbers, and wildlife lovers. The park contains over 350 miles of hiking trails and 114 peaks over 10,000 feet, including Longs Peak, Colorado's most frequently climbed fourteener. One-third of the park is above tree line, so the majority of trails climb to mountain lakes and ridgelines with fabulous views of this glaciated landscape. The park also has the highest continuous paved highway in the country, Trail Ridge Road. A trip to the park isn't complete without a drive along this route, which traverses the park and crosses the Continental Divide. With so many attractions, Rocky Mountain is a busy destination in the summer, but the crowds thin out dramatically in the winter and fall. Winter sports here include snowshoeing, cross-country skiing, and even mountaineering.

Timber Creek is the only front-country campground on the west side of the park. It has four loops in an evergreen forest near the Colorado River, with views of Baker Mountain, Mount Stratus, and Mount Nimbus. From the campground, hikers can take the Colorado Trail to Lulu City (the remains of an old mining town) and La Poudre Pass. Fishing is restricted on the river to protect a growing population of greenback cutthroat trout. The campground is full on weekends but not as busy midweek as the campgrounds on the east side of the park. There are four loops in the campground: Aspen, Beaver, Columbine, and Dogwood. Dogwood (sites 76–100) is for tents only. Sites 77–82, 84, and 85 have good views. Sites 47, 49, 51, 52, and 70–73 are also tent-only sites with good views. Sites 29–34, 58–62, and 90–96 are very close to the road.

Campsites, facilities: There are 71 sites for

tents and RVs up to 35 feet and 26 tent-only sites. Sites 22, 24, 25, and 39 are wheelchair accessible. There are no hookups. Sites 5, 7, 19, 41, 60, 68, 69, and 74 are pull-through. Picnic tables, grills, fire rings, and tent pads are provided. Vault toilets, drinking water, service sinks, pay phones, and campfire programs are available. Leashed pets are permitted in the campground but are not allowed on trails.

Reservations, fees: Reservations are not accepted. The fee is $20 per night for six people and two camping units. There is an additional park entrance fee of $20 per vehicle. Golden Age and Golden Access Passports are accepted. Cash or check only. Open year-round.

Directions: From Grand Lake, take U.S. Highway 34 north for 9.8 miles. The campground entrance is on the left.

Contact: Rocky Mountain National Park, 970/586-1206, www.nps.gov/romo.

11 WINDING RIVER RESORT

🚶 🚴 🎣 🐕 ⛺ 🚐 ⛺

Scenic rating: 7

in Grand Lake

BEST (

Winding River is an excellent destination for families and snowbirds looking for a long-term campground outside of Rocky Mountain National Park. The campground is on the west side of the park, next to the Colorado River. The resort is a full-service destination with hookups, cabins, trail rides, and even a petting zoo. The loops are dispersed in lodgepole and aspen forests. The sites are unusually private for a commercial campground. Hikers and horseback riders will enjoy the trail access, including the Continental Scenic Divide, Valley, Supply, and River Trails. The campground is also a short drive from the park entrance and from the fishing and boating opportunities on Lake Granby and Shadow Mountain.

Campsites, facilities: There are 107 sites

for tents and RVs up to 40 feet and 43 tent-only sites. Full and partial hookups are available. Picnic tables, fire rings, restrooms with flush toilets and showers, drinking water, and dump stations are provided. A laundry room, convenience store, playground, horse corrals, petting zoo, softball, volleyball, baseball, horseshoes, trail rides, ice-cream socials, hay rides, and chuck wagon breakfasts are available. Leashed pets are permitted.

Reservations, fees: Reservations are accepted at 970/627-3215 and 303/623-1121. The tent fee is $25 per night, and the RV fee is $30–32 per night (includes two people). Additional people cost $4 per night. Open May 15–October 1.

Directions: From Grand Lake, take U.S. Highway 34 north for 1.4 miles. Turn left on County Road 120. The resort is on the left in 1.4 miles.

Contact: Winding River Resort, 970/627-3215, www.windingriverresort.com.

12 DENVER CREEK

🎣 🐕 🚐 ⛺

Scenic rating: 6

north of Granby

This campground mainly attracts residents of the Front Range who are seeking a respite from summer heat. There are two loops in a lodgepole pine forest. The second loop, on the west side of the road beside meandering Willow Creek, is more popular and fills up on weekends. The first loop is on the east side of the road; sites 1–3 have pretty views down the valley. There are no trails nearby, and fishing is fair to poor depending on the time of year.

Campsites, facilities: There are 22 sites for tents and RVs up to 25 feet. There are no hookups. Sites 5 and 11 are pull-through. Picnic tables, grills, and fire rings are provided. Sites 3 and 8 have tent pads. Vault toilets and drinking water are available. Leashed pets are permitted.

Reservations, fees: Reservations are not accepted. The fee is $12 per night (includes eight people). Golden Age and Golden Access Passports are accepted. Cash or check only. Open late May–mid-October.

Directions: From Granby, take U.S. Highway 40 north to Highway 125 north. The campground is on the right in 12.5 miles.

Contact: Arapaho National Forest, 970/887-4100, www.fs.fed.us/r2/arnf/.

13 SAWMILL GULCH

Scenic rating: 7

north of Granby

This tiny campground is on the east shore of Willow Creek, a meandering stream with a gravel bed in a narrow valley surrounded by evergreen forests. The sites are shaded by pine trees and willow bushes, and they are far from each other and the road. Privacy is exceptional. There are no hiking or biking trails nearby, so this destination is best for campers who just want to cast a line in the creek and put up their feet.

Campsites, facilities: There are six sites for tents and RVs up to 32 feet. There are no hookups. Site 3 is pull-through. Picnic tables, grills, and fire rings are provided. Vault toilets and drinking water are available. Leashed pets are permitted.

Reservations, fees: Reservations are not accepted. The fee is $11 per night (includes eight people). Golden Age and Golden Access Passports are accepted. Cash or check only. Open late May–mid-October.

Directions: From Granby, take U.S. Highway 40 north to Highway 125 north. The campground is on the left in 10.5 miles.

Contact: Arapaho National Forest, 970/887-4100, www.fs.fed.us/r2/arnf/.

14 STILLWATER

Scenic rating: 8

on Lake Granby

BEST (

Lake Granby is part of the Arapaho National Recreation Area, a 36,000-acre district that contains four other major lakes: Shadow Mountain Reservoir, Monarch Lake, Willow Creek Reservoir, and Meadow Creek Reservoir. The Lake Granby area adjoins Rocky Mountain National Park and the Indian Peaks Wilderness, making it the vacation equivalent of a Grand Slam. The campgrounds around the lakes are busy throughout July and August. It's possible to find a site midweek, but reservations are highly recommended on weekends. The stocked lake has record mackinaw and kokanee salmon, as well as some rainbow and cutthroat trout. Anglers can fish from boats or from the shore in many areas. There are several hiking trails on the east side of the lake, but none on the west side. In the fall, hunters flock to the lake for the waterfowl and big game.

Stillwater is the largest and most modern campground at Lake Granby. It has three loops on a small promontory with amazing views of the Indian Peaks. It can be a maze, but if you find a site on the lakeshore, it's a great place to spend a week with the family. The sites are 10–25 feet apart with a few exceptions. They are either shaded by lodgepole pine or on the sagebrush flats. The following sites have lake views: 12, 24–35, 37–42, 62–92, and 103–123. The worst sites (0–10) overlook the boat ramp and parking lot.

Campsites, facilities: There are 129 sites for tents and RVs up to 45 feet. Sites 24–29, 32–35, 56–58, 67–75, 111–118, and 120–122 are walk-ins. Sites 29, 32, and 121 are wheelchair accessible. Water and electrical hookups are available at 20 sites. Sites 2, 3, 9, 84–86, and 95 are pull-through. Sites 41, 42, and 86 are double sites. Picnic tables, grills, fire rings, and tent pads are provided. Restrooms with flush toilets and showers, drinking water, dump stations, a boat ramp, amphitheater, and pay phone are available. Leashed pets are permitted.

Reservations, fees: Reservations are accepted at 877/444-6777 and www.reserveusa.com. Single sites are $17 per night, single lakefront sites are $20 per night, double sites are $33 per night, and sites with hookups are $22 per night (includes eight people). Vehicles must also have a daily pass ($5) or weekly pass ($15) for the Arapaho National Recreation Area. Golden Age and Golden Access Passports are accepted. Cash or check only. Open mid-May–early November.

Directions: From Granby, take U.S. Highway 34 north for 8.5 miles and turn right into the campground.

Contact: Arapaho National Forest, 970/887-4100, www.fs.fed.us/arnf.

15 CUTTHROAT BAY GROUP

Scenic rating: 8

on Lake Granby

Cutthroat Bay is an attractive group campsite on the north shore of Lake Granby. There's something for the whole family here: fishing, boating, hiking, wildlife viewing, sightseeing, and trail riding. Rocky Mountain National Park is a short drive away, and the Indian Peaks Wilderness beckons hardy hikers. (There are no trails from the campground because the surrounding land is private property.) The campground is in a lodgepole pine forest on a hill overlooking the lake. The trees obscure the views from the campsites, but there is a scenic overlook with views of the high peaks of the Continental Divide. There are two group sites with picnic pavilions. There's plenty of room for large groups to spread out. (For more information on Lake Granby, see the Stillwater listing earlier in this chapter.)

Campsites, facilities: There are two group sites with tent camping for up to 50 people. The parking area can accommodate RVs up to 32 feet. There are no hookups. Picnic tables, grills, fire rings, and tent pads are provided. Vault toilets, drinking water, picnic pavilions, lantern hooks, and horseshoe pits are available. Leashed pets are permitted.

Reservations, fees: Reservations are required and accepted at 877/444-6777 and www.reserveusa.com. The fee is $70 per night. Vehicles must also have a daily pass ($5) or weekly pass ($15) for the Arapaho National Recreation Area. Golden Age and Golden Access Passports are accepted. Open late May–early September.

Directions: From Granby, take U.S. Highway 34 north for 9.9 miles. Turn right on County Road 64. The campground is on the right in 0.3 mile. **Contact:** Arapaho National Forest, 970/887-4100, www.fs.fed.us/arnf.

16 GREEN RIDGE

Scenic rating: 7

near Lake Granby

Green Ridge is at the south end of Shadow Mountain Lake, not far from impressive Lake Granby. The campground is in a lodgepole pine forest below the dam, so there are no views from the campsites of the surrounding mountains or the lake. The dam is an easy fishing spot for kids. Wakeless boating is allowed on the lake. Hikers will be pleased to find that a Continental Divide trailhead is nearby. There are two loops with sites 10–25 feet apart. Sites 61–74 are on the edge of the forest next to a pretty valley. (For more information on the Lake Granby area, see the Stillwater listing earlier in this chapter.)

Campsites, facilities: There are 77 sites for tents and RVs up to 35 feet. Sites 18–22 are walk-in sites. There are no hookups. Sites 7, 10, 24, 29, 31, 41, and 52 are pull-through.

Picnic tables, grills, fire rings, and tent pads are provided. Vault toilets, drinking water, a boat ramp, and amphitheater are available. The facilities are wheelchair accessible. Leashed pets are permitted.

Reservations, fees: Reservations are not accepted. A single site costs $14 per night (includes eight people), and a double site costs $28 per night. Vehicles must also have a daily pass ($5) or a weekly pass ($15) for the Arapaho National Recreation Area. Golden Age and Golden Access Passports are accepted. Open mid-May–early November.

Directions: From Granby, take U.S. Highway 34 north for 11.7 miles. Turn right on County Road 66. The campground is on the left in 1.3 miles.

Contact: Arapaho National Forest, 970/887-4100, www.fs.fed.us/arnf.

17 WILLOW CREEK
🏕🛶🚣🐕♿🚙⛰

Scenic rating: 7

near Lake Granby

Willow Creek Reservoir is part of the Arapaho National Recreation Area, a 36,000-acre district that contains four other major lakes: Shadow Mountain Lake, Monarch Lake, Lake Granby, and Meadow Creek Reservoir. Willow Creek is much quieter than the busy campgrounds on the shores of Lake Granby. The views aren't quite as spectacular, but the tips of the Indian Peaks are visible to the east, and the lake is surrounded by hills covered in sagebrush, pine, and aspen. The lake is also home to several pairs of osprey every year. The campground is on the south shore of the lake. The sites are about 50 feet apart and have partial shade. A trail around the lake provides easy fishing access. Sites 1 and 4 are very close to the road. Sites 13–15, 19, 24, 26, 28, and 30–32 have the best lake views.

Campsites, facilities: There are 34 sites for tents and RVs up to 25 feet. Sites 2, 6, and

32 are doubles. There are no hookups. Picnic tables, grills, fire rings, tent pads, lantern hooks, and food lockers are provided. Vault toilets, drinking water, and a boat ramp are available. The facilities are wheelchair accessible. Leashed pets are permitted.

Reservations, fees: Reservations are not accepted. The fee is $14 per night for a single site and $28 per night for a double site. Vehicles must also have a daily pass ($5) or a weekly pass ($15) for the Arapaho National Recreation Area. Golden Age and Golden Access Passports are accepted. Cash or check only. Open mid-May–mid-November.

Directions: From Granby, take U.S. Highway 34 north for 5.2 miles. Turn left on County Road 40. In 2.6 miles, turn left at the dam. The campground is on the right in one mile.

Contact: Arapaho National Forest, 970/887-4100, www.fs.fed.us/r2/arnf/.

18 WILLOW CREEK GROUP
🏕🛶🚣🐕♿⛰

Scenic rating: 7

near Lake Granby

Willow Creek Reservoir is part of the Colorado–Big Thompson Diversion Project that transports water from the west side of the Front Range to the rapidly growing communities on the east side. Willow Creek Reservoir is one of four major lakes in Arapaho National Recreation Area. It is a peaceful alternative to the busy campgrounds on the shores of nearby Lake Granby. The group site is adjacent to the larger campground on the south shore of the lake. A trail provides easy access to the shoreline. The tent pads are shaded by pines and aspen. The scenery includes rolling hills and glimpses of the Indian Peaks to the east.

Campsites, facilities: There is one group site for tent camping for up to 20 people. Picnic tables, grills, fire rings, tent pads, lantern hooks, and food lockers are provided. Vault toilets, drinking water, and a boat ramp are available. The facilities are wheelchair accessible. Leashed pets are permitted.

Reservations, fees: Reservations are required and accepted at 877/444-6777 and www.reserveusa.com. The fee is $60 per night. Vehicles must also have a daily pass ($5) or a weekly pass ($15) for the Arapaho National Recreation Area. Golden Age and Golden Access Passports are accepted. Cash or check only. Open mid-May–mid-November.

Directions: From Granby, take U.S. Highway 34 north for 5.2 miles. Turn left on County Road 40. In 2.6 miles, turn left at the dam. The campground is on the right in one mile.

Contact: Arapaho National Forest, 970/887-4100, www.fs.fed.us/r2/arnf/.

19 SUNSET POINT

Scenic rating: 6

on Lake Granby

Sunset Point is near the dam on the south shore of Lake Granby. This first-come, first-served campground doesn't have the awesome views of Stillwater and Lakeview, but it is a comfortable location for late arrivals. The campground is in a lodgepole pine forest that provides privacy and shade. There is a short but steep slope down to the water. The following sites are lakeside: 1–4, 6, 7, 10, 11, 17, 18, 20, and 21. (For more information on Lake Granby, see the Stillwater listing earlier in this chapter.)

Campsites, facilities: There are 25 sites for tents and RVs up to 35 feet. Sites 14–16 are walk-in tent sites. Sites 9, 19, 23, and 25 are doubles. There are no hookups. Picnic tables, grills, fire rings, tent pads, and lantern posts are provided. Vault toilets, drinking water, dump stations, and a boat ramp are available. The facilities are wheelchair accessible. Leashed pets are permitted.

Reservations, fees: Reservations are not accepted. A single site costs $17 per night, and a double site costs $34 per night. Vehicles must also have a daily pass ($5) or a weekly pass ($15) for the Arapaho National Recreation Area. Golden Age and Golden Access Passports are accepted. Open mid-May–early September.

Directions: From Granby, take U.S. Highway 34 north for 5.4 miles. Turn right on Forest Route 125/Arapaho Bay Road. In 0.9 mile, turn left at the Sunset Point Complex sign. The campground is on the left in 0.2 mile.

Contact: Arapaho National Forest, 970/887-4100, www.fs.fed.us/arnf.

20 ARAPAHO BAY

Scenic rating: 9

on Lake Granby

BEST (

Arapaho Bay is on the eastern tip of the long arm of Lake Granby, beneath the magnificent Indian Peaks. This wilderness area contains 110 miles of trails, 18 miles of the Continental Divide, and nearly 50 high-altitude lakes, as well as a few ice fields, remnants of the glaciers that carved the serrated ridgelines. Because of its proximity to Denver and Boulder, the trails on the eastern side are extremely busy in the summer (so busy that the Forest Service requires permits for backcountry camping), but the west side is much quieter. The Roaring Fork, Monarch Lake, and Strawberry Lake Trails begin near the campground and connect with the Buchanan Pass, Cascade Creek, and Continental Divide Trails, making several overnight loops possible. Anglers will be as happy as hikers. They can fish for mackinaw or kokanee salmon from the shore or by boat.

Arapaho Bay is the most remote and attractive of the four campgrounds around the lake. It has three loops in a lodgepole pine forest. The Big Rock Loop (sites 1–22) is the least impressive. Many of the sites are by the road, and there are no views. The Moraine Loop (sites 23–51) is a half mile away and dramatically different. It is closer to the lake, and most sites have good views. Sites 25–33 are lakeside. Sites 30–33 have their own small loop and are great for groups. The Roaring Fork Loop (sites 52–84) is even better. The views are awesome and a hilly topography makes the sites more private. Sites 55, 57–62, 64–66, and 70–78 overlook the water.

Campsites, facilities: There are 84 sites for tents and RVs up to 35 feet. Sites 57–62 and 64–66 are walk-in sites. Sites 69, 71, and 73 are doubles. There are no hookups. Picnic tables, grills, fire rings, and tent pads are provided. Vault toilets, drinking water, and a boat ramp are available. The facilities are wheelchair accessible. Leashed pets are permitted.

Reservations, fees: Reservations are accepted at 877/444-6777 and www.reserveusa.com. A single site costs $14 per night (includes eight people), and a double site costs $28 per night. Vehicles must also have a daily pass ($5) or a weekly pass ($15) for the Arapaho National Recreation Area. Golden Age and Golden Access Passports are accepted. Open mid-May–mid-November.

Directions: From Granby, take U.S. Highway 34 north for 5.4 miles. Turn right on Forest Route 125/Arapaho Bay Road. The campground is on the left in 8.7 miles.

Contact: Arapaho National Forest, 970/887-4100, www.fs.fed.us/arnf.

21 WILLOWS

Scenic rating: 5

on Green Mountain Reservoir

Green Mountain Reservoir is on the Blue River, between the Williams Fork Mountains and the Gore Range, one of the most striking of Colorado's mountain ranges. The mountains create a rain shadow, so the land

around the lake is high desert. The reservoir is five miles long and holds over 2,000 surface acres of water. Personal watercraft and water skis are allowed at Green Mountain (but not nearby Dillon Reservoir), so this lake attracts a big water-sports crowd. There are no official trails around the lake, but hikers can drive to nearby Lower Cataract Lake to hike the Surprise and Eaglesmere Trails in the north end of the Eagles Nest Wilderness.

Willows offers dispersed camping along the north end of the reservoir. It's a madhouse on weekends with RVs, ATVs, and personal watercraft zipping in and out of the campground. Extended families encamp for the weekend, many of them almost on top of each other. If you love solitude, head elsewhere. If you want to play in the water and don't mind a scene, this is your place.

Campsites, facilities: There are approximately 35 sites for tents and RVs of any length. Vault toilets are available. Leashed pets are permitted.

Reservations, fees: Reservations are not accepted. The fee is $5 per night. Golden Age and Golden Access Passports are accepted. Cash or check only. Open May–October.

Directions: From Silverthorne, take Highway 9 north for 17.5 miles. Turn left on Heeney Road. The campground is on the right in 9.8 miles.

Contact: White River National Forest, 970/468-5400, www.fs.fed.us/whiteriver.

22 COW CREEK NORTH

Scenic rating: 5

on Green Mountain Reservoir

Cow Creek North is almost indistinguishable from the adjacent campground Cow Creek South. They are both on the east shore of Green Mountain Reservoir, a five-mile-long lake with over 2,000 surface acres of water. The campground is in a high desert setting, but it has excellent views of the Gore Range to the west and Green Mountain. Cow Creek North is a little smaller. There is about a half mile of dispersed camping for about 15 groups, but on weekends, when one group of RVs and tents blends into the next, it's difficult to tell how many groups are there. The lake is so popular because personal watercraft are allowed on Green Mountain Reservoir but not at nearby Dillon Reservoir. Personal watercraft owners can put in at the boat ramp and then moor near their campsite. There are no official trails around the lake, but hikers can drive to nearby Lower Cataract Lake to hike the Surprise and Eaglesmere Trails in the north end of the Eagles Nest Wilderness.

Campsites, facilities: There are approximately 30 sites for tents and RVs. Vault toilets are available. Leashed pets are permitted.

Reservations, fees: Reservations are not accepted. The fee is $5 per night. Golden Age and Golden Access Passports are accepted. Cash or check only. Open May–October.

Directions: From Silverthorne, take Highway 9 north for 23.7 miles. The campground is on the left.

Contact: White River National Forest, 970/468-5400, www.fs.fed.us/whiteriver.

23 COW CREEK SOUTH

Scenic rating: 5

on Green Mountain Reservoir

Cow Creek South is on the east shore of Green Mountain Reservoir, a five-mile-long lake with over 2,000 surface acres of water. The campground is in a high desert setting, but it has excellent views of the Gore Range to the west and Green Mountain. There is almost a mile of dispersed camping for about 30 groups. The lake is very popular because personal watercraft are allowed on Green Mountain Reservoir but not at nearby Dillon Reservoir. Personal watercraft owners can put

in at the boat ramp and then moor near their campsite. On weekends in July and August, it can be a madhouse. There are no official trails around the lake, but hikers can drive to nearby Lower Cataract Lake to hike the Surprise and Eaglesmere Trails in the north end of the Eagles Nest Wilderness.

Campsites, facilities: There are approximately 30 sites for tents and RVs. Vault toilets are available. Leashed pets are permitted.

Reservations, fees: Reservations are not accepted. The fee is $5 per night. Golden Age and Golden Access Passports are accepted. Cash or check only. Open May–October.

Directions: From Silverthorne, take Highway 9 north for 23.4 miles. The campground is on the left.

Contact: White River National Forest, 970/468-5400, www.fs.fed.us/whiteriver.

24 ELLIOT CREEK

Scenic rating: 5

on Green Mountain Reservoir

Green Mountain Reservoir is on the Blue River, between the Williams Fork Mountains and the Gore Range, one of the most striking of Colorado's mountain ranges. Since the mountains create a rain shadow, the land around the lake is high desert. The five-mile-long reservoir attracts a big water-sports crowd. There are no official trails around the lake, but hikers can drive to nearby Lower Cataract Lake to hike the Surprise and Eaglesmere Trails in the north end of the Eagles Nest Wilderness. Elliot Creek has primitive camping near the dam at the northwest corner of the lake with views of the dam, the Williams Fork Mountains, and Green Mountain. The sites are dispersed in three levels along a steep shore. Some sites are shaded by evergreens and cottonwoods, others are in the sagebrush flats, and others are right next to a large parking lot. This campground attracts large groups and young people. It's a party scene on weekends.

Campsites, facilities: There are approximately 24 sites for tents and RVs. Vault toilets are available. Leashed pets are permitted.

Reservations, fees: Reservations are not accepted. The fee is $5 per night. Golden Age and Golden Access Passports are accepted. Cash or check only. Open May–October.

Directions: From Silverthorne, take Highway 9 north for 17.5 miles. Turn left on Heeney Road. The campground is on the right in eight miles.

Contact: White River National Forest, 970/468-5400, www.fs.fcd.us/whitcrivcr.

25 CATARACT CREEK
🚶 🛶 🐕 🚙 ⛺

Scenic rating: 9

near Green Mountain Reservoir

BEST (

Cataract Creek is a rare gem in a region of oversized and overcrowded campgrounds. This tiny campground overlooks the lovely Cataract Creek valley (almost free of development) and the Williams Fork Mountains. The sites are large and shaded by mature spruce and fir, but they still have good views (except site 5). They're also very private. Several trails begin at Lower Cataract Lake, including a 2.3-mile loop around the lake and the Surprise and Eaglesmere Trails. The Surprise Trail is one of the most popular routes into the Eagles Nest Wilderness. It travels through spruce forests past lakes and wetlands with views of the Gore Range. There are side trips to alpine lakes and the crest of the Gore Range. Predictably, this campground is very popular. If you're visiting on a summer weekend, arrive on Wednesday or Thursday to bag a spot.

Campsites, facilities: There are five sites for tents and RVs up to 21 feet. Picnic tables, fire rings, and grills are provided. Leashed pets are permitted.

Reservations, fees: Reservations are not accepted. The fee is $5 per night. Golden Age and Golden Access Passports are accepted. Cash or check only. Open late May–mid-September.

Directions: From Silverthorne, take Highway 9 north for 17.5 miles. Turn left on Heeney Road. In 5.3 miles, turn left on Cataract Creek Road. The campground is on the left in 2.2 miles.

Contact: White River National Forest, 970/468-5400, www.fs.fed.us/whiteriver.

26 DAVIS SPRINGS
🛶 🚙 🐕 ⛺

Scenic rating: 5

on Green Mountain Reservoir

There are seven campgrounds at Green Mountain Reservoir, and Davis Springs is the smallest and quietest of them all. Located near the inlet, it's also the best choice for anglers who want to fish on the Blue River, offering primitive camping on the lakeshore. The sites are shaded by cottonwoods and aspen and have views of the highway and the Williams Fork foothills. The views are not as impressive as at the north end of the reservoir. This campground fills up quickly on weekends. The vault toilets are extremely run-down.

Campsites, facilities: There are three sites for tents. Fire rings and vault toilets are provided. Leashed pets are permitted.

Reservations, fees: Reservations are not accepted. The fee is $5 per night. Golden Age and Golden Access Passports are accepted. Cash or check only. Open May–October.

Directions: From Silverthorne, take Highway 9 north for 17.5 miles. Turn left on Heeney Road. The campground is on the right in 1.6 miles.

Contact: White River National Forest, 970/468-5400, www.fs.fed.us/whiteriver.

27 MCDONALD FLATS

Scenic rating: 4

on Green Mountain Reservoir

On the west shore of Green Mountain Reservoir, McDonald Flats has views of the Williams Fork Mountains and the highway. It is a very popular weekend destination, especially for water-sports enthusiasts. The lake is almost five miles long and has over 2,000 surface acres. Water-skiers and personal watercraft take over the lake on weekends. Anglers might have better luck on the Blue River, a Gold Medal fishery, or at nearby Dillon Reservoir. The campground is in the sagebrush flats, so there is no shade or privacy. The sites are very close together. Sites 10–13 are closest to the water. The views are not as good at this campground as on the east shore, but it's smaller and quieter than those campgrounds.

Campsites, facilities: There are 13 sites for tents and RVs up to 21 feet. Picnic tables, fire rings, and grills are provided. Vault toilets, a boat ramp, and pay phone are available. Leashed pets are permitted.

Reservations, fees: Reservations are not accepted. The fee is $10 per night (includes 10 people and two vehicles). Additional vehicles cost $5 per night. Golden Age and Golden Access Passports are accepted. Cash or check only. Open May–October.

Directions: From Silverthorne, take Highway 9 north for 17.5 miles. Turn left on Heeney Road. The campground is on the right in two miles.

Contact: White River National Forest, 970/468-5400, www.fs.fed.us/whiteriver.

28 PRAIRIE POINT

Scenic rating: 4

on Green Mountain Reservoir

Prairie Point is on the east shore of Green Mountain Reservoir, a five-mile-long reservoir on the Blue River, between the Williams Fork Mountains and the Gore Range. The lake attracts mainly water-sports enthusiasts, but the Blue River is also a Gold Medal fishery. There are no official trails around the lake, but hikers can drive to nearby Lower Cataract Lake to hike the Surprise and Eaglesmere Trails in the north end of the Eagles Nest Wilderness. The campground has views of the foothills of the Williams Fork and the tips of the Gore Range. It's in a high desert setting with a few cottonwoods and willows along the shore. This campground has designated sites, so it's much calmer than neighboring Cow Creek, but it still lacks privacy because the sites are just 10 feet apart. Sites 1–8 and 17–33 are right on the water.

Campsites, facilities: There are 33 sites for tents and RVs up to 20 feet. Picnic tables, fire rings, and grills are provided. Vault toilets and drinking water are available. Leashed pets are permitted.

Reservations, fees: Reservations are not accepted. The fee is $10 per night (includes 10 people and two vehicles). Additional vehicles cost $5 per night. Golden Age and Golden Access Passports are accepted. Cash or check only. Open May–October.

Directions: From Silverthorne, take Highway 9 north for 19.1 miles. The campground is on the left.

Contact: White River National Forest, 970/468-5400, www.fs.fed.us/whiteriver.

29 HORSESHOE

Scenic rating: 6

south of Hot Sulphur Springs

Horseshoe campground sits between the Williams Fork Mountains to the west and the Vasquez Mountains to the east. The campground is small and not especially scenic—a pine beetle infestation has turned the surrounding hills red and increased logging traffic in the area. However, ATV riders love the network of Forest Service roads in the Vasquez Mountains, and backpackers appreciate the proximity to Byers Peak Wilderness and Ptarmigan Peak Wilderness. Williams Peak Trail is the nearest hiking and pack trail.

The campground is on the west bank of the Williams Fork River in a forest of spruce, fir, and aspen. Sites 2–5 are riverside and shaded. The sites are 30–60 feet apart. Weekdays are quiet, but weekends can be busy with a four-wheeling crowd.

Campsites, facilities: There are seven sites for tents and RVs up to 23 feet. There are no hookups. Sites 1, 4, and 5 are pull-through. Picnic tables, grills, and fire rings are provided. Vault toilets are available. Trash must be packed out. Leashed pets are permitted.

Reservations, fees: Reservations are not accepted. The fee is $6 per night (includes eight people). Golden Age and Golden Access Passports are accepted. Cash or check only. Open late May–mid-October.

Directions: From Hot Sulphur Springs, take U.S. Highway 40 west for 4.5 miles. Turn left on County Road 3/Forest Route 138. In 15.5 miles, turn left on Forest Route 139. The campground is on the left before the bridge.

Contact: Arapaho National Forest, 970/887-4100, www.fs.fed.us/r2/arnf/.

30 ST. LOUIS CREEK

Scenic rating: 6

near Fraser

St. Louis Creek is in the Fraser Experimental Forest, a 20,000-acre biosphere reserve where scientists have spent 60 years studying subalpine forests in the Rocky Mountains. This campground is packed all summer with mountain bikers of all ages. The Fraser Valley has an extensive trail network between Fraser and Winter Park and in the Winter Park Resort. Bikers can take a dirt trail from the campground into Fraser and beyond. Hikers enjoy ridge hiking in the Byers Peak Wilderness. The 8.6-mile Byers Peak Trail is a difficult but rewarding route which begins near the campground. The campground is a loop in a lodgepole pine forest. The forest is thin, the campground is very flat, and the sites are 25–50 feet apart, so there's not much privacy. Nevertheless, it's packed on weekends, so arrive early. Sites 8, 10, 12, 13, and 15 are creekside.

Campsites, facilities: There are 17 sites for tents and RVs up to 32 feet. Site 17 and the facilities are wheelchair accessible. There are no hookups. Sites 4, 6, 10, and 11 are pull-through. Picnic tables, grills, and fire rings are provided. Vault toilets and drinking water are available. Leashed pets are permitted.

Reservations, fees: Reservations are not accepted. The fee is $12 per night (includes two vehicles). Additional vehicles cost $6 each. Golden Age and Golden Access Passports are accepted. Cash or check only. Open late May–mid-September.

Directions: From Fraser, take County Road 72 west for 0.2 mile. Turn right on County Road 721. In 0.7 mile, turn left on County Road 73. The campground entrance is on the left in 2.2 miles.

Contact: Arapaho National Forest, 970/887-4100, www.fs.fed.us/arnf.

31 BYERS CREEK

Scenic rating: 7

near Fraser

Byers Creek is in the Fraser Experimental Forest, a 20,000-acre biosphere reserve where scientists have spent 60 years studying subalpine forests in the Rocky Mountains. The campground is near the confluence of Byers and St. Louis Creeks. (Sites 2, 3, and 4 overlook the creek.) It's a small, quiet loop that attracts mainly mountain bikers and hikers. Bikers can take Byers Creek Road to the network of trails in the Fraser Valley. Hikers enjoy alpine ridge hiking in the Byers Peak Wilderness via the St. Louis Lakes and Byers Peak Trails. The wilderness area is just 8,000 acres, but it's part of a 100,000-acre roadless area that includes the Vasquez Peak and Ptarmigan Peak wilderness areas.

Campsites, facilities: There are six sites for tents and RVs up to 25 feet. There are no hookups. Site 5 is pull-through. Picnic tables, grills, and fire rings are provided. Vault toilets are available. Leashed pets are permitted.

Reservations, fees: Reservations are not accepted. The fee is $12 per night (includes two vehicles). Additional vehicles cost $6 each. Golden Age and Golden Access Passports are accepted. Cash or check only. Open late May–mid-September.

Directions: From Fraser, take County Road 72 west for 0.2 mile. Turn right on County Road 721. In 0.7 mile, turn left on County Road 73. In 6.5 miles, stay left at the fork to enter the campground.

Contact: Arapaho National Forest, 970/887-4100, www.fs.fed.us/arnf.

32 IDLEWILD

Scenic rating: 5

near Winter Park

Idlewild is just outside of Winter Park, so it is packed throughout July and August with the standard summer assortment of families, grandparents, and spandex-clad mountain bikers shouting "On your left!" The Fraser River Trail runs through the campground and connects to an extensive network of mountain biking trails, including the ski runs in Winter Park Resort. Hikers can explore the Byers Peak and Vasquez wilderness areas, part of a 100,000-acre roadless area. Several trailheads are a short drive away. The campground is divided into an upper and lower loop. The upper loop (sites 16–25) is very close to the busy highway, and the sites are on a hill, so there's limited tent space. The lower loop (sites 6–25) is in a spruce-fir forest beside the river and the trail.

Campsites, facilities: There are 24 sites for tents and RVs up to 32 feet. There are no hookups. Sites 2, 5, and 18 are pull-through. Picnic tables, grills, fire rings, and tent pads are provided. Vault toilets and drinking water are available. The facilities are wheelchair accessible. Leashed pets are permitted.

Reservations, fees: Reservations are not accepted. The fee is $12 per night (includes two vehicles). Additional vehicles cost $6 each. Golden Age and Golden Access Passports are accepted. Cash or check only. Open late May–mid-September.

Directions: From the Winter Park visitors center, drive south on U.S. Highway 40 for 1.3 miles. The campground entrance is on the left across from the Winter Park north entrance.

Contact: Arapaho National Forest, 970/887-4100, www.fs.fed.us/arnf.

33 ROBBER'S ROOST

Scenic rating: 5

near Winter Park

Robber's Roost is a stopover campground on the road to Winter Park. It's in a spruce-fir forest adjacent to the Fraser River and U.S. Highway 40. There is a lot of traffic noise. The only activity at the campground is fishing, but the Fraser Valley's extensive trail network attracts hordes of mountain bikers. This campground is very busy in the summer and usually full on weekends. Sites 6–10 are farthest from the road. The sites are about 30 feet apart. There is lots of shade but limited privacy.

Campsites, facilities: There are 11 sites for tents and RVs up to 45 feet. There are no hookups. Site 11 is pull-through. Picnic tables, grills, and fire rings are provided. Vault toilets are available. The facilities are wheelchair accessible. Leashed pets are permitted.

Reservations, fees: Reservations are not accepted. The fee is $12 per night (includes two vehicles). Additional vehicles cost $6 each. Golden Age and Golden Access Passports are accepted. Cash or check only. Open late May–mid-September.

Directions: From the Winter Park visitors center, drive south on U.S. Highway 40 for 6.8 miles. The campground entrance is on the left.

Contact: Arapaho National Forest, 970/887-4100, www.fs.fed.us/arnf.

34 SOUTH FORK

Scenic rating: 5

south of Hot Sulphur Springs

South Fork campground is in the Williams Fork Valley between the Williams Fork Mountains to the west and the Vasquez Mountains

to the east, downstream of the large Henderson Mill site. This formerly pleasant campground has been decimated by a pine beetle infestation. The sites are only 25–50 feet apart, so once the dead trees are harvested, privacy and shade will be poor. However, riders and hikers will continue to use this campground for its proximity to the Byers Peak Wilderness. The Darling Creek Trail begins nearby and climbs six miles to the Continental Divide and St. Louis Divide Trail. The South Fork Loop also begins nearby in the Sugarloaf campground. This 27-mile trail is the most popular in the valley with backpackers, riders, and mountain bikers.

Campsites, facilities: There are 21 sites for tents and RVs up to 23 feet. There are no hookups. Sites 5, 6, 9, 12, 17, and 19 are pull through. Picnic tables, grills, and fire rings are provided. Vault toilets, drinking water, and two horse corrals are available. The facilities are wheelchair accessible. Leashed pets are permitted.

Reservations, fees: Reservations are not accepted. The fee is $12 per night (includes eight people) and $36 per night for the group site. Golden Age and Golden Access Passports are accepted. Cash or check only. Open late May–mid-September.

Directions: From Hot Sulphur Springs, take U.S. Highway 40 west for 4.5 miles. Turn left on County Road 3/Forest Route 138. In 18.2 miles, stay left on Forest Route 138/County Road 30. In 5.6 miles, turn left and go through the tunnel, then veer right. The campground is on the right in 0.1 mile.

Contact: Arapaho National Forest, 970/887-4100, www.fs.fed.us/r2/arnf/.

35 SUGARLOAF

Scenic rating: 6

south of Hot Sulphur Springs

Sugarloaf is the most attractive campground in the Williams Fork Valley and the most remote. Located on the South Fork of the Williams River, the campground is in an evergreen forest that has been affected by the pine beetle epidemic, although the damage is not as dramatic as in nearby South Fork campground. The sites are 30–60 feet apart and shaded. A wheelchair-accessible boardwalk provides fishing access on the river. The 27-mile South Fork Loop begins and ends in the campground and offers challenging backpacking and riding trips.

Campsites, facilities: There are 11 sites for tents and RVs up to 23 feet. There are no hookups. Site 10 is pull-through. Picnic tables, grills, fire rings, and tent pads are provided. Vault toilets, drinking water, and horseshoe pits are available. The facilities are wheelchair accessible. Leashed pets are permitted.

Reservations, fees: Reservations are not accepted. The fee is $12 per night (includes eight people). Golden Age and Golden Access Passports are accepted. Cash or check only. Open late May–mid-September.

Directions: From Hot Sulphur Springs, take U.S. Highway 40 west for 4.5 miles. Turn left on County Road 3/Forest Route 138. In 18.2 miles, stay left on Forest Route 138/County Road 30. In 5.6 miles, turn left and go through the tunnel, then veer right. The road ends in 0.6 mile at the campground.

Contact: Arapaho National Forest, 970/887-4100, www.fs.fed.us/r2/arnf/.

36 BLUE RIVER
🎣 ⛵ 🏕 ♿ 🚐 ⛺

Scenic rating: 5

on Green Mountain Reservoir

Between Dillon Reservoir and Green Mountain Reservoir, the Blue River is a Gold Medal trout stream. This little campground on the west bank is popular with anglers and families looking to enjoy the shopping in Silverthorne and Frisco. There are three loops. The upper

loop (sites 1–4) is right by the highway and has limited shade. The middle loop is a little lower and has more privacy, but everyone heads for the lower loop beside the river. This loop is shaded by aspen, pine, and cottonwood. The far bank is the foothills of the Williams Fork Mountain. Sites 10, 12–15, and 17–20 are right on the water. The sites are small, but this campground is very busy on weekends. In addition to fishing, kayakers will find three miles of Class III water on the Blue River below the campground.

Campsites, facilities: There are 24 sites for tents and RVs up to 25 feet. Picnic tables, grills, and fire rings are provided. Site 19 has a tent pad. Vault toilets, drinking water, and a pay phone are available. The facilities are wheelchair accessible. Leashed pets are permitted.

Reservations, fees: Reservations are not accepted. The fee is $12 per night (includes 10 people and two vehicles). Additional vehicles cost $5 per night. Golden Age and Golden Access Passports are accepted. Cash or check only. Open late May–mid-October.

Directions: From Silverthorne, take Highway 9 north for 8.5 miles. The campground is on the right.

Contact: White River National Forest, 970/468-5400, www.fs.fed.us/whiteriver.

37 GORE CREEK
🚶 🚴 🎣 🏕 🐕 ♿ 🚐 ⛺

Scenic rating: 6

near Vail

Gore Creek campground isn't especially scenic, but it has two things going for it: proximity to Vail and the Eagles Nest Wilderness. It's a perfect destination for enjoying the town (including numerous summer festivals) and exploring Eagles Nest, one of the most easily accessible wilderness areas. From I-70, there's no hint at the beauty and wildness that awaits just north of the campground, but the adjacent trailheads climb steeply through lush valleys that dead-end at alpine lakes beneath the serrated ridges of the Gore Range. The Deluge Lake Trail is a four-mile ascent (one of the steepest in Eagles Nest) with views of the Vail Valley and Gore Range. The Gore Creek Trail climbs for 6.5 miles to Gore Lake and Red Buffalo Pass, where it connects with the Gore Range Trail. Gore Creek is the most popular trail in the area, so you can expect company in the summer. Both of these trails are closed to bikes, but mountain bikers can follow Bighorn Road to its terminus and the Two Elk trailhead. This National Scenic Trail has panoramic views of the Gore and Sawatch Ranges and passes by the back bowls of Vail. There is fair fishing for brook and cutthroat trout in Gore Creek. Downstream of Exit 180, Gore Creek is a Class III–IV white water run with numerous play spots.

The campground is a gravel loop beside Gore Creek. Most sites are shaded by aspen and spruce-fir groves. The sites are 50 feet apart and screened from each other but not the road. Sites 9–14, 16, and 17 are creekside. In 2005, this campground had bear problems and was closed in late July and August to tents and pop-ups. Normal operation will resume in 2006, but please be bear aware.

Campsites, facilities: There are 25 sites for tents and RVs up to 40 feet. There are no hookups. Picnic tables, grills, and fire rings are provided. Vault toilets and drinking water are available. The facilities are wheelchair accessible. Leashed pets are permitted.

Reservations, fees: Reservations are not accepted. The fee is $14 per night (includes 10 people and two vehicles). Additional vehicles cost $5 per night. Golden Age and Golden Access Passports are accepted. Cash or check only. Open late May–mid-September.

Directions: From Exit 180 in Vail, take Bighorn Road east for 2.3 miles and turn left into the campground.

Contact: White River National Forest, 970/827-5715, www.fs.fed.us/r2/whiteriver/.

38 TIGIWON

Scenic rating: 9

south of Minturn

BEST (

At 10,100 feet, Tigiwon will take your breath away. The drive and the altitude are not for the faint of heart, but there are two good reasons to go: the views of the Gore Range and Tigiwon Community House. The views speak for themselves, but the community house needs more explanation. This log cabin lodge was built in 1933 by CCC volunteers. It's available by reservation for private groups. Weddings frequently take place there (once the snow melts). With the campground just a few steps away, guests can party until they poop out. There are no hiking trails accessible from the campground. Cross Creek, about four miles down the road, sees heavy traffic throughout the summer. The Halfmoon Pass trailhead is located two miles up the road and provides access to the Holy Cross Wilderness.

The campground is a small loop in a spruce forest. Sites 0–2 are protected by trees which also block their views. Site 3 has stunning views of the Gore Range. Site 5 is also popular because it's large and sits below the road, which makes it very private. Site 8 is also very private.

Campsites, facilities: There are nine sites for tents and RVs up to 30 feet. There are no hookups or pull-throughs. Picnic tables, grills, and fire rings are provided. Vault toilets are available. Leashed pets are permitted.

Reservations, fees: Reservations are not accepted. The fee is $10 per night (includes 10 people and two vehicles). Additional vehicles cost $5 per night. Golden Age and Golden Access Passports are accepted. Cash or check only. Open late June–September.

Directions: From Vail, take I-70 west for five miles to Exit 171. Go south on U.S. Highway 24. In 4.7 miles, turn right on Tigiwon Road/Forest Route 707. It is six miles to the Tigiwon

Community House. The campground is after the lodge on the right.

Contact: White River National Forest, 970/827-5715, www.fs.fed.us/r2/whiteriver/.

39 HALF MOON
👫 🐕 ♿ 🚐 ⛺

Scenic rating: 6

south of Minturn

BEST ☾

This high-altitude campground is used for the most part by hikers and backpackers exploring the Holy Cross Wilderness area. The Holy Cross Wilderness contains five glacial valleys and 25 thirteeners, as well as the landmark Mount of the Holy Cross. First photographed and painted in 1873 by members of the Hayden Expedition, this mountain draws hordes of visitors every summer who want to see the snowy cross on its north face. In 1924, a shelter was built on Notch Mountain to accommodate the pilgrims. The shelter is still accessible via the Notch Mountain Trail, which climbs 3,000 feet in five miles. Campers at Halfmoon can take the Fall Creek Trail to the Notch Mountain Trail, or they can take the Half Moon Pass Trail to explore the wilderness. The 3.75-mile trail features views of the Sawatch Range, Mount of the Holy Cross, the Gore Range, and the Mosquito Range. If possible, visit midweek when traffic is moderate.

The campground is a small loop in a spruce forest beside Fall Creek. Sites 1, 6, and 7 are closest to the creek. The sites are 50–100 feet apart, and the dense forest provides ample privacy.

Campsites, facilities: There are seven sites for tents and RVs up to 20 feet. There are no hookups or pull-throughs. Picnic tables and fire rings are provided. Vault toilets are available and are wheelchair accessible. Trash must be packed out. Leashed pets are permitted.

Reservations, fees: Reservations are not accepted. The fee is $10 per night (includes 10 people and two vehicles). Additional vehicles cost $5 per night. Golden Age and Golden Access Passports are accepted. Cash or check only. Open late June–September.

Directions: From Vail, take I-70 west for five miles to Exit 171. Go south on U.S. Highway 24. In 4.7 miles, turn right on Tigiwon Road/Forest Route 707. In 8.4 miles the road ends at the Halfmoon Pass trailhead. Just before the parking area, turn left into the campground. This road is very narrow and potted. High-clearance vehicles are recommended but not required.

Contact: White River National Forest, 970/827-5715, www.fs.fed.us/r2/whiteriver/.

40 HORNSILVER
🎣 🐕 🚐 ⛺

Scenic rating: 6

south of Minturn

Hornsilver is a clean, convenient stopover on the Top of the Rockies Scenic Byway, a 75-mile Y-shaped travel route. The first section, Dowd Junction to Leadville, features the historic mining towns of Minturn, Gilman, and Redcliff, and access to the Holy Cross Wilderness. Hornsilver is about halfway between Dowd Junction and Leadville. There were once two loops here. Only the upper loop remains, but the sites are still numbered 6–12. It occupies a flat area about 20 feet above the highway. Traffic is audible but not heavy. The large sites are about 30 feet apart. Sites 8 and 9 are in a small aspen glen and have the most privacy. In 2005, many of the trees were affected by pine beetles.

Campsites, facilities: There are seven sites for tents and RVs up to 30 feet. There are no hookups or pull-throughs. Picnic tables, grills, fire rings, and tent pads are provided. Vault toilets are available. Leashed pets are permitted.

Reservations, fees: Reservations are not accepted. The fee is $12 per night (includes 10 people and two vehicles). Additional vehicles cost $5 per night. Golden Age and Golden Access Passports are accepted. Cash or check only. Open late June–September.

Directions: From Vail, take I-70 west for five miles to Exit 171. Go south on U.S. Highway 24. The campground is on the left in 11.5 miles, just after Homestake Picnic Area.

Contact: White River National Forest, 970/827-5715, www.fs.fed.us/r2/whiteriver/.

41 BLODGETT

Scenic rating: 7

south of Minturn

Like Hornsilver, Blodgett is a convenient stopover between Leadville and Vail on the Top of the Rockies Scenic Byway, but it's more scenic, and there's excellent fly-fishing on Homestake Creek. Public access extends intermittently from the bridge upstream for about 12 miles. On summer days, there seems to be more anglers than nymphs on the water. Following a pine beetle infestation, the campground closed in 2005 for hazard removal. It's scheduled to reopen in May 2006. Unfortunately, hazard removal requires cutting down many trees. Sites 2 and 5 lost almost all of their trees (and privacy). Sites 1 and 3 are still sheltered by tall pines, and they have excellent views of the valley and the peaks of the Holy Cross Wilderness.

Campsites, facilities: There are six sites for tents and RVs up to 30 feet. There are no hookups or pull-throughs. Picnic tables and fire rings are provided. Vault toilets and drinking water are available. Leashed pets are permitted.

Reservations, fees: Reservations are not accepted. The fee is $12 per night (includes 10 people and two vehicles). Additional vehicles cost $5 per night. Golden Age and Golden Access Passports are accepted. Cash or check only. Open late May–September.

Directions: From Vail, take I-70 west for five miles to Exit 171. Go south on U.S. Highway 24. In 12.7 miles, turn right on Homestake Road/Forest Route 703. The campground is on the left in 0.4 mile.

Contact: White River National Forest, 970/827-5715, www.fs.fed.us/r2/whiteriver/.

42 HEATON BAY

Scenic rating: 6

on Dillon Reservoir

Located in the heart of Summit County, Dillon Reservoir is an extremely popular summer destination. It has 24.5 miles of shoreline and 3,300 surface acres of water open to boating and windsurfing (but not personal watercraft and swimming). There are four boat ramps, and hiking and biking trails circle the lake and connect the campgrounds to the towns of Silverthorne, Frisco, and Dillon. Three rivers feed the reservoir: the Snake River, Blue River, and Tenmile Creek. Tenmile Creek has Class III–V whitewater for creek kayakers from for about four miles upstream of the reservoir. The valley is ringed by impressive peaks, including the Gore Range, the Williams Fork Mountains, and the Tenmile Range. The Eagles Nest and Ptarmigan Peak wilderness areas offer some of the best high-altitude hiking in the state, and the Continental Divide snakes along the south horizon.

Heaton Bay is on the north shore of the reservoir in a lodgepole pine forest that's been thinned by pine beetles. There are five loops with 10–25 sites in each loop. The sites are close together with very little privacy. Loops B and D (sites 10–26 and 30–54) have the best views of the peaks. Loop E was recently renovated. It has tent pads and hookups and attracts big RVs. Sites 18, 19, 21, 43, 44, and 48–52 are lakeside.

Campsites, facilities: There are 72 sites for tents and RVs up to 90 feet. Site 10 and the facilities are wheelchair accessible. Sites 55–70 have electrical hookups. Sites 3, 4, 9, 12, 25, 39, and 44 are pull-through. Picnic tables, grills, and fire rings are provided. Sites 10 and 55–72 have tent pads. Vault toilets and drinking water are available. Leashed pets are permitted.

Reservations, fees: Reservations are accepted for Loops B, D, and E at 877/444-6777 and www.reserveusa.com. The fee is $14 per night for sites without hookups and $19 per night for sites with hookups (includes 10 people and two vehicles). Additional vehicles cost $5 per night. Golden Age and Golden Access Passports are accepted. Cash or check only. Open late May–early October.

Directions: From Main Street in Frisco, take Summit Boulevard north for one mile. Turn right on Dillon Dam Road. The campground is on the right in 2.2 miles.

Contact: White River National Forest, 970/468-5400, www.fs.fed.us/whiteriver.

43 LOWRY

Scenic rating: 5

on Dillon Reservoir

There are six campgrounds around the 24 miles of shoreline at Dillon Reservoir. Lowry is the only one that's not on the water, but it's a short drive to the boat ramps and fishing access. Bike trails circle the lake and connect the campground with the towns of Silverthorne, Dillon, and Frisco. On nearby Sapphire Point, there is a short hiking trail and great views of the lake and mountains. The campground used to be part of Lowry Air Force Base. It hasn't been renovated, so the sites are small and close together. They're in a lodgepole pine forest that provides some shade but no privacy. Nevertheless, the campground is full on summer weekends. Sites 25–27 used to be walk-in sites and have the most privacy. Sites 14, 15, and 17 are also good tent sites. (For

more information on Dillon Reservoir, see the Heaton Bay listing in this chapter.)

Campsites, facilities: There are 29 sites for tents and RVs up to 40 feet. Sites 2–24 have electric hookups. Sites 7, 16, and 20 are pull-through. Picnic tables, grills, and fire rings are provided. Vault toilets and drinking water are available. Leashed pets are permitted.

Reservations, fees: Reservations are accepted for sites 1–14 at 877/444-6777 and www.reserveusa.com. The fee is $13 per night for sites without hookups and $18 per night for sites with hookups (includes 10 people and two vehicles). Additional vehicles cost $5 per night. Golden Age and Golden Access Passports are accepted. Cash or check only. Open late May–mid-September.

Directions: From Main Street in Frisco, take Summit Boulevard/Highway 9 south for 3.1 miles. Turn left on Swan Mountain Road/Summit High School Road. The campground entrance is on the right in 3.1 miles.

Contact: White River National Forest, 970/468-5400, www.fs.fed.us/whiteriver.

44 PEAK ONE

Scenic rating: 6

on Dillon Reservoir

Peak One shares a peninsula on the south shore of Dillon Reservoir with the Frisco Nordic and Recreation Center. The Crown Point Trail connects the peninsula to the trail network that circles the lake. This family campground has three loops in a lodgepole pine forest that has been thinned by the pine beetle epidemic. The sites are 20–50 feet apart and offer very little privacy. Sites 44–50 have the best views. Sites 41–60 and 68–70 are close to the water. (For more information on Dillon Reservoir, see the Heaton Bay listing in this chapter.)

Campsites, facilities: There are 79 sites for tents and RVs up to 50 feet. Sites 2, 21, 72, and 76 are pull-through. Picnic tables, grills, and fire rings are provided. Vault toilets, drinking water, and an amphitheater are available. A skate park and ball fields are available by reservation at the Nordic Center. Leashed pets are permitted.

Reservations, fees: Reservations are accepted for Loop B at 877/444-6777 and www.reserveusa.com. The fee is $14 per night (includes 10 people and two vehicles). Additional vehicles cost $5 per night. Golden Age and Golden Access Passports are accepted. Cash or check only. Open late May–mid-September.

Directions: From Main Street in Frisco, take Summit Boulevard/Highway 9 south for 1.1 mile. Turn left on Peninsula Drive. The campground is on the left in one mile.

Contact: White River National Forest, 970/468-5400, www.fs.fed.us/whiteriver.

45 PINE COVE
🚶 🚴 ⛴ 🛶 🐕 🚐 ⛺

Scenic rating: 5

on Dillon Reservoir

Pine Cove shares a peninsula with the Peak One campground and Frisco Nordic Center and Recreation Area. This campground is for boaters and late arrivals. It's a parking lot with tent camping on the sandy shoreline. Sites 1–16 are on the water. Lodgepole pines provide a little shade, but with the sites just 10 feet apart, there is no privacy. The best feature is the views of the surrounding peaks. The long ridgelines and bare peaks of the Gore Range, Tenmile Range, and Williams Fork Mountains scream Colorado. The Crown Point Trail connects the campground with the trails that circle the lake and connect Frisco, Dillon, and Silverthorne. (For more information on Dillon Reservoir, see the Heaton Bay listing in this chapter.)

Campsites, facilities: There are 55 sites for tents and RVs up to 50 feet. There are no hookups. Picnic tables, grills, and fire rings

are provided. Vault toilets and a boat ramp are available. Leashed pets are permitted.

Reservations, fees: Reservations are accepted for Loop B at 877/444-6777 and www.reserveusa.com. The fee is $12 per night (includes 10 people and two vehicles). Additional vehicles cost $5 per night. Golden Age and Golden Access Passports are accepted. Cash or check only. Open late May–mid-September.

Directions: From Main Street in Frisco, take Summit Boulevard/Highway 9 south for 1.1 miles. Turn left on Peninsula Drive. The campground is on the left in 1.2 miles.

Contact: White River National Forest, 970/468-5400, www.fs.fed.us/whiteriver.

46 PROSPECTOR
🚶 🚴 ⛴ 🛶 🐕 🚐 ⛺

Scenic rating: 5

on Dillon Reservoir

Located on the southeast shore of Dillon Reservoir, Prospector is a busy campground full of families. With five loops in a lodgepole pine forest, it's a bit of a maze. The sites are close together and offer no privacy. The Windy Point Trail connects the campground to the shoreline. Nearby Sapphire Point has excellent views of the lake and the surrounding mountains. Sites 95–98 are next to a meadow and have the best views in the campground. (For more information on Dillon Reservoir, see the Heaton Bay listing in this chapter.)

Campsites, facilities: There are 108 sites for tents and RVs up to 32 feet. There are no hookups. Sites 1, 2, 6–11, 14–19, 22, 23, 25, 37, 41, 55, 58, 70, 103, and 105 are pull-through. Picnic tables, grills, and fire rings are provided. Site 40 has a tent pad. Vault toilets and drinking water are available. Leashed pets are permitted.

Reservations, fees: Reservations are accepted for Loops D and E at 877/444-6777 and www.reserveusa.com. The fee is $13 per night (includes 10 people and two vehicles). Additional vehicles cost $5 per night. Golden Age and Golden Access Passports are accepted. Cash or check only. Open late May–mid-September.

Directions: From Main Street in Frisco, take Summit Boulevard/Highway 9 south for 3.1 miles. Turn left on Swan Mountain Road/ Summit High School Road. In three miles, turn left at the campground sign and continue 0.5 mile to the fee station.

Contact: White River National Forest, 970/468-5400, www.fs.fed.us/whiteriver.

47 WINDY POINT GROUP

Scenic rating: 6

on Dillon Reservoir

Windy Point is a group campground on the southeast shore of Dillon Reservoir. The forest site is on the shore and has views of the lake and Dillon. It has a large picnic pavilion, and scattered lodgepole pines provide partial shade. The second site is in a lodgepole pine forest a short distance from the water. There are limited views from the campground, but the Windy Point Trail connects the campground to the shore and offers panoramic views of the surrounding mountain ranges. (For more information on Dillon Reservoir, see the Heaton Bay listing in this chapter.)

Campsites, facilities: There are two group sites for tent camping. RVs can park in the parking lot. Picnic tables, grills, and fire rings are provided. Vault toilets, drinking water, and a picnic pavilion are available. The facilities are wheelchair accessible. Leashed pets are permitted.

Reservations, fees: Reservations are required and accepted at 877/444-6777 and www.reserveusa.com. The fee is $60–200 per night. Golden Age and Golden Access Passports are accepted. Cash or check only. Open late May–early September.

Directions: From Main Street in Frisco, take

Summit Boulevard/Highway 9 south for 3.1 miles. Turn left on Swan Mountain Road/ Summit High School Road. The gated entry is in three miles. The campground is 0.5 mile past the gate.

Contact: White River National Forest, 970/468-5400, www.fs.fed.us/whiteriver.

48 GOLD PARK

Scenic rating: 7

south of Minturn

BEST (

Gold Park is seven miles upstream of Blodgett. The long drive to get here deters many campers, but there seems to be a regular following. The campground can accommodate RVs, but it attracts mostly tent campers and families with young children. Situated in a pine forest next to Homestake Creek, every site has plenty of flat space for pitching pavilion-size tents, and there's no shortage of shade. It's possible to fish from the campground, but the fish are tiny. Anglers will have more luck driving downstream and working their way up to the campground or driving up to Homestake Reservoir. Several hiking trails begin a short drive away, including the Whitney Lake, Missouri Lakes, and Fancy Pass Trails, all of which explore the Holy Cross Wilderness. Four-wheeling is also a popular pastime. The Holy Cross Jeep Trail is one of the toughest roads in Colorado. Forest Route 704 is an easier road to the ghost town.

Campsites, facilities: There are 11 sites for tents and RVs up to 30 feet. Picnic tables, grills, and fire rings are provided. Vault toilets and drinking water are available. Leashed pets are permitted.

Reservations, fees: Reservations are not accepted. The fee is $12 per night (includes 10 people and two vehicles). Additional vehicles cost $5 per night. Golden Age and Golden Access Passports are accepted. Cash or check only. Open late May–September.

Directions: From Vail, take I-70 west for five miles to Exit 171. Go south on U.S. Highway 24. In 12.7 miles, turn right on Homestake Road/Forest Route 703. Continue seven miles to the campground entrance on the left. This is a wide gravel road with a lot of washboarding.

Contact: White River National Forest, 970/827-5715, www.fs.fed.us/r2/whiteriver/.

49 CAMP HALE MEMORIAL
🚶 🚵 💧 🏕 ♿ 🚐 ⛺

Scenic rating: 8

south of Minturn

During World War II, Eagle Park was the site of Camp Hale, the training grounds of the elite 10th Mountain Division, the only specialized mountain/ski soldiers in the United States Army. Up to 14,000 soldiers lived in this valley and trained in the surrounding mountains, developing mountaineering and cold weather survival skills that they used to battle the Germans in the Italian Alps. After the war, members of the 10th Mountain Division returned to Colorado and founded the first recreational ski resorts. Little remains of the base, but interpretive displays help visitors imagine life in this valley during the war. In the summer, the Forest Service offers interpretive programs on Saturday afternoons.

The campground is in a fir-spruce forest at the south end of the park. It offers expansive views of the valley and surrounding ridgelines. You could spend a whole day just watching the clouds go by, or go fishing on the Eagle River or hiking or mountain biking on the Colorado Trail. All of the sites are large and spaced about 100 feet apart. Sites 11, 14, 15, and 17–21 have the best views, but they are also more exposed. Sites 1–4, 7, 8, 10, 12, 13, and 16 are screened by lots of trees. The campground is usually full on weekends, but five sites are first-come, first-served.

Campsites, facilities: There are 21 sites for tents and RVs up to 60 feet. There are no hookups or pull-throughs. The facilities are wheelchair accessible. Picnic tables, grills, and fire rings are provided. Vault toilets and drinking water are available. Leashed pets are permitted.

Reservations, fees: Reservations are accepted at 887/444-6777 and www.reserveusa.com. The fee is $12 per night (includes 10 people and two vehicles). Additional vehicles cost $5 per night. The reservation fee is $9. Golden Age and Golden Access Passports are accepted. Cash or check only. Open late May–September.

Directions: From Vail, take I-70 west for five miles to Exit 171. Go south on U.S. Highway 24. In 16.6 miles, turn left at the Camp Hale Memorial sign. Turn left at the stone gate and drive 0.2 mile to the T intersection. Turn right on B Street and continue 1.2 miles to the fee station.

Contact: White River National Forest, 970/827-5715, www.fs.fed.us/r2/whiteriver/.

50 CAMP HALE EAST FORK
🚶 🚵 💧 🏕 ♿ ⛺

Scenic rating: 6

south of Minturn

This is a very private group campground, perfect for church groups, scout groups, and family reunions. The access road Forest Route 726 is also part of the Colorado Trail, which is open to hikers, bikers, and ATV riders. The campground is in a narrow valley beside the East Fork of the Eagle River, which is just a creek at this point. Campers can go fishing here or in Eagle Park, the site of Camp Hale, a World War II training base for the 10th Mountain Division. Rock climbing is also available on the east side of Eagle Park.

Campsites, facilities: This is a group site with dispersed tent camping for up to 200 people. The facilities are wheelchair accessible. Picnic tables, grills, and fire rings are provided.

Vault toilets and drinking water are available. Leashed pets are permitted.

Reservations, fees: Reservations are required and can be made at 887/444-6777 and www.reserveusa.com. The fee is $70–145 per night, depending on group size. Open late May–September.

Directions: From Vail, take I-70 west for five miles to Exit 171. Go south on U.S. Highway 24 for about 19 miles. After the South Fork bridge, turn left into a large gravel pullout. Forest Route 726 is at the end of the pullout (there is no sign). Drive north for three miles and then make a sharp left into the campground.

Contact: White River National Forest, 970/827-5715, www.fs.fed.us/r2/whiteriver/.

SOUTH CENTRAL MOUNTAINS

© SARAH RYAN

BEST CAMPGROUNDS

This is one of my favorite areas in Colorado. You can visit all the highlights in a week, or return every summer to enjoy the majestic mountains and friendly towns of central Colorado.

Leadville, aka "Cloud City," is a good place to begin your adventures. It has the dual distinction of being the highest town in the country (elevation 10,430 feet) and a historic mining district. Leadville has been slow to trade its mining past for resort status. It's smaller and more authentic than the resort towns of Summit County. The historic buildings of the main drag have been turned into locally owned hotels, restaurants, cafés, and gift shops. They're surrounded by gun-shot cottages, which are in turn surrounded by the Fryer Hill, Carbonate Hill, and Oro City mining districts. You can tour these areas by foot or bike on the 12-mile Mineral Belt Trail.

Leadville is an unparalleled destination for outdoor athletes. In addition to hosting the annual Leadville 100 endurance race, it's the perfect base camp for summiting Colorado's highest peaks, Mount Elbert and Mount Massive. Most peak-baggers stay at the Elbert Creek or Halfmoon campgrounds because of their proximity to the trail. After summiting, hikers can drive into town and reward themselves at the excellent Tennessee Pass Café.

Turquoise Lake is another big draw. At the northern base of Mount Massive, this 780-surface-acre reservoir has eight campgrounds around its shore, and many of them have amazing views of the Sawatch Range. The boating and fishing are also excellent, and it's a short drive to shopping and dining in Leadville.

Twin Lakes Reservoir is south of Leadville at the base of Mount Elbert. There are three campgrounds on the lakeshore and two on the road to Independence Pass, an unforgettable drive. The Colorado Trail circumnavigates the lake, providing hiking and mountain biking opportunities.

South of Twin Lakes, the Arkansas River enters a wide valley with the Collegiate Peaks on the west side and the hills of San Isabel National Forest on the east side. This is Chaffee County, and the sight of this arid valley enclosed by the snowy peaks of the Sawatch Range explains the county's clever slogan: "Now *this* is Colorado."

For hiking, biking, fishing, and soaking in hot springs, head to the mountains and the numerous scenic campgrounds. For Colorado's best whitewater, head for the river. The state park system operates three campgrounds along this stretch of river (Ruby Mountain's my favorite). You can sign up for a rafting trip in Buena Vista (pronounced Byoo-na Vista), Salida, or at any of the rafting companies along U.S. Highway 24.

Salida is home to the FIBArk Whitewater Race, a festival that attracts over 25,000 visitors annually. It also has some of the best eating in the central mountains. West of town, hikers and mountain bikers can hop on both the Colorado and Continental Divide Trails. East of town, they can take the 100-mile Rainbow Trail along the eastern flank of the Sangre de Cristos, one of Colorado's most stunning mountain ranges. From Salida to Cañon City, the Arkansas River continues its torturous trek east, culminating in the Class V rapids of the Royal Gorge.

South Park is the other half of this region. This expansive grassland is one of four intermountain valleys in Colorado. (The others are North Park, Middle Park, and the San Luis Valley.) It's enclosed by the Mosquito Range and Buffalo Peaks Wilderness to the west and the Tarryall Mountains and Lost Creek Wilderness to the east. The mining history of the park is preserved at the towns of Fairplay and Como.

The campgrounds in Pike National Forest on the west side of the park are just an hour or two from Denver but, with a few exceptions, they're rarely crowded. There's challenging hiking and four-wheeling along these slopes. On the east side of the park, the Lost Creek Wilderness is a gentler landscape of granite peaks and high meadows with a hundred miles of trails and numerous backpacking loops.

The majority of South Park's visitors head for Eleven Mile State Park. There are nine campgrounds on the shores of this vast reservoir, considered an angler's paradise, as long as you can handle the strong winds and intense sun. These campgrounds are best suited for RVs, with the exception of the hike-in/boat-in backcountry sites.

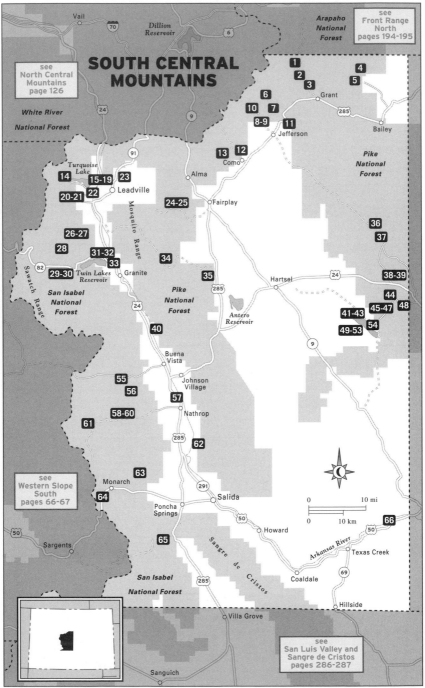

1 GENEVA PARK

🏠 🚐 ⛺

Scenic rating: 6

north of Grant

Geneva Park is a large loop in lodgepole pine forest on the quiet side of Guanella Pass. The park has a history of mining. In the 1850s, prospectors moved into the basin and worked at three nearby mines. Mining ceased by 1900, and no trace remains of the towns. The campsites here are 30–60 feet apart, and privacy is moderate. Geneva Creek is a short walk away, but fishing is poor and there are no trails near the campground. Sites 1–3 have views of the area around the pass.

Campsites, facilities: There are 26 sites for tents and RVs up to 20 feet. There are no hookups. Site 26 is pull-through. Picnic tables, grills, and fire rings are provided. Vault toilets and drinking water are available. Leashed pets are permitted.

Reservations, fees: Reservations are not accepted. The fee is $11 per night (includes one vehicle). Additional vehicles cost $5 per night. Golden Age and Golden Access Passports are accepted. Cash or check only. Open late May–early September.

Directions: From Grant, take County Road 62 north 6.8 miles. Turn left on Forest Route 119. The campground is on the left in 0.3 mile.

Contact: Pike National Forest, 303/275-5610, www.fs.fed.us/r2/psicc/.

2 BURNING BEAR

🚶 🚵 🏠 🚐 ⛺

Scenic rating: 6

north of Grant

Geneva Basin is a lovely, wide, green valley on the west side of Mount Evans Wilderness. Burning Bear is a small loop on the edge of the valley that blends into a thin forest of pine, spruce, and fir. The sites are 50–100 feet apart, and privacy

is moderate. Hikers can take the Abyss Trail up Scott Gomer Creek to Abyss Lake, at the base of the fourteeners Mount Evans and Mount Bierstadt. Bighorn sheep and mountain goats are frequently sighted in this area, which is notable as being one of the few areas of arctic tundra south of the Arctic Circle. Hikers can also make a loop by connecting Abyss Trail, Rosalie Trail, and Threemile Creek Trail. Mountain bikers can explore Bear Creek Trail.

Campsites, facilities: There are 13 sites for tents and RVs up to 20 feet. There are no hookups. Site 1 is pull-through. Picnic tables, grills, and fire rings are provided. Vault toilets and drinking water are available. Leashed pets are permitted.

Reservations, fees: Reservations are not accepted. The fee is $12 per night (includes one vehicle). Additional vehicles cost $5 per night. Golden Age and Golden Access Passports are accepted. Cash or check only. Open late May–early September.

Directions: From Grant, take County Road 62 north for 5.4 miles. Turn right into the campground.

Contact: Pike National Forest, 303/275-5610, www.fs.fed.us/r2/psicc/.

3 WHITESIDE

🎣 🏠 ⛺

Scenic rating: 5

north of Grant

Whiteside is a good stopover for tent campers traveling between Denver and Fairplay. It's convenient and cozy. There are five walk-in sites on the far side of Geneva Creek and two tent sites close to the parking lot. The campground is in a spruce-fir forest that provides shade and some privacy, although the sites are only about 25 feet apart. A horse trail wanders through the campground. Threemile Creek Trail begins a short distance up the road and climbs to the base of Tahana Mountain in the Mount Evans Wilderness. From there, hikers can make a loop by connecting Rosalie and Abyss Trails, or continue farther into the wilderness area to fourteeners Mount Evans and Mount Bierstadt.

Campsites, facilities: There are seven tent sites. Sites 2–4, 6, and 7 are walk-in. Picnic tables and fire rings are provided. Vault toilets are available. Leashed pets are permitted.

Reservations, fees: Reservations are not accepted. The fee is $11 per night (includes two vehicles). Additional vehicles cost $5 per night. Golden Age and Golden Access Passports are accepted. Cash or check only. Open late May–early September.

Directions: From Grant, take County Road 62 north for 2.4 miles and turn left into the campground.

Contact: Pike National Forest, 303/275-5610, www.fs.fed.us/r2/psicc/.

4 MERIDIAN

Scenic rating: 6

north of Bailey

Meridian is a dirt loop in a forest of ponderosa pine with scattered aspen. The campground has a slight slope and lots of sunshine. The sites are 50–100 feet apart. The campground is almost empty on weekdays, but it can fill up with locals on weekends. There is not a lot of privacy, but the sites accommodate multiple tents. Trail 604 begins nearby and climbs into the Mount Evans Wilderness area where it intersects Cub Creek Trail. The wilderness area is famous for the fourteeners Mount Evans and Mount Bierstadt and healthy populations of bighorn sheep and mountain goat.

Campsites, facilities: There are 18 sites for tents and RVs up to 20 feet. Picnic tables, grills, and fire rings are provided. Vault toilets and drinking water are available. Leashed pets are permitted.

Reservations, fees: Reservations are not accepted. The fee is $11 per night (includes 10 people and two vehicles). Additional vehicles

cost $5 per night. Golden Age and Golden Access Passports are accepted. Cash or check only. Open late May–early September.

Directions: From Bailey, take U.S. Highway 285 east about three miles and turn north on County Road 43. At 6.8 miles, stay right at the fork on County Road 47. The campground is on the left in 0.9 mile.

Contact: Pike National Forest, 303/275-5610, www.fs.fed.us/r2/psicc/.

5 DEER CREEK

Scenic rating: 6

north of Bailey

The only exceptional feature of the Deer Creek campground is its proximity to the Mount Evans Wilderness, which begins 1.5 miles away and is accessible via Trails 603 and 636. It is about six miles from the trailhead to Beartrack Lakes, a string of paternoster lakes created by glacial activity around the fourteener Mount Evans. The lakes are an excellent overnight destination. The campground is a small, quiet loop in an open forest of pine, spruce, fir, and aspen. The sites are 20–50 feet apart. Sites 3–5 and 10–12 are creekside.

Campsites, facilities: There are 13 sites for tents and RVs up to 20 feet. Picnic tables, grills, and fire rings are provided. Vault toilets and drinking water are available. Leashed pets are permitted.

Reservations, fees: Reservations are not accepted. The fee is $11 per night (includes 10 people and two vehicles). Additional vehicles cost $5 per night. Golden Age and Golden Access Passports are accepted. Cash or check only. Open late May–early September.

Directions: From Bailey, take U.S. Highway 285 east about three miles and turn north on County Road 43. At 6.8 miles, stay left at the fork. The campground is in another 1.3 miles on the left.

Contact: Pike National Forest, 303/275-5610, www.fs.fed.us/r2/psicc/.

6 HALL VALLEY

🏃 🚵 🐕 🚙 ⛺

Scenic rating: 8

west of Grant

This campground is in a scenic little valley with aspen groves and views of Handcart Peak. The rough road deters many campers, but it's a worthwhile destination. Most of the sites are in the spruce-fir forest beside the creek. They are private and shaded. Sites 3, 8, and 9 are in the meadow. Hikers and bikers can take the Gibson Lake Trail 2.5 miles to remote Gibson Lake, in the shadow of Whale Peak. Mountain bikers and ATV owners can also take Forest Route 121 to Webster Pass.

Campsites, facilities: There are nine sites for tents and RVs up to 20 feet. Picnic tables, grills, and fire rings are provided. Vault toilets and drinking water are available. Trash must be packed out. Leashed pets are permitted.

Reservations, fees: Reservations are not accepted. The fee is $12 per night (includes 10 people and two vehicles). Additional vehicles cost $5 per night. Golden Age and Golden Access Passports are accepted. Cash or check only. Open late May–early September.

Directions: From Grant, take U.S. Highway 285 west about three miles to County Road 60 and turn right. Continue north for 5.2 miles. The last half mile requires high clearance. The campground entrance is on the left.

Contact: Pike National Forest, 303/275-5610, www.fs.fed.us/r2/psicc/.

7 HANDCART

🏃 🚵 🏕 ⛺

Scenic rating: 7

west of Grant

Handcart is a shady, quiet tent campground on the banks of the Lake Fork of the South Platte River. Located in a mature spruce-fir forest, the campground offers privacy and solitude. The Gibson Lake Trail begins in the campground and climbs gradually for 2.5 miles to Gibson Lake in the cirque below Whale Peak. In the late 1800s, this area was home to mining towns and prospectors, but little remains of the old ghost towns. Four-wheelers and mountain bikers can take Forest Route 121 to Webster Pass. All of the sites are walk-ins, but sites 9 and 10 are close to the parking lot. Sites 1–3 and 6–8 are creekside. Sites 6–8 are the most attractive.

Campsites, facilities: There are 10 sites for tents. Picnic tables, grills, and fire rings are provided. Vault toilets and drinking water are available. Trash must be packed out. Leashed pets are permitted.

Reservations, fees: Reservations are not accepted. The fee is $12 per night (includes 10 people and two vehicles). Additional vehicles cost $5 per night. Golden Age and Golden Access Passports are accepted. Cash or check only. Open late May–early September.

Directions: From Grant, take U.S. Highway 285 west about three miles and head north on County Road 60 for 4.8 miles. The road is rough but does not require high clearance. The campground is on the left.

Contact: Pike National Forest, 303/275-5610, www.fs.fed.us/r2/psicc/.

8 LODGEPOLE

🏃 🚵 🎣 🐕 ♿ 🚙 ⛺

Scenic rating: 6

north of Jefferson

Lodgepole is in the Jefferson Creek Recreation Area, a popular weekend destination for anglers and families. Lodgepole is the least appealing of the three campgrounds on this road because it's farthest from the lake and the least scenic. The best feature is the Colorado Trail, which passes through the campground and continues west across the Continental Divide and down into Summit

County. The campground is a large loop in a coniferous forest surrounded by pine-covered hills and one rocky crag. The road separates the campground from the creek. Sites 2, 5, and 32–35 are near the road. The sites are 20–50 feet apart.

Campsites, facilities: There are 35 sites for tents and RVs up to 25 feet. There are no hookups. Sites 6, 8, and 27 are pull-through. Picnic tables, grills, and fire rings are provided. Vault toilets and drinking water are available. The facilities are wheelchair accessible. Leashed pets are permitted.

Reservations, fees: Reservations are accepted at 877/444-6777 and www.reserveusa.com. The fee is $10 per night (includes eight people and two vehicles). Additional vehicles cost $5 per night. Golden Age and Golden Access Passports are accepted. Cash or check only. Open late May–early September.

Directions: From Jefferson, take County Road 35 north for two miles. Turn right on County Road 37. The campground entrance is on the left in 2.5 miles.

Contact: Pike National Forest, 719/836-2031, www.fs.fed.us/r2/psicc/.

9 ASPEN

north of Jefferson

Scenic rating: 7

Aspen is the second campground in Jefferson Creek Recreation Area, a popular weekend destination for families and anglers. The campground is about two miles from Jefferson Lake, but fishing is available on the creek and in the beaver ponds. The Colorado Trail passes through the campground and offers hiking and mountain biking over the Continental Divide. The campground is a small loop in a spruce-fir forest with scattered aspen and wildflowers. Sites 1 and 2 are next to the road. Sites 4–6 are creekside. Sites 5–8 are the best sites; they're large and sheltered

by aspen. The campground is about half full midweek. Reservations are highly recommended on weekends.

Campsites, facilities: There are 12 sites for tents and RVs up to 25 feet. There are no hookups. Site 1 is pull-through. Picnic tables, grills, and fire rings are provided. Vault toilets and drinking water are available. The facilities are wheelchair accessible. Leashed pets are permitted.

Reservations, fees: Reservations are accepted at 877/444-6777 and www.reserveusa.com. The fee is $10 per night (includes eight people and two vehicles). Additional vehicles cost $5 per night. Golden Age and Golden Access Passports are accepted. Cash or check only. Open late May–early September.

Directions: From Jefferson, take County Road 35 north for two miles. Turn right on County Road 37. The campground entrance is on the right in 2.7 miles.

Contact: Pike National Forest, 719/836-2031, www.fs.fed.us/r2/psicc/.

10 JEFFERSON CREEK

north of Jefferson

Scenic rating: 6

Jefferson Creek is the last campground on the road to Jefferson Lake, a small reservoir with excellent trout fishing. The campground is about a mile from the lake. Fishing is also possible on the creek. Hiking and mountain biking are available on 3.5-mile West Jefferson Trail and on the Colorado Trail, which climbs to the Continental Divide. The campground is a small lollipop in a spruce-fir forest. The sites are about 30 feet apart, and privacy is poor. The campground is not as popular as Aspen, but reservations are recommended on weekends.

Campsites, facilities: There are 17 sites for tents and RVs up to 25 feet. There are no hookups. Site 12 is pull-through. Picnic tables, grills, and fire rings are provided. Vault toilets and drinking water are available. The facilities are wheelchair accessible. Leashed pets are permitted.

Reservations, fees: Reservations are accepted at 877/444-6777 and www.reserveusa.com. The fee is $10 per night (includes eight people and two vehicles). Additional vehicles cost $5 per night. Golden Age and Golden Access Passports are accepted. Cash or check only. Open late May–early September.

Directions: From Jefferson, take County Road 35 north for two miles. Turn right on County Road 37. The campground entrance is on the left in 3.6 miles.

Contact: Pike National Forest, 719/836-2031, www.fs.fed.us/r2/psicc/.

11 KENOSHA PASS

Scenic rating: 6

west of Grant

Location is the best feature of Kenosha Pass, "The Gateway to South Park." This road was an important route into the Rockies for the Utes and the miners. The Denver, South Park, and Pacific Railroad carried supplies and tourists to the early settlements in South Park. The railroad is gone, but the highway is still the fastest route from Denver into the southern Rockies. The campground is a convenient stopover, and it's popular with hikers and mountain bikers who want to explore the Colorado Trail, which passes through the campground and continues west across the Continental Divide into Summit County. The main campground is a figure eight in a spruce-fir forest. The sites are about 60 feet apart. Across the highway, an old picnic area has been turned into an additional campground. This loop is mostly forested with aspen, and the sites are much closer together. Twin Cone Road leads east from the campground to dispersed camping. Traffic is audible from both loops.

Campsites, facilities: There are 37 sites for tents and RVs up to 20 feet. There are no hookups. Sites 3 and 22 are pull-through. Picnic tables, grills, and fire rings are provided. Vault toilets and drinking water are available. Leashed pets are permitted.

Reservations, fees: Reservations are not accepted. The fee is $13 per night (includes 10 people and two vehicles). Additional vehicles cost $5 per night. Golden Age and Golden Access Passports are accepted. Cash or check only. Open late May–early September.

Directions: From Grant, take U.S. Highway 285 west about seven miles to Kenosha Pass. The campground entrance is on the right.

Contact: Pike National Forest, 303/275-5610, www.fs.fed.us/r2/psicc/.

12 MICHIGAN CREEK

Scenic rating: 8

north of Jefferson

This campground consists of a big meadow ringed by aspen and bordered by Michigan Creek on one side. Most sites have views of the Continental Divide to the west. The campground was recently renovated, and the facilities are very modern. Sites 6–12 sit in or around the meadow. Sites 6–10 are also sheltered by aspen. Sites 1–3 have the best shade. The sites are about 100 feet apart and fairly private. This campground is popular with mountain bikers and ATV owners. 4WD forest routes climb to Georgia Pass and panoramic views of South Park. Fishing is also available on Michigan Creek.

Campsites, facilities: There are 12 sites for tents and RVs up to 25 feet. There are no hookups. Sites 4 and 5 are pull-through. Picnic tables, grills, fire rings, and tent pads are provided. Vault toilets and drinking water are available. Leashed pets are permitted.

Reservations, fees: Reservations are accepted at 877/444-6777 and www.reserveusa.com.

The fee is $8 per night (includes eight people and two vehicles) or $16 per night for a double site (sites 1 and 8). Golden Age and Golden Access Passports are accepted. Cash or check only. Open late May–early September.

Directions: From Jefferson, take County Road 35 north for three miles. Turn right on County Road 54. The campground is on the left in three miles.

Contact: Pike National Forest, 719/836-2031, www.fs.fed.us/r2/psicc/.

13 SELKIRK

Scenic rating: 7

north of Como

Selkirk is an excellent destination campground for history buffs, mountain bikers, and four-wheelers. The campground is on the road to Boreas Pass, a former railroad route from South Park into Breckenridge. Nearby Como was a mining and railroad town and has become a self-reliant community of artists. Mountain bikers and ATV riders will enjoy the ride up to Boreas Pass and panoramic views of Summit County and South Park. Anglers can fish for trout on Tarryall Creek. The campground loop is in a mature spruce-fir forest. The sites are about 50 feet apart. Sites 7 and 8 are closest to the creek and the beaver pond. The campground is usually empty midweek and rarely fills up.

Campsites, facilities: There are 15 sites for tents and RVs up to 25 feet. There are no hookups. Picnic tables, grills, and fire rings are provided. Vault toilets and drinking water are available. Leashed pets are permitted.

Reservations, fees: Reservations are not accepted. The fee is $7 per night (includes eight people and two vehicles). Golden Age and Golden Access Passports are accepted. Cash or check only. Open late May–early September.

Directions: In Como, turn left on County Road 33. In 3.8 miles, turn right on Forest Route 33. In 3.5 miles, turn left on Forest Route 406. The campground is in 1.5 miles.

Contact: Pike National Forest, 719/836-2031, www.fs.fed.us/r2/psicc/.

14 MAY QUEEN

Scenic rating: 9

Turquoise Lake

BEST (

May Queen is the only campground at the west end of Turquoise Lake and it is truly special. The views are as spectacular as on the east side, but the bedlam is missing. This campground also has the best access to the hiking opportunities in the Holy Cross and Mount Massive wilderness areas as well as the Colorado Trail, which passes by the campground entrance. Four-wheelers and ATV riders enjoy driving up Hagerman Pass, but ATVs cannot unload in the campground due to road restrictions (which keeps the campground very quiet). Canoes and kayaks can be carried down to the lake. The nearest boat ramp is the Matchless Ramp, about six miles away. (For more information on Turquoise Lake and activities, see the Belle of Colorado listing in this chapter.)

There are 12 walk-in tent sites. Most of them are widely distributed away from the road in a coniferous forest, but sites 4, 6, and 21–23 are too close to the road and lack privacy. The following tent and RV sites lack trees but they have fantastic views: 10, 12, 13, 15, 17, and 22. Sites 21–23 are close to the lake.

Campsites, facilities: There are 17 sites for tents and RVs up to 32 feet and 12 walk-in tent sites. There are no hookups. Sites 10–17, 19, 20, and 22 are pull-through. Picnic tables, grills, and fire rings are provided. Tent pads are provided at sites 10–13, 16, 17, 19, 20, and 22. Flush toilets and drinking water are available. Facilities are wheelchair-accessible. Leashed pets are permitted.

Reservations, fees: Reservations are accepted at 887/444-6777 and www.reserveusa.com. The fee is $14 per night (includes 10 people and 2 vehicles). Additional vehicles cost $5 per night. The reservation fee is $9. Golden Age and Golden Access Passports accepted. Cash or check only. Open Memorial Day–Labor Day.

Directions: In Leadville, from the intersection of U.S. Highway 24 and 6th Street, drive south on 6th Street. Turn right on McWethy Road/County Road 4 and follow this road for 1 mile. Turn right on County Road 9 (unmarked) and in 1.5 miles turn left on another unmarked road. In 0.5 mile turn right on Forest Route 104. In 7.5 miles, turn left at the May Queen sign and continue downhill a half mile to the fee station.

Contact: Pike and San Isabel National Forest, 719/486-0749, www.fs.fed.us/r2/psicc/.

15 BELLE OF COLORADO

🥾 🚲 🛶 🏊 🚗 🐕 ⛰

Scenic rating: 8

on Turquoise Lake

BEST (

Turquoise Lake is a 780-surface-acre reservoir on the Lake Fork of the Arkansas River. The setting is absolutely spectacular. On the west half of the lake, the shores climb steeply to the Continental Divide. On the east half, the land rises gently towards Leadville, a National Historic Landmark District. To the south, the tallest peaks in Colorado, Mount Massive and Mount Elbert, tower over the valley. They are inside the Mount Massive Wilderness area, and trails on the north side of the lake head into the Holy Cross Wilderness.

Turquoise Lake has it all: fishing, boating, swimming, water sports, hiking, mountain biking, fourteeners, and four-wheeling. The lake is stocked with rainbow trout and kokanee salmon and contains brown, cutthroat, brook, and lake trout. There are a few sandy beaches for frigid swimming and three boat ramps. The Turquoise Lake Trail, which circles the lake, is accessible from every campground and is popular with hikers, bikers, horseback riders, and even strollers (but it's not paved). The Colorado Trail passes within a mile of the inlet. The Hagerman Pass Road is a major four-wheeling and ATV destination, and it crosses the Continental Divide Trail. There is enough to do to fill a whole summer, but be warned—it's no secret. The eight campgrounds are busy (and packed on the weekends) from late June–August. If you want privacy, stay away. If you don't mind the crowds, then bring the family, a hammock, and your fishing pole.

Belle of Colorado is the first campground on the east side and my personal favorite. It's the smallest and quietest campground on the lake, and every campsite is a short walk away from the water. It's also one of the only first-come, first-served campgrounds, so you can show up on Friday and still bag a site. Like all of the other campgrounds (except May Queen), it's in a lodgepole pine forest that affords lots of shade and glimpses of shimmering water, but not heaps of privacy. Campers can choose between proximity to their cars and proximity to the lake. Sites 1, 6, 8, 9, 13, 18, and 19 are close to the road. Sites 2–4, 7, 11, 15, 16, and 17 are close to the water.

Campsites, facilities: There are 19 walk-in sites for tents. Picnic tables, grills, and fire rings are provided. Flush toilets and drinking water are available. Leashed pets are permitted.

Reservations, fees: Reservations are not accepted. The fee is $14 per night (includes 10 people and two vehicles). Additional vehicles cost $5 per night. Golden Age and Golden Access Passports are accepted. Cash or check only. Open Memorial Day–Labor Day.

Directions: In Leadville, from the intersection of U.S. Highway 24 and 6th Street, drive south on 6th Street. Turn right on McWethy Road/County Road 4 and follow this road for one mile. Turn right on County Road 9 (unmarked) and in 1.5 miles turn left on another unmarked road. In 0.5 mile, turn right on Forest Route 104. In 0.1 mile, turn left at the Belle of Colorado sign.

Contact: Pike and San Isabel National Forest, 719/486-0749, www.fs.fed.us/r2/psicc/.

16 FATHER DYER

Scenic rating: 7

on Turquoise Lake

Father Dyer is upslope of popular Baby Doe. It's neither as scenic nor appealing as Baby Doe, but it's much quieter. It's a fairly flat campground in a lodgepole pine forest, which provides plenty of shade. The sites are 20–50 feet apart, and most of them are very close to the campground road. The following sites are removed from the road and more private: 6, 10, 11, 14, 16, 17, 21, 22, and 25. There is a footpath to the lake, so fishing and swimming are accessible, but it's a little too far to comfortably carry a canoe or kayak. (For more information on Turquoise Lake, see the Belle of Colorado listing earlier in this chapter.)

Campsites, facilities: There are 25 sites for tents and RVs up to 32 feet. There are no hookups. Sites 2, 8, 11, 12, 16, and 26 are pull-through. Picnic tables, grills, and fire rings are provided. Flush toilets and drinking water are available. The Tabor Boat Ramp is a half mile away. Leashed pets are permitted.

Reservations, fees: Reservations are accepted at 887/444-6777 and www.reserveusa.com. The fee is $14 per night (includes 10 people and two vehicles). Additional vehicles cost $5 per night. The reservation fee is $9. Golden Age and Golden Access Passports are accepted. Cash or check only. Open Memorial Day–Labor Day.

Directions: In Leadville, from the intersection of U.S. Highway 24 and 6th Street, drive south on 6th Street. Turn right on McWethy Road/County Road 4 and follow this road for one mile. Turn right on County Road 9

(unmarked) and in 1.5 miles turn left on another unmarked road. In 0.5 mile, turn right on Forest Route 104. In 0.7 mile, turn left at the Baby Doe sign and in 0.1 mile turn right into the campground.

Contact: Pike and San Isabel National Forest, 719/486-0749, www.fs.fed.us/r2/psicc/.

17 BABY DOE

Scenic rating: 7

on Turquoise Lake

Baby Doe is the hub of the activity at Turquoise Lake. One camp host, describing the weekend scene, called it "bedlam." The campground is so popular because it has a sandy beach that's easily accessible from all of the sites. There are two loops in a lodgepole pine forest, which provides ample shade. The bottom loop (sites 1–27) is closer to the lake, and sites 4, 6, 8, 10, 11, and 14 are just a stone's throw from the beach. The top loop (sites 28–50) is terraced into three levels which offer glimpses of water through the trees. If you are visiting on the weekend, reservations are highly recommended. (For more information on Turquoise Lake and activities in the area, see the Belle of Colorado listing earlier in this chapter.)

Campsites, facilities: There are 50 sites for tents and RVs up to 32 feet. There are no hookups. Site 24 is pull-through. Picnic tables, grills, and fire rings are provided. Tent pads are provided at sites 4, 7, 11, 28, and 41. Flush toilets and drinking water are available. The Tabor Boat Ramp is a mile away. Facilities are wheelchair accessible. Leashed pets are permitted.

Reservations, fees: Reservations are accepted at 887/444-6777 and www.reserveusa.com. The fee is $14 per night (includes 10 people and two vehicles). Additional vehicles cost $5 per night. The reservation fee is $9. Golden Age and Golden Access Passports are accepted. Cash or check only. Open Memorial Day–Labor Day.

Directions: In Leadville, from the intersection of U.S. Highway 24 and 6th Street, drive south on 6th Street. Turn right on McWethy Road/County Road 4 and follow this road for one mile. Turn right on County Road 9 (unmarked) and in 1.5 miles turn left on another unmarked road. In 0.5 mile, turn right on Forest Route 104. In 0.7 mile, turn left at the Baby Doe sign and continue downhill a half mile to the fee station.

Contact: Pike and San Isabel National Forest, 719/486-0749, www.fs.fed.us/r2/psicc/.

18 TABOR

Scenic rating: 6

on Turquoise Lake

Tabor is mainly a boating and overflow campground, but it looks more like a parking lot than a campground. It's busy during Leadville Boom Days in August, but otherwise there is very little traffic. The campsites are around the edge of two large parking lots. Sites 1–8 are on a narrow strip of land between the upper parking lot and the road. Sites 9 and 10 are on the opposite side of this parking lot and are quieter. Sites 11–15 are RV sites. They are numbered on the fence along the lower edge of the bottom parking lot. They have stairs down to the rocky beach, but there are no flat sites for tents. The campground is adjacent to the Lady of the Lake picnic area. (For more information on Turquoise Lake, see the Belle of Colorado listing earlier in this chapter.)

Campsites, facilities: There are 20 sites for tents and RVs up to 37 feet. There are no hookups or pull-throughs. Picnic tables, grills, and fire rings are provided at sites 1–10. Flush toilets, drinking water, a boat ramp, and picnic area are available. The facilities are wheelchair accessible. Leashed pets are permitted.

Reservations, fees: Reservations are not accepted. The fee is $14 per night (includes 10 people and two vehicles). Additional vehicles cost $5 per night. Golden Age and Golden Access Passports are accepted. Cash or check only. Open Memorial Day–Labor Day.

Directions: In Leadville, from the intersection of U.S. Highway 24 and 6th Street, drive south on 6th Street. Turn right on McWethy Road/County Road 4 and follow this road for one mile. Turn right on County Road 9 (unmarked) and in 1.5 miles turn left on another unmarked road. In 0.5 mile, turn right on Forest Route 104. In 1.2 miles, turn left at the Tabor Boat Ramp sign and in 0.1 mile turn right into the campground.

Contact: Pike and San Isabel National Forest, 719/486-0749, www.fs.fed.us/r2/psicc/.

19 PRINTER BOY

Scenic rating: 7

on Turquoise Lake

Printer Boy is a favorite location for family reunions. Like the other Turquoise Lake campgrounds, it's in a hilly lodgepole pine forest, but it's about a two-mile drive to the water. This campground can accommodate four groups at a time. The hills help separate the groups, and the recreational and cooking facilities are excellent. Nearby activities will keep every group member happy. There is a hiking and mountain biking trail around the lake. More trails access the Mount Massive and Holy Cross wilderness areas, and ambitious hikers can try several nearby fourteeners. There are three boat ramps on the lake, which contains kokanee salmon and rainbow, brown, and lake trout. History buffs and shoppers will love Leadville, a National Historic Landmark District. (For more information on Turquoise Lake and nearby activities, see the Belle of Colorado listing earlier in this chapter.)

Campsites, facilities: There are four group sites with walk-in tent camping and parking areas for RVs up to 32 feet. There are no hookups or pull-throughs. Picnic tables, grills, and fire rings are provided. Flush toilets, drinking water, volleyball, softball, horseshoe pits, and a community cook house and picnic area are available. Leashed pets are permitted.

Reservations, fees: Reservations are required and are accepted at 887/444-6777 and www.reserveusa.com. The fee is $50–100 depending on group size. The sites can accommodate up to 75 people. The reservation fee is $9. Open Memorial Day–Labor Day.

Directions: In Leadville, from the intersection of U.S. Highway 24 and 6th Street, drive south on 6th Street. Turn right on McWethy Road/County Road 4 and follow this road for 1 mile. Turn right on County Road 9 (unmarked) and in 1.5 miles turn left on another unmarked road. In 0.5 mile turn right on Forest Route 104. In 3 miles turn right into the campground.

Contact: Pike and San Isabel National Forest, 719/486-0749, www.fs.fed.us/r2/psicc/.

20 SILVER DOLLAR

🚶 🚴 🏊 🛶 🚤 🐕 🚗 ⛺

Scenic rating: 7

on Turquoise Lake

Like almost all of the Turquoise Lake campgrounds, Silver Dollar sprawls through a lodgepole pine forest on the hilly shores of the lake. Unlike the other campgrounds, the narrow road and short spurs deter many RV drivers, so this campground tends to be quieter than the campgrounds to the north. Most sites are near the road, but they are grouped in threes and fours, so it doesn't feel like you're surrounded. As a result, these sites feel more private than at many of the other campgrounds. Sites 3, 4, and 13 have the most privacy. A foot trail to the lake begins next to site 18. (For more information on Turquoise Lake, see the Belle of Colorado listing earlier in this chapter.)

Campsites, facilities: There are 43 sites for tents and RVs up to 22 feet. There are no hookups or pull-throughs. Picnic tables, grills, and fire rings are provided. Tents pads are provided at sites 1, 2, 8, 13–16, 24, 27, 33, 37, 40, 42, and 43. Flush toilets, drinking water, a boat ramp, and picnic area are available. Leashed pets are permitted.

Reservations, fees: Reservations are accepted at 887/444-6777 and www.reserveusa.com. The fee is $14 per night (includes 10 people and two vehicles). Additional vehicles cost $5 per night. The reservation fee is $9. Golden Age and Golden Access Passports are accepted. Cash or check only. Open late June–Labor Day.

Directions: In Leadville, from the intersection of U.S. Highway 24 and 6th Street, drive south on 6th Street. Turn right on McWethy Road/County Road 4 and follow this road for one mile. Turn right on County Road 9 (unmarked) and in 1.5 miles turn left on another unmarked road. In a half mile, turn left on Forest Route 104. In 1.5 miles, turn right at the Matchless Boat Ramp sign. The fee station is straight ahead in 0.7 mile. Loop B is on the left, and Loop A is on the right.

Contact: Pike and San Isabel National Forest, 719/486-0749, www.fs.fed.us/r2/psicc/.

21 MOLLY BROWN

🚶 🚴 🏊 🛶 🚤 🐕 ♿ 🚗 ⛺

Scenic rating: 7

on Turquoise Lake

Like almost all of the Turquoise Lake campgrounds, Molly Brown sprawls through a lodgepole pine forest on the hilly shores of the lake. The sites are 50–100 feet apart, and most of them are close to the road. There are two paved loops. Loop A (sites 27–49) does not have water access so campers have to walk to Loop B to reach the shore. Sites 35–38, 41, and 44 are on the outside of the loop and have the most privacy. In Loop B, sites 2–16 are on the bottom of the loop and have views of the water. Site 4, 6, 8, 10, 12, and 13 are separated from the shore by a few trees. These are very popular sites and usually require reservations. The Turquoise Lake Trail, which circles the lake, is accessible to hikers and bikers. Anglers can fish from the beach, carry boats down to the water, or drive 1.5 miles to the Matchless Boat Ramp. (For more information on Turquoise Lake, see the Belle of Colorado listing earlier in this chapter.)

Campsites, facilities: There are 49 sites for tents and RVs up to 32 feet. There are no hookups or pull-throughs. Picnic tables, grills, and fire rings are provided. Flush toilets, drinking water, and a dump station are available. Facilities are wheelchair accessible. Leashed pets are permitted.

Reservations, fees: Reservations are accepted at 887/444-6777 and www.reserveusa.com. The fee is $14 per night (includes 10 people and vehicles). Additional vehicles cost $5 per night. The reservation fee is $9. Golden Age and Golden Access Passports are accepted. Cash or check only. Open Memorial Day–Labor Day.

Directions: In Leadville, from the intersection of U.S. Highway 24 and 6th Street, drive south on 6th Street. Turn right on McWethy Road/County Road 4 and follow this road for one mile. Turn right on County Road 9 (unmarked) and in 1.5 miles turn left on another unmarked road. In a half mile, turn left on Forest Route 104. In 0.3 mile, turn right at the Molly Brown sign. The fee station is in a half mile. Loop A is on the left, and Loop B is on the right.

Contact: Pike and San Isabel National Forest, 719/486-0749, www.fs.fed.us/r2/psicc/.

22 SUGAR LOAFIN'

🚶 🚴 🏊 🛶 🚤 🐕 ♿ 🚐 ⛺

Scenic rating: 6

on Turquoise Lake

Turquoise Lake is a very popular Colorado destination, and Sugar Loafin' is the only campground where campers can stay for longer than two weeks. The campground is one mile from the dam and lake. (It's an easy walk if you're in

shape.) Hiking, biking, fishing, swimming, and boating are all available at the lake. The Holy Cross and Mount Massive wilderness areas are nearby, and four-wheeling is available at Hagerman Pass. Leadville is a National Historic Landmark District and great day trip for history buffs and shoppers. Visitors can also go for a ride on the Colorado and Southern Railroad, or hike or bike on the 12-mile Mineral Belt Trail.

The campground is in a thin coniferous forest. The facilities are excellent, but the sites are very close together. The following sites have unobstructed views of Mount Massive and Mount Elbert: 9, 10, 17, 18, 32, 33, 43–46. Sites 70–77 can accommodate tents and small RVs in a denser grove of trees. The best tent sites, A–R, are in a dense coniferous forest and slightly apart from the RV part of the campground.

Campsites, facilities: There are 71 sites for tents and RVs up to 45 feet and 27 sites for tents only. Full and partial hookups are available. Site 19 is wheelchair accessible. Picnic tables, grills, and fire rings are provided. Tent pads are available at sites A–R. Restrooms with flush toilets and showers, drinking water, dump stations, laundry facilities, a store, playground, propane, pet walk, and pay phones are available. There is also a recreation room with a fireplace, arcade games, and a pool table. Leashed pets are permitted but cannot be left alone.

Reservations, fees: Reservations are accepted at 719/486-1031 and www.leadville.com/sugarloafin. The tent fee is $24.45 per night for two people, and the RV fee is $29–30 per night for two people. Additional adults (over 12 years) cost $3 per night. Additional children (ages 4–12) cost $2 per night. Additional camping units and vehicles cost $6 per night. Good Sam, AAA, and senior citizen discounts are accepted. Open mid-May–late September.

Directions: In Leadville, from the intersection of U.S. Highway 24 and 6th Street, drive west on 6th Street. Turn right on McWethy Road/County Road 4. The campground is on the right in 2.7 miles.

Contact: Don and Edith Seppi, 719/486-1031, www.leadville.com/sugarloafin.

23 LEADVILLE HOSTEL

Scenic rating: 7

Leadville

Okay, it's not a campground, but so many campers stay at the Leadville Hostel that it deserves a listing. This is the place to stop for hikers on the Continental Divide and Colorado Trails who need a hot shower, laundry, and a movie night. Ultrarunners flock here for the Leadville 100, and every bed is booked when Ride the Rockies passes through town. Leadville is a high-altitude sports mecca, and the Leadville Hostel is the place to get advice on the area or a big pasta meal. The owner Wild Bill serves up inexpensive, very tasty dinners and breakfasts when the house is full. Trailhead shuttles are also available. From the hostel, hikers and bikers can explore the Mineral Belt Trail, a 12-mile loop through historic Leadville.

Campsites, facilities: Both dorm rooms and private rooms are available. Restrooms with flush toilets and showers, drinking water, laundry facilities, a community kitchen, recreation room, TV room, and Internet access are available. Leashed pets are permitted.

Reservations, fees: Reservations are accepted at 719/486-9334 and leadvillehostel@amigo.net. The fee is $15–30 per night. Credit cards are accepted. Open year-round.

Directions: From U.S. Highway 24 and 7th Street, turn east on 7th Street. The hostel is on the southwest corner in five blocks.

Contact: Leadville Hostel, 719/486-9334, www.leadvillehostel.com.

24 HORSESHOE

Scenic rating: 7

south of Fairplay

Fourmile Creek Road is a historic tour through a mining district that boomed in the late 1880s and went bust in the early 1900s. The 1.6-mile Limber Grove Trail connects Horseshoe and Fourmile campgrounds, and passes by a living pine that's over 1,500 years old. Mountain bikers can travel up Fourmile Creek Road to Leavick townsite and views of South Park and the Continental Divide. The campground loop is in a spruce-fir forest with abundant young aspen next to a small meadow and the creek. The sites are about 60 feet apart and a little less private than at Fourmile. Sites 1 and 2 have the best views. Sites 9–11 are walk-ins. Sites 18 and 19 are next to the meadow and have views of the road.

Campsites, facilities: There are 19 sites for tents and RVs up to 25 feet. There are no hookups. Site 5 is pull-through. Picnic tables, grills, and fire rings are provided. Vault toilets and drinking water are available. Trash must be packed out. Leashed pets are permitted.

Reservations, fees: Reservations are accepted at 877/444-6777 and www.reserveusa.com. The fee is $10 per night (includes eight people and two vehicles). Golden Age and Golden Access Passports are accepted. Cash or check only. Open early May–early October.

Directions: From Fairplay, take U.S. Highway 285 south for 1.2 miles. Turn right on County Road 18. The campground is on the left in 6.7 miles.

Contact: Pike National Forest, 719/836-2031, www.fs.fed.us/r2/psicc/.

25 FOURMILE

Scenic rating: 7

south of Fairplay

The road up Fourmile Creek to the Horseshoe Mine is an interesting historic tour of the mining area that served the Last Chance, Hilltop, and Dauntless Mines. The road has amazing views of the Continental Divide and South Park. The cirque below Horseshoe Mountain is an almost perfect half-circle. Mountain bikers can head up Fourmile Creek Road or take Forest Route 423 to the ghost town Sacramento. Hikers should stretch their legs on the 1.6-mile Limber Grove Trail. The trail passes by a living pine that's over 1,500 years old. Fishing is available on Fourmile Creek. The campground is in a spruce-fir forest in the shadow of Sheep Mountain. The sites are about 75 feet apart. This campground is rarely used, so privacy is excellent. Site 1 has the best views down the valley.

Campsites, facilities: There are 14 sites for tents and RVs up to 22 feet. There are no hookups. Picnic tables, grills, and fire rings are provided. Vault toilets and drinking water are available. Leashed pets are permitted.

Reservations, fees: Reservations are not accepted. The fee is $10 per night (includes eight people and two vehicles). Golden Age and Golden Access Passports are accepted. Cash or check only. Open early May–early October.

Directions: From Fairplay, take U.S. Highway 285 south for 1.2 miles. Turn right on County Road 18. The campground is on the right in 7.9 miles.

Contact: Pike National Forest, 719/836-2031, www.fs.fed.us/r2/psicc/.

26 HALFMOON EAST
🚶‍♂️ 🚴 🎣 🚐 🐴 🚙 ⛺

Scenic rating: 6

near Leadville

Halfmoon East has a group of regulars from southern Colorado who return every few weeks. Most of them are Golden Age pass holders, so it's a quiet campground. The Mount Elbert, Mount Massive, and Colorado Trails are nearby, but most of these campers just make the short hike to Emerald Lake, which is stocked with trout. Hand-powered and electric motor boats are allowed on the lake. The campground is in a coniferous forest beside Elbert Creek. All of the sites are just 10–30 feet from the lake. Sites 1 and 4 are

walk-ins. Site 1 is below the road and has the most privacy.

Campsites, facilities: There are six sites for tents and RVs up to 16 feet. There are no hookups or pull-throughs. Picnic tables, grills, and fire rings are provided. Vault toilets and drinking water are available. Leashed pets are permitted.

Reservations, fees: Reservations are not accepted. The fee is $11 per night (includes 10 people and two vehicles). Additional vehicles cost $5 per night. Golden Age and Golden Access Passports are accepted. Cash or check only. Open Memorial Day–Labor Day.

Directions: From U.S. Highway 24 and 6th Street in Leadville, take U.S. 24 south four miles. Turn right on Highway 300. In 0.8 mile, turn left on Halfmoon Road. In 1.2 miles, turn right on County Road 11. The campground is on the right in four miles. This dirt road has potholes and washboarding but does not require 4WD.

Contact: San Isabel National Forest, 719/486-0749, www.fs.fed.us/r2/psicc/.

27 HALFMOON WEST
🚶‍♂️ 🚴 🎣 🚐 🐴 🚙 ⛺

Scenic rating: 7

near Leadville

Like Elbert Creek, Halfmoon West is a quiet campground surrounded by excellent recreational opportunities, but it's barely used. The only busy time is in August during the Leadville 100 ultramarathon, when the campground is turned into a medical station. Halfmoon Road is the first climb, and any runners who can't pass a medical exam are not allowed to continue. The rest of the year, this campground is virtually unused. It contains three loops in a lodgepole pine forest. The sites are large and mostly far apart from each other. The first loop (sites 1–4) is very close to the road. The second loop (sites 5–11) affords more privacy. The back loop (sites 12–16) is on a hill above the rest of the campground. These are the most secluded sites in the campground.

Campsites, facilities: There are 16 sites for tents and RVs up to 16 feet. There are no hookups. Site 14 is pull-through. Picnic tables, grills, and fire rings are provided. Vault toilets and drinking water are available. Leashed pets are permitted.

Reservations, fees: Reservations are not accepted. The fee is $11 per night (includes 10 people and two vehicles). Additional vehicles cost $5 per night. Golden Age and Golden Access Passports are accepted. Cash or check only. Open Memorial Day–Labor Day.

Directions: From U.S. Highway 24 and 6th Street in Leadville, take U.S. 24 south four miles. Turn right on Highway 300. In 0.8 mile, turn left on Halfmoon Road. In 1.2 miles, turn right on County Road 11. The campground is on the left in 4.1 miles. This dirt road has potholes and washboarding but does not require 4WD.

Contact: San Isabel National Forest, 719/486-0749, www.fs.fed.us/r2/psicc/.

28 ELBERT CREEK
🚶 🚴 🏊 🛶 🐕 🚙 ⛺

Scenic rating: 6

near Leadville

BEST (

Elbert Creek is a quiet campground surrounded by outstanding recreational opportunities. Most of the campers at Elbert Creek are there to climb Colorado's highest peaks, Mount Elbert and Mount Massive. They go to bed early, get up early, hike all day, and leave the next day. A few campers stay long enough to enjoy mountain biking on the South Halfmoon Creek and Mount Champion Trails or fishing on Emerald Lake, which is stocked with trout. It's also a stopover on the Colorado Trail. The only time this campground is full is on holiday weekends. It parallels Elbert Creek, and the sites are large and spaced about 60–100 feet apart. The conif-

erous forest is not dense, but there is adequate privacy. Sites 1, 4, 7, 8, 10, 13, and 14 are next to the road. Sites 2, 5, 6, 9, 11, 12, and 15–17 are next to the creek. Site 17 is the only site with views of the Continental Divide.

Campsites, facilities: There are 17 sites for tents and RVs up to 16 feet. There are no hookups or pull-throughs. Picnic tables, grills, and fire rings are provided. Vault toilets and drinking water are available. Leashed pets are permitted.

Reservations, fees: Reservations are not accepted. The fee is $11 per night (includes 10 people and two vehicles). Additional vehicles cost $5 per night. Golden Age and Golden Access Passports are accepted. Cash or check only. Open Memorial Day–Labor Day.

Directions: From U.S. Highway 24 and 6th Street in Leadville, take U.S. 24 south four miles. Turn right on Highway 300. In 0.8 mile, turn left on Halfmoon Road. In 1.2 miles, turn right on County Road 11. The campground is on the right in five miles. This dirt road has potholes and washboarding but does not require 4WD.

Contact: San Isabel National Forest, 719/486-0749, www.fs.fed.us/r2/psicc/.

29 TWIN PEAKS
🚶 🚴 🐕 🚙 ⛺

Scenic rating: 6

south of Leadville

The Twin Peaks campground and neighboring Parry Peak campground are about five miles upstream from Twin Lakes and the associated mayhem. Travelers frequently use these campgrounds as a stopover on their way up Independence Pass, but they're not a bad selection for campers who want a quiet vacation near Twin Lakes. Twin Peaks contains two gravel loops between the highway and Lake Creek. The sites are 50–100 feet apart and are forested with pine and aspen. Sites 14, 16, 18, 19, 22, and 23 are next to the creek. Walk-in sites 34–37 are also next to the creek. Sites 6, 27, 29, and 31–33 are next to the road. Traffic can be quite heavy in July and August. From the Parry Peak campground, hikers and mountain bikers can take the Interlocken Loop Trail to Twin Lakes and the Colorado Trail. The Black Cloud trailhead is one mile upstream. This trail climbs 4.4 miles to the summit of Mount Elbert.

Campsites, facilities: There are 33 sites for tents and RVs up to 32 feet and four walk-in tent sites. There are no hookups or pull-throughs. Picnic tables, grills, and fire rings are provided. Vault toilets and drinking water are available. Leashed pets are permitted.

Reservations, fees: Reservations are not accepted. The fee is $12 per night (includes 10 people and two vehicles). Additional vehicles cost $5 per night. Golden Age and Golden Access Passports are accepted. Cash or check only. Open Memorial Day–Labor Day.

Directions: From the intersection of U.S. Highway 24 and 6th Street in Leadville, take U.S. 24 south for 15 miles. Turn right on Highway 82. In 10 miles, turn left into the campground.

Contact: Pike and San Isabel National Forest, 719/486-0749, www.fs.fed.us/r2/psicc/.

30 PARRY PEAK
🥾 🚲 🐕 🚐 ⛺

Scenic rating: 6

south of Leadville

Parry Peak is in a flat area below the highway, so there's less traffic noise than at Twin Peaks, but the sites are closer together. The campground has two loops on both sides of Lake Creek. The habitat is subalpine spruce and fir with some sagebrush. Sites 1, 4, 5, and 7 are very close to the road. Sites 16–26 are across the bridge in an aspen grove. They are great for both tent and RV camping. Sites 14, 16, and 24–26 are next to the creek. Sites 35 and 26 are walk-in tent sites. Hikers and mountain bikers can take the Interlocken Loop Trail to Twin Lakes and the Colorado Trail.

Campsites, facilities: There are 26 sites for tents and RVs up to 32 feet. There are no hookups. Sites 6, 8, and 20 are pull-through. Picnic tables, grills, and fire rings are provided. Tent pads are provided at sites 6, 8–11, 14, 16–18, and 22–24. Vault toilets and drinking water are available. Leashed pets are permitted.

Reservations, fees: Reservations are not accepted. The fee is $12 per night (includes 10 people and two vehicles). Additional vehicles cost $5 per night. Golden Age and Golden Access Passports are accepted. Cash or check only. Open Memorial Day–Labor Day.

Directions: From the intersection of U.S. Highway 24 and 6th Street in Leadville, take U.S. 24 south for 15 miles. Turn right on Highway 82. In nine miles, turn left into the campground.

Contact: Pike and San Isabel National Forest, 719/486-0749, www.fs.fed.us/r2/psicc/.

31 WHITE STAR
🥾 🚲 🏊 🚣 🎣 🐕 🚐 ⛺

Scenic rating: 8

south of Leadville

White Star is a huge campground, but it doesn't feel that big because the three loops are completely separated from each other. Most of the campers are tourists heading over Independence Pass and southern Colorado residents who enjoy fishing. The campground is full on the weekends with boaters and anglers. If you want a good campsite, make a reservation. (For more information on Twin Lakes, see the Dexter Point listing later in this chapter.)

Sage Loop (sites 1–28) is right on the water and offers outstanding views of Twin Peaks, Mount Hope, and Quail Mountain. It's an arid habitat of sagebrush and pine, and shade and privacy are in short supply. Sites 6, 7, 10, 12, and 16 are closest to the water. Site 3 has a lot of shade.

Ridge Loop (sites 30–45) feels cramped,

but there is more shade than in Sage Loop. It's a first-come, first-served area on a ridge overlooking Twin Lakes, but only a few sites (33, 35, 37, and 38) have good views. Sites 36–38 are walk-in. Sites 30, 31, 35, 37, 38, 43, and 44 have tent pads.

Valley Loop (sites 46–66) is farthest from the water and the least crowded of the three loops. The habitat is sagebrush with some pine and aspen in a shallow dell. Sites 46, 48, 51, and 60–66 are shaded. Sites 63–66 are walk-in tent sites. Site 54 has nice views across the Arkansas River valley.

Campsites, facilities: There are 66 sites for tents and RVs up to 32 feet. There are no hookups. Sites 25, 56, and 59 are pull-through. Picnic tables, grills, and fire rings are provided at all sites. Tent pads are provided in the Sage Loop and at some sites in the Ridge Loop. Vault toilets, drinking water, a dump station, and boat ramp are available. Leashed pets are permitted.

Reservations, fees: Reservations are accepted for the Sage and Valley Loops at 887/444-6777 and www.reserveusa.com. The fee is $12 per night (includes 10 people and two vehicles). Additional vehicles cost $5 per night. The reservation fee is $9. Golden Age and Golden Access Passports are accepted. Cash or check only. Open Memorial Day–late September.

Directions: From the intersection of U.S. Highway 24 and 6th Street in Leadville, take U.S. 24 south for 15 miles. Turn right on Highway 82. In 5.5 miles, turn left into the campground.

Contact: Pike and San Isabel National Forest, 719/486-0749, www.fs.fed.us/r2/psicc/.

32 LAKEVIEW

Scenic rating: 7

south of Leadville

Lakeview contains eight terraced loops on a steep hill overlooking Twin Lakes. Each loop has its own personality. This campground is popular with tent campers and pop-up owners. The Colorado Trail passes by the campground, and hikers and mountain bikers can take it to the Mount Elbert and Interlocken Loop Trails. Fishing, boating, and swimming are a mile away at Twin Lakes. (For more information on Twin Lakes, see the Dexter Point listing in this chapter.)

Loop A has 14 sites in a young, dense pine forest. It can be hard to find enough flat spots for several tents, but sites 7–9, 12, and 14 have tent pads. Site 10 has views of Twin Peaks. Loop B has five sites, all with views of Twin Peaks and Twin Lakes. Sites 2 and 5 have tent pads. Loop C has eight sites packed tightly together. There is no privacy or views. Sites 3 and 8 have tent pads. Loop D has seven cozy sites in an aspen grove. It's great for large group reservations. Sites 2 and 4–6 have good views. Loop E is my favorite. There are 13 roomy sites, most with excellent views. Site 9 is the best. Loop F is equally inviting but smaller and more private. Sites 3 and 6 have good views. Loop G is in a more mature pine forest. Sites 1, 2, 4, and 6 have good views. Loop H is similar to Loop G, but it's next to the Colorado and Mount Elbert Trails. Sites 3, 7, and 10 have good views.

Campsites, facilities: There are 59 sites for tents and RVs up to 32 feet. There are no hookups. Site C2 is pull-through. Picnic tables, grills, fire rings and some tent pads are provided. Vault toilets and drinking water are available. Leashed pets are permitted.

Reservations, fees: Reservations are accepted at 887/444-6777 and www.reserveusa.com. The fee is $12 per night (includes 10 people and two vehicles). Additional vehicles cost $5 per night. The reservation fee is $9. Golden Age and Golden Access Passports are accepted. Cash or check only. Open Memorial Day–Labor Day.

Directions: From the intersection of U.S. Highway 24 and 6th Street in Leadville, take U.S. 24 south for 15 miles. Turn right on Highway 82. In four miles, turn right on

County Road 24. In one mile, turn left into the campground.

Contact: Pike and San Isabel National Forest, 719/486-0749, www.fs.fed.us/r2/psicc/.

33 DEXTER POINT

🥾 🚵 🏊 ⛷ 🚣 🐕 🚙 🏕

Scenic rating: 5

south of Leadville

The Twin Lakes reservoir is at the foot of Mount Elbert in the Arkansas River valley. It's been a popular summer vacation destination since the 1860s, when a resort was built on the shore of Colorado's largest glaciated lake. In the late 1890s, a dam was built and the lake became a reservoir. Today, it's a summer destination for boaters, water-sports enthusiasts, anglers, hikers, and mountain bikers. The scenery and recreation are outstanding, but the weekend crowds can be overwhelming.

Dexter Point is a campground for boaters and desperate campers who can't find a spot anywhere else at the popular Twin Lakes reservoir. The campground is a large gravel parking lot surrounded by sagebrush. On the lakeside, there are 12 walk-in tent sites with picnic tables, grills, and fire rings. A few sites are on a hill overlooking the lake and have excellent views. Sites 12–24 are on the far side of the parking lot and do not have tables or tent sites. They are strictly for RV camping. Hikers and mountain bikers have access to the 12-mile Interlocken Loop around the lake.

Campsites, facilities: There are 12 sites for tents and 12 sites for RVs up to 37 feet. There are no hookups. Picnic tables, grills, and fire rings are provided at sites 1–12. Vault toilets, drinking water, and a boat ramp are available. Leashed pets are permitted.

Reservations, fees: Reservations are not accepted. The fee is $10 per night (includes 10 people and two vehicles). Additional vehicles cost $5 per night. Golden Age and Golden

Access Passports are accepted. Cash or check only. Open Memorial Day–Labor Day.

Directions: From the intersection of U.S. Highway 24 and 6th Street in Leadville, take U.S. 24 south for 15 miles. Turn right on Highway 82. In 2.3 miles, turn left into the campground.

Contact: Pike and San Isabel National Forest, 719/486-0749, www.fs.fed.us/r2/psicc/.

34 WESTON PASS

🥾 ⛷ 🐕 🚙 🏕

Scenic rating: 7

south of Fairplay

It's a long drive to Weston Pass, but this remote campground is a worthwhile destination for hikers interested in exploring the Buffalo Peaks Wilderness. With only 43,410 acres and no fourteeners, this wilderness area receives fewer visitors than the Collegiate Peaks Wilderness across the Arkansas River valley. The wilderness is dominated by the volcanic domes of East and West Buffalo Peak, which are surrounded by open meadows and gentle forests. From the campground, hikers can make a 12-mile loop by connecting the trails along Rich Creek and Rough and Tumbling Creek. Fishing is possible on the South Fork of South Platte and in the numerous beaver ponds along local creeks. The campground is a lollipop in a spruce-fir forest with a few scattered aspen. The sites are 30–60 feet apart. Sites 5, 7–9, and 12 overlook the creek and the road.

Campsites, facilities: There are 14 sites for tents and RVs up to 25 feet. There are no hookups. Picnic tables and grills are provided. Vault toilets and drinking water are available. Trash must be packed out. Leashed pets are permitted.

Reservations, fees: Reservations are not accepted. The fee is $10 per night (includes eight people and two vehicles). Golden Age and

Golden Access Passports are accepted. Cash or check only. Open late May–early October.
Directions: From Fairplay, take U.S. Highway 285 south for 4.7 miles. Turn right on County Road 5. The campground is on the left in 11.2 miles.
Contact: Pike National Forest, 719/836-2031, www.fs.fed.us/r2/psicc/.

35 BUFFALO SPRINGS
🐕 🚐 ⛺

Scenic rating: 7

south of Fairplay

Buffalo Springs is in a small, arid valley a few miles from the Buffalo Peaks Wilderness. The high domes of East and West Buffalo Peaks are impressive landmarks in South Park and the Arkansas River valley. The campground is a large loop in a mature forest of pine, spruce, and fir with scattered aspen. Many trees have been struck by the pine beetle epidemic and are slated for logging. The sites are about 100 feet apart, and privacy is fair. There are no trails near the campground, so it is mainly a stopover between Fairplay and Salida, or a destination for snowbirds.
Campsites, facilities: There are 18 sites for tents and RVs up to 25 feet. There are no hookups. Sites 7 and 18 are pull-through. Picnic tables, grills, and fire rings are provided. Vault toilets and drinking water are available. Leashed pets are permitted.
Reservations, fees: Reservations are accepted at 877/444-6777 and www.reserveusa.com. The fee is $10 per night (includes eight people and two vehicles). Golden Age and Golden Access Passports are accepted. Cash or check only. Open early May–early October.
Directions: From Fairplay, take U.S. Highway 285 south for 13 miles. Turn right on County Road 76/Forest Route 431. The campground is on the left in 0.8 mile.
Contact: Pike National Forest, 719/836-2031, www.fs.fed.us/r2/psicc/.

36 TWIN EAGLES
🚶 🐕 🚐 ⛺

Scenic rating: 6

north of Lake George

Twin Eagles sits beside the southwestern boundary of the Lost Creek Wilderness, a landscape of granite domes and buttresses. There are three mountain ranges in the wilderness: Tarryall Mountains, Kenosha Mountains, and Platte River Mountains. The mountains are covered in dense forests and open parks. Twin Eagles is an afterthought of a campground at the Twin Eagles trailhead. From this location, hikers heading into the wilderness have several options. They can complete a 16-mile loop around Lake Park, which has some of the best views in the wilderness, or they can head north on the Brookside-McCurdy Trail. This 31-mile trail traverses the entire length of the wilderness and crosses all three mountain ranges. It can be connected with several other trails to make a loop hike.
Campsites, facilities: There are four sites for tents and RVs up to 22 feet. There are no hookups. Picnic tables, grills, and fire rings are provided. Vault toilets and drinking water are available. Trash must be packed out. Leashed pets are permitted.
Reservations, fees: Reservations are not accepted. The fee is $7 per night (includes eight people and two vehicles). Additional vehicles cost $5 per night. Golden Age and Golden Access Passports are accepted. Cash or check only. Open May–October.
Directions: From Woodland Park, take U.S. Highway 24 west to Lake George. Go north on County Road 77 for 16.2 miles. Turn right at the trailhead sign.
Contact: Pike National Forest, 719/836-2031, www.fs.fed.us/r2/psicc/.

37 SPRUCE GROVE

Scenic rating: 7

north of Lake George

Spruce Grove is larger and nicer than nearby Twin Eagles. The campground sits on Tarryall Creek in a small park with granite outcroppings and views of South Tarryall Peak. The sites are in the willows beside the creek or in the meadow at the base of a granite cliff. There are scattered pine trees but not much shade. This is a high-use campground on weekends. Many visitors are there to explore the Lost Creek Wilderness, a 120,000-acre landscape of granite domes and spires with three mountain ranges and numerous high-altitude parks. From the Twin Eagles trailhead, hikers can complete a 16-mile loop around Lost Park or head north on the Brookside-McCurdy Trail, a 31-mile route that traverses the length of the wilderness. The area is home to a healthy bighorn population, as well as bear, mountain lion, and elk.

Campsites, facilities: There are 27 sites for tents and RVs up to 35 feet. Sites 3–10 are walk-ins. There are no hookups. Sites 22, 25, and 27 are pull-through. Picnic tables, grills, fire rings, and tent pads are provided. Vault toilets and drinking water are available. Leashed pets are permitted.

Reservations, fees: Reservations are not accepted. The fee is $10 per night (includes eight people and two vehicles). Additional vehicles cost $5 per night. Golden Age and Golden Access Passports are accepted. Cash or check only. Open May–October.

Directions: From Woodland Park, take U.S. Highway 24 west to Lake George. Go north on County Road 77 for 13.7 miles. Turn right at the campground sign and then right after the cattle guard.

Contact: Pike National Forest, 719/836-2031, www.fs.fed.us/r2/psicc/.

38 HAPPY MEADOWS

Scenic rating: 6

north of Lake George

Happy Meadows is a dirt bike and fishing destination north of the popular Eleven Mile Recreation Area. The campground is in a valley on the South Platte River, surrounded by forested ridgelines and rocky outcroppings. Privacy is fair to poor in this small campground. Sites 1, 2, 4, and 7–10 are creekside, and sites 7/8 and 9/10 are buddy sites. In addition to fishing on the river, anglers can drive to Eleven Mile for lake fishing or to the nearby Lost Creek Wilderness for backcountry hiking and climbing.

Campsites, facilities: There are 10 sites for tents and RVs up to 22 feet. There are no hookups. Picnic tables, grills, and fire rings are provided. Vault toilets and drinking water are available. Leashed pets are permitted.

Reservations, fees: Reservations are not accepted. The fee is $10 per night (includes eight people and two vehicles). Additional vehicles cost $5 per night. Golden Age and Golden Access Passports are accepted. Cash or check only. Open May–October.

Directions: From Woodland Park, take U.S. Highway 24 west to Lake George. Go north on County Road 77 for 1.3 miles. Turn right at the campground sign. The campground is on the right in one mile.

Contact: Pike National Forest, 719/836-2031, www.fs.fed.us/r2/psicc/.

39 ROUND MOUNTAIN

Scenic rating: 6

north of Lake George

Round Mountain is a stopover campground between Colorado Springs and South Park. The campground is on a low hill in a forest of scattered pines and grassland. The sites are about 100 feet apart around a large gravel loop. ATV owners make up most of the traffic at this campground. They can explore a network of Jeep trials in the Puma Hills and Tarryall Mountains. There are no hiking or biking trails nearby.

Campsites, facilities: There are 16 sites for tents and RVs up to 30 feet. There are no hookups. Picnic tables, grills, and fire rings are provided. Vault toilets and drinking water are available. Trash must be packed out. Leashed pets are permitted.

Reservations, fees: Reservations are accepted at 877/444-6777 and www.reserveusa.com. The fee is $10 per night (includes eight people and two vehicles). Additional vehicles cost $5 per night. Golden Age and Golden Access Passports are accepted. Cash or check only. Open May–October.

Directions: From Woodland Park, take U.S. Highway 24 west to Lake George. The campground is 5.7 miles west of Lake George on the north side of the highway.

Contact: Pike National Forest, 719/836-2031, www.fs.fed.us/r2/psicc/.

40 RAILROAD BRIDGE

Scenic rating: 7

north of Buena Vista

The Arkansas Headwaters Recreation Area stretches from the headwaters of the Arkansas River (at Fremont Pass and Tennessee Pass) all the way to Lake Pueblo State Park. It contains some of the finest whitewater in the state, as well as the Collegiate Peaks and portions of the Sawatch Range. From Leadville to Salida, the semiarid Arkansas River valley has endless vistas of fourteeners and fascinating weather patterns. Buena Vista and Salida, with their restaurants, art galleries, bars, and sports stores, are great towns to hang out in for a weekend.

Colorado State Parks manages six campgrounds on the river. Railroad Bridge is the first of the six. Located at the take-out for the Numbers, a classic Class IV white-water run, this campground is often swamped with commercial rafting companies. Railroad Bridge is also the put-in for the mellower Fractions/Frog Rock Run. Campers who are lucky enough to bag a walk-in site (sites 9–14) or sites 7 and 8 will be content. Sites 1–6 are a lot less appealing, lacking shade and privacy.

Campsites, facilities: There are 14 sites for tents and RVs up to 40 feet and six tent-only sites. Site 3 and the facilities are wheelchair accessible. There are no hookups. Sites 1, 2, and 4 are pull-through. Picnic tables, grills, fire rings, and tent pads are provided. Vault toilets, changing rooms, and a boat ramp are available. Trash must be packed out. Leashed pets are permitted.

Reservations, fees: Reservations are accepted (and recommended in July and August) at 800/678-2267 and www.parks.state.co.us. The fee is $12 per night (includes six people). There is an additional $8 reservation fee. Campers must also purchase a Daily Parks Pass ($2) or an Annual Parks Pass ($55). The Aspen Leaf Annual Pass is accepted. Open year-round.

Directions: In Buena Vista, drive east on Main Street. Turn left on Colorado Avenue. In 6.2 miles, turn left into the campground.

Contact: Arkansas Headwaters Recreation Area, 719/539-7289, www.parks.state.co.us.

41 ROCKY RIDGE

Scenic rating: 7

in Eleven Mile State Park

BEST (

Eleven Mile State Park is an angler's paradise surrounded by Pike National Forest. Located on the southern edge of South Park, the 3,400-surface-acre reservoir is fed by the South Platte River as well as Cross, Prudence, Union, Balm-of-Gilead, Simms, and Spring Creeks. These creeks drain Thirtynine Mile Mountain to the south and the Tarryall Mountains to the north. Every spot in the park offers scenic vistas of the lake, the grasslands, and the mountains, which seem to change constantly with time of day and season. The views and recreational opportunities make this park a year-round destination. The lake offers trophy fishing for kokanee salmon, cutthroat, rainbow trout, northern pike, and carp. Water sports include boating, windsurfing, and personal-watercraft riding (but swimming is prohibited). Winter visitors go ice fishing, ice-skating, ice boating, and cross-country skiing. The park also has five miles of trails open to hiking, biking, and riding, including a 1.4-mile interpretive trail. The climate is arid and subalpine, so trees are few and far between, clinging to spots of soil around boulders and outcroppings. There are nine campgrounds at the park. They all have excellent views but little shade and shelter.

Rocky Ridge is the largest and most developed of the campgrounds with five loops. Loop A (sites 1–10) is closest to the campers' services building. It has hookups but no views and mainly attracts RVs. Loop B (sites 11–26) also has electric hookups. It's in a low spot that obscures the other loops, but the lake is still visible. Loop C (sites 27–73) surrounds a granite outcropping. It has great views and some shade at sites 28, 33, 44, 47, 53, 56, and 73. Loop D (sites 74–99) is very flat. It has views but no shade or privacy. Loop E (sites 100–144) is also decked with large boulders and outcroppings, but it's farthest from the lake. The walk-in sites (117–120) are more private and have shade.

Campsites, facilities: There are 144 sites for tents and RVs up to 35 feet. Sites 117–120 are walk-in tent sites. Sites 1 and 2 and the facilities are wheelchair accessible. Sites 1–26 and 74–99 have electric hookups. Picnic tables, grills, and fire rings are provided. Restrooms with flush toilets and showers, vault toilets, drinking water, dump stations, and laundry

facilities are available. At North Shore campground, there is a marina with rentals and a boat ramp, a playground, and amphitheater. Leashed pets are permitted.

Reservations, fees: Reservations are accepted at 800/678-2267 and www.parks.state.co.us. The fee is $12–16 per night (includes six people and one camping unit). Vehicles must also have a Daily Parks Pass ($5) or Annual Parks Pass ($55). The Aspen Leaf Pass is accepted. Loop A is open year-round. The other loops are open from late spring to early fall.

Directions: From Lake George, take County Road 90 south for 4.1 miles. Turn left on County Road 92. The park office is in six miles. The campground is behind the park office.

Contact: Eleven Mile State Park, 719/748-3401, email: eleven.mile.park@state.co.us.

42 NORTH SHORE

Scenic rating: 7

in Eleven Mile State Park

North Shore is the campground for avid boaters and anglers. Located on the north shore, next to the marina, it has fantastic views of the lake and surrounding mountains but very little protection from the strong winds and intense sunshine that are typical of this park. There are almost no trees in this campground because the arid, subalpine climate does not provide adequate soil. Most of the sites are on a grassland interrupted by granite outcroppings. Loop A (sites 201–217) is next to the parking lot and is the least appealing. Loop B (sites 218–239) is a little hillier and rockier than the other loops. Loop C (sites 240–249) is on a rocky promontory overlooking the lake. Loop D and Loop E (sites 250–281) are surrounded by short, dry grass. (For more information on Eleven Mile State Park, see the Rocky Ridge listing in this chapter.)

Campsites, facilities: There are 81 sites for

tents and RVs up to 35 feet. Site 239 is wheel-chair accessible. There are no hookups. Sites 226, 228, 229, 240–243, 245, 251, 254, 256, 265, and 266 are pull-through. Picnic tables, grills, and fire rings are provided. Vault toilets and drinking water are available. A marina with a boat ramp and rentals, a playground, and amphitheater are also available. Restrooms with flush toilets and showers, dump stations, and laundry facilities are available at the park office. Leashed pets are permitted.

Reservations, fees: Reservations are accepted at 800/678-2267 and www.parks.state.co.us. The fee is $12 per night (includes six people and one camping unit). Vehicles must also have a Daily Parks Pass ($5) or Annual Parks Pass ($55). The Aspen Leaf Pass is accepted. Open year-round.

Directions: From Lake George, take County Road 90 south for 4.1 miles. Turn left on County Road 92. The park office is in six miles. The campground is across from the park office.

Contact: Eleven Mile State Park, 719/748-3401, email: eleven.mile.park@state.co.us.

43 STOLL MOUNTAIN
🏊 🛶 ❄ 🐾 🚐 ⛺

Scenic rating: 7

in Eleven Mile State Park

Stoll Mountain is on the north shore of Elevenmile Reservoir, about halfway between the park office and Spinney Mountain State Park. This is the smallest campground on the north shore, and for that reason, it's attractive to some campers and unattractive to others. It has two gravel loops close to the water, and the gentle shoreline is perfect for fishing from the shore and launching canoes. The views are amazing, but there is no privacy. The campground is in a short grass prairie with absolutely no trees, and the sites are just 15–30 feet apart. Mostly small RVs and pop-ups use this campground. Sites 305–308 and

319–325 are closest to the water. (For more information on Eleven Mile State Park, see the Rocky Ridge listing in this chapter.)

Campsites, facilities: There are 25 sites for tents and RVs up to 35 feet. There are no hookups. Sites 313, 316, and 320–323 are pull-through. Picnic tables, grills, and fire rings are provided. Sites 311, 313, and 315 have sun shelters. Vault toilets and drinking water are available. Restrooms with flush toilets and showers, dump stations, and laundry facilities are available at the park office. Leashed pets are permitted.

Reservations, fees: Reservations are accepted at 800/678-2267 and www.parks.state.co.us. The fee is $12 per night (includes six people and one camping unit). Vehicles must also have a Daily Parks Pass ($5) or Annual Parks Pass ($55). The Aspen Leaf Pass is accepted. Open year-round.

Directions: From Lake George, take County Road 90 south for 4.1 miles. Turn left on County Road 92. The park office is in six miles, and the campground is on the left 1.9 miles past the park office.

Contact: Eleven Mile State Park, 719/748-3401, email: eleven.mile.park@state.co.us.

44 RIVERSIDE
🏊 🐾 🚐 ⛺

Scenic rating: 6

in Eleven Mile Canyon Recreation Area

Eleven Mile Canyon is a surprising find in the gentle rolling hills east of South Park. From Elevenmile Reservoir to the town of Lake George, the South Platte River descends 500 feet, carving a narrow, wild canyon out of Pikes Peak granite. The steep walls, huge boulders, and cascading river are a dramatic sight, and when the water is high enough, anglers will find good fishing along the banks.

Riverside is the first of four campgrounds in the canyon. Fishing access is excellent, but like all of these campgrounds, Riverside is squeezed into a narrow area between the canyon walls and the river, so the sites are close to each other and the road. The RV sites in the meadow have minimal privacy. Tent campers will be pleasantly surprised, however, by walk-in sites located among pine trees on a slight hill.

Campsites, facilities: There are 19 sites for tents and RVs up to 25 feet. Sites 2–6 and 14–19 are walk-in. There are no hookups. Sites 10 and 13 are pull-through. Picnic tables, grills, and fire rings are provided. Vault toilets and drinking water are available. Leashed pets are permitted.

Reservations, fees: Reservations are accepted at 877/444-6777 and www.reserveusa.com. The fee is $10 per night (includes eight people and two vehicles). Additional vehicles cost $5 per night. Golden Age and Golden Access Passports are accepted. Cash or check only. Open May–October.

Directions: From Woodland Park, take U.S. Highway 24 west to Lake George. Go south on County Road 96. The fee station is in one mile. The campground is on the left one mile after the station.

Contact: Pike National Forest, 719/836-2031, www.fs.fed.us/r2/psicc/.

45 SPRINGER GULCH

Scenic rating: 7

in Eleven Mile Canyon Recreation Area

There are four campgrounds in Elevenmile Canyon. The second, Springer Gulch, is farthest from the river, but it's also very scenic. Sites 1–3 are near the road and lack shade, but the other sites are in a narrow gulch decked with pine trees and huge granite boulders. It's a great place for rock scrambling, and it has more shade than the other campgrounds. Sites 7–10, at the back of the campground, are the most appealing. (For more information on Eleven Mile Canyon, see the Riverside listing in this chapter.)

Campsites, facilities: There are 15 sites for tents and RVs up to 25 feet. There are no hookups. Picnic tables, grills, and fire rings are provided. Vault toilets and drinking water are available. Leashed pets are permitted.

Reservations, fees: Reservations are accepted at 877/444-6777 and www.reserveusa.com. The fee is $10 per night (includes eight people and two vehicles). Additional vehicles cost $5 per night. Golden Age and Golden Access Passports are accepted. Cash or check only. Open May–October.

Directions: From Woodland Park, take U.S. Highway 24 west to Lake George. Go south on County Road 96. The fee station is in one mile. The campground is on the right 5.5 miles after the station.

Contact: Pike National Forest, 719/836-2031, www.fs.fed.us/r2/psicc/.

46 COVE

Scenic rating: 6

in Eleven Mile Canyon Recreation Area

The third campground in Eleven Mile Canyon, Cove, is small and sweet. Set in a slight widening of the canyon, Cove has four riverside sites. Site 1 is a walk-in with privacy and the best river access. Sites 3 and 4 are located next to one of the granite outcroppings that characterize the canyon and are screened by trees and boulders. Site 2 is closest to the road and the least appealing. Because of its size, this campground is very popular, and reservations are highly recommended. (For more information on Eleven Mile Canyon, see the Riverside listing in this chapter.)

Campsites, facilities: There are four sites for tents and RVs up to 16 feet. There are no hookups. Picnic tables, grills, and fire rings are provided. Vault toilets and drinking water are available. Leashed pets are permitted.

Reservations, fees: Reservations are accepted at 877/444-6777 and www.reserveusa.com.

The fee is $10 per night (includes eight people and two vehicles). Additional vehicles cost $5 per night. Golden Age and Golden Access Passports are accepted. Cash or check only. Open May–October.

Directions: From Woodland Park, take U.S. Highway 24 west to Lake George. Go south on County Road 96. The fee station is in one mile. The campground is on the right 8.1 miles after the station.

Contact: Pike National Forest, 719/836-2031, www.fs.fed.us/r2/psicc/.

47 SPILLWAY

Scenic rating: 7

in Eleven Mile Canyon Recreation Area

Spillway is the last and largest campground in Eleven Mile Canyon. The scenery is dramatic. It includes the dam, surrounded by tall granite cliffs, and the boulders and outcroppings that form the mouth of the canyon. A half-mile trail climbs steeply to an overlook with panoramic views of the reservoir and the Tarryall Mountains. The sites are fairly close together, and the campground is usually busy. Sites 3–6 and 11–13 are walk-ins. Sites 13 and 14 have enviable views of the river. Sites 16–18, 20, 22, and 24 are also close to the water. (For more information on Eleven Mile Canyon, see the Riverside listing in this chapter.)

Campsites, facilities: There are 24 sites for tents and RVs up to 25 feet. There are no hookups. Sites 17–18, 20, 22, and 24 are pull-through. Picnic tables, grills, and fire rings are provided. Vault toilets, drinking water, and an amphitheater are available. Leashed pets are permitted.

Reservations, fees: Reservations are accepted at 877/444-6777 and www.reserveusa.com. The fee is $10 per night (includes eight people and two vehicles). Additional vehicles cost $5 per night. Golden Age and Golden Access

Passports are accepted. Cash or check only. Open May–October.

Directions: From Woodland Park, take U.S. Highway 24 west to Lake George. Go south on County Road 96. The fee station is in one mile. The campground is on the right 8.4 miles after the station.

Contact: Pike National Forest, 719/836-2031, www.fs.fed.us/r2/psicc/.

48 BLUE MOUNTAIN

Scenic rating: 6

in Eleven Mile Canyon Recreation Area

Blue Mountain is a small, quiet campground slightly removed from the tumult of Eleven Mile Canyon and Eleven Mile State Park. The campground is in a dense pine forest on a slightly rolling landscape. Sites 1, 10, and 19–21 have nice views of the surrounding valley and the ridgelines of the Tarryall Mountains to the north. The Hard Rock Trail leads from the campground to a canyon overlook. Fishing is a short drive away in the canyon and at the state park. Campers also take day trips to the mining museums and casinos of Cripple Creek and Victor. Florissant Fossil Beds National Monument is also nearby. Visitors can see the fossilized remains of plants, insects, and small mammals preserved in ash that fell on the ancient lake bed. The ash probably came from the Thirtynine Mile volcanic field at the southern end of South Park. Although quiet midweek, this campground usually fills up by Friday night.

Campsites, facilities: There are 21 sites for tents and RVs up to 35 feet. There are no hookups. Sites 2 and 19 are pull-through. Picnic tables, grills, and fire rings are provided. Vault toilets and drinking water are available. Leashed pets are permitted.

Reservations, fees: Reservations are accepted at 877/444-6777 and www.reserveusa.com. The fee is $10 per night (includes eight people and two vehicles). Additional vehicles cost $5 per night. Golden Age and Golden Access Passports are accepted. Cash or check only. Open mid-May–late October.

Directions: From Woodland Park, take U.S. Highway 24 west to Lake George. Go south on County Road 96. In 0.9 mile, turn left on County Road 61. The campground is on the right in 0.6 mile.

Contact: Pike National Forest, 719/836-2031, www.fs.fed.us/r2/psicc/.

49 CROSS CREEK

Scenic rating: 7

in Eleven Mile State Park

There are five small campgrounds on the south shore of massive Elevenmile Reservoir. Cross Creek is at the west end of the lake, near the South Platte inlet, so anglers can try river and lake fishing at this location. The campground is protected by a low ridge to the south, and it has great views of Spinney Mountain to the west and the Tarryall Range to the north. The landscape is rolling grasslands, and there isn't a tree in sight. The nearest boat ramp is about six miles away, but canoes can launch from the shoreline. There are two loops. The second loop (sites 408–415) is next to Cross Creek and close to the ridge. Walk-in sites 411 and 412 are about 150 feet away from the rest of the campground. (For more information on Eleven Mile State Park, see the Rocky Ridge listing earlier in this chapter.)

Campsites, facilities: There are 15 sites for tents and RVs up to 35 feet. Sites 411 and 412 are walk-in tent sites. There are no hookups. Sites 408 and 414 are pull-through. Picnic tables, grills, and fire rings are provided. Vault toilets and drinking water are available. Leashed pets are permitted.

Reservations, fees: Reservations are accepted at 800/678-2267 and www.parks.state.co.us. The fee is $12 per night (includes six people

and one camping unit). Vehicles must also have a Daily Parks Pass ($5) or Annual Parks Pass ($55). The Aspen Leaf Pass is accepted. Open year-round.

Directions: From Lake George, take County Road 90 south for 4.1 miles. Turn left on County Road 92. The park office is in six miles. From the office, drive west on County Road 92 for 5.3 miles. Turn left on County Road 59. The campground is on the left in 2.8 miles.

Contact: Eleven Mile State Park, 719/748-3401, email: eleven.mile.park@state.co.us.

50 LAZY BOY

Scenic rating: 7

in Eleven Mile State Park

There are five small campgrounds on the south shore of Elevenmile Reservoir. Lazy Boy and Rocking Chair are on a promontory near the middle of the lake. They are located on an arid, grassy plain without trees or shade, but the views of the Tarryall Range and the 3,400-surface-acre lake are outstanding. Lazy Boy has two loops. The first loop (sites 501–507) is close to the water and a walkway to an island that is closed to protect nesting birds. The second loop (sites 508–514) is farther from the water, near the anglers' parking. (For more information on Eleven Mile State Park, see the Rocky Ridge listing earlier in this chapter.)

Campsites, facilities: There are 14 sites for tents and RVs up to 35 feet. There are no hookups. Sites 501–503, 506, and 507 are pull-through. Picnic tables, grills, and fire rings are provided. Vault toilets and drinking water are available. Leashed pets are permitted.

Reservations, fees: Reservations are accepted at 800/678-2267 and www.parks.state.co.us. The fee is $12 per night (includes six people and one camping unit). Vehicles must also have a Daily Parks Pass ($5) or Annual Parks

Pass ($55). The Aspen Leaf Pass is accepted. Open year-round.

Directions: From Lake George, take County Road 90 south for 4.1 miles. Turn left on County Road 92. The park office is in six miles. From the office, drive west on County Road 92 for 5.3 miles. Turn left on County Road 59. In 5.5 miles, turn left at the campground sign. In 0.3 mile, turn left at the stop sign. The campground is in 0.4 mile.

Contact: Eleven Mile State Park, 719/748-3401, email: eleven.mile.park@state.co.us.

51 ROCKING CHAIR

Scenic rating: 7

in Eleven Mile State Park

There are five small campgrounds on the south shore of Elevenmile Reservoir. Lazy Boy and Rocking Chair are on a promontory near the middle of the lake. They are located on an arid, grassy plain without trees or shade, but Rocking Chair has 360-degree views of the Tarryall Range, Thirtynine Mile Mountain, and the lake. The nearest boat ramp is at Witcher Cove, but the gentle shoreline is open to fishing and launching hand-powered boats. Rocking Chair has two loops. The first loop (sites 601–609) is closest to the water. Only self-contained camping units are allowed at the second loop (sites 610–613) because there is no vault toilet. (For more information on Eleven Mile State Park, see the Rocky Ridge listing earlier in this chapter.)

Campsites, facilities: There are 13 sites for tents and RVs up to 35 feet. There are no hookups. Site 601 is pull-through. Picnic tables, grills, and fire rings are provided. Sites 604 and 609 have sun shelters. Vault toilets and drinking water are available. Leashed pets are permitted.

Reservations, fees: Reservations are accepted at 800/678-2267 and www.parks.state.co.us. The fee is $12 per night (includes six people

and one camping unit). Vehicles must also have a Daily Parks Pass ($5) or Annual Parks Pass ($55). The Aspen Leaf Pass is accepted. Open year-round.

Directions: From Lake George, take County Road 90 south for 4.1 miles. Turn left on County Road 92. The park office is in six miles. From the office, drive west on County Road 92 for 5.3 miles. Turn left on County Road 59. In 5.5 miles, turn left at the campground sign. In 0.3 mile, turn right at the stop sign. The campground is in 0.4 mile.

Contact: Eleven Mile State Park, 719/748-3401, email: eleven.mile.park@state.co.us.

52 HOWBERT POINT

Scenic rating: 7

in Eleven Mile State Park

Howbert Point is on a small promontory near the middle of Elevenmile Reservoir. The campground is on an arid grassland with views of the east end of the lake and the Tarryall Range. There are no trees, and the sites are just 10–20 feet apart, so privacy is in short supply. Sites 709 and 710 are slightly apart from the rest of the campground and are the most appealing. The nearest boat ramp is two miles away at Witcher Cove. (For more information on Eleven Mile State Park, see the Rocky Ridge listing earlier in this chapter.)

Campsites, facilities: There are 10 sites for tents and RVs up to 35 feet. There are no hookups. Picnic tables, grills, and fire rings are provided. Vault toilets and drinking water are available. Leashed pets are permitted.

Reservations, fees: Reservations are accepted at 800/678-2267 and www.parks.state.co.us. The fee is $12 per night (includes six people and one camping unit). Vehicles must also have a Daily Parks Pass ($5) or Annual Parks Pass ($55). The Aspen Leaf Pass is accepted. Open year-round.

Directions: From Lake George, take County

Road 90 south for 4.1 miles. Turn left on County Road 92. The park office is in six miles. From the office, drive west on County Road 92 for 5.3 miles. Turn left on County Road 59. The campground is on the left in seven miles.

Contact: Eleven Mile State Park, 719/748-3401, email: eleven.mile.park@state.co.us.

53 WITCHER COVE

Scenic rating: 7

in Eleven Mile State Park

There are five campgrounds on the south shore of Elevenmile Reservoir. At the east end of the lake, Witcher Cove sprawls along the shoreline, allowing more privacy than at most of the other campgrounds. The views include the rocky north shore and the Tarryall Range. Sites 802 and 803 are close to the boat ramp and slightly separate from the rest of the campground. Sites 804–807 are surrounded by short grass prairie with granite outcroppings. Sites 809–812 are on a slight rise with awesome views. Sites 818–822 are in a small loop almost a mile from the first sites. They are close to the water and have good views. (For more information on Eleven Mile State Park, see the Rocky Ridge listing earlier in this chapter.)

Campsites, facilities: There are 22 sites for tents and RVs up to 35 feet. There are no hookups. Sites 801, 809, and 810 are pull-through. Picnic tables, grills, and fire rings are provided. Vault toilets, drinking water, dump stations, and a boat ramp are available. Leashed pets are permitted.

Reservations, fees: Reservations are accepted at 800/678-2267 and www.parks.state.co.us. The fee is $12 per night (includes six people and one camping unit). Vehicles must also have a Daily Parks Pass ($5) or Annual Parks Pass ($55). The Aspen Leaf Pass is accepted. Open year-round.

Directions: From Lake George, take County Road 90 south for 4.1 miles. Turn left on County Road 92. The park office is in six miles. From the office, drive west on County Road 92 for 5.3 miles. Turn left on County Road 59. In 8.5 miles, turn left at the Witcher Cove sign.

Contact: Eleven Mile State Park, 719/748-3401, email: eleven.mile.park@state.co.us.

54 BACKCOUNTRY

Scenic rating: 9

in Eleven Mile State Park

BEST (

Backcountry is one of the best features of Eleven Mile State Park. Designed for walk-in and boat-in tent camping, this campground is on a rocky promontory between Corral Cove and Fresh Water Cove on the north shore of Elevenmile Reservoir. Granite outcroppings and pine, spruce, aspen, and fir trees interrupt the grassland that dominates the rest of the park. Corral Cove is considered one of the most beautiful locations in the park, especially at sunrise and sunset. The sites are grouped in twos and threes and are screened and shaded by trees and boulders. Most of them have excellent views of the south shore and east end of the lake. Sites 910, 911, 916, and 922 are alone and have the most privacy. In addition to fishing and hiking, campers can enjoy hiking and biking on the five miles of trails on the promontory, including the 1.5-mile Coyote Ridge Interpretive Trail. Midland, the longest trail, circumnavigates a large wetland. (For more information on Eleven Mile State Park, see the Rocky Ridge listing earlier in this chapter.)

Campsites, facilities: There are 22 walk-in and boat-in tent sites. Picnic tables, grills, and fire rings are provided. Vault toilets and drinking water are available. Leashed pets are permitted.

Reservations, fees: Reservations are accepted

at 800/678-2267 and www.parks.state.co.us. The fee is $12 per night (includes six people and one camping unit). Vehicles must also have a Daily Parks Pass ($5) or Annual Parks Pass ($55). The Aspen Leaf Pass is accepted. Open year-round.

Directions: From Lake George, take County Road 90 south for 4.1 miles. Turn left on County Road 92. The park office is in six miles. Turn left out of the parking lot. In 0.3 mile, turn right at the Coyote Ridge sign. The parking area is in 0.4 mile.

Contact: Eleven Mile State Park, 719/748-3401, email: eleven.mile.park@state.co.us.

55 COLLEGIATE PEAKS
Scenic rating: 7
west of Buena Vista

Collegiate Peaks is halfway between Buena Vista and Cottonwood Pass (elevation 12,126 feet). It's an ideal base camp for hikers interested in summiting Mount Yale, Mount Harvard, and Mount Columbia. The Colorado Trail passes less than two miles south of the campground, and the Browns Pass Trail, which connects to the Mount Yale and Hartenstein Lake Trails, begins nearby. Middle Cottonwood Creek borders the campground and offers good trout fishing. The campground is popular with tent and RV campers and is very busy on weekends and holidays. Most of the sites are in a spruce/fir forest. The roomy sites are about 100 feet apart. The back loop (sites 24–34) is in a young aspen grove, and the sites are closer together. Sites 29 and 31 have views up the valley. The following sites are next to the creek: 8, 10, 12, 15, 16, 19, 20, 22, 29, 31, 33, A, B, D, E, G, I, and J.

Campsites, facilities: There are 56 sites for tents and RVs up to 35 feet. There are no hookups. Sites O and 14 are pull-through. Picnic tables, grills, and fire rings are pro-

vided. Vault toilets and drinking water are available. Leashed pets are permitted.

Reservations, fees: Reservations are accepted at 887/444-6777 and www.reserveusa.com. The fee is $12 per night (includes 10 people and two vehicles). Additional vehicles cost $5 per night. The reservation fee is $9. Golden Age and Golden Access Passports are accepted. Cash or check only. Open late May–early September.

Directions: From Buena Vista, take Cottonwood Pass Road/County Road 306 west for 4.1 miles. The campground entrance is on the left. There is a tent sign, but it's easy to miss.

Contact: San Isabel National Forest, 719/539-3591, www.fs.fed.us/r2/psicc/.

56 COTTONWOOD LAKE
Scenic rating: 7
west of Buena Vista

Cottonwood Lake was renovated in 2005, and the new campground is a very appealing destination. There are enough activities to keep the whole family happy. The lake and South Cottonwood Creek offer good fishing and hand-powered boating. The Colorado Trail, open to hikers and bikers, is a short drive away. ATVs and four-wheeling are very popular north of the lake. The campground is a large gravel loop in an aspen grove on a hill that slopes toward the lake. The large sites are terraced and many have stairs. The sites on the top of the loop have good views and more privacy. Those on the bottom of the loop are close to the road and ATV traffic.

Campsites, facilities: There are 28 sites for tents and RVs up to 40 feet. There are no hookups. Picnic tables, grills, fire rings, lantern posts, and tent pads are provided. Vault toilets and drinking water are available. Leashed pets are permitted.

Reservations, fees: Reservations are accepted at 887/444-6777 and www.reserveusa.com.

The fee is $12 per night (includes 10 people and two vehicles). Additional vehicles cost $5 per night. The reservation fee is $9. Golden Age and Golden Access Passports are accepted. Cash or check only. Open late May–early September.

Directions: From Buena Vista, take Cottonwood Pass Road/County Road 306 west for seven miles. Turn left on Forest Route 344. The campground is on the right in four miles.

Contact: San Isabel National Forest, 719/539-3591, www.fs.fed.us/r2/psicc/.

57 RUBY MOUNTAIN
🏃 🚵 🛶 🎣 🏕 ♿ 🚐 ⛺

Scenic rating: 8

south of Buena Vista

BEST (

The Arkansas Headwaters Recreation Area stretches from the headwaters of the Arkansas River (at Fremont Pass and Tennessee Pass) all the way to Lake Pueblo State Park. Colorado State Parks manages six campgrounds on the Arkansas River. Ruby Mountain is the second of the six. Like the other campgrounds, it attracts heaps of kayakers and rafters. Ruby Mountain is a put-in for Brown's Canyon, possibly the most popular Class III run in all of Colorado. But Ruby Mountain also appeals to hikers, mountain bikers, and ATV riders interested in exploring the BLM–managed Four Mile Recreation Area. With all this recreation, the campground can be quite a scene on summer weekends, but the views of Mount Princeton and Mount Antero are absolutely stunning and worth every overheard conversation. Campers should bring a tarp for shade. If you're not lucky enough to get a spot on the river, it can get very hot on a sunny day.

Sites 1–8 have great views but no shade. Sites 5–7 also have excellent views, and they are terraced and have a little more privacy. Sites 12–14 are right next to the parking lot and should be avoided. Sites 15–19 are walk-in sites beside the river in the shade of the cottonwoods. Sites 21 and 22 are in a small canyon a short walk from the river. These secluded sites have heaps of privacy and shade.

Campsites, facilities: There are 16 sites for tents and RVs up to 40 feet and five tent-only sites. Site 11 and the facilities are wheelchair accessible. There are no hookups. Site 9 is pull-through. Picnic tables, grills, fire rings, and tent pads are provided. Vault toilets, changing rooms, a boat ramp, and small amphitheater are available. Trash must be packed out. Leashed pets are permitted.

Reservations, fees: Reservations are accepted (and strongly recommended in July and August) at 800/678-2267 or www.parks.state.co.us. The fee is $12 per night (includes six people). There is an additional $8 reservation fee. Campers must also purchase a Daily Parks Pass ($2) or an Annual Parks Pass ($55). The Aspen Leaf Annual Pass is accepted. Open year-round.

Directions: In Buena Vista, from the intersection of U.S. Highway 24 and Cottonwood Pass Road, travel south on Highway 24 for 5.9 miles. Turn left on County Road 301. In 0.5 mile, turn right on County Road 300. The Ruby Mountain Recreation Site is on the right in 2.3 miles.

Contact: Arkansas Headwaters Recreation Area, 719/539-7289, www.parks.state.co.us.

58 MOUNT PRINCETON
🏃 🚵 🛶 🏕 ♿ 🚐 ⛺

Scenic rating: 6

west of Buena Vista

Mount Princeton is the first campground on the road to St. Elmo, and it fills up fast with both tent and RV campers. There are many hiking and mountain biking opportunities nearby, and the surrounding cliffs are home to bighorn sheep and mountain goats, which the very observant camper might spot.

Campers shouldn't miss the family-oriented Mount Princeton Hot Springs, four miles down the road. The landscape is fairly arid, and the ponderosa pines provide good shade but limited privacy. Sites 12, 13, and 15 solve the privacy problem with terracing. Sites 2–5, 7, 9, 11, and 12 are creekside and have lots of shade. Sites 1, 16, 18, and 19 are near the road and get a lot of traffic noise.

Campsites, facilities: There are 19 sites for tents and RVs up to 40 feet. Sites 16, 18, and 19 and the facilities are wheelchair accessible. There are no hookups. Site 4 is pull-through. Picnic tables, grills, fire rings, and tent pads are provided. Vault toilets and drinking water are available. Leashed pets are permitted.

Reservations, fees: Reservations are accepted at 887/444-6777 and www.reserveusa.com. The fee is $12 per night (includes 10 people and two vehicles). Additional vehicles cost $5 per night. The reservation fee is $9. Golden Age and Golden Access Passports are accepted. Cash or check only. Open late May–late September.

Directions: From Buena Vista, take Cottonwood Pass Road west for 0.7 mile. Turn south on County Road 321. In eight miles, turn right on County Road 162. In 3.9 miles, turn left into the campground.

Contact: San Isabel National Forest, 719/539-3591, www.fs.fed.us/r2/psicc/.

59 CHALK LAKE

Scenic rating: 7

west of Buena Vista

Chalk Lake campground is in a peaceful grove of ponderosa pines and cottonwoods on the banks of Chalk Creek. It's the best destination on the road to St. Elmo for tent campers because there are nine walk-in tent sites (11–15 and 6–9) beside the creek. They are close together, so privacy is limited, but the road and the mayhem just disappear. Sites 3–5 are also near the creek, but they share one

long tent pad right next to the parking spaces. Sites 16–21 are close to the road and have little or no shade. Site 2 is the best one for RVs. There are several hiking and mountain biking opportunities nearby. The 0.5-mile trail to Agnes Vail Falls begins across the road. The Narrow Gauge Trail connects to the Colorado Trail. Mountain bikers should also explore the forest roads and trails above the historic town of St. Elmo. Kids enjoy pulling brook trout out of the creek.

Campsites, facilities: There are 12 sites for tents and RVs up to 35 feet and nine walk-in tent sites. Sites 17 and 18 and the facilities are wheelchair accessible. There are no hookups or pull-throughs. Picnic tables, grills, fire rings, and tent pads are provided. Vault toilets and drinking water are available. Leashed pets are permitted.

Reservations, fees: Reservations are accepted at 887/444-6777 and www.reserveusa.com. The fee is $12 per night (includes 10 people and two vehicles). Additional vehicles cost $5 per night. The reservation fee is $9. Golden Age and Golden Access Passports are accepted. Cash or check only. Open late May–late September.

Directions: From Buena Vista, take Cottonwood Pass Road west for 0.7 mile. Turn south on County Road 321. In eight miles, turn right on County Road 162. In 4.3 miles, turn left into the campground.

Contact: San Isabel National Forest, 719/539-3591, www.fs.fed.us/r2/psicc/.

60 CASCADE

Scenic rating: 7

west of Buena Vista

Cascade is the highest developed campground on the road to St. Elmo. A dense spruce and aspen forest offers more privacy than either Chalk Lake or Mount Princeton, but the creek is across the road. Hiking, mountain biking, and four-wheeling are all available nearby, but there are no trails accessible from the campground, and ATVs cannot unload in the campground. Nevertheless, this is a very popular family-oriented campground, and reservations are highly recommended from July 4th through the rest of the summer. All of the sites have ample shade except for sites 16 and 17, which have the best views. Site 18 is very close to the road.

Campsites, facilities: There are 20 sites for tents and RVs up to 35 feet. Site 15 and the facilities are wheelchair accessible. There are no hookups. Site 10 is pull-through. Picnic tables, grills, fire rings, and tent pads are provided. Vault toilets and drinking water are available. Leashed pets are permitted.

Reservations, fees: Reservations are accepted at 887/444-6777 and www.reserveusa.com. The fee is $12 per night (includes 10 people and two vehicles). Additional vehicles cost $5 per night. The reservation fee is $9. Golden Age and Golden Access Passports are accepted. Cash or check only. Open late May–late September.

Directions: From Buena Vista, take Cottonwood Pass Road west for 0.7 mile. Turn south on County Road 321. In eight miles, turn right on County Road 162. In 5.1 miles turn left into the campground.

Contact: San Isabel National Forest, 719/539-3591, www.fs.fed.us/r2/psicc/.

61 IRON CITY

Scenic rating: 6

west of Buena Vista

Iron City is the highest of the four campgrounds on the road to St. Elmo. The distance deters many campers, but it is very popular with ATV riders who can unload their vehicles in this campground but not at the others. Mountain bikers will also love this location. The network of forest roads and trails provides access to alpine valleys and the Continental Divide. To many mountain bikers, these lung-busting rides are as good as it gets. Hikers should take advantage of the 6.5-mile Poplar Gulch Trail, which offers vistas of the Sawatch Range. There is good fishing in Chalk Creek between Alpine Lake and St. Elmo, especially in the western branch. The well-preserved ghost town of St. Elmo is just up the road, and it's a very popular tourist destination. Except for toilets and water, the campground is undeveloped and attracts mostly tent campers. The campsites overlook Chalk Creek, but the bank is steep, so flat space can be hard to find. Sites 13 and 15 are the largest sites.

Campsites, facilities: There are 15 sites for tents and RVs up to 35 feet. Picnic tables, grills, and fire rings are provided. Vault toilets and drinking water are available. The facilities are wheelchair accessible. Leashed pets are permitted.

Reservations, fees: Reservations are not accepted. The fee is $10 per night (includes 10 people and two vehicles). Additional vehicles cost $5 per night. The reservation fee is $9. Golden Age and Golden Access Passports are accepted. Cash or check only. Open late May–early September.

Directions: From Buena Vista, take Cottonwood Pass Road west for 0.7 mile. Turn south on County Road 321. In eight miles, turn right on County Road 162. In 11.2 miles, make a very sharp right onto Forest Route 292. The campground is in one mile. High clearance vehicles are recommended.

Contact: San Isabel National Forest, 719/539-3591, www.fs.fed.us/r2/psicc/.

62 HECLA JUNCTION

Scenic rating: 7

south of Buena Vista

BEST (

Hecla Junction, aka the International Harbor of Hecla, is the third of six campgrounds managed by the State Parks system on the Arkansas River. It is the take-out for Brown's Canyon, a very popular Class III run, and it's one of only two campgrounds open to commercial groups. Despite the activity, the Hecla campground can be quieter than Ruby Mountain and Railroad Bridge because it's farther from the boat ramp and parking lot than those two campgrounds. There are no views of the Collegiate Peaks, but the piñon-juniper canyons are quite scenic. From the campground, anglers can hike up or down the river for excellent fishing, especially in the evening when the rafts are gone. Sites 1–4 and 6–12 overlook the river. Sites 5 and 19 are in the middle of the campground and have no privacy. Sites 3, 6, 11, and 13 have partial shade. Bring a tarp in case you don't bag a site with shade.

Campsites, facilities: There are 22 sites for tents and RVs up to 40 feet. Site 19 and the facilities are wheelchair accessible. There are no hookups. Site 13 is pull-through. Picnic tables, grills, fire rings, and tent pads are provided. Vault toilets, changing rooms, and a boat ramp are available. Trash must be packed out. Leashed pets are permitted.

Reservations, fees: Reservations are accepted at 800/678-2267 or www.parks.state.co.us. The fee is $12 per night (includes six people). There is an additional $8 reservation fee. Campers must also purchase a Daily Parks Pass ($2) or an Annual Parks Pass ($55). The Aspen Leaf Annual Pass is accepted. Open year-round.

Directions: From the junction of Highways 285 and 291, drive north on U.S. Highway 285 for 1.4 miles. Turn right onto County Road 194. The campground is in 2.7 miles, past the parking lot and boat ramp area. The road is narrow and steep.

Contact: Arkansas Headwaters Recreation Area, 719/539-7289, www.parks.state.co.us.

63 ANGEL OF SHAVANO

Scenic rating: 6

west of Salida

Shavano appeals to hikers and campers looking for a small, primitive campground near the Collegiate Peaks. Except for a few regulars who like the seclusion, very few people know this campground is here, so it's never full. If you can't find a spot at popular Monarch Park, Shavano is a decent backup, although it's a little out of the way for a stopover. The Colorado Trail passes through camp, and the Mount Shavano trailhead is across the road. There is a small beaver pond for fishing or, if you have 4WD, you can drive six miles to the North Fork Reservoir for some alpine fishing. On weekends, a ranger leads scavenger hunts for kids.

The setting is a young spruce and aspen forest beside the North Fork of the Arkansas, which is a small creek at this elevation. At some sites, it's hard to find enough flat space for more than one tent. The best sites for space and privacy are beside the creek: 6, 8, 10, 12, and 14. Site 3 is also very large. Site 6 is in a small aspen grove near the creek and is quite pretty.

Campsites, facilities: There are 20 sites for tents and RVs up to 35 feet and one group site. There are no hookups. Sites 6, 12, 14, and 17 are pull-through. Picnic tables, grills, and fire rings are provided. Vault toilets and drinking water are available. Leashed pets are permitted.

Reservations, fees: Reservations are not accepted for the main campground. The fee is $12 per night (includes 10 people and two vehicles). Additional vehicles cost $5 per night. Golden Age and Golden Access Passports are accepted. Cash or check only. Reservations are required for the group site and are accepted at 887/444-6777 and www.reserveusa.com. Open late May–mid-September.

Directions: From the intersection of U.S.

Highways 50 and 285 in Poncha Springs, take U.S. 50 west for 6.8 miles. In Maysville, turn right on County Road 240. The campground is on the left in four miles.

Contact: San Isabel National Forest Salida District, 719/539-3591, www.fs.fed.us/r2/psicc/.

64 MONARCH PARK

Scenic rating: 8

west of Salida

Monarch Park is a busy campground for some very good reasons. The setting is beautiful—a subalpine spruce forest in a park with several creeks, beaver ponds, and views of Taylor Mountain. It's also just three miles from the top of Monarch Pass and the Continental Divide Trail. Visitors can take a tram or hike to the summit for vistas that stretch as far as Pike's Peak to the east and Utah to the west. The Monarch Crest Trail traverses 12 miles from Monarch Pass to Marshall Pass. Another 28 miles of single-track are accessible on the Rainbow Trail, making this loop one of the best advanced fat tire rides in this part of the state. Hiking and mountain biking are also available across the highway from the campground entrance. Trail 1417 climbs steeply for 1.6 miles to Waterdog Lakes, which contain good-sized cutthroat trout. Kids love fishing on the beaver ponds, which have been enhanced by the Department of Wildlife to improve fish habitat.

The mature spruce forest provides plenty of shade at all of the sites. The sites are large enough for several tents and are spaced 30–60 feet apart. The creekside sites go first: 4–8, 10–13, 15, 17, 19, 21, 24, 26, 28–30, 32, 34, and 36. Sites 2, 22, 23, and 38 have impressive views of Taylor Mountain. Sites 4 and 5 are in a dead-end spur which provides lots of privacy. Site 4 is walk-in.

Campsites, facilities: There are 38 sites for tents and RVs up to 40 feet. There are no

hookups. Sites 1, 24, and 25 are pull-through. Picnic tables, grills, and fire rings are provided. Vault toilets and drinking water are available. Leashed pets are permitted.

Reservations, fees: Reservations are accepted at 887/444-6777 and www.reserveusa.com. The fee is $12 per night (includes 10 people and two vehicles). Additional vehicles cost $5 per night. The reservation fee is $9. Golden Age and Golden Access Passports are accepted. Cash or check only. Open mid-June–early September.

Directions: From the intersection of U.S. Highways 50 and 285 in Poncha Springs, take U.S. 50 west for 15.3 miles. Turn left on Forest Route 231. The road ends at the campground in one mile.

Contact: San Isabel National Forest, 719/539-3591, www.fs.fed.us/r2/psicc/.

65 O'HAVER LAKE

Scenic rating: 6

south of Poncha Springs

O'Haver Lake is on the flanks of Mount Ouray at an elevation of 8,700 feet. This small lake is a fishing favorite with kids. It is usually stocked, and the still waters just beckon canoes. ATV-riding is also a common pastime, especially on the road to Marshall Pass and the Colorado Trail. The Marshall Pass Road is also considered an excellent beginning mountain bike trail. Hikers have to drive to the nearest trailhead, Starvation Creek. The campground encircles one half of the lake. All of the sites are within 50 yards of the water, but the lakeside sites are most popular: 8, 10, 11, 12, 15A, 16, 19, 20, 23–26, 28, and 29. The habitat is a mixed sage and spruce/fur forest, which provides ample shade at most sites. This is a very popular weekend destination, so reservations are recommended.

Campsites, facilities: There are 29 sites for tents and RVs up to 35 feet. There are no hookups. Site 21 is pull-through. Picnic tables, grills, and fire rings are provided. Site 15A has a tent pad. Vault toilets and drinking water are available. The facilities are wheelchair accessible. Leashed pets are permitted.

Reservations, fees: Reservations are accepted at 877/444-6777 and www.reserve-usa.com. The fee is $12 per night (includes 10 people and two vehicles). Additional vehicles cost $5 per night. The reservation fee is $9. Golden Age and Golden Access Passports are accepted. Cash or check only. Open late May–late September.

Directions: From the intersection of U.S. Highways 50 and 285 in Poncha Springs, take U.S. 285 south for five miles. Turn right on Forest Route 200. In 2.3 miles, turn right on O'Haver Lake Road, which is very narrow and winding. The campground entrance is in 1.3 miles.

Contact: San Isabel National Forest, 719/539-3591, www.fs.fed.us/r2/psicc/.

66 FIVE POINTS

🐟 🛶 🐴 ♿ 🚐 ⛺

Scenic rating: 5

east of Texas Creek

Five Points is in the McIntyre Hills, on the south bank of the Arkansas River, Colorado's premier white-water run. Five Points is the most eastern of the six campgrounds managed by the State Parks system on the Arkansas River. This stretch of the river—from Pinnacle Rock to Parkdale—is a popular Class III–IV run that's easy to scout from the highway. A footpath under the highway connects the campground with the day-use area. The campground is not especially appealing, but bighorn sheep are sometimes sighted on the surrounding hills. Sites 1–3, 15, 16, 18, and 19 are next to the road. The only sites with shade are 4, 14, and 15. There is very little privacy.

Campsites, facilities: There are 20 sites for tents and RVs up to 40 feet. Site 10 and the facilities are wheelchair accessible. There are no hookups. Picnic tables, grills, fire rings, and tent pads are provided. Vault toilets and drinking water are available. Trash must be packed out. Leashed pets are permitted.

Reservations, fees: Reservations are accepted at 800/678-2267 and www.parks.state.co.us. The fee is $12 per night (includes six people). There is an additional $8 reservation fee. Campers must also purchase a Daily Parks Pass ($2) or an Annual Parks Pass ($55). The Aspen Leaf Annual Pass is accepted. Open year-round.

Directions: From Cañon City, take U.S. Highway 50 west 19 miles. The campground is on the left at mile marker 260.

Contact: Arkansas Headwaters Recreation Area, 719/539-7289, www.parks.state.co.us.

FRONT RANGE NORTH

© SARAH RYAN

BEST CAMPGROUNDS

The High Plains end abruptly at the Front Range,

a massive uplifted block of Precambrian granite that soars some 7,000 feet above the plains. These mountains, one of the most recognizable symbols of the Rockies, are the eastern edge of the Rocky Mountains. Miners were daunted by – but not turned back by – this barrier. They prospected during the brief summer and spent the long winter encamped along the foothills and rivers of the Colorado Piedmont, the hilly region that separates the mountains from the plains.

Over half of the state's population lives in the northern Front Range, north from Denver to Fort Collins and west to the Continental Divide. Those early settlements became today's urban centers: Denver, Boulder, Golden, and Colorado Springs, and the toll roads the miners built have become the highways that transport natives and non-natives into the mountains, the largest continuous playground in the country.

Denver is often called the "Mile High City," and the 13th step of the capitol building is exactly one mile above sea level. Traditionally, Denver went through boom and bust cycles because of its dependency on a natural resources market. In the 1990s, the city became a high-tech center, an economic shift that brought a huge population boom and urban renewal.

Denver has the largest city park system in the nation. There are 205 parks within city limits and 20,000 acres in the nearby mountains. Popular spots include Echo Lake on Mount Evans and Red Rocks Park, the most beloved concert venue in the state. Within city limits, Cherry Creek State Park has a lake, riding stable, shooting range, campground, and hiking and biking trails. It's an amazing urban resource for visitors and residents alike.

On Friday mornings in the winter, I-70 becomes a migratory route from the city to the ski resorts. Within a half hour of the city, the interstate passes the historic mining districts turned bedroom communities of Idaho Springs and Georgetown. The summit of Mount Evans (elevation 14,264 feet) is also within a half hour of the city, thanks to Highway 103, the highest paved road in the country.

Black Hawk and Golden are north of I-70. Black Hawk is a gambling destination with a few national forest campgrounds nearby for multitask-ers. Golden, former gold rush town and capital of the Colorado Territory, is now home to the Colorado School of Mines and Coors Brewery. Nearby Golden Gate Canyon State Park has three campgrounds and 35 miles of trails for hiking, mountain biking, and horseback riding.

Boulder has a reputation for being the most liberal, freethinking, po-litically correct city in conservative Colorado. (Thus the nickname "The People's Republic of Boulder.") Recreation has always been one of the primary appeals in Boulder. The city's backdrop, the Flatirons, provide hik-ing and climbing opportunities within walking distance of downtown.

The Indian Peaks Wilderness is just 25 miles west of Boulder. It's heavily visited by Front Range residents, but the national forest manages use with backcountry permits. Visitors will find a glaciated landscape dotted with almost 50 alpine lakes and a handful of lingering glaciers. There are over 100 miles of trails in this wilderness area, including the Continental Divide Trail (CDT).

The CDT continues north into Rocky Mountain National Park, the jewel of the Front Range. There are over 265,000 acres in the park, including 355 miles of trails and 114 peaks over 10,000 feet. You could spend a whole summer in the park exploring the backcountry by foot or horseback. If you don't have that much time, take a day to drive Trail Ridge Road, which bisects the park. Longs Peak is the other great attrac-tion. This peak is the most frequently climbed fourteener in Colorado. The Keyhole Route is the only nontechnical route to the summit, but it's no afternoon stroll. To complete the 16-mile hike, campers at the Longs Peak campground have to rise around 2 A.M. and set off by flashlight.

North of Fort Collins, the Cache la Poudre is Colorado's only National Wild and Scenic River. This gorgeous canyon is home to a vibrant white-water scene. Local kayakers take to the water with the snowmelt in the spring, and commercial outfitters offer half-day and full-day rafting trips. The trout fishing is also excellent. The upper Poudre (pronounced POO-der) flows from the Comanche Peak, Rawah, and Neota wilder-ness areas. There is excellent camping the whole length of the river and along the borders of the wilderness areas.

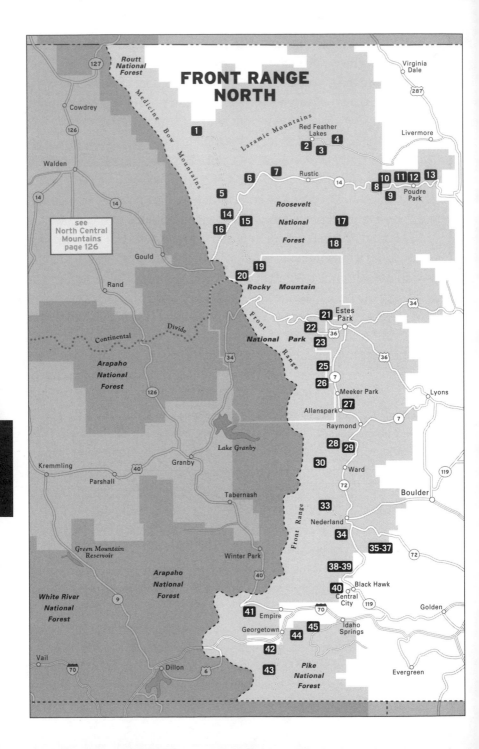

FRONT RANGE NORTH

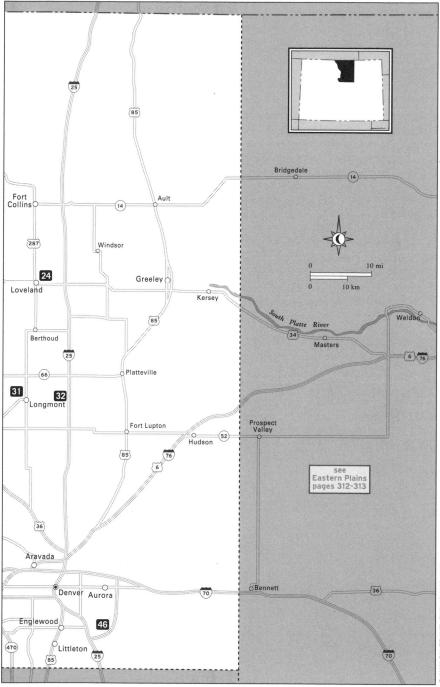

Front Range North

25
85
Bridgedale
14
Fort Collins
14 Ault
287
Windsor
24
Loveland
Greeley
Kersey
85
South Platte River
Weldon
34
Masters
6 76
Berthoud
25
66
Platteville
31
32 Longmont
Fort Lupton
Prospect Valley
85
6 76
Hudson
52
see
Eastern Plains
pages 312-313
36
Aravada
70 Bennett
36
Denver Aurora
Englewood
46
470
Littleton
85 25
70

0   10 mi
0   10 km

1 BROWNS PARK

Scenic rating: 6

in Poudre Canyon

Browns Park is in the Laramie River valley, adjacent to the Rawah Wilderness, an area of granite peaks and remote valleys. The campground is a dirt loop in an evergreen and aspen forest. The sites are just 20–50 feet apart. The campground is a long drive from the Front Range, but it's fairly busy on weekends, with a diverse crowd of old couples, young couples, and serious backpackers. Most campers are there for the hiking. The McIntyre and Link Trails begin at the campground and climb about seven miles to the Medicine Bow Trail on the crest of the Medicine Bow Mountains. The views of North Park and the Laramie River valley are outstanding. These trails can be turned into an overnight loop or combined with other trails for a longer route.

Campsites, facilities: There are 28 sites for tents and RVs up to 38 feet. There are no hookups. Site 28 is pull-through. Picnic tables, grills, fire rings, and tent pads are provided. Vault toilets and drinking water are available. Trash must be packed out. Leashed pets are permitted.

Reservations, fees: Reservations are not accepted. The fee is $11 per night. Golden Age and Golden Access Passports are accepted. Cash or check only. Open early June–early November.

Directions: From Fort Collins, take U.S. Highway 287 north to Ted's Place and take Highway 14 west for 51.7 miles. Turn right on County Road 103/Laramie River Road and drive north for 15.8 miles. Turn left on County Road 190. The campground is on the left in 2.5 miles.

Contact: Roosevelt National Forest, 970/295-6796, www.fs.fed.us/arnf.

2 BELLAIRE LAKE

Scenic rating: 6

at Red Feather Lakes

Bellaire Lake seems like an unlikely body of water. This small lake is surrounded by the granite outcroppings and rolling hills of the Red Feather Lakes region. The sandy shore is excellent for shore fishing, and there's a wheelchair-accessible fishing pier. The lake and campground are surrounded by lodgepole pine. Most visitors enjoy fishing and boating (hand-powered only), as well as day trips to Wyoming and the Cache la Poudre canyon. The campground has two loops. The sites are large and spaced 25–50 feet apart. The back loop (sites 23–27) is smaller and quieter than the front loop, which is very popular with families and RVers.

Campsites, facilities: There are 26 sites for tents and RVs up to 60 feet. Electric hookups are available at sites 1–22. Sites 4, 14, and 26 are doubles. Sites 8, 10, 18, and 20 are pull-throughs. Picnic tables, grills, fire rings, and tent pads are provided. Flush toilets, drinking water, and a small amphitheater are available. The facilities are wheelchair accessible. Leashed pets are permitted.

Reservations, fees: Reservations are not accepted. The fee is $15 per night. Electric hookups cost $5 per night. Golden Age and Golden Access Passports are accepted. Cash or check only. Open mid-May–early October.

Directions: From Fort Collins, take U.S. Highway 287 north for about 21 miles. Go west on Red Feather Lakes Road/County Road 74E for 34.1 miles and turn left on County Road 162. In 2.1 mile, turn right on Forest Route 163. In 0.4 mile, turn left on Forest Route 163A. The campground is in 0.3 mile.

Contact: Roosevelt National Forest, 970/295-6796, www.fs.fed.us/arnf.

🖪 WEST LAKE

🛶 🎣 🏠 ♿ 🚐 ⛺

Scenic rating: 6

at Red Feather Lakes

The Red Feather Lakes area is inexplicably popular. There are no soaring mountains here, but the rolling hills and low ridgelines, covered in grasslands and ponderosa pine, and numerous fishing lakes attract a devoted following of weekend campers. The campground has two loops on the south shore of a small, stocked lake. The sites are about 30 feet apart. Privacy is poor, and this campground mostly attracts RVs. Sites 6, 7, 9, 10, 12, 14, 15, 17, 18, 20, 23, and 25–28 have lake views. Sites 25–28 also have views of the small town of Red Feather. Site 35 is on a small knoll with 360-degree views. There is a fishing trail around the lake, which is open to hand-powered boats.

Campsites, facilities: There are 35 sites for tents and RVs up to 50 feet. Sites 1–5 are walk-ins. Electric hookups are available. Picnic tables, grills, fire rings, and tent pads are provided. Vault toilets, drinking water, and a boat ramp are available. The facilities are wheelchair accessible. Leashed pets are permitted.

Reservations, fees: Reservations are accepted at 877/444-6777 and www.reserveusa.com. The fee is $15 per night or $23 for double sites and $5 for electricity. Golden Age and Golden Access Passports are accepted. Cash or check only. Open mid-May–early October.

Directions: From Fort Collins, take U.S. Highway 287 north for about 21 miles. Go west on Red Feather Lakes Road/County Road 74E for 22.4 miles and turn right at the West Lake sign.

Contact: Roosevelt National Forest, 970/295-6796, www.fs.fed.us/arnf.

🖪 DOWDY LAKE

🚶 🚴 🛶 🎣 ✳ 🏠 🚐 ⛺

Scenic rating: 6

at Red Feather Lakes

The Red Feather Lakes area is inexplicably popular. There are no soaring mountains here, but the rolling hills and low ridgelines, covered in grasslands and ponderosa pine, and numerous fishing lakes attract a devoted following of weekend campers. The campground has five loops around the south and west shores of the lake. Most sites have lake views. They are just 10–20 feet apart, so privacy is poor, especially on weekends, when this campground usually fills up. Sites 2, 7, 8, 50, 51, 53, and 54 are doubles. Hikers and bikers can take an old logging road to the Mount Margaret Trail, an easy four-mile hike to a rocky peak. In the winter, the Mount Margaret Trail is open for cross-country skiing and snowshoeing.

Campsites, facilities: There are 62 sites for tents and RVs up to 40 feet. Sites 12–21 are walk-ins. Hookups and pull-throughs are not available. Picnic tables, grills, fire rings, and tent pads are provided. Vault toilets, drinking water, and an amphitheater are available. Leashed pets are permitted.

Reservations, fees: Reservations are accepted at 877/444-6777 and www.reserveusa.com. The fee is $13 per night. Golden Age and Golden Access Passports are accepted. Cash or check only. Open year-round.

Directions: From Fort Collins, take U.S. Highway 287 north for about 21 miles. Go west on Red Feather Lakes Road/County Road 74E for 22.7 miles and turn right on Dowdy Lake Road. The campground is on the right in 0.6 mile.

Contact: Roosevelt National Forest, 970/295-6796, www.fs.fed.us/arnf.

5 TUNNEL

Scenic rating: 6

in Poudre Canyon

Tunnel is a big, sprawling campground in a pine forest on the west bank of the Laramie River, adjacent to the Rawah Wilderness. The wilderness contains 73,000 acres in the Mummy Range, an area of granite peaks and glacial lakes. From the campground, the West Branch Trail climbs through aspen and pine to Grassy Pass and the Rawah Lakes Basin. Campers can also go fishing on the river and biking and four-wheeling in the Roosevelt National Forest. The campground is in a thin pine forest and the sites are just 25 feet apart, so privacy is poor, but the campground is busy during the summer. Sites 4, 10, 20, 21, 24, and 25 are riverside. The valley is beautiful, but only sites 8 and 14 have views of the aspen-covered ridges.

Campsites, facilities: There are 49 sites for tents and RVs up to 40 feet. There are no hookups. Sites 3, 4, 21, and 35 are pull-through. Picnic tables, grills, fire rings, and tent pads are provided. Vault toilets and drinking water are available. Leashed pets are permitted.

Reservations, fees: Reservations are not accepted. The fee is $13 per night. Golden Age and Golden Access Passports are accepted. Cash or check only. Open mid-May–late October.

Directions: From Fort Collins, take U.S. Highway 287 north to Ted's Place and take Highway 14 west for 51.7 miles. Turn right on County Road 103/Laramie River Road. The campground is on the left in 6.5 miles.

Contact: Roosevelt National Forest, 970/295-6796, www.fs.fed.us/arnf.

6 SLEEPING ELEPHANT

Scenic rating: 6

in Poudre Canyon

Sleeping Elephant is a small loop separated from the river by the highway. The impressive granite summit of Sleeping Elephant Mountain towers over the far bank. The campground is basically a stopover. The sites are in a forest of aspen and spruce and spaced about 30 feet apart. The nearest hiking trail is Roaring Creek, about three miles downstream. The river has excellent trout fishing.

Campsites, facilities: There are 15 sites for tents and RVs up to 20 feet. There are no hookups. Picnic tables, grills, and fire rings are provided. Vault toilets and drinking water are available. The facilities are wheelchair accessible. Leashed pets are permitted.

Reservations, fees: Reservations are not accepted. The fee is $12 per night. Golden Age and Golden Access Passports are accepted. Cash or check only. Open mid-May–early October.

Directions: From Fort Collins, take U.S. Highway 287 north to Ted's Place and take Highway 14 west for 44 miles. The campground is on the right.

Contact: Roosevelt National Forest, 970/295-6796, www.fs.fed.us/arnf.

7 BIG BEND

Scenic rating: 7

in Poudre Canyon

Big Bend doesn't suffer from the rambunctious summer crowds that the downstream campgrounds receive, and it can lay claim to one of the grandest sites on the Cache la Poudre River. The canyon opens up here and the formerly narrow river becomes braided. As you might guess from the number of anglers casting up and down the river, it's prime trout habitat. If you don't enjoy fishing, bring your binoculars and try spotting bighorn sheep in the meadow that borders the campground or on the steep hillsides across the road. In early spring, ewes and lambs are often seen munching on western wheatgrass and sulphur flower. Hunting and disease eliminated bighorn sheep from the canyon by 1900, but the Department of Wildlife reintroduced them in 1950, and they presently number about 95. You can also spot bighorn on the scenic Roaring Creek Trail. The trailhead is a half mile west of the campground. The one thing Big Bend can't boast about is privacy. There are no trees separating the drive-in sites, and even the walk-in sites are too close to the road.

Campsites, facilities: There are six sites for tents and RVs up to 20 feet and three walk-in tent sites. There are no hookups. Picnic tables, grills, and fire rings are provided. Vault toilets and drinking water are available. Leashed pets are permitted.

Reservations, fees: Reservations are not accepted. The fee is $12 per night. Golden Age and Golden Access Passports are accepted. Cash or check only. Open year-round.

Directions: From Fort Collins, take U.S. Highway 287 north to Ted's Place and take Highway 14 west for 40.2 miles. The campground is on the left.

Contact: Roosevelt National Forest, 970/295-6796, www.fs.fed.us/arnf.

8 KELLY FLATS

Scenic rating: 6

in Poudre Canyon

Kelly Flats straddles both banks of the wild Cache la Poudre River. This campground is a great destination for families because the river widens and slows as it flows across a nice gravel bar here. Anglers can fish for trout on this excellent fishery, and kayakers and rafters can take to the river. Upstream of the campground, the Lower and Upper Rustic

runs offer scenic Class III boating. The lower Poudre is tougher and closer to the highway.

The campground has three spurs. In the first spur, sites 1–6 are in a meadow with no trees. These are the least popular sites. Sites 9–13 are for tents only. Sites 20–30 are across the river. Every site except 7 is riverside. Sites 15–17, 20, and 21 are walk-ins.

Campsites, facilities: There are 29 sites for tents and RVs up to 40 feet. Sites 15–17, 20, and 21 are walk-ins. There are no hookups. Picnic tables, grills, fire rings, and tent pads are provided. Vault toilets and drinking water are available. The facilities are wheelchair accessible. Leashed pets are permitted.

Reservations, fees: Reservations are not accepted. The fee is $15 per night. Golden Age and Golden Access Passports are accepted. Cash or check only. Open mid-May–early October.

Directions: From Fort Collins, take U.S. Highway 287 north to Ted's Place and take Highway 14 west for 25.4 miles. The campground is on the left.

Contact: Roosevelt National Forest, 970/295-6796, www.fs.fed.us/arnf.

9 MOUNTAIN PARK

Scenic rating: 6

in Poudre Canyon

Mountain Park is the largest campground on the Cache la Poudre River. As Colorado's only Wild and Scenic River, the Poudre attracts hordes of campers all summer long with excellent fishing, white-water, and hiking opportunities. Mountain Park is one of the most popular campgrounds, in part because it has hookups, and it's adjacent to the Mount McConnell Trail, the only trail in the Cache la Poudre Wilderness area. This strenuous four-mile loop climbs 1,300 feet to an overlook of the Little South Fork canyon, even wilder and more rugged than the main fork. The trail also has sweeping views of the Mummy

Range and Storm Peaks. It's a must-do for visitors to the Poudre.

The campground has four loops and a group area in a pine forest on the south bank of the river. The sites are just 15–30 feet apart, so privacy is poor, but shade is excellent. The campground is packed all summer with snowbirds and families. The Bear and McConnell Loops (sites 1–32) have electric hookups. The Crown and Comanche Loops (sites 33–57) are riverside, but they are also within sight of the road.

Campsites, facilities: There are 55 sites for tents and RVs up to 50 feet and one group site. Electric hookups are available at sites 1–32. Sites 31–33 are pull-through. Sites 24, 37, 38, 40, and 42 are doubles. Picnic tables, grills, fire rings, and tent pads are provided. Showers, vault toilets, drinking water, horseshoe pits, volleyball courts, a playground, and an amphitheater are available. The facilities are wheelchair accessible. Leashed pets are permitted.

Reservations, fees: Reservations are accepted at 877/444-6777 and www.reserveusa.com. The tent fee is $15 per night for a single and $30 per night for a double. Electric sites are $20 per night or $40 per night for a double. The group site costs $75 per night (includes 30 people). Golden Age and Golden Access Passports are accepted. Cash or check only. Open mid-May–early October.

Directions: From Fort Collins, take U.S. Highway 287 north to Ted's Place and take Highway 14 west for 23.5 miles. Turn left and cross the river. The campground is on the left.

Contact: Roosevelt National Forest, 970/295-6796, www.fs.fed.us/arnf.

10 DUTCH GEORGE
🏊 ⛵ 🐕 ♿ 🚐 ⛺

Scenic rating: 6

in Poudre Canyon

Dutch George is a popular campground beside the Cache la Poudre, Colorado's only Wild and Scenic River. The campground is across from the Cache la Poudre Wilderness area, an almost impenetrable area of granite gorges and rocky creeks. Anglers fish for trout on the main fork of the Poudre and on the Little South Fork. There is river running above and below the campground. Most sites have views of Sheep Mountain. The riverside sites, 1–13 and 19–21, are shaded by cottonwoods. Sites 14–18 are too close to the road and lack shade and privacy. Sites 10 and 13 are doubles.

Campsites, facilities: There are 21 sites for tents and RVs up to 35 feet. Sites 8–15 are walk-ins. There are no hookups. Sites 8, 13, and 15 are pull-through. Picnic tables, grills, fire rings, and tent pads are provided. Vault toilets and drinking water are available. The facilities are wheelchair accessible. Leashed pets are permitted.

Reservations, fees: Reservations are not accepted. The fee is $14 per night. Golden Age and Golden Access Passports are accepted. Cash or check only. Open mid-May–early October.

Directions: From Fort Collins, take U.S. Highway 287 north to Ted's Place and take Highway 14 west. The campground is on the left in 21.6 miles.

Contact: Roosevelt National Forest, 970/295-6796, www.fs.fed.us/arnf.

11 NARROWS
🏊 ⛵ 🐕 ♿ 🚐 ⛺

Scenic rating: 7

in Poudre Canyon

BEST (

The Narrows is named for the gnarly Class IV–V+ white-water run that begins just downstream of the campground. Only advanced kayakers can tackle this run, which becomes unboatable when the Cache la Poudre is swollen. The river is the only designated Wild and Scenic River in Colorado; the waters are also protected by the wilderness area to the south of the river. The river has carved a deep gorge through the granite of the Front Range. The wilderness area is almost impenetrable. There is only one four-mile loop trail into the wilderness, but anglers have created a strenuous use trail up the Little South Fork of the Poudre. Fishing and whitewater are the primary attractions on this stretch of the canyon.

The campground has two loops at a place where the canyon widens. The upper loop (sites 1–7) is next to the put-in. The sites are exposed to the road and each other. The lower loop (sites 8–15) has walk-in tent sites in a grove of ponderosa pines. The sites are about 25 feet apart. Shade is good and privacy is fair. Sites 1–6 and 11–15 are riverside.

Campsites, facilities: There are 15 sites for tents and RVs up to 30 feet. Sites 8–15 are walk ins. There are no hookups. Picnic tables, grills, fire rings, and tent pads are provided. Vault toilets and drinking water are available. The facilities are wheelchair accessible. Leashed pets are permitted.

Reservations, fees: Reservations are not accepted. The fee is $14 per night. Golden Age and Golden Access Passports are accepted. Cash or check only. Open mid-May–late October.

Directions: From Fort Collins, take U.S. Highway 287 north to Ted's Place and take Highway 14 west. The lower campground is on the left in 20.3 miles. The upper campground is on the left in 20.5 miles.

Contact: Roosevelt National Forest, 970/295-6796, www.fs.fed.us/arnf.

12 STOVE PRAIRIE

🛶 ♿ 🐕 🚐 ⛺

Scenic rating: 6

in Poudre Canyon

The Cache la Poudre (pronounced poo-der by locals) is Colorado's only Wild and Scenic River, a designation that has helped to protect superior fishing and whitewater on the upper stretches of the river. According to legend, the river was named by a group of fur trappers

who had to lighten their load when they hit a snowstorm in the canyon. They were told to "cache la poudre" or "hide the powder" in the banks. Today, trappers have been replaced by rafters and kayakers. Stove Prairie is just downstream of the Upper Landing and Steven's Gulch put-ins at the beginning of the Upper Mishawaka run. This three-mile section is a classic Class IV run. Boaters can take-out at the Mishawaka Inn and grab a burger, or keep running down the Lower Mishawaka and Poudre Park runs.

The campground is a small loop in a wide spot of the canyon. The walk-in sites are in a grove of cottonwoods and pine trees by the river. The drive-in sites are grouped around a meadow. They lack shade and privacy.

Campsites, facilities: There are nine sites for tents and RVs up to 30 feet. Sites 3–6 are walk-ins. There are no hookups. Picnic tables, grills, fire rings, and tent pads are provided. Vault toilets and drinking water are available. Leashed pets are permitted.

Reservations, fees: Reservations are not accepted. The fee is $14 per night. Golden Age and Golden Access Passports are accepted. Cash or check only. Open mid-May–late October.

Directions: From Fort Collins, take U.S. Highway 287 north to Ted's Place. Take Highway 14 west for 16.8 miles. The campground is on the right.

Contact: Roosevelt National Forest, 970/295-6796, www.fs.fed.us/arnf.

13 ANSEL WATROUS

🚶 🚴 🛶 ♿ 🐕 ♿ 🚐 ⛺

Scenic rating: 6

in Poudre Canyon

BEST (

From Memorial Day–Labor Day, Ansel Watrous is a hot bed of activity. As the easternmost campground on Colorado's only National Wild and Scenic River, Ansel Watrous fills up fast and early with rafters, kayakers, anglers, families, and groupies. It's the perfect base camp for an early morning launch, and if you don't have your own boat, there are three rafting companies in Fort Collins to choose from. Rafting begins in May and ends in August when the river nearly dries up. The best times to go are early in the season when the snowmelt is cold but abundant. If you prefer to stay on dry land, you can watch the rafters from the porch of the Mishawaka Inn, a short walk upstream. The "Mish" serves the best burgers in the canyon, and it's a popular concert venue, favored by the likes of String Cheese Incident, Yonder Mountain, and Indigo Girls. The Greyrock trailhead is located four miles to the east. This strenuous trail summits Greyrock Mountain at 7,613 feet. The climb is worth it for the views of the plains and the Front Range. The easier 4.7-mile Young Gulch Trail begins across from the campground. It's open to bikes as well as hikers.

Ansel Watrous has two loops sandwiched between the highway and the river, so the sound of traffic is constant on a summer day. Tall pines provide shade but not much privacy because the sites are just 15–20 feet apart. Trails lead down to the water and a nice swimming hole at the lower loop. Sites 1–10 and 14–19 are riverside sites.

Campsites, facilities: There are 19 sites for tents and RVs up to 30 feet. Sites 8–10 are walk-ins, and sites 11–19 are recommended for tents. There are no hookups. Picnic tables, grills, fire rings, and tent pads are provided. Vault toilets and drinking water are available. The facilities are wheelchair accessible. Leashed pets are permitted.

Reservations, fees: Reservations are not accepted. The fee is $14 per night. Golden Age and Golden Access Passports are accepted. Cash or check only. Open year-round.

Directions: From Fort Collins, take U.S. Highway 287 north to Ted's Place. Take Highway 14 west for 12.6 miles. The campground is on the right.

Contact: Roosevelt National Forest, 970/295-6796, www.fs.fed.us/arnf.

14 ASPEN GLEN

🏃 🛶 🏠 🚐 ⛺

Scenic rating: 6

in Poudre Canyon

Aspen Glen is a small loop in a spruce-fir and aspen forest on Joe Wright Creek. The campground is surrounded by the rocky ridges of the Upper Poudre Canyon. There is a fair amount of traffic noise, but the sites are large and well spaced. Site 6 has the most privacy. The campground is less than a mile away from the Big South trailhead. This 10-mile trail travels into the Comanche Peak Wilderness along the Big South Fork of the Poudre, a tantalizing trout stream characterized by frequent cascades and pools.

Campsites, facilities: There are nine sites for tents and RVs up to 30 feet. There are no hookups. Site 4 is pull-through. Picnic tables, grills, fire rings, and tent pads are provided. Vault toilets and drinking water are available. Leashed pets are permitted.

Reservations, fees: Reservations are not accepted. The fee is $11 per night. Golden Age and Golden Access Passports are accepted. Cash or check only. Open mid-May–early October.

Directions: From Fort Collins, take U.S. Highway 287 north to Ted's Place and take Highway 14 west for 50.2 miles. The campground is on the right.

Contact: Roosevelt National Forest, 970/295-6796, www.fs.fed.us/arnf.

15 BIG SOUTH

🏃 🛶 🛶 🏠 🚐 ⛺

Scenic rating: 7

in Poudre Canyon

Big South is a tiny little campground at the junction of the Big South Fork and the main fork of the Cache la Poudre River. The campground is adjacent to the Big South Trail, a 10-mile trek into the Comanche Peak Wilderness. The wilderness encompasses about 67,000 acres of spruce-fir forests and granite peaks in the Mummy Range. The scenic cascades and pools of the Big South are extremely popular with anglers and hikers. The Big South is also a Class V white-water route for steep creek boaters.

Campsites, facilities: There are four sites for tents and RVs up to 25 feet. There are no hookups. Picnic tables, grills, and fire rings are provided. Vault toilets are available. Leashed pets are permitted.

Reservations, fees: Reservations are not accepted. The fee is $14 per night. Golden Age and Golden Access Passports are accepted. Cash or check only. Open mid-May–early October.

Directions: From Fort Collins, take U.S. Highway 287 north to Ted's Place and take Highway 14 west for 49 miles. The campground is on the left.

Contact: Roosevelt National Forest, 970/295-6796, www.fs.fed.us/arnf.

16 CHAMBERS LAKE
🏃 🛶 🐕 🚐 🏕

Scenic rating: 7

in Poudre Canyon

At 9,200 feet, Chambers Lake is a high-altitude reservoir surrounded by Roosevelt National Forest. From the campground, hikers can take Blue Lake Trail north for seven miles through the Rawah Wilderness to the West Fork Trail. This route offers panoramic views of the Mummy Range and Rocky Mountain National Park. It is the most popular trail in the Rawah.

This large campground has two paved loops in a spruce-fir forest on the south shore of Chambers Lake. The sites are 20–40 feet apart, and privacy varies from fair to poor. The lower loop (sites 1–20) is not very appealing. The upper loop (sites 21–51) overlooks the lake from a high ridge. Sites 21, 23, 32, 34, 37, and 41–51 have the best views of the lake.

Campsites, facilities: There are 52 sites for tents and RVs up to 30 feet. Sites 45–51 are walk-in tent sites. Sites 6, 7, 9, 24, 25, 31, 34, 35, and 38 are doubles. There are no hookups. Picnic tables, grills, fire rings, and tent pads are provided. Vault toilets, drinking water, a boat ramp, and amphitheater are available. Leashed pets are permitted.

Reservations, fees: Reservations are accepted at 877/444-6777 and www.reserveusa.com. The fee is $15 per night or $30 per night for doubles. Golden Age and Golden Access Passports are accepted. Cash or check only. Open early June–early October.

Directions: From Fort Collins, take U.S. Highway 287 north to Ted's Place and take Highway 14 west for 52.5 miles. Turn right at the Chambers Lake sign. The campground is in 0.6 mile.

Contact: Roosevelt National Forest, 970/295-6796, www.fs.fed.us/arnf.

17 JACK'S GULCH
🐕 ♿ 🚐 🏕

Scenic rating: 7

in Pingree Park

Jack's Gulch is on the eastern boundary of the Comanche Peak Wilderness. The campground was built in 1995 to reduce the impact of recreation on the Little South Fork of the Cache la Poudre. There are no trailheads at the campground, but it's a short drive to the Flowers, Fish Creek, and Little Beaver Trails. The area is also popular with ATV owners and hunters. The campground is in a ponderosa pine forest with scattered meadows and aspen. The walk-in sites are especially attractive. The Paintbrush Loop has modern, roomy equestrian sites.

Campsites, facilities: There are 70 sites for tents and RVs up to 50 feet and 10 walk-in sites. There is also a group site. Most sites and facilities are wheelchair accessible. Electric hookups are available at sites 1–29 and the group site. Picnic tables, grills, fire rings, and tent pads are provided. Vault toilets, drinking water, corrals, and a small amphitheater are available. Leashed pets are permitted.

Reservations, fees: Reservations are not accepted for the main campground. The fee is $15–20 per night. Reservations can be made for the group site at 970/498-2770. The group site costs up to $100 per night for up to 60 people. Golden Age and Golden Access Passports are accepted. Cash or check only. Open mid-May–early November.

Directions: From Fort Collins, take U.S. Highway 287 north to Ted's Place and take Highway 14 west for 26.5 miles. Turn left on Pingree Park Road/County Road 63E. In 6.3 miles, turn right into Jack's Gulch Recreation Area. The main loop is on the left, and the group and equestrian loops are on the right.

Contact: Roosevelt National Forest, 970/295-6796, www.fs.fed.us/arnf.

18 TOM BENNETT

Scenic rating: 5

in Pingree Park

Tom Bennett is a short drive away from the Pingree Park Campus of Colorado State University. This research site once belonged to a homesteading family; their house and several outhouses have been preserved and restored. They offer an interesting glance into the lonely lives of the pioneers in this region. The campground is a cramped affair in a spruce-fir forest beside a small creek. The privacy and scenery are poor, so the campground mainly serves as an overnight destination for hikers. Three trails begin nearby: Beaver Creek, Emmaline Lake, and Stormy Peaks Pass. Emmaline Lake Trail climbs through the Comanche Peak Wilderness to the Cirque and Emmaline Lakes basin. The views merit an overnight trip. Stormy Peaks Pass is equally impressive.

Campsites, facilities: There are 12 sites for tents and RVs up to 20 feet. Site 6 is pull-through. Picnic tables, grills, and fire rings are provided. Vault toilets are available. Leashed pets are permitted.

Reservations, fees: Reservations are not accepted. The fee is $10 per night. Golden Age and Golden Access Passports are accepted. Cash or check only. Open mid-May–late October.

Directions: From Fort Collins, take U.S. Highway 287 north to Ted's Place and take Highway 14 west for 26.5 miles. Turn left on Pingree Park Road/County Road 63E. In 15.8 miles, turn right on Forest Route 145. The campground is on the left at the bottom of the hill.

Contact: Roosevelt National Forest, 970/295-6796, www.fs.fed.us/arnf.

19 LONG DRAW

Scenic rating: 6

in Poudre Canyon

Long Draw is a small loop in a spruce-fir forest. The sites are small and tightly packed. In the fall, this campground is overrun with hunters. Campers can go hiking on the Big South and Corral Creek Trails. The Big South travels through the Comanche Peak Wilderness area, a stunning landscape of dense forests and glaciated peaks. There are no views from the campground, but the valley and the reservoir are quite scenic.

Campsites, facilities: There are 25 sites for tents and RVs up to 30 feet. There are no hookups. Site 9 is pull-through. Picnic tables, grills, and fire rings are provided. Vault toilets and drinking water are available. The facilities are wheelchair accessible. Trash must be packed out. Leashed pets are permitted.

Reservations, fees: Reservations are not accepted. The fee is $11 per night. Golden Age and Golden Access Passports are accepted. Cash or check only. Open late June–early November.

Directions: From Fort Collins, take U.S. Highway 287 north to Ted's Place and take Highway 14 west for 53.9 miles. Turn left on Long Draw Road. The campground is on the left in 8.8 miles.

Contact: Roosevelt National Forest, 970/295-6796, www.fs.fed.us/arnf.

20 GRANDVIEW
🥾 🚤 🚐 🐴 ⛺

Scenic rating: 8

in Poudre Canyon

Grandview occupies an enviable position between the Neota Wilderness and Rocky Mountain National Park. The campground is at the south end of Long Draw Reservoir, in a spruce grove on a steep shore. The campground is small, cozy, and off the beaten track. The large reservoir, wide park, and surrounding ridgelines are impressive. Campers can go fishing or carry a boat down to the reservoir. The nearest hiking trails are Neota Creek and La Poudre Pass Trails, which begin at the end of Long Draw Road. Neota Creek Trail is an unmaintained track through wetlands to the base of Iron Mountain. La Poudre Pass Trail enters Rocky Mountain National Park and meets up with the Colorado River.

Campsites, facilities: There are nine sites for tents only. There are no hookups. Picnic tables, grills, and fire rings are provided. Vault toilets and drinking water are available. Trash must be packed out. Leashed pets are permitted.

Reservations, fees: Reservations are not accepted. The fee is $11 per night (includes two tents). Golden Age and Golden Access Passports are accepted. Cash or check only. Open late June–early November.

Directions: From Fort Collins, take U.S. Highway 287 north to Ted's Place and take Highway 14 west for 53.9 miles. Turn left on Long Draw Road. The campground is on the left in 11.9 miles.

Contact: Roosevelt National Forest, 970/295-6796, www.fs.fed.us/arnf.

21 ASPENGLEN
🥾 🚤 🐴 ♿ 🚐 ⛺

Scenic rating: 7

in Rocky Mountain National Park

Rocky Mountain National Park is a renowned destination for hikers, climbers, and wildlife lovers. The park contains over 350 miles of hiking trails and 114 peaks over 10,000 feet, including Longs Peak, Colorado's most frequently climbed fourteener. One-third of the park is above tree line, so the majority of trails climb to mountain lakes and ridgelines with fabulous views of this glaciated landscape. The park also has the highest continuous paved highway in the country, Trail Ridge Road. A trip to the park isn't complete without a drive along this route, which traverses the park and crosses the Continental Divide. With so many attractions, Rocky Mountain is a busy destination in the summer, but the crowds thin out dramatically in the winter and fall. There are four front-country campgrounds on the east side of the park and one on the west side. Aspenglen is the smallest and quietest campground for tents and RVs, but the views aren't nearly as spectacular as at nearby Moraine Park. The Horseshoe Park and Deer Mountain Trails are accessible from the campground, and the Lawn Lake trailhead is a short drive away. Horseshoe Park is a popular location for viewing elk and bighorn sheep.

The campground has four loops. Loop A (1–5 and A–E) has drive-in and walk-in tent sites in an evergreen forest. The walk-in sites are across the old Fall River channel and have views of Bighorn Mountain. Loop B (6–20) has drive-in tent sites shaded by tall ponderosa pines with views of Bighorn Mountain. Loop C (21–50) is for both tents and RVs. Sites 31–34 and 50 are in a small draw without views. Sites 35–49 are in a meadow with views of Bighorn Mountain. Privacy is poor, so mostly RVs use this site.

Campsites, facilities: There are 55 sites for tents and RVs up to 40 feet. There are 25 sites for tents only. The facilities are wheelchair accessible. Picnic tables, grills, fire rings, and tent pads are provided. Flush toilets, drinking water, dishwashing sinks, food lockers, campfire programs, an amphitheater, and a riding stable are available. Leashed pets are permitted in the campground, but pets are not allowed on trails.

Reservations, fees: Reservations are not accepted. The fee is $20 per night (includes six people and two tents). Vehicles must also have a $20 entrance pass. Golden Age and Golden Access Passports are accepted. Open mid-May–late September.

Directions: From Estes Park, take U.S. Highway 34 west to the Fall River entrance station. In 0.1 mile, turn left at the Aspenglen sign. The campground is in 0.5 mile.

Contact: Rocky Mountain National Park, 970/586-1206, www.nps.gov/romo.

22 MORAINE PARK
🧍‍♀️ 🚣 ❄️ 🐎 🚐 ⛺

Scenic rating: 9

in Rocky Mountain National Park

BEST (

Moraine Park is the largest of the four campgrounds on the east side of Rocky Mountain National Park. (For more information on the park, see the Aspenglen listing in this chapter.) The setting is incredible—the campground is in a grassy parkland enclosed on three sides by the high peaks of the Continental Divide. The campground is like a small village, busy with RVs coming and going, and everyone from toddlers to old-timers running around, but the crowds are worth the setting. The Fern Lake and Cub Lake trailheads are nearby. These trails can be turned into a loop of about 14 miles

with the Bear Lake Trail, providing a tour of the park's many ecosystems. Anglers can fish for native trout on the Big Thompson River. Cross-country skiing is excellent in the park, but visitors should be prepared for frigid temperatures and howling winds.

There are five loops in a montane habitat. The tall ponderosa pines and scattered aspen provide fair shade and allow excellent views. The sites are color coded: brown for tents, blue for vans and pickups, yellow for trailers under 18 feet and small RVs, and green for trailers over 18 feet and large RVs. Loop A (1–140) attracts tents and RVs of all sizes. Loop B (170–225) is more cramped and attracts mostly RVs with some tents. Most of the sites in Loop C (226–247) have nice views. Loop D (141–169) is largely reserved for tent campers. This loop has excellent views as well.

Campsites, facilities: There are 246 sites for tents and RVs up to 40 feet. There are no hookups. Sites 129, 219, 226, 238, 239, and 242 are pull-through. Picnic tables, grills, fire rings, and tent pads are provided. Flush toilets, drinking water, dishwashing sinks, dump stations, pay phones, food lockers, campfire programs, and an amphitheater are available. Leashed pets are permitted, but pets are not allowed on trails.

Reservations, fees: Reservations are accepted from late May–late September at 800/365-CAMP. The fee is $20 per night (includes six people and two tents). Vehicles must also have a $20 entrance pass. Golden Age and Golden Access Passports are accepted. The B loop is open year-round. The other loops are open late spring to early fall. Water is not available from mid-September–mid-May.

Directions: From Estes Park, take U.S. Highway 36 west to the Beaver Meadow entrance station. In 0.2 mile, turn left on Bear Lake Road. In 1.2 miles, turn right at the campground sign.

Contact: Rocky Mountain National Park, 970/586-1206, www.nps.gov/romo.

23 GLACIER BASIN
🏕 🎣 ♿ 🚐 ⛺

Scenic rating: 8

in Rocky Mountain National Park

Glacier Basin is a sprawling front-country campground on the east side of Rocky Mountain National Park. (For more information on the park, see the Aspenglen listing in this chapter.) The campground is in a dense lodgepole forest that's very monotonous, but the basin is surrounded by the peaks of the Continental Divide, including Longs Peak, Storm Peak, Half Mountain, Taylor Peak, Otis Peak, and Flattop Mountain. There are numerous hiking trails, too. The Sprague Lake, Storm Pass, and Bierstadt Lake Trails begin nearby, and a trail connects the campground to the YMCA. Winter visitors will have very little company and can enjoy frigid snowshoeing and mountaineering in the park.

The campground has four loops and 14 group sites. The sites are just 15–30 feet apart, and the lodgepoles provide good shade but little privacy. The following sites have the best views: 69, 71, 72, 93, 94, 99, 120, 121, 149, and 150. The group sites have dispersed tent camping (without tent pads) in a lodgepole forest. Sites 1, 3, and 5 are next to a beautiful meadow.

Campsites, facilities: The sites are color-coded: brown for tents, blue for vans and pickups, yellow for trailers under 18 feet and small RVs, and green for trailers over 18 feet and large RVs. There are 150 sites for tents and RVs up to 40 feet, with 63 sites for tents only. There are also 14 group sites. Sites 33, 35, 60, and 61 and the facilities are wheelchair accessible. Picnic tables, grills, fire rings, and tent pads are provided. Flush toilets, drinking water, dishwashing sinks, dump stations, pay phones, food lockers, campfire programs, an amphitheater, and a riding stable are available. Leashed pets are permitted, but pets are not allowed on trails.

Reservations, fees: Reservations are accepted from late May–late September at 800/365-CAMP. The fee is $20 per night (includes six people and two tents). Vehicles must also have a $20 entrance pass. Golden Age and Golden Access Passports are accepted. Open June–mid-September.

Directions: From Estes Park, take U.S. Highway 36 west to the Beaver Meadow entrance station. In 0.2 mile, turn left on Bear Lake Road. In 4.8 miles, turn left at the Glacier Basin sign.

Contact: Rocky Mountain National Park, 970/586-1206, www.nps.gov/romo.

24 BOYD LAKE STATE PARK
🏕 🚴 🏊 🛶 ⛵ 🎣 ❄ 🦌 ♿ 🚐 ⛺

Scenic rating: 5

in Loveland

Boyd Lake is a "water sports haven" and a busy summer destination. The park is on the western edge of the plains; to the west, Longs Peak and the Indian Peaks dominate the horizon. The 1,700-surface-acre lake is open to boating, windsurfing, waterskiing, and swimming. A busy multiuse trail circles the lake, and the wetlands are open to wildlife viewing and waterfowl hunting. Anglers catch bass, catfish, perch, crappie, walleye, and trout. Winter activities include ice fishing and cross-country skiing.

The campground is on the western shore. With six identical paved loops, it's a mega-complex. Privacy is poor (the sites are just 10 feet apart), but the campground is extremely popular on weekends, so reservations are highly recommended. Many sites have partial shade, and a few sites have lake views. Loop A is closest to the swim beach. Loop F has more mature trees and it borders a grassland, so it's a little more quiet and private than the other loops.

Campsites, facilities: There are 148 sites for tents and RVs up to 60 feet. Sites 47, 76, 97, and 131 and the facilities are wheelchair accessible. Electric hookups are available at all sites, and all sites are pull-through. Picnic tables, grills, and fire rings are provided. Restrooms with flush toilets and showers, drinking water, dump stations, a laundry room, boat ramp, amphitheater, marina with rentals, horseshoe pits, and a basketball court are available. Leashed pets are permitted.

Reservations, fees: Reservations are accepted at 800/678-2267 and www.parks.state.co.us. The fee is $16–18 per night. Vehicles must also have a Daily Parks Pass ($5) or Annual Parks Pass ($55). The Aspen Leaf Pass is accepted. Cash or check only. Open year-round.

Directions: From I-25, take Exit 257/U.S. Highway 34 west for 3.4 miles. Turn north on Madison Avenue. In 1.5 miles, turn right on 37th Street. The park entrance is on the right in one mile.

Contact: Boyd Lake State Park, 970/669-1739, email: boyd.lake@state.co.us.

25 LONGS PEAK

Scenic rating: 7

in Rocky Mountain National Park

BEST (

There are four front-country campgrounds on the east side of Rocky Mountain National Park. (For more information on the park, see the Aspenglen listing in this chapter.) Longs Peak is the smallest and the only tent-only campground. This is the starting point for the challenging ascent of Longs Peak (14,259 feet). Hikers begin at 3:00 A.M. to complete the 12–15-hour climb. The only nontechnical route, the Keyhole, is about 16 miles round-trip. Many hikers are turned back by strong winds, thunderstorms, and ice, but Longs Peak remains the most frequently climbed fourteener in the state. The campground is a small loop in a dense spruce-fir forest. The sites are just 10–20 feet apart. There is plenty of camaraderie and very little privacy. Sites 1, 3, 4, 6, 8, 9, and 11 have views of Sheep Mountain. Stays are limited to three days during the summer season.

Campsites, facilities: There are 26 tent sites. Picnic tables, grills, fire rings, and tent pads are provided. Wheelchair-accessible vault toilets, drinking water, pay phones, and food lockers are available. Leashed pets are permitted.

Reservations, fees: Reservations are not accepted. The fee is $20 per night (includes six people and two tents). Golden Age and Golden Access Passports are accepted. Cash or check only. Open year-round. Water is not available from mid-September–mid-May.

Directions: From U.S. Highway 36 in Estes Park, take Highway 7 south for nine miles. Turn right at the Longs Peak sign. Go uphill 0.9 mile to the campground.

Contact: Rocky Mountain National Park, 970/586-1206, www.nps.gov/romo.

26 MEEKER PARK

Scenic rating: 7

south of Estes Park

Meeker Park is a campground au naturel. With the cheapest rates in town, it's usually considered an overflow campground. Although this is the least developed campground near Rocky Mountain National Park, it can fill up on Friday and Saturday nights with tent campers. It has three loops in a thin pine forest. Sites 1–5 are walk-ins near the busy highway. Sites 6–8 are in an aspen grove that is also near the highway. The back loop (sites 15–29) requires a high-clearance vehicle to access it, but it's the best place to camp. Sites 17–19, 21, and 24 have views of Sheep Mountain. Sites 27–29 are especially rocky, but they also have views of Mount Meeker.

Campsites, facilities: There are 29 sites for tents and RVs up to 25 feet. There are no hookups. Sites 1–5 and 9 are pull-through. Grills, fire rings, and portable toilets are provided. Leashed pets are permitted.

Reservations, fees: Reservations are not accepted. The fee is $8 per night (includes eight

people). Golden Age and Golden Access Passports are accepted. Cash or check only. Open mid-June–Labor Day.
Directions: From Estes Park, take Highway 7 south for 11 miles. The campground is on the right about a half mile before the town of Meeker.
Contact: Arapaho Roosevelt National Forest, 303/444-6600, www.fs.fed.us/r2/arnf/.

27 OLIVE RIDGE

Scenic rating: 7

south of Estes Park

Olive Ridge is just outside the southeast corner of Rocky Mountain National Park, at the entryway to the Wild Basin, a vast area of dense woods, tumbling streams, and high cirques. From the Wild Basin trailhead, hikers can follow St. Vrain Creek to Ouzel Lake (an excellent fishing destination), Bluebird Lake, and Thunder Lake. This large, pleasant campground is in a pine forest with scattered boulders. The sites are 30–50 feet apart and practically identical, with a few exceptions. Sits 37, 39, and 40 have views of the Wild Basin. Sites 50 and 52 have views of the valley. Sites 26 and 40 are oversized.
Campsites, facilities: There are 56 sites for tents and RVs up to 30 feet. There are no hookups. Site 50 is pull-through. Picnic tables, grills, fire rings, and tent pads are provided. Vault toilets and drinking water are available. Leashed pets are permitted.
Reservations, fees: Reservations are accepted at 877/444-6777 and www.reserve-usa.com. The fee is $14 per night (includes eight people). Oversized sites cost $17 per night (includes 10 people and two tent pads). Golden Age and Golden Access Passports are accepted. Cash or check only. Open mid-May–early October.
Directions: From Lyons, take Highway 7 west to Allenspark. Continue 1.3 miles past Al-

lenspark and turn left at the campground sign and then another left to reach the fee station.
Contact: Arapaho Roosevelt National Forest, 303/444-6600, www.fs.fed.us/r2/arnf/.

28 CAMP DICK

Scenic rating: 7

north of Ward

Camp Dick is a popular destination for families and hikers. The Buchanan Pass Trail runs from the campground into the heart of the Indian Peaks Wilderness, where serrated peaks and alpine lakes await the hardy hiker. The campground consists of two loops in a meadow ringed by a spruce-fir forest beside the Middle St. Vrain Creek. Mountain bikers and ATV riders can explore the Bunce School Road, Coney Flats Road, and South Vrain Road. Anglers can pick brookies out of the Middle St. Vrain Creek. Most sites are close to the road and not screened, so privacy is poor, but modern facilities and great hiking brings in the crowd. Half of the sites are nonreservable, but those fill up quickly on weekends, so arrive early if you don't have a reservation. Sites 1, 3, 4, 7–10, and 12–16 are creekside. Sites 1, 3, and 4 are walk-ins. Sites 7, 11, 12, 21, 26, 28, 39, and 40 are oversized.
Campsites, facilities: There are 41 sites for tents and RVs up to 55 feet. There are no hookups. Site 16 is pull-through. Picnic tables, grills, fire rings, and tent pads are provided. Vault toilets and drinking water are available. The facilities are wheelchair accessible. Leashed pets are permitted.
Reservations, fees: Reservations are accepted at 877/444-6777 and www.reserve-usa.com. The fee is $14 per night (includes eight people). Oversized sites cost $17 per night (includes 10 people and two tent pads). Golden Age and Golden Access Passports are accepted. Cash or check only. Open mid-May–late October.

Directions: From Peaceful Valley, take County Road 92 west for 0.8 mile to the campground.
Contact: Arapaho Roosevelt National Forest, 303/444-6600, www.fs.fed.us/r2/arnf/.

29 PEACEFUL VALLEY
🚶🚵🛶🐕🏕️♿🚐⛺

Scenic rating: 7

north of Ward

Peaceful Valley is a great campground for R&R. It's about four miles east of the Indian Peaks Wilderness boundary. From nearby Camp Dick, hikers can take the Buchanan Pass Trail into the wilderness to the Middle St. Vrain Trail, the St. Vrain Glaciers, Red Deer Lake, and Buchanan Pass. These are challenging hikes and many require a night in the backcountry. Because of the popularity of the wilderness, permits are required for backcountry camping. Mountain bikers and ATV riders can explore the Bunce School Road, Coney Flats Road, and South Vrain Road. Anglers can pick brookies out of the Middle St. Vrain Creek.

The campground is in a spruce-fir forest on the banks the creek. The road runs through the middle of the campground, so it can be very busy on the weekends, when every site is full. About half of the sites are nonreservable, but they're usually full by Thursday afternoon. Sites 1–3, 7, 8, and 11–14 are creekside. Sites 11–14 are walk-ins with views up the valley. Site 17 is oversized.
Campsites, facilities: There are 17 sites for tents and RVs up to 55 feet. There are no hookups. Picnic tables, grills, fire rings, and tent pads are provided. Vault toilets and drinking water are available. The facilities are wheelchair accessible. Leashed pets are permitted.
Reservations, fees: Reservations are accepted at 877/444-6777 and www.reserve-usa.com. The fee is $14 per night (includes eight people). Oversized sites cost $17 per night (includes 10 people and two tent pads). Golden Age and Golden Access Passports are accepted. Cash or check only. Open mid-May–late October.
Directions: From Peaceful Valley, take County Road 92 west for 0.2 mile to the campground.
Contact: Arapaho Roosevelt National Forest, 303/444-6600, www.fs.fed.us/r2/arnf/.

30 PAWNEE
🚶🛶🚐🐕🚐⛺

Scenic rating: 9

west of Ward

BEST (

Pawnee is the best campground for accessing the Indian Peaks Wilderness from the east side, not to mention it has some of the very best scenery of any national forest campground. Predictably, it's incredibly popular and reservations are highly recommended on weekends. However, half the sites (the evens) are first-come, first-served, so even late arrivals can land a site. The campground is on the shore of Lake Brainard, in a basin ringed by Pawnee Peak, Mount Toll, Mount Audubon, Pauite Peak, Shoshone Peak, and Navajo Peak—all over 12,000 feet. The Navajo and Isabelle glaciers are visible on these jagged peaks. The Mount Audubon, Mitchell and Blue Lakes, Pawnee Pass, and Beaver Creek Trails are all accessible from the two trailheads at the campground. Pawnee Pass is on the Continental Divide. There is also good trout fishing on Brainard and Red Rock Lakes, which are open to hand-powered boats.

The campground is a figure eight in a dense spruce-fir forest. The trees closest to the lake have been bent and twisted by strong winds into krummholz. The sites are about 50 feet apart and fairly private. Sites 16–18, 20, 24, 27, and 28 are near the road. Sites 20–30 and 39–42 have the best views of the Continental

Divide. Sites 43–55 are excellent tent sites. Sites 52 and 54 have double tables.

Campsites, facilities: There are 55 sites for tents and RVs up to 45 feet. There are no hookups. Sites 22 and 26 are pull-through. Picnic tables, grills, fire rings, and tent pads are provided. Vault toilets and drinking water are available. Leashed pets are permitted.

Reservations, fees: Reservations are accepted at 877/444-6777 and www.reserveusa.com. The fee is $14 per night (includes eight people). Campers must also purchase a Brainard Lake Recreation Fee for $7 (five days) or $25 (season). Golden Age and Golden Access Passports are accepted. Cash or check only. Open late June–mid-September.

Directions: From Ward, take County Road 102 west for 4.8 miles. The campground is on the right.

Contact: Arapaho Roosevelt National Forest, 303/444-6600, www.fs.fed.us/r2/arnf/.

31 BOULDER COUNTY FAIRGROUND

Scenic rating: 2

in Longmont

This utilitarian campground on the county fairgrounds has a distinctive smell—elephant ears, popcorn, and livestock. The campground is primarily used by fair participants, but it's open to anyone. It's set up like an RV park with rows of parallel parking spots. There are few trees and no shade or privacy. Tent camping is not recommended. Fair visitors will find the location very convenient—it's across from the arenas and adjacent to trailer parking.

Campsites, facilities: There are 96 sites for tents and RVs up to 60 feet. Water and electric hookups are available. Restrooms with flush toilets and showers, drinking water, dump stations, and pay phones are available. Leashed pets are permitted.

Reservations, fees: Reservations are accepted at 303/678-1525. The tent fee is $15 per night, and the RV fee is $20–25 per night. Cash or check only. Open year-round, but there is no water after October.

Directions: From I-25, take Highway 119 west 8.5 miles. Turn right on Hover Street, then left on Nelson Road. The campground is on the right.

Contact: Boulder County Fairgrounds, 303/678-1525.

32 ST. VRAIN STATE PARK

Scenic rating: 4

in Longmont

St. Vrain State Park is a bit of a mud hole on the floodplain of the St. Vrain River. This state park has just 80 acres of water and 50 acres of land, but it's trying hard to be more than it is. Despite its proximity to the interstate (spitting distance), it's a popular afternoon fishing hole for residents of Longmont, and it even attracts a large crowd of weekend campers looking for a very quick getaway. The three stocked ponds are open to hand-powered boats and electric motors. The Muskrat Run Nature Trail is half a mile long.

There are three loops around the fishing ponds. The West Loop was completely renovated in 2005 and has partial hookups and new tent pads and sun shelters. The East Loop (sites 24–42) is in a cottonwood grove and has the best shade. The North Loop is closest to the interstate and is a last resort.

Campsites, facilities: There are 60 sites for tents and RVs up to 40 feet. Site 45, the facilities, and the fishing pier are wheelchair accessible. Water and electric hookups are available in the West Loop (sites 1–25). Picnic tables, grills, and fire rings are provided. Vault toilets, drinking water, dump stations, and an amphitheater are available. Leashed pets are permitted.

Reservations, fees: Reservations are accepted at 800/678-2267 and www.parks.state.co.us. Group reservations are accepted at 303/699-3860, ext. 721. The tent fee is $12 per night, and the RV fee is $16 per night (includes six people and two camping units). Vehicles must also have a Daily Parks Pass ($5) or Annual Parks Pass ($55). The Aspen Leaf Pass is accepted. Cash or check only. Open year-round, but the park is unattended from October–March.

Directions: From I-25, take Highway 119 west for 1.1 miles. Turn right on County Road 7/County Road 24.5. The park entrance is in 0.9 mile.

Contact: St. Vrain State Park, 303/678-9402, email: st.vrain.park@state.co.us.

33 RAINBOW LAKES

Scenic rating: 8

north of Nederland

BEST (

Rainbow Lakes is a high-altitude campground with access to the Indian Peaks Wilderness. The serrated ridgeline of the Indian Peaks runs from Longs Peak to James Peak and contains gorgeous alpine lakes and a handful of glaciers. This wilderness is easily accessible from Denver, Boulder, and Fort Collins, making it incredibly popular. Usage is closely monitored, and permits are required for backcountry camping. Campers can take the Arapaho Glacier Trail for six miles to awesome views of the glacier, and two miles farther to Arapaho Pass. The campground is in a spruce-fir forest below the basin that holds Rainbow Lakes. Sites 4–10 are next to a rocky stream. Site 15 has a double table.

Campsites, facilities: There are 16 sites for tents and RVs up to 20 feet. There are no hookups. Site 3 is pull-through. Picnic tables, grills, and fire rings are provided. Vault toilets and drinking water are available. The facilities are wheelchair accessible. Trash must be packed out. Leashed pets are permitted.

Reservations, fees: Reservations are not accepted. The fee is $8 per night (includes eight people). Golden Age and Golden Access Passports are accepted. Cash or check only. Open late June–early October.

Directions: From Nederland, take Highway 72/Peak to Peak Byway north for 7.1 miles. Turn left on Forest Route 298. The campground is in 4.9 miles.

Contact: Arapaho Roosevelt National Forest, 303/444-6600, www.fs.fed.us/r2/arnf/.

34 KELLY DAHL

Scenic rating: 6

south of Nederland

Kelly Dahl is a convenient campground for exploring the Front Range from Estes Park to Black Hawk, with a combination of back-country and grown-up options to keep any multigenerational family happy. The campground has three loops in a shady pine forest. The Aspen Loop (sites 1–20) is shady. Sites 10, 11, 14, and 15 are on a slope that's not good for tents. Sites 16 has good views to the north. Fir Loop (sites 21–27) is more open. It surrounds a meadow and has scattered pines. Pine Loop (sites 28–46) is similar to Aspen Loop. Sites 28 and 30 are next to the playground.

Campsites, facilities: There are 46 sites for tents and RVs up to 40 feet. There are no hookups. Site 11 is pull-through. Picnic tables, grills, and fire rings are provided. Vault toilets, drinking water, and a playground are available. Leashed pets are permitted.

Reservations, fees: Reservations are accepted at 877/444-6777 and www.reserveusa.com. The fee is $14 per night (includes eight people). Golden Age and Golden Access Passports are accepted. Cash or check only. Open late May–October.

Directions: From Nederland, take Highway 119 south for 3.7 miles. The campground is on the left.

Contact: Arapaho Roosevelt National Forest, 303/444-6600, www.fs.fed.us/r2/arnf/.

35 REVEREND'S RIDGE
🚶 🚴 🛶 ❄️ 🐎 ♿ 🚐 ⛺

Scenic rating: 6

in Golden Gate Canyon State Park

Golden Gate Canyon State Park has 12,000 acres of pine forests, hills, and meadows just 16 miles northwest of Golden. This busy campground serves Front Range residents as well as out-of-staters. Activities include hiking, biking, and horseback riding on 35 miles of trails. Ralston Creek and all of the ponds are stocked by the Department of Wildlife. The park's facilities—especially the Red Barn and Panorama Point—are frequently reserved for special events like reunions and weddings. Winter activities include cross-country skiing, snowshoeing, and ice fishing and skating.

Reverend's Ridge is in the northwestern corner of the park. It is the largest campground in the area. The Elk, Mule Deer, and Raccoon Trails all pass through the campground. It has 10 loops in a seemingly endless lodgepole pine forest. The sites are 20–50 feet apart, so privacy is at a minimum in most of the loops. Loops A–E (sites 1–59) have electric hookups and are used mainly by RVs. Loops H, I, and J are for tents only.

Campsites, facilities: There are 97 sites for tents and RVs up to 35 feet. Loops F, G, and J are for tents only. Sites 21, 56, and 72 and the facilities are wheelchair accessible. Electric hookups are available at Loops A–E. Sites 9–24 and 44–59 are pull-through. There are also five cabins and two yurts. Picnic tables, grills, and fire rings are provided. Restrooms with flush toilets and showers, drinking water, dump stations, a laundry room, amphitheater, campfire programs, and pay phones are available. Leashed pets are permitted.

Reservations, fees: Reservations are accepted at 800/678-2267 and www.parks.state.co.us. The fee is $12–18 per night. Vehicles must also have a Daily Parks Pass ($5) or Annual Parks Pass ($55). The Aspen Leaf Pass is accepted. Loop C is open year-round. The other loops are open from late spring to early fall.

Directions: From Golden, take Highway 46 west about 20 miles. Go north on Highway 119 for 3.3 miles. Turn right on Gap Road. In 1.1 mile, turn left at the campground sign. Camper registration is in 0.4 mile.

Contact: Golden Gate Canyon State Park, 303/582-3707, www.parks.state.co.us.

36 ASPEN MEADOW
🚶 🚴 🛶 🐎 ⛺

Scenic rating: 7

in Golden Gate Canyon State Park

Aspen Meadow is in the northwestern corner of 12,000-acre Golden Gate Canyon State Park. This tent-only campground is a quieter, more primitive alternative to oversized Reverend's Ridge. The Snowshoe Hare and Mule Deer Trails are accessible from the campground, and Dude's Fishing Hole is a short hike away. The first loop, Meadow, has walk-in and drive-in sites in a spruce-fir forest with a small aspen grove next to a meadow. Sites 2–5 and 9–14 are walk-ins. The Rimrock Loop (sites 15–23) can accommodate horses and horse trailers. Sites 17–20 are walk-ins. The Twin Creek Loop has just two sites a short distance from the road. The Conifer Loop (sites 26–35) is the most attractive, with all of the sites walk-ins. Sites 29–35 follow a small creek up a slight rise with an aspen grove and a small meadow. This is a great location for families, since small kids can explore without going near the parking lot. Sites 30, 32, and 34 and creekside. All of the sites are shaded. (For more information on Golden Gate Canyon State Park, see the Reverend's Ridge listing in this chapter.)

Campsites, facilities: There are 35 sites for

tents. Picnic tables, grills, fire rings, and tent pads are provided. Vault toilets and drinking water are available. Leashed pets are permitted.

Reservations, fees: Reservations are accepted at 800/678-2267 and www.parks.state.co.us. The fee is $12 per night. Vehicles must also have a Daily Parks Pass ($5) or Annual Parks Pass ($55). The Aspen Leaf Pass is accepted. Closed in winter.

Directions: From Golden, take Highway 46 west about 20 miles. Go north on Highway 119 for 3.3 miles. Turn right on Gap Road. The campground entrance is on the right in three miles.

Contact: Golden Gate Canyon State Park, 303/582-3707, www.parks.state.co.us.

37 RIFLEMAN PHILLIPS GROUP

Scenic rating: 6

in Golden Gate Canyon State Park

This group campground is in the northern half of Golden Gate Canyon State Park in a pine and aspen forest with dispersed tent camping. There are lots of dead trees and the ground is rocky, so it's not the most appealing group site, but the park's group facilities are excellent. The Red Barn and Panorama Point can be reserved for group functions. Panorama Point has an extensive deck with views from Idaho Springs to Estes Park. The Red Barn's picnic area can accommodate up to 150 people, and it has a volleyball court, fishing ponds, and horseshoe pits. It's a long drive from the campground to the Red Barn, but ambitious groups can hike there on the Buffalo Trail. The Snowshoe Hare Trail also passes by the campground and provides access to Dude's Fishing Hole.

Campsites, facilities: There is dispersed tent camping for up to 75 people. Picnic tables, grills, fire rings, and tent pads are provided.

Vault toilets and drinking water are available. Leashed pets are permitted.

Reservations, fees: Reservations are accepted at 800/678-2267 and www.parks.state.co.us. The fee is $48 per night (includes 24 people). Six additional people cost $12 per night. Vehicles must also have a Daily Parks Pass ($5) or Annual Parks Pass ($55). Open February–October.

Directions: From Golden, take Highway 46 west about 20 miles. Go north on Highway 119 for 3.3 miles. Turn right on Gap Road. The campground entrance is on the right in 3.8 miles.

Contact: Golden Gate Canyon State Park, 303/582-3707, www.parks.state.co.us.

38 PICKLE GULCH GROUP

Scenic rating: 6

near Black Hawk

Pickle Gulch is a group campground in a lodgepole pine forest with a few aspen. The six sites each have dispersed tent camping around a central eating area. The sites are well spaced and fairly private. Sites 4 and 5 are farthest from the parking lot. The primary draw here is the proximity to the cities of the Front Range, but without views or any activities except cooking and eating, this campground is not very appealing.

Campsites, facilities: There are six group areas for tent camping. Sites 1–5 can accommodate up to 30 people. Site 6 can accommodate up to 15 people. Picnic tables, grills, fire rings, and tent pads are provided. Vault toilets, drinking water, and an amphitheater are available. Leashed pets are permitted.

Reservations, fees: Reservations are required and accepted at 877/444-6777 and www.reserveusa.com. The fee is $30–45 per night. Open year-round.

Directions: From Black Hawk, take Highway 119 north for 3.5 miles. Turn left on Missouri

Gulch Road. In 0.8 mile, turn left at the Pickle Gulch sign.

Contact: Arapaho Roosevelt National Forest, 303/567-3000, www.fs.fed.us/r2/arnf/.

39 COLD SPRINGS

Scenic rating: 6

north of Black Hawk

Cold Springs is a great stopover campground for travelers exploring the Front Range. The campground is in a forest of spruce, fir, and aspen, with several small clearings. It's a scenic spot with some good views of the high peaks to the east and west, especially from the overlook. The nearest hiking and biking trails are in Golden Gate Canyon State Park. The only drawback is the ever-present traffic noise. Sites 6–8, 14–17, 32, and 33 have excellent views of the high peaks to the south. The tent sites (20–22) are very close to each other and the road. Sites 26–30 are in the aspen grove, and sites 35–38 overlook the highway. Steep stairs climb up to sites 1–5.

Campsites, facilities: There are 38 sites for tents and RVs up to 50 feet. Sites 20–22 are for tents only. Site 23 and the facilities are wheelchair accessible. There are no hookups. Sites 1–5, 9, 10, 35, 36, and 38 are pull-through. Picnic tables, grills, fire rings, and tent pads are provided. Vault toilets, drinking water, and a playground are available. Leashed pets are permitted.

Reservations, fees: Reservations are accepted at 877/444-6777 and www.reserveusa.com. The fee is $13 per night (includes eight people). Golden Age and Golden Access Passports are accepted. Cash or check only. Open mid-May–early October.

Directions: From Black Hawk, take Highway 119 north for 5.1 miles. Turn left into the campground.

Contact: Arapaho Roosevelt National Forest, 303/567-3000, www.fs.fed.us/r2/arnf/.

40 COLUMBINE

Scenic rating: 5

near Black Hawk

Columbine is the gambler's choice campground. A shortcut makes it possible to get from the campground to Black Hawk's casinos in less than 15 minutes. The historic mining and gambling town is the main reason to come to this campground, which is otherwise unextraordinary. It's a large loop in an evergreen forest. There are no views, and the sites are just 25–50 feet apart. The rocky ground makes it hard to find multiple tent sites. This campground is rarely busy.

Campsites, facilities: There are 47 sites for tents and RVs up to 30 feet. There are no hookups. Picnic tables, grills, and fire rings are provided. Vault toilets and drinking water are available. The facilities are wheelchair accessible. Leashed pets are permitted.

Reservations, fees: Reservations are accepted at 877/444-6777 and www.reserveusa.com. The fee is $12 per night (includes eight people). Golden Age and Golden Access Passports are accepted. Cash or check only. Open mid-May–early October.

Directions: From Black Hawk, take Highway 119 west for 1.9 miles. Turn left on Apex Valley Road. In 2.3 miles, turn left on Upper Apex Road. In 2.4 miles, turn right on Bald Mountain Road. The campground is on the right in 1.3 miles.

Contact: Arapaho Roosevelt National Forest, 303/567-3000, www.fs.fed.us/r2/arnf/.

41 MIZPAH

Scenic rating: 5

south of Winter Park

Mizpah is on busy U.S. Highway 40 between I-70 and Winter Park. There is a lot of traffic noise from the highway, but the campground frequently fills up on weekends because it's a good place for exploring Summit County. It's in a spruce-fir forest next to the West Fork of Clear Creek. Sites 1–3 are close to the river. There are good coffee shops and an excellent burger joint in nearby Empire.

Campsites, facilities: There are 10 sites for tents and RVs up to 20 feet. There are no hookups. Sites 6 and 9 are pull-through. Picnic tables, grills, and fire rings are provided. Vault toilets and drinking water are available. The facilities are wheelchair accessible. Leashed pets are permitted.

Reservations, fees: Reservations are not accepted. The fee is $11 per night. Golden Age and Golden Access Passports are accepted. Cash or check only. Open late May–early September.

Directions: From the Winter Park visitors center, drive south on U.S. Highway 40 for 20.8 miles. The campground entrance is on the right.

Contact: Arapaho National Forest, 303/567-3000, www.fs.fed.us/arnf.

42 CLEAR LAKE

Scenic rating: 6

south of Georgetown

Clear Lake campground is a short drive from the historic mining district of Georgetown, and it's on the western boundary of Mount Evans Wilderness area. The campground is very popular on weekends when it fills up with ATV owners and Front Range residents looking for a quick getaway. It's in a narrow valley forested with spruce, fir, and aspen and about a mile above Lower Cabin Creek Reservoir. The sites are large and spaced about 80 feet apart. Sites 1, 2, and 5 are next to the road.

Campsites, facilities: There are eight sites for tents and RVs up to 15 feet. There are no

hookups. Picnic tables, grills, and fire rings are provided. Vault toilets and drinking water are available. Leashed pets are permitted.

Reservations, fees: Reservations are not accepted. The fee is $11 per night. Golden Age and Golden Access Passports are accepted. Cash or check only. Open late May–early September.

Directions: From the Georgetown visitors center, turn right on Argentine Street and then left on 6th Street. On 0.1 mile, turn right on Rose Street/Guanella Pass Road. The campground is on the right in 5.8 miles.

Contact: Arapaho National Forest, Clear Creek Ranger District, 303/567-3000, www.fs.fed.us/r2/arnf/.

43 GUANELLA PASS

Scenic rating: 7

south of Georgetown

This campground is on the west side of the Mount Evans Wilderness area and a short drive from the spectacular views at the top of the pass. Due to its proximity to Denver, Guanella Pass is frequently full during the summer, and reservations are highly recommended. Anglers can fish for brookies on the creek or hike up a 1.5-mile trail to Silver Dollar Lake. Hikers have several options in Mount Evans Wilderness, which has two fourteeners, alpine tundra, arctic tundra, and Mount Goliath Natural Area, a large stand of bristlecone pines. On the east side of the wilderness area, the Mount Evans Byway, the highest paved road in the country, summits Mount Evans, but from Guanella Pass, the Bierstadt Trail climbs to Mount Bierstadt, the other fourteener. From that peak, hikers can follow a horseshoe-shaped ridge another two miles to Mount Evans. Bighorn sheep and mountain goats are frequently sighted in this area.

The campground has two loops. The first loop (sites 1–7) is on the west side of the road, and the sites are first-come first-served. The second loop (sites 8–18) is on the east side of the road beside Cabin Creek. Sites 2, 3, 7, and 14–16 have good views down the valley. Sites 8, 10, and 11 are creekside. Sites 9–12, 14, and 15 are walk-in tent sites.

Campsites, facilities: There are 18 sites for tents and RVs up to 35 feet. Sites 9–12, 14, and 15 are for tents only. There are no hookups. Picnic tables, grills, fire rings, and tent pads are provided. Vault toilets and drinking water are available. The facilities are wheelchair accessible. Leashed pets are permitted.

Reservations, fees: Reservations are accepted at 877/444-6777 and www.reserveusa.com. The fee is $12 per night (includes eight people). Golden Age and Golden Access Passports are accepted. Cash or check only. Open late May–early September.

Directions: From the Georgetown visitors center, turn right on Argentine Street and then left on 6th Street. On 0.1 mile, turn right on Rose Street/Guanella Pass Road. The campground is in 8.7 miles. Sites 1–7 are on the right, and sites 8–18 are on the left.

Contact: Arapaho National Forest, Clear Creek Ranger District, 303/567-3000, www.fs.fed.us/r2/arnf/.

44 WEST CHICAGO CREEK
🏞️ 🛶 🐕 🚙 ⛰️

Scenic rating: 6

south of Idaho Springs

West Chicago Creek flows out of the Mount Evans Wilderness area down a narrow valley. The campground is a short distance from the Hells Hole trailhead, which follows the creek to the meadows at its headwaters beneath Gray Wolf Mountain. West Chicago Creek is a quick getaway from Denver, so it's very popular throughout the summer. It usually fills up on Thursday evening, but there are five nonreservable sites. The campground is a small loop in pine trees. An aspen grove bor-

ders one side of the campground and covers the slope down to the creek. The sites are just 25–50 feet apart. Sites 11 and 12 have views up the valley of Sugarloaf Peak. Sites 1 and 13–16 are next to the road, which receives a fair amount of traffic on weekends.

Campsites, facilities: There are 16 sites for tents and RVs up to 30 feet. There are no hookups. Site 10 is pull-through. Picnic tables, grills, and fire rings are provided. Vault toilets and drinking water are available. Leashed pets are permitted.

Reservations, fees: Reservations are accepted at 877/444-6777 and www.reserveusa.com. The fee is $11 per night (includes eight people). Golden Age and Golden Access Passports are accepted. Cash or check only. Open late May–early October.

Directions: From Idaho Springs, take Highway 103 south for 6.7 miles. Turn right on Forest Route 188. The campground is on the left in 2.8 miles.

Contact: Arapaho Roosevelt National Forest, 303/567-3000, www.fs.fed.us/r2/arnf/.

45 ECHO LAKE
🏞️ 🛶 🐕 🚙 ⛰️

Scenic rating: 7

south of Idaho Springs

BEST (

Echo Lake is on the northern edge of the Mount Evans Wilderness. The Mount Evans Byway is the highest paved road in North America. It climbs from the lake to the peak and features frequent sightings of bighorn sheep and mountain goats. Campers who want some exercise can take the Resthouse Trail to the Summit Lake Trail to Mount Evans. Most of the wilderness is above timberline, and the landscape is rugged glacial terrain pockmarked by alpine lakes and arctic tundra. The views plus the wildlife and proximity to Denver make this wilderness extremely popular. Reservations are highly recommended during the summer.

The campground is in a spruce-fir forest beside the highway and a short distance from the lake, which is owned by the City of Denver and open for fishing. The terraced sites are very close together, and the campground is a bit cramped. Sites 11 and 14 have the most privacy.

Campsites, facilities: There are 18 sites for tents and RVs up to 20 feet. Sites 1–4 are walk-ins. There are no hookups. Picnic tables, grills, fire rings, and tent pads are provided. Vault toilets and drinking water are available. There is a small store at Echo Lake Lodge. Leashed pets are permitted.

Reservations, fees: Reservations are accepted at 877/444-6777 and www.reserveusa.com. The fee is $12 per night (includes eight people). Golden Age and Golden Access Passports are accepted. Cash or check only. Open late May–early September.

Directions: From Idaho Springs, take Highway 103 south for 13.3 miles. Turn right after Echo Lake Lodge and then make the first left to enter the campground.

Contact: Arapaho Roosevelt National Forest, 303/567-3000, www.fs.fed.us/r2/arnf/.

46 CHERRY CREEK STATE PARK

🥾 🚲 🏊 🎣 🚤 ❄️ 🐎 ♿ 🚐 ⛺

Scenic rating: 5

in Denver

BEST (

Cherry Creek State Park is remarkable for its size and proximity to downtown Denver. The park has 4,200 acres of land and an 880-surface-acre lake. The marina is on the west shore of the lake, a large wetland preserve surrounds the south shore and Cherry Creek, and the campground is on the east shore. This campground is popular all summer long with Colorado residents and out-of-staters who are visiting the city and exploring the Front Range. Campers can go horseback riding, swimming, fishing, boating, and hiking or biking on the trail system. The 24-mile Cherry Creek Regional Trail connects the park with Castlewood Canyon State Park to the south. Winter visitors can go ice fishing or cross-country skiing. There's also a model airplane field and shooting range. Plus, the lakeshore offers excellent views of the Front Range.

The campground is very pleasant considering its size. There are six loops in the main campground, plus three group loops. There are no views of the mountains, but large cottonwoods provide shade at many of the loops. The loops are mostly designed for RVs, with the exception of the Cottonwood Loop (sites 76–102), which attracts mainly tent campers. The only loop with mountain views is Gold Rush (sites 103–125), but this loop has less shade than its neighbors. It's a real family scene, with kids of all ages taking over the grove on weekends. The sites are close together, but there's room for multiple tents.

Campsites, facilities: There are 120 sites for tents and RVs up to 80 feet. Sites 1, 15, 20, 60, and 70 and the facilities are wheelchair accessible. Full hookups are available at sites 1–75 and 103–125. Picnic tables, grills, and fire rings are provided. Restrooms with flush toilets and showers, drinking water, dump stations, a laundry room, boat ramp, amphitheater, pay phones, and a volleyball court are available. The park also offers interpretive programs, a riding stable, shooting range, and swim beach. Leashed pets are permitted.

Reservations, fees: Reservations are accepted at 800/678-2267 and www.parks.state.co.us. Group reservations are accepted at 303/699-3860, ext. 721. The tent fee is $12 per night, and the RV fee is $20 per night (includes six people and two camping units). Vehicles must also have a Daily Parks Pass ($5) or Annual Parks Pass ($55). The Aspen Leaf Pass is accepted. Open year-round.

Directions: From I-25 in Denver, take I-225 east for four miles. Go south on Highway 83. The park entrance is on the right in about three miles. The campground is 0.8 mile after the visitors center.

Contact: Cherry Creek State Park, 303/690-1166, email: cherry.creek.park@state.co.us.

FRONT RANGE SOUTH

BEST CAMPGROUNDS

❰ Fourteeners
Mueller State Park, **page 232**

❰ Weddings
Mueller State Park, **page 232**

The southern Front Range extends from the edge of the Denver area to Pueblo. It includes the cities of Castle Rock, Colorado Springs, and Pueblo, as well as the southern half of the Front Range Mountains, a giant uplift of Precambrian granite that soars thousands of feet above the High Plains.

These mountains are divided into chains of smaller ranges. Their local names are the Rampart Range, Platte River Mountains, Kenosha Mountains, Tarryall Mountains, and, of course, the Pikes Peak massif, which marks the southern end of the Front Range. Pikes Peak towers over the 9,000-foot Rampart Range. South of Pikes Peak, the isolated Wet Mountains rise west of Pueblo.

A good place to begin a tour of the area is at Chatfield State Park, an inexplicably popular camping destination in the southwest corner of Denver. The campgrounds are large and unattractive, but the lake is a convenient weekend destination for Denverites. The park is also the northern terminus of the Colorado Trail, a 470-mile multiuse trail that ends in Durango.

From Chatfield, Highway 121 follows the South Platte corridor into Pike National Forest. This is a region of low peaks and narrow valleys that's especially popular for four-wheeling and dirt bikes. The Rampart Range Motorized Recreation Area has over 100 miles of trails open to dirt bikes and ATVs. The most popular hiking destination in this area is the Devils Head Lookout, a still-functional fire tower. There's a pretty but extremely busy campground at the trailhead.

Actually, all of the campgrounds in this region are extremely busy in the summer. In the South Platte region, many campgrounds were closed after the Hayman Burn of 2002, the largest forest fire in Colorado's history. The remaining campgrounds are crowded because of the fishing. These are Gold Medal Waters, so anglers are limited to artificial flies and lures.

The campgrounds in Manitou Park also fill up quickly on weekends, in large part because of their proximity to Colorado Springs, Pikes Peaks, and the Garden of the Gods. Pikes Peak (elevation 14,109 feet) is a granite massif that's named for explorer Zebulon Pike, the first white man to try to summit the peak. During the gold rush, a common miners' slogan was "Pike's Peak or Bust," and in 1893, a trip to the summit inspired Katherine Lee Bates to write "America the Beautiful." Instead of hiking, you can take the Pikes Peak Cog Railway or the Toll Road to the peak.

Garden of the Gods is the colorful name for an area of fascinating sandstone formations. You can drive or bike the one-way loop through the park, hike through the formations, or even join the climbers after registering at the visitors center.

The Florissant Fossil Beds National Monument and Mueller State Park are the primary attractions west of Pikes Peak. The national monument protects 35-million-year-old fossils that were created when volcanic ash repeatedly covered a vast lake, preserving mammals, birds, and plants. Mueller State Park has the best camping in the area. A series of loops on densely forested ridges, many of the sites have fantastic views of Pikes Peak. There is also an excellent group site at this state park.

Heading south from Colorado Springs (the antithesis of liberal Boulder), I-25 continues to Pueblo and Lake Pueblo State Park, possibly the most popular water-sports destination in the state. This reservoir was built to control flooding on the Arkansas River. With over 4,500 surface acres, two marinas, and a large swim beach, its three campgrounds are packed to capacity in the summer. Nearby Pueblo isn't very attractive, but the city hosts several excellent festivals, especially Cinco de Mayo and Bluegrass on the River.

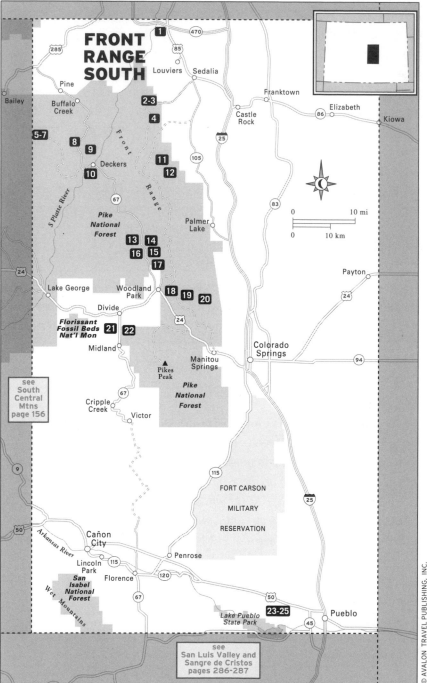

FRONT
RANGE
SOUTH

285
Bailey
Pine
Buffalo
Creek
Louviers
Sedalia
Franktown
Elizabeth
Kiowa
86
Castle
Rock
25
105
83
Deckers
S Platte River
Front Range
Pike
National
Forest
67
Palmer
Lake
Payton
24
24
Lake George
Woodland
Park
Divide
Florissant
Fossil Beds
Nat'l Mon
Midland
94
Colorado
Springs
Pikes
Peak
Manitou
Springs
Pike
National
Forest
67
Cripple
Creek
Victor
115
9
FORT CARSON
MILITARY
RESERVATION
25
50
Arkansas River
Cañon
City
115
Lincoln
Park
San
Isabel
National
Forest
Wet Mountains
Florence
120
67
50
Penrose
Lake Pueblo
State Park
45
Pueblo

0   10 mi
0   10 km

1
2-3
4
5-7
8
9
10
11
12
13 14
16 15
17
18 19 20
21 22
23-25

470
85

see
South
Central
Mtns
page 156

see
San Luis Valley and
Sangre de Cristos
pages 286-287

⬛ CHATFIELD STATE PARK

🚶 🚴 🏊 🛶 ⛴ 🐕 🚵 ♿ 🚗 ⛺

Scenic rating: 5

near Denver

Chatfield State Park is in Littleton, on the southern edge of the Denver metropolitan area. This is a full-service state park, from the riding stables to the marina to the hiking and biking trails. It's also a popular park—there are nearly 1.5 million visitors annually, so if you're visiting on a summer weekend, make reservations. The lake is open to boating, fishing, and swimming. It's stocked with rainbow trout and other species. Bass, catfish, perch, and crappie are common catches in the summer. The park is also a popular hot-air balloon launch site. Wake up around sunrise to catch a glimpse of these beauties taking off.

The campground contains four large loops and 10 group sites on the south shore of the lake. It's overwhelming, to say the least. The loops have a few trees, but shade and privacy are virtually nonexistent. When they're full, all four loops look almost identical. The most prominent feature is the Star Trek–looking toilets. The nicest feature is the views of the foothills and glimpses of the lake. The swim beach is a three-mile walk away.

Campsites, facilities: There are 197 sites for tents and RVs up to 45 feet and 10 group sites. Sites 33, 50, 51, 99, 102, 148, 151, 155–157, 176, and 177 and the facilities are wheelchair accessible. Sites 1–51, 66–78, 88–96, 100–102, and 154–197 have full hookups, and all other sites have electric hookups. All sites are pull-through. Picnic tables, grills, and fire rings are provided. Loop D has tent pads. Restrooms with flush toilets and showers, vault toilets, drinking water, dump stations, a laundry room, amphitheater, playground, pay phones, volleyball net, and horseshoe pits are available. The park also has a horse stable, model airplane field, restaurant, swim beach, and marina with a store and boat ramp. Leashed pets are permitted.

Reservations, fees: Reservations are accepted at 800/678-2267 and www.parks.state.co.us. Group reservations are accepted at 303/791-7275. The tent fee is $16–20 per night (includes six people and one camping unit). Group sites cost $64 per night for 32 people. Vehicles must also have a Daily Parks Pass ($5) or Annual Parks Pass ($55). The Aspen Leaf Pass is accepted. Cash or check only. Open year-round.

Directions: From Denver, take U.S. Highway 85 south for 10.5 miles. Take I-470 west for 2.5 miles to Highway 121/Wadsworth Boulevard south. The park entrance is on the left in one mile. Make the first right after the entrance station. The campground is on the left in 3.5 miles.

Contact: Chatfield State Park, 303/791 7275, www.parks.state.co.us.

⬛ INDIAN CREEK

🚶 🚴 🐕 🚗 ⛺

Scenic rating: 7

north of Deckers

Indian Creek is at the northern end of the Rampart Range, a granite uplift that demarcates the eastern edge of the Front Range Mountains between Denver and Colorado Springs. This area of low peaks and steep, forested valleys extends west to the Lost Creek and Mount Evans wilderness areas. Panoramic vistas are few and far between, but there's good fishing in the creeks and moderate hiking and riding on the trails. Indian Creek is a beautiful little campground full of ponderosa pine, aspen, and wildflowers. The sites are about 50–100 feet apart, encircling two small meadows. Go straight to the back loop for the best combination of scenery and privacy. Sites 5–8 have views of Devil's Head. The Indian Creek Trail is open to hikers, bikers, and riders. This campground is so close to the Denver area that it fills up on Thursday nights, but midweek it's almost deserted.

Campsites, facilities: There are 11 sites for tents and RVs up to 20 feet. There are no hookups. Picnic tables, grills, and fire rings are provided. Vault toilets and drinking water are available. Leashed pets are permitted.

Reservations, fees: Reservations are not accepted. The fee is $13 per night (includes 10 people and two vehicles). Additional vehicles cost $5 per night. Golden Age and Golden Access Passports are accepted. Cash or check only. Open early May–early October.

Directions: From Denver, take U.S. Highway 85 south to Sedalia. Go west on Highway 67 for 10.4 miles. The campground is on the right.

Contact: Pike National Forest, 303/275-5610, www.fs.fed.us/r2/psicc/.

❸ INDIAN CREEK EQUESTRIAN

🏃 🚲 🐴 🚙 ⛺

Scenic rating: 6

north of Deckers

Indian Creek is at the northern end of the Rampart Range, a granite uplift that demarcates the eastern edge of the Front Range Mountains between Denver and Colorado Springs. This area of low peaks and steep, forested valleys extends west to the Lost Creek and Mount Evans wilderness areas. Panoramic vistas are few and far between, but there's good fishing in the creeks and moderate hiking and riding on the trails. Indian Creek Equestrian is in a small clearing surrounded by ponderosa pines. The middle of the loop can accommodate corrals. The sites on the outside of the loop are about 100 feet apart and shady. The Indian Creek Trail is open to hikers, bikers, and riders. The neighboring campground is so close to the Denver area that it fills up on Thursday nights, so the equestrian campground, which usually only has one or two groups, doubles as an overflow campground.

Campsites, facilities: There are eight sites for tents and RVs up to 60 feet. There are no hookups. Picnic tables, grills, fire rings, and hitch racks are provided. Vault toilets and drinking water are available. Leashed pets are permitted.

Reservations, fees: Reservations are accepted at 877/444-6777 and www.reserveusa.com. The fee is $15 per night (includes 10 people and two vehicles). Additional vehicles cost $5 per night. Golden Age and Golden Access Passports are accepted. Cash or check only. Open early May–early October.

Directions: From Denver, take U.S. Highway 85 south to Sedalia. Go west on Highway 67 for 10.4 miles and turn right at the campground entrance, then left. Drive through the day-use area to the equestrian sites.

Contact: Pike National Forest, 303/275-5610, www.fs.fed.us/r2/psicc/.

❹ FLAT ROCKS

🚲 🐴 ♿ 🚙 ⛺

Scenic rating: 6

northeast of Deckers

Flat Rocks is near the northern end of the Rampart Range, a granite uplift that demarcates the eastern edge of the Front Range Mountains between Denver and Colorado Springs. This area of low peaks and narrow, forested valleys extends west to the Lost Creek and Mount Evans wilderness areas. There's good fishing in the creeks and moderate hiking and riding on the trails, but the biggest draw is the motorized trails. There are over 100 miles of trails open to ATVs and dirt bikes in the Rampart Range Motorized Recreation Area, so Flat Rocks and other nearby campgrounds are packed on weekends with families, trailers, and four-wheelers.

Flat Rocks is on a long, narrow ridge forested with pine trees and scattered aspen. Because of the steep terrain, there is limited tent space at the sites. Sites 2 and 3 are the roomiest sites. There are great views of the plains from the Flat Rocks overlook. Sites 2, 3, 8, 10, 12, 13, 18, and 19 have partial views to the west.

Campsites, facilities: There are 19 sites for tents and RVs up to 20 feet. Site 3 and the facilities are wheelchair accessible. There are no hookups. Picnic tables, grills, and fire rings are provided. Vault toilets and drinking water are available. Leashed pets are permitted.

Reservations, fees: Reservations are not accepted. The fee is $13 per night (includes 10 people and two vehicles). Additional vehicles cost $5 per night. Golden Age and Golden Access Passports are accepted. Cash or check only. Open early May–early October.

Directions: From Denver, take U.S. Highway 85 south to Sedalia. Go west on Highway 67 for 10 miles. Turn left on Rampart Range Road. The campground is on the right in 4.6 miles.

Contact: Pike National Forest, 303/275-5610, www.fs.fed.us/r2/psicc/.

5 GREEN MOUNTAIN

Scenic rating: 6

northwest of Deckers

Green Mountain is on South Fork Creek, a short distance downstream of Wellington Lake. The campground is in a spruce-fir forest. The sites are large and about 75 feet apart. On the map, this campground looks like it's in the middle of nowhere, but it's actually just about an hour from Denver, and it's just outside the Lost Creek Wilderness. The wilderness has almost 120,000 acres of dense forests, granite domes, and high parks. Mule deer, elk, bobcat, bear, and a healthy bighorn herd thrive there, and there are 100 miles of trails to explore. The Colorado Trail runs past the campground and into the middle of the wilderness area. It connects with the Rolling Creek, Payne Creek, and Brookside-

McCurdy Trails. This is a great jumping-off point for exploring both the north and south ends of the wilderness, which may explain the campground's popularity. It frequently fills up midweek.

Campsites, facilities: There are six tent sites. Picnic tables, grills, and fire rings are provided. Vault toilets and drinking water are available. Leashed pets are permitted.

Reservations, fees: Reservations are not accepted. The fee is $12 per night (includes 10 people and two vehicles). Additional vehicles cost $5 per night. Golden Age and Golden Access Passports are accepted. Cash or check only. Open May–September.

Directions: From Deckers, take County Road 126 northwest for 11.5 miles. Turn left on Forest Route 550. In 5.4 miles, stay left at the fork on Forest Route 543. The campground is on the left in 1.6 miles.

Contact: Pike National Forest, 303/275-5610, www.fs.fed.us/r2/psicc/.

6 MEADOWS GROUP

Scenic rating: 8

northwest of Deckers

As the name indicates, Meadows Group is in a large meadow dotted with pines and bands of aspen. It's a gorgeous location, surrounded by low ridges, with views of Buffalo Peak. The peak is inside the Lost Creek Wilderness, a landscape of granite domes and buttresses that encompasses the Tarryall Mountains, Platte River Mountains, and Kenosha Mountains. Desp Despite the number of peaks, the habitat rarely enters the alpine zone. There are numerous broad valleys and small, steep creeks. Mule deer, elk, bobcat, bear, and a healthy bighorn herd inhabit the dense woods. There are 100 miles of trails to explore as well, and several loops are possible. The Colorado Trail runs through the campground and into the middle of the wilderness area. It connects with the Rolling Creek, Payne Creek, and Brookside-McCurdy Trails. This is a great jumping-off point for exploring both the north and south ends of the wilderness.

Campsites, facilities: There are two group sites for up to 150 people each. There are no hookups. Picnic tables, grills, and fire rings are provided. Vault toilets and drinking water are available. Leashed pets are permitted.

Reservations, fees: Reservations are accepted at 877/444-6777 and www.reserveusa.com. The fee is $75–175 per night. Open May–September.

Directions: From Deckers, take County Road 126 northwest for 11.5 miles. Turn left on Forest Route 550. The campground is on the left in 5.1 miles.

Contact: Pike National Forest, 303/275-5610, www.fs.fed.us/r2/psicc/.

7 BUFFALO

Scenic rating: 6

northwest of Deckers

Buffalo is about three miles east of the Lost Creek Wilderness, a landscape of granite domes and buttresses that encompasses the Tarryall Mountains, Platte River Mountains, and Kenosha Mountains. The broad valleys and dense forests provide habitat for healthy populations of elk and bighorn as well as some bobcat and bear. The extensive trail system, including a long portion of the Colorado Trail can be used for week-long backpacking trips. The Colorado Trail runs through the campground and into the middle of the wilderness area. It connects with the Rolling Creek, Payne Creek, and Brookside-McCurdy Trails. This is a great jumping-off point for exploring both the north and south ends of the wilderness.

The campground is a large gravel loop on a gentle slope. Tall, scattered pines provide shade but not a ton of privacy. The sites are 50–100 feet apart. The only landmark is the large, granite formation across the valley.

Campsites, facilities: There are 41 sites for tents and RVs up to 30 feet. There are no hookups. Sites 2, 10, 11, 28, 30, and 31 are pull-through. Picnic tables, grills, and fire rings are provided. Vault toilets and drinking water are available. Leashed pets are permitted.

Reservations, fees: Reservations are accepted at 877/444-6777 and www.reserveusa.com. The fee is $12 per night (includes 10 people and two vehicles). Additional vehicles cost $5 per night. Golden Age and Golden Access Passports are accepted. Cash or check only. Open early May–early October.

Directions: From Deckers, take County Road 126 northwest for 11.5 miles. Turn left on Forest Route 550. The campground is on the left in 4.9 miles.

Contact: Pike National Forest, 303/275-5610, www.fs.fed.us/r2/psicc/.

8 KELSEY

Scenic rating: 6

north of Deckers

Kelsey is in a no-man's-land west of the Rampart Range and east of the Lost Creek Wilderness, in a landscape of forested ridgelines and narrow valleys. There are no activities at the campground, but the South Platte River is a short drive away, and the Colorado Trail crosses the highway a few miles to the north. The campground is in a forest of pine, spruce, and fir with some traffic noise from the nearby road. The campground is a paved loop with dirt spurs. The sites are about 50 feet apart, and privacy is good except in the middle of the loop. This is a low-use campground.

Campsites, facilities: There are 17 sites for tents and RVs up to 20 feet. Site 16 is pull-through. Picnic tables, grills, and fire rings are provided. Vault toilets are available. Leashed pets are permitted.

Reservations, fees: Reservations are not accepted. The fee is $12 per night (includes 10 people and two vehicles). Additional vehicles cost $5 per night. Golden Age and Golden Access Passports are accepted. Cash or check only. Open late May–early September.

Directions: From Deckers, take County Road 126 west for eight miles. The campground is on the left.

Contact: Pike National Forest, 303/275-5610, www.fs.fed.us/r2/psicc/.

9 PLATTE RIVER

Scenic rating: 7

east of Deckers

The South Platte watershed supplies over 60 percent of Denver's water supply. The water quality is closely monitored by the state, and, as a result, the South Platte has been designated a Gold Medal trout fishery. This campground is in the floodplain and on a hillside overlooking the river, which is wide and slow at this point. It's a soothing place to pitch a tent and cast a line from the fishing platform or the shore. Only artificial flies and lures are allowed because of the Gold Medal designation. Sites 1 and 2 are next to the parking lot. Sites 3–8 are on the hill and shaded by scattered pine. Sites 9 and 10 are right next to the water. This campground can be very busy on weekends, but it's quiet midweek.

Campsites, facilities: There are 10 walk-in tent sites. Site 10 and the facilities are wheelchair accessible. Picnic tables, grills, and fire rings are provided. Sites 1–3, 9, and 10 have tent pads. Vault toilets and drinking water are available. Leashed pets are permitted.

Reservations, fees: Reservations are not accepted. The fee is $12 per night (includes 10 people and two vehicles). Additional vehicles

cost $5 per night. Golden Age and Golden Access Passports are accepted. Cash or check only. Open late May–early September.

Directions: From Deckers, take County Road 67 north for 3.9 miles. The campground is on the right.

Contact: Pike National Forest, 303/275-5610, www.fs.fed.us/r2/psicc/.

10 LONE ROCK

Scenic rating: 6

near Deckers

Lone Rock is in a small meadow with scattered ponderosa pines on the banks of the South Platte River. These are Gold Medal Waters, so fishing is limited to artificial flies and lures. This campground is popular because of its proximity to the Front Range, It fills up by Thursday evening, usually with families and large groups. Nearby Cheesman Reservoir used to be a popular destination, but the Hayman Fire—the largest in Colorado history—closed many trails and campgrounds in this area. Sites 4 and 7–11 are riverside. Sites 14 and 16–19 are in the middle of the loop. The sites are 50–100 feet apart and set back a bit from the campground road.

Campsites, facilities: There are 19 sites for tents and RVs up to 30 feet. Sites 13 and 16 are wheelchair accessible. There are no hookups. Sites 8–10, 12, 13, 15, and 16 are pull-through. Picnic tables, grills, and fire rings are provided. Sites 13, 15, and 16 have tent pads. Vault toilets and drinking water are available. Leashed pets are permitted.

Reservations, fees: Reservations are accepted at 877/444-6777 and www.reserveusa.com. The fee is $13 per night (includes 10 people and two vehicles). Additional vehicles cost $5 per night. Golden Age and Golden Access Passports are accepted. Cash or check only. Open year-round.

Directions: From Deckers, take County Road

126 west for 0.7 mile. The campground is on the left.

Contact: Pike National Forest, 303/275-5610, www.fs.fed.us/r2/psicc/.

11 DEVIL'S HEAD

🏃 🚲 🐕 🚐 ⛺

Scenic rating: 7

east of Deckers

Devil's Head, reported to be the hideout of bandits and outlaws in the 1800s, is a prominent peak on the Rampart Range between Castle Rock and Colorado Springs. It's most notable for the lookout tower on the summit, the last functioning lookout tower in Pike National Forest. The views from the tower extend from Pikes Peak in the south to the highest peaks of Rocky Mountain National Park in the north. A steep, 1.4-mile out-and-back trail climbs the peak. It can be combined with Zinn Trail to make a 3.75-mile loop. The trail is very busy, so bikers should ride with caution.

The campground is quieter but just as busy as the ATV hubs to the north. It attracts mainly tent campers and a large group of regulars from the Front Range. It has two loops in a forest of pine and aspen dotted with huge granite boulders. The top loop has five walk-in sites. Site 5 has the best views of Devil's Head. The road to the lower loop (sites 10–21) is very rough, but the sites can accommodate larger groups.

Campsites, facilities: There are 21 sites for tents and RVs up to 20 feet. There are no hookups. Sites 6, 17, and 18 are pull-through. Picnic tables, grills, and fire rings are provided. Vault toilets and drinking water are available. Leashed pets are permitted.

Reservations, fees: Reservations are not accepted. The fee is $13 per night (includes 10 people and two vehicles). Additional vehicles cost $5 per night. Golden Age and Golden Access Passports are accepted. Cash or check only. Open early May–early October.

Directions: From Denver, take U.S. Highway 85 south to Sedalia. Go west on Highway 67 for 10 miles. Turn left on Rampart Range Road. The road forks in nine miles. Stay right on Forest Route 300. The Devil's Head Recreation Area and campground are in 0.3 mile.

Contact: Pike National Forest, 303/275-5610, www.fs.fed.us/r2/psicc/.

12 JACKSON CREEK

🐕 🚐 ⛺

Scenic rating: 6

east of Deckers

Jackson Creek is in a quiet little valley that's almost hidden from the Rampart Range Motorized Recreation Area. It's near the Devil's Head Recreation Area and often functions as an overflow campground when Devil's Head fills up. The campground is in a pine and aspen forest. The sites are small and very close together, but this campground receives fewer visitors than its neighbors. Sites 2, 3, 5, 7, and 8 are creekside.

Campsites, facilities: There are nine sites for tents and RVs up to 16 feet. There are no hookups or pull-throughs. Picnic tables, grills, and fire rings are provided. Vault toilets and drinking water are available. Leashed pets are permitted.

Reservations, fees: Reservations are not accepted. The fee is $13 per night (includes 10 people and two vehicles). Additional vehicles cost $5 per night. Golden Age and Golden Access Passports are accepted. Cash or check only. Open early May–early October.

Directions: From Denver, take U.S. Highway 85 south to Sedalia. Go west on Highway 67 for 10 miles. Turn left on Rampart Range Road. The road forks in nine miles. Stay right on Forest Route 300. In five miles, turn left on Forest Route 502. The campground is on the right in 1.5 miles.

Contact: Pike National Forest, 303/275-5610, www.fs.fed.us/r2/psicc/.

13 PAINTED ROCKS

Scenic rating: 7

north of Woodland Park

The Manitou Park Recreation Area is heavily used year-round. The five-acre Manitou Lake is a family fishing hole encircled by a hiking trail. Another trail connects the campgrounds and picnic area, and the Centennial Bike Trail runs into Woodland Park. The park's grasslands and pine stands are not especially scenic, but visitors appreciate the proximity to Garden of the Gods, Pikes Peak, Florissant Fossil Beds National Monument, and Colorado Springs. Painted Rocks is the smallest and most attractive campground in the park. It has the same pine and grassland habitat of the other campgrounds, but it's away from the roads, and there are some interesting rock outcroppings in the adjacent meadow. The large sites are about 100 feet apart and are shaded, except for 11–13. Sites 9 and 12–18 have the best views. This campground fills up on weekends with a crowd of regulars.

Campsites, facilities: There are 18 sites for tents and RVs up to 30 feet. There are no hookups. Site 15 is pull-through. Picnic tables, grills, and fire rings are provided. Vault toilets and drinking water are available. Leashed pets are permitted.

Reservations, fees: Reservations are accepted at 877/444-6777 and www.reserveusa.com. The fee is $15 per night (includes 10 people and two vehicles). Additional vehicles cost $5 per night. Golden Age and Golden Access Passports are accepted. Cash or check only. Open mid-May–early September.

Directions: From Woodland Park, take Highway 67 north for 6.3 miles. Turn left on Painted Rocks Road/County Road 78. The campground is on the left in 0.4 mile.

Contact: Pike National Forest, 719/636-1602, www.fs.fed.us/r2/psicc/.

14 COLORADO

Scenic rating: 6

north of Woodland Park

Colorado is the largest campground in the Manitou Park Recreation Area, a broad valley with grasslands and abundant ponderosa pines. This valley is pleasant but not extremely scenic. Nevertheless, it's busy year-round because of the proximity to the Colorado Springs area. This campground usually fills up on weekends. It has two large paved loops in a thin pine forest that provides shade but not much privacy. The sites are 50–100 feet apart and large enough for multiple tents. Sites 5, 11, and 56 are doubles. Sites 1–10 are very close to the road.

Campsites, facilities: There are 81 sites for tents and RVs up to 30 feet. There are no hookups. Picnic tables, grills, and fire rings are provided. Vault toilets, drinking water, and an amphitheater are available. The facilities are wheelchair accessible. Leashed pets are permitted.

Reservations, fees: Reservations are accepted at 877/444-6777 and www.reserveusa.com. The fee is $15 per night (includes 10 people and two vehicles). Additional vehicles cost $5 per night. Golden Age and Golden Access Passports are accepted. Cash or check only. Open early May–early September.

Directions: From Woodland Park, take Highway 67 north for six miles. The campground is on the right.

Contact: Pike National Forest, 719/636-1602, www.fs.fed.us/r2/psicc/.

15 PIKE COMMUNITY GROUP

Scenic rating: 6

north of Woodland Park

Pike Community Group is a large group campground with a steady stream of reservations from the Colorado Springs area.

Church groups, scout groups, and family reunions enjoy this location with its proximity to Pike's Peak, Florissant Fossil Beds National Monument, Garden of the Gods, and the Air Force Academy. The campground is in a grassland with scattered ponderosa pines. It has dispersed tent camping and a large kitchen area. There is frequent traffic noise from the highway. Across the highway, the Centennial Trail connects the campground to Woodland Park and Manitou Lake. The five-acre reservoir is a family fishing destination with a multiuse trail around the shoreline. The views are not exceptional, but there are glimpses of a small peak to the north. This is not wilderness—but it is a good destination for a diverse group.

Campsites, facilities: There is dispersed tent camping for up to 150 people and parking spaces for 48 vehicles. There are no hookups. Picnic tables, grills, and fire rings are provided. Vault toilets, drinking water, dump stations, a playground, volleyball court, softball field, and horseshoe pits are available. Leashed pets are permitted.

Reservations, fees: Reservations are accepted at 877/444-6777 and www.reserveusa.com. The fee is $75–175 per night. Open May–late September.

Directions: From Woodland Park, take Highway 67 north for 5.3 miles. Turn right at the campground sign. The campground is in 0.5 mile.

Contact: Pike National Forest, 719/636-1602, www.fs.fed.us/r2/psicc/.

16 SOUTH MEADOWS
🥾 🚲 🐕 🚐 ⛺

Scenic rating: 6

north of Woodland Park

South Meadows is the second-largest campground in Manitou Park Recreation Area, and it was completely renovated in 2005. It doesn't have views, but the pine forest provides lots of shade and some privacy. The sites are 50–100 feet apart and a nice distance from the road. Hikers and bikers can take the Centennial Trail to Manitou Lake, a family fishing hole, or south to Woodland Park. For more entertainment, campers drive to the Colorado Springs area and Pikes Peak. This campground is extremely busy in the summer because of its proximity to so many Front Range attractions.

Campsites, facilities: There are 64 sites for tents and RVs up to 30 feet. There are no hookups. Picnic tables, grills, and fire rings are provided. Vault toilets and drinking water are available. Leashed pets are permitted.

Reservations, fees: Reservations are accepted at 877/444-6777 and www.reserveusa.com. The fee is $15 per night (includes 10 people and two vehicles). Additional vehicles cost $5 per night. Golden Age and Golden Access Passports are accepted. Cash or check only. Open mid-May–early September.

Directions: From Woodland Park, take Highway 67 north for 5.2 miles. The campground is on the left across from the Pike Community Group campground.

Contact: Pike National Forest, 719/636-1602, www.fs.fed.us/r2/psicc/.

17 RED ROCKS GROUP
🥾 🚲 🐕 🚐 ⛺

Scenic rating: 5

north of Woodland Park

Red Rocks is located in a dense pine forest just a few miles north of Woodland Park. It's farther from the road than nearby Pike Community Group, but there is still a lot of traffic noise, and there are no scenic views. However, the six group picnic areas have a nice communal atmosphere. The nearest activity is the Centennial Trail, a paved hiking and biking trail that connects Woodland Park to the Manitou Lake picnic area. Also, Red Rocks Trail leads to some unusual sandstone formations. Most groups select this site for its location—it's a short drive from Pike's Peak, Florissant Fossil Beds National Monument, Garden of the Gods, and Colorado Springs.

Campsites, facilities: There is dispersed tent camping for up to 125 people. There are no hookups. Picnic tables, grills, and fire rings are provided. Vault toilets and drinking water are available. Leashed pets are permitted.

Reservations, fees: Reservations are accepted at 877/444-6777 and www.reserveusa.com. The fee is $75–150 per night. Open early May–late October.

Directions: From Woodland Park, take Highway 67 north about three miles. Turn right on Forest Route 335. The campground entrance is on the left in 0.2 mile.

Contact: Pike National Forest, 719/636-1602, www.fs.fed.us/r2/psicc/.

18 SPRINGDALE

Scenic rating: 7

east of Woodland Park

The highlight of Springdale is the drive there with its awesome views of Pikes Peak. The campground is in a forest of pine and aspen beside a grassland plateau. All of the sites have good shade and privacy. Sites 7 and 8 feature views across the grassland. Rampart Reservoir Recreation Area is a few miles away. Fishing, hiking, and boating are available in the recreation area, but there are no activities at the campground. It has a weekend crowd of locals and regulars, but it's very quiet midweek.

Campsites, facilities: There are 13 sites for tents and RVs up to 16 feet. Site 7 is walk-in. There are no hookups. Site 6 is pull-through. Picnic tables, grills, and fire rings are provided. Vault toilets and drinking water are available. Leashed pets are permitted.

Reservations, fees: Reservations are not accepted. The fee is $10 per night (includes 10 people and two vehicles). Additional vehicles

cost $5 per night. Golden Age and Golden Access Passports are accepted. Cash or check only. Open May–September.

Directions: From Woodland Park, take Kelly's Road east for one mile. Turn left on Rampart Range Road. In 1.6 miles, stay right at the fork. The campground is on the left in 2.2 miles.

Contact: Pike National Forest, 719/636-1602, www.fs.fed.us/r2/psicc/.

19 MEADOW RIDGE

Scenic rating: 7

east of Woodland Park

Located in Rampart Reservoir Recreation Area, Meadow Ridge is a modern campground with decent recreational opportunities. The 500-surface-acre lake stores water for Colorado Springs, so it can get quite low during drought years. When it's full enough, it's open to wakeless boating and fishing for trout, bass, and perch. There are several hiking trails around the lake, including the Rainbow Gulch, Rampart Reservoir, Aspen Grove, and Nichols Trails. Rampart and Rainbow are also popular with mountain bikers. A one-mile trail connects the campground to the reservoir. The boat ramp is about three miles away.

The campground is on a ridge overlooking the reservoir in a forest of aspen and pine. The sites are terraced and many have stairs. They are 50–100 feet apart. The campground is booked on weekends, and there is only one first-come, first-served site. Sites 7–11 have the most privacy.

Campsites, facilities: There are 19 sites for tents and RVs up to 35 feet. There are no hookups. Sites 6, 14, 16, and 18 are pull-through. Picnic tables, grills, fire rings, tent pads, and lantern hooks are provided. Vault toilets and drinking water are available. The facilities are wheelchair accessible. Leashed pets are permitted.

Reservations, fees: Reservations are accepted

at 877/444-6777 and www.reserveusa.com. The fee is $15 per night (includes 10 people and two vehicles). Additional vehicles cost $5 per night. Golden Age and Golden Access Passports are accepted. Cash or check only. Open May–September.

Directions: From Woodland Park, take Kelly's Road east for one mile. Turn left on Rampart Range Road. In 1.6 miles, stay right at the fork. In 5.3 miles, turn left into the Rampart Reservoir Recreation Area. In 0.8 mile, turn left at the entrance station. The campground is in 0.6 mile.

Contact: Pike National Forest, 719/636-1602, www.fs.fed.us/r2/psicc/.

20 THUNDER RIDGE
Scenic rating: 7

east of Woodland Park

Thunder Ridge is in an aspen and pine forest overlooking Rampart Reservoir. It has less shade than nearby Meadow Ridge, but better views. Sites 7, 9, and 10 have views of the foothills, and sites 11–13 have lake views. The sites are just 25–50 feet apart. Privacy would be poor, but the topography is quiet hilly. A short trail leads down to the lake where there are more trails for hiking and biking and good shore fishing. The boat ramp is about two miles away. (For more information on the Rampart Reservoir Recreation Area, see the Meadow Ridge listing in this chapter.)

Campsites, facilities: There are 21 sites for tents and RVs up to 35 feet. There are no hookups. Sites 6, 10, and 11 are pull-through. Picnic tables, grills, fire rings, tent pads, and lantern hooks are provided. Vault toilets and drinking water are available. The facilities are wheelchair accessible. Leashed pets are permitted.

Reservations, fees: Reservations are accepted at 877/444-6777 and www.reserveusa.com. The fee is $15 per night (includes 10 people and two vehicles). Additional vehicles cost

$5 per night. Golden Age and Golden Access Passports are accepted. Cash or check only. Open May–October.

Directions: From Woodland Park, take Kelly's Road east for one mile. Turn left on Rampart Range Road. In 1.6 miles, stay right at the fork. In 5.3 miles, turn left into the Rampart Reservoir Recreation Area. Turn left in 0.9 mile. The campground is in 0.2 mile.

Contact: Pike National Forest, 719/636-1602, www.fs.fed.us/r2/psicc/.

21 MUELLER STATE PARK
Scenic rating: 8

south of Woodland Park

BEST (

Mueller Park is a 6,000-acre game preserve west of Pikes Peak. Its forested ridges are home to bear, elk, bighorn, and mule deer. The area was settled by pioneers in the 1860s. Logging and cattle ranching supported residents until the former owners, the Mueller family, turned it into a game preserve. The park is a great destination for families who like hiking and biking; there are 55 miles of trails in the park. Other attractions include nearby Florissant Fossil Beds National Monument and the Pikes Peak massif. Other activities include pond fishing, cross-country skiing, and snowshoeing.

The campground has seven loops, but the ridgeline topography and dense woods separate the loops and make the campground seem smaller than it really is. Most of the loops are best for RV camping, but Turkey Meadow and Prospector Ridge are reserved for walk-in tent camping. Peak View (sites 1–5) and Turkey Meadow (sites 100–109) have views of Pikes Peak. Pisgah Point (sites 70–80) is a group site that's available by reservation only. It's next to the camper services building and the amphitheater, so it's a great choice for family reunions and weddings.

Campsites, facilities: There are 110 sites for

tents and RVs up to 60 feet. There are 22 tent-only sites (sites 55–66 and 100–109). Sites 12 and 22 and the facilities are wheelchair accessible. All other sites have electric hookups and most sites are pull-through. Picnic tables, grills, and fire rings are provided. Tent pads of various sizes are provided at most sites. Restrooms with flush toilets and showers, vault toilets, drinking water, dump stations, a laundry room, amphitheater, playground, and interpretive programs are available. Leashed pets are permitted in the campground but are not allowed on trails or in the backcountry.

Reservations, fees: Reservations are accepted at 800/678-2267 and www.parks.state.co.us. Group reservations are accepted at 719/687-2366. The tent fee is $14 per night, and the RV fee is $18 per night (includes six people and one camping unit). Vehicles must also have a Daily Parks Pass ($5) or Annual Parks Pass ($55). The Aspen Leaf Pass is accepted. Cash or check only. Sites 1–22 and 81–90 are open year-round. The rest of the campground is open only in the summer.

Directions: From Woodland Park, take U.S. Highway 24 west for seven miles. Go south on Highway 67. In 0.9 mile, turn right at the park entrance. The campground is two miles past the fee station.

Contact: Mueller State Park, 719/687-2366, www.parks.state.co.us.

22 THE CRAGS

Scenic rating: 6

south of Woodland Park

Located between Pikes Peak and Mueller State Park, The Crags looks remote on the map, but it's a high-use campground in the summer. It's in a spruce-fir forest with outcroppings of Pikes Peak granite and a small creek running through it. Most sites are creekside. Sites 15 and 17 are next to The Crags trailhead, a short hike to a rock outcropping with impressive views of the Rockies. Sites 5–7 are walk-ins. Besides the hike, the other nearby attractions are the 55 miles of trails in Mueller State Park and the historic mining towns of Cripple Creek and Victor.

Campsites, facilities: There are 17 sites for tents and RVs up to 20 feet. There are no hookups. Sites 3 and 11 are pull-through. Picnic tables, grills, and fire rings are provided. Vault toilets and drinking water are available. Leashed pets are permitted.

Reservations, fees: Reservations are not accepted. The fee is $10 per night (includes 10 people and two vehicles). Additional vehicles cost $5 per night. Golden Age and Golden Access Passports are accepted. Cash or check only. Open May–September.

Directions: From Woodland Park, take U.S. Highway 24 west to Highway 67 south. In 4.3 miles, turn left on Forest Route 383. This road is very rough. The campground is on the left in 3.1 miles.

Contact: Pike National Forest, 719/636-1602, www.fs.fed.us/r2/psicc/.

23 NORTHERN PLAINS

Scenic rating: 6

in Lake Pueblo State Park

Lake Pueblo State Park is west of Pueblo on the Arkansas River. It is one of the most popular destinations in the state for water sports. The 4,546-surface-acre reservoir is open to waterskiing, sailing, swimming, and fishing. There are two marinas, two boat ramps, and a swim beach with a five-story water slide. Fish species include trout, walleye, large and smallmouth bass, crappie, bluegill, and yellow perch, and below the dam there is a stocked fishing pond for the kids. There are also 18 miles of trails for hiking, biking, and riding. The park's backdrop includes the Sangre de Cristo and Wet Mountains and Pikes Peak to the north.

The campground is at the west end of the lake near the Northshore marina and the inlet. The campground includes three loops: Prairie Ridge, Yucca Flats, and Kettle Creek. The Prairie Ridge and Yucca Flats loops are large and fairly cramped. The Kettle loop (sites 187–214) does not have electricity and attracts mainly tent campers. Sites 24–42, 59–75, and 151–184 are closest to the water. Sites 84–100 are reserved for group camping.

Campsites, facilities: There are 214 sites for tents and RVs up to 45 feet and seven walk-in tent sites. Sites 10, 32, 71, 107, 128, and 179 and the facilities are wheelchair accessible. Electric hookups and pull-throughs are available. Picnic tables, grills, fire rings, and tent pads are provided. Restrooms with flush toilets and showers, vault toilets, drinking water, dump stations, laundry facilities, an amphitheater, playground, and campfire programs are available. Leashed pets are permitted.

Reservations, fees: Reservations are accepted at 800/678-2267 and www.parks.state.co.us. Group reservations can be made at 719/561-9320. The tent fee is $7–12 per night, and the RV fee is $12–18 per night (includes six people and one camping unit). Vehicles must also have a Daily Parks Pass ($5) or Annual Parks Pass ($55). The Aspen Leaf Pass is accepted. Open May–September.

Directions: From I-25 in Pueblo, take U.S. Highway 50 west for four miles. Turn south on Pueblo Boulevard and go four miles to Thatcher Avenue. Turn west and drive six miles to the park entrance.

Contact: Pueblo Lake State Park, 719/561-9320, email: lake.pueblo.park@state.co.us.

24 JUNIPER BREAKS

Scenic rating: 6

in Lake Pueblo State Park

Juniper Breaks is on the north shore of Lake Pueblo, a reservoir on the Arkansas River with nearly 5,000-surface acres. Predictably, it's one of the most popular water sports destinations in the state. The campground sits on the bluffs overlooking the lake and is surrounded by prairie grass. Most sites have good views of the lake and the Sangre de Cristo Mountains, but shade and privacy are poor. It's a short drive from the campground to the sailboat launching area. (For more information on Lake Pueblo State Park, see the Northern Plains listing in this chapter.)

Campsites, facilities: There are 84 sites for tents and RVs up to 40 feet. Sites 15, 17, 58, and 19 and the facilities are wheelchair accessible. There are no hookups. Sites 75 and 79 are pull-throughs. Picnic tables, grills, fire rings, and tent pads are provided. Vault toilets and drinking water are available. Leashed pets are permitted.

Reservations, fees: Reservations are accepted at 800/678-2267 and www.parks.state.co.us. Group reservations can be made at 719/561-9320. The tent fee is $12 per night, and the RV fee is $12–18 per night (includes six people and one camping unit). Vehicles must also have a Daily Parks Pass ($5) or Annual Parks Pass ($55). The Aspen Leaf Pass is accepted. Open year-round.

Directions: From I-25 in Pueblo, take U.S. Highway 50 west for four miles. Turn south on Pueblo Boulevard and go four miles to Thatcher Avenue. Turn west and drive six miles to the park entrance.

Contact: Pueblo Lake State Park, 719/561-9320, email: lake.pueblo.park@state.co.us.

25 ARKANSAS POINT

Scenic rating: 6

in Lake Pueblo State Park

Arkansas Point is on the rocky south shore of the 11-mile long Lake Pueblo, a massive reservoir that's also one of the most popular watersports destinations in the state. This campground is less scenic than the Northern Plains and Juniper Breaks campgrounds on the north shore, but it is next to the Southshore marina, so it stays busy all summer. It's packed with RVs and families, and can be quite loud on summer weekends.

Campsites, facilities: There are 92 sites for tents and RVs up to 40 feet. Sites 13, 31, 51, and 85 and the facilities are wheelchair accessible. Electric hookups and pull-throughs are available. Picnic tables, grills, fire rings, and tent pads are provided. Restrooms with flush toilets and showers, vault toilets, drinking water, dump stations, laundry facilities, and a playground are available. Leashed pets are permitted.

Reservations, fees: Reservations are accepted at 800/678-2267 and www.parks.state.co.us. Group reservations can be made at 719/561-9320. The tent fee is $12 per night, and the RV fee is $12–18 per night (includes six people and one camping unit). Vehicles must also have a Daily Parks Pass ($5) or Annual Parks Pass ($55). The Aspen Leaf Pass is accepted. Sites 1–29 are open year-round. The rest of the campground is open May–September.

Directions: From I-25 in Pueblo, take U.S. Highway 50 west for four miles. Turn south on Pueblo Boulevard and go four miles to Thatcher Avenue. Turn west and drive six miles to the park entrance.

Contact: Pueblo Lake State Park, 719/561-9320, email: lake.pueblo.park@state.co.us.

FOUR CORNERS AND THE SAN JUAN MOUNTAINS

© SARAH RYAN

BEST CAMPGROUNDS

In a state full of contrasts, no other region is as
distinctive as the southwestern corner, where the lush, rugged San Juans tower above the arid mesas and canyons of the Four Corners.

Even in Colorado, the geology of the San Juans is remarkable. These mountains were created during a volcanic period that lasted for 30 million years. Massive eruptions interspersed with collapsing, faulting, and erosion followed by glaciation resulted in the jagged peaks and U-shaped valleys that earned these mountains the moniker "Alps of America." But the San Juans are not entirely volcanic. Geologists have found canyons of Precambrian sedimentary rocks (quartzite and shale), and the Needle Mountains are Precambrian granite and gneiss.

To the south and west, the mountains give way to the sedimentary rocks that characterize the Four Corners. In this region of canyons and mesas, the Ancestral Puebloans built complex communities from A.D. 450 to 1100, and then disappeared. The reasons for their departure are a puzzle that has intrigued archaeologists since the first scientific expedition in 1874.

This region was also important to the Navajos and Utes. In the southern San Juans, Mount Hesperus, or *Dibé Nitsaa* (Obsidian Mountain), was the Sacred Mountain of the North to the Navajo. From an overlook at McPhee Reservoir, one can also see Mount Taylor in New Mexico (the Sacred Mountain of the South) and the San Francisco Peaks in Arizona (the Sacred Mountain of the West).

The Ute Nation traditionally roamed throughout Colorado and the Four Corners. A series of treaties in the 1800s forced the Utes onto increasingly smaller portions of land, until they were limited to the Uintah Reservation in Northern Utah and the Ute Mountain and Southern Ute Indian Reservations in the Four Corners area.

The single greatest reason for the U.S. government to force the Utes out of the mountains was the presence of gold and silver. Volcanic activity made minerals more abundant and accessible in the San Juans than anywhere else in Colorado. The natural resources of the San Juans dictated the ebb and tide of white settlement. Where gold, silver, lead, copper, or zinc was discovered, a new town was born. In this harsh climate, most of those towns died as well, but the railroad saved a few, and today Ouray, Silverton, Durango, Telluride, Lake City, and Creede survive on tourism instead of mining.

Most travelers begin a tour of the San Juans in Ouray, the Switzerland of America. Settled in 1875, the town is in a precipitous box canyon between Mount Sneffels and Wetterhorn Peak. The location makes Ouray an important destination for rock and ice climbers, and the hiking in the Mount Sneffels and Uncompahgre wilderness areas is unparalleled.

Near Durango, the geology begins to change from volcanic mountains to sandstone and shale hills. The Animas River runs through downtown and has excellent fly-fishing and whitewater that ranges from Class II-V. The La Plata Mountains west of town contain the southern terminus of the Colorado Trail, a multiuse trail that traverses 500 miles between Denver and Durango. It takes four to six weeks to through-hike this multiuse trail, or it can be hiked in shorter segments in combination with other trails. Junction Creek campground is at the trailhead.

From Durango, the San Juan Skyway continues west into the Four Corners. Ancestral Puebloan ruins are preserved at Mesa Verde National Park, the Ute Mountain Tribal Park, Hovenweep National Monument, Anasazi Heritage Center, and Chimney Rock Archaeological Area. Haunting and thought provoking, the cliff dwellings and towers of the ancient people are a must-see.

The mining town of Telluride is a neverland of steep skiing and killer real estate deals. Most mortals can't afford to stay in Telluride in the winter, but in the summer, it's irresistible.

From Telluride, the skyway returns to Ouray through Ridgway, completing a scenic loop that gives a good picture of the San Juans, but not a complete one. The whole eastern half of the San Juans awaits. This area includes the La Garita and Powderhorn wilderness areas, the headwaters of the Rio Grande, the quaint towns of the Lake City and Creede, the mineral hot springs of Pagosa Springs, and the South San Juan Wilderness, where Colorado's last confirmed grizzly sighting took place. This region sees far fewer visitors than the popular San Juan Skyway, but the beauty of the Rio Grande Valley, which is sublime in Creede, only increases as one approaches the headwaters in the Weminuche Wilderness.

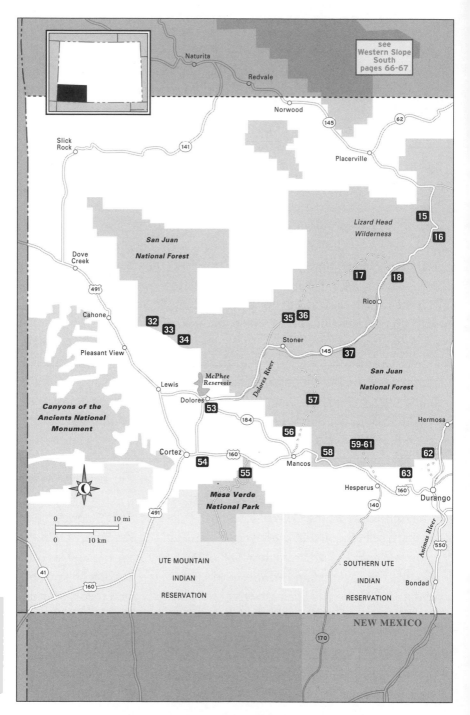

see
Western Slope
South
pages 66-67

Naturita

Redvale

Norwood

145

62

Slick
Rock

141

Placerville

Lizard Head
Wilderness

15

16

San Juan

National Forest

Dove
Creek

491

17

18

Cahone

32

Rico

35 **36**

33

34

Stoner

145

37

Pleasant View

San Juan

National Forest

Lewis

McPhee
Reservoir

Dolores River

Dolores

53

184

57

Hermosa

Canyons of the
Ancients National
Monument

56

Cortez

160

58

59-61

62

54

Mancos

63

55

Hesperus

160

Durango

Mesa Verde
National Park

140

491

Animals River

0   10 mi

0   10 km

UTE MOUNTAIN

INDIAN

RESERVATION

SOUTHERN UTE

INDIAN

RESERVATION

Bondad

550

41

160

NEW MEXICO

170

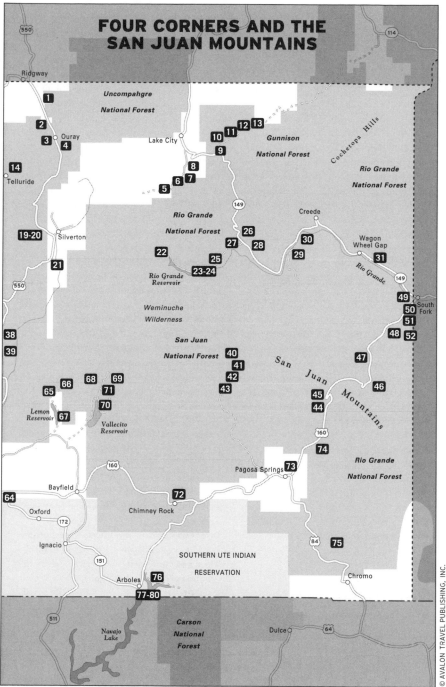

FOUR CORNERS AND THE
SAN JUAN MOUNTAINS

1 ORVIS HOT SPRINGS

Scenic rating: 4

near Ridgway

Orvis is a commercial hot springs in the Uncompahgre Valley with eight pools, ponds, and tubs with water temperatures ranging 103–127°F. The main attraction is The Pond, a 40-foot-by-5-foot natural spring pool, but visitors can also dip into The Lobster Pot and several pools with waterfalls. The facilities are available all night to overnight guests. Clothing is optional, but this is a family-oriented environment. The campsites are in a gravel lot (next to an AmeriGas facility) with pleasant views of the valley and the San Juan Mountains. There are eight wooden tent pads and two ground pads. The springs attract a large regular crowd in the summer, so reservations are recommended.

Campsites, facilities: There are 10 tent sites. Tent pads and a group picnic table and grill are provided. Restrooms with flush toilets and showers and drinking water are available. Leashed pets are permitted only in the campsites.

Reservations, fees: Reservations are accepted at 970/626-5324. The fee for camping only is $15. The fee for camping and soaking is $24 per person per night. Open year-round.

Directions: From Ridgway, drive south on U.S. Highway 550 for about 2.5 miles. Turn right at County Road 3. The resort is on the right.

Contact: Orvis Hot Springs, 970/626-5324, www.orvishotsprings.com.

2 OURAY KOA

Scenic rating: 4

north of Ouray

Ouray is the northern gateway to the San Juans, which makes this KOA a destination campground. It's packed all summer, so reservations are strongly recommended, especially for RVs. Church groups, tour groups, and snowbirds make the most of easy access to the San Juan Scenic Byway and the historic town of Ouray (not to mention the public hot springs which are four miles south of the campground). From June 15 to August 15, the campground offers Texas-style all-you-can-eat barbecues and live bluegrass music on weekends. Jeep rentals and guided tours are also available. This campground consists of multiple loops on both sides of a small stream. There is not much privacy, but some sites are wooded and others have views of the mountains. The best tent sites, 47–50, are situated in an aspen grove.

Campsites, facilities: There are 80 sites for RVs up to 50 feet and 50 tent-only sites. The cabins and some facilities are wheelchair accessible. Full and partial hookups and pull-through sites are available. Picnic tables, grills, and fire rings are provided. Restrooms with flush toilets and showers, drinking water, dump stations, laundry facilities, a store, and playground are available. A hot tub, horseshoe pits, volleyball court, and restaurant are also available. Leashed pets are permitted with some breed restrictions.

Reservations, fees: Reservations are accepted at 970/325-4736. The tent fee is $24 per night for two people. The RV fee is $27–32 per night for two people. Additional people cost $4.50 per night. The KOA Valu Kard and AAA are accepted. Open May–late September.

Directions: From the Ouray Hot Springs Pool, drive north on I-550 for four miles. Turn west on County Road 225. The campground entrance is in 0.2 mile.

Contact: Ouray KOA, 970/325-4736, email: koaouray1@mindspring.com.

3 4J+1+1

🚶 🚵 🏊 🎣 🎿 🏕 🐕 🚐 ⛺

Scenic rating: 5

in Ouray

Ouray is a historic mining town turned summer destination in the San Juan Mountains. The opportunities for outdoor recreation are almost endless, including hiking, mountain biking, rock climbing, four-wheeling, and fishing. Ouray is famous for its Hot Springs Pool, a public outdoor park with a lap pool, several soaking pools, a diving area, and a water slide. (From the campground, the hot springs are accessible via a footbridge across the river.) The 4J+1+1 is a good destination for RVers and families with a variety of interests. From this convenient downtown location, it's as easy to rent a Jeep or sign up for a trail ride as it is to go shopping or visit the art galleries. (There are about 20 galleries, pottery studios, and silversmiths in town.) The campground is a gravel loop beside the river without much privacy. The tent sites (across the road on a narrow strip of grass) are equipped with wooden privacy screens.

Campsites, facilities: There are 53 sites for tents and RVs of any length and 15 sites for tents only. Full and partial hookups and pull-through sites are available. Picnic tables are provided at every site. Grills and fire rings are provided at tent sites. Restrooms with flush toilets and showers, drinking water, laundry facilities, and a playground are available. Leashed pets are permitted.

Reservations, fees: Reservations are accepted at 970/325-4418. The tent fee is $18 per night. The RV fee is $20–24 per night. Open May–October.

Directions: From Main Street in Ouray, drive west on 7th Avenue. After the bridge, follow the road to the right. The campground is on the right.

Contact: 4J+1+1, 970/325-4418, www.coloradodirectory.com/4j11rvpark.

4 AMPHITHEATRE

🚶 🚵 🏊 🎿 🏕 ♿ 🚐 ⛺

Scenic rating: 9

near Ouray

BEST (

This is one of the busiest campgrounds in the state, especially on July 4th, when the town of Ouray sets off fireworks in the amphitheater which looms impressively over the town. The campground is on a steep hill below the amphitheater. The terraced sites are set in a forest of aspen and evergreens and many feature views of Mount Sneffels and the surrounding thirteeners. (Sites 7–14 have the best views. Sites 5, 12, and 16 have no view.) From the overlook, there is a vertigo-inducing view of tiny Ouray, where campers can browse art galleries, visit the railroad museum, or take a dip in the famous hot springs. Nearby trails include Portland, Baby Bathtubs, and Upper Cascade Falls. Campers should also head down the hill and across I-550 to Box Cañon Falls Park to view the Canyon Creek waterfall. Many visitors rent Jeeps or mountain bikes to explore the numerous mining towns and four-wheel-drive roads in the area. One of the most popular (and difficult) routes is the Camp Bird Road up to Imogene Pass and then down to Telluride. This route takes about four hours and requires a detailed map.

Campsites, facilities: There are 32 sites for tents and RVs up to 22 feet. Sites 6–14 can only accommodate very small vehicles. Sites 9, 19, 26, and 27 are hike-in sites (and very private). Sites 17 and 28–30 are wheelchair accessible. Picnic tables, grills, fire rings, and tent pads are provided. Vault toilets and drinking water are available. Leashed pets are permitted.

Reservations, fees: Reservations are accepted at 877/444-6777 and www.reserveusa.com. Some sites are first-come, first-served. The fee is $14 per night (incudes one vehicle). Additional vehicles cost $7 per night. Golden Age and Golden Access Passports are accepted. Cash or check only. Open mid-May–mid-September.

Directions: In Ouray, from the intersection of Third Avenue and I-550/Main Avenue, drive south on I-550 for one mile. Turn left at the National Forest sign. It is one mile up a very narrow paved road to the campground entrance.

Contact: Uncompahgre National Forest, 970/874-6600, www.fs.fed.us/r2/gmug.

5 MILL CREEK

Scenic rating: 7

west of Lake City

The Lake City area is extremely popular with ATV riders and four-wheelers heading out on the Alpine Loop Backcountry Byway, a 65-mile 4WD route that connects Lake City, Ouray, and Silverton. The setting is the high San Juans, dotted with the remnants of the mining boom and basins of wildflowers in July and August. Mountain bikers also travel the Alpine Loop, rated by *Outside* magazine as one of the 10 best rides in the country. The entire route takes bikers four to five days to complete, but day trips to Carson City, Sherman, and beyond are also possible. ATVs can unload in the Mill Creek campground, so they're a common sight. Anglers also come to Mill Creek for the fishing. North of the campground there is a willow-filled park known for brookies. Waders are helpful. The water adjacent to the campground is faster, and the fishing is excellent.

The campground is on a slope above the Lake Fork of the Gunnison. Most sites are wooded with aspen and spruce, so there is plenty of shade. Sites are about 50 feet apart, but the campground is usually only half full, so privacy isn't much of an issue. Sites 10–17 have great views.

Campsites, facilities: There are 22 sites for tents and RVs up to 25 feet. There are no hookups or pull-throughs. Picnic tables, grills, fire rings, vault toilets, and drinking water are provided. Leashed pets are permitted.

Reservations, fees: Reservations are not accepted. The fee is $7 per night. Golden Age and Golden Access Passports are accepted. Cash or check only. Open early June–late September.

Directions: From 2nd Street in Lake City, take Highway 149 south for 2.3 miles. Turn right on County Road 30. The campground is on the left in 10.8 miles.

Contact: BLM Gunnison, 970/641-0471, www.blm.gov.

6 CASTLE LAKES RESORT

Scenic rating: 7

west of Lake City

BEST (

This campground is on the Alpine Loop Backcountry Byway, a 65-mile 4WD route through the San Juans. It's beautiful high mountain country with excellent fishing, hiking, mountain biking, and especially four-wheeling. ATVs can unload in the campground, which attracts many long-term visitors escaping the heat of the South and Midwest. The other main attraction is the stocked fishing ponds, one of which is reserved for catch-and-release fly-fishing. Sites 2–20 are on top of each other like most RV resorts, but the rest of the sites are in a wooded area with an unusual amount of privacy and shade. Sites 35–43 and 48–50 are next to the pond and have excellent views. The tent sites are also next to the pond and shielded by aspen and spruce. This is one of the nicest private campgrounds in the state.

Campsites, facilities: There are 45 sites for RVs up to 45 feet and five tent sites. Full and partial hookups are available, and many sites are pull-through. Picnic tables, grills, and fire rings are provided. Restrooms with flush toilets and showers, drinking water, laundry facilities, a playground, pavilion, and store are available. Horseshoe pits, stocked fishing ponds, Jeep rentals, a recreation room, and video rentals are also available. Leashed pets are permitted.

Reservations, fees: Reservations are accepted at 970/944-2622. The tent fee is $20 per night for two people. The RV fee is $23–27 per night for two people. Each additional person costs $1–2 per night. Open May 15–October 1.

Directions: From 2nd Street in Lake City, take Highway 149 south for 2.3 miles. Turn right on County Road 30. The campground is on the right in 8.1 miles.

Contact: Castle Lakes Resort, 970/944-2622, www.castlelakes.com.

7 WILLIAMS CREEK
Scenic rating: 6

west of Lake City

Williams Creek is the closest national forest campground to Lake City, so it sees a fair amount of stopover traffic. There are also lots of long-term campers here who come to enjoy the Alpine Loop Backcountry Byway, miles of hiking and biking trails, fishing on the Lake Fork of the Gunnison and Lake San Cristobal, and sightseeing in this historic mining district. ATVs cannot unload in this campground, so it tends to be quieter than Mill Creek. Anglers will enjoy the canyon on the Lake Fork which extends from the Wupperman bridge upstream for two miles. It's full of deep pools and fair-sized rainbows and brookies. Anglers can also try Williams Creek, but it's brushy and tight. The Williams Creek Trail connects with the Alpine Gulch Trail. Across the road, Camp Trail climbs steeply to join the Colorado Trail.

The campground is on a hill with views down the valley towards Lake San Cristobal. It is pretty but not jaw-dropping. Sites 6–10 have the best views. The sites are about 50 feet

apart in an aspen and spruce-fir forest. Privacy is moderate but not great for tent campers.

Campsites, facilities: There are 23 sites for tents and RVs up to 20 feet. There are no hookups. Picnic tables, grills, and fire rings are provided. Vault toilets and drinking water are available. Leashed pets are permitted.

Reservations, fees: Reservations are not accepted. The fee is $12 per night (includes one vehicle). Additional vehicles cost $6 per night. Golden Age and Golden Access Passports are accepted. Cash or check only. Open May–September.

Directions: From 2nd Street in Lake City, take Highway 149 south for 2.3 miles. Turn right on County Road 30. In four miles, turn left on County Road 33. The campground is on the right in 6.8 miles.

Contact: Gunnison National Forest, 970/641-0471, www.fs.fed.us/r2/gmug.

8 WUPPERMAN
Scenic rating: 7

near Lake City

Lake San Cristobal is the second largest natural lake in the state. It was formed about a thousand years ago by the three-mile-long Slumgullion Earthflow, which is still moving a few feet a year. The lake contains mostly brook and rainbow trout, plus some monster browns and mackinaw. The Wupperman campground is on the high bluffs on the eastern shore of the lake. There are five loops in a semiarid setting. The sites are either shaded or very exposed with great views. It can be hard to find a flat tent site with shade. Sites 26–31 are in the flats beside the water and have the best fishing and boating access.

Campsites, facilities: There are 28 sites for tents and RVs up to 25 feet and three tent-only sites. Sites 7 and 8 are wheelchair accessible. There are no hookups. Picnic tables, grills, and fire rings are provided.

Vault toilets, drinking water, a boat ramp, and a dump station are available. Leashed pets are permitted.

Reservations, fees: Reservations are not accepted. The fee is $10 per night. There is a $5 fee to use the dump station. Cash or check only. Open late May–September.

Directions: From 2nd Street in Lake City, take Highway 149 south for 2.3 miles. Turn right on County Road 30. In four miles, turn left on County Road 33. The campground is on the left in 0.8 mile.

Contact: Lake City Chamber of Commerce, 970/944-2527.

⑨ SLUMGULLION
🐕 🚐 ⛺

Scenic rating: 6

east of Lake City

At 11,200 feet, Slumgullion is the highest developed campground in the state. Most people don't want to camp at this altitude, which could explain the "ghost town" feel of the campground. On a weekend in July, the campground was empty, despite its proximity to the Silver Thread Scenic Byway, a historic 75-mile route from South Fork to Lake City. The sound of traffic also deters campers, but if you're looking for an easy stopover between Lake City and Creede, Slumgullion is a decent option. There are two loops in a spruce-fir grove. The loops are paved, but not the spurs (except site 11). The sites are 20–50 feet apart and would feel cramped if it were a busy campground, but it isn't. Sites 1–3 have great views of the San Juans and Continental Divide.

Campsites, facilities: There are 19 sites for tents and RVs up to 30 feet. There are no hookups. Sites 15–17 are pull-through. Picnic tables, grills, and fire rings are provided. Vault toilets and drinking water are available. Leashed pets are permitted.

Reservations, fees: Reservations are not ac-

cepted. The fee is $10 per night (includes one vehicle). Additional vehicles cost $5 per night. Golden Age and Golden Access Passports are accepted. Cash or check only. Open June–September.

Directions: From 2nd Street in Lake City, take Highway 149 south for 9.6 miles. Turn left on Forest Route 788 (before Slumgullion Pass). The campground is in 0.1 mile.

Contact: Gunnison National Forest, 970/641-0471, www.fs.fed.us/r2/gmug.

⑩ DEER LAKES
🥾 🚴 🛶 🎣 🐕 🦽 🚐 ⛺

Scenic rating: 9

east of Lake City

The drive up to Deer Lakes, from Forest Route 788 to the campground, offers spectacular views of the peaks of the La Garita Wilderness to the east. The campground is almost as scenic and just as magical. Tucked into an area of rolling hills and small parks between the Powderhorn and La Garita wilderness areas, Deer Lakes campground is in an aspen and spruce forest beside a series of small stocked fishing ponds. Tall trees block the best views, but they also offer abundant privacy. The area is remote, rugged, and quiet. Hikers and anglers will appreciate this campground, which rarely fills up. The artificially constructed lakes are perfect learning ponds for kids. More advanced anglers can explore Cebolla Creek or hike up to Devils Lake. The Deer Lakes Cutoff (open to bikes) reaches from Deer Lakes to the Powderhorn Wilderness boundary, where it connects with the Cañon Inferno and Calf Creek Plateau Trails (closed to bikes). Sites 7 and 8 are close to the lakes. Sites 4 and 5 offer outstanding privacy and scenery.

Campsites, facilities: There are 12 sites for tents and RVs up to 30 feet. Site 8 and the facilities are wheelchair accessible. There are no hookups. Sites 10 and 12 are pull-through. Picnic tables, grills, and fire rings are provided at all sites. Sites 1, 4–6, and 12 have tent pads. Vault toilets and drinking water are available. Leashed pets are permitted.

Reservations, fees: Reservations are not accepted. The fee is $12 per night (includes one vehicle). Additional vehicles cost $6 per night. Golden Age and Golden Access Passports are accepted. Cash or check only. Open mid-May–October.

Directions: From 2nd Street in Lake City, take Highway 149 south for 9.6 miles. Turn left on Forest Route 788 (before Slumgullion Pass). In 2.7 miles, turn left at the tent sign. The campground is in 0.8 mile.

Contact: Gunnison National Forest, 970/641-0471, www.fs.fed.us/r2/gmug.

11 HIDDEN VALLEY

Scenic rating: 5

east of Lake City

Hidden Valley isn't half as enchanting as the name implies. There are four tent sites on the banks of Cebolla Creek. Three of them are accessible via a small footbridge. Scattered spruce provide some shade but not much privacy. There is fair to poor fishing for brook trout on this portion of the stream. Hiking trails into the La Garita and Powderhorn wilderness areas are a short drive away, but not within walking distance. The biggest attraction here is solitude. There are few visitors to this remote part of the state, and even fewer visitors to this campground. For more information on the La Garita and Powderhorn wilderness areas, see the Cebolla listing later in this chapter.

Campsites, facilities: There are four tent sites. There are no hookups or pull-throughs. Picnic tables, grills, and vault toilets are provided. Leashed pets are permitted.

Reservations, fees: Reservations are not accepted. The fee is $8 per night (includes one vehicle). Additional vehicles cost $4 per

night. Golden Age and Golden Access Passports are accepted. Cash or check only. Open May–September.

Directions: From 2nd Street in Lake City, take Highway 149 south for 9.6 miles. Turn left on Forest Route 788 (before Slumgullion Pass). The campground is on the right in 7.3 miles.

Contact: Gunnison National Forest, 970/641-0471, www.fs.fed.us/r2/gmug.

12 SPRUCE

Scenic rating: 7

east of Lake City

Spruce campground is in the northern portion of the La Garita Wilderness. The Powderhorn Wilderness begins a few miles away. This remote area offers a true wilderness experience to the adventurous camper, but the narrow, winding road deters the majority of visitors. The creek has good brook trout fishing for experienced anglers in the canyons. Novice anglers will have better luck in the numerous beaver ponds. The campground is in a small park on Cebolla Creek, surrounded by dramatic rock formations. The willowy undergrowth provides more privacy than at Cebolla campground downstream. The sites are 50–100 feet apart and offer lots of room for large groups to spread out. Sites 2, 3, 5, and 6 have abundant shade and privacy. For more information on the Powderhorn and La Garita wilderness areas, see the Cebolla listing later in this chapter.

Campsites, facilities: There are nine sites for tents and RVs up to 15 feet. There are no hookups or pull-throughs. Picnic tables, grills, and fire rings are provided. Vault toilets and drinking water are available. Leashed pets are permitted.

Reservations, fees: Reservations are not accepted. The fee is $8 per night (includes one vehicle). Additional vehicles cost $4 per night. Golden Age and Golden Access Passports are accepted. Cash or check only. Open May–September.

Directions: From 2nd Street in Lake City, take Highway 149 south for 9.6 miles. Turn left on Forest Route 788 (before Slumgullion Pass). The campground is on the right in 8.4 miles.

Contact: Gunnison National Forest, 970/641-0471, www.fs.fed.us/r2/gmug.

13 CEBOLLA

Scenic rating: 6

east of Lake City

This remote little campground is on Cebolla Creek, between the Powderhorn Wilderness to the north and the La Garita Wilderness to the south. The Powderhorn Wilderness ranges in elevation from 8,600–12,600 feet. Most of it is a plateau, the largest relatively flat expanse of alpine tundra in the continental United States. This area was summer hunting grounds for the Utes, and was used for cattle and sheep ranching in the early 1900s, but it was never widely settled. It's home to beaver, bobcat, mountain lion, bear, mule deer, and elk, as well as bighorn sheep and the occasional moose. The best way to access the interior is with pack animals. The Powderhorn Lakes trailhead is a short drive east of the campground. The Rough Creek Trail begins near the campground and extends 7.5 miles into the La Garita Wilderness. Anglers can fish for brookies, brownies, and rainbows on Cebolla Creek. Young anglers will have an easier time on the beaver ponds upstream.

The campground is in a spruce-fir forest on the banks of Cebolla Creek in a steep-walled canyon. The sites are about 50 feet apart. There is plenty of shade, and the sun doesn't penetrate the canyon until late morning. Visitors are few and far between, but the campground has a small following of regulars.

Campers should come prepared for a wilderness experience.

Campsites, facilities: There are four sites for tents and RVs up to 15 feet. There are no hookups or pull-throughs. Picnic tables, grills, and fire rings are provided. Vault toilets and drinking water are available. Leashed pets are permitted.

Reservations, fees: Reservations are not accepted. The fee is $8 per night (includes one vehicle). Additional vehicles cost $4 per night. Golden Age and Golden Access Passports are accepted. Cash or check only. Open May–September.

Directions: From 2nd Street in Lake City, take Highway 149 south for 9.6 miles. Turn left on Forest Route 788. The campground is on the right in 9.3 miles.

Contact: Gunnison National Forest, 970/641-0471, www.fs.fed.us/r2/gmug.

14 TELLURIDE TOWN PARK

Scenic rating: 7

in downtown Telluride

Telluride's social calendar would give Martha Stewart a conniption fit. A typical summer lineup includes the celebrated Bluegrass Festival, Bike Week, Wine Festival, Jazz Celebration, Mushroom Fest, and the Film Festival. Add to that the endless hiking, mountain biking, and fishing opportunities of the San Juans (and all that Main Street shopping), and finding a place to pitch your tent in a town with only one campground can be pretty tough. If you want to camp at the town park, arrive early. If there's a festival going on, call ahead to check availability. If you do manage to snag a spot, you can sit back and enjoy the scene: deadheads, dirt bags, prayer flags, family reunions, and VW buses are typical sights. The park is adjacent to Bear Creek Preserve, a 381-acre open space. The San Miguel River Trail and Bear Creek Trail are accessible from the campground. There is no privacy in this campground, but privacy is not the point. Camping in Telluride is a social event, so bring your hiking boots, your hammock, and your happy face.

Campsites, facilities: There are 29 sites for tents and RVs up to 20 feet and five primitive hike-in sites. There are no hookups. Picnic tables, grills, restrooms with flush toilets and showers, and drinking water are provided. The park also contains a swimming pool, playground, volleyball and basketball courts, baseball fields, tennis courts, a fishing pond, skateboard ramp, disc golf course, and festival stage. Leashed pets are permitted, and leash laws are strictly enforced.

Reservations, fees: Reservations are not accepted. The fee for primitive sites is $12 per night. All other sites cost $15 per night (includes one vehicle). Additional vehicles cost $4 each. The senior rate is $8 per night. Cash only. Open mid-May–mid-October.

Directions: The town park is located at the east end of Telluride at 500 East Colorado Avenue. Highway 145 (the only road into town) turns into Colorado Avenue/Main Street. The park entrance is at the Maple Street bridge.

Contact: Telluride Parks and Recreation Department, 970/728-2173, www.town.telluride.co.us.

15 SUNSHINE
🚶 🚴 🛶 🐕 ♿ 🚐 ⛺

Scenic rating: 8

south of Telluride

Sunshine is the closest national forest campground to Telluride, and it's on the San Juan Skyway, so the earlier you arrive at this first-come, first-served campground, the better. The campground is a paved loop through a pretty aspen grove. A 50-yard trail leads to an overlook with views of the South Fork valley and the snowbound peaks of the Lizard Head Wilderness. And that's just the beginning.

From Sunshine, campers can hike or drive up to Alta Lakes. And just a short drive away is a Nature Conservancy Preserve on the South Fork of the San Miguel with excellent catch-and-release fishing. The historic town of Ophir, the Ophir needle, and wall and crack climbing are a 15-minute drive to the south. And cyclists shouldn't miss the heart-stopping climb up Lizard Head Pass. Sites 1–3 are next to a small wetland. Sites 8 and 9 are next to the overlook trail. Sites 10–12 are right next to the road, but sites 11 and 12 also have the best views of the mountains.

Campsites, facilities: There are 17 sites for tents and RVs up to 35 feet. Sites 2–4 and 12–14 are wheelchair accessible. There are no hookups. Picnic tables, fire rings, grills, and tent pads are provided. Vault toilets and drinking water are available. Leashed pets are permitted.

Reservations, fees: Reservations are not accepted. The fee is $14 per night (includes one vehicle). Additional vehicles cost $7 per night. Golden Age and Golden Access Passports are accepted. Cash or check only. Open May–October.

Directions: From the San Miguel River bridge just west of Telluride, take Highway 145 south for six miles. The campground entrance is on the right.

Contact: San Juan National Forest, 970/247-4874, www.fs.fed.us/r2/sanjuan/.

16 MATTERHORN
🚶 🚴 🛶 🐕 🚐 ⛺

Scenic rating: 9

south of Telluride

BEST (

Matterhorn is named for the awe-inspiring views of Sheep Mountain to the south. It's a large loop located in an aspen grove between North Fork Creek and Yellow Mountain. This is a gorgeous location. The only drawbacks are the sound of the highway and chilly nights, but at this altitude, the stargazing is unbeatable, and, with a little patience, you'll see several shooting stars. It's a short hike from the campground to Trout Lake, where the rainbows are biting all summer. The historic town of Ophir and the Ophir Needles are a brief drive away. The Lizard Head Wilderness is on the opposite side of the highway. Several trailheads into the wilderness are located on the other side of Lizard Head Pass. RV drivers appreciate the full hookups, and tent campers won't want to miss the hike-in sites. Site 1 is the only unattractive location because of its proximity to the entrance. Sites 10, 17, 19, and 21 are in the middle of the loop and less private than the rest of the campground.

Campsites, facilities: There are 25 sites for tents and RVs up to 35 feet and three hike-in tent sites. Full hookups are available at sites 5, 7, 20, and 22–26. Picnic tables, fire rings, and grills are provided. Tent pads are available at sites 7, 8, 11–14, and 17. Restrooms with flush toilets and showers and drinking water are available. Trash must be packed out. Leashed pets are permitted.

Reservations, fees: Reservations are accepted at 887/444-6777 and www.reserveameri-ca.com. The fee is $16 per night for tent sites and $24 per night for sites with full hookups. Additional vehicles cost $8 per night. Golden Age and Golden Access Passports are accepted. Cash or check only. Open May–October.

Directions: From the San Miguel River bridge just west of Telluride, take Highway 145 south for 12 miles. The campground entrance is on the left.

Contact: San Juan National Forest, 970/247-4874, www.fs.fed.us/r2/sanjuan/.

17 BURRO BRIDGE

🏃 🚴 🛶 🎣 🐕 🚐 ⛺

Scenic rating: 8

north of Dolores

BEST (

Burro Bridge is the third campground on West Dolores Road. It is a long haul to get here, but if you prize scenery and solitude over acces-

sibility, then keep driving. (There are rarely crowds because the long dirt road deters most people.) Burro Bridge is the ideal base camp for exploring the Lizard Head Wilderness. The Navajo Lake trailhead is a mile up the road. From the lakes, three fourteeners are accessible to experienced mountaineers. Mountain biking is not allowed in the wilderness area, but there are advanced trails south of the campground. The river is about a hundred feet down a steep slope; anglers will have to scout for access sites. The campground is full of ponderosa pine and aspen, which are incredibly beautiful when the colors change in the fall. Many sites have views of Mount Wilson.

Campsites, facilities: There are 12 sites for tents and RVs up to 35 feet. There are no hookups. Only sites 7 and 8 are pull-through. Picnic tables, grills, and fire rings are provided. Vault toilets, drinking water, and a horse corral are available. Trash must be packed out. Leashed pets are permitted.

Reservations, fees: Reservations are not accepted. The fee is $12 per night (includes one vehicle). Additional vehicles cost $6 per night. Electricity costs $3 per night. Golden Age and Golden Access Passports are accepted. Cash or check only. Open mid-May–mid-October.

Directions: From Dolores, take Highway 145 north for about 13 miles. Turn left on Forest Route 535/West Dolores Road. In 22.5 miles, stay right at the fork. The campground entrance is on the right in 1.2 miles.

Contact: San Juan National Forest, 970/247-4874, www.fs.fed.us/r2/sanjuan.

18 CAYTON

🏃 🚴 🛶 🎣 🐕 🚐 ⛺

Scenic rating: 6

south of Telluride

At 9,400 feet, Cayton can be a chilly place to wake up. It's not unusual to find patches of snow in June. As a result, this is a quiet summer destination, frequented mostly by backpackers and hikers heading into the rugged Lizard Head Wilderness. The wilderness encompasses 41,000 acres in the San Miguel Mountains, including three fourteeners and several thirteeners. The Navajo Lake and Lizard Head Trails are popular destinations. Outside of the wilderness, ATVs and snowmobilers enjoy the Barlow Creek and Divide Roads. There are 60 miles of snowmobiling trails in the Roaring Forks and Barlow Creek Snowmobile Area. Sites 11–14 and 19, 21, and 22 are next to the Dolores River. The prettiest sites in the campground are 8 and 22. Sites are fairly private in this uncrowded destination.

Campsites, facilities: There are 22 sites for tents and RVs up to 35 feet. Sites 6, 7, 9, and 18 are pull-through. There are no hookups. Picnic tables and grills are provided. Vault toilets, drinking water, and a group picnic area are available. Leashed pets are permitted.

Reservations, fees: Reservations are not accepted. The fee is $12 per night (includes one vehicle). Additional vehicles cost $6 per night. Golden Age and Golden Access Passports are accepted. Cash only. Open May–October.

Directions: Take Highway 145 south from Telluride. The campground entrance is nine miles past Lizard Head Pass. Turn left onto Forest Route 578 and cross the bridge. In 0.3 mile, stay right at the fork and enter the campground.

Contact: San Juan National Forest, 970/882-7296, www.fs.fed.us/r2/sanjuan/.

19 SOUTH MINERAL
🚶 🚲 🛶 🐕 🚐 ⛺

Scenic rating: 8

near Silverton

In July and August, it can be tough to find an empty campsite in this gorgeous valley formed by volcanic activity. The surrounding mountains are colorful and dotted with waterfalls and alpine lakes. The most popular hike, Ice Lake Trail, is a strenuous 4.5-mile climb to a lake surrounded by thirteeners. Clear Lake Trail is equally challenging and rewarding. The Rico-Silverton Trail can be accessed by following South Mineral Road past the campground to Bandora Mine. The eight-mile trail climbs two passes and provides access to Grizzly Peak, Rolling Mountain, and Graysill Mountain. Mountain bikers and ATV owners will enjoy exploring the forest routes. When you're ready for some culture, it's a short drive to Silverton, a National Historic District with good restaurants and mining attractions. The campground is a dirt loop in an evergreen forest. Sites 4–6 and 18–20 have the best views. Sites 5, 8, 9, 11, and 14–16 are on the banks of South Mineral Creek. Site 10 is hike-in. Be sure to bring your air mattress—the ground can be quite rocky—and arrive early to beat out the large crowd of regulars.

Campsites, facilities: There are 26 sites for tents and RVs up to 25 feet. There are no hookups. Sites 2, 15, 16, and 30 are pull-through. Picnic tables, grills, fire rings, vault toilets, and drinking water are provided. Leashed pets are permitted.

Reservations, fees: Reservations are not accepted. The fee is $14 per night (includes two vehicles). Additional vehicles cost $7 per night. Golden Age and Golden Access Passports are accepted. Cash or check only. Open late May–mid-September.

Directions: From the intersection of I-550 and Highway 110 in Silverton, take I-550 north for two miles. Turn left on County Road 7/South Mineral Road. Continue 4.6 miles to the campground.

Contact: San Juan National Forest, 970/247-4874, www.fs.fed.us/r2/sanjuan.

20 SOUTH MINERAL DISPERSED
🚶 🚲 🛶 🐕 🚐 ⛺

Scenic rating: 9

near Silverton

In July and August, it can be tough to find an empty campsite in this gorgeous volcanic valley. If the developed campground at the end of South Mineral Road is packed with regulars, look for a campsite at four pull-offs along the road (two beside the creek, two across the road). You won't be missing out. The floodplain has numerous beaver ponds and amazing views of the igneous peaks and sparkling waterfalls. Two hikes begin at the end of the road. Ice Lake Trail is a strenuous 4.5-mile climb to an alpine lake basin surrounded by thirteeners. Clear Lake Trail is equally challenging and rewarding. Mountain bikers and ATV owners can explore the forest routes. Silverton, a National Historic District with good restaurants and mining attractions, is a short drive to the east. This is free camping at its best.

Campsites, facilities: There are four dispersed camping areas for tents and RVs up to 25 feet. A vault toilet is available at the last pull-off. Leashed pets are permitted.

Reservations, fees: Reservations are not accepted, and camping is free. Open May–October.

Directions: From the intersection of I-550 and Highway 110 in Silverton, take I-550 north for two miles. Turn left on County Road 7/South Mineral Road. The pull-offs are located at mile 0.5, 0.9, 1.3, and 3.

Contact: San Juan National Forest, 970/247-4874, www.fs.fed.us/r2/sanjuan.

21 MOLAS LAKE PUBLIC PARK

Scenic rating: 9

south of Silverton

BEST (

This is a campground of superlatives. At 10,680 feet, Molas Lake is the highest campground in the continental U.S., and the views are nothing short of awesome. The park is surrounded by BLM property (north and east) and national forest (west and south), including the Weminuche Wilderness, the largest wilderness area in Colorado. Molas Lake is cradled by high peaks: Engineer Mountain, Twin Sisters, Sultan Mountain, Whitehead Peak, and Snowdon Peak. The drive here on I-550 is part of the San Juan Scenic Byway, often called the most beautiful drive in the country. Every traveler on the byway should reserve at least one night for Molas Lake. There's fishing and boating on the lake and excellent hiking around the lake as well as on the Colorado Trail. With a shuttle, backpackers can hike 20 miles one-way from Molas Pass to Bolam Pass or make a loop with several connecting trails. Molas Trail leads east from the pass into the Weminuche. It's four miles one-way, and it connects with Elk Creek, the most popular trail in the wilderness area. The Upper Animas, from Silverton to Rockwood Railroad Depot, is considered one of the finest Class IV–V white-water adventures in the country. It's enjoyed by advanced kayakers and commercial rafting companies.

The campground itself is not as impressive as the surroundings, but it's still a comfortable place to pitch your tent, and it will only improve. Silverton has received a grant to renovate and enlarge the facilities in 2006. The campsites are dispersed around the north and east sides of the lake, and they are very diverse. Campers can choose from forest, meadows, and lakefront. Weekends get very crowded, but there is ample privacy midweek.

Campsites, facilities: There are 50 sites for tents and very small RVs or pop-ups and 10 sites which can accommodate RVs of any length. There are no hookups. Picnic tables and fire rings are provided. Vault toilets, coin showers, drinking water, dump stations, a fish-cleaning station, and a small store are available. Most facilities are wheelchair accessible. Leashed pets are permitted.

Reservations, fees: Reservations are accepted at 800/752-4494. The fee is $16 per night. Cash or check only. Open Memorial Day–Labor Day.

Directions: From Silverton, take I-550 south for 5.2 miles and turn left at the Molas Lake

Public Park sign and continue a half mile to the office. The dirt road can be very bad when wet.

Contact: Silverton Chamber of Commerce, 800/752-4494, www.silvertoncolorado.com.

22 LOST TRAIL

Scenic rating: 10

West of Creede

BEST (

This campground is on Lost Trail Creek, about a mile upstream of the confluence with the Rio Grande. It's a long, narrow, bumpy road to get there, but it's worth every bit of washboard. Every site has outstanding views of the surrounding ridgelines, which include the thirteeners Pole Creek Mountain and Ute Ridge, as well as the spires of Finger Mesa. The Continental Divide lies to the north of the campground, and the Weminuche Wilderness boundary is just south of the road. This destination campground attracts hikers, anglers, horseback riders, and four-wheelers. The Lost Creek Trail begins near the campground and connects with the West Lost Creek, Heart Lake, Continental Divide, and Colorado Trails. These trails feature open parks, aspen groves, panoramic views, bighorn sheep, and good fishing. Backpackers will find good camping along West Lost Creek and at Heart Lake. The Ute Creek Trail begins a mile east of the campground. This 12-mile trail is a popular route into the Weminuche Wilderness. The Ute Basin has four good fishing lakes below the Continental Divide. There are also views of The Window and the Rio Grande Pyramid. Four-wheelers can take Forest Route 520 to Stony Pass (the old toll road to Silverton) or Forest Route 506 to Beartown and Kite Lake. When you're done exploring, you can kick up your feet at this quiet campground and listen to the bubbling of Lost Trail Creek.

Campsites, facilities: There are seven sites for tents and RVs up to 25 feet. There are no hookups. Picnic tables, grills, and fire rings are provided. Vault toilets and drinking water are available. Leashed pets are permitted.

Reservations, fees: Camping is free, and reservations are not accepted. Closed only by seasonal snow. No water is available after Labor Day.

Directions: From First Street in Creede, take Highway 149 west for 20.7 miles. Turn left on Forest Route 520. The campground is on the left in 18 miles. This is a rough road, but it is 2WD. It is not recommended for long trailers or RVs.

Contact: Rio Grande National Forest, 719/658-2556, www.fs.fed.us/r2/riogrande/.

23 THIRTY MILE

Scenic rating: 7

west of Creede

Thirty Mile is a short walk from the east end of the Rio Grande Reservoir, a 1,196-acre lake with an earthen boat ramp which can accommodate only canoes, rafts, and small fishing boats. Fishing is also possible on the Rio Grande, Squaw Creek, Weminuche Creek, and Little Squaw Creek, all of which are within walking distance of the campground. Two trails being at the campground and access the Weminuche Wilderness. The popular Weminuche Creek Trail is an easy five-mile climb to Weminuche Pass, the lowest point on the Continental Divide within the wilderness area. The Squaw Creek Trail parallels the creek for 10 miles from the campground to the Continental Divide. There is good fishing and frequent elk sightings on this trail. Because of the variety of activities and accessibility, Thirty Mile is a very popular campground, and reservations are recommended. It has four loops in a spruce/fir forest. The sites are large and spaced 25–75 feet apart. Privacy is fairly limited. Sites 2, 3, 5, 6, and 24–26 are next to the river.

Campsites, facilities: There are 39 sites for tents and RVs up to 32 feet. There are no hookups. Sites 4, 5, 7, 9, 11, 12, 19, 21, 27, 29, 32, and 33 are pull-through. Picnic tables, grills, and fire rings are provided. Vault toilets, drinking water, and a pavilion/slide-show area are available. Leashed pets are permitted.

Reservations, fees: Reservations are accepted at 877/444-6777 or www.reserveusa.com. The fee is $14 per night (includes one vehicle). Additional vehicles cost $5 per night. Golden Age and Golden Access Passports are accepted. Cash or check only. Open mid-May–early September with services. Open for hunting season without services.

Directions: From First Street in Creede, take Highway 149 west for 20.7 miles. Turn left on Forest Route 520. The campground is on the left in 11.2 miles.

Contact: Rio Grande National Forest, 719/658-2556, www.fs.fed.us/r2/riogrande/.

24 RIVER HILL

Scenic rating: 7

west of Creede

River Hill is at the confluence of Little Squaw Creek and the Rio Grande, which offer fair stream fishing. The kayaking is also excellent. The six-mile stretch from the campground to Trail 816 offers Class III whitewater when water is being released from the reservoir in May and June. The nearest hiking trails are Weminuche Creek and Squaw Creek, which begin at the Thirty Mile campground and access the Weminuche Wilderness and Continental Divide.

The campground is in the riparian zone between the forest route and the river. It has a blend of meadows and spruce/fir forests. Most of the sites are well shaded. The best sites, 5, 6, and 8–12, are next to the river. This campground us smaller than Thirty Mile and offers more privacy. It's very popular with return

campers, and stays about three-quarters full throughout the summer.

Campsites, facilities: There are 20 sites for tents and RVs up to 32 feet. There are no hookups. Sites 2, 7, 11, and 13 are pull-through. Picnic tables, grills, and fire rings are provided. Vault toilets, drinking water, volleyball, and horseshoe pits are available. Leashed pets are permitted.

Reservations, fees: Reservations are accepted at 877/444-6777 or www.reserveusa.com. The fee is $14 per night (includes one vehicle). Additional vehicles cost $5 per night. Golden Age and Golden Access Passports are accepted. Cash or check only. Open late May–early September.

Directions: From First Street in Creede, take Highway 149 west for 20.7 miles. Turn left on Forest Route 520. The campground is on the left in 9.8 miles.

Contact: Rio Grande National Forest, 719/658-2556, www.fs.fed.us/r2/riogrande/.

25 ROAD CANYON

Scenic rating: 4

west of Creede

This unattractive campground is squeezed between Forest Route 520 and the Road Canyon Reservoir, and it's easy to miss. It looks more like a picnic area than a campground. There are no trees or shade, and the campsites are totally exposed to the road. When the campgrounds upstream are full, there are usually vacancies at Road Canyon. The reservoir has an earthen boat ramp suitable for small boats and canoes. Most of the campers are there for four-wheeling in House Canyon and up Stony Pass, the historic toll road to Silverton. Fishing is poor on the reservoir. Better fishing is available on the Rio Grande and the Rio Grande Reservoir.

Campsites, facilities: There are six sites for tents and RVs up to 30 feet. There are no hookups. Sites 3 and 4 are pull-through. Picnic tables, grills, and fire rings are provided. Vault toilets are available. Trash must be packed out. Leashed pets are permitted.

Reservations, fees: Camping is free, and reservations are not accepted. The campground only closes due to heavy snow.

Directions: From First Street in Creede, take Highway 149 west for 20.7 miles. Turn left on Forest Route 520. The campground is on the left in 6.3 miles.

Contact: Rio Grande National Forest, 719/658-2556, www.fs.fed.us/r2/riogrande/.

26 NORTH CLEAR CREEK

Scenic rating: 6

west of Creede

North Clear Creek is an easily accessible destination for travelers interested in exploring the Rio Grande valley. The campground is in a little park beside North Clear Creek, ringed by a forest of spruce, fir, and aspen. The meadow in the middle accommodates two volleyball courts. The best feature of the scenery is the views of Table Mountain and Snow Mesa. Anglers can fish for brookies on the creek. The sites are well spaced, and the campground seems smaller than it is. Sites 10–20 have the best creek access and shade. Sites 4–8 and 21–25 border the meadow and have partial shade but nice views. Sites 1 and 2 share an aspen grove on a small hill overlooking the meadow. Site 20 is a family site with an extra large picnic table and room for several tents.

Campsites, facilities: There are 25 sites for tents and RVs up to 32 feet. There are no hookups. Sites 10–13, 15, 19, 21, 22, 24, and 25 are pull-through. Picnic tables, grills, and fire rings are provided. Vault toilets and drinking water are available. Leashed pets are permitted.

Reservations, fees: Reservations are not accepted. The fee is $12 per night (includes one vehicle). Additional vehicles cost $5 per night. Golden Age and Golden Access Passports are accepted. Cash or check only. Open Memorial Day–Labor Day.

Directions: From First Street in Creede, take Highway 149 west for 22.9 miles. Turn right on Forest Route 510. The campground is on the right in two miles.

Contact: Rio Grande National Forest, 719/658-2556, www.fs.fed.us/r2/riogrande/.

27 SILVER THREAD

Scenic rating: 6

west of Creede

Silver Thread is a stopover on the Silver Thread Scenic Byway, a 75-mile route from South Fork to Lake City. The scenery of the Rio Grande valley around Creede is spectacular, so if you're heading east on the byway near nightfall, spend the night at Silver Thread so you don't miss some of the best sites on the route. The campground contains open meadows and aspen groves below a hairpin turn in the highway. There is a foot trail to the impressive North Clear Creek Falls, where the creek tumbles over volcanic tuff. The only drawback is the proximity of the road. Traffic noise deters many campers, so there are always open sites. Sites 1–4 are in a meadow near the highway. Sites 5, 6, and 9–11 are in an aspen grove.

Campsites, facilities: There are 11 sites for tents and RVs up to 30 feet. There are no hookups. Sites 1–4, 7, 9, and 11 are pull-through. Picnic tables, grills, and fire rings are provided. Vault toilets are available. Leashed pets are permitted.

Reservations, fees: Reservations are not accepted. The fee is $12 per night (includes one vehicle). Additional vehicles cost $5 per night. Golden Age and Golden Access Passports are accepted. Cash or check only. Open mid-May–early September.

Directions: From First Street in Creede, take Highway 149 west for 24.3 miles. The campground is on the right, across from Forest Route 515.

Contact: Rio Grande National Forest, 719/658-2556, www.fs.fed.us/r2/riogrande/.

28 BRISTOL HEAD

Scenic rating: 7

west of Creede

Bristol Head is named for the 12,706-foot peak to the east of the campground. Most sites have excellent views of this landmark, which marks the northwestern boundary of the Creede Caldera, a 10-mile-wide caldera that was formed 30 million years ago during a massive volcanic eruption. BASE jumpers sometimes use this peak for parachuting into the Rio Grande valley, a surprising sight to most campers. (BASE is an acronym for Building Antennae Span Earth, the four kinds of fixed objects from which BASE jumpers hurl themselves with small parachutes.) Activities include fishing for brookies on South Clear Creek and hiking a short footpath to an overlook with views of North Clear Creek Falls and the North and South Clear Creek Canyons, also formed by volcanic activity and erosion. In addition to these activities, most campers are inclined to just cook and visit. There are two loops that border a meadow. The second loop, sites 9–16, has more trees and shade. The campground is about half full most of the summer.

Campsites, facilities: There are 16 sites for tents and RVs up to 32 feet. There are no hookups. Sites 2–7, 9, and 11–15 are pull-through. Picnic tables, grills and fire rings are provided. Vault toilets and drinking water are available. Leashed pets are permitted.

Reservations, fees: Reservations are not accepted. The fee is $12 per night (includes one vehicle). Additional vehicles cost $5 per night. Golden Age and Golden Access Passports are accepted. Cash or check only. Open Memorial Day–Labor Day.

Directions: From First Street in Creede, take Highway 149 west for 22.9 miles. Turn right on Forest Route 510/North Clear Creek Road. The campground is on the right in 0.2 mile.

Contact: Rio Grande National Forest, 719/658-2556, www.fs.fed.us/r2/riogrande/.

29 RIO GRANDE

Scenic rating: 5

west of Creede

This campground has four undeveloped sites on the north bank of the Rio Grande. Spruce trees and willows provide limited shade but no privacy. The campground is completely hidden from the highway, and there is no traffic noise. It's a good destination for small groups interested in fishing, rafting, or tubing on the river. The river has large rainbow trout, brown trout, and native cutthroat, but special fishing regulations apply. The road is not suitable for long trailers or RVs.

Campsites, facilities: There are four sites for tents and RVs up to 21 feet. There are no hookups or pull-throughs. Picnic tables, grills, and fire rings are provided. Vault toilets are available. Trash must be packed out. Leashed pets are permitted.

Reservations, fees: Camping is free, and reservations are not accepted. Open year-round. No water is available after Labor Day.

Directions: From First Street in Creede, take Highway 149 west for nine miles. Turn left on an unmarked dirt road. The campground is in 0.6 mile.

Contact: Rio Grande National Forest, 719/658-2556, www.fs.fed.us/r2/riogrande/.

🗐 MARSHALL PARK
🦌🚗🏕

Scenic rating: 6

west of Creede

Marshall Park is on the north bank of the Rio Grande, just seven miles from Creede. This popular campground stays full for most of the summer. The majority of campers stay for a night, but there are also snowbirds who spend several weeks enjoying the Creede area. There is good fishing for rainbow, brown, and native cutthroat, but special regulations apply. The campground is a paved loop around a small meadow. The middle sites (1–3, 8, and 15) are exposed and have no shade. Cottonwoods, spruce, and fir provide shade and privacy at the riverside sites (4–7 and 9–14). Mornings are cool and afternoons are hot.

Campsites, facilities: There are 15 sites for tents and RVs up to 32 feet. There are no hookups. Picnic tables, grills, and fire rings are provided. Vault toilets and drinking water are available. Leashed pets are permitted.

Reservations, fees: Reservations are accepted at 877/444-6777 or www.reserveusa.com. The fee is $14 per night (includes one vehicle). Additional vehicles cost $5 per night. Golden Age and Golden Access Passports are accepted. Cash or check only. Open late May–early September.

Directions: From First Street in Creede, take Highway 149 west for 6.7 miles. Turn left on Forest Route 623. In 0.2 mile, turn left after the bridge and into the campground.

Contact: Rio Grande National Forest, 719/658-2556, www.fs.fed.us/r2/riogrande/.

🗐 PALISADE
🦆🦌🚗🏕

Scenic rating: 6

east of Creede

Palisade campground is two miles downstream of Wagon Wheel Gap and the former location of the Hot Springs Hotel on Goose Creek, now privately owned. As the only campground on the Silver Thread Scenic Byway between Creede and South Fork, Palisade receives a lot of stopover activity, but if you have time to cast a line, the fishing is excellent. This stretch of the Rio Grande is not known for its whitewater, but beginning kayakers and rafters may wish to float it. There are no hiking or biking trails within walking distance, but snowmobilers will enjoy Forest Route 600. This road goes to the Wheeler Geological Area, an area of volcanic ash carved into tepees and hoodoos by erosion. The road is groomed in the winter, but snowmobilers should check trail conditions at www.sledcity.com. Big cottonwoods as well as willows, spruce, and fir provide ample shade at sites 9–13. Sites 1, 4–6, and 8 are next to the river. Site 1 is a walk-in tent site.

Campsites, facilities: There are 11 sites for tents and RVs up to 32 feet and one walk-in tent site. There are no hookups. Sites 5–8 and 13 are pull-through. Picnic tables, grills, and fire rings are provided. Vault toilets and drinking water are available. Open year-round. Services are provided from late May–early September.

Reservations, fees: Reservations are not accepted. The fee is $14 per night (includes one vehicle). Additional vehicles cost $5 per night. Golden Age and Golden Access Passports are accepted. Cash or check only. Open late May–early September.

Directions: From Creede, take Highway 149 east for 12 miles. Turn right at the campground sign.

Contact: Rio Grande National Forest, 719/658-2556, www.fs.fed.us/r2/riogrande/.

32 BRADFIELD

Scenic rating: 7

west of McPhee Reservoir

The Dolores River was named by the Franciscan friars/explorers Dominquez and Escalante in honor of our Our Lady of Sorrows. From its headwaters in the San Juan Mountains, it flows northwest 200 miles to the Colorado River. Below the McPhee Reservoir, the Dolores traverses John Wayne country—beautiful sandstone canyons where cowboys and their herds used to winter. This campground is named for the Bradfield Ranch, which owned the land until the 1970s. It's set in an appealing meadow with a boat ramp for the river runners—commercial and private—who float downriver on single and multiday trips. The last take-out, Bedrock, is 97 miles (and a few Class IV rapids) downstream. The fishing is good, too. From McPhee Dam to Bradfield Bridge, the Dolores is very popular with anglers looking for native trout. There are very few trees in the campground, but the sites are spaced 100–200 feet apart, which affords some privacy. Site 5 is the best. It's next to the river and surrounded by shade trees.

Campsites, facilities: There are 22 sites for tents and RVs up to 30 feet. Sites 1, 3, and 10 are wheelchair accessible. Picnic tables, grills, fire rings, and shelters are provided. Vault toilets, drinking water, a boat ramp, and group picnic area are available. Trash must be packed out. Leashed pets are permitted.

Reservations, fees: This is a first-come, first-served campground. The fee is $8 per night. Golden Age and Golden Access Passports are accepted. Cash only. Open early April–late October.

Directions: From Cortez, take I-491 north. From the intersection with Highway 184, continue north on I-491 for 10.6 miles to County Road DD/County Road 15. Turn right on County Road DD and then left on County Road 16. In 2.7 miles, turn right on S Road. In one mile, turn left at the Bradfield Recreation Site sign. The campground is in 0.5 mile.

Contact: Dolores Public Lands Office, 970/882-7296, www.co.blm.gov/sjra/sjdolores.htm.

33 CABIN CANYON

Scenic rating: 7

west of McPhee Reservoir

From McPhee Dam to Bradfield Bridge, the Dolores River is considered Gold Medal Water. Colorado River rainbow trout, Snake River cutthroat trout, and brown trout thrive in these waters. Fishing is limited to artificial flies and lures and catch-and-release. The campground, located next to the river in a steep sandstone canyon, feels like a forgotten place, haunted by the wind and the birds. Bald eagles nest in the tall cottonwood trees in the winter. The whole campground is forested, and the campsites are about 200 feet apart. There is ample quiet and solitude for the angler or bird-watcher. (For more information on the Dolores River, see the Bradfield listing in this chapter.)

Campsites, facilities: There are 11 sites for tents and RVs up to 45 feet. Site 7 and the riverside trail are wheelchair accessible. Picnic tables and grills are provided. Vault toilets, drinking water, and dump stations are available. Trash must be packed out. Leashed pets are permitted.

Reservations, fees: This is a first-come, first-served campground. The fee is $10 per night for one vehicle. Additional vehicles cost $5 per night. Golden Age and Golden Access Passports are accepted. Cash only. Open year-round.

Directions: From Cortez, take I-491 north. From the intersection with Highway 184, continue north on I-491 for 10.6 miles to County Road DD/County Road 15. Turn

right on Country Road DD and then left on County Road 16. In 2.7 miles, turn right on S Road. In one mile, turn right on Forest Route 504. The campground is in 3.1 miles on the right.
Contact: Dolores Public Lands Office, 970/882-7296, www.co.blm.gov/sjra/sjdolores.htm.

34 FERRIS CANYON

Scenic rating: 7

west of McPhee Reservoir

Ferris Canyon is a smaller version of Cabin Canyon to the west, except it is about 400 yards from the campground to the Dolores. It's about six miles from Ferris Canyon to the McPhee dam. This whole stretch of river is managed by the San Juan National Forest and is open to anglers. It's very popular with anglers who fly-fish for Colorado River rainbow trout, Snake River cutthroat trout, and brown trout in these waters. Fishing is limited to artificial flies and lures and catch-and-release. The campground is a densely wooded loop with very few users.

Campsites, facilities: There are seven sites for tents and RVs up to 45 feet. Site 4 is wheelchair accessible. Picnic tables, grills, and fire rings are provided. Vault toilets, drinking water, and a dump station are available. Trash must be packed out. Leashed pets are permitted.

Reservations, fees: This is a first-come, first-served campground. The fee is $10 per night for one vehicle. Additional vehicles cost $5 per night. Golden Age and Golden Access Passports are accepted. Cash only. Open year-round.

Directions: From Cortez, take I-491 north. From the intersection with Highway 184, continue north on I-491 for 10.6 miles to County Road DD/County Road 15. Turn right on Country Road DD and then left

on County Road 16. In 2.7 miles, turn right on S Road. In one mile, turn right on Forest Route 504. The campground is in 6.4 miles on the right.
Contact: Dolores Public Lands Office, 970/882-7296, www.co.blm.gov/sjra/sjdolores.htm.

35 MAVREESO

Scenic rating: 6

north of Dolores

Mavreeso is a narrow campground that parallels the West Dolores River. The sites are distributed throughout an evergreen forest. The best riverside sites, 6 and 11, are at opposite ends of the campground. Site 14 is the most appealing RV site. The campground isn't striking, but the location is excellent for hikers, mountain bikers, and ATVers, and it's a decent stopover for travelers on the San Juan Skyway. Mountain bikers can do a 25-mile intermediate to advanced loop on the Stoner Mesa Trail and West Dolores Road. Hikers can also explore the Stoner Mesa and Stoner Creek area by trail. Anglers can fish for stocked rainbow, brown, and cutthroat trout along the West Fork, the largest tributary of the Dolores, as well as in Stoner Creek, accessible only by trail.

Campsites, facilities: There are 18 sites for tents and RVs up to 35 feet. Electric hookups are available at sites 15–18, 10, 13, and 14. Picnic tables, grills, and fire rings are provided. Vault toilets, drinking water, and a group picnic area are available. Leashed pets are permitted.

Reservations, fees: Reservations are not accepted. The fee is $12 per night for one vehicle. Additional vehicles cost $6 per night. Electricity costs $3 per night. Golden Age and Golden Access Passports are accepted. Cash or check only. Open May–October.

Directions: From Dolores, take Highway 145

north for about 13 miles. Turn left on Forest Route 535/West Dolores Road. The campground is on the right in six miles.
Contact: San Juan National Forest, 970/247-4874, www.fs.fed.us/r2/sanjuan.

36 WEST DOLORES
🚶 🚲 🎣 🐕 ♿ 🚐 ⛺

Scenic rating: 7

north of Dolores

West Dolores is in a beautiful setting on the banks of the West Fork of the Dolores, a first-rate trout fishery. It's a quiet destination during the week, but on weekends, the riverside sites fill up quickly with a mostly local crowd. Hikers will enjoy the miles of trails in the San Juan National Forest. The Stoner Mesa, Stoner Creek, Fish Creek, Calico, and Navajo Lake Trails are accessible from this campground. Mountain bikers can also explore these intermediate to advanced trails. ATV and Jeep owners frequent this campground as well and explore the Forest Service roads up to Groundhog Reservoir and Lone Cone State Wildlife Area. Riverside sites are 3, 4, 8, 9, 11, and 12. Sites 12 and 12A can accommodate large groups. Site 15 lacks trees and is the least appealing.
Campsites, facilities: There are 18 sites for tents and RVs up to 35 feet. Electric hookups are available at sites 3–6 and 14. Site 12 is pull-through. Sites 1, 9, and 14 are double sites can be double-rented. Picnic tables, grills, and fire rings are provided. Vault toilets and drinking water are available. The picnic tables and toilets are wheelchair accessible. Leashed pets are permitted.
Reservations, fees: Reservations are not accepted. The fee is $12 per night (includes one vehicle). Additional vehicles cost $6 per night. Electricity costs $3 per night. Golden Age and Golden Access Passports are accepted. Cash or check only. Open mid-May–mid-October.
Directions: From Dolores, take Highway 145

north for about 13 miles. Turn left on Forest Route 535/West Dolores Road. The campground is on the right in 7.2 miles.
Contact: San Juan National Forest, 970/247-4874, www.fs.fed.us/r2/sanjuan.

37 PRIEST GULCH
🚶 🎣 🐕 ♿ 🚐 ⛺

Scenic rating: 5

south of Telluride

Priest Gulch made the *Trailer Life* Top 100 Campgrounds of 2005. It is very popular with the RV crowd, many of whom have semipermanent residences with sprinklers, bird feeders, and wind socks. The location encourages long-term visits. Campers are able to explore the Four Corners region as well as the San Juan Mountains. The campground lines both sides of the Dolores River. Sites are very close together and are separated by a few evergreen trees. The most popular sites are on the river. The tent sites are across the river from the office and at the end of the road. The Priest Gulch and Calico Trails begin across the highway. The 17.5-mile Calico Trail climbs up to Sockrider Peak and ends in The Meadows on Forest Route 471. This trail is difficult and should only be attempted by advanced backpackers. Anglers will enjoy the Dolores River, named one of the 50 Best Trout Streams in America by *Trout Magazine*. It is stocked between Stoner and Dolores.
Campsites, facilities: There are 88 sites for RVs of any length and five tent sites. Full and partial hookups are available. Picnic tables and fire rings are provided. Restrooms with flush toilets and showers, drinking water, dump stations, laundry facilities, a store, playground, wireless Internet, and propane gas are available. Leashed pets are permitted.
Reservations, fees: Reservations are accepted at 970/562-3810. The tent fee is $20 per night, and the RV fee is $27–29 per night (includes two people). Each additional person

costs $2 per night. Good Sam cards are accepted. Open May–October.

Directions: From Rico, take Highway 145 south for about 20 miles. The campground entrance is on the left.

Contact: Priest Gulch Campground, 970/562-3810, www.priestgulch.com.

38 HAVILAND LAKE

Scenic rating: 7

north of Durango

BEST (

Haviland Lake is an attractive destination in its own right, and it's a short drive away from Durango, so it's a convenient stopover on the Million Dollar Highway. The lake is stocked and practically lined with kids fishing with power bait and hauling out trout. It's a good lake for fly-fishing and a beautiful place to paddle a canoe. There's a short interpretive trail for hikers. This is a modern, well-designed facility. There are four interlaced gravel loops on a hillside overlooking the lake. The sites are terraced and have large pull-ins, so they work well for tent camping and RVs. Most of them are screened by aspen, so even when the campground is full, it's easy to find privacy. The campground fills up quickly on the weekends, so arrive early if possible. Most of the campers are retirees and families, but it can get a little rowdy until 10 P.M. when the camp hosts enforce quiet hours.

Campsites, facilities: There are 45 sites for tents and RVs up to 45 feet. Some sites and all facilities are wheelchair accessible. Sites 8, 12, 21, 23, 39, and 43 are double sites. Sites 10–16, 19–21, 31, 32, and 39–43 have electric hookups. Picnic tables, grills, and fire rings are provided. Vault toilets and drinking water, a boat ramp, and group picnic area are available. Leashed pets are permitted.

Reservations, fees: This is a first-come, first-served campground. The fee is $14 per night for one vehicle. Additional vehicles

cost $7 per night. Lakeside sites cost $18 per night. Golden Age and Golden Access Passports are accepted. Cash or check only. Open May–October.

Directions: From Durango, take I-550 north for about 24 miles. Turn right at the Haviland Lake sign onto an unmarked road. Stay left at the fork. The campground is in 0.3 mile.

Contact: San Juan National Forest, 970/247-4874, www.fs.fed.us/r2/sanjuan.

39 CHRIS PARK

Scenic rating: 6

north of Durango

This group campground is in a sheltered hollow full of ponderosa pines. It's a perfect location for a family reunion, scouting trip, or church event. The three sites have large gravel lots for RVs and dispersed tent camping in the woods. Haviland Lake is accessible via the short Wagon Road Historic Trail. The trout fishing on the lake is good, and it's a nice place to paddle a canoe. Durango is just 30 minutes away, and the Trimble Hot Springs are just outside of town. There are no mountain views from the campground, but the lake is very scenic.

Campsites, facilities: There are three group sites for tents and RVs up to 35 feet. Some sites and all facilities are wheelchair accessible. Picnic tables, grills, and fire rings are provided. Vault toilets and drinking water, an event pavilion, horseshoe pits, and a volleyball court are available. Leashed pets are permitted.

Reservations, fees: Reservations are required. At sites 1 and 2, the fee is $40–60. At site 3, the fee is $100–175. Open May–October.

Directions: From Durango, take I-550 north for about 24 miles. Turn right at the Haviland Lake sign onto an unmarked road. Stay right at the fork. The campground is in one mile.

Contact: San Juan National Forest, 970/247-4874, www.fs.fed.us/r2/sanjuan.

40 CIMARRONA
🏃 🐕 🚗 ⛺

Scenic rating: 10

north of Pagosa Springs

At the north end of the Williams Creek valley, Cimarrona campground has spectacular views of the lake and the surrounding peaks: Toner Mountain, Sugarloaf Mountain, and Cimarrona Peak. The Cimarrona Creek trailhead is adjacent to the campground. The first two miles are easy, but then it climbs steeply past Cimarrona Peak to Squaw Pass and the Continental Divide. Williams Creek Trail begins at the end of the road and continues for 14 miles through the Weminuche Wilderness to the Continental Divide. At three miles, the trail passes through an area that looks like a walled garden with unusual rock formations, which could explain the Spanish name for Williams Creek: Huerto, or gardenlike. Both of these trails are closed to mountain bikes, but they are very popular with horseback riders, and the Forest Service has plans to open an additional campground designed for horse trailers in 2006.

Sites 1–5, 7, 20, and 21 are in a meadow with a young aspen grove. These sites have limited shade but the best views. Sites 8 and 10–19 are in a forest of spruce, fir, and cottonwoods. They have ample shade and a little more privacy. Sites 11, 13, 16, and 17 are next to Cimarrona Creek. Site 13 is a family site. The sites are about 100 feet apart. The campground is usually about half full, so it's easy to find a site.

Campsites, facilities: There are 21 sites for tents and RVs up to 35 feet. There are no hookups. Sites 12, 13, and 17 are pull-through. Picnic tables, grills, and fire rings are provided. Vault toilets and drinking water are available. Leashed pets are permitted.

Reservations, fees: Reservations are not accepted. The tent fee is $10 per night, and the RV fee is $12 per night (includes one vehicle). Additional vehicles cost $5 per night.

Golden Age and Golden Access Passports are accepted. Cash or check only. Open June–September.

Directions: From U.S. Highway 160 in Pagosa Springs, take Piedra Road/County Road 600/Forest Route 631 north for 22 miles. At the fork, stay right on Forest Route 640. The campground is on the right in four miles.

Contact: San Juan National Forest, 970/264-2268, www.fs.fed.us/r2/sanjuan.

41 TEAL
🛶 🚤 🐕 🚗 ⛺

Scenic rating: 10

north of Pagosa Springs

BEST (

Teal campground perches on the western shore of Williams Creek Reservoir and features dramatic views of the San Juans towering above the lake. Cimarrona Peak, Chief Mountain, and Toner Mountain dominate the horizon to the north. To the east, Rock Mountain juts out of the surrounding slopes. If you look closely, you can see the profile of the Wounded Warrior peering up at the sky from the south face. Behind the campground, the slopes are covered in aspen groves. Unlike the nearby Cimarrona campground, Teal is almost always full because of the 343-acre reservoir, which has good trout and kokanee salmon fishing in early summer. Small sailboats and canoes and kayaks are frequently on the lake. Hikers can drive to the Williams Creek and Cimarrona trailheads.

The campground has two loops. The right loop has just five sites, all with excellent views and lots of shade. The left loop has 11 sites close to the lake. Sites 6–13 overlook the water. These sites are closer together and have less shade.

Campsites, facilities: There are 16 sites for tents and RVs up to 35 feet. There are no hookups. Picnic tables, grills, and fire rings are provided. Vault toilets, drinking water, and a boat ramp are available. The dump station is 1.6 miles away. Leashed pets are permitted.

Reservations, fees: Reservations are not accepted. The tent fee is $10 per night, and the RV fee is $12 per night (includes one vehicle). Additional vehicles cost $5 per night. Golden Age and Golden Access Passports are accepted. Cash or check only. Open mid-May–mid-September and without services during hunting season.

Directions: From U.S. Highway 160 in Pagosa Springs, take Piedra Road/County Road 600/Forest Route 631 north for 22 miles. At the fork, stay right on Forest Route 640. The campground is on the right in 1.6 miles.

Contact: San Juan National Forest, 970/264-2268, www.fs.fed.us/r2/sanjuan.

42 WILLIAMS CREEK

Scenic rating: 7

north of Pagosa Springs

Williams Creek campground is the biggest and busiest in the area. It has six loops on both sides of the creek in a forest of pine, spruce, fir, and aspen. There are excellent views of the San Juans from the road, but not from the campground. It's the least appealing of the four campgrounds in this valley, but it's such a social scene that it's very popular with families and retirees. Anglers can try stream fishing on Williams Creek, or drive one mile to the reservoir for better luck. The Piedra River is also an excellent trout fishery, but anglers will need to drive south to the bridge on Forest Route 631. Trail 583 begins nearby and is open to hikers and bikers.

Loop E (sites 1–4, 12, and 13) is in a forest of ponderosa pine on the edge of the meadow. It's popular with RVers. Loop G (sites 5–11) is also popular with RVers. The rest of the loops are in the spruce/fir forest with good shade and moderate privacy. Sites 50–66 are very close together. Sites 9–11 have the best creek

access. Sites 29–49 are in a hilly area which offers the best privacy.

Campsites, facilities: There are 67 sites for tents and RVs up to 45 feet. Water and sewer hookups are available at sites 1–4 and 6–8. Sites 3, 5, 9, 10, 12, 16, 18, 19, 21–23, 27, 29, 37, and 40 are pull-through. Picnic tables, grills, and fire rings are provided. Vault toilets and drinking water are available. The dump station is 0.4 mile away. Leashed pets are permitted.

Reservations, fees: Reservations are not accepted. The tent fee is $10 per night, and the RV fee is $12 per night or $15 for sites with hookups (includes one vehicle). Additional vehicles cost $5 per night. Golden Age and Golden Access Passports are accepted. Cash or check only. Open mid-May–mid-September.

Directions: From U.S. Highway 160 in Pagosa Springs, take Piedra Road/County Road 600/Forest Route 631 north for 22 miles. At the fork, stay right on Forest Route 640. The campground is on the right in 0.4 mile.

Contact: San Juan National Forest, 970/264-2268, www.fs.fed.us/r2/sanjuan.

43 BRIDGE

Scenic rating: 9

north of Pagosa Springs

Bridge is the least-used campground on Piedra Road, but it shouldn't be overlooked, especially by hikers, kayakers, and anglers, because it has the best access to the Piedra River. The Piedra River Trail begins a couple miles to the south, where Forest Route 631 crosses this river. This trail is 14 miles one-way. Most hikers just hike 3.5 miles to the footbridge and then turn around, but if you continue, the trail passes through two box canyons. The 10-mile stretch of river from the bridge through the Second Box Canyon has Class III whitewater. Only advanced kayakers should continue through the First Box Canyon. Anglers will enjoy fly-fishing for trout on the river. Access begins at the bridge and extends to the lower boundary of the Tres Piedras Ranch.

The campground is a mile-long spur on the west bank of Williams Creek. This riparian zone is lush with cottonwoods and willows, and many sites have excellent views of the San Juan Mountains to the north. Site 6 is the most secluded. Site 7 has the best views.

Campsites, facilities: There are 19 sites for tents and RVs up to 50 feet. There are no hookups. Picnic tables, grills, and fire rings are provided. Vault toilets and drinking water are available. The dump station is three miles up the road. Leashed pets are permitted.

Reservations, fees: Reservations are not accepted. The tent fee is $10 per night, and the RV fee is $12 per night (includes one vehicle). Additional vehicles cost $5 per night. Golden Age and Golden Access Passports are accepted. Cash or check only. Open mid-May–mid-September.

Directions: From U.S. Highway 160 in Pagosa Springs, take Piedra Road/County Road 600/Forest Route 631 north for 19 miles. The campground is on the right.

Contact: San Juan National Forest, 970/264-2268, www.fs.fed.us/r2/sanjuan.

44 WOLF CREEK

Scenic rating: 6

north of Pagosa Springs

Most campers at Wolf Creek are there to fish and relax. The main campground is on the south bank of Wolf Creek, and there are stocked fishing ponds at the end of the campground. (Sites 1–11 are near the creek.) Besides fishing, the main activity (if you're under 12) is riding a bike around the loop. There is a smaller separate campground that's perfect for larger groups. This family campground sees little use, perhaps because it hasn't been updated in many years and cannot accommodate the big rig RVs. It's in an old spruce-fir forest that is overgrown with moss and underbrush. There are many dead trees that are slowly being removed by the concessionaire. It's very shady but can also be a little gloomy, and the high trees obscure views of the beautiful valley. The nearest trailhead, West Fork/Rainbow Trail, is three miles away. There's a natural hot springs about three miles up the trail, but most campers will just head for The Springs in Pagosa Springs.

Campsites, facilities: There are 26 sites for tents and RVs up to 35 feet. There are no hookups. Sites 9, 10, 13, 14, 16, 17, and 20 are pull-through. Picnic tables, grills, and fire rings are provided. Vault toilets and drinking water are available. Leashed pets are permitted.

Reservations, fees: Reservations are not accepted. The tent fee is $10 per night, and the RV fee is $12 per night (includes one vehicle). Additional vehicles cost $5 per night. Golden Age and Golden Access Passports are accepted. Cash or check only. Open late May–early September.

Directions: From U.S. Highway 84 in Pagosa Springs, take U.S. Highway 160 north for 13.6 miles. Turn left on Forest Route 648. The campground is on the right in 0.5 mile.

Contact: San Juan National Forest, 970/264-2268, www.fs.fed.us/r2/sanjuan.

45 WEST FORK

Scenic rating: 6

north of Pagosa Springs

West Fork is north of Pagosa Springs, on the road to Wolf Creek Pass. The campground is in an old forest of spruce and fir, so overgrown with hanging moss that it feels almost primeval. The campground also looks a bit run-down, but the sites are still large and fairly private. The West Fork of the San Juan River runs nearby but is not visible from the campground. Sites 4–19 are closest to the river. The surrounding valley is gorgeous, but the high trees obscure the views. The river has good-sized rainbow and cutthroat trout. There is also good fishing along the West Fork/Rainbow Trail. (The trailhead is at the end of Forest Route 648.) This trail passes a waterfall and hot springs in the first three miles before continuing to the Continental Divide. Most of the trail is in the San Juan Wilderness and is closed to bikes. On the way out of the campground, there is an excellent view of Treasure Falls.

Campsites, facilities: There are 26 sites for tents and RVs up to 35 feet. There are no hookups. Sites 1, 7, 12–17, 20, 21, and 26 are pull-through. Picnic tables, grills, and fire rings are provided. Vault toilets and drinking water are available. Leashed pets are permitted.

Reservations, fees: Reservations are not accepted. The tent fee is $10 per night, and the RV fee is $12 per night (includes one vehicle). Additional vehicles cost $5 per night. Golden Age and Golden Access Passports are accepted. Cash or check only. Open late May–early September.

Directions: From U.S. Highway 84 in Pagosa Springs, take U.S. Highway 160 north for 13.6 miles. Turn left on Forest Route 648. The campground is on the left in 1.6 miles.

Contact: San Juan National Forest, 970/264-2268, www.fs.fed.us/r2/sanjuan.

46 TUCKER PONDS
🛶�'t🏠🚻♿🚐🔺

Scenic rating: 8

south of South Fork

Tucker Ponds are two tiny reservoirs with a total of four surface acres of water. They offer good amateur bait fishing for rainbows. The trail and fishing pier have been designed to accommodate wheelchairs, and the lake is open to hand-powered boats. The adjacent campground is a quiet family destination. The campground is a loop in a mature spruce-fir forest which affords excellent privacy. Site 1 has views of the lake. Sites 3 and 5–7 border a sunny clearing in the middle of the woods. Sites 3 and 5, and 9 and 10, are grouped closely together and best suited for a larger group. There are few visitors midweek, and the campground is only half full on weekends.

Campsites, facilities: There are 16 sites for tents and RVs up to 35 feet. There are no hookups. Sites 3, 5, 8, and 11–13 are pull-through. Picnic tables, grills, and fire rings are provided. Vault toilets, drinking water, and a wheelchair-accessible fishing pier are available. Leashed pets are permitted.

Reservations, fees: Reservations are not accepted. The fee is $12 per night (includes one vehicle). Additional vehicles cost $5 per night. Golden Age and Golden Access Passports are accepted. Cash or check only. Open late May–early September.

Directions: From Highway 149 in South Fork, take U.S. Highway 160 south for 13.2 miles. Turn left on Forest Route 390/Pass Creek Road. The campground is on the right in 2.7 miles.

Contact: Rio Grande National Forest, 719/658-2556, www.fs.fed.us/r2/riogrande.

47 BIG MEADOWS
🏕️🛶🚍🏠🚻♿🚐🔺

Scenic rating: 7

south of South Fork

This is a busy campground adjacent to popular Big Meadows Reservoir, the largest lake in the South Fork area. There is fair fishing for stocked rainbow, brook, and native cutthroat trout, and a paved boat ramp that can accommodate small motor boats. Anglers can also hike seven miles to Archuleta Lake, near the Continental Divide in the Weminuche Wilderness. The alpine lake has medium-sized native trout. There is also a two-mile hiking trail around the lake and a quarter-mile trail to Cascade Falls. ATVs can unload in the campground. Many ATV riders travel from the campground on Forest Route 430 to nearby Shaw Lake.

The campground is in a dense spruce/fir forest that limits views of the scenic valley. Privacy varies widely from site to site. There are three meandering loops on a steep hillside. Sites 1–16 are closest to the lake. Sites 17–43 are more widely spaced. Sites 44–56 are farthest from the lake. The campground stays busy all summer, but more than a quarter of the sites are nonreservable, so it's usually possible to show up on the weekend and find a site.

Campsites, facilities: There are 56 sites for tents and RVs up to 35 feet. Sites 6–8 and the facilities are wheelchair accessible. There are no hookups. Sites 12, 13, 18, 24, 29, 32, and 48 are pull-through. Picnic tables, grills, and fire rings are provided. Vault toilets, drinking water, a boat ramp, fishing pier, and small amphitheater are available. Leashed pets are permitted.

Reservations, fees: Reservations are accepted at 877/444-6777 or www.reserveusa.com. The fee is $14 per night (includes one vehicle). Additional vehicles cost $5 per night. Golden Age and Golden Access Passports are accepted. Cash or check only. Open late May–early September and without services during hunting season.

Directions: From Highway 149 in South Fork, take U.S. Highway 160 south for 11.3 miles. Turn right on Forest Route 410. Stay left at the fork. The campground is in 2.5 miles.

Contact: Rio Grande National Forest, 719/658-2556, www.fs.fed.us/r2/riogrande/.

48 PARK CREEK

Scenic rating: 5

south of South Fork

This campground is a half mile upstream of the confluence of the South Fork of the Rio Grande and Park Creek. Most sites are on the west bank of the South Fork, which offers excellent trout fishing. The campground has cottonwoods, willows, spruce, and fir trees. The river sites are well shaded and large enough to accommodate several tents. The sites are 50–100 feet apart but not well screened from each other. Traffic noise from the busy highway can be annoying.

Campsites, facilities: There are 13 sites for tents and RVs up to 35 feet. There are no hookups. Sites 1, 10, 11, and 13 are pull-through. Picnic tables, grills, and fire rings are provided. Vault toilets and drinking water are available. Leashed pets are permitted.

Reservations, fees: Reservations are not accepted. The fee is $13 per night (includes one vehicle). Additional vehicles cost $5 per night. Golden Age and Golden Access Passports are accepted. Cash or check only. Open late May–early September.

Directions: From Highway 149 in South Fork, take U.S. Highway 160 south for 7.6 miles. The campground is on the left after Park Creek Road.

Contact: Rio Grande National Forest, 719/658-2556, www.fs.fed.us/r2/riogrande/.

49 HIGHWAY SPRINGS

Scenic rating: 6

near South Fork

Except for accessibility, there is little to recommend this stopover campground between South Fork and Pagosa Springs and, in fact, five sites are no longer in use. Unfortunately, these sites have the best views of the South Fork of the Rio Grande valley. The upper loop, sites 1–6, overlook the road and have very little shade. The lower loop, sites 9–11, are away from the road but very close together. They also lack shade. Site 8, located between the two loops, has the best combination of views and privacy. Good fly-fishing is available on the South Fork.

Campsites, facilities: There are 11 sites for tents and RVs up to 35 feet. There are no hookups or pull-throughs. Picnic tables, grills, and fire rings are provided. Vault toilets are available. Leashed pets are permitted.

Reservations, fees: Reservations are not accepted. The fee is $9 per night (includes one vehicle). Additional vehicles cost $5 per night. Golden Age and Golden Access Passports are accepted. Cash or check only. Open Memorial Day–Labor Day.

Directions: From Highway 149 in South Fork, take U.S. Highway 160 south for four miles. The campground is on the left.

Contact: Rio Grande National Forest, 719/658-2556, www.fs.fed.us/r2/riogrande/.

50 UPPER BEAVER CREEK

Scenic rating: 6

south of South Fork

Upper Beaver Creek is a pleasant family destination. Except for playing or fishing in the creek, there is little to do in the campground, but there are several trails a short drive away and good lake fishing and boating on Beaver Creek Reservoir, about two miles upstream. Hikers, bikers, and ATV riders can drive to the Tewksberry and Cross Creek trailheads. Despite the limited activities, this campground fills up frequently with regulars from Texas, Kansas, Missouri, and Colorado, perhaps because all of the sites are next to the creek. Sites 1–6 and 10–13 have good shade. The road is visible from sites 4–9. The best tent sites are 2 and 11–13.

Campsites, facilities: There are six sites for tents and RVs up to 35 feet and seven walk-in tent sites. There are no hookups or pull-throughs. Picnic tables, grills, and fire rings are provided. Vault toilets and drinking water are available.

Reservations, fees: Reservations are not accepted. The fee is $13 per night (includes one vehicle). Additional vehicles cost $5 per night. Golden Age and Golden Access Passports are accepted. Cash or check only. Open late May–early September with services and without services during hunting season.

Directions: From Highway 149 in South Fork, take U.S. Highway 160 south for 1.3 miles. Turn left on Forest Route 360/Beaver Creek Road. The campground is on the right in 3.8 miles.

Contact: Rio Grande National Forest, 719/658-2556, www.fs.fed.us/r2/riogrande/.

51 LOWER BEAVER CREEK

Scenic rating: 6

south of South Fork

This campground is popular with families with young children. Set in the narrow valley of Beaver Creek, the campground is lightly wooded with mature ponderosa pine, spruce, and fir. Interesting boulders dot the landscape as well, and steep, forested hills ring the horizon. Most sites have good shade. Sites 10, 12, 14, 16, and 18 are next to the creek, but the bank is very steep. Sites 13 and 14 are a small group site, and sites 19 and 20 are on a spur very close to the road. Tewksberry Trail begins at the end of Forest Route 355 and offers five miles of moderate climbing to Meadow Pass, between Cattle Mountain and Demijohn Peak. This rarely used trail is open to hikers, bikers, horseback riders, and ATVs. The scenery is best viewed in the fall. Fair trout fishing is available from the campground on Beaver Creek, and lake fishing is available a few miles upstream on Beaver Creek Reservoir.

Campsites, facilities: There are 20 sites for tents and RVs up to 35 feet. There are no hookups. Sites 8, 9, 11, and 16 are pull-through. Picnic tables, grills, and fire rings are provided. Vault toilets and drinking water are available.

Reservations, fees: Reservations are not accepted. The fee is $13 per night (includes one vehicle). Additional vehicles cost $5 per night. Golden Age and Golden Access Passports are accepted. Cash or check only. Open late May–early September and without services during hunting season.

Directions: From Highway 149 in South Fork, take U.S. Highway 160 south for 1.3 miles. Turn left on Forest Route 360/Beaver Creek Road. In three miles, turn right on Forest Route 355. Make an immediate left into the campground.

Contact: Rio Grande National Forest, 719/658-2556, www.fs.fed.us/r2/riogrande/.

52 CROSS CREEK

Scenic rating: 6

south of South Fork

Cross Creek campground is at the south end of Beaver Creek Reservoir, near the inlet and adjacent to the Cross Creek trailhead. The lake contains rainbow, brown, and cutthroat trout as well as kokanee salmon. The boat ramp is suitable for small boats and rafts. Fishing is best in May and June, and ice fishing is excellent in the winter. Cross Creek Trail, open to hikers, bikers, and ATVs, is a moderate four-mile climb to Willow Park, with nice views of Del Norte Peak. This trail is popular with big game hunters in the fall, and the forest routes in this area are groomed for snowmobilers in the winter. The campground is split into two small loops on either side of Cross Creek. Sites 1–3 have views of the reservoir and partial shade. Sites 6–8 are walk-in tent sites in a grassy area with mature spruce and fir. They have limited shade and privacy. Sites 10–12 are best for RVs. This campground sees moderate use throughout the summer. It usually fills up on the weekends.

Campsites, facilities: There are nine sites for tents and RVs up to 30 feet and three walk-in tent sites. There are no hookups or pull-throughs. Picnic tables, grills, and fire rings are provided. Vault toilets, drinking water, and a small boat ramp are available. Open late May–early September and without services during hunting season.

Reservations, fees: Reservations are not accepted. The fee is $13 per night (includes one vehicle). Additional vehicles cost $5 per night. Golden Age and Golden Access Passports are accepted. Cash or check only. Open late May–November 15. There are no services after Labor Day.

Directions: From Highway 149 in South Fork, take U.S. Highway 160 south for 1.3 miles. Turn left on Forest Route 360/Beaver Creek Road. The campground is on the left in 6.2 miles.

Contact: Rio Grande National Forest, 719/658-2556, www.fs.fed.us/r2/riogrande/.

53 MCPHEE RESERVOIR

Scenic rating: 7

west of Dolores

McPhee Reservoir, the second largest lake in Colorado, offers warm- and cold-water fishing. It is stocked with rainbow trout, kokanee salmon, bass, catfish, and pan fish. Shoreline fishing, waterskiing, and canoeing are all popular water sports at McPhee. Fly-fishing and rafting take place on the Dolores River above and below the reservoir. When you're tired of playing in the water, you can explore the numerous cultural and archaeological attractions in the Four Corners region. Mesa Verde National Park, Hovenweep National Monument, Ute Mountain Tribal Park, and the Anasazi Heritage Center are all day trips from McPhee. In the winter, hunters use McPhee as a base camp for hunting elk and deer at higher elevations.

The campground consists of two loops, Pinyon and Juniper, on a hilltop overlooking the lake. Pinyon and juniper trees throughout provide more privacy than shade. It can get quite hot in the summer. The sites on the outside of the loops tend to have more coverage and privacy. The walk-in sites are removed from the main loops and have the best views of the lake. The campground is quiet and attracts families and retirees.

Campsites, facilities: There are 64 campsites for tents and RVs up to 40 feet and 12 walk-in tent sites. There are also three group campsites that can accommodate 25 people. Juniper 21 and Pinyon 10 are wheelchair accessible. Partial and full hookups are available. Picnic tables, grills, and fire rings are provided. In the Pinyon loop, sites 7, 20, and 31 have sun shelters. In the Juniper loop, site 29 has a sun shelter. Restrooms with flush toilets and showers, drinking water, dump stations, laundry facilities, fish-cleaning stations, and boat ramps are available. Leashed pets are permitted.

Reservations, fees: Reservations are accepted for the Pinyon loop at 800/678-2267 and www.reserveamerica.com. Walk-in sites are $10, and all other sites are $12. The group sites are $45 per day. Electric hookups cost $3–4, and full hookups cost $5. Showers cost $2. Golden Age and Golden Access Passports are accepted. Cash or check only. Juniper is open year-round, and Pinyon is open May–October.

Directions: From Dolores, take Highway 184 west for 4.2 miles. Turn right at the McPhee Reservoir sign. Follow the signs 2.1 miles to the campground entrance.

Contact: San Juan National Forest, 970/247-4874, www.fs.fed.us/r2/sanjuan.

54 CORTEZ/MESA VERDE KOA

Scenic rating: 5

in Cortez

This KOA is a popular stopover for travelers in the Four Corners region. From this location, Mesa Verde National Park, Four Corners Monument, and Hovenweep National Monument are easy day trips. The San Juan Skyway is also accessible. McPhee Reservoir, 10 miles to the north, is a fishing and watersports destination, and several outfitters run rafting trips on the Dolores River. Cortez is also the last large town before entering Utah. This campground has excellent views of Sleeping Ute Mountain and the blue ridge of Mesa Verde. Otherwise, it follows the KOA pack-em-in model. It is convenient and comfortable, but not scenic or secluded.

Campsites, facilities: There are 140 sites for tents and RVs up to 80 feet. Full and partial hookups are available. Picnic tables, grills, and fire rings are provided. Tent pads are provided at some sites. Restrooms with flush toilets and showers, vault toilets, drinking water, dump stations, laundry facilities, a store, pool, hot tub, and playground are available. There is also a gift store, horseshoe pits, volleyball and basketball courts, a game room, and wireless Internet. Leashed pets are permitted. Some dog breeds are prohibited.

Reservations, fees: Reservations are accepted at 800/562-3901. The tent fee is $21–31 per night for two people. The RV fee is $29–35 per night (includes two people). Each additional person costs $3 per night. The KOA Valu Kard, Good Sam card, and AAA are accepted. Open April 1–October 15.

Directions: From the intersection of Highway 145 and U.S. Highway 160 in Cortez, take U.S. Highway 160 east for 0.5 mile. At the KOA sign, turn right onto an unmarked gravel road. It ends at the campground.

Contact: Cortez/Mesa Verde KOA, 970/565-9301, www.cortezkoa.com.

55 MOREFIELD

Scenic rating: 4

in Mesa Verde National Park

Mesa Verde National Park contains over 4,000 archaeological sites, including 600 cliff dwellings of the Ancestral Puebloans. Discovered by cowboys in the late 19th century, the cliff dwellings have amazed archaeologists, photographers, and tourists with the story they tell about the lives of these ancient people. If only Morefield were as impressive as the rest of the park. The campground feels like an overblown, abandoned subdivision. The sites are small, cramped, and overgrown, and the facilities are dated. The campground is in a small valley without views, and the surrounding hillsides were ravaged by forest fires. It's a grim place to camp. The best features are the three hiking trails which begin at the campground. The visitors center is 11 miles away, and the nearest accessible ruins are six miles past that.

The campground consists of four large paved loops: Pueblo Road, Hopi Road, Ute Road, and Apache Road. Pueblo Road has tent pads. Ute Road has hookups at some sites. The campsites are 15–30 feet apart. Some of them are well protected by small trees and shrubs; most are not. Campers must drive around for a while to find privacy.

Campsites, facilities: There are 395 sites for tents and RVs up to 40 feet. Full and partial hookups are available. Picnic tables, grills, and fire rings are provided. Restrooms with flush toilets and showers, drinking water, dump stations, a laundry room, store, café, amphitheater, and telephones are available. Leashed pets are permitted in the campground but are not allowed on trails.

Reservations, fees: Reservations are not accepted. The fee is $20 per night for sites without hookups, $25 per night for sites with full hookups. Group camping costs $5 per person. The park entrance fee is $5 per vehicle. Golden Age and Golden Access Passports are accepted. Open year-round.

Directions: From the intersection of Highway 145 and I-190 in Cortez, take U.S. Highway 160 east for nine miles. Exit at Mesa Verde National Park. Turn right off the ramp and stop at the entrance station to purchase a park pass. The campground is four miles past the entrance station.

Contact: Mesa Verde National Park, 970/529-4465, www.visitmesaverde.com.

56 MANCOS STATE PARK

🚶 🚴 🛶 ❄ 🐴 ♿ 🚐 ⛰

Scenic rating: 6

east of Cortez

Mancos State Park has 300 acres of land and a 216-surface-acre reservoir. The park isn't half as spectacular as its surroundings, but it's a great place for children to learn to fish. The reservoir is stocked with rainbow trout, and the dam is often packed with kids casting power bait. Wakeless boating is allowed on the lake. The park also has a five-mile trail system open to hiking and mountain biking, and it is adjacent to San Juan National Forest. Mancos Lake Ranch, located just outside the park, offers one-day and multiday trail rides into the national forest. "Dudes" practice in the park before heading up the mountain. This small park can get very busy on weekends with a largely local crowd. The campground is divided into two loops. The larger loop near the entrance station is situated in a forest of ponderosa pine and Gambel's oak. The sites are large and fairly private. On the far side of the lake, there are nine sites intended for tent camping, but small RVs and pop-ups can also access this area. (Drinking water is not available on this side of the lake.) The tent sites have views of the San Juans to the east, and each site has room for several tents. The campground is open year-round and there is snowshowing around the lake and snowmobiling in the national forest.

Campsites, facilities: There are 30 sites for tents and RVs up to 35 feet and two yurts. Sites 1, 9, 16, 25, and 26 are pull-through, but there are no hookups. Site 24A and the facilities are wheelchair accessible. Picnic tables, fire rings, and grills are provided. Vault toilets, drinking water, dump stations, a boat ramp, horseshoe pits, volleyball court, and group picnic area are available. Leashed pets are permitted.

Reservations, fees: Reservations are accepted (and recommended on weekends) at 800/678-2267 and www.parks.state.co.us. The fee is $12 per night. The yurts sleep six and cost $60 per night. Campers must also purchase a Daily Parks Pass ($5) or an Annual Parks Pass ($55). The Aspen Leaf Annual Pass is accepted. Open year-round.

Directions: From Cortez, take U.S. Highway 160 east to Mancos. Drive north on Highway 184 for 0.3 mile and then turn right on County Road 42. In 4.2 miles, turn left on N Road. The campground is at the end of the road.

Contact: Mancos State Park, 970/882-2213, email: mancos.park@state.co.us.

57 TRANSFER
🚶 🚴 🐎 🚙 ⛺

Scenic rating: 7

north of Mancos

Transfer is a secluded campground on the west slope of the La Plata Mountains. The weddings that take place there several times a summer are a testament to the beauty and tranquility of this campground. It sits in a grove of aspen trees and wildflowers and couldn't be more peaceful, except on Friday mornings when the local dude ranch uses the horse corral. From the campground, backpackers, mountain bikers, horse owners, and ATV riders can explore the La Platas via the West Mancos, Box Canyon, Sharkstooth, Morrison, and Bear Creek Trails, totaling nearly 50 miles of trails. The 40-mile Aspen Loop Trail, specifically designed for ATVs, is also open to bikes and horses. Most of the traffic in Transfer consists of tent and pop-up campers who rarely stay just one night, in part because of the remote location, but also because there's so much to do.

Campsites, facilities: There are 12 sites for tents and RVs up to 35 feet. There are no hookups. Picnic tables, grills, and fire rings are provided. Vault toilets, drinking water, a group picnic area, volleyball court (bring your own net), and horse corral are available. Trash must be packed out. Leashed pets are permitted.

Reservations, fees: This is a first-come, first-served campground. The fee is $10 per night (includes one vehicle). Additional vehicles cost $5 per night. Golden Age and Golden Passport cards are accepted. Cash or check only. Open late May–early September.

Directions: From Cortez, take U.S. Highway 160 east to Mancos. Drive north on Highway 184 for 0.3 mile and then turn right on County Road 42/Forest Route 561. This is a gravel and dirt road and can be rough, but it is passable by a passenger vehicle. In 10 miles, turn right at the Transfer sign. Turn left after the overlook to enter the campground.

Contact: San Juan National Forest, 970/247-4874, www.fs.fed.us/r2/sanjuan/.

58 TARGET TREE
🚶 🚴 🐎 🚙 ⛺

Scenic rating: 6

east of Mancos

This site was formerly a Ute camp. The campground is named for the trees they used for target practice, and it is still possible to find ponderosa pines with scars from arrowheads and rifles. The abandoned Rio Grande Southern Railroad is nearby; hikers and bikers may enjoy exploring the grade. After exhausting those recreation opportunities, most campers will move on. Target Tree is a convenient stopover between Durango and Cortez, but it's not a destination.

Campsites, facilities: There are 25 sites for tents and RVs up to 35 feet. A third of the sites are pull-through. Picnic tables, grills, fire rings, and tent pads are provided. Vault toilets, drinking water, and a group picnic area are available. Leashed pets are permitted.

Reservations, fees: This is a first-come, first-served campground. The fee is $12 per night (includes one vehicle). Additional vehicles cost $6 per night. Golden Age and Golden Access Passports are accepted. Cash or check only. Open May–October.

Directions: From Mancos, take U.S. Highway 160 east for seven miles. Shortly after the La Plata County line, turn left at the Target Tree Recreation Area sign. The campground is in 0.4 mile.

Contact: San Juan National Forest, 970/247-4874, www.fs.fed.us/r2/sanjuan.

59 BAY CITY

Scenic rating: 5

west of Durango

There are three campgrounds in the La Plata Canyon. Snowslide is the most appealing, Kroeger is second, and Bay City is a distant third. This is a primitive campground. Minimal improvement has been done here. The pull-ins are rough, and the campsites are small. It's good for a group, but there's not enough privacy or scenery to make it appealing to individual campers. If you do choose to stay here, there are steep fire roads nearby for exploring, and at the end of County Road 124 the Kennebec trailhead provides access to Indian Ridge and the Colorado Trail. There is fishing on the La Plata.

Campsites, facilities: There are four sites for tents and RVs up to 35 feet. There are no hookups. Grills and fire rings are provided. Leashed pets are permitted.

Reservations, fees: Camping is free, and reservations are not accepted. Open May–October.

Directions: From Durango, take U.S. Highway 160 west for about 12 miles. At the Kennebec Café, turn north on County Road 124 and drive up the La Plata Canyon for five miles to the Bay City sign. The entrance is on the right.

Contact: San Juan National Forest, 970/247-4874, www.fs.fed.us/r2/sanjuan.

60 SNOWSLIDE

Scenic rating: 7

west of Durango

The La Plata Mountains were named by Spaniards for the silver ore they found here. Appropriately, the La Plata canyon has a rich mining history, as evidenced by the historic town of Mayday, which has become a bedroom community of Durango. Enclosed by 12,000-foot peaks, the canyon is narrow and cool. Hikers and mountain bikers can explore several very steep fire roads or drive to the Kennebec trailhead at the end of County Road 124 and take Sharkstooth Trail to Indian Ridge Trail (a part of the Colorado Trail). The views of the Animas valley are spectacular. The campground is the largest and most appealing of three campgrounds on this road. There are two very nice tent-only sites by the river, and most of the sites have good views of the La Plata peaks at the end of the canyon. The avalanche path for which the campground is named is just north of the site. There is fishing on the La Plata.

Campsites, facilities: There are nine sites for tents and RVs up to 35 feet and two tent-only sites. There are roomy pull-ins for RVs but no hookups. Picnic tables, grills, and fire rings are provided. Vault toilets and a group picnic area are available. Leashed pets are permitted.

Reservations, fees: This is a first-come, first-served campground. The fee is $10 per night (includes one vehicle). Additional vehicles cost $5 per night. Golden Age and Golden Access Passports are accepted. Cash only. Open May–October.

Directions: From Durango, take U.S. Highway 160 west for about 12 miles. At the Kennebec Café, turn north on County Road 124 and drive up the La Plata Canyon for 5.6 miles to the Snowslide sign. The campground is on both sides of the road.

Contact: San Juan National Forest, 970/247-4874, www.fs.fed.us/r2/sanjuan.

61 KROEGER

Scenic rating: 6

west of Durango

There are three campgrounds in the La Plata Canyon. They are all fairly secluded. Snowslide is the most appealing, and Kroeger is the next best. It is not quite as roomy or private as Snowslide, and it lacks the excellent views of the La Plata peaks. But if you're looking for a quiet place to pitch the tent or want a base camp for exploring the La Plata peaks, then Kroeger might be perfect for you. (Due to snow and rain, it can stay muddy until July.) There is fishing on the La Plata.

Campsites, facilities: There are 10 sites for tents and RVs up to 35 feet. There are no hookups. Picnic tables, grills, and fire rings are provided. Vault toilets and a group picnic area are available. Leashed pets are permitted.

Reservations, fees: This is a first-come, first-served campground. The fee is $10 per night (includes one vehicle). Additional vehicles cost $5 per night. Golden Age and Golden Access Passports are accepted. Cash only. Open May–October.

Directions: From Durango, take U.S. Highway 160 west for about 12 miles. At the Kennebec Café, turn north on County Road 124 and drive up the La Plata Canyon for six miles to the Kroeger sign.

Contact: San Juan National Forest, 970/247-4874, www.fs.fed.us/r2/sanjuan.

62 JUNCTION CREEK

Scenic rating: 6

near Durango

This campground is hopping all summer long with hikers, bikers, and horseback riders heading out on the Colorado Trail. This 470-mile multiuse trail is the pride and joy of the Colorado trail system. It travels from Durango to Chatfield State Park in the Denver area. The campground is in a pine forest with ample shade and fair privacy. It was renovated in 2005, so the facilities are brand new.

Campsites, facilities: There are 34 sites for tents and RVs up to 50 feet. There are no hookups or pull-throughs. Picnic tables, grills, fire rings, and tent pads are provided. Vault toilets and drinking water are available. The facilities are wheelchair accessible. Leashed pets are permitted.

Reservations, fees: Reservations are not accepted. The fee is $14 per night (includes one vehicle). Additional vehicles cost $7 per night. Golden Age and Golden Access Passports are accepted. Cash or check only. Open May–September.

Directions: From downtown Durango, take I-550 north. Turn left on Junction Creek Road/25th Street/County Road 204. In three miles, stay left at the fork. The campground is on the left in two miles.

Contact: San Juan National Forest, 970/247-4874, www.fs.fed.us/r2/sanjuan.

63 LIGHTNER CREEK

Scenic rating: 4

near Durango

This is a family-run campground/RV park on the banks of Lightner Creek, northwest of Durango. Proximity to the city and its environs is the main attraction here. Durango is the largest city in southwestern Colorado and an outdoor mecca. The five-mile section of the Animas River that runs through town is a Class III white-water destination with a permanent slalom course. From Lightner Creek to Purple Cliffs, the Animas is a Gold Medal trout fishery. The hiking in this area is also spectacular; the southern head of the Colorado Trail begins north of town at Junction Creek. All of these activities are a short drive from the campground.

Campsites, facilities: There are 67 sites with full hookups for RVs up to 35 feet and 33 tent sites, as well as nine cabins. Sites 1–3 and some facilities are wheelchair accessible. Picnic tables, grills, restrooms with flush toilets and showers, drinking water, and dump stations are provided. Laundry facilities, a store, pool, playground, propane gas, group picnic area, game room, pet walk, horseshoe pits, and a basketball court are available. Leashed pets are permitted but cannot be left unattended.

Reservations, fees: Reservations are accepted at 970/247-5406. The tent fee is $23 per night for two people, and the RV fee is $33–36 per night for two people. Additional people cost $4 per night. Open May–September.

Directions: From the intersection of I-550 and U.S. Highway 160 in Durango, take U.S. Highway 160 west for 3.4 miles. Turn right on Dry Creek Road/County Road 207. The campground entrance is on the left in 1.6 miles.

Contact: Lightner Creek Campground, 970/247-5406, www.webcamplightner-creek.com.

64 DURANGO EAST KOA
🏊 🏕 🚵 ♿ 🚐 ⛺

Scenic rating: 5

near Durango

This KOA stands out because its tent sites are more private than at most KOAs. The campground consists of a series of gravel loops in a piñon-sage environment. The setting isn't spectacular, but the proximity to downtown shopping, hiking, and lake and river fishing is hard to beat. In 2005, a dirt bike park was built across the highway.

Campsites, facilities: There are 65 sites with full and partial hookups for RVs of any length. There are also 23 tent sites and 14 cabins. Some facilities are wheelchair accessible. Picnic tables, grills, restrooms with flush toilets and showers, and drinking water are provided. Dump stations, coin laundry, a gift store, pool, playground, propane gas, game room, dog walk, miniature golf, and cable TV are available. Pancake breakfasts and evening movies are offered all summer. Leashed pets are permitted.

Reservations, fees: Reservations are accepted at 800/562-0793. Tent fees are $20–25, and RV fees are $28–38 per night for two people. Additional people cost $4 per night. The KOA Valu Kard is accepted. Open May 1– October 15.

Directions: From the intersection of U.S. Highway 160 and I-550 in Durango, drive east on U.S. Highway 160 for seven miles and turn right at the KOA sign.

Contact: Durango East KOA, 970/247-0783, email: durango.east.koa@compuserve.com.

65 FLORIDA
🏃 🏕 🚐 ⛺

Scenic rating: 6

near Lemon Reservoir

Florida is two miles past the north end of Lemon Reservoir, which makes it a great compromise for families with hikers and anglers. The campground is a small loop in a pine forest alongside the Florida River. Sites 12 and 13 are next to the river. The sites are small, but dense vegetation affords ample privacy. It is quiet and clean but not especially appealing. Two hikes are accessible nearby. The Lost Lake Trail, a half-mile trail to a scenic alpine lake, begins two miles up East Florida Road. The Burnt Timber Trail, which begins at Transfer Park, climbs into the Weminuche Wilderness and connects with Vallecito Creek Trail.

Campsites, facilities: There are 20 sites for tents and RVs up to 35 feet and one group site. There are no hookups, but some sites are pull-through. Picnic tables, grills, fire rings, vault toilets, and drinking water are provided. The group site, available by reservation, can accommodate up to 100 people. Leashed pets are permitted.

Reservations, fees: Reservations are not accepted (except for the group site). The cost is $12 per night (includes two vehicles). Additional vehicles cost $6 per night. The fee for the group site is $40–60. Golden Age and Golden Access Passports are accepted. Cash or check only. Open May–October.

Directions: From Durango, drive east on Florida Road/County Road 240 for 14 miles. At Helen's Store, turn left on County Road 243. In seven miles, turn left at the Florida sign. The campground is in 0.3 mile.

Contact: San Juan National Forest, 970/247-4874, www.fs.fed.us/r2/sanjuan.

66 TRANSFER PARK

Scenic rating: 6

near Lemon Reservoir

Transfer Park is a historic site where miners transferred ores and supplies from wagons to pack mules. The campground has two loops separated by a small meadow. The small sites are fairly close together, but there are so few visitors that it's easy to find a bit of privacy. It's a quiet destination for families and large groups. Fishing and boating are available four miles away on Lemon Reservoir. Hikers and horseback riders can head north on the Burnt Timber Trail into the Weminuche Wilder-

ness. While enjoying this area, be aware of burn hazards from the Missionary Ridge fire of 2002, which burned 70,000 acres. Fire-damaged trees can fall without warning after strong winds or thunderstorms.

Campsites, facilities: There are 25 sites for tents and RVs up to 35 feet. There are no hookups. Picnic tables, grills, fire rings, and vault toilets are provided. Drinking water is available at the Florida campground. Leashed pets are permitted.

Reservations, fees: Reservations are not accepted. The cost is $12 per night (includes two vehicles). Additional vehicles cost $6 per night. Golden Age and Golden Access Passports are accepted. Cash or check only. Open May–October.

Directions: From Durango, drive east on Florida Road/County Road 240 for 14 miles. At Helen's Store, turn left on County Road 243. In seven miles, turn left at the Florida sign on an unmarked road. Bear left through the Florida campground. The road becomes very rough. The campground is in 1.2 miles.

Contact: San Juan National Forest, 970/247-4874, www.fs.fed.us/r2/sanjuan.

67 MILLER CREEK

Scenic rating: 5

on Lemon Reservoir

Located in the Florida River drainage, Lemon Reservoir is much less developed than Vallecito Reservoir to the east. The fishery was decimated by the Missionary Ridge forest fire in 2002, but with the help of the Department of Wildlife, it's recovering. There is good shoreline fishing at the north end of the lake and a concrete boat ramp. The lake is also a great place to learn to roll a kayak. The sites at the campground are close together and offer little privacy.

Campsites, facilities: There are six sites for RVs up to 35 feet and six walk-in tent sites along the shore. There are no hookups. Picnic tables, grills, fire rings, vault toilets, and drinking water are provided. A boat ramp is available. Leashed pets are permitted.

Reservations, fees: Reservations are not accepted. The cost is $12 per night (includes two vehicles). Additional vehicles cost $6 per night. Golden Age and Golden Access Passports are accepted. Cash or check only. Open May–October.

Directions: From Durango, drive east on Florida Road/County Road 240 for 14 miles. At Helen's Store, turn left on County Road 243. The campground is on the left in 3.5 miles.

Contact: San Juan National Forest, 970/247-4874, www.fs.fed.us/r2/sanjuan.

68 VALLECITO

Scenic rating: 7

near Vallecito Reservoir

Many people don't realize this campground exists, and they're missing out. Following the Missionary Ridge forest fire of 2002, Vallecito was closed off and on for several years. It's up and running again, and it makes a great destination for families and backpackers who want a quiet weekend getaway with wilderness access. The Weminuche Wilderness (encompassing nearly 500,000 acres) begins a half mile up the Vallecito Creek Trail. The 15-mile trail climbs 3,840 feet to Rock Lake and offers waterfalls, wildlife viewing, and wildflowers in late summer. It can also be linked with the Pine River Trail to form a 50-mile loop. Anglers can fish for trout on Vallecito Creek or drive to the north end of Vallecito Reservoir about four miles away.

The campground consists of four loops in a mature ponderosa pine forest: Bear, Wapiti, Deer, and Chipmunk. In Bear Loop, the sites are large enough for multiple tents, and sites 1–10 and 12 are next to Vallecito Creek. In

Chipmunk, the sites are closer together, but this smaller loop is much quieter. Wapiti, located next to the trailhead parking, is the least private of all the loops. There were no hookups in 2005, but the Forest Service is considering installing hookups in 2006 or 2007.

Campsites, facilities: There are 79 sites for tents and RVs up to 35 feet. There are no hookups, but many sites are pull-through. Picnic tables, grills, and fire rings are provided. Vault toilets, drinking water, and a group picnic area are available. Leashed pets are permitted.

Reservations, fees: Reservations are not accepted. The cost is $12 per night (includes two vehicles). Additional vehicles cost $6 per night. Golden Age and Golden Access Passports are accepted. Cash or check only. Open mid-May–mid-September.

Directions: From Durango, drive east on U.S. Highway 160 for about 18 miles. Turn north on Vallecito Road/County Road 501. In Columbus, stay right at the fork, continuing on Vallecito Road along the west shore of the reservoir. At 9.7 miles past Columbus, turn left on County Road 500. The campground entrance is in 2.6 miles.

Contact: San Juan National Forest, 970/247-4874, www.fs.fed.us/r2/sanjuan.

69 PINE RIVER

Scenic rating: 7

near Vallecito Reservoir

Like Vallecito campground to the west, Pine River is a gateway to the 487,912-acre Weminuche Wilderness. Backpackers and horseback riders use Pine River Trail to access Weminuche Pass and 10 other trails. It can also be linked with the Vallecito Creek Trail to form a 50-mile loop. Except for the trailhead traffic, this is a very quiet place, and you might not even notice the campground at first. The primitive sites are dispersed on a hillside overlooking a ranching valley with impressive granite cliffs soaring overhead.

Campsites, facilities: There are two sites for RVs up to 20 feet and four walk-in tent sites. There are no hookups. Picnic tables, grills, fire rings, and vault toilets are provided. There is also a parking lot for hikers and horseback riders. Leashed pets are permitted.

Reservations, fees: Reservations are not accepted. The cost is $10 per night (includes two vehicles). Additional vehicles cost $5 per night. Golden Age and Golden Access Passports are accepted. Cash or check only. Open May–September.

Directions: From Durango, drive east on U.S. Highway 160 for about 18 miles. Turn north on Vallecito Road/County Road 501. In Columbus, stay right at the fork, continuing on Vallecito Road. At 4.5 miles past Columbus, turn right on Forest Route 603. At Middle Mountain, turn right on Forest Route 602. In 3.8 miles, the road ends at the campground.

Contact: San Juan National Forest, 970/247-4874, www.fs.fed.us/r2/sanjuan.

70 PINE POINT

Scenic rating: 7

on Vallecito Reservoir

In 2002, the Missionary Ridge forest fire closed all of the five campgrounds on the east side of Vallecito Reservoir. Middle Mountain and Pine Point were reopened in 2005, and Pine Point is the most appealing of the two. It is a small lakeside loop in a mature pine forest with views of the snowy San Juan peaks to the north. Sites 11, 13, 15, 17, and 18 are lakeside. Before the forest fire, record-holding pike and brown trout were caught on the lake, but fish populations were suffocated by organic materials released into the water during and after the fire. Today, the lake is stocked with native trout species. Some anglers fish from the shore, but most fish from boats. There is

a trail to the lake but no place to moor boats. Hiking is available less than a mile south of the campground on the North Canyon Trail, which climbs to the ridgeline and features scenic vistas of the reservoir and San Juans. (This trail may be closed due to fire hazards.) A small store, restaurant, and dump station are available at the 5 Ranches RV Park just north of the campground.

Campsites, facilities: There are 30 sites for tents and RVs up to 35 feet. There are no hookups. Picnic tables, grills, fire rings, drinking water, and vault toilets are provided. Leashed pets are permitted.

Reservations, fees: Reservations are not accepted. The fee is $12–14 per night (includes two vehicles). Additional vehicles cost $6 per night. Golden Age and Golden Access Passports are accepted. Cash or check only. Open May–October.

Directions: From Durango, drive east on U.S. Highway 160 for about 18 miles. Turn north on Vallecito Road/County Road 501. In Columbus, stay right at the fork, continuing on Vallecito Road for 4.5 miles. Turn right on Forest Route 603. The campground is on the left in four miles.

Contact: San Juan National Forest, 970/247-4874, www.fs.fed.us/r2/sanjuan.

71 MIDDLE MOUNTAIN

Scenic rating: 7

on Vallecito Reservoir

Middle Mountain campground is in an aspen and pine forest on the eastern shore of Vallecito Reservoir. Before the Missionary Ridge burn of 2002, record pike and brown trout were caught on the lake, but fish populations were suffocated by organic materials released into the water during and after the fire. Today, the lake is stocked with native trout species. Fishing is possible from the shore, but most prefer fishing from boats. An interesting half-day trip involves following Middle Mountain Road/Forest Route 724 up the Bear Creek drainage to the old mining town of Tuckerville. Additionally, nearby outfitters offer trail-riding excursions. The sites at the campground are large and set about 50 feet apart, but they are not very private. All of the sites have excellent views of the lake and surrounding ridgelines.

Campsites, facilities: There are 24 sites for tents and RVs up to 40 feet. There are no hookups. Picnic tables, grills, fire rings, vault toilets, and drinking water are provided. Leashed pets are permitted.

Reservations, fees: Reservations are not accepted. The cost is $12–14 per night (includes two vehicles). Additional vehicles cost $6 per night. Golden Age and Golden Access Passports are accepted. Cash or check only. Open mid-May–mid-September.

Directions: From Durango, drive east on U.S. Highway 160 for about 18 miles. Turn north on Vallecito Road/County Road 501. In Columbus, stay right at the fork, continuing on Vallecito Road for 4.5 miles. Turn right on Forest Route 603. In five miles (the road goes through 5 Ranches RV Park), turn left on Forest Route 602. The campground is on the left in 0.2 mile.

Contact: San Juan National Forest, 970/247-4874, www.fs.fed.us/r2/sanjuan.

72 LOWER PIEDRA

Scenic rating: 7

between Durango and Pagosa Springs

Lower Piedra is a very pretty primitive campground in a mixed evergreen and deciduous forest on the banks of the sparkling Piedra River. The sites are wooded and widely spaced. Sites 1–7 are next to the river. Sites 7 and 9–11 have the most privacy. Sites 13–15 are set apart from the rest of the campground and perfect for a large group. Located be-

tween Durango and Pagosa Springs, this campground makes a good base camp for exploring the southern San Juans. Kayakers and hikers will enjoy the Piedra River. North of the campground, there is a 19-mile stretch of Class IV–V whitewater early in the boating season. Hikers can check out the river and its interesting geology by setting up a shuttle for Trail 596 (14 miles one-way). From north to south, this is a long but easy hike with access to the Lower Weminuche and Sand Creek Trails.

Campsites, facilities: There are 17 sites for tents and RVs up to 35 feet. There are no hookups. Sites 1–7 are pull-through. Picnic tables, grills, fire rings, and vault toilets are provided. Trash must be packed out. Leashed pets are permitted.

Reservations, fees: Reservations are not accepted. The tent fee is $10 per night, and the RV fee is $12 per night. Additional vehicles cost $5 per night. Cash or check only. Open May–October.

Directions: From Durango, take U.S. Highway 160 east for 37.2 miles. Turn north on Forest Route 621. (If you cross the Piedra River, you've missed it.) In 0.2 mile, turn left and follow the signs to the campground.

Contact: San Juan National Forest, 970/247-4874, www.fs.fed.us/r2/sanjuan.

73 SAN JUAN MOTEL

Scenic rating: 2

in Pagosa Springs

This motel allows tent camping in a grassy area beside the San Juan River and Highway 160. The cottonwoods offer plenty of shade, but forget about privacy. Trucks heading into town provide an early morning wake-up call. The best feature about this campground, and the reason it has campers every night of the summer, is the proximity to the hot springs. You can soak until 1 A.M. and then walk back to your campsite. Kayakers can also use this as a staging ground for boating the East Fork and the San Juan. There's a popular "surf spot" across from the hot springs.

Campsites, facilities: There are about 10 dispersed tent sites. Picnic tables and a portable toilet are provided. Pets are permitted.

Reservations, fees: Reservations are accepted at 800/765-0250. The fee is $15 plus tax per night. Open year-round.

Directions: The campground is on the east side of U.S. Highway 160, one mile north of the hot springs.

Contact: San Juan Motel, 970/264-2262.

74 EAST FORK

🚶 🚴 🏊 ⛵ 🐴 ♿ 🚐 ⛺

Scenic rating: 7

north of Pagosa Springs

East Fork is in a forest of pine, Gambel's oak, spruce, and fir with dense underbrush which provides ample privacy. This is the closest public campground to Pagosa Springs, which is a good reason in itself to stay here. Despite its proximity to town, this campground is usually only half full, so it's easy to find a site that suits you. The Sand Creek and Coal Creek Trails begin two miles up the road. Mountain bikers frequently ride the East Fork Road up to the Silver Falls guard station, a round-trip of 16 miles. The road travels through the dramatic East Fork Canyon and a pristine high mountain valley. Four-wheelers can continue on this route across Elwood Pass and down into Platoro. In the spring and early summer, kayakers boat from the East Fork confluence down to Pagosa Springs. This nine-mile run has Class IV whitewater. Anglers can scramble down to the river for some fishing. The best route is a footpath that begins between sites 14 and 15.

Campsites, facilities: There are 26 sites for tents and RVs up to 35 feet. There are no hookups. Sites 1, 3, 6, 7, 13, 16, 17, 20, and 24–26 are pull-through. Picnic tables, grills, and fire rings are provided. Vault toilets and drinking water are available. The facilities are wheelchair accessible. Leashed pets are permitted.

Reservations, fees: Reservations are not accepted. The tent fee is $10 per night, and the RV fee is $12 per night (includes one vehicle). Additional vehicles cost $5 per night. Golden Age and Golden Access Passports are accepted. Cash or check only. Open late May–early September.

Directions: From U.S. Highway 84 in Pagosa Springs, take U.S. Highway 160 north for 9.6 miles. Turn right on Forest Route 667/East Fork Road. The campground is on the right in 0.7 mile.

Contact: San Juan National Forest, 970/264-2268, www.fs.fed.us/r2/sanjuan.

75 BLANCO RIVER

🏊 🐴 🚐 ⛺

Scenic rating: 7

south of Pagosa Springs

This campground is a small loop beside the Rio Blanco. Most sites are shaded by ponderosa pine, spruce, or cottonwoods, and there is a small meadow in the middle of the loop. There are very few visitors to this campground, so it is a quiet place to stay while exploring the Pagosa Springs area. For an interesting day trip, take Lower Blanco Road west to Trujillo Road to Carracas Road, and then return to Pagosa Springs on Highway 151. This route will take you through an area that seems more like New Mexico than Colorado, past the old settlements of Trujillo and Juanita, the landmark Lone Tree Catholic Church, Navajo State Park, and Chimney Rock Archaeological Area. In 2005, a forest fire burned a large area north of the campground, but the Forest Service used a prescribed burn to stop the fire in Deadman Canyon before it reached the campground.

Campsites, facilities: There are six sites for tents and RVs up to 35 feet. There are no hookups. Picnic tables, grills, and fire rings are provided. Vault toilets and drinking water are available. Leashed pets are permitted.

Reservations, fees: Reservations are not accepted. The tent fee is $10 per night, and the RV fee is $12 per night (includes one vehicle). Additional vehicles cost $5 per night. Golden Age and Golden Access Passports are accepted. Cash or check only. Open late May–early September.

Directions: From U.S. Highway 160 in Pagosa Springs, take U.S. Highway 84 south for 15 miles. Turn left on Forest Route 656. In 2.2 miles, turn left into the picnic ground. The campground is on the far side of the picnic area.

Contact: San Juan National Forest, 970/264-2268, www.fs.fed.us/r2/sanjuan.

76 ARBOLES POINT
🚶 🚴 ♨ 🛶 🎣 ⛵ 🐕 ♿ 🚐 ⛰️

Scenic rating: 6

in Navajo State Park

This primitive campground offers three tent sites in the piñon-sage flats at the north end of the reservoir, and one RV site in the parking area beside the vault toilet. This is a popular destination for sunbathing teenagers and water-sports enthusiasts. There are views of the western shore and the Arboles community. The tent sites are far apart, partly shaded, and very private. For more information on Navajo State Park and activities, see the Rosa listing in this chapter.

Campsites, facilities: There are three walk-in tent sites and one site for a small RV. There are no hookups. Picnic tables, grills, vault toilets, drinking water, and an earthen boat ramp are provided. Restrooms with flush toilets and showers, laundry facilities, and a dump station are available at the Rosa campground. Leashed pets are permitted.

Reservations, fees: Reservations are accepted at 800/678-2267 and www.parks.state.co.us. The fee is $7 per night. A Daily Park Pass ($5) or Annual Parks Pass ($55) is also required. The Aspen Leaf Pass is accepted. Open year-round.

Directions: From Pagosa Springs, take U.S. Highway 160 west for 17 miles. Take Highway 151 south for about 15 miles. Turn left on County Road 500/Carracas Road. In 3.5 miles, turn right at the Arboles Point sign. The campground is in 0.3 mile.

Contact: Navajo State Park, 970/883-2208, www.parks.state.co.us.

77 ROSA
🚶 🚴 ♨ 🛶 🏊 ⛵ 🐕 ♿ 🚐 ⛰️

Scenic rating: 7

in Navajo State Park

BEST (

The 35-mile-long Navajo Reservoir straddles the Colorado–New Mexico border. Three thousand of the 15,000 surface acres are on the Colorado side. This warm-water fishery is also a boating mecca, and everything from houseboats to sailboats plies the waters. Water sports are also very popular. The reservoir is so large that even on holidays it's possible to find a secluded cove for fishing. In shallow waters, there are northern pike, bluegill, catfish, and smallmouth bass. In deeper waters, there are kokanee salmon and lake trout. If you cross the state line, don't forget to follow New Mexico fishing and boating regulations, which are available at the park headquarters and the marina. There are five trails for hiking and biking. Wildlife includes deer, beavers, muskrat, raccoons, fox, and, of course, shorebirds. Bald eagles nest in the park during the winter. Beginning kayakers and rafters can boat Class I–II water on the Piedra and San Juan Rivers.

This full-service loop is very popular with RVers, but tent campers shouldn't overlook the walk-in tent sites. This campground has the best views in the park. Sites 130–147 have lake views. The setting is piñon-juniper and sagebrush. The only shade is provided by the shade shelters.

Campsites, facilities: There are 39 sites for tents and RVs up to 45 feet and eight walk-in tent sites. Sites 103, 105, 108, 121, 128, and 130 and the facilities are wheelchair accessible. There are full hookups, and most sites are pull-through. Picnic tables, grills, fire rings, and tent pads are provided at all sites. Sites 103, 105, 107, 108, 115, 121, 123, 125, 126, 128, 130, 136, 140, and 144 have shade shelters. Restrooms with flush toilets and showers, drinking water, a laundry room, and small amphitheater are available. A boat ramp, store, water sports rentals, and a fish-cleaning station are available at the marina. Leashed pets are permitted.

Reservations, fees: Reservations are accepted at 800/678-2267 and www.parks.state.co.us. The tent fee is $12, and the RV fee is $20. A Daily Park Pass ($5) or Annual Parks Pass ($55) is also required. The Aspen Leaf Pass is accepted. Open year-round.

Directions: From Pagosa Springs, take U.S. Highway 160 west for 17 miles. Take Highway 151 south for 17.8 miles. Turn left on County Road 982. Continue 1.6 miles to the visitors center. Rosa is across from the visitors center.

Contact: Navajo State Park, 970/883-2208, www.parks.state.co.us.

are nice views of the surrounding hills. The setting is piñon-juniper and sagebrush, and the only shade is provided by the sun shelters. For more information on Navajo State Park, see the Rosa listing in this chapter.

Campsites, facilities: There are 40 sites for tents and RVs up to 45 feet. Sites 75, 84, 85, and 88 and the facilities are wheelchair accessible. Electric hookups are available, and many sites are pull-through. Picnic tables, grills, fire rings, and tent pads are provided at all sites. Sites 51, 57, 61, 64, 67, 70, 75, 84, 85, and 88 have sun shelters. Restrooms with flush toilets and showers, drinking water, and a small amphitheater are available. Laundry facilities and a dump station are available at the Rosa campground. A boat ramp, store, water sports rentals, and a fish cleaning station are available at the marina. Leashed pets are permitted.

Reservations, fees: Reservations are accepted at 800/678-2267 and www.parks.state.co.us. The fee is $16 per night. A daily park pass ($5) or Annual Parks Pass ($55) are also required. The Aspen Leaf Pass is accepted. Open year-round.

Directions: From Pagosa Springs, take U.S. Highway 160 west for 17 miles. Take Highway 151 south for 17.8 miles. Turn left on County Road 982. Continue 1.6 miles to the visitors center. Turn right out of the parking lot and stay right at the boat ramp. The campground is on the left in 0.5 mile.

Contact: Navajo State Park, 970/883-2208, www.parks.state.co.us.

78 CARRACAS

🚶 🚴 🏊 🛶 ⛴ 🛥 🐕 ♿ 🚐 ⛰

Scenic rating: 6

in Navajo State Park

This paved loop is popular with both RV and tent campers. Like Rosa, it attracts a boating crowd because of its proximity to the boat ramp. Sites 60–75 are on the lake side. There

79 TIFFANY

🚶 🚴 🏊 🛶 ⛴ 🛥 🐕 ♿ 🚐 ⛰

Scenic rating: 6

in Navajo State Park

Tiffany is the original campground at Navajo State Park, but it's been updated with sun shelters and tent pads and is comfortable for tent and RV campers. Sites 22–26 overlook the lake. Sites 27–32 are next to the cabins. The setting is piñon-juniper and sagebrush, and the only shade is provided by the sun shelters. (For more information on Navajo State Park and activities, see the Rosa listing in this chapter.)

Campsites, facilities: There are 24 sites for tents and RVs up to 45 feet and six walk-in tent sites. There are also three cabins. Sites 13, 21, 31, and 32 and the facilities are wheelchair accessible. There are no hookups, but pull-throughs are available. Picnic tables, grills, fire rings, and tent pads are provided at all sites. Sites 1, 13, 18, 20, 21, and 32 have sun shelters. Restrooms with flush toilets and showers, drinking water, and a small amphitheater are available. Laundry facilities and a dump station are available at the Rosa campground. A boat ramp, store, water-sports rentals, and a fish-cleaning station are available at the marina. Leashed pets are permitted.

Reservations, fees: Reservations are accepted at 800/678-2267 and www.parks.state.co.us. The fee is $12 per night for tents and RVs. Cabins cost $80 per night. A Daily Park Pass ($5) or Annual Parks Pass ($55) is also required. The Aspen Leaf Pass is accepted. Open year-round.

Directions: From Pagosa Springs, take U.S. Highway 160 west for 17 miles. Take Highway 151 south for 17.8 miles. Turn left on County Road 982. Continue 1.6 miles to the visitors center. Turn right out of the parking lot and stay right at the boat ramp. The campground is on the left in 0.7 mile.

Contact: Navajo State Park, 970/883-2208, www.parks.state.co.us.

80 WINDSURF BEACH

Scenic rating: 7

in Navajo State Park

This primitive campground is adjacent to the rocky shoreline of Navajo Reservoir, a 35-mile-long lake that straddles the Colorado–New Mexico border. There's no sandy beach here, but the proximity to the water attracts windsurfers, personal watercraft riders, and kids. The campground has views of the steep slopes at the north end of the reservoir. The habitat is piñon-juniper and sagebrush. (For more information on Navajo State Park and activities, see the Rosa listing in this chapter.)

Campsites, facilities: There are 15 sites for tents and RVs up to 20 feet. There are no hookups. Picnic tables, grills, and vault toilets are provided. Restrooms with flush toilets and showers, laundry facilities, and a dump station are available at the Rosa campground. Leashed pets are permitted.

Reservations, fees: Reservations are accepted at 800/678-2267 and www.parks.state.co.us. The fee is $7 per night. A Daily Park Pass ($5) or Annual Parks Pass ($55) is also required. The Aspen Leaf Pass is accepted. Open year-round.

Directions: From Pagosa Springs, take U.S. Highway 160 west for 17 miles. Take Highway 151 south for 17.8 miles. Turn left on County Road 982. Continue 1.6 miles to the visitors center. Turn left out of the parking lot and continue 0.7 mile. Turn right at the Windsurf Beach sign. The campground is at the end of the road.

Contact: Navajo State Park, 970/883-2208, www.parks.state.co.us.

SAN LUIS VALLEY AND SANGRE DE CRISTOS

© SARAH RYAN

BEST CAMPGROUNDS

The San Luis valley is a truly magical place. With an average rainfall of eight inches, it is Colorado's only true desert. Nevertheless, the valley floor is a patchwork of farms, irrigated by deep artesian wells, and wetland wildlife refuges. This intriguing paradox is enclosed by the Cochetopa Hills and San Juan Mountains to the west and the Sangre de Cristo ("Blood of Christ") Mountains to the east.

The valley has a long history of Spanish culture. Spanish settlers established San Luis, the oldest permanent town in Colorado, in 1851. The majority of towns in the valley share the rich heritage and agricultural economy of San Luis.

The Rio Grande flows from the San Juans south through the valley and into New Mexico. The valley is actually an extension of the Rio Grande Rift valley. When the Sangre de Cristos and Rocky Mountains uplifted about 28 million years ago, the valley remained relatively stable. The real floor is buried under thousands of feet of sediment washed into the valley from the surrounding peaks. At the southern end of the valley, the river forms a deep canyon through soft volcanic rock.

The campgrounds on the east side of the southern San Juans are included in this region because they are only accessible from the San Luis valley. No roads divide the vast expanse of the South San Juan Wilderness, now considered the last possible home for grizzlies in Colorado. There are 180 miles of trails through these dense forests and U-shaped valleys. Many of them are accessible from Conejos River canyon, which has world-class trout fishing and several scenic campgrounds. This is also home to the still-functioning Cumbres and Toltec Scenic Railroad, the highest and longest narrow-gauge steam railroad in the country.

Across the valley, the Great Sand Dunes National Park contains one of the most surprising sights in all of Colorado. At the base of the San-gre de Cristo, a 46,000-acre dune field contains 700-foot sand dunes, including Star Dune, the tallest sand dune in North America. These dunes were formed by strong winds picking up sand from the valley floor and depositing it in a protected area north of Blanca Peak. The dunes are a fascinating ecosystem to explore. The campground in the park is excellent for tents and pop-ups; large RVs will appreciate the modern facilities (and the views) at nearby San Luis Lakes State Park.

The park abuts the Sangre de Cristo Wilderness, a 70-mile-long area that protects the high peaks and steep valleys of this precipitous range. The peaks soar 7,000 feet above the San Luis and Wet Mountain valleys, but the range is only six-eight miles wide. Hiking is excellent but extremely challenging. Climbing is technical and dangerous. Mountain biking is mostly limited to the Rainbow Trail, a 100-mile multiuse trail along the eastern border of the wilderness.

The Wet Mountains lie to the east of the Sangre de Cristos. Part of the San Isabel National Forest, this range is a weekend destination for residents of the Front Range. The Lake Isabel Recreation Area is the most popular area for families and campers.

The Sangre de Cristos extend south into New Mexico. The mountains south of La Veta Pass are locally called the Culebras. The most interest-ing feature is the Spanish Peaks on the east side. The Utes called these massive volcanic peaks *wahatoya,* or "Breasts of the World." They are also protected by a wilderness designation, but there are only a few miles of trails around these peaks. The nearby campgrounds are nice destinations for fishing and trail riding. East of the mountains, Trinidad State Park and the historic town of Trinidad are the last stop before New Mexico.

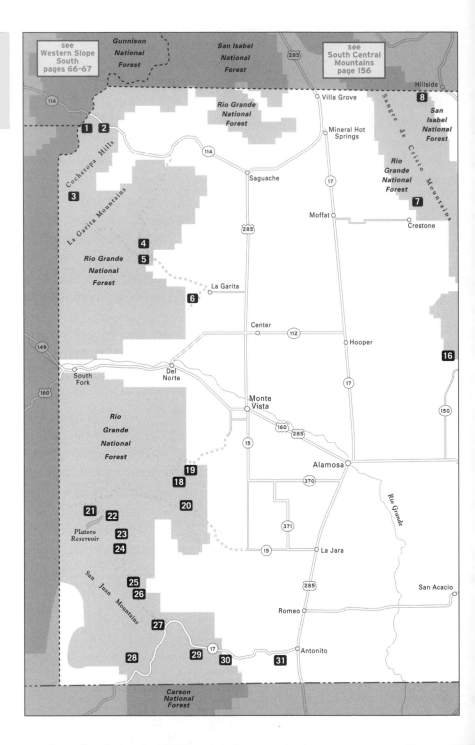

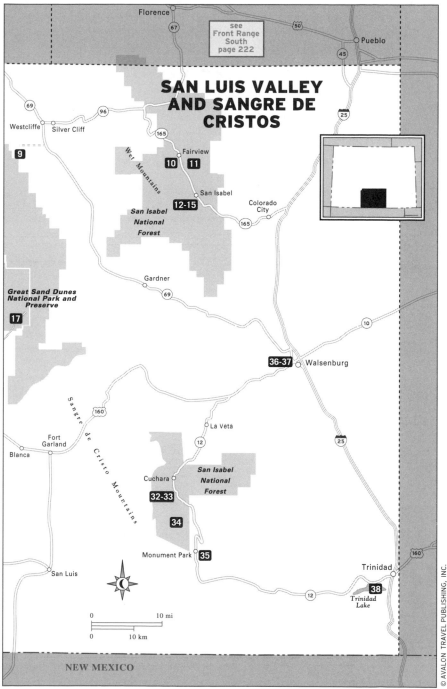

SAN LUIS VALLEY AND SANGRE DE CRISTOS

Florence

see Front Range South page 222

Pueblo

Westcliffe
Silver Cliff

9

Wet Mountains

Fairview

10 **11**

San Isabel

12-15

Colorado City

San Isabel National Forest

Gardner

Great Sand Dunes National Park and Preserve

17

Sangre de Cristo Mountains

Walsenburg

36-37

La Veta

Fort Garland

Blanca

Cuchara

San Isabel National Forest

32-33

34

Monument Park **35**

San Luis

Trinidad

38

Trinidad Lake

0   10 mi

0   10 km

NEW MEXICO

© AVALON TRAVEL PUBLISHING, INC.

1 LUDERS CREEK
🚲 🏕 ♿ 🚐 ⛰

Scenic rating: 8

west of Saguache

Luders Creek campground is a rare find. Surrounded by the rolling hills and diverse forests of the Cochetopa Hills, the campground is sublimely scenic, small, and remote. The campground is in a wide park banded with aspen and tall pines. Sites 3–6 are next to the meadow and have good views of the layered hills, an especially scenic sight at sunset. Just a mile to the west, mountain bikers and ATV riders can cross the Continental Divide and hop on the Colorado Trail. This is perhaps the least-used portion of the trail because it lacks the altitude and views of many other segments, but the mountain biking in this area is excellent. Forest routes make several loops possible around Archuleta Creek and Luders Creek. A good topo map is a must-have on these roads.

Campsites, facilities: There are six sites for tents and RVs up to 25 feet. There are no hookups. Sites 2, 4, and 6 are pull-through. Picnic tables, grills, and fire rings are provided. Wheelchair-accessible vault toilets are available. Leashed pets are permitted.

Reservations, fees: Reservations are not accepted. The fee is $5 per night. Golden Age and Golden Access Passports are accepted. Cash or check only. Open May–November.

Directions: From Saguache, take Highway 114 west for 21.4 miles. Turn left on County Road NN14. The campground is on the right in 8.7 miles.

Contact: Rio Grande National Forest, 719/655-2547, www.fs.fed.us/r2/riogrande/.

2 BUFFALO PASS
🏕 ♿ 🚐 ⛰

Scenic rating: 7

west of Saguache

The Cochetopa Hills are a rolling landscape of diverse forests and meadows between the Elk and Sawatch ranges to the north and the San Juans to the south. The Continental Divide winds through this area, but the landscape rarely rises above the timberline. Stunning panoramas are visible from Long Branch Baldy (11,974 feet) and Middle Baldy (11,685 feet)—but these peaks are in the heart of an 80,000-acre roadless area and are only accessible via a long hike on the Continental Divide/Colorado Trail.

The Buffalo Pass campground is typical of the Cochetopa Hills landscape: towering ponderosa pines intermingled with quaking aspen and arid sagebrush meadows. The sites are about 100 feet apart and have partial shade. Sites 3, 17–19, and 23 have the best views of the surrounding hills, which are scenically silhouetted at sunrise and sunset. The campground is almost empty midweek but can get quite busy on weekends with a local crowd. The area's network of 4WD roads attracts ATV riders and mountain bikers. The Colorado Trail is open to hikers, bikers, and four-wheelers. The trail is accessible about four miles west on Highway 114.

Campsites, facilities: There are 23 sites for tents and RVs up to 30 feet. There are no hookups. Sites 1 and 24 are pull-through. Picnic tables, grills, and fire rings are provided. Wheelchair-accessible vault toilets are available. Leashed pets are permitted.

Reservations, fees: Reservations are not accepted. The fee is $5 per night. Golden Age and Golden Access Passports are accepted. Cash or check only. Open May–November.

Directions: From Saguache, take Highway 114 west for 26 miles. The campground entrance is on the left.

Contact: Rio Grande National Forest, 719/655-2547, www.fs.fed.us/r2/riogrande/.

🟦 STONE CELLAR
🚴 🏠 🚐 ⛺

Scenic rating: 7

west of Saguache

Stone Cellar is in Saguache Park between the Cochetopa Hills to the north and the La Garita Mountains to the south. The gentle terrain of this area is home to thriving herds of elk, deer, and bighorn sheep. Expect abundant wildlife and very few people in this remote campground. The La Garita Wilderness lies to the south of the campground and offers long backpacking loops through alpine terrain, as well as several virgin spruce-fir forests and the Wheeler Geologic Area, a unique natural formation where wind and rain have carved volcanic tuff into pinnacles and spires. Hikers will have to drive several miles south to the Halfmoon Creek and South Fork Saguache trailheads. Mountain bikers and ATV owners can explore a network of Jeep trails from the campground. A good topo map is a necessity in this remote backcountry.

Stone Cellar is beautiful and isolated. It sits in a meadow with scattered aspen and pine, and a small creek runs through the campground. There are few visitors to this location, which attracts mainly ATV owners and horseback riders.

Campsites, facilities: There are five sites for tents and RVs up to 25 feet. There are no hookups. Picnic tables, grills, and fire rings are provided. Vault toilets and drinking water are available. Trash must be packed out. Leashed pets are permitted.

Reservations, fees: Reservations are not accepted. The fee is $7 per night. Golden Age and Golden Access Passports are accepted. Cash or check only. Open May–November.

Directions: From Saguache, take Highway 114 west for 21.4 miles. Go west on County Road NN14/Forest Route 750 for 18.7 miles and then south for 16.4 miles to the campground.

Contact: Rio Grande National Forest, 719/655-2547, www.fs.fed.us/r2/riogrande/.

🟦 STORM KING
🏠 🚐 ⛺

Scenic rating: 6

west of La Garita

Storm King is a weekend destination for local ATV owners. A network of mining and logging trails crisscrosses the eastern flank of the La Garita Mountains and connects the area to the rolling Cochetopa Hills to the north. The campground is a little run-down, but the quaking aspen and tall pines provide plenty of shade. The sites are just 25 feet apart, so privacy is poor on a busy weekend, but midweek the campground is often deserted. The neighboring stream is not fishable.

Campsites, facilities: There are 11 sites for tents and RVs up to 25 feet. There are no hookups. Picnic tables, grills, and fire rings are provided. Vault toilets and drinking water are available. Trash must be packed out. Leashed pets are permitted.

Reservations, fees: Reservations are not accepted. The fee is $7 per night. Golden Age and Golden Access Passports are accepted. Cash or check only. Open May–November.

Directions: From La Garita, take County Road G west about one mile and turn right on County Road 41-G/Carnero Creek Road and continue 14.5 miles to the campground.

Contact: Rio Grande National Forest, 719/655-2547, www.fs.fed.us/r2/riogrande/.

🟦 POSO
🏊 🏠 ♿ 🚐 ⛺

Scenic rating: 6

west of La Garita

Poso is in a narrow canyon on the South Fork of Carnero Creek. The fishing on the creek and in the beaver ponds is fair but challenging. Poso is in better shape than nearby Storm King, and it's popular with local church and scout groups. The sites are shaded by pine and a few aspen and are spaced from 30–60 feet apart. Located on the eastern flank of the La Garita Mountains, there are abundant elk in the area, as well as some moose and bear. Consequently, the campground is very popular with hunters in the fall and winter. There are numerous Jeep trails in the area, but no hiking trails within walking distance.

Campsites, facilities: There are eight sites for tents and RVs up to 25 feet. There are no hookups. Picnic tables, grills, and fire rings are provided. Wheelchair-accessible vault toilets and a group picnic area are available. Leashed pets are permitted.

Reservations, fees: Reservations are not accepted. The fee is $5 per night. Golden Age and Golden Access Passports are accepted. Cash or check only. Open May–November.

Directions: From La Garita, take County Road G west about one mile and turn right on County Road 41-G. In 10 miles, turn left on Forest Route 675. The campground is on the left in 1.5 miles.

Contact: Rio Grande National Forest, 719/655-2547, www.fs.fed.us/r2/riogrande/.

6 PENITENTE CANYON
🏃 🚴 🐴 ♿ 🚐 ⛺

Scenic rating: 8

west of La Garita

Penitente Canyon is a nationally renowned destination for sport climbers. The eerie landscape of rhyolite canyons and rock gardens offers mountain biking, hiking, and challenging rock climbing (but watch out for rattlesnakes!). The south-facing walls are climbable year-round. The canyon's proximity to tiny La Garita is also an attractive feature. This historic Hispanic town has a chapel on the National Register of Historic Places and a cooperative art gallery. There is a gas station but no grocery store, so campers should stock up in Del Norte or Center.

The campground is very busy—and hot—

in the summer. The best time to visit is in the fall. Piñon and juniper provide limited shade. There are group sites and several walk-in sites. Watch for petroglyphs and traces of the Old Spanish Trail in the canyons.

Campsites, facilities: There are five drive-in sites for tents and RVs up to 25 feet, 18 walk-in sites, and two group sites. There are no hookups. Picnic tables, grills, and fire rings are provided. Vault toilets and drinking water are available. The facilities are wheelchair accessible. Leashed pets are permitted.

Reservations, fees: Reservations are not accepted. The fee is $5 per night for a single site (two-tent limit) and $15 per night for a group site (five-tent limit). Golden Age and Golden Access Passports are accepted. Cash or check only. Open April–November, but drinking water is only available May–October.

Directions: From La Garita, take County Road G west to County Road 38. Veer left on County Road 38. The main road turns south in one mile. Stay right and take the middle of three dirt roads. Follow the signs to the campground.

Contact: Bureau of Land Management, 719/655-2547, www.blm.gov.

7 NORTH CRESTONE
🏃 🛶 🎿 🐴 ♿ 🚐 ⛺

Scenic rating: 9

north of Crestone

BEST (

North Crestone is a one-of-a-kind camping experience. The campground is on the western flank of the Sangre de Cristo range, in the northern San Luis valley, at the base of Venable Peak, just north of the hamlet of Crestone. Founded as a mining town in 1880, Crestone has undergone a unique transformation. Nicknamed the "Shambala of the Rockies," Crestone is considered a spiritual center and is home to a wide variety of religious and spiritual institutions. South of town, the 200,000-acre Baca Grande subdivision is a complex of shrines, ashrams, churches, monasteries, retreats, and homes. You can get a chakra massage, a tarot-card reading, or a spiritual awakening in these foothills, or you can stick to the campground and the challenging trails of the Sangre de Cristo Wilderness. These peaks—part of the only fault-block range in Colorado—tower 7,000 feet above the valley floor. The contrasts are amazing. The valley is an arid agricultural landscape, while the foothills are covered in piñon-juniper woodlands that rapidly become pine, aspen, and spruce-fir forests laced with steep creeks and cascades. Glacial cirques with alpine lakes are at the top of most creeks, offering good backcountry fishing. The fourteeners south of the campground—especially Crestone Needle and Crestone Peak—should only be attempted by experienced mountaineers. However, hikers and anglers with strong lungs will enjoy the challenging hike up North Crestone Creek, which can be connected with trails down Cotton Creek and Rito Alto Creek. Afterwards, take a dip in the Valley View Hot Springs about a half-hour drive to the north.

The campground has a wild reputation. It attracts climbers, anglers, and hikers, as well as its fair share of hippies, yogis, and nudists. A modern-day hermit lives in a cave on adjacent private property and sometimes visits the campground, which is packed on summer weekends—especially during the annual music festival—so arrive early in the week to grab a shady, creekside site.

Campsites, facilities: There are 13 sites for tents and RVs up to 25 feet. There are no hookups. Picnic tables, grills, and fire rings are provided. Wheelchair-accessible vault toilets and drinking water are available. Leashed pets are permitted.

Reservations, fees: Reservations are not accepted. The fee is $9 per night. Golden Age and Golden Access Passports are accepted. Cash or check only. Open May–November.

Directions: From Crestone, take Forest Route 950 north for 1.2 miles to the campground.

Contact: Rio Grande National Forest, 719/655-2547, www.fs.fed.us/r2/riogrande/.

8 LAKE CREEK

Scenic rating: 7

north of Westcliffe

Lake Creek is in the foothills of the Sangre de Cristo range, at the north end of the grasslands of the Wet Mountain valley. This gorgeous area is not as well known as Colorado's central mountains, but it is popular with southern Colorado residents as well as tourists from Texas and Oklahoma. This campground is just a spur in a dense thicket of Gambel's oak and aspen. The majority of sites are well screened and very private, but there are no views from these sites. The campground is best for tents and small RVs. Hikers and bikers can explore the Rainbow Trail, a 100-mile route through the Sangre de Cristo foothills from Music Pass to Salida. This trail skirts the wilderness boundary. Hikers and climbers who want to explore the wilderness are better off staying at Alvarado campground.

Campsites, facilities: There are 12 sites for tents and RVs up to 29 feet. Site 1 is pull-through. Picnic tables, grills, and fire rings are provided. Vault toilets and drinking water are available. The facilities are wheelchair accessible. Leashed pets are permitted.

Reservations, fees: Reservations are not accepted. The fee is $11 per night (includes two cars and 10 people). Additional vehicles cost $5 per night. Golden Age and Golden Access Passports are accepted. Open late May–early September.

Directions: From Westcliffe, take Highway 69 north for 12.7 miles. Turn left on County Road 198. The campground is on the right in 2.9 miles.

Contact: San Isabel National Forest, 719/269-8500, www.fs.fed.us/r2/psicc/.

9 ALVARADO

🏃 🚵 🐕 ♿ 🚐 ⛺

Scenic rating: 7

north of Westcliffe

Alvarado is located where the Sangre de Cristo range meets the Wet Mountain valley, a 35-mile-wide grassland with a ranching history. The campground is a short drive from the twin towns of Westcliffe and Silver Cliff, and it sits just outside the Sangre de Cristo Wilderness, so this campground can be very popular in the summer. It consists of several loops and spurs in a dense spruce-fir forest with scattered aspen groves. Sites 1–4, 15–17, 26, and 27 are in the aspens. Sites 1–3 are horse sites on a small spur with access to Venable Trail. Sites 28–47 are on a long spur at the back of the campground and have the most privacy. The sites are 20–50 feet apart and shaded.

Venable is one of the best-known trails in the wilderness. Open to hikers and riders, the trail can be turned into a 16-mile loop with Comanche Trail. Mountain bikers and ATVers frequent the Rainbow Trail, a 100-mile route through the Sangre de Cristo foothills from Music Pass to Salida.

Campsites, facilities: There are 47 sites for tents and RVs up to 35 feet and three horse sites. There are no hookups. Site 41 is pull-through. Picnic tables, grills, and fire rings are provided. Vault toilets and drinking water are available. The facilities are wheelchair accessible. Leashed pets are permitted.

Reservations, fees: Reservations are accepted at 877/444-6777 and www.reserveusa.com. The fee is $12 per night (includes two cars and 10 people) or $15 for a horse site. Additional vehicles cost $5 per night. Golden Age and Golden Access Passports are accepted. Cash or check only. Open late May–early September.

Directions: From Westcliffe, take Highway 69 south for 3.4 miles. Turn right on Schoolfield Road/County Road 140. In 4.6 miles, turn left on County Road 141. The campground is in two miles.

Contact: San Isabel National Forest, 719/269-8500, www.fs.fed.us/r2/psicc/.

10 OPHIR CREEK

🏕 ♿ 🚐 ⛺

Scenic rating: 7

west of Colorado City

Ophir Creek is a remote campground in the Wet Mountains, a narrow range to the east of the Sangre de Cristos. These mountains receive abundant rainfall, and the forests are lush and diverse. This campground has two loops. The lower loop is creekside, and sites 1–6 are in a meadow. Sites 14–16 are walk-ins accessible via a footbridge. The upper loop (sites 23–31) is all walk-in sites. There are no hiking or biking trailheads at the campground, so many of the campers bring ATVs and explore the forest routes that connect this campground with the Lake San Isabel area.

Campsites, facilities: There are 31 sites for tents and RVs up to 40 feet. Sites 8, 9, 14–16, and 20–31 are walk-ins. Picnic tables, grills, and fire rings are provided. Vault toilets and drinking water are available. The facilities are wheelchair accessible. Leashed pets are permitted.

Reservations, fees: Reservations are not accepted. The fee is $12 per night (includes two cars and 10 people). Additional vehicles cost $5 per night. Golden Age and Golden Access Passports are accepted. Open late May–early September.

Directions: From Colorado City, take Highway 165 west for 25.2 miles. Turn left on Forest Route 360 and then left in front of the fire station. The campground is in 0.3 mile.

Contact: San Isabel National Forest, 719/269-8500, www.fs.fed.us/r2/psicc/.

⓫ DAVENPORT

Scenic rating: 6

west of Colorado City

Davenport is a small, isolated campground in the Wet Mountains, a long narrow range east of the Sangre de Cristos. The campground is in a meadow surrounded by spruce and aspen, and the campsites line Davenport Creek. Hikers and bikers will be very happy here. There are several easy to moderate multiuse trails in the area. Squirrel Creek Trail begins at the campground and connects with the Dome Rock, Middle Creek, and Second Mace Trails and Pueblo Mountain Park. Sites 1–8 are walk-ins that are accessible via a footbridge. Site 9 is a double. The campground receives heavy use on weekends, but it's virtually deserted on weekdays.

Campsites, facilities: There are 12 sites for tents and RVs up to 25 feet. Picnic tables, grills, and fire rings are provided. Vault toilets are available. Leashed pets are permitted.

Reservations, fees: Reservations are not accepted. The fee is $11 per night (includes two cars and 10 people). Additional vehicles cost $5 per night. Golden Age and Golden Access Passports are accepted. Open late May–early September.

Directions: From Colorado City, take Highway 165 west for 23.9 miles. Turn right on Forest Route 382 and continue 1.3 miles to the campground.

Contact: San Isabel National Forest, 719/269-8500, www.fs.fed.us/r2/psicc/.

⓬ LA VISTA

Scenic rating: 7

west of Colorado City

Lake San Isabel is a 37-acre reservoir on the eastern side of the Wet Mountains. The lake is stocked, and the shoreline is easily accessible with open areas that are perfect for kids learning to fish. Hiking and mountain biking are available on the Cisneros and Charles Trails and on a footpath around the lake. Because of its mountain setting and accessibility, the lake is a very popular weekend destination for families from Pueblo to Trinidad. Reservations are highly recommended in the summer, especially at La Vista, the most modern and scenic campground at the lake.

La Vista has two loops on a promontory overlooking the lake. The lower loop (sites 1–16) is mostly wooded with pine and aspen. Sites 1–10 are attractive walk-in tent sites with good privacy. RV sites 11–16 are very close together. The upper loop (sites 17–29) has mainly RV camping. It has nice views of the surrounding ridgelines.

Campsites, facilities: There are 19 sites for tents and RVs up to 50 feet and 10 sites for tents only. Sites 11–29 have electric hookups. Site 15 is pull-through. Picnic tables, grills, fire rings, and tent pads are provided. Vault toilets and drinking water are available. Leashed pets are permitted.

Reservations, fees: Reservations are accepted at 877/444-6777 and www.reserveusa.com. The fee is $13–18 per night (includes two cars and 10 people). Additional vehicles cost $5 per night. A daily recreation area pass is also required ($5 per vehicle). Golden Age and Golden Access Passports are accepted. Cash or check only. Open mid-April–mid-October.

Directions: From Colorado City, take Highway 165 west for 18 miles. Turn left at the Lake Isabel Recreation Area. The campground is on the right in 0.9 mile.

Contact: San Isabel National Forest, 719/269-8500, www.fs.fed.us/r2/psicc/.

⓭ ST. CHARLES

Scenic rating: 7

west of Colorado City

St. Charles is a small loop on the banks of

St. Charles Creek. The forest is especially lush and dense at this campground. Anglers can hike to Lake San Isabel, a 37-acre stocked reservoir, or try fishing on the creek. The campground is very close to the Cisneros trailhead, a 9.5-mile trail open to hiking, biking, and riding. This trail connects with the St. Charles Trail, a 9.5-mile route that passes by St. Charles Peak. The campground has good privacy and shade. Sites 1–10 are creekside. The best sites for privacy are 2–5 and 11. This area is very popular with Front Range residents, so reservations are highly recommended on weekends.

Campsites, facilities: There are 15 sites for RVs up to 35 feet. Sites 6, 10, and 15 are pull-through. There are no hookups. Picnic tables, grills, and fire rings are provided. Sites 4, 5, 13, and 15 have tent pads. Vault toilets and drinking water are available. Leashed pets are permitted.

Reservations, fees: Reservations are accepted at 877/444-6777 and www.reserveusa.com. The fee is $13 per night (includes two cars and 10 people). Additional vehicles cost $5 per night. A daily recreation area pass is also required ($5 per vehicle). Golden Age and Golden Access Passports are accepted. Cash or check only. Open late May–early September.

Directions: From Colorado City, take Highway 165 west for 18 miles. Turn left at the Lake Isabel Recreation Area. In 0.8 mile, turn left at the campground sign. The campground is on the right in 0.2 mile.

Contact: San Isabel National Forest, 719/269-8500, www.fs.fed.us/r2/psicc/.

14 PONDEROSA AND SPRUCE GROUP

Scenic rating: 7

west of Colorado City

These group campsites offer dispersed tent camping in a spruce, fir, and aspen forest beside St. Charles Creek. The sites are extremely popular with church and scout groups as well as family reunions and company events. The campground is a short walk from Lake San Isabel, a 35-acre stocked reservoir with an easily accessible shoreline. The campground is also very close to the Cisneros trailhead, a 9.5-mile trail that connects with the St. Charles Trail. Both trails are open to hiking, biking, and riding. Spruce has a wheelchair-accessible picnic pavilion.

Campsites, facilities: These group sites have tent camping for up to 60 people. Small RVs can park in the lot. Picnic tables, grills, and fire rings are provided. Vault toilets and drinking water are available. Leashed pets are permitted.

Reservations, fees: Reservations are required and accepted at 877/444-6777 and www.reserveusa.com. The fee is $75 per night (includes 60 people). A daily recreation area pass is also required ($5 per car and $15 per van or bus). Open late May–early September.

Directions: From Colorado City, take Highway 165 west for 18 miles. Turn left at the Lake Isabel Recreation Area. In 0.8 mile, turn left at the campground sign. The group sites are on the left in 0.5 mile.

Contact: San Isabel National Forest, 719/269-8500, www.fs.fed.us/r2/psicc/.

15 SOUTHSIDE

Scenic rating: 4

west of Colorado City

Southside is the last resort campground at Lake San Isabel. Nevertheless, it's frequently full on summer weekends with campers who forgot to make a reservation. The campground is essentially a small parking lot with islands that separate the RV pull-ins. Campers can pitch a tent on the islands at sites 1, 7, and 8, but it's not recommended for tent camping. The campground is surrounded by a dense spruce-fir forest, and there are no views of the pretty lake that's a short walk away. The 35-acre reservoir is stocked, and a footpath around the shore makes it very accessible. Hand-powered boats are allowed on the lake as well. Hiking and biking are available on the Cisneros Trail, a 9.5-mile trail through the Wet Mountains.

Campsites, facilities: There are eight sites for RVs up to 30 feet. All sites are pull-through. There are no hookups. Picnic tables, grills, and fire rings are provided. Vault toilets are available. Leashed pets are permitted.

Reservations, fees: Reservations are accepted at 877/444-6777 and www.reserveusa.com. The fee is $12 per night (includes two cars and 10 people). Additional vehicles cost $5 per night. A daily recreation area pass is also required ($5 per vehicle). Golden Age and Golden Access Passports are accepted. Cash or check only. Open mid-April–mid-October.

Directions: From Colorado City, take Highway 165 west for 18 miles. Turn left at the Lake Isabel Recreation Area. The campground is on the left in 0.3 mile.

Contact: San Isabel National Forest, 719/269-8500, www.fs.fed.us/r2/psicc/.

16 MOSCA

Scenic rating: 8

in San Luis Lakes State Park

San Luis Lakes State Park is usually overlooked by visitors to the San Luis valley, but with spectacular views and excellent facilities, it's the best destination in the valley if you plan on staying more than a week. There are three loops in a high desert setting with views of Blanca Peak and the Great Sand Dunes National Park. Shade is nonexistent, and privacy is poor when the park is busy, but otherwise it's a great base camp for exploring this unique landscape. The San Luis valley was first settled by Spanish farmers

in the 1800s, and it remains an agricultural landscape surrounded by the dramatic peaks of the Sangre de Cristo range to the east and the southern San Juans to the south. Hikers and climbers face endless challenges in the Sangre de Cristo Wilderness, and anglers who enjoy backcountry fishing will find numerous alpine lakes at the heads of the steep valleys. More sedentary campers can visit the national park, the nearby gator farm, and the alien viewing platform in Hooper, or just sit and watch the storm clouds build.

The park has two lakes and a wetlands area that are important for migrating birds. Water levels fluctuate dramatically, so boaters and anglers should call ahead to make sure the boat ramp is open. The four-mile hiking/biking trail is often closed to protect nesting waterfowl. It usually opens after July 4th. Loop A is very popular with RVers, and Loop C is the best loop for tent campers because it's separated from the other loops and has great views. In Loop A, the best tent sites are 10, 11, and 15–17. In Loop B, the best tent sites are 25, 27, 30, 33, and 37–39. In Loop C, the best tent sites are 41, 42, 44, and 47–51.

Campsites, facilities: There are 51 sites for tents and RVs up to 45 feet. All sites have electric hookups. Sites 1–7, 11–15, 18–40, 42–47, and 51 are pull-through. Picnic tables, grills, fire rings, and shade shelters are provided. Sites 10, 15, 16, 34, and 41 have tent pads. Restrooms with flush toilets and showers, vault toilets, drinking water, laundry facilities, dump stations, a boat ramp, and basketball court are available. Leashed pets are permitted.

Reservations, fees: Reservations are accepted at 800/678-2267 and www.parks.state.co.us. The fee is $16 per night. A Daily Park Pass ($3 per vehicle) is also required. The Aspen Leaf Pass is accepted. Cash or check only. Open mid-May–mid-September.

Directions: From Alamosa, take Highway 17 north. About one mile past Mosca, turn east on 6N Lane. In 7.7 miles, turn left into the state park. The campground is on the left, 0.8 mile after the entrance station.

Contact: San Luis Lakes State Park, 719/378-2020, www.parks.state.co.us.

17 PINYON FLATS

Scenic rating: 9

in Great Sand Dunes National Park

BEST (

Formerly a national monument, the Sand Dunes became a national park in 2004, extending protection to the watersheds and mountains that are an integral part of this unique ecosystem. The park includes a 30-square-mile dune field surrounded by grasslands and wetlands and bordered on the east by the high peaks of the Sangre de Cristo—the only fault-block range in Colorado—where the life zones range from montane forest to alpine tundra. The park is a unique experience for hikers, four-wheelers, and birders and naturalists. Most visitors spend a day exploring the dune field and trying to reach Star Dune, the tallest sand dune in North America. Visitors with 4WD shouldn't miss the Medano Pass Road, a very rough 22-mile road that connects the sand dunes with the Wet Mountain valley. Hardened backpackers can take the Sand Ramp Trail to the Sand Creek Trail to several alpine lakes. Winter visitors might find enough snow for cross-country skiing, but they should call ahead. The park also offers excellent campfire programs for all ages.

The main campground has two loops in a piñon-juniper woodland with sites that are 25–50 feet apart. The piñon-juniper provides some privacy, but the sites are small, and most can only accommodate one tent. Loop 1 (sites 1–44) is closer to the dunes and has tent pads. Loop 2 (sites 45–88) overlooks the lower loop and the dunes. Sites 20, 41, 63, 66, and 72 have amazing views. The group loop has three sites with dispersed tent camping. Sites B and C have better views. Groups should bring a large tent to provide shade in the picnic area.

Campsites, facilities: There are 88 sites for tents and RVs up to 25 feet and three group sites. Sites 10, 61A, and 63 and the facilities are wheelchair accessible, and dune-accessible wheelchairs are available at the visitors center. Picnic tables, grills, fire rings, tent pads, and food lockers are provided. Flush toilets, drinking water, dump stations, an amphitheater, pay phones, and interpretive programs are available. Leashed pets are permitted.

Reservations, fees: Reservations are not accepted for the single sites. Reservations are required for the group sites and are accepted at 719/378-6399. The fee is $12 per night for single sites (includes six people). The group sites cost $3 per person per night. Golden Age and Golden Access Passports are accepted. Cash or check only. Loop 1 is open year-round. The rest of the campground is open from late spring to early fall.

Directions: From Alamosa, take Highway 17 north. About one mile past Mosca, turn east on 6N Lane. In 16.2 miles, turn north on Highway 150 and continue 5.4 miles to the campground.

Contact: Great Sand Dunes National Park, 719/378-6399, www.nps.gov/grsa.

18 COMSTOCK

Scenic rating: 6

west of Monte Vista

Comstock campground is in a shady forest of spruce and fir on the south bank of Rock Creek. There is fair fishing in the creek, but the area is most popular with hunters. Hikers and bikers can take the Alamosa–Rock Creek Trail for five miles past Silver Mountain to the Alamosa River. At about three miles, this trail intersects the Silver Mountain Trail, which continues west to Sheep Mountain and has excellent views. A horse or ATV is recommended for really rewarding day trips into the mountains. The campground is remote and a bit run-down, but it offers quiet and solitude.

Campsites, facilities: There are eight sites for tents and RVs up to 30 feet. There are no hookups. Picnic tables, grills, and fire rings are provided. Vault toilets are available. Trash must be packed out. Leashed pets are permitted.

Reservations, fees: Reservations are not accepted, and there is no camping fee. Open Memorial Day–Labor Day and without services during hunting season.

Directions: From Monte Vista, take Highway 15 south for four miles. Turn right on County Road 29. In 4.5 miles, turn left on County Road 28/Forest Route 265. The campground is on the left in 11.6 miles.

Contact: Rio Grande National Forest, 719/657-3321, www.fs.fed.us/r2/riogrande/.

19 ROCK CREEK

Scenic rating: 6

west of Monte Vista

Rock Creek campground is in a big aspen grove on the south bank of Rock Creek. There is fair fishing in the creek, but the area is most popular with hunters, and horses or ATVs are necessary for rewarding day trips into the mountains. There is lots of shade and heaps of privacy at this rarely used, slightly run-down campground.

Campsites, facilities: There are 23 sites for tents and RVs up to 30 feet. There are no hookups. Picnic tables, grills, and fire rings are provided. Vault toilets are available. Trash must be packed out. Leashed pets are permitted.

Reservations, fees: Reservations are not accepted, and there is no camping fee. Open year-round but may be closed due to heavy snows.

Directions: From Monte Vista, take Highway 15 south for four miles. Turn right on County

Road 29. In 4.5 miles, turn left on County Road 28/Forest Route 265. The campground is on the left in nine miles.

Contact: Rio Grande National Forest, 719/657-3321, www.fs.fed.us/r2/riogrande/.

20 ALAMOSA

Scenic rating: 5

west of Alamosa

This campground is on the north bank of the Alamosa River. It's a free campground because there are very few overnight visitors to this valley. Natural contaminants and mining activities have made the Alamosa unfit for recreation, as the red waters will demonstrate. Most of the traffic in this area consists of four-wheelers headed for Elwood Pass and the Continental Divide, the traditional route west for settlers until Wolf Creek Pass opened in 1916. Wildlife-watching is the other main attraction. A herd of about 30 bighorn sheep live on the ridgelines above the river and sometimes come down to the road in search of water. The campground is a small loop shaded by spruce, fir, and cottonwood. Due to low use, it's fairly run-down.

Campsites, facilities: There are 10 sites for tents and RVs up to 25 feet. There are no hookups. Several sites are pull-through. Picnic tables and grills are provided. Vault toilets and drinking water are available. Leashed pets are permitted.

Reservations, fees: Reservations are not accepted, and there is no camping fee. Open late May–early September.

Directions: From Alamosa, take U.S. Highway 285 south to Highway 370. Go west on Highway 370 and then south on Highway 15 for two miles. Go west on County Road 12S/Forest Route 12S for 12.7 miles. Turn left into the campground.

Contact: Rio Grande National Forest, 719/274-8971, www.fs.fed.us/r2/riogrande/.

21 STUNNER

Scenic rating: 9

west of Alamosa

In its heyday, 150 people lived in Stunner, and there were 219 mines in the area. But mining never made anyone in Stunner rich, and by 1916, the town was abandoned. Today, almost no traces of the town remain, but the campground merits a visit, and the area is especially interesting for amateur geologists. North of the campground, the mineral-rich slopes of Big and Little Red Mountain are a vivid collage of orange, yellow, and red. The runoff from these mountains dyes the Alamosa River almost maroon. (It was these colors that attracted those miners who were ultimately disappointed.) The campground circles a small meadow above the Alamosa. The sites are shaded by spruce and aspen trees. Due to the remote location, campers here are guaranteed solitude. Most of the traffic in this area is four-wheelers heading for Elwood Pass on the Continental Divide, the same route used by settlers and the military before the opening of Wolf Creek Pass in 1916. Mountain bikers also traverse this route, and hikers can take Iron Creek Trail to Elwood Pass.

Campsites, facilities: There are nine sites for tents and RVs up to 25 feet and one walk-in site. There are no hookups. Several sites are pull-throughs. Picnic tables, grills, and fire rings are provided. Vault toilets and drinking water are available. Leashed pets are permitted.

Reservations, fees: Reservations are not accepted, and there is no camping fee. Open late June–early September.

Directions: From Antonito, take Highway 17 west for 22 miles. Continue west on Forest Route 250 for 28.5 miles. Turn left on Forest Route 380. The campground is on the left in 0.3 mile.

Contact: Rio Grande National Forest, 719/274-8971, www.fs.fed.us/r2/riogrande/.

22 MIX LAKE

Scenic rating: 9

in Conejos Canyon

At 10,000 feet, Mix Lake campground is above the town of Platoro, near the top of the Conejos Canyon. The Conejos River (*conejos* means "rabbit" in Spanish) is a tributary of the Rio Grande and an outstanding trout fishery, protected from overfishing by its remote location. Fly-fishing is the primary activity in the canyon, but hiking is also popular. Campers can fish on the river and Mix Lake, or drive two miles to the 6,000-acre Platoro Reservoir for fishing and boating. A small trail for hikers and bikers connects the campground to the dam.

The campground contains two loops in a forest of aspen, spruce, and fir with several small clearings. The first loop (sites 1–4) is separated from the top loop by a long walk. The whole top loop (sites 5–22) has views of Stunner Pass and the surrounding ridgelines. Sites 5–7, 21, and 22 also have views of Platoro. The sites are close to the campground road but are well spaced. Shade varies widely. Site 21 has an extralarge table.

Campsites, facilities: There are 22 sites for tents and RVs up to 25 feet. There are no hookups. Sites 5–8 and 15 are pull-through. Picnic tables, grills, and fire rings are provided. Vault toilets and drinking water are available. Leashed pets are permitted.

Reservations, fees: Reservations are not accepted. The camping fee is $12 per night (includes one vehicle). There is a $5 fee per additional vehicle. Golden Age and Golden Access Passports are accepted. Cash or check only. Open late May–early September.

Directions: From Antonito, take Highway 17 west for 22 miles. Continue west on Forest Route 250 for 23 miles. Turn left on an unmarked dirt road. The campground entrance is on the right in 0.4 mile.

Contact: Rio Grande National Forest, 719/274-8971, www.fs.fed.us/r2/riogrande/.

23 LAKE FORK

🚶‍♂️ 🚵 🛶 ⛵ 🐕 🚐 ⛺

Scenic rating: 7

in Platoro Canyon

Lake Fork is a family campground in a forest of aspen, spruce, and fir beside the Conejos River, a first-rate trout fishery. This remote canyon is in the southern San Juans. The long ridgelines and 12,000-foot peaks are not as dramatic as the "Alps of America" (the northern San Juans), but the aspen forests and pristine rivers are full of recreation opportunities, and the history of Spanish settlement is also interesting. This canyon attracts repeat visitors from Texas and Oklahoma, and many of these families return to the canyon year after year. In all of the campgrounds in the canyon, it's possible to find three generations of a family enjoying their summer vacation together. In addition to fishing, hikers and bikers can enjoy day trips on the Lake Fork Creek and Bear Lake Trails. Kayakers and rafters can put in at Saddle Creek and boat six miles of Class III–IV water through Pinnacle Gorge. The whitewater below the gorge is mellower Class II boating.

Sites 11–17 are next to the river. These large sites have the best shade and privacy and are usually occupied. Sites 1–6, 8, and 9 are in an aspen grove and have partial shade. Site 10 has an extra-large table.

Campsites, facilities: There are 18 sites for tents and RVs up to 25 feet. There are no hookups. Sites 9, 11, 13, 15, 16, and 19 are pull-through. Picnic tables, grills, and fire rings are provided. Vault toilets and drinking water are available. Leashed pets are permitted.

Reservations, fees: Reservations are not accepted. The camping fee is $12 per night (includes one vehicle). There is a $5 fee per additional vehicle. Golden Age and Golden Access Passports are accepted. Cash or check only. Open late May–early September and without services during hunting season.

Directions: From Antonito, take Highway 17 west for 22 miles. Continue west on Forest Route 250 for 17 miles. The campground entrance is on the left.

Contact: Rio Grande National Forest, 719/274-8971, www.fs.fed.us/r2/riogrande/.

24 TRAIL CREEK DISPERSED

🚶‍♂️ 🚵 🛶 ⛵ 🐕 🚐 ⛺

Scenic rating: 9

in Conejos Canyon

The area surrounding the confluence of Trail Creek and Conejos River is set aside for primitive camping. There are several dispersed sites for tents and small RVs in a forest of spruce and fir. The campsites are a short distance from the road, but they are completely screened from traffic. It's a gorgeous location above the Pinnacle Gorge portion of the Conejos, but it's a steep scramble down to the river. The mountains across the river are in the South San Juan Wilderness, and there are beautiful views down the valley. The trailhead for the five-mile Valdez Trail is a mile away. Farther down the road, the popular South Fork Conejos Trail begins a 10-mile trek into the wilderness area. The attractions on this trail include narrow canyons, high lakes, and the scenery of a glacial valley. Experienced whitewater enthusiasts can put in for The Pinnacles at Saddle Creek and boat six miles of Class III–IV whitewater down to the South Fork.

Campsites, facilities: This is primitive dispersed camping. There are no services or facilities. Leashed pets are permitted.

Reservations, fees: Reservations are not accepted, and there is no fee for camping. Open year-round.

Directions: From Antonito, take Highway 17 west for 22 miles. Continue west on Forest Route 250 for 14.2 miles and turn left at the Trail Creek sign. High-clearance vehicles are recommended for this road.

Contact: Rio Grande National Forest, 719/274-8971, www.fs.fed.us/r2/riogrande/.

25 CONEJOS

Scenic rating: 7

in Conejos Canyon

Conejos is about halfway up the scenic and remote Conejos Canyon. This area attracts families from Texas and Oklahoma who return year after year for the fishing and hiking. The Conejos is an outstanding trout fishery, and there are two hiking trails nearby. The Spectacle Lake Trail is a moderate 1.5-mile day hike that connects with the Valle Victoria and Notch Trails. The Ruybalid Trail is a steep climb through the South San Juan Wilderness to a subalpine lake.

The campground is a riverside loop shaded by spruce, fir, willow, and cottonwood. Sites 3–6 have the best river access. Sites 10–15 have the best shade but less privacy.

Campsites, facilities: There are 16 sites for tents and RVs up to 25 feet. There are no hookups. Site 1 is pull-through. Picnic tables, grills, and fire rings are provided. Vault toilets and drinking water are available. Leashed pets are permitted.

Reservations, fees: Reservations are not accepted. The camping fee is $12 per night (includes one vehicle). There is a $5 fee per additional vehicle. Golden Age and Golden Access Passports are accepted. Cash or check only. Open late May–early September and without services during hunting season.

Directions: From Antonito, take Highway 17 west for 22 miles. Continue west on Forest Route 250 for 6.5 miles. The campground entrance is on the left.

Contact: Rio Grande National Forest, 719/274-8971, www.fs.fed.us/r2/riogrande/.

26 SPECTACLE LAKE

Scenic rating: 7

in Conejos Canyon

Like nearby Conejos campground, Spectacle Lake attracts families from Texas and Oklahoma with its good fishing and nearby trails. Anglers will enjoy the Conejos River, and kids love tiny Spectacle Lake. There are two hiking trails within walking distance. The Spectacle Lake Trail is a moderate 1.5-mile day hike that connects with the Valle Victoria and Notch Trails. The Ruybalid Trail is a steep climb through the South San Juan Wilderness to a subalpine lake.

The campground is a riverside loop that is usually less than half full. The sites are shaded by spruce, fir, cottonwoods, and willows. Sites 7–11 are the most private because of dense undergrowth. The sites are 50–75 feet apart, and all have partial shade and nice views of the cliffs on the surrounding ridgelines. Perhaps the only drawback is the open range which surrounds the campground. You might wake up to a cow sedately munching the grasses beside your tent.

Campsites, facilities: There are 24 sites for tents and RVs up to 25 feet. Sites 3 and 4 and the facilities are wheelchair accessible. There are no hookups. Sites 7, 8, 12, 13, 18, 20, and 24 are pull-through. Picnic tables, grills, and fire rings are provided at all sites. Sites 3 and 4 have tent pads. Vault toilets and drinking water are available. Leashed pets are permitted.

Reservations, fees: Reservations are not accepted. The camping fee is $12 per night (includes one vehicle). There is a $5 fee per additional vehicle. Golden Age and Golden Access Passports are accepted. Cash or check only. Open late May–early September and without services during hunting season.

Directions: From Antonito, take Highway 17 west for 22 miles. Continue west on Forest Route 250 for 6.2 miles. The campground entrance is on the left.

Contact: Rio Grande National Forest, 719/274-8971, www.fs.fed.us/r2/riogrande/.

27 ELK CREEK

Scenic rating: 7

in Conejos Canyon

Elk Creek flows from the Continental Divide through a series of meadows to the Conejos River. The campground is in the small park at the confluence of the two rivers, an attractive location with access to the South San Juan Wilderness via the Elk Creek and Duck Lake Trails. The former is a 13.5-mile trail through the Elk Creek valley to the Conejos Plateau. The latter is a 3.5-mile day hike with scenic vistas and several fishing lakes. Both trails are popular with anglers.

The recently renovated campground has three loops shaded by pine, spruce, fir, and aspen. Small meadows occupy the middle of the loops. The sites are 25–50 feet apart and have moderate privacy. This campground is popular with RVers and families from Texas and Oklahoma. The camaraderie amongst the regulars (campers who return year after year) will appeal to some and deter others. There are also many campers who are just stopping for the weekend. Sites 11, 13, and 14 are next to the creek. Site 8 has an extralarge table.

Campsites, facilities: There are 34 sites for tents and RVs up to 25 feet. The facilities are wheelchair accessible. There are no hookups. Sites 2, 4, 5, 13, 21, 25, and 28 are pull-through. Picnic tables, grills, and fire rings are provided at all sites. Vault toilets and drinking water are available. Leashed pets are permitted.

Reservations, fees: Reservations are not accepted. The camping fee is $14 per night (includes one vehicle). There is a $5 fee per additional vehicle. Golden Age and Golden Access Passports are accepted. Cash or check

only. Open late May–late October. There are no services after Labor Day.

Directions: From Antonito, take Highway 17 west for 23 miles. Just after the Conejos River, turn right on an unmarked dirt road. In 0.1 mile, turn left. The campground entrance is on the right in 0.3 mile.

Contact: Rio Grande National Forest, 719/274-8971, www.fs.fed.us/r2/riogrande/.

28 TRUJILLO MEADOWS

Scenic rating: 8

in Platoro Canyon

This is a destination campground beside the Trujillo Meadows Reservoir in the Rio de los Pinos valley. This U-shaped glacial valley offers wide meadows, subalpine forests, wildflowers, and solitude for hikers and anglers. Forest Route 118 continues for four miles past the reservoir to the Los Pinos trailhead. (This section of the road is a rough Jeep trail that is more suitable for hikers and bikers than cars.) This two-mile trail climbs through the South San Juan Wilderness to the Jarosa Mesa and excellent views. The Continental Divide Trail and the Cumbres and Toltec Scenic Railroad cross Highway 17 at the turnoff for the reservoir. Bikers can ride to the trailhead, but hikers will want to drive.

Both loops are in a dense forest of spruce and fir. The sites are grouped in threes and fours, so privacy isn't a problem. The first loop (sites 1–24) is more popular with RVs. The second loop has a scenic overlook of a small waterfall. Site 49 overlooks the lake.

Campsites, facilities: There are 49 sites for tents and RVs up to 25 feet. Site 21 and the facilities are wheelchair accessible. There are no hookups. Sites 12 and 19 are pull-through. Picnic tables and grills are provided at all sites. Sites 41 and 42 have tent pads. Vault toilets and drinking water are available. A boat ramp and wheelchair-accessible fishing pier are 1.5 miles away. Leashed pets are permitted.

Reservations, fees: Reservations are not accepted. The camping fee is $14 per night (includes one vehicle). There is a $5 fee per additional vehicle. Golden Age and Golden Access Passports are accepted. Cash or check only. Open late May–early September.

Directions: From Antonito, take Highway 17 west to Cumbres. Go north on Forest Route 118. The campground is on the right in 2.1 miles.

Contact: Rio Grande National Forest, 719/274-8971, www.fs.fed.us/r2/riogrande/.

29 ASPEN GLADE

Scenic rating: 7

in Conejos Canyon

Aspen Glade campground is a series of loops on the north bank of the Conejos River, an outstanding trout fishery. It can fill up on weekends, but there are usually sites available. Campers go there for the fishing and the hiking. The Sheep Creek and Bear Creek Trails begin at the campground and can be made into a backpacking loop around Osier Mountain.

The A Loop (sites 1–10) is in a meadow near the road. It hasn't been renovated and is the least attractive and private of the loops. The B Loop (sites 11–19) is in a meadow with mature ponderosa pines that overlooks the river. Sites 16–19 have the best views in the loop and more shade. The C Loop (sites 20–32) is beside the river. The sites are shaded by pine and aspen. Sites 20–22 and 24–26 have the best river access and fill up quickly. Sites 8, 11, 17, and 22 have extralarge tables.

Campsites, facilities: There are 34 sites for tents and RVs up to 25 feet. There are no hookups. Sites 4, 11, 13, 18, and 26 are pull-through. Picnic tables, grills, and fire rings are provided at all sites. Sites 1–19 have tent pads. Vault toilets and drinking water are available. A boat ramp and wheelchair-accessible fishing pier are 1.5 miles away. Leashed pets are permitted.

Reservations, fees: Reservations are accepted at 877/444-6777 and www.reserveusa.com. The camping fee is $14 per night (includes one vehicle). There is a $5 fee per additional vehicle. Golden Age and Golden Access Passports are accepted. Cash or check only. Open mid-May–early September.

Directions: From Antonito, take Highway 17 west for 15 miles. The campground entrance is on the left.

Contact: Rio Grande National Forest, 719/274-8971, www.fs.fed.us/r2/riogrande/.

30 MOGOTE

Scenic rating: 6

west of Antonito

Mogote is the first public campground in the Conejos Canyon, but most campers continue up the canyon to Aspen Glade. The valley is much wider at this point than it is upstream, and summer days can be very hot. The first loop (sites 1–21) is in a grassy meadow with tall ponderosa pines. There is not much shade or privacy in this loop. The more popular lower loop (sites 22–41) is beside the river, and the sites are shaded by spruce and aspen. Dense undergrowth provides privacy. Sites 24, 26, and 28–30 are on the river. There are also two group loops (Piñon and Juniper) on the meadows above the river. Scattered ponderosa pines provide partial shade for dispersed tent camping. It's a short walk from these loops to the fishing access. The campground gate is closed from 9 P.M. to 7 A.M.

Campsites, facilities: There are 40 sites for tents and RVs up to 25 feet and two group sites. There are no hookups. Many sites are pull-through. Picnic tables and grills are provided at all sites. Fire rings are provided at some sites. Vault toilets and drinking water are available. Leashed pets are permitted. **Reservations, fees:** Reservations are accepted at 877/444-6777 and www.reserveusa.com. The camping fee is $14 per night (includes one vehicle). There is a $5 fee per additional vehicle. The group rate is $85–95 per night. Golden Age and Golden Access Passports are accepted. Cash or check only. Open mid-May–early September. **Directions:** From Antonito, take Highway 17 west for 13 miles. Turn left at the Mogote sign. The campground is on the right in 0.2 mile. **Contact:** Rio Grande National Forest, 719/274-8971, www.fs.fed.us/r2/riogrande/.

31 MOGOTE MEADOW

Scenic rating: 3

west of Antonito

Mogote Meadow is a private campground in the San Luis valley, the highest agricultural valley in the country, just outside of Antonito, one of the oldest towns in the country. The campground is an RV park with a grassy area for tent camping beneath several large cottonwoods. Nearby attractions include the Cumbres and Toltec Scenic Railroad, fishing on the Conejos River, and hiking in the South San Juan Wilderness. With its mild climate and Christian emphasis, the campground attracts mostly snowbirds.
Campsites, facilities: There are 45 sites for RVs up to 45 feet and five tent sites. There are full hookups. Picnic tables are provided. Restrooms with flush toilets and showers, drinking water, laundry facilities, a small store, playground, pay phones, and propane are available. There are also potlucks and pancake breakfasts. Leashed pets are permitted.
Reservations, fees: Reservations are accepted at 900/877-2133. The tent fee is $16 per night, and the RV fee is $22 per night (includes two

people). There is a $1–3 fee per additional person. Weekly and monthly rates are also available. AAA cards are accepted. Cash or check only. Open May 1–October 15.
Directions: From Antonito, take Highway 17 west for five miles. The campground entrance is on the right.
Contact: Mogote Meadows, 719/376-5774, email: mogotemeadow@amigo.com.

32 BLUE LAKE

Scenic rating: 6

south of La Veta

The Utes called the Spanish Peaks *wahatoya*, or "Breasts of the World," a fitting name for these unique peaks that have guided Native Americans and settlers across the plains for hundreds of years. The peaks were formed by molten rock that rose beneath sedimentary rocks, filling vertical fractures. The sedimentary rocks eroded away over millions of years, revealing the volcanic stocks and the rock walls, or dikes, that radiate out from the peaks like giant fins. This area gained wilderness designation in 2000. The peaks are the prominent landmark as visitors drive down Highway 12, "The Highway of Legends," to the Cuchara area on the west side of the wilderness area. There are three campgrounds on the eastern flank of the Sangre de Cristo: Bear Lake, Blue Lake, and Purgatoire.

Blue Lake is in a spruce-fir forest about a mile upstream of its namesake. Cuchara Creek runs through the middle of the campground, and some sites have glimpses of Boyd Mountain, Sheep Mountain, and Trinchera Peak. There are two loops. The smaller loop, sites 14–16, is secluded in a slightly denser wood. Sites 1, 2, and 11–13 are creekside. The campground always fills up on weekends, mostly with Front Range residents and some Texans escaping summer heat waves. Campers enjoy fishing on the creek and on Bear

Lake, as well as hiking and mountain biking on North Fork Trail and Indian Trail.

Campsites, facilities: There are 16 sites for tents and RVs up to 40 feet. There are no hookups. Picnic tables, grills, and fire rings are provided. Vault toilets and drinking water are available. The facilities are wheelchair accessible. Leashed pets are permitted.

Reservations, fees: Reservations are not accepted. The fee is $12 per night (includes two cars and 10 people). Additional vehicles cost $5 per night. Golden Age and Golden Access Passports are accepted. Cash or check only. Open late May–early October.

Directions: From U.S. Highway 160, take Highway 12 south for 20 miles. Turn right on Forest Route 422. The campground is on the right in four miles.

Contact: San Isabel National Forest, 719/269-8500, www.fs.fed.us/r2/psicc/.

33 BEAR LAKE

Scenic rating: 7

south of La Veta

Bear Lake is an appealing campground on the eastern flank of the Sangre de Cristo range, not far from the Spanish Peaks Wilderness area. (For more information on the Spanish Peaks, see the Blue Lake listing in this chapter.) The campground is in a meadow ringed by a spruce-fir forest. A creek runs alongside the campground, and Bear Lake is a short walk away. The meadow is circled by the forested slopes of Sheep Mountain, Teddy's Peak, and Boyd Mountain.

Campers will enjoy fishing on the stocked lake and hiking and mountain biking on the Indian, Baker, and Dodgetown Trails. Sites 5–12 are in the meadow and have excellent views. Sites 2, 3, and 13 are creekside. Site 9 is next to the Indian trailhead.

Campsites, facilities: There are 14 sites for tents and RVs up to 40 feet. There are no hookups. Picnic tables, grills, and fire rings are provided. Vault toilets and drinking water are available. Leashed pets are permitted.

Reservations, fees: Reservations are not accepted. The fee is $12 per night (includes two cars and 10 people). Additional vehicles cost $5 per night. Golden Age and Golden Access Passports are accepted. Cash or check only. Open late May–early October.

Directions: From U.S. Highway 160, take Highway 12 south for 20 miles. Turn right on Forest Route 422. The road ends at the campground in 5.5 miles.

Contact: San Isabel National Forest, 719/269-8500, www.fs.fed.us/r2/psicc/.

34 PURGATOIRE

Scenic rating: 8

south of La Veta

Purgatoire is on the North Fork of Purgatoire Creek, just a few miles from the North Lake State Wildlife Area. This quiet campground is in a spruce-fir forest with aspen groves and small meadows. The campground is divided into three loops. The upper loop (sites 5–10) overlooks a large meadow and has the most appealing sites with aspen groves and good views down the valley. Sites 11–15 and 17 are horse sites next to a meadow where horses can graze. Riding and hiking are popular activities, mainly on North Fork Trail, a five-mile trail that links the Purgatoire campground with the Cuchara Creek area. Fishing is also good on North Lake, but only artificial flies and lures are allowed.

Campsites, facilities: There are 23 sites for tents and RVs up to 40 feet. There are no hookups. Picnic tables, grills, and fire rings are provided. Tent pads are provided at sites 1–10. Vault toilets and drinking water are available. Leashed pets are permitted.

Reservations, fees: Reservations are accepted at 877/444-6777 and www.reserveusa.com.

The fee is $12 per night (includes two cars and 10 people). Additional vehicles cost $5 per night. Golden Age and Golden Access Passports are accepted. Cash or check only. Open late May–early October.

Directions: From U.S. Highway 160, take Highway 12 south for 31 miles. Turn right on Forest Route 411/North Fork Road. The road ends at the campground in 4.2 miles.

Contact: San Isabel National Forest, 719/269-8500, www.fs.fed.us/r2/psicc/.

35 MONUMENT LAKE PARK

Scenic rating: 5

south of La Veta

Monument Lake Park is a small summer resort on the Highway of Legends (Highway 12) between La Veta and Trinidad. The park has excellent views of the Spanish Peaks, massive volcanic stocks with rock walls, or dikes, radiating out from them like giant fins. The stocked reservoir offers excellent fishing and boating opportunities, and families enjoy the boat rentals and the restaurant and bar at the southwestern-style lodge. There's RV and tent camping in an evergreen forest on a hillside above the lake. The sites are only about 15 feet apart, so privacy is poor, but many guests are regulars who return every year and meet up with old friends. The campground is busy throughout the summer, and reservations are recommended. The tent sites are creekside.

Campsites, facilities: There are 48 sites for tents and RVs up to 45 feet. Full and partial hookups are available. Picnic tables are provided. Restrooms with flush toilets and showers, drinking water, dump stations, a laundry room, playground, boat ramp, convenience store, and restaurant are available. Leashed pets are permitted.

Reservations, fees: Reservations are accepted at 719/868-2112. The tent fee is $12 per night. The RV fee is $16–26 per night. The dump station fee is $5. Open mid-May–mid-September.

Directions: From U.S. Highway 160, take Highway 12 south for 33.2 miles. Turn left at the campground entrance.

Contact: Monument Lake Park, 719/868-2226, www.monumentlakepark.com.

36 YUCCA

Scenic rating: 6

in Lathrop State Park

Yucca offers basic tent camping at Lathrop State Park. (For more information on Lathrop, see the Piñon listing in this chapter.) Located beneath the Martin Lake dam, the campground has two small loops in a piñon-juniper setting, as well as two group sites. It's a short walk to the swim beach and the Hogback Trail, but the boat ramp is driving distance. The top of the loop (sites 10–13 and 21) is very close to the highway. The best sites for privacy are 6, 7, 19, and 20. Group site A has walk-in tent camping shaded by large trees. Group site B can accommodate RVs and has a covered picnic shelter.

Campsites, facilities: There are 21 sites for tents and RVs up to 45 feet and two group sites. There are no hookups or pull-throughs. Picnic tables, grills, fire rings, and vault toilets are provided. Restrooms with flush toilets and showers, drinking water, dump stations, laundry facilities, a playground, golf course, interpretive programs, and amphitheater are available at Piñon campground. Leashed pets are permitted.

Reservations, fees: Reservations are accepted at 800/678-2267 and www.parks.state.co.us. The fee is $12 per night (includes six people). A Daily Park Pass ($5) or Annual Parks Pass ($55) is also required. The Aspen Leaf Pass is accepted. Cash or check only. Open year-round.

Directions: From I-25 in Walsenberg, take

U.S. Highway 160 west for 4.7 miles. Turn right into the park and follow the signs 0.4 mile to the campground on the right.
Contact: Lathrop State Park, 719/738-2388, email: lathrop@csn.net.

37 PIÑON

🏃 🚴 🏊 🎣 🚤 🐕 ⛷ ♿ � ⛺

Scenic rating: 6

Lathrop State Park

Lathrop was Colorado's first state park. It has two small lakes and about 1,500 acres of high plains grassland. To the south, the Spanish Peaks dominate the horizon. The Utes called these volcanic peaks *wahatoya,* or "Breasts of the World." The land surrounding the peaks was called the Valley of the Rising Sun, and the Utes believed that gods and demons inhabited the area. Lathrop is a weekend destination for residents of Walsenberg and Trinidad. The lakes are stocked with rainbow trout, catfish, muskie, bass, walleye, and bluegill, and they're open to boating, waterskiing, wind surfing, and sailing. There's also a swimming beach, a paved trail for hiking and biking, and a municipal golf course.

Piñon was renovated in 2005, and the campsites and facilities got a facelift. The campground has scattered piñon and juniper trees, but privacy is poor. There are four loops. Loop A (sites 22–42) is closest to the water but not recommended for tent camping because the sites are so close together. Loop D (sites 79–103) has the best tent camping.

Campsites, facilities: There are 79 sites for tents and RVs up to 45 feet. Electric hookups are available. Picnic tables, grills, fire rings, and tent pads are provided. Restrooms with flush toilets and showers, drinking water, dump stations, laundry facilities, a playground, golf course, interpretive programs, and amphitheater are available. Leashed pets are permitted.

Reservations, fees: Reservations are accepted at 800/678-2267 and www.parks.state.co.us. The fee is $12 per night (includes six people) for sites without hookups and $16 per night for sites with hookups. A Daily Park Pass ($5) or Annual Parks Pass ($55) is also required. The Aspen Leaf Pass is accepted. Cash or check only. Open year-round.

Directions: From I-25 in Walsenberg, take U.S. Highway 160 west for 4.7 miles. Turn right into the park and follow the signs 1.1 miles to the campground on the north side of the lake.

Contact: Lathrop State Park, 719/738-2388, email: lathrop@csn.net.

38 CARPIOS RIDGE

🏃 🚴 🎣 🚤 🐕 ♿ � ⛺

Scenic rating: 6

in Trinidad Lake State Park

Trinidad Lake is an 800-surface-acre reservoir stocked with walleye, catfish, trout, bass, and perch. The lake is on the Purgatoire River, west of the historic mining town of Trinidad, where the brick-paved downtown, called the Corazon de Trinidad, is a designated National Historic District with several museums dedicated to local history. The park is a local fishing and boating destination with 10 miles of hiking and biking trails. It's also a convenient stopover between Denver and Albuquerque.

The campground consists of two loops in a piñon-juniper wood on the north shore of the lake. Privacy is poor, but the views of the Sangre de Cristos are excellent. The second loop (sites 25–62) is closer to the lake. It has better privacy and views. The Reilly Canyon Trail connects the campground with the old mining town Cokedale.

Campsites, facilities: There are 62 sites for tents and RVs up to 45 feet. Sites 13, 33, 42, and 50 are wheelchair accessible. Electric hookups are available at sites 1–6, 9–11, 13, 19–25, 27–35, and 37–59. Sites 5, 12, 33, 36, 42, and 60 are pull-through. Picnic tables, grills, fire rings, and tent pads are provided. Restrooms with flush toilets and showers, drinking water, dump stations, a laundry room, playground, boat ramp, group picnic area, interpretive programs, and amphitheater are available. Leashed pets are permitted.

Reservations, fees: Reservations are accepted at 800/678-2267 and www.parks.state.co.us. The fee is $12 per night for sites without hookups and $16 per night for sites with hookups (includes six people). A Daily Park Pass ($5) or Annual Parks Pass ($55) is also required. The Aspen Leaf Pass is accepted. Cash or check only. Sites 1–24, 61, and 62 are open year-round (without services in the winter), and sites 25–60 are open from April 15–October 15.

Directions: From Trinidad, take Highway 12 west for four miles. Turn left into the park. The campground is on the right in 0.5 mile.

Contact: Trinidad Lake State Park, 719/846-6951, email: trinidad.lake@state.co.us.

EASTERN PLAINS

The High Plains extend from near the Rocky Mountains

to Kansas and Nebraska, and reach as far north as Wyoming and as far south as Pueblo, Colorado. They are a sloping apron of shale, gravel, and sandy soil deposited over millennia by mountain erosion and ancient seas. The South Platte, Republican, Arkansas, and Purgatoire Rivers have carved through these lands, creating canyons, valleys, and sand dunes which haven't changed much for thousands of years.

Geological time may move slowly here, but this region has seen almost constant social change since the 1800s: the arrival of plains Indians pushed west by American expansion, the advent of trading forts, the decimation of the bison herds, the Mexican American War, the Civil War, the establishment of cattle farms, the Gold Rush, the arrival of homesteaders, railroad construction, the Dust Bowl devastation, irrigation, and oil exploration. It challenges the imagination to stand on top of the restored Old Bent Fort and imagine the scene that Charles Bent might have surveyed in 1835: the Cheyenne and Arapaho camped along the Arkansas River, a wagon train approaching from St. Louis, chiefs assembling for a peace council, and Kit Carson striding through the courtyard. Just 40 years later, the Native Americans were gone and railroad barons were already replacing cattle lords.

One thing is constant here – the wind. Every highway has a "Road Closed" sign to protect drivers from the strong winds that roar across the plains in the winter, spring, summer, and fall. Blizzards are common, and it is still possible to drive into a sandstorm, although nothing to rival the black clouds that engulfed the Great Plains during the Dust Bowl years of the 1930s, burying farms and driving away thousands of homesteaders.

Today the farmers have returned and the "Colorado Outback" is once again a vital contributor to the country's bread basket, thanks in large part to the Ogallala Aquifer, a vast reservoir of groundwater that underlies much of the Great Plains. The region has thrived because of deep wells and modern irrigation. Most urban areas are located next to the railroad to facilitate moving crops and cattle to market. This is a land of small towns and big churches, of county fairs, rodeos, barbecues, and pancake breakfasts.

History buffs will enjoy the Santa Fe Trail Scenic and Historic Byway, which travels 188 miles from Holly to the Colorado-New Mexico border. The old Santa Fe Trail was a trading route that traversed five states and linked Franklin, Missouri, with Santa Fe, New Mexico. It was a crossroads for Anglo, American Indian, and Hispanic cultures, and it played an important part in the westward expansion of the United States. There is an auto tour on the Mountain Branch from Lamar to Trinidad. To listen, tune your car AM radio to 1590 or 1610. And don't miss Bent's Old Fort near La Junta. The restored trading post is a gem and a key to understanding the rich history of the High Plains.

Bird-watchers, hikers, and hunters will delight in the Pawnee and Comanche National Grasslands. These prairies were created by the federal government as part of a soil conservation program. The native grasses provide habitat for antelope, deer, fox, and coyote as well as about 300 bird species. The best months for bird-watching are May and June. Hikers can also visit prehistoric American Indian rock art in Vogel, Picketwire, Carrizo, and Picture Canyons and dinosaur tracks in the Comanche Grassland. Mountain bikers may also enjoy the dirt roads that traverse these remote areas. But come prepared – services are few and far between.

Anglers and water-sports enthusiasts flock to the warm waters and sandy beaches of the reservoirs bordering the Arkansas and South Platte Rivers. These lakes are an oasis on the plains during the hot summers. The John Martin, Sterling Lake, and Bonny Lake Reservoirs are especially scenic.

Reservoirs also offer the best destination camping in the region, so these campgrounds fill up quickly in the summer with hordes of people looking to escape the heat. If you're headed for the mountains and need a place to stay overnight on I-70, the Strasburg KOA is a great place to rest up before climbing the Front Range. On Highway 50, the John Martin Reservoir is both convenient and scenic. On I-76, Jackson Lake State Park is the closest public campground to the interstate. These campgrounds can't compare to the majestic mountain settings that await you, but if you bring a fishing pole, they'll suffice for a night or two.

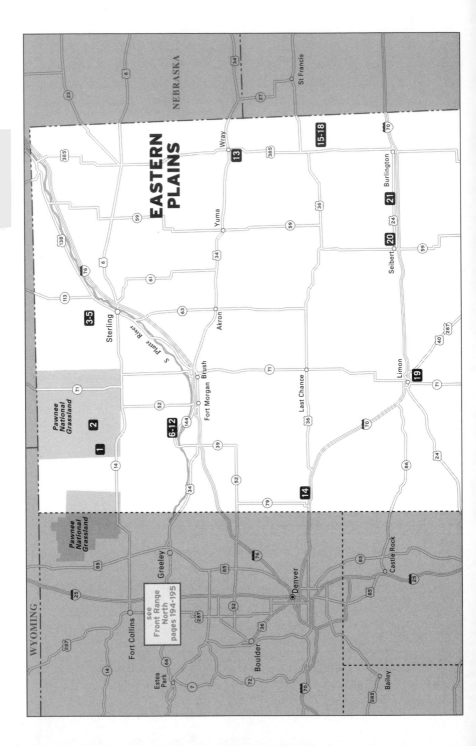

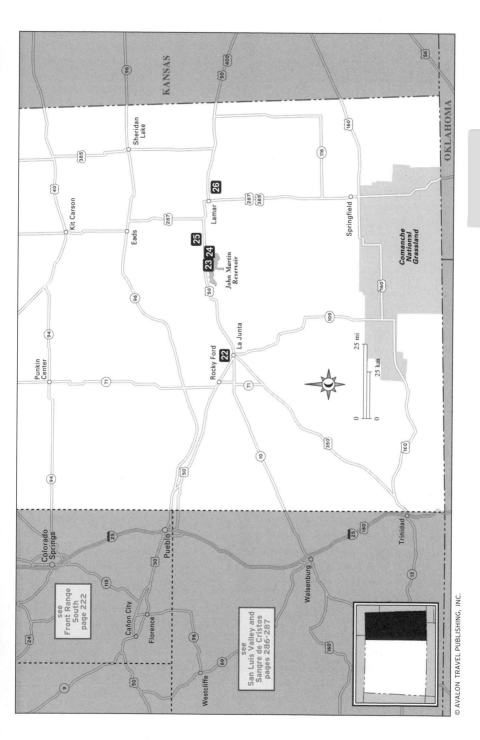

◼ CROW VALLEY RECREATION AREA

🏃 🚴 🐕 ♿ 🚐 ⛺

Scenic rating: 6

in Pawnee National Grassland

After the Homestead Act of 1962, homesteaders flocked to this area to claim free land. They plowed up the native grasses, planted wheat, and raised cattle on this harsh landscape. In the 1930s, a series of droughts and characteristic strong winds turned this region, along with rest of the southern Great Plains, into the Dust Bowl. Topsoil was carried away by wind erosion, burying homes and ruining farms. Many of the settlers gave up their land and migrated west. The federal government instituted new conservation measures, including buying land and planting it with native short grasses. As a result, Pawnee National Grassland was created in 1954.

The Grassland contains 193,00 acres of public land interspersed with private wheat fields and pastures. It is a haven for migrating birds (and bird-watchers); 301 species have been sighted here. The best months for bird-watching (and good weather) are May and June. A birding checklist and a brochure detailing a 36-mile tour for cars and mountain bikes are available at the campground. A popular and worthwhile hike to Pawnee Buttes is a half-hour drive to the northeast. The campground is small, scenic, and quiet when there are no large groups present. It is also remote; be sure to stock up before entering the Grasslands.

Campsites, facilities: On the main loop, there are 10 sites for tents and RVs up to 60 feet. Sites 4–6 are oversized and can hold four vehicles and 15 people. Site 5 is wheelchair accessible. The second loop has three group sites that hold up to 30 people. There is one educational site available by reservation. Picnic tables, fire rings, and grills are provided. Vault toilets and drinking water are available. Horseshoe pits, a group picnic area, an outdoor farm museum, and baseball field are also available. Leashed pets are permitted.

Reservations, fees: Reservations are only accepted for the group and educational sites at 877/444-6777 or www.reserveusa.com. The fee is $10 for five people for one night. The oversized lots cost $14 per night. The Golden Age Passport is accepted. Cash only. Open year-round.

Directions: From Fort Collins, take Highway 14 to Briggsdale. Turn north on County Road 77. The camp entrance is on the left in 0.2 mile.

Contact: Pawnee National Grassland, 970/346-5000, www.fs.fed.us/r2/arnf/.

◼ PAWNEE BUTTES

🏃 🚴 🐕 ⛺

Scenic rating: 7

in Pawnee National Grassland

Pawnee National Grassland is the result of soil conservation policies enacted by the federal government after the devastating Dust Bowl years. When drought and agriculture turned the High Plains prairies into a virtual desert in the 1930s, this region lost several inches of topsoil and most of its homesteaders. Since then, the government has planted native grasses in an effort to restore the land. The birds are thriving here—over 300 species have been sighted in this area. The best months for bird-watching (and good weather) are May and June. A birding checklist and a brochure detailing a 36-mile tour for cars or mountain bikes are available at Crow Valley Recreation Area (see listing in this chapter).

Plains tribes like the Arapaho, Cheyenne, and Sioux hunted buffalo and antelope in this area. Today, it's a popular hiking destination for Front Range residents. The buttes are the sandstone remains of an ancient sea eroded by wind and rain. You may be tempted to try rock climbing, but the pinkish sandstone is far too soft. A 2.5-mile trail travels from the parking area to the East Butte. A shorter trail heads north to an overlook with views of both buttes. Some of the trail crosses private land—these areas are clearly marked and should not be camped on. The best camping is around the West Butte. Camping is prohibited within 100 feet of the parking lot and windmills and 200 feet of the overlook.

Campsites, facilities: This is a primitive hike-in campsite in a remote area. There are no facilities or drinking water available. Stock up on gas and water before heading into the Grasslands. Leashed pets are permitted.

Reservations, fees: Reservations are not accepted. There is no fee for camping here. Open year-round, but weather conditions are unpleasant in winter and midsummer.

Directions: From Briggsdale, drive east on Highway 14 for 15 miles. Turn north on County Road 105. In 10 miles, turn right on County Road 104. In three miles, turn left on Country Road 111. The trailhead and parking lot are on the right in five miles.

Contact: Pawnee National Grassland, 970/346-5000, www.fs.fed.us/r2/arnf/.

3 ELKS

Scenic rating: 5

in North Sterling State Park

North Sterling State Park consists of a 3,000-acre lake and 1,500 acres of land. The reservoir occupies the valley carved by Cedar and Darby Creek, tributaries of the South Platte. The surrounding sandstone bluffs were first seen by settlers traveling west on the Overland Trail in the mid-1800s. Today, the bluffs are enjoyed by boaters exploring the many inlets of the lake. The hills in this area are sand dunes that were deposited millennia ago by winds from the Rocky Mountains and have since been covered by prairie grass and uncovered by agriculture. On windy days, it can feel more like the Sahara than the High Plains.

Located next to the marina, Elks is very popular with boaters and anglers. Sites 5–7,

27–32, and 41–49 are closest to the water and have the best views. Sites 1–21 have tent pads. There are few trees here and very little privacy. The campsites are generally 50–100 feet apart.

Campsites, facilities: There are 50 sites for tents and RVs. All of the sites have electrical hookups, and the majority are pull-through. Site 15 is wheelchair accessible. Picnic tables, fire rings, grills, and wind shelters are provided. Restrooms with flush toilets and showers, drinking water, and laundry facilities are available. Propane gas, a boat ramp, and a convenience store are available at the marina. Leashed pets are permitted.

Reservations, fees: Reservations are accepted at 800/678-CAMP (800/678-2267) and www.reserveamerica.com. The fee for sites without hookups is $12 per night. The fee for sites with electricity is $16 per night. Campers are limited to six people per campsite. There is an additional $2 fee per night for waterfront campsites. Campers must also purchase a Daily Parks Pass ($5) or an Annual Parks Pass ($55). The Aspen Leaf Annual Pass is accepted. Open year-round.

Directions: From Sterling, take 7th Avenue/ County Road 37 north for 10 miles. Turn left on County Road 46. The park entrance and campground are on the left in 3.9 miles.

Contact: North Sterling State Park, 970/522-3657, www.parks.state.co.us.

4 CHIMNEY VIEW

Scenic rating: 5

in North Sterling State Park

Chimney View occupies a barren hilltop with grand views of the lake and the surrounding farms. Due to the proximity and abundance of sites, the campground looks a bit like a prairie dog colony. On windy days, the hilltop turns into a dust farm. But if you hit it on a calm day, it's a pleasant place for tent camping with all the amenities. The shelter with the laundry and restrooms is large and clean. The swimming beach is a short walk downhill, and there are several hiking trails leading from the campground down to the water. At night, campers can enjoy stargazing and the nostalgic whistle of the train crossing the plains to the east. Sites 51, 53, 55, 57, 59, 61, 63, and 65 are closest to the lake and have the most unobstructed views.

Campsites, facilities: There are 43 pull-through sites without hookups. Picnic tables, fire rings, grills, tent pads, and shade shelters are provided. Restrooms with flush toilets and showers, vault toilets, drinking water, a dump station, and laundry facilities are available. A playground and picnic pavilion are a short walk away. A boat ramp and propane gas are available at the marina. Leashed pets are permitted.

Reservations, fees: Reservations are accepted at 800/678-CAMP (800/678-2267) and www.reserveamerica.com. The fee for sites without hookups is $12 per night for up to six people. Campers must also purchase a Daily Parks Pass ($5) or an Annual Parks Pass ($55). The Aspen Leaf Annual Pass is accepted. Closed November 1–April 1.

Directions: From Sterling, drive north on 7th Avenue/County Road 37 for 10 miles. Turn left on County Road 46. In 1.9 miles, turn left into the south park entrance. In 0.1 mile, pass the dump stations on the left and turn right into the campground.

Contact: North Sterling State Park, 970/522-3657, www.parks.state.co.us.

5 INLET GROVE
🏃 ⛵ 🦢 🛶 🐕 🛟 🚐 ⛺

Scenic rating: 5

in North Sterling State Park

North Sterling Reservoir is a 3,000-acre lake with many coves and abundant wildlife. It's subject to very hot summers and strong winds, but the weather doesn't deter water-sports enthusiasts and anglers. As the name implies, Inlet Grove is situated on an inlet, downhill of Chimney View campground. It is very close to the shore; sites 116–132 are practically touching the water. The campground is a large loop set up for RV camping, fishing, and birding. The South Shoreline Trail begins at the southern end of the campground and follows the south shore of the lake to the end of County Road 29 and a parking lot where hikers who want to do a shuttle can leave a car. Another trail leads up to Chimney View and down to the swimming beach.

Campsites, facilities: There are 46 pull-through sites with electrical hookups for tents and RVs. Picnic tables, fire rings, grills, tent pads, and shade shelters are provided. Vault toilets, drinking water, and a dump station are available. A boat ramp and propane gas are available at the marina. Leashed pets are permitted.

Reservations, fees: Reservations are accepted at 800/678-CAMP (800/678-2267) and www.reserveamerica.com. The fee is $16 per night for up to six people. Waterfront sites cost an additional $2 per night. Campers must also purchase a Daily Parks Pass ($5) or an Annual Parks Pass ($55). The Aspen Leaf Annual Pass is accepted. Closed November 1–April 1.

Directions: From Sterling, drive north on 7th Avenue/County Road 37 for 10 miles. Turn left on County Road 46. In 1.9 miles, turn left into the south park entrance. The campground entrance is straight ahead in 0.2 mile.

Contact: North Sterling State Park, 970/522-3657, www.parks.state.co.us.

6 LAKESIDE
🏃 ⛵ 🦢 🛶 🐕 ♿ 🚐 ⛺

Scenic rating: 4

in Jackson Lake State Park

Jackson Lake is a large, shallow reservoir with 11 miles of shoreline. It's popular for its warm water and sandy beaches. Summer weekends can be *very* crowded with water-sports enthusiasts. Water-skiers zip around the lake, and anglers fish for trout, walleye, catfish, perch, and crappie. It's also a convenient stopover for travelers on I-76. The seven campgrounds on the western shore are close together—many of them share facilities—and it can be difficult to tell which campground you're in. Quiet hours are 10 P.M.–6 A.M., but weekend crowds can be quite rowdy. On the lakeside is a grassy park with more trees than any of the other campgrounds. All of the sites are within 25 yards of the water and very popular with anglers.

Campsites, facilities: There are 58 sites with electrical hookups for tents and RVs, and four sites (49–52) for tents only. Most sites are pull-through. Site 35 is wheelchair accessible. Picnic tables, fire rings, and grills are provided. Restrooms with flush toilets and showers, vault toilets, drinking water, a dump station, laundry facilities, and horseshoe pits are available. A convenience store, propane gas, ATM, boat ramp, and water-sports rentals are available at the marina. Interpretive programs are offered at the visitors center. Leashed pets are permitted.

Reservations, fees: Reservations are accepted (and recommended in the summer) at 303/470-1144 or 800/678-2267 and www.parks.state.co.us. The fee is $12 per night for sites without hookups and $18 per night for sites with hookups. Campers must also purchase a Daily Parks Pass ($5) or an Annual Parks Pass ($55). The Aspen Leaf Annual Pass is accepted. Closed in winter.

Directions: From Fort Morgan, go west on I-76 for 13 miles. Turn north on Highway 39. In seven miles, the road ends at County Road Y.5. Go west for 3.5 miles to the entrance station. Lakeside is the first campground on the right.

Contact: Jackson Lake State Park, 970/645-2551, www.parks.state.co.us.

7 COVE

Scenic rating: 4

in Jackson Lake State Park

Cove is a small campground with almost no trees, but it's very popular because it has a sandy swimming beach. It's also a day-use area, so there's not much privacy here. Dense underbrush along the shore obstructs views of the lake. (For more information on Jackson Lake, see the Lakeside listing in this chapter.)

Campsites, facilities: There are 16 sites with electrical hookups for tents and RVs. Picnic tables, fire rings, shade shelters, and grills are provided. Restrooms with flush toilets and showers, drinking water, a dump station, horseshoe pits, and an amphitheater are available. A convenience store, propane gas, ATM, boat ramp, and water-sports rentals are available at the marina. Interpretive programs are offered at the visitors center. Leashed pets are permitted.

Reservations, fees: Reservations are accepted (and recommended in the summer) at 303/470-1144 or 800/678-2267 and www.parks.state.co.us. The fee is $12 per night for sites without hookups and $18 per night for sites with hookups. Campers must also purchase a Daily Parks Pass ($5) or an Annual Parks Pass ($55). The Aspen Leaf Annual Pass is accepted. Closed in winter.

Directions: From Fort Morgan, go west on I-76 for 13 miles. Turn north on Highway 39. In seven miles, the road ends at County Road Y.5. Go west for 3.5 miles to the entrance station. Cove is the second campground on the right.

Contact: Jackson Lake State Park, 970/645-2551, www.parks.state.co.us.

🖸 PELICAN
🚶 🏊 🎣 ⛴ 🐕 🚐 ⛺

Scenic rating: 4

in Jackson Lake State Park

Pelican is very close to the marina, and most of the sites are lakeside. It's usually packed with RVers, water-skiers, and anglers. It's also a short walk away from the swim beach at Cove campground. The tent-only sites are close to the road but have excellent views of the lake, which can be almost glorious at sunset. (For more information on Jackson Lake, see the Lakeside listing in this chapter.)

Campsites, facilities: There are 33 sites with electrical hookups for tents and RVs and four sites (1–4) for tents only. Sites 5–11 are pull-through. Picnic tables, fire rings, and grills are provided. Restrooms with flush toilets and showers, vault toilets, drinking water, a dump station, volleyball court, and horseshoe pits are available. A convenience store, propane gas, ATM, boat ramp, and water-sports rentals are available at the marina. Interpretive programs are offered at the visitors center. Leashed pets are permitted.

Reservations, fees: Reservations are accepted (and recommended in the summer) at 303/470-1144 or 800/678-2267 and www.parks.state.co.us. The fee is $12 per night for sites without hookups and $18 per night for sites with hookups. Campers must also purchase a Daily Parks Pass ($5) or an Annual Parks Pass ($55). The Aspen Leaf Annual Pass is accepted. Open year-round.

Directions: From Fort Morgan, go west on I-76 for 13 miles. Turn north on Highway 39. In seven miles, the road ends at County Road Y.5. Go west for 3.5 miles to the entrance station. Pelican is the third campground on the right.

Contact: Jackson Lake State Park, 970/645-2551, www.parks.state.co.us.

🖸 SANDPIPER
🚶 🏊 🎣 ⛴ 🐕 🚐 ⛺

Scenic rating: 4

in Jackson Lake State Park

Sandpiper is a medium-sized loop located just north of the marina. The west swim beach is a short walk away at Cove campground. The sites here are roomy, but there is no shade. All of the outside sites are long pull-throughs. Sites 13–15 are lakeside. The ground here is not level, so it's a poor choice for tent camping. (For more information on Jackson Lake, see the Lakeside listing in this chapter.)

Campsites, facilities: There are 28 sites with electrical hookups for tents and RVs. Picnic tables, fire rings, and grills are provided. Restrooms with flush toilets and showers, drinking water, a dump station, laundry facilities, and horseshoe pits are available. A convenience store, propane gas, ATM, boat ramp, and water-sports rentals are available at the marina. Interpretive programs are offered at the visitors center. Leashed pets are permitted.

Reservations, fees: Reservations are accepted (and recommended in the summer) at 303/470-1144 or 800/678-2267 and www.parks.state.co.us. The fee is $12 per night for sites without hookups and $18 per night for sites with hookups. Campers must also purchase a Daily Parks Pass ($5) or an Annual Parks Pass ($55). The Aspen Leaf Annual Pass is accepted. Closed in winter.

Directions: From Fort Morgan, go west on I-76 for 13 miles. Turn north on Highway 39. In seven miles, the road ends at County Road Y.5. Go west for 3.5 miles to the entrance station. Sandpiper is the fourth campground on the right.

Contact: Jackson Lake State Park, 970/645-2551, www.parks.state.co.us.

10 FOX HILLS

Scenic rating: 4

in Jackson Lake State Park

Fox Hills is the largest and the most unappealing campground at Jackson Lake State Park. The sites are close together, and there are no trees. Tent campers will probably be uncomfortable here and should head to Northview, Pelican, or Lakeside campgrounds. On the positive side, most of the sites have views of the lake. The swimming beach at Cove campground is a short walk to the south. (For more information on Jackson Lake, see the Lakeside listing in this chapter.)

Campsites, facilities: There are 87 sites without hookups for tents and RVs. Picnic tables, fire rings, and grills are provided. Restrooms with flush toilets and showers, vault toilets, drinking water, a dump station, laundry facilities, and horseshoe pits are available. A convenience store, propane gas, ATM, and water-sports rentals are available at the marina. Interpretive programs are offered at the visitors center. Leashed pets are permitted.

Reservations, fees: Reservations are accepted (and recommended in the summer) at 303/470-1144 or 800/678-2267 and www.parks.state.co.us. The fee is $12 per night. Campers must also purchase a Daily Parks Pass ($5) or an Annual Parks Pass ($55). The Aspen Leaf Annual Pass is accepted. Closed in winter.

Directions: From Fort Morgan, go west on I-76 for 13 miles. Turn north on Highway 39. In seven miles, the road ends at County Road Y.5. Go west for 3.5 miles to the entrance station. Fox Hills is the fifth campground on the right.

Contact: Jackson Lake State Park, 970/645-2551, www.parks.state.co.us.

11 NORTHVIEW

Scenic rating: 5

in Jackson Lake State Park

Northview is the last campground on the western shore of Jackson Lake, and it's the smallest and most appealing in the state park. These sites have the best views of the lake, so it's a very popular campground. Because the ground is uneven, it's more appropriate for RVs than tent camping. (For more information on Jackson Lake, see the Lakeside listing in this chapter.)

Campsites, facilities: There are 10 sites with electrical hookups for tents and RVs. Picnic tables, fire rings, grills, and shade shelters are provided. Vault toilets and drinking water are available, and a dump station for registered campers is at the park entrance. A convenience store, propane gas, ATM, boat ramp, and water-sports rentals are available at the marina. Interpretive programs are offered at the visitors center. Leashed pets are permitted.

Reservations, fees: Reservations are accepted (and recommended in the summer) at 303/470-1144 or 800/678-2267 and www.parks.state.co.us. The fee is $12 per night for sites without hookups and $18 per night for sites with hookups. Campers must also purchase a Daily Parks Pass ($5) or an Annual Parks Pass ($55). The Aspen Leaf Annual Pass is accepted. Open year-round.

Directions: From Fort Morgan, go west on I-76 for 13 miles. Turn north on Highway 39. In seven miles, the road ends at County Road Y.5. Go west for 3.5 miles to the entrance station. Northview is the last campground on the right.

Contact: Jackson Lake State Park, 970/645-2551, www.parks.state.co.us.

12 DUNES GROUP

🏃 ≋ 🚣 🛶 🐴 🚐 ⛺

Scenic rating: 4

in Jackson Lake State Park

Dunes is the only group campground at Jackson Lake. Separated from the string of six campgrounds on the west shore, it's more secluded and private than the other sites. This is an excellent destination for family reunions. The south swim beach is a short walk away, and the warm waters of the 2,700-acre reservoir are popular with anglers and waterskiers. There are also interpretive programs at the visitors center. The campground has a large fire pit where as many as 25 people can gather for s'mores and ghost stories. There are also sand dunes bordering the campground where kids romp on sunny days, but beware of windy days when dunes can turn into a miniature Dust Bowl.

Campsites, facilities: There are 16 sites with electrical hookups for tents and RVs. Picnic tables, fire rings, and grills are provided. Restrooms with flush toilets and showers, drinking water, a group picnic area, and horseshoe pits are available. A dump station is available for registered campers at the north park entrance. A convenience store, propane gas, ATM, and water-sports rentals are available at the marina to the north. Leashed pets are permitted.

Reservations, fees: Reservations are required. Stop by the visitors center or call 970/645-2551. The fee is $12 per night for sites without hookups and $18 per night for sites with hookups. There is an additional $8 reservation fee. Closed in winter.

Directions: From Fort Morgan, go west on I-76 for 13 miles. Turn north on Highway 39. In seven miles, the road ends at County Road Y.5. Go west for three miles and turn right at the south entrance to the park. Dunes Group is 0.3 mile past the entrance station.

Contact: Jackson Lake State Park, 970/645-2551, www.parks.state.co.us.

13 HITCH 'N POST CAMPGROUND AND RV PARK

≋ 🐴 🚐 ⛺

Scenic rating: 2

south of Wray

The Hitch 'n Post is a quiet, orderly stopover that is geared towards RVs. The large gravel lot that surrounds the owner's house is a quiet place to rest overnight. Wray is a good place to stock up on supplies, grab an ice-cream cone, or go swimming at the large public pool.

Campsites, facilities: There are 19 sites for RVs up to 100 feet and five tent sites on a small grassy area. Full hookups are available at all RV sites. Picnic tables and grills are provided. Restrooms with flush toilets and showers, drinking water, dump stations, laundry facilities, and horse corrals are available. Leashed pets are permitted.

Reservations, fees: Reservations are not accepted. The fee is $20 per night. Cash only. Open year-round.

Directions: From the intersection of Highway 385 and Highway 34 in Wray, drive south on 385 for one mile. The campground is on the east side of the highway.

Contact: Noble Burns, 34172 Highway 385, Wray, CO, 80758, 970/332-3128, email: hitchn@centurytel.net.

14 DENVER EAST/ STRASBURG KOA

≋ 🐴 🚶 🚐 ⛺

Scenic rating: 2

east of Denver on I-70

Strasburg is a small, safe town, and so is the KOA. In fact, on a busy summer afternoon, this campground may seem larger than Strasburg. This convenient stopover on the way to or from the mountains is a beehive of activity with its pool, hot tub, large playground, and busy game room (featuring arcade games, pool table, and

Ping Pong). In the summer, there's also a pancake breakfast on Saturday mornings and free movies in the evenings. It's a popular place for family reunions, in part because the friendly owners offer the meeting room for free to groups with at least 10 RVs. It's fortunate that there's so much to do at the campground because there's not much to do in Strasburg, and the scenery leaves much to be desired (unless you consider granaries and railroads breathtaking). However, there are plenty of trees on-site, providing much-needed shade during the hot summers.

Campsites, facilities: There are 56 RV sites, 22 tent sites near the playground and along the north perimeter, and one large group site. There are also seven rustic cabins that sleep 4–6 people. Picnic tables, fire rings, grills, wireless Internet, and an adults-only hot tub are provided. There is a pool, playground, basketball and volleyball courts, a large game room, and a meeting room. There are flush toilets, showers, and drinking water, as well as laundry facilities and a store. Bike rentals and propane are available. The management is very pet friendly, but pets should be leashed.

Reservations, fees: Reservations are accepted year-round. The two-person rate is $20–22 per night for tent sites and $29–36 per night for RV sites. Kids under 10 stay free. Cabins cost $40–58 per night. The KOA Value Kard is accepted.

Directions: From Denver, go east on I-70 for 35 miles. In Strasburg, take exit 310. Turn left off the ramp, then right onto Frontage Road. Turn left on Monroe Street, and the campground is immediately on the right.

Contact: Jeff and Tracy Hastings, 303/622-9274, email: deneastkoa@direcway.com.

15 WAGON WHEEL

Scenic rating: 5

in Bonny Lake State Park

Bonny Lake is a reservoir on the South Fork of the Republican River. In the summer, families flock here to enjoy water sports and fishing on the 1,900-acre lake. In the fall, hunters search for turkey and deer in the surrounding woods and ravines. This supersized campground is popular with boaters because of its proximity to the marina. It fills up quickly in the summer, but campers have it almost to themselves between Labor Day and Memorial Day. Most of the sites are grassy and pleasant. The A and B loops are closest to the water. They are also good tent sites. Sites 71–73 are nicely situated in a shady pine tree grove adjacent to the amphitheater. Loop E is shaded by large cottonwood trees. The swimming beach is 0.4 mile away.

Campsites, facilities: There are 87 sites for tents and RVs up to 40 feet. All sites have electrical hookups, and water is centrally located at each loop. Sites 48–61 and 69–80 are pull-through. Picnic tables, grills, fire rings, and wind shelters are provided. Restrooms with flush toilets and showers, vault toilets, drinking water, dump stations, propane gas, and laundry facilities are available. The group picnic area is available by reservation only. Site 80 is wheelchair accessible. The marina has a store with fishing and boating supplies and offers boat and personal-watercraft rentals. Boat ramps are available when water levels permit. The park offers campfire programs on Saturday and Sunday mornings and Friday evenings. Leashed pets are permitted.

Reservations, fees: Reservations are accepted at 800/678-CAMP (800/678-2267) and www.reserveamerica.com. The fee for tents and RVs without hookups is $12 per night. The fee for sites with electricity is $16 per night. Campers are limited to six people per campsite. Campers must also purchase a Daily Parks Pass ($5) or an Annual Parks Pass ($55). The Aspen Leaf Annual Pass is accepted. Open year-round.

Directions: From Burlington, take Highway 385 North for 20 miles. Turn right on County Road 2. Drive 3.3 miles to a stop sign and turn left on County Road JJ. Follow the signs

for a half mile to the park headquarters and purchase a pass. The entrance to the campground is just past the headquarters.
Contact: Bonny Lake State Park, 970/354-7306, email: bonny@plains.net.

16 EAST BEACH

Scenic rating: 5

in Bonny Lake State Park

Located beneath the dam, East Beach is more remote and much quieter than the busy Wagon Wheel campground. All of the sites are less than a hundred yards from the sandy beaches, but no swimming is allowed here. It's popular with tent campers and anglers as well as birders who can enjoy bald eagle viewing November–March. Summer temperatures are intense, and the only shaded sites are the walk-in tent sites. Sites 19–25 are closest to the water, and sites 14–34 are fairly uninviting. The only pull-through sites are 14, 29–31, and 35.

Campsites, facilities: There are 35 sites total, including 10 walk-in tent sites (4–13). Site 28 is wheelchair accessible. There are no hookups. Picnic tables, grills, fire rings, and wind shelters are provided. Vault toilets and drinking water are available. Leashed pets are permitted.

Reservations, fees: Reservations are accepted at 800/678-CAMP (800/678-2267) and www.reserveamerica.com. The fee for tents and RVs without hookups is $12 per night. Campers are limited to six people per campsite. Campers must also purchase a Daily Parks Pass ($5) or an Annual Parks Pass ($55). The Aspen Leaf Annual Pass is accepted. Open year-round.

Directions: From Burlington, take Highway 385 North for 20 miles. Turn right on County Road 2. Drive 3.3 miles to a stop sign and turn left on County Road JJ. Follow the signs for a half mile to the park headquarters where

you can purchase a pass. From the headquarters, turn right at the stop sign and then make an immediate left on an unnamed dirt road. The campground entrance is in 1.8 miles.
Contact: Bonny Lake State Park, 970/354-7306, email: bonny@plains.net.

17 FOSTER GROVE

Scenic rating: 5

in Bonny Lake State Park

Foster Grove is located a quarter mile from the shoreline and seven miles from the marina. It is an ideal campground for families and groups more interested in wildlife than water sports. Depending on the season, campers might see whitetail deer, wild turkey, red-tailed hawks, and pheasants. This campground's best features are the numerous cottonwoods shading most of the sites and the cool breeze that blows through in the evenings. One minus is the irrigated alfalfa fields that partially surround the campground and provide a perfect breeding ground for mosquitoes. The campground is laid out as a large loop that encircles a smaller loop. The facilities are within the inner loop, so those sites (9–29) see a lot more traffic. Sites 22–37 have the best shade trees.

Campsites, facilities: There are 42 sites for tents and RVs. Electrical hookups are available at sites 1–4, 14–18, 25, and 40–42. The only pull-through sites are 30–33 and 38–42. Site 25 is wheelchair accessible. Picnic tables, grills, and fire rings are provided. Restrooms with flush toilets and showers are available April–October. Vault toilets, drinking water, and a dump station are available all year. Leashed pets are permitted.

Reservations, fees: Reservations are accepted at 800/678-CAMP (800/678-2267) and www.reserveamerica.com. The fee for tents and RVs without hookups is $12 per night. The fee for sites with electricity is $16 per night. Campers are limited to six people per campsite. Campers must also purchase a Daily Parks Pass ($5) or an Annual Parks Pass ($55). The Aspen Leaf Annual Pass is accepted. Camping and park permits can be purchased here or at the park headquarters. Open year-round.

Directions: From Burlington, drive north on Highway 385 for 21 miles. Turn right on County Road 3. In 1.7 miles, turn right into the campground.

Contact: Bonny Lake State Park, 970/354-7306, email: bonny@plains.net.

18 NORTH COVE

Scenic rating: 5

in Bonny Lake State Park

North Cove is the smallest and most remote campground in Bonny Lake State Park, so it is the best destination for anglers and birders. Under normal conditions, all of the sites are 50 yards or less from the shoreline, but drought conditions can turn this cove into a marsh. In early 2005, the boat ramp was nearly a quarter mile away from the water. Bird-watchers can take advantage of these conditions by hiking in the marsh or on the half-mile nature trail that begins in the campground. It is not uncommon to see great blue herons, white pelicans, and osprey in this area. The campground itself is very spartan, but the scenery and solitude are outstanding.

Campsites, facilities: There are 21 sites for tents and RVs up to 60 feet. There are no hookups. Sites 11–21 are pull-through. Site 16 is wheelchair accessible. There is also a group site for five units or 30 people available by reservation. Picnic tables, grills, and fire rings are provided. Vault toilets, drinking water, and a horseshoe pit are available. The boat ramp is intermittently available. Leashed pets are permitted.

Reservations, fees: Reservations are ac-

cepted at 800/678-CAMP (800/678-2267) and www.reserveamerica.com. The fee for tents and RVs without hookups is $12 per night. Campers are limited to six people per campsite. Campers must also purchase a Daily Parks Pass ($5) or an Annual Parks Pass ($55). The Aspen Leaf Annual Pass is accepted. Closed November 1–January 31 for waterfowl migration.

Directions: From Burlington, drive north on Highway 385 for 21 miles. Turn right on County Road 3. In 5.7 miles, turn right into the campground. Camping and park permits can be bought here or at the park headquarters.

Contact: Bonny Lake State Park, 970/354-7306, email: bonny@plains.net.

19 LIMON KOA

Scenic rating: 2

in Limon

The tiny town of Limon (pop. 2,400) is a spartan stopover point for travelers on I-70. Summer temperatures here regularly top 100°F, and there are few distractions from the heat except for the campground pool, fast-food restaurants, and the Limon Heritage Museum Depot, a short drive away in downtown Limon. There is also a bike path along the river, a golf course on the west end of town, and the Doug Kissel Fishing Pond, a tiny, stocked pond beside the railroad. This family-oriented KOA is very close to the highway and surrounded by fields. There are numerous trees to provide some relief from the heat, but very little privacy. The owners serve a pancake breakfast every day in the summer.

Campsites, facilities: There are 10 sites for tents and 59 sites with full hookups for RVs up to 70 feet. Picnic tables and grills are provided. Restrooms with flush toilets and showers, drinking water, dump stations, laundry facilities, a convenience store, diner, propane gas, volleyball, tetherball, a playground, and game room are available. Leashed pets are permitted.

Reservations, fees: Reservations are accepted. The tent fee is $20–25 per night for two people. The RV fee is $25–32 per night for two people. Additional adults cost $4 each, and kids over five cost $3. The KOA Value Kard is accepted. Open mid-March–October 31.

Directions: Take I-70 to Limon and take Exit 361 West. At the Pizza Hut, turn right onto Colorado Avenue (the sign is usually knocked down by semis). The campground is behind the Flying J.

Contact: Limon KOA, 719/775-2152 or 800/562-2129, www.koa.com.

20 SHADY GROVE

Scenic rating: 2

in Siebert

This family-run campground is located in a residential neighborhood in Siebert, the kind of small town where everyone waves as you drive by. The family who runs the campground lives in the house in the middle of the park, a dirt lot with numerous shade trees. Despite the lack of privacy, the setting is peaceful. Most campers are families traveling to the mountains, and in the summer, there's the occasional harvesting or pipeline crew. The only recreation in town is one block away at the large public playground with basketball courts. Like many of the farming communities in eastern Colorado, Siebert's main street is struggling to stay alive. There is a small food co-op where travelers can purchase supplies. During the summer, the family shows movies in the evening.

Campsites, facilities: There are 30 RV sites with full hookups and 10 tent sites. Picnic tables, grills, and fire rings are provided. Restrooms with flush toilets and showers,

drinking water, dump stations, laundry facilities, bike rentals, a foosball table, library shelf, and hot tub are available. Cable TV and Internet access are free. Pets are welcomed.

Reservations, fees: Reservations are accepted. The tent fee is $15 per night, and the RV fee is $22 per night. There is an additional charge of $4 for 50-amp hookups. One cabin is available for $25 per night. Cash only. Most discount cards are honored. Open year-round.

Directions: From I-70, take Exit 405 and drive north on Highway 59. In 0.2 mile, turn right on 4th Street. In 0.3 mile, turn left at the stop sign. The campground entrance is on the right.

Contact: Shady Grove Campground, 970/664-2218, email: shadygrove@plains-tel.com.

21 MARSHALL ASH VILLAGE

Scenic rating: 1

in Stratton

This RV park is a large gravel lot just a stone's throw from the interstate. It is utilitarian but clean and well maintained. All of the RV sites are pull-through sites separated by grass dividers with small shade trees. Sites 6–16 have picnic tables. There is a grassy area for tent camping that can comfortably hold six tents. The only recreational opportunities in Stratton are the golf course and possibly storm-chasing during the tornado season (May–July).

Campsites, facilities: There are 32 sites with full hookups for RVs of any length and a grassy area for tents. Picnic tables are provided. Restrooms with flush toilets and showers, drinking water, dump stations, a dog run, and a laundry room are available. Leashed pets are permitted.

Reservations, fees: Reservations are accepted. The tent fee is $20 per night for up to four people. The RV fee is $24–49 per night for up to four people. The cost for each additional person is $3 per night. Campers receive a discount on gas purchases. Open year-round.

Directions: From I-70, take exit 419 north. In 0.1 mile, turn left at the Conoco station. The campgrounds are behind the gas station.

Contact: Marshall Ash Village, 719/348-5501 or 719/348-5141.

22 LA JUNTA KOA

Scenic rating: 2

in La Junta

Thanks to the glowing lights of Wal-Mart, flashlights aren't a necessity at this busy KOA. There are a few semipermanent residents, but this park is mainly for overnighters who need to restock and don't mind the close quarters. What the campground lacks in wilderness and privacy, it makes up for with its proximity to fascinating historical sights along the Santa Fe Trail (Highway 50) and in Comanche National Grassland. Bent's Old Fort, eight miles to the east, was a center of the fur trade in the mid-1800s and a military fort during the Mexican-American War. Today, the restored adobe fort is a national historic site with tour guides in period clothing. In the Grassland, hikers in Vogel and Picket Wire Canyons can see prehistoric Native American rock art, abandoned homesteads, and the largest dinosaur track site in North America.

Campsites, facilities: There are three tent sites, 41 sites with full hookups for RVs up to 66 feet, and two cabins. Picnic tables, grills, and fire rings are provided. Restrooms with flush toilets and showers, drinking water, dump stations, a store, propane gas, miniature golf, horseshoes, basketball courts, a playground, swimming pool, meeting room, recreation room, and cable TV are available. Leashed pets are permitted, but some dog breeds are restricted.

Reservations, fees: Reservations are accepted. Tent fees are $21–23.50 per night, and RV fees are $22–30 per night for up to four people. Additional campers over the age of 10 cost $2.50 each. The KOA Value Kard is accepted. Open year-round.

Directions: From the junction of U.S. 50 and Highway 71 in Limon, drive west on Highway 50 for one mile. The campground is on the left at 26680 Highway 50.

Contact: La Junta KOA, 719/384-9580 or 800/KOA-9501, website: www.lajunta-koa.com.

23 LAKE HASTY

Scenic rating: 4

in John Martin Reservoir State Park

John Martin Reservoir State Park deserves its moniker "an oasis on the plains." Campers regularly travel from five states to enjoy boating, fishing, bird-watching, and hunting on and around the lake. Hikers and birders will enjoy the Red Shin Hiking Trail (4.5 miles), which begins below the dam, traverses shortgrass prairie and wetland environments, and ends at the Santa Fe Trail marker on the north shore. The lake provides nesting habitat for the threatened piping plover and the endangered interior least tern, and it's an important migratory stop for waterfowl and bald eagles. This campground closes in the winter to protect the bald eagles that nest in the large trees scattered throughout the campground.

Located in the shadow of the dam, the campground is a short walk away from two stocked fishing ponds and a sandy swimming beach. Sites 1–29 are the closest to the dam and the least appealing, in part because there are no shade trees at this end of the campground. Sites 30–109 have more shade, and they are closer to the swimming beach. Most of the picnic tables at this campground have shelters, a useful feature when the winds kick up, which they often do. There is very little privacy when it's crowded. Reservations are recommended if you are traveling here in the summer, but you will have the campground almost to yourself in the off-season.

Campsites, facilities: There are 109 sites for tents or RVs up to 60 feet. Sites 59 and 60 are wheelchair accessible. Every site has electric hookups. Picnic tables, grills, and fire rings are provided. Restrooms with flush toilets and showers, drinking water, dump stations, coin-operated laundry facilities, a playground, and a fish-cleaning station are available. Boat ramps are available at the reservoir. Group camping and picnic areas are available by reservation. Leashed pets are permitted.

Reservations, fees: Reservations are accepted at 800/678-CAMP (800/678-2267) and www.reserveamerica.com. The fee is $16 per night for up to six people. Campers must also purchase a Daily Park Pass ($5) or an Annual Parks Pass ($55). The Aspen Leaf Annual Pass is accepted. This campground is closed November 1–March 31.

Directions: From Lamar, drive west on U.S. 50 for 20 miles. In the tiny town of Hasty, turn south on County Road 24. Follow the signs 2.2 miles to the visitors center where you can purchase a park pass and camping permit. After the visitors center, the go left at the fork. The campground entrance is on the right in 0.9 mile.

Contact: John Martin Reservoir State Park, 719/829-1801, email: john.martin.park@state.co.us.

24 POINT

Scenic rating: 6

in John Martin Reservoir State Park

This campground is popular with anglers, hunters, and birders who travel from five states to enjoy this oasis on the plains, a year-round migration stop for waterfowl and birds of prey. Located on a peninsula on the north shore, this campground has dramatic views of the lake and the seemingly barren short-grass prairie. Don't let first impressions fool you. The habitat is home to deer, coyote, rabbits, raccoons, and prairie dogs. For wildlife viewing, try the Red Shin Hiking Trail (4.5 miles), which begins at the Santa Fe Trail marker and ends below the dam. Swimmers must scramble down sandstone cliffs to reach the water, and life jackets are required. There's more room between the sites here than at the Lake Hasty campground, but no trees, a serious drawback when temperatures regularly top 100°F in the summer.

Campsites, facilities: There are 104 sites for tents and RVs up to 45 feet, but there are no hookups. Gravel tent pads, picnic tables, grills, fire rings, and vault toilets are provided. The boat ramps are nearby. Group camping and picnic sites are available by reservation. Leashed pets are permitted.

Reservations, fees: Reservations are accepted at 800/678-CAMP (800/678-2267) and www.reserveamerica.com. The fee is $12 per night for up to six people. Campers must also purchase a Daily Park Pass ($5) or an Annual Parks Pass ($55). The Aspen Leaf Annual Pass is accepted. This campground is closed November 1–mid-March for the waterfowl migration.

Directions: From Lamar, drive west on U.S. 50 for 20 miles. In the tiny town of Hasty, turn south on County Road 24. Follow the signs 2.2 miles to the visitors center where you can purchase a park pass and camping permit. After the visitors center, follow the Point campground signs for 2.6 miles. Before the boat ramps, turn right onto the dirt road. In one mile, turn left at the T intersection. The campground is on both sides of the road in one mile.

Contact: John Martin Reservoir State Park, 719/829-1801, email: john.martin.park@state.co.us.

25 HUD'S CAMPGROUND

🏃 🏊 🛶 ⛴ 🐕 🚐 ⛰️

Scenic rating: 2

west of Lamar

This family-run campground is a summer stopover for most campers. It's also popular with boaters and family reunions because of the recreation opportunities at nearby John Martin Reservoir State Park. A 10-minute drive away, the state park offers swimming, fishing, boating, and birding. This humble campground has a few scattered trees, and the sites are too close together to allow any privacy, but the owners are friendly and accommodating.

Campsites, facilities: There are 10 tent sites and 20 sites with full hookups for RVs of any length. Picnic tables, grills, and a few fire rings are provided. Restrooms with flush toilets and showers, drinking water, laundry facilities, a dump station, and a convenience store are available. Pets are permitted.

Reservations, fees: Reservations are accepted. The tent fee for two people is $14 per night. The RV fee for two people is $19 per night. Additional people cost $3 per night. Cash only. Open year-round.

Directions: From Lamar, drive west on U.S. 50 for 15 miles. The campground is on the northwest corner at the intersection of U.S. 50 and Highway 196.

Contact: Bob and Patty Boyer, 29995 U.S. 50, McClave, CO, 81057, 719/829-4344.

26 COUNTRY ACRES RV PARK AND MOTEL

🐕 🚐 ⛰️

Scenic rating: 1

in Lamar

Lamar is just 32 miles west of Kansas which makes this family-owned RV park a convenient stopover for tired travelers. It is a large gravel parking lot surrounded by fields and adjacent to an old-fashioned motel. There is a small, grassy plot for tent camping, although campers might be disturbed at night by the constant sound of the highway. Complimentary coffee and newspapers help early risers get a head start on the road. The nearest recreation areas are the Lamar golf course and John Martin Reservoir State Park. The Colorado Welcome Center, at the corner of Main and Beech, is a great resource for vacation information.

Campsites, facilities: There are 22 pull-through sites with full hookups for RVs of any length and 10 tent sites. Picnic tables are provided. Flush toilets and showers are available in a motel room reserved for tent campers. A dump station, laundry room, and wireless Internet are also available. Leashed pets are permitted.

Reservations, fees: Reservations are accepted. The tent fee is $11 per night, and the RV fee is $24 per night. Major credit cards are accepted. The KOA Value Kard and AARP are accepted. Open year-round.

Directions: From the junction of U.S. 50/Highway 385 and Highway 287, drive south on Highway 287/385 for 5.5 miles. The RV park is on the north side of the road.

Contact: Country Acres RV Park & Motel, 719/366-1031 or 866/336-1031, email: rooms@lamarcountryacres.com.

RESOURCES

Resources

NATIONAL RESOURCES

Browns Park National Wildlife Refuge
1318 Highway 318
Maybell, CO 81640
970/365-3613
www.fws.gov/brownspark

Bureau of Land Management
Colorado State Office
2850 Youngfield Street
Lakewood, CO 80215
303/239-3600

Colorado Canyons National Conservation Area
2815 H Road
Grand Junction, CO 81506
970/244-3000

Gunnison Gorge National Conservation Area
2465 S. Townsend Avenue
Montrose, CO 81401
303/239-3600

Rocky Mountain Arsenal National Wildlife Refuge
U.S. Fish and Wildlife Service
Building 121
Commerce City, CO 80022
303/289-0232
www.fws.gov/rockymountainarsenal

Rocky Mountain Research Station
Natural Resources Research Center
2150 Centre Avenue, Building A
Fort Collins, CO 80526
970/295-5926
www.fs.fed.us/rm

San Luis Valley National Wildlife Refuge
8249 Emperius Road
Alamosa, CO 81101
719/589-4705
http://alamosa.fws.gov

National Forests

Arapaho and Roosevelt National Forests and Pawnee National Grassland
2150 Centre Avenue
Building E
Fort Collins, CO 80526-8119
970/295-6600
www.fs.fed.us/r2/arnf/

Grand Mesa, Uncompahgre, and Gunnison National Forests
250 Highway 50
Delta, CO 81416
970/874-6600
www.fs.fed.us/r2/gmug/

Pike and San Isabel National Forests and Comanche National Grassland
2840 Kachina Drive
Pueblo, CO 81008
719/553-1400
www.fs.fed.us/r2/psicc/coma/

Rio Grande National Forest
1803 W. Highway 160
Monte Vista, CO 81144
719/852-5941
www.fs.fed.us/r2/riogrande/

Routt National Forest
2468 Jackson Street
Laramie, WY 82070
307/745-2300
www.fs.fed.us/r2/mbr/

San Juan National Forest
15 Burnett Court
Durango, CO 81301
970/247-4874
www.fs.fed.us/r2/sanjuan/

White River National Forest
900 Grand Avenue
P.O. Box 948
Glenwood Springs, CO 81602
970/945-2521
www.fs.fed.us/r2/whiteriver/

National Parks and Monuments
Black Canyon of the Gunnison National Park
Park Headquarters
102 Elk Creek
Gunnison, CO 81230
970/641-2337
www.nps.gov/blca/

Canyons of the Ancients National Monument & Anasazi Heritage Center
27501 Highway 184
Dolores, CO 81323
970/882-4811

Colorado National Monument
Colorado National Monument
Fruita, CO 81521
970/858-3617
www.nps.gov/dino

Curecanti National Recreation Area
102 Elk Creek
Gunnison, CO 81230
970/641-2337
www.nps.gov/cure/

Dinosaur National Monument
4545 E. Highway 40
Dinosaur, CO 81610
970/374-3000
www.nps.gov/dino

Florissant Fossil Beds National Monument
P.O. Box 185
15807 Teller County 1
Florissant, CO 80816
719/748-3253
www.nps.gov/flfo/

Great Sand Dunes National Park Visitors Center
11999 Highway 150
Mosca, CO 81146
719/378-6399
www.nps.gov/grsa/

Hovenweep National Monument
McElmo Route
Cortez, CO 81321
970/562-4282
www.nps.gov/hove/

Mesa Verde National Park
P.O. Box 8
Mesa Verde, CO 81330
970/529-4465
www.nps.gov/meve/

Rocky Mountain National Park
1000 Highway 36
Estes Park, CO 80517
970/586-1206
www.nps.gov/romo/

STATE RESOURCES
CDOT Traveler Information
303/639-1111
877/315-7623
www.cotrip.org

Colorado Avalanche Information Center
325 Broadway, WS1
Boulder, CO 80305
http://geosurvey.state.co.us/avalanche/

Colorado Division of Wildlife
6060 Broadway
Denver, CO 80216
303/297-1192
http://wildlife.state.co.us

Colorado State Government Website
www.colorado.gov/colorado-visiting-activities

State Parks
High Plains Region Office
1313 Sherman Street #618
Denver, CO 80203
303/866-3437
http://parks.state.co.us

Rocky Mountain Region Office
P.O. Box 700
Clifton, CO 81520
970/434-6862
http://parks.state.co.us

Southeast Region Office
4255 Sinton Road
Colorado Springs, CO 80907
719/227-5250
http://parks.state.co.us

LOCAL RESOURCES AND NONPROFITS
The Access Fund
P.O. Box 17010
Boulder, CO 80308
303/545-6772
www.accessfund.org

Colorado Fourteeners Initiative
710 Tenth Street, Suite 220
Golden, CO 80401
303/278-7525
www.coloradofourteeners.org

Colorado Mountain Club
710 10th Street, #200
Golden, CO 80401
303/279-3080
www.cmc.org

Colorado Trail Foundation
710 10th Street#210
Golden, CO 80401
303/384-3729
www.coloradotrail.org

The Forest Conservancy
P.O. Box 3136
Aspen, CO 81612
970/963-8071
www.wriainfo.org

Volunteers for Outdoor Colorado
600 South Marion Parkway
Denver, CO 80209
303/715-1010
800/925-2220
www.voc.org

Colorado Outdoor Recreation Search and Rescue (CORSAR)
A CORSAR card offers the benefit of covering the costs of your rescue if you should require search-and-rescue services when hiking. A one-year card costs $3.00, and a five-year card costs $12. If interested, you may purchase a CORSAR card by calling 970/248-7313, or by visiting one of 300 vendors in the state of Colorado. A current vendor list is available at www.state.co.us/searchandrescue.

Acknowledgments

First and foremost, thanks to my husband and best camping buddy, Travis Schmidt. Without your love, encouragement, patience, and fish whispering skills it wouldn't have happened. Thanks as well to my next best camping buddy and cheerleader, Emily Ruell, and to Claudia Capitini and Maggie Stanislawski.

I owe a huge debt to the members of the Old Town Writing Group for their wisdom and humor. Laura Katers, Kim Lipker, Leslie Patterson, Laura Resau, and Joan Schmid. Thank you!

Thanks to Velma Yarrow of the Rio Grande National Forest for being there in a pinch. I hope we meet again in the backcountry.

To all of the public servants and volunteers who help to preserve and protect our public lands, thank you for hard work and dedication. I saw it every day I was out there, and I am so grateful.

Last but far from least, thanks and high-fives to my editors at Avalon Travel Publishing, Elizabeth McCue and Rebecca Browning, for investing in and encouraging a new writer.

Index

www.moon.com

For helpful advice on planning a trip, visit www.moon.com for the **TRAVEL PLANNER** and get access to useful travel strategies and valuable information about great places to visit. When you travel with Moon, expect an experience that is uncommon and truly unique.

OUTDOORS

"A smart new look provides just one more reason to travel with Moon Outdoors. Well written, thoroughly researched, and packed full of useful information and advice, these guides really do get you into the outdoors."

—GORP.COM

ALSO AVAILABLE AS FOGHORN OUTDOORS ACTIVITY GUIDES:

101 Great Hikes of the
   San Francisco Bay Area
250 Great Hikes in
   California's National Parks
Baja Camping
Bay Area Biking
California Beaches
California Camping
California Fishing
California Golf
California Hiking
California Recreational
   Lakes & Rivers
California Waterfalls
California Wildlife
Camper's Companion
Easy Biking in Northern
   California

Easy Hiking in Northern
   California
Easy Hiking in Southern
   California
Florida Beaches
Florida Camping
Georgia & Alabama Camping
Great Lakes Camping
Maine Hiking
Massachusetts Hiking
Montana, Wyoming & Idaho
   Camping
New England Biking
New England Cabins
   & Cottages
New England Camping
New England Hiking
New Hampshire Hiking

Northern California Biking
Oregon Hiking
Pacific Northwest Hiking
Southern California
   Cabins & Cottages
Tom Stienstra's Bay Area
   Recreation
Utah Camping
Utah Hiking
Vermont Hiking
Washington Boating
   & Water Sports
Washington Fishing
Washing Hiking
West Coast RV Camping

MOON COLORADO CAMPING

Avalon Travel Publishing
An Imprint of
Avalon Publishing Group, Inc.

AVALON
publishing group incorporated

1400 65th Street, Suite 250
Emeryville, CA 94608, USA
www.moon.com

Editor: Elizabeth McCue
Series Manager: Sabrina Young
Acquisitions Manager: Rebecca K. Browning
Copy Editor: Donna Leverenz
Graphics Coordinator: Elizabeth Jang
Production Coordinators: Darren Alessi,
 Elizabeth Jang
Cover Designer: Gerilyn Attebery
Interior Designer: Darren Alessi
Map Editor: Kevin Anglin
Cartographer: Kat Bennett
Cartography Manager: Mike Morgenfeld
Indexer: Greg Jewett

ISBN-10: 1-56691-546-5
ISBN-13: 978-1-56691-546-5
ISSN: 1098-8262

Printing History
1st Edition—1998
3rd Edition—April 2006
5 4 3 2 1

KEEPING CURRENT

We are committed to making this book the most accurate and enjoyable camping guide to Colorado. You can rest assured that every campground in this book has been carefully reviewed in an effort to keep this book as up-to-date as possible. However, by the time you read this book, some of the fees listed herein may have changed and campgrounds may have closed unexpectedly.

If you have a favorite gem you'd like to see included in the next edition, or see anything that needs updating, clarification, or correction, please drop us a line. Send your comments via email to feedback@moon.com, or use the address above.